WESTERN CIVILIZATION

WESTERN CIVILIZATION

The Continuing Experiment

SECOND EDITION

Thomas F. X. Noble
University of Virginia

Barry S. Strauss
Cornell University

Duane J. Osheim
University of Virginia

Kristen B. Neuschel
Duke University

William B. Cohen
Indiana University

David D. Roberts
University of Georgia

Houghton Mifflin Company   Boston   New York

Executive Editor: Patricia A. Coryell
Senior Basic Book Editor: Elizabeth M. Welch
Senior Project Editor: Christina M. Horn
Editorial Assistant: Stewart S. Jester
Senior Production/Design Coordinator: Sarah Ambrose
Senior Manufacturing Coordinator: Marie Barnes
Marketing Manager: Sandra McGuire

Chapter opener credits begin on page A-1. Text credits begin on page A-1.

Volume B cover image: The Surrender of Breda (to the Spanish General Spinola, 1625). Diego Rodríguez Veláquez (1599–1660), Spanish. Museo del Prado, Madrid. © Superstock.

Cover designer: Tony Saizon

Printed in the U.S.A.

Library of Congress Catalog Card Number: 97-93648

ISBN: 0-395-87066-6

1 2 3 4 5 6 7 8 9-VH-01 00 99 98 97

Brief Contents

Contents

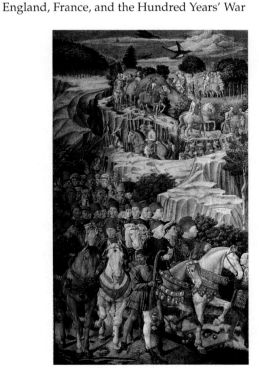

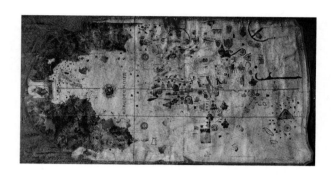

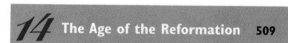

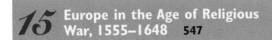

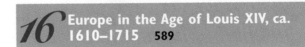

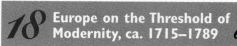

Maps

Documents

Chronologies, Genealogies, and Charts

Weighing the Evidence

Preface

Miles Davis was once asked what he thought jazz musicians would be playing in ten years, and he said that if he knew that, he would already be playing it. The authors of this book are committed teachers who never lost the thrill of being history students. We do not claim that we have seen into the future, but we can say with real conviction that we have tried to do better, for both instructors and students, than has been done in the past. And as we look back over nearly a decade, to the time when we were planning the first edition of *Western Civilization: The Continuing Experiment,* we can say with a mixture of pride and humility that we anticipated quite well what kind of history would be "playing" in ten years.

The purpose of a Western civilization textbook is to anchor a course that aims to inform students about essential developments within a tradition that has powerfully, although not always positively, affected everyone who is alive today. Although each of us finds something to admire in all of the existing textbooks, none of us was fully happy with any of them. We were disappointed with books that claimed "balance" but actually stressed a single kind of history. We regretted that so many texts were uneven in their command of recent scholarship. Although convinced of both the inherent interest of Western civilization and the importance of teaching the subject, we were disconcerted by the celebratory tone of some books, which portray the West as resting on its laurels instead of creatively facing its future.

As we were planning this book, momentous changes shook the Western world. Most obviously, the Soviet Union collapsed and the communist regimes of Eastern Europe tumbled one after another. Those who reflect on the West today must take account of Islamic minorities in the Slavic Balkans, Turkish workers in Germany, and African workers in France. Unprecedented economic prosperity—to be sure, unevenly distributed—marks all the lands from Ireland to Russia. Thus, the study of Western civilization at the dawn of a new millennium cannot focus narrowly on the peoples of Europe's western fringe, and it cannot take its bearings from a historical landscape whose most prominent features are the Depression of the 1930s, the world wars, and a global population divided by the iron curtain.

We decided to try very hard to produce a book that is balanced and coherent; that addresses the full range of subjects that a Western civilization text needs to address; that provides the student reader with interesting, timely material; that is up-to-date in terms of scholarship and approach; and that is handsome to look at—in short, a book that helps the instructor to teach and the student to learn. We have kept our common vision fresh through frequent meetings, correspondence, E-mail, critical mutual readings, and expert editorial guidance. Six authors have come together as one, and because each of us focused on his or her own area of specialization, we believe we have attained a rare blend of competence, confidence, and enthusiasm.

CENTRAL THEMES AND APPROACH

Western civilization is a story. We therefore aimed at a strong chronological narrative line. Our experience as teachers tells us that students appreciate this clear but gentle orientation. Our experience tells us, too, that an approach that is more chronological than thematic will leave instructors plenty of room to adapt our narrative to their preferred organization.

Although we maintain the familiar, large-scale divisions of a Western civilization book, we also present some innovative adjustments in arrangement. For instance, Chapter 2 treats early Greece together with the whole eastern Mediterranean region in the period from about 1500 to 750 B.C. This approach both links kindred cultures and respects chronological flow better than customary treatments, which take western Asia to a certain point and backtrack to deal with early Greece. We focus an entire chapter on Late Antiquity, the tumultuous and fascinating period from about A.D. 300 to 600 that witnessed the transformation of the Roman Empire into three successors: Byzantine, Islamic, and European. We introduce and analyze the industrial transformation in the middle of the nineteenth century, when it was at its high point, instead of scattering its account through several chapters. Our twentieth-century chapters reflect an understanding of the century formed in its closing years rather than in its middle decades. What is new in our organization represents adjustments grounded in the best scholarship, and what is old represents time-tested approaches.

A chronological narrative that respects the traditional divisions of ancient, medieval, early modern, and modern will inevitably reflect great people and great events. We make no apology for this, and we urge no particular ideology in doing it. Marx was surely right when he said that women and men make history without knowing they are doing so, but it is nonetheless true that Alexander, Charlemagne, Elizabeth I, Napoleon, and Hitler have had a more decisive impact on the development of the West than most ordinary individuals. That is true, but not interesting to teachers or to students until we say why it is true.

This book takes as its point of departure *power* in all its senses: public and private; economic, social, political, and cultural; symbolic and real. We continually ask who had power, and who did not. Through what public and private means was power gained, lost, and exercised in a given time and place? How did people talk about power? What kinds of rituals, ceremonies, or celebrations displayed power? What relationships existed among economic, social, political, and cultural power?

By using power, not old-fashioned high politics, as our organizing principle we believe we have achieved the kind of balance and integration that are frequently promised but seldom attained. We have deliberately avoided putting the occasional paragraph or section on women, children, families, religious minorities, eating habits, or marriage patterns in the middle of a discussion of something else entirely. We maintain a sustained interest in the history of women, often using gender as a tool of analysis and explanation, and we discuss such subjects as diet, clothing, or dwellings when Europeans themselves talked about them, or when there were important changes in these areas. Women are not relegated to a separate section in our account of the Middle Ages, for example, but instead are situated in accounts of politics, society, religion, and culture. Nineteenth-century women appear as workers, writers, or political activists and not under a single heading that would deprive them of contextual participation in their contemporary world.

Our focus on power permits a continuous, nuanced treatment of intellectual history. Major thinkers and key intellectual traditions are consistently integrated into the story rather than treated independently as if they were *the* story of Western civilization, or else a sideshow to the main event. Any understanding of Plato and Aristotle, for instance, must begin in the Greek *polis*. Renaissance humanism cannot be understood apart from its late medieval Italian, urban context. We anchor the Scientific Revolution to Renaissance and Reformation intellectual life, court societies, patronage networks, and the expanding world created by Europe's first overseas empires. We root romanticism in its urban, industrial, nationalistic, and politically restless nineteenth-century world, and we treat existentialism as one response to modern war and totalitarianism.

We thought hard about another issue that textbooks usually take for granted: What is the West? This book was conceived and written after the end of the cold war and the fall of communist regimes in Eastern Europe. Both the West's understanding of itself at any point in time and the historical understanding of the West through succeeding generations have changed in interesting and important ways, never more so than today. Thus, we continually invite our readers to think about the precise object of their study.

In fashioning our picture of the West, we took two unusual steps. First, our West is bigger than the one found in most textbooks. We treat the Celtic world, Scandinavia, and the Slavic world as integral parts of the story. We look often at the lands that border the West—Anatolia/Turkey, western Asia, North Africa, the Eurasian steppes—in order to show the to-and-fro of peoples, ideas, technologies, and products. Second, we continually situate the West in its global context. We must be clear: This is not a world history book. But just as we recognize that the West has influenced the rest of the world, so too we carefully acknowledge that the rest of the world has influenced the West. We begin this story of mutual interaction with the Greeks and Romans, carry it through the European Middle Ages, focus on it in the age of European exploration and conquest, and analyze it closely in the modern world of industry, empire, diplomacy, and questions of citizenship and identity.

We ask, finally, that you note the subtitle of the book: "The Continuing Experiment." It was carefully chosen to convey our resolve to avoid a deterministic approach. For students and teachers, an appreciation of continuity and change, of unity and diversity, can foster sympathetic participation in our often bewildering world. We try to give individual actors, moments, and movements the sense of drama, possibility, and contingency that they actually possessed.

We, with faultless hindsight, always know how things came out. Contemporaries often hadn't a clue. We respect them. Much of the fascination, and the reward, of studying Western civilization lies precisely in its richness, diversity, changeability, unpredictability.

DISTINCTIVE FEATURES

To make this text as accessible as possible to students, we have constantly been aware of its place in a program of teaching. Each chapter begins with a thematic introduction that engages the reader's interest while pointing clearly and in some detail to what will follow. Chronologies help to organize and review major developments. Careful chapter summaries draw together major topics and themes and link the present chapter to the one that follows. To help students strike out on their own to new historical discoveries, we provide for each chapter an annotated reading list of scholarly classics and exciting new works.

In addition to a sound pedagogical framework, and to an engaging full-color design that clarifies and animates the illustrations and text, we have thoroughly integrated all the elements of the book. Our maps, for example, support the text in both traditional and novel ways. Teachers will find "old friends" among them but will make many new acquaintances too. Our diverse array of boxed primary sources—five per chapter—are referred to and tightly anchored in the text and support their surrounding discussion. Here again, classic documents are blended with fresh newcomers. Our photographs, many of which have not previously appeared in textbooks, are never merely decorative, and their captions seek to extend the discussions that they complement.

An example may help to illustrate this integration. The central theme of Chapter 9, which treats Europe from 900 to 1150, is "expansion." Thus the chapter explores population growth, economic development, and foreign military adventures—chiefly the Crusades. But this theme of expansion is developed to reinforce the book's central, unifying themes—power and the West within the wider world. For example, the text discusses the kinds of social and institutional structures that were created or refined to accommodate the expansion of territorial power and responsibility. The maps provide clear evidence of the territorial expansion of both old

states (England, France, Germany) and new ones (in Celtic, Scandinavian, and Slavic areas). The pictures illustrate power in several ways. Kings are depicted on thrones, wearing crowns, holding orbs and scepters, and receiving gifts and obeisance. In other words, their symbolic and ceremonial manifestations of power are displayed. Castles, one of the great military and political technologies of the time, appear in Welsh, French, and Polish forms. A woman of immense power in central Italy is shown receiving the earnest entreaties for help of a German emperor. Boxed documents illustrate personal bonds of homage and fealty, key issues in the period's clashes between secular and ecclesiastical officials, and, on a lesser scale, the division of goods in Welsh law between men and women after a divorce. The various components of this chapter, as of all the chapters, continually reinforce one another, for a careful integration that promotes discussion and enhances learning.

Another important component of this book is the two-page feature "Weighing the Evidence," presented at the end of each chapter. These features introduce students to the fascinating variety of sources that historians use and invite them to think critically about the nature of historical information and inquiry. Each opens with a description of the evidence reproduced in the feature—sources ranging from images of Cleopatra, the Ravenna mosaics, Reformation woodcuts, eighteenth-century political symbols, the layout of the British Museum, and the poetry of World War I—and then discusses how the professional historian examines this evidence to reconstruct the past. When Samuel Butler said that God cannot change history but that historians can and often do, he meant that history itself arises from new or different acts of interpretation. With "Weighing the Evidence," students look over the shoulder of the historian to become active participants in this interpretive process. The sources examined are interesting and instructive in their own right, but the "Weighing the Evidence" features also contribute to the teaching program of the book. As always, they are carefully integrated into the text: There are references to them at appropriate points in the narrative; they themselves contain cross-references where appropriate to other sections or illustrations; and they support ongoing discussions.

This book is also flexible in format as well as substantive organization. Because schools use different academic calendars, organize Western civilization courses according to different chronologies, and require or recommend different parts of the course, we issue this book in four formats, three of which embrace the complete work:

- One-volume hardcover edition (Chapters 1–30)
- Two-volume paperback, Volume I: To 1715 (Chapters 1–17), Volume II: Since 1560 (Chapters 15–30)
- Three-volume paperback, Volume A: To 1500 (Chapters 1–12), Volume B: 1300–1715 (Chapters 11–19), Volume C: Since 1789 (Chapters 19–30)
- And new to this edition, Since 1300 (Chapters 11–30)

Volume II opens with a comprehensive introduction that situates the student reader in the late sixteenth century and surveys the course of Western civilization from ancient times to the early centuries of the modern era. This introduction is designed particularly for students who did not take the first semester of the course, or who are new to this book.

CHANGES IN THE NEW EDITION

In preparing our second edition we thought hard about our own experiences in using the book, and we paid strict attention to the advice given us by many instructors, including those who used the book and those who did not. Five main lines of revision guided our changes:

Organizational Changes

The most obvious change here is that we shrank our book from thirty-two to thirty chapters. The first-edition chapter on "The Frontiers of Latin Europe" was deleted, and its most important conceptual perspectives and substantive material were redistributed among Chapters 8, 9, and 10. Two chapters on later medieval Europe were tightened in focus and organization and turned into one new chapter (11). By cutting out two first-edition chapters in Volume I, it became possible to include Chapter 17 on the Scientific Revolution in both Volumes I and II, a change that accommodates many syllabuses.

Many other organizational changes are less visible but still significant. The revolution from the Gracchi to Caesar in Republican Rome has been moved to Chapter 5, which permits Chapter 6 to have a sharper focus on the crisis of the late Republic and the emergence of the Roman Empire. Some material on medieval church-state controversies that was earlier distributed over several chapters is now

consolidated in Chapter 10. Discussions of the late medieval economy are now sharply focused in Chapter 11, and former sections on late medieval and Renaissance art are now found together in Chapter 12. Sections treating the English Revolution, the French Revolution, and the revolutions of 1848 have undergone significant reorganization and revision. The book's final chapters have been rearranged and revised in light of shifting perspectives on postcommunist Eastern Europe.

Thematic Integration

Users and reviewers praised our book's two major themes—power and the shape of the West within the wider world—but in preparing this edition we felt we could do even better. Specifically, we saw opportunities to treat the second theme in more detail and to sharpen our use of gender as a means of explanation. Accordingly, we began at the beginning, so to speak, and incorporated material on Neolithic and Copper Age Europe to complement our treatment of the Mesopotamian and Mediterranean worlds. We paid more attention to the shifting frontiers of medieval Europe. In revising our account of the immensely important political and diplomatic history of the period from about 1500 to 1800, we included more extensive coverage of both Europe's immediate frontiers and the wider world. Our nineteenth-century chapters contain an expanded account of the growing power of the United States and the global significance of European emigration. Our nineteenth- and twentieth-century chapters now contain additional coverage of the mutual relations between Europe and its colonies. The Depression of the 1930s is anchored more firmly in a global context, and the multicultural implications of vast population movements in the late twentieth century are carefully considered.

From the start, our book paid serious attention to the experiences of women and to the exciting possibilities of using gender as a tool of analysis. We were very pleased that users and reviewers affirmed our intentions and achievements. Still, in revising we believed that we could improve our coverage. Readers of the first edition will detect many changes, as in the sections on the Roman Empire, Late Antiquity, the High Middle Ages, exploration and discovery, the Scientific Revolution, nineteenth-century ideologies and social movements, the welfare state, and the problems of identity politics in the very recent past.

New Primary-Source Chapter Feature

To help us achieve our goal of thematic integration, in this edition we have added the primary-source feature "Encounters with the West." Every chapter contains one readily identifiable document that portrays other people commenting on westerners or westerners commenting on the world around them. In these documents, students meet Egyptians and Romans reacting to foreigners, a Franciscan missionary telling about the Mongols, an Inca nobleman describing his civilization, the wife of a wealthy plantation owner stating her views on Haiti's slave revolt, a Moroccan commenting on French press freedoms, Gandhi talking about nonviolence, and the controversial, influential Edward Said discussing "Orientalism."

Improved Chapter Features

We have also revised our existing pedagogical framework to take every opportunity to tighten the book's integration and to enhance its teachability. Every chapter now opens with an arresting full-color illustration that is specifically referenced in the introduction on the facing page. This visual and textual device expresses the main themes and issues raised in that chapter and captures the interest and provokes the imagination of the student reader. To continue our book's close integration of text and artwork, we have replaced about one-third of the in-text illustrations. Each new picture and drawing was chosen specifically to enhance the book's pedagogical force. All maps were scrutinized for accuracy and pedagogical value, and many were revised in subtle ways. We incorporated a number of new boxed documents that work to illustrate or extend our themes. Most chapters, moreover, now contain at least one document that lends itself to a "gendered" reading to help students familiarize themselves with gender as a tool of analysis. About one-third of the "Weighing the Evidence" features are new in this edition. Some of the newcomers are attributable to exciting discoveries, such as "The Ice Man's World." Others, on topics ranging from the invention of modern cartography to the Crystal Palace and pop art, serve to bolster our themes and to provoke discussion.

Incorporation of Recent Scholarship

One important advantage of a six-person author team is that we can keep track of the latest publications across the whole course of Western civilization. Natu-rally, few periods or problems have been the subject of massive reinterpretation since our first edition, but many small changes in perspective have turned up all over. In line with the most recent, sound work, we have especially revised sections on the Greek phalanx and polis, the Etruscans and early Rome, Jesus and early Christianity, Late Antiquity, the Slavic world, vernacular culture in the Renaissance, the origins of the Reformation, the English Revolution, Napoleon, many aspects of the nineteenth century, the cold war, and the fall of Soviet communism. To incorporate recent findings and perspectives, we have updated all the lists of suggested readings.

SUPPLEMENTS

We have thoroughly revised our array of text supplements provided to aid students in learning and instructors in teaching. These supplements, including a *Study Guide*, a *Computerized Study Guide*, an *Instructor's Resource Manual*, *Test Items*, *Computerized Test Items*, *Map Transparencies*, a *Videodisc* and *Videodisc Guide*, and two new multimedia supplements: a *Power Presentation Manager* and a CD-ROM of interactive maps, are tied closely to the text and to one another, to provide a tightly integrated program of teaching and learning.

The *Study Guide*, written by Miriam Shadis of Ohio University, includes an introductory essay on how to make the best use of your Western Civilization course. For each chapter it gives learning objectives, an annotated outline of the chapter, multiple-choice questions keyed to the text, essay questions with guidelines, analytical questions, and map exercises. The *Study Guide* is published in two volumes, to correspond with Volumes I and II of the text: Volume I contains Chapters 1–17 and Volume II contains Chapters 15–30. The *Study Guide* is also available in a computerized version for use with IBM® PC or compatible computers. This *Computerized Study Guide* contains text page references for all questions and rejoinders to each multiple-choice question that explain why the student's response is or is not correct.

The *Instructor's Resource Manual*, prepared by Janice Liedl of Laurentian University, contains useful teaching strategies and tips for getting the most out of the text. Each chapter includes a summary and outline, learning objectives, lecture suggestions, discussion questions, recommended outside reading, and writing assignment and paper topics. For the new edition we have expanded the *Instructor's Resource Manual* to include recommended film, video, and multimedia resources, as well as collaborative learning activities for students.

Each chapter of the *Test Items,* written by Diane Moczar of Northern Virginia Community College, offers a list of 20 to 30 key terms, 10 to 15 short-answer and essay questions, 2 to 3 map questions, and 40 to 50 multiple-choice questions. Answers to the multiple-choice questions are located at the end of the *Test Items.* We also offer a computerized version of the *Test Items* for use with IBM® PC or compatible computers, to enable teachers to alter, replace, or add questions. Each item in the computerized test item file is numbered according to the printed test item file to ease the creation of customized tests.

An exciting addition to our map program is a CD-ROM of thirty interactive maps, available to both instructors and students. We also offer *The Western Civilization Videodisc/Videotape/Slide* program, a multimedia collection of visual images, as well as a set of full-color *Transparencies* of all the maps in the text.

In addition, we are pleased to provide the *Power Presentation Manager,* a software tool that enables teachers to prepare visual aids for lectures electronically, using both textual and visual materials. Instructors can customize their lectures by incorporating their own material onto the PPM and combining it with the electronic resources provided, including adaptable chapter outlines, tables, illustrations, and maps from the text.

Finally, we are proud to announce the creation of our on-line primary-source collection, *BiblioBase™: Custom Coursepacks in Western Civilization.* This resource will allow instructors to select from over 600 primary-source documents to create their own customized reader.

ACKNOWLEDGMENTS

From the first draft to the last, the authors have benefited from repeated critical readings by many colleagues. We have tried very hard to profit from the vast fund of experience and knowledge that has been placed generously at our disposal. Our thanks to the following instructors: **Lawrence Backlund,** Montgomery County Community College; **John Battick,** University of Maine—Orono; **F. E. Beemon,** Middle Tennessee State University; **Christopher M. Bellitto,** St. Joseph's Seminary, Dunwoodie; **Wayne Bledsoe,** University of Missouri—Rolla; **Donna Bohanan,** Auburn University; **RaGena De Aragon,** Gonzaga University; **Peter Diehl,** Western Wash-

ington University; **Katherine J. Haldane,** The Citadel; **Boyd Hill,** University of Colorado—Boulder; **James Lehning,** University of Utah; **Daniel Lewis,** California State Polytechnic University at Pomona; **Janice Liedl,** Laurentian University; **Raymond Mentzner,** Montana State University; **John Nicols,** University of Oregon; **Byron Nordstrom,** Gustavus Adolphus College; **Beth Plummer,** Wingate University; **Janet Polasky,** University of New Hampshire; **Donald Pryce,** University of South Dakota; **John Rosser,** Boston College; **Arnold Sherman,** Champlain College; **Tom Taylor,** Seattle University; and **James Walter,** Sinclair Community College.

Each of us has also benefited from the close readings and valuable criticisms of our coauthors, although we all assume responsibility for our own chapters. Barry Strauss has written Chapters 1–6; Thomas Noble, Chapters 7–10; Duane Osheim, Chapters 11–14; Kristen Neuschel, Chapters 15–19; William Cohen, Chapters 20–24; and David Roberts, Chapters 25–30.

Many colleagues, friends, and family members have helped us develop this work as well. Thomas Noble wishes to thank Linda L. Noble for her patience and kindness over the years devoted to this project. He is also grateful to John Contreni, Wendy Davies, Thomas Head, Elizabeth Meyer, Richard Sullivan, John Van Engen, Robert Wilken, and Ian Wood.

Barry Strauss is grateful to colleagues at Cornell and at other universities who offered advice and encouragement and responded to scholarly questions. He would also like to thank Sandra Kisner and Elaine Scott for their invaluable assistance. Most important has been the support and forbearance of his family. His daughter, Sylvie, his son, Michael, and, above all, his wife, Marcia, have truly been sources of inspiration.

Duane Osheim wishes to thank his family for support during the writing and revising of this book. He is also grateful to colleagues at the University of Virginia, who helped to clarify the many connections between Western civilization and the wider world. He would specifically like to thank Erik Midelfort, Arthur Field, Janis Gibbs, and Beth Plummer for comments and advice.

Kristen Neuschel thanks her colleagues at Duke University for sharing their expertise. She is especially grateful to Sy Mauskopf, Bill Reddy, John Richards, Tom Robisheaux, Alex Roland, John J. TePaske, Julius Scott, and Peter Wood. She also thanks her husband and fellow historian, Alan Williams, for his wisdom about Western civilization and his support throughout the project, and her children, Jesse and Rachel, for their patience, joy, and curiosity.

William Cohen thanks his wife, Christine Matheu, and his daughters, Natalie, Leslie, and Laurel, for their support and encouragement over the many years that this project has matured.

David Roberts wishes to thank Bonnie Cary, Linda Green, and Nancy Heaton for their able assistance and Joshua Cole, Karl Friday, Thomas Ganschow, John Haag, John Morrow, Miranda Pollard, Ronald Rader, William Stueck, Eve Troutt Powell, and Kirk Willis, colleagues at the University of Georgia, for sharing their expertise in response to questions. He also thanks Beth Roberts for her constant support and interest and her exceedingly critical eye, and Ellen, Trina, and Anthony, for their college-age perspective and advice.

All the authors wish to thank the thousands of students who helped us to learn and to teach Western civilization. Their questions and concerns have shaped much of this work.

We also wish to acknowledge and thank the editors who did so much to bring this book into being. Elizabeth Welch, our Senior Basic Book Editor, sifted our thoughts, sharpened our focus, and smoothed our prose. Christina Horn, our Senior Project Editor, displayed boundless patience and professionalism as she assembled this book from all its constituent parts. Carole Frohlich, our tireless and enterprising picture researcher, often knew better than we did just what we wanted. To Jean Woy, Editor-in-Chief for Social Sciences (and our original Sponsoring Editor), we are grateful for confidence in this project, and in us. Sean Wakely was the Sponsoring Editor who steered this ship safely into port on its first voyage. Patricia Coryell is on the bridge now. We are grateful to them both for smooth passages.

Thomas F. X. Noble

The authors (left to right): Kristen Neuschel, Bill Cohen, David Roberts, Tom Noble (in back), Duane Osheim, Barry Strauss.

About the Authors

Thomas F. X. Noble

After receiving his Ph.D. from Michigan State University, Thomas Noble has taught at Albion College, Michigan State University, Texas Tech University, and since 1980 at the University of Virginia. He is the author of *The Republic of St. Peter: The Birth of the Papal State, 680–825, Religion, Culture and Society in the Early Middle Ages,* and *Soldiers of Christ: Saints and Saints' Lives from Late Antiquity and the Early Middle Ages.* Noble's articles and reviews have appeared in many leading journals, including the *American Historical Review, Byzantinische Zeitschrift, Catholic Historical Review, Revue d'histoire ecclésiastique, Speculum,* and *Studi medievali.* He has also contributed chapters to several books and articles to three encyclopedias. Noble, who was a member of the Institute for Advanced Study in 1994, has been awarded fellowships by the National Endowment for the Humanities (twice) and by the American Philosophical Society.

Barry S. Strauss

Professor of history and Classics at Cornell University, where he is also Director of the Peace Studies Program, Barry S. Strauss holds a Ph.D. from Yale in history. He has been awarded fellowships by the National Endowment for the Humanities, the American School of Classical Studies at Athens, and the Killam Foundation of Canada. He is the recipient of the Clark Award for excellence in teaching from Cornell. His many publications include *Athens After the Peloponnesian War: Class, Faction, and Policy, 403–386 B.C.; Fathers and Sons in Athens: Ideology and Society in the Era of the Peloponnesian War; The Anatomy of Error: Ancient Military Disasters and Their Lessons for Modern Strategists* (with Josiah Ober); and *Hegemonic Rivalry from Thucydides to the Nuclear Age* (co-edited with R. Ned Lebow).

Duane J. Osheim

A Fellow of the American Academy in Rome with a Ph.D. in History from the University of California, Davis, Duane Osheim is a professor of history at the University of Virginia. A specialist in late Medieval and Renaissance social and institutional history, he is author of *A Tuscan Monastery and Its Social World* and *An Italian Lordship: The Bishopric of Lucca in the Late Middle Ages,* as well as numerous studies of religious values and rural life in late Medieval Italy.

Kristen B. Neuschel

Associate professor of history at Duke University, Kristen B. Neuschel received the Ph.D. from Brown University. She is the author of *Word of Honor: Interpreting Noble Culture in Sixteenth-Century France* and articles on French social history and European women's history. In 1988 she received the Alumni Distinguished Undergraduate Teaching Award, which is awarded annually on the basis of student nominations for excellence in teaching at Duke.

William B. Cohen

After receiving his Ph.D. at Stanford University, William Cohen has taught at Northwestern University and Indiana University, where he is now professor of history. At Indiana, he served as chairman of the West European Studies and History departments. A previous president of the Society for French Historical Studies, Cohen has received several academic fellowships, among them a National Endowment for the Humanities and a Fulbright fellowship. Among his many publications are *Rulers of Empire, The French Encounter with Africans, European Empire Building, Robert Delavignette and the French Empire, The Transformation of Modern France,* and *Urban Government and the Rise of the City.*

David D. Roberts

After taking his Ph.D. in modern European history at the University of California, Berkeley, David Roberts taught at the Universities of Virginia and Rochester before becoming professor of history at the University of Georgia in 1988. At Rochester he chaired the Humanities Department of the Eastman School of Music, and he has chaired the History Department at Georgia since 1993. A recipient of Woodrow Wilson and Rockefeller Foundation fellowships, he is the author of *The Syndicalist Tradition and Italian Fascism, Benedetto Croce and the Uses of Historicism,* and *Nothing but History: Reconstruction and Extremity after Metaphysics,* as well as numerous articles and reviews.

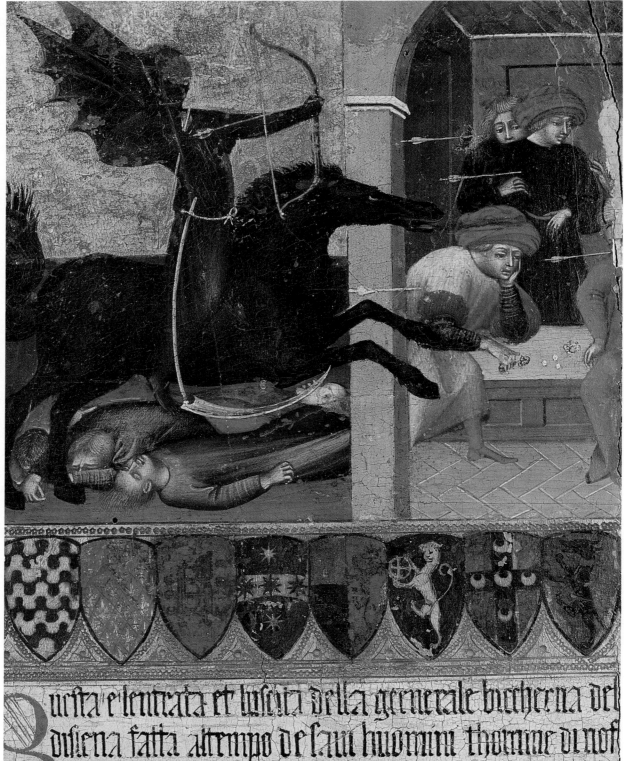

Questa e lentrata et lusoia della generale bicchena del
disiena fatta attempo de sani huomini thomme di nos
chamarlengho per uno anno chominando adi p̄mo digiēnā

CHAPTER 11

The Transformation of Medieval Civilization, 1300–1500

I n the fourteenth century, Europeans sang an old Franciscan hymn, "Day of Wrath, Day of Burning," which described the fear and disorder that would accompany the end of the world and God's judgment of the saved and the damned. Images of God's judgment and the terrible fates awaiting sinners were constantly on the minds of Christians. As we see in the facing illustration, sinners, like these gamblers, fell victim to deadly plague carried by arrows shot by the winged angel of death. The flood, fire, and pestilence that ravaged late medieval Europe were thought to be premonitions of coming judgment.

The late Middle Ages (ca. 1300–1500) is often described as a period of continued crisis and decline that saw the end of the growth and expansion of the previous three centuries. In truth, however, this period was an age of transformation, of both crisis and recovery, that witnessed not only dislocation but also growth. In this chapter we discuss the roots of the crisis and the later economic, social, and political recovery in the fifteenth century. The cultural and intellectual changes that accompanied the crisis and recovery are the focus of Chapter 12, "The Renaissance."

Military, political, religious, economic, and social crises burdened Europe in the fourteenth and early fifteenth centuries. Between 1337 and 1453, France and England fought what was in effect a world war. The Hundred Years' War, as it has come to be known, was primarily fought over English

Painted cover for a fifteenth-century government account book from Siena, Italy, showing symbols of death—arrows, a scythe, and a horse—to carry the angel of death from place to place.

claims to traditionally French lands. Social and political disruptions and the economic burdens of the war allowed the nobles of England and France to limit royal power and made local administration more difficult. Both monarchies transformed themselves in the aftermath of political strife, however, in ways that preserved and even increased royal power.

Problems were not confined to England and France. Although by 1300 the monarchies, the city-states of Italy, and the papacy had the legal systems, tax structures, and traditions of representation that were to be the foundations of modern European government and representative institutions, aristocrats in many parts of Europe challenged the hereditary rights of their rulers. In the towns of Germany and Italy, patrician classes moved to reduce the influence of artisans and laborers in government, instituting oligarchies or even aristocratic dictatorships in place of more democratic governments.

Questions of power and representation also affected the Christian church as ecclesiastical claims to authority came under attack. Secular governments challenged church jurisdictions. Disputed papal elections led to the so-called Great Schism, a split between rival centers of control in Rome and Avignon (a city in what is now the south of France). In dealing with the schism and with more general problems of moral reform, the church hierarchy was challenged by those who argued that authority resided in the whole church and not just with its head, the pope. In the aftermath of the crisis, the papacy was forced to redefine its place in both the religious and the political life of Europe.

A series of economic and demographic shocks worsened these political and religious difficulties. Part of the problem was structural: The population of Europe grew too large to be supported by the resources available. Famine and the return of the bubonic plague in 1348 sent the economy into long-term decline. In almost every aspect of political, religious, and social life, then, the fourteenth and early fifteenth centuries marked a pause in the expansion and consolidation that had characterized the previous century and a half and the growth that was to mark the sixteenth century.

Yet some of the seeds of that future growth were planted during this period. Two empires quite unlike the monarchical states of the twelfth and thirteenth centuries appeared in the fifteenth century. The marriage of the sovereigns of Aragon and Castile formed a new Spanish Empire that would become the most powerful government in sixteenth-century Europe, while at the other end of the Mediterranean, a new Muslim Turkish empire replaced the weakened Byzantine Empire. Neither state had existed in 1300, and the future seemed to belong to them.

THE CRISIS OF THE WESTERN CHRISTIAN CHURCH

Early in the fourteenth century, the Christian church endured a series of shocks that began a debate about the nature of church government and the role of the church in society. First, the popes moved from their traditional seat of authority in central Italy to Avignon. Then, in the wake of a disputed election, two and later three rivals claimed the papal throne. Simultaneously, the church hierarchy faced challenges from radical reformers who wished to change it. At various times all the European powers got involved in the problems of the church. By the mid-fifteenth century, the papacy realized that it needed a stronger, independent base. In response it transformed itself into a major political power in central Italy.

The French attack on Pope Boniface VIII in 1303 (see page 387) had exposed the weakness of the papacy as a political power and also revealed the deep splits within the Christian community. Although Philip IV's agents were excommunicated for their deeds, Boniface's successors, many of whom were from French-speaking lands, tried to reach an accommodation with the king. It was, in fact, largely because of Philip that the French archbishop of Bordeaux was elected Pope Clement V (r. 1305–1314). Clement chose to remain north of the Alps in order to seek an end to warfare between France and England and to protect, to the extent possible, the wealthy religious order of the Templars, which Philip was in the process of suppressing (see page 317). He hoped also to prevent the king from carrying through his threatened posthumous heresy trial of Boniface. After the death of Boniface, it was clear that the governments of Europe had no intention of recognizing papal authority as absolute.

The Babylonian Captivity, 1309–1377

Clement's pontificate marked the beginning of the so-called Babylonian Captivity, a period during which the pope resided almost continuously in what is now the south of France. In 1309, Clement moved the papal court to Avignon, on the Rhône River in a region that was technically part of the Holy Roman Empire (the name that by the fourteenth century was given to the medieval empire whose origin reached back to Charlemagne). Initially there had been no plan to remain outside of Italy, but by the 1330s the popes had created a large and brilliant court in Avignon, perhaps the largest in Europe. Pope John XXII (r. 1316–1334) set the tone for the court. To celebrate the marriage of his grandniece in 1324, for example, he ordered a wedding feast during which numerous guests consumed 4012 loaves of bread, 8¾ oxen, 55¼ sheep, 8 pigs, 4 boars, and vast quantities of fish, capons, chickens, partridges, rabbits, ducks, and chickens. The repast was topped off with 300 pounds of cheese, 3000 eggs, and assorted fruits. The guests washed down this feast with about 450 liters of wine.

It is indicative of the changed circumstances of the popes that although the thirteenth-century papal administration required only two hundred or so officials, the bureaucracy grew to about six hundred in Avignon. It was not just the pope's immediate circle that expanded the population of Avignon. Artists, writers, lawyers, and merchants from across Europe were drawn to the new center of administration and patronage. Kings, princes, towns, and ecclesiastical institutions needed representatives at the papal court. Papal administrators continued to intervene actively in local ecclesiastical affairs, and revenues that the popes claimed in the form of annates (generally a portion of the first year's revenues from an ecclesiastical office

Papal Avignon During the pontificate of Benedict XII the papal palace was begun in Avignon. It became the center of the most brilliant and politically important court in fourteenth-century Europe. *(Altitude, Paris)*

THE CRISIS OF THE WESTERN CHURCH

1302	Boniface VIII issues *Unam sanctam*
1303	Boniface VIII is attacked at Anagni and dies
1305	Election of Clement V
1309	Clement V moves the papal court to Avignon; beginning of the Babylonian Captivity
1377	End of the Babylonian Captivity
1378	Death of Gregory XI in Rome
1378	Elections of rival popes: Urban VI and Clement VII; start of the Great Schism
1409	Council of Pisa elects a third pope
1414–1417	Council of Constance deposes all three papal claimants
1415	Council of Constance condemns and executes John Hus
1417	Election of Martin V by the Council of Constance; end of the Great Schism
1438	Pragmatic Sanction of Bourges gives French kings influence in the French church

granted by papal letter), court fees, and provisioning fees continued to grow.

Not everyone approved of this situation. It was the Italian poet and philosopher Francesco Petrarch (1304–1374) who first referred to a "Babylonian Captivity of the papacy." Recalling the exile of the Israelites and the image of Babylon as a center of sin and immorality, he complained of

[an] unholy Babylon, Hell on Earth, a sink of iniquity, the cesspool of the world. There is neither faith, nor charity, nor religion, nor fear of God, nor shame, nor truth, nor holiness, albeit the residence . . . of the supreme pontiff should have made it a shrine and the very stronghold of religion.[1]

To Petrarch and to others, the exile of the papacy from its traditional see in Rome stood as an example of all that was wrong with the church.

Those who came to the court were practical and worldly. Many people renowned for their piety, like Saint Catherine of Siena and Saint Bridget of Sweden, appealed to the pope to return to simpler ways and to Rome, his episcopal city. (See the box, "Saint Catherine and the Avignon Papacy.")

Late in 1377, Pope Gregory XI (r. 1370–1378) did return to Rome. He found churches and palaces in ruin and the city violent and dangerous. He would have retreated to Avignon had he not died a few months later. In a tumultuous election during which the Roman populace threatened to break into the conclave, the cardinals finally elected a compromise candidate acceptable both to the French cardinals and to the Roman mob. Urban VI (r. 1378–1389) was an Italian cleric from a French-controlled part of Italy. He was also violent, intemperate, and eager to reduce the privileges of the clerical hierarchy. Many cardinals soon feared for their own safety. Some immediately questioned the legitimacy of the election, which they believed had been conducted under duress. Within months they deposed Urban and elected in his place a French cardinal who took the name Clement VII (r. 1378–1394). Urban responded by denouncing the cardinals and continuing to rule in Rome. There were now two popes.

After some hesitation, Western Christians divided into two camps, initiating the Great Schism, a period of almost forty years during which no one knew for sure who was the true pope. Each side found ready supporters among the states of Europe; however, support for one pope or the other often had more to do with political rivalries than with religious conviction. The French supported Clement, who eventually resettled in Avignon. The English, together with the Italians and most of the German Empire, supported Urban, the pope in Rome. Scotland, a mortal enemy of the English, and Castile sided with the French.

The crisis gave impetus to new discussions about church government: Should the pope be considered the sole head of the church? Debates within the church followed lines of thought already expressed in the towns and kingdoms of Europe. Representative bodies—the English Parliament, the French Estates General, the Swedish Riksdag—already claimed the right to act for the realm, and in the city-states of Italy ultimate authority was thought to reside in the body of citizens. Canon lawyers and theologians similarly ar-

Saint Catherine and the Avignon Papacy

Like most of her female contemporaries, Catherine Benincasa (1347–1380) was given no formal education. Nonetheless, because of her piety and spirituality, she was named a "Doctor of the Church"—a title granted only to the most important and influential theologians. Catherine surrounded herself with a "spiritual family" of men and women from many parts of Italy and used her influence to pressure the popes to return to Rome and to reform the church. She was also more than willing to use her influence to bring about political reconciliation between the papacy and Italian governments. This letter to Pope Gregory XI was probably dictated (Catherine was illiterate) in 1376. It was instrumental in his decision to return to Rome.

My soul longs with inestimable love that God in His infinite mercy will take from you each passion and all tepidity of heart and will reform you into another man by rekindling in you an ardent and burning desire, for in no other way can you fulfill the will of God and the desires of all His servants. Alas, my sweetest Babbo [literally "Daddy"], pardon my presumption in what I have said and am saying—the sweet and primal Truth forces me. This is His will, Father; He demands this of you. He demands that you require justice in the multitude of iniquities committed by those nourished and sheltered in the garden of the Holy Church; He declares that beasts should not receive men's food. Because He has given you authority and because you have accepted it, you ought to use your virtue and power. If you do not wish to use it, it might be better for you to resign what you have accepted; it would give more honor to God and health to your soul.

In addition, His will demands that you make peace with all Tuscany where now you have strife. Receive all your wicked and rebellious sons whenever you can peacefully do so—but punish them as a father would an offending son. . . . [T]hat which appears impossible to you is possible to the sweet goodness of God who has ordained and willed that it be so. Beware, as you hold your life dear, that you are not negligent in this nor treat lightly the works of the Holy Spirit. . . . You can have peace by avoiding the perverse pomps and delights of the world and by preserving God's honor and the Holy Church's rights.

Source: Robert Coogan, *Babylon on the Rhone: A Translation of Letters by Dante, Petrarch, and Catherine of Siena on the Avignon Papacy* (Potomac, Md.: Studia Humanitatis, 1983), p. 115.

gued that authority resided in the whole church, which had the right and duty to come together in council to correct and reform the church hierarchy. The most conservative of these "conciliarists" said merely that although the pope normally ruled the church on earth, the "Universal Church" had the right to respond in periods of heresy or schism. More radical conciliarists argued that the pope as bishop of Rome was merely the first among equals in the church hierarchy and he, like any other bishop, could be corrected by a gathering of his peers—that is, by a general council of the church.

As more and more churchmen assumed one or another of the conciliarist positions, the rival popes found themselves under increased pressure to end the schism. The issue seemed on its way to resolution when the two parties agreed to meet in northern Italy in 1408. In the end, though, the meeting never took place, and in retrospect many doubted whether either party had been negotiating in good faith. In exasperation the cardinals, the main ecclesiastical supporters of the rival popes, agreed to call a general council of the church. Meeting in Pisa in 1409, the council deposed both popes and elected a new pope. The council, however, lacked the power to force the rivals to accept deposition, and so the only result was that three men now claimed to be the rightful successor of Saint Peter and the Vicar of Christ. The outcome of the Council of Pisa demonstrated that the conciliarists, by themselves, could not heal the split in the church. A workable solution would not come until secular rulers were willing to enforce it.

Heresy, Reunion, and Reform

The Holy Roman emperor, Sigismund (r. 1411–1437), vigorously lobbied the other European powers to support a call for a council. When the other rulers agreed, the rival popes had to accept. The third papal claimant, John XXIII (r. 1410–1415), even felt compelled to call a general council of the church. Resolution of the schism was but one of the items on the agenda of the churchmen attending the council, which met from 1414 to 1417 in the German imperial city of Constance under the auspices of Sigismund.

Sigismund needed a council because he faced a religious civil war in Bohemia, the most important part of his family's traditional lands (see Map 11.3). Bohemia and its capital, Prague, were Czech-speaking. But Prague was also the seat of the Luxembourg dynasty of German emperors and the site of the first university in the German world. The issue centered on the preaching of Czech reformer John Hus (ca. 1370–1415). As preacher in the Bethlehem Chapel in Prague and theologian at the university, Hus was the natural spokesman for the non-German townsmen in Prague and the Czech minority at the university. His criticisms of the church hierarchy, which in Prague was primarily German, fanned the flames of Czech national feeling. It was Sigismund's hope that a council might heal the rift within the church of Bohemia.

The council's response to the issue of heresy was based on the church's experience with heresy over the previous forty years. In the 1370s, John Wyclif (1329–1384), an Oxford theologian and parish priest, began to criticize in increasingly vitriolic terms the state of the clergy and the depredations of the church hierarchy. By 1387, Wyclif's ideas had been declared heretical and his followers suffered ecclesiastical persecution. Wyclif's criticisms had been especially dangerous because he denied the position of the priest as an interme-

diary between God and believers. Wyclif believed that the church could be at once a divine institution and an earthly gathering of individuals. Thus, in his opinion, the pronouncements of the church hierarchy had no magisterial status. Wyclif gave that special status to Scripture, to the Bible. Wyclif once claimed that he had a number of "poor priests" spreading his doctrines in the countryside. He did gather about himself followers called Lollards, who emphasized Bible-reading and popular piety and supported public preaching by women. According to one, "every true man and woman being in charity is a priest."[2] Because of their attacks on the ecclesiastical hierarchy, Lollards were popular among the nobility of England, and especially at the court of Richard II during the 1390s. In the first two decades of the fifteenth century, however, their influence waned.

Wyclif's most lasting impact was probably his influence on John Hus and the Husite movement that he inspired. Following the teachings of Wyclif, Hus attacked clerical power and privileges. By 1403 the German majority in the university had condemned Hus's teaching as Wyclifite, thus initiating almost a decade of struggle between Czechs and Germans, Husites and Catholics. In an effort to break the impasse, Sigismund offered Hus a safe-conduct pass to attend the Council of Constance. The emperor fully expected some sort of reconciliation that would absolve Hus and thus reduce the possibility of civil war in Bohemia. As matters progressed, however, it became clear that the councilors and Hus himself were in no mood to compromise. The council revoked the pledge of safe conduct and ordered Hus to recant his beliefs. He refused. The council condemned him as a heretic and burned him at the stake on July 6, 1415.

Far from ending Sigismund's problems with the Bohemians, the actions of the council provided the Czechs with a martyr and hero. The Husite movement continued to gather strength. Radical Husites argued that the true church was the community of spiritual men and women. They had no use for ecclesiastical hierarchy of any kind. The German emperors were unable to defeat a united Husite movement. So from 1430 to 1433 the emperor and moderate Husites negotiated an agreement that allowed the Husites to continue some of their practices while returning to the church. The Husite war engulfed all of Bohemia and dragged on until 1436. Bohemia remained a center of religious dissent, and the memory of the execution of Hus at a church council would have a chilling effect on discussions of church reform during the Reformation in the sixteenth century.

The council was more successful in dealing with the schism, which to most Europeans seemed the most pressing issue before it. Gregory XII (r. 1406–1415), the Roman pope, soon realized that he had lost all his support. Although Pope John had convened the council, Gregory was allowed to issue a new call for the council (as a rightful pope should do). His call was immediately followed by his letter of resignation. John still hoped to survive as the one legitimately elected pope, but the council deposed him on May 29, 1415. The council also deposed Benedict III (r. 1394–1417), the pope in Avignon, in 1417. The council justified its actions in what was perhaps its most important decree, *Haec sancta synodus* (This sacred synod):

This sacred synod of Constance . . . declares . . . that it has its power immediately from Christ, and that all men, of every rank and position, including even the pope himself are bound to obey it in those matters that pertain to the faith.[3]

The Great Schism had ended. In the final sessions of the Council of Constance, Odo of Colonna, member of an old Roman noble family, was elected pope of the newly reunified church. Taking the name of Martin V (r. 1417–1431), he presided over an institution that had changed dramatically since the papacy of Boniface VIII a hundred years earlier. Popes could no longer expect to remain unchallenged if they made claims of absolute dominion similar to those made by Boniface in *Unam sanctam* (see page 388). And ecclesiastical rights and jurisdictions increasingly were matters for negotiation between popes and the governments of Europe. As we will see in Chapter 12 (see page 466) popes depended on their Italian lands for wealth and on the image of Rome for a historical explanation for their status and authority.

The Reformed Papacy

The issue of papal reform was complex. Critics agreed that the pope no longer behaved like the "Servant of the Servants of Christ" but instead acted like the "Lord of Lords." Cardinals claimed to represent the church at large as counterweights

Pope Martin Receiving the Crown from a Council Delegates to the Council of Constance stated that even the pope had to accept the decrees of a council sitting for the whole church. *(From* Chronik des Konstanzen Konzils, *1414–1418. Courtesy, Rosgartenmuseum, Constance)*

to papal abuse, but as the nobility of the church, they and other members of the hierarchy required multiple benefices to maintain their presence at the papal court. Both the cardinals and the popes viewed any reforms to the present system as potential threats to their ability to function. The council, however, recognized the need for further reforms. In the decree *Frequens* (Frequently), the council mandated that reform councils be called regularly, and a reform council met at Basel from 1431 to 1449, but with little success. It tried again to reduce papal power, but it received no support from European governments.

Because of the continuing conciliarist threat, the papacy was forced to accept compromises on the issues of reform, ecclesiastical jurisdictions and immunities, and rights to papal revenues. It continued to claim highest jurisdiction, but lay rulers viewed their own religious role as special. Various governments argued that it was they, and not the pope, who should be responsible for ecclesiastical institutions and jurisdictions within their territories.

Lay rulers focused on several issues. They wanted church officials in their territories to be from local families. They wanted ecclesiastical institutions to be subject to local laws and administration. And by the 1470s, it was clear that they wanted to have local prelates named as cardinal-protectors, churchmen who could serve as mediators between local government and the papacy. The most famous of these new political cardinals is Cardinal Thomas Wolsey of England (ca. 1470–1530), who was an important supporter of King Henry VII and chancellor of England under Henry VIII.

One of the most important compromises between the papacy and the monarchs was the Pragmatic Sanction of Bourges of 1438, by which the French crown established a claim to a church largely independent of papal influence. The agreement abolished papal rights to annates, limited appeals to the papal court, and reduced papal rights to appoint clergy within France without the approval of the local clergy or the Crown. The Pragmatic Sanction was the first of a number of claims for a unique "Gallican church," a national church free from outside interference. There were similar treaties throughout Europe. Perhaps the most momentous was a bull issued in 1478 by Pope Sixtus IV (r. 1471–1484) that allowed Ferdinand and Isabella of Aragon and Castile to institute a church court, the Spanish Inquisition, under their own authority (see page 430).

The papal concessions signaled a changed relationship between the papacy and the governments of Europe. With reduced revenues from jurisdictions, annates, and appointments, the papacy of the fifteenth century was forced to derive more and more of its revenue and influence from its traditional Papal States in central Italy. By the late 1420s, the Papal States produced about half of the annual income of the papacy. Papal interests increasingly centered on protecting the papacy's influence among the Italian states. Thus, the papacy had to deal with many of the jurisdictional, diplomatic, and military challenges that faced medieval governments.

THE CHALLENGE TO MEDIEVAL GOVERNMENTS

A lawyer who served King Philip IV of France (r. 1285–1314) observed that "everything within the limits of his kingdom belongs to the lord king, especially protection, high justice and dominion."[4] Royal officials in England and France generally believed that "liberties"—that is, individual rights to local jurisdictions—originated with the king. At almost the same time, however, an English noble challenged royal claims on his lands, saying, "Here, my lords, is my warrant," as he brandished a rusty longsword. "My ancestors came with William the Bastard [that is, with William the Conqueror in 1066] and conquered their lands with the sword, and by the sword I will defend them against anyone who tries to usurp them."[5] The old earl clearly believed that the rights and traditions of the aristocracy limited even royal attempts to centralize authority.

The issue throughout Europe in the late Middle Ages was whether central, regional, or even local authorities should dominate political and social life. In England and France traditional elites initially limited royal power, but by 1500 it was firmly re-established. From Italy through central Europe and into Scandinavia, however, late medieval monarchies found themselves hard-pressed to dominate political life. Yet as the development of the grand duchy of Tuscany, the independent feeling of the Swiss states, the free peasantry of Scandinavia, and the rise of Moscovy demonstrate, political order and stability may characterize territorial states as well as centralized monarchies.

England, France, and the Hundred Years' War

In the twelfth and thirteenth centuries, as we have seen, centralization of royal power proceeded almost without interruption. In the fourteenth century, matters changed. Charles IV of France died in 1328 without heirs, and his successor soon faced a long war that brought into question the king's control of most of France. And in England after the death of Edward I in 1307, monarchs found their power limited by forces largely beyond their control.

Fears arising from the growing power of the Crown and the weakness of an easily influenced king brought issues to a head during the reign of Edward II (r. 1307–1327). By the early fourteenth century, resident justices of the peace were replacing the expensive and inefficient eyre system of traveling justices (see page 365). In theory, they were royal officials doing the king's bidding. In reality, these unpaid local officials were modestly well-to-do gentry who were often clients of local magnates. Justices were known to use their office to carry out local vendettas and feuds and to protect the interests of the wealthy and powerful.

The barons, the titled lords of England, were interested in controlling more than just local justices. Fearing that Edward II would continue many of the centralizing policies of his father and ignore what the barons considered their traditional place as the king's natural advisers, the barons forced the king to accept the Ordinances of 1311. These statutes required a greatly expanded role for Parliament, and especially for the barons sitting in Parliament. According to the ordinances, the king could no longer wage war, leave the realm, grant lands or castles, or appoint chief justices and chancellors without the approval of the barons in Parliament. All funds raised by special taxes or subsidies were to be paid to the public Exchequer rather than into the king's private household treasury. Some of the ordinances were later voided, but the basic principle of parliamentary consent remained central to English constitutional history. In spite of Parliament's power to limit royal acts, kings used Parliament because it had the power to vote new taxes and generally did so when funds were necessary for the defense of the realm—a common occurrence during these centuries. Thus, Parliament grew in power because it usually did what the monarchy asked.

The baronial influence grew because Edward II was a weak and naive king, easily influenced by his court favorites. He suffered a humiliating defeat at the hands of the Scots at the Battle of Banockburn (1314), and his position steadily deteriorated until he was deposed in 1327 by a coalition of barons led by Queen Isabella. After a short regency, his son, Edward III (r. 1327–1377), assumed the throne. He was a cautious king, ever aware of the volatility of the baronage.

Observing the civil strife and open rebellion that characterized England in the early fourteenth

ENGLAND AND FRANCE IN THE LATE MIDDLE AGES

1259	Treaty of Paris grants Aquitaine to Henry III of England as a French fief
1311	English barons force Edward II to accept the Ordinances of 1311
1327	Parliament deposes Edward II
1328	The last Capetian king dies; French nobles elect Philip of Valois king of France (Philip VI)
1340	Edward III of England formally claims the French crown
1346	Battle of Crécy
1356	Battle of Poitiers
1399	Abdication of Richard II; accession of Henry IV
1415	Battle of Agincourt
1420	Treaty of Troyes
1422	Charles VI of France and Henry V of England die
1431	Joan of Arc is tried and executed
1453	The last battle of the Hundred Years' War
1483	Death of Edward IV; death of Edward V and his brother in the Tower of London
1485	Death of Richard III at the battle of Bosworth Fields
1491	Charles VIII reclaims French control of Brittany by marrying Anne of Brittany
1494	Charles VIII invades Italy

century, French thinkers prided themselves on the stability of the French monarchy. "The government of the earth," the royal lawyer Jean of Jandun proclaimed, "belongs rightly to the august and sovereign House of France." Nonetheless, the French monarchy in the early fourteenth century also found its prerogatives limited. As in England, there were institutional limits to the power of the kings; and again, as in England, these limits were compounded by events that were to lead to virtual civil war within the kingdom.

A series of relatively weak kings during the fourteenth century made clear the limits of French

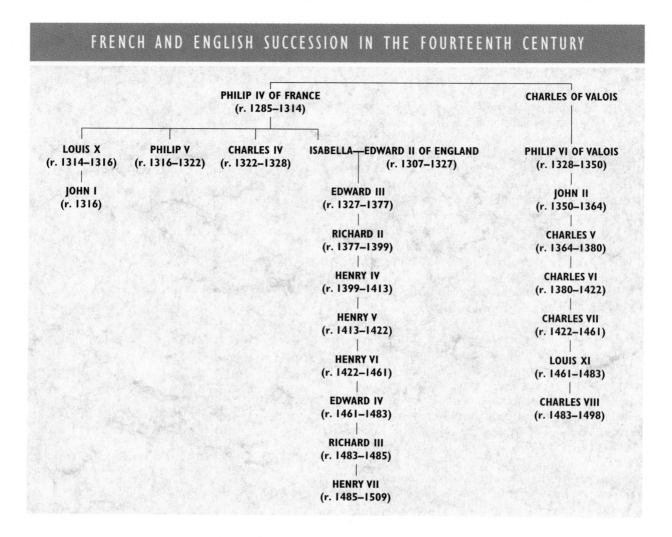

FRENCH AND ENGLISH SUCCESSION IN THE FOURTEENTH CENTURY

PHILIP IV OF FRANCE
(r. 1285–1314)

CHARLES OF VALOIS

LOUIS X
(r. 1314–1316)

PHILIP V
(r. 1316–1322)

CHARLES IV
(r. 1322–1328)

ISABELLA—EDWARD II OF ENGLAND
(r. 1307–1327)

PHILIP VI OF VALOIS
(r. 1328–1350)

JOHN I
(r. 1316)

EDWARD III
(r. 1327–1377)

JOHN II
(r. 1350–1364)

RICHARD II
(r. 1377–1399)

CHARLES V
(r. 1364–1380)

HENRY IV
(r. 1399–1413)

CHARLES VI
(r. 1380–1422)

HENRY V
(r. 1413–1422)

CHARLES VII
(r. 1422–1461)

HENRY VI
(r. 1422–1461)

LOUIS XI
(r. 1461–1483)

EDWARD IV
(r. 1461–1483)

CHARLES VIII
(r. 1483–1498)

RICHARD III
(r. 1483–1485)

HENRY VII
(r. 1485–1509)

kingship. Philip IV was succeeded by his three sons, each of whom died without a legitimate male heir. In 1328 the direct Capetian line, which had provided the kings of France since the election of Hugh Capet in 987, finally died out. The last Capetians did produce daughters, but since the fourteenth century it was customary that the French crown should pass through the male line only. Thus, the French nobility selected as king Philip of Valois (Philip VI; r. 1328–1350), a cousin of the last king through the male line. He was chosen in preference to the daughters of the last kings and, more significantly, in preference to King Edward III of England, whose mother was the daughter of the late king Philip IV.

In 1340, Edward III of England formally claimed the title "king of France." As a grandson of Philip IV, he claimed he was the rightful heir of the last Capetian king. Although Edward's claim to the French throne was certainly part of the reason for the Hundred Years' War, the issue of the crown merely worsened diplomatic and political tensions between the two monarchies. There were numerous other problems: the long-standing claims of the English kings to territories in France, the fragmented nature of the French monarchy itself, and the volatile nature of international politics.

Since the mid-thirteenth century Treaty of Paris, the French had recognized English control of the duchy of Aquitaine, which the English king

Ransoming Captives One English strategy during the first stages of the Hundred Years' War was seizing and ransoming French knights such as Charles of Blois, whose capture is illustrated here. *(Bibliothèque Nationale)*

was to hold as a vassal of the French king (see Map 11.1). This created two insoluble problems. First, the French kings claimed that as dukes of Aquitaine, the English kings owed *liege homage*—that is, while kneeling before the French king, they had to swear to provide military aid whenever the French king asked for it. The French king could use liege homage to humiliate the English king and to limit English diplomatic relations with other kingdoms. Second, the treaty implied French sovereignty over Aquitaine, an area in which the French previously had enjoyed little influence. French kings claimed the rights to hear judicial appeals from the area. To the French kings, these appeals were a normal part of the process of judicial centralization. To the English kings, they were an unacceptable subversion of English jurisdiction and a sign that acknowledging French claims in Aquitaine had been a mistake. In frustration, Edward finally made his fateful claim to the French throne, thus igniting the war.

The Hundred Years' War was a series of short raids and expeditions punctuated by a few major battles and marked off by truces or ineffective treaties. The relative strengths of the two kingdoms dictated the sporadic nature of the struggle.

With a population of about sixteen million, France was far richer and more populous than England. On at least one occasion the French managed to field an army of over 50,000; at most the English mustered only 32,000. These armies were easily the largest ever assembled by a medieval kingdom. In almost every engagement the English were outnumbered. The most successful English strategy was to avoid pitched battles and engage in a series of quick, profitable raids during which they stole what they could, destroyed what they could not steal, and captured enemy knights to hold for ransom.

The war can be divided into four stages (Map 11.1). The first stage, from 1337 to 1360, was characterized by English raids led by the crown prince Edward, later called "the Black Prince" because of the black armor he once wore. The few pitched battles, Crécy (1346) and Poitiers (1356), for example, were resounding victories for the English, who took advantage of an individualistic French chivalric ethos according to which, in the words of one knight, "Who does the most is worth the most." In both battles, smaller English armies in excellent defensive positions used longbowmen to

ENGLAND
Southampton • Calais • FLANDERS
PONTHIEU
English Channel

NORMANDY
Paris • CHAMPAGNE
BRITTANY
MAINE HOLY
ANJOU ROMAN
TOURAINE BURGUNDY EMPIRE
POITOU
AUVERGNE
AQUITAINE
Bordeaux • DAUPHINÉ
Saint-Sardos •
GASCONY LANGUEDOC
• Toulouse
SPAIN
1337
(before the Battle of Crécy)
  English holdings
  French holdings
  Extent of English holdings
  after Treaty of Paris, 1259
Mediterranean Sea

ENGLAND
Calais • FLANDERS
English Channel Crécy 1346

NORMANDY Rouen •
Paris • CHAMPAGNE
BRITTANY
MAINE HOLY
ANJOU ROMAN
TOURAINE BURGUNDY EMPIRE
Poitiers 1356
POITOU
AUVERGNE
AQUITAINE
Bordeaux • DAUPHINÉ
GASCONY LANGUEDOC
• Toulouse
SPAIN
1360
(after the Battle of Poitiers)
  English holdings
  French holdings
  ✕ Major battles
Mediterranean Sea

ENGLAND
Calais • FLANDERS HOLY
Agincourt 1415 ROMAN
English Channel EMPIRE

Rouen •
Reims •
NORMANDY Paris • CHAMPAGNE
BRITTANY Domrémy •
MAINE Orléans •
ANJOU
Bourges • DUCHY OF COUNTY OF
TOURAINE BURGUNDY BURGUNDY
POITOU
AUVERGNE
AQUITAINE
Bordeaux • DAUPHINÉ
GASCONY LANGUEDOC
• Toulouse
SPAIN
ca. 1429
(after the siege of Orléans)
  English holdings
  French holdings
  Burgundian lands allied
  with England to 1435
  ✕ Major battle
Mediterranean Sea

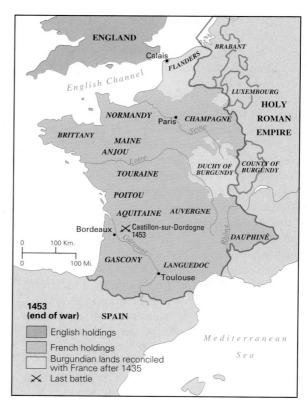

ENGLAND
Calais • FLANDERS BRABANT
English Channel
LUXEMBOURG
HOLY
NORMANDY Paris • CHAMPAGNE ROMAN
EMPIRE
BRITTANY
MAINE DUCHY OF COUNTY OF
ANJOU BURGUNDY BURGUNDY
TOURAINE
POITOU
AQUITAINE AUVERGNE
Bordeaux • Castillon-sur-Dordogne 1453 DAUPHINÉ
GASCONY LANGUEDOC
• Toulouse
1453 SPAIN
(end of war)
  English holdings
  French holdings
  Burgundian lands reconciled
  with France after 1435
  ✕ Last battle
Mediterranean Sea

their best advantage. In the second phase of the war, from 1360 to 1396, careful French leaders managed to regain control of much of the land they had lost. Edward III's grandson, Richard II (r. 1377–1399), could not afford the expensive French war and in 1396 signed an unpopular truce. Three years later he was forced to abdicate; he died, probably murdered, a year later.

The most fateful shift occurred in the third stage, from 1396 to 1422. Because King Charles VI (r. 1380–1422) of France suffered bouts of insanity throughout his long reign, effective French resistance to the English was almost impossible. Political power fell into the hands of dukes of Burgundy and of Orléans, whose political maneuvering led to civil war in France. With the aid of the Burgundian factions, the English king Henry V (r. 1413–1422) renewed his family's claim to the French throne. At Agincourt in 1415, the English (led this time by Henry) again enticed a larger French army into attacking a fortified English position, and again a hail of arrows from English longbows shattered the advance. With Burgundian aid, Henry gained control over Normandy, Paris, and much of northern France. By the terms of the Treaty of Troyes (1420), Henry married Catherine, the daughter of Charles VI, and became the heir to the French throne. A final English victory seemed assured, but both Charles VI and Henry V died in 1422, leaving the infant Henry VI with claims to both kingdoms.

The kings' deaths ushered in the final stage of the war, the French reconquest, from 1422 to 1453. In 1428, military and political power seemed firmly in the hands of the English and the great aristocrats. Charles VI's successor, the dauphin (or crown prince) Charles VII (r. 1422–1461), was derisively called "the king of Bourges," after the town south of the Loire where he remained under the protection and virtual control of a court faction. Yet in a stunning series of events, the French were able to reverse the situation.

In 1429, with the aid of the mysterious Joan of Arc (d. 1431), the king was able to raise the Eng-

Map 11.1 England and France in the Hundred Years' War The succession of maps depicts both why hit-and-run tactics worked for the English early in the war and why the English were ultimately unable to defeat the French and take control of all of France.

lish siege of Orléans and begin the reconquest of the north of France. Joan was the daughter of prosperous peasants. Like other late medieval mystics she reported regular visions of divine revelation. Her "voices" told her to go to the king and aid him in driving out the English. Dressed as a man, she was Charles's most charismatic and feared military leader. With Joan's aid the king was crowned in the cathedral at Reims, the traditional site of French coronations. Joan was captured during an audacious attack on Paris itself. Charles, however, refused to ransom "the Maid," as she was known, and eventually she fell into English hands. Because of her "unnatural dress" and her claim to divine illumination, she was condemned and burned as a heretic in 1431. A heretic only to the English and their supporters, Joan almost instantly became a symbol of French resistance. Pope Calixtus III reversed the condemnation in 1456, and in 1920 she was canonized. (See the box, "The Inquisition of Joan of Arc.") The heretic became Saint Joan, patron of France.

Despite Joan's capture, the French advance continued. By 1450 the English had lost all their major centers except Calais. In 1453, the French armies captured the fortress of Castillon-sur-Dordogne in what was to be the last battle of the war (see Map 11.1). There was no treaty, only a cessation of hostilities.

The Results of the War

The war touched almost every aspect of life in late medieval Europe: political, religious, economic, and social. It ranged beyond the borders of France as Scotland, Castile, Aragon, and German principalities were drawn at various times into the struggle. French and English support for rival popes prevented early settlement of the Great Schism in the papacy (see page 398). Further, the war caused a general rise in the level of violence in society. As Henry V casually observed, "War without fire is as bland as sausages without mustard."[6] And because of the highly profitable quick raids, the war was never bland. Soldiers regularly stole or ransomed all they could take. What could not be carried was burned. During periods of truce soldiers went in search of work as mercenaries in other parts of Europe. The English mercenary Sir John Hawkwood (d. 1394), for example, finished his life as "ser Giovanni Acuto," a heralded military

The Inquisition of Joan of Arc

Between January and May 1431, Joan of Arc was investigated by an inquisitorial commission. The minutes of the trial were later translated into Latin and copies were retained by the king of England and the Dominican inquisitor, among others. An important question was whether Joan's acts had any authoritative value: Were her voices from God or the Devil? The judges wanted to demonstrate to their own satisfaction that Joan was one of "the sowers of deceitful inventions" of which the Gospels warned. They fully expected that external signs could indicate internal dispositions. She was found guilty and burned alive as a heretic.

The following memorandum is a summation of the commission's case against the maid.

You said that you wore and still wear man's dress at God's command and to His good pleasure, for you had instruction from God to wear this dress, and so you put on a short tunic, jerkin, and hose with many points. You even wear your hair cut above the ears, without keeping about you anything to denote your sex, save what nature has given you. . . . The clergy declare that you blaspheme against God, despising Him and His sacraments, that you transgress divine law, Holy Scripture and the canons of the Church, that you think evil and err from the faith, that you are full of vain boasting, that you are given to idolatry and worship of yourself and your clothes, according to the customs of the heathen.

You have declared that you know well that God loves certain living persons better than you, and that you learned this by revelation from St. Catherine and St. Margaret; also that those saints speak French, not English, as they are not on the side of the English. And since you knew that your voices were for your king, you began to dislike the Burgundians.

Such matters the clergy pronounce to be a rash and presumptuous assertion, a superstitious divination, a blasphemy uttered against St. Catherine and St. Margaret, and a transgression of the commandment to love our neighbors.

And you have said . . . that you know that all the deeds of which you have been accused in your trial were wrought according to the command of God and that it was impossible for you to do otherwise. . . . Wherefore the clergy declare you to be schismatic, an unbeliever in the unity and authority of the Church, apostate and obstinately erring from the faith. . . . [The inquisitor admonished her,] "You have believed in apparitions lightly, instead of turning to God in devout prayer to grant you certainty; and you have not consulted prelates or learned ecclesiastics to enlighten yourself: although, considering your condition and the simplicity of your knowledge, you ought to have done so."

Source: The Trial of Jeanne d'Arc, trans. W. P. Barrett (New York: Gotham House, 1932), pp. 331–338.

captain for the Italian city of Florence. Other mercenary captains pillaged freely across Europe, kidnapping municipal officials and even laying siege to entire towns in order to extort money. Truces did not necessarily mean peace in fourteenth-century Europe.

The war also helped consolidate the French monarchy's power. A key to French military successes had been the creation of a paid professional army, which replaced the feudal host and mercenary companies of the fourteenth century. Charles VII created Europe's first standing army, a cavalry of about 8000 nobles under the direct control of royal commanders. Charles also expanded his judicial claims. He and his son, Louis XI (r. 1461–1483), created new provincial parlements, or law courts, at Toulouse, Grenoble, Bordeaux, and Dijon. They also required that local laws and customs be registered and approved by these local parlements.

French kings attacked the power of the great aristocratic families in two ways. First, ducal power was based on land. In 1477, when Charles the Bold of Burgundy was killed, Louis quickly seized his duchy, ridding himself of the greatest independent power in the kingdom. The process of consolidation was completed in 1491 when Charles VIII (r. 1483–1498), Louis's son, married Anne of Brittany, the heiress of the last independent duke of Brittany.

A second key to maintaining royal influence was the rise of the French court as a political and financial center. Through careful appointments and judicious offers of annuities and honors, Charles VII and Louis XI drew the nobility to the royal court and made the nobles dependent on it. "The court," complained a frustrated noble, "is an assembly of people who, under the pretense of acting for the good of all, come together to diddle each other; for there's scarcely anyone who isn't engaged in buying and selling and exchanging . . . and sometimes for their money we sell them our . . . humanity."[7] One of Louis XI's advisers noted that Charles VII never had revenues greater than 18,000 francs in a single year but that Louis collected 4.7 million. By the end of the fifteenth century, France had recovered from the crisis of war. It was once again a strong and influential state.

In England during the fifteenth century, the Hundred Years' War became the backdrop for a series of struggles over royal power. Although the English generally agreed that the king could institute new taxes to pay for foreign wars, theorists and parliamentary leaders alike held that the king should live off the income of his traditional rights and properties and honor the influence of the aristocracy.

It was fear of the king's power that contributed to the downfall of King Richard II in 1399. Recognizing the dangers of noble influence, Richard tried to insulate himself from the peers of the realm by choosing advisers from the lesser nobility and the middle classes as well as from the peerage. Simmering unrest overflowed, and leaders of the peers captured and forced Richard to abdicate. Parliament then elected as king Henry IV (r. 1399–1413), the first of the Lancastrian line.

In the beginning the Lancastrians were quite successful. Henry IV avoided war taxes and was careful not to alienate the magnates. Henry V, perhaps the most charismatic of the late medieval English kings, gave the Lancastrians their greatest moments: the victory at Agincourt in 1415 and the Treaty of Troyes in 1420, designed to unify the French and English crowns. Within a decade, however, the French were beginning to force the English out of France, and Henry VI (r. 1422–1461) turned out to be weak-willed, immature, and prone to bouts of insanity.

The infirmity of Henry VI and the loss of virtually all French territories in 1453 led to factional battles called the Wars of the Roses—the red rose was the symbol of the Lancastrian dynasty and the white rose signified the Yorkist opposition. Edward of York eventually deposed Henry and claimed the crown for himself as Edward IV (r. 1461–1483). He faced little opposition because there seemed to be few alternatives. English public life was again thrown into confusion, however, at the death of Edward IV. The late king's brother, Richard, duke of Gloucester, claimed the protectorship over the 13-year-old king, Edward V (r. April–June 1483), and his brother. He seized the boys, who were placed in the Tower of London and never seen again. An Italian diplomat reported what little was known:

All the attendants who waited upon the king were debarred access to him. He and his brother were withdrawn into the inner apartments of the Tower proper, and day by day began to be seen more rarely behind the bars and windows till at length they ceased to appear altogether. . . . Whether, however, [the king] has been done away with, and by what manner of death, so far I have not at all discovered.[8]

Richard proclaimed himself king and was crowned Richard III (r. 1483–1485). The new king attempted to consolidate his control at the local level. He withstood early challenges to his authority but in 1485 was killed in the battle of Bosworth Fields, near Coventry, by Henry Tudor, a leader of the Lancastrian faction. Henry married Elizabeth, the surviving child of the late Edward IV. Symbolically at least, the struggle between the rival claimants to the crown appeared over.

Like his predecessor, Edward IV, Henry VII (r. 1485–1509) recognized the importance of avoiding war and taxation. Like the French kings, he created a patronage network of local officials to secure allies for his dynasty. Royal power, however, was not based on a transformation of the institutions of government. Following Edward IV's example, Henry VII controlled local affairs through the traditional system of royal patronage. He also imitated Edward in emphasizing the dignity of the royal office. Though careful with his funds, he was willing to buy jewels and clothing if they added to the brilliance of his court. As one courtier summed up his reign, "His hospitality was splendidly generous. . . . He knew well how to maintain his majesty and all which pertains to kingship." Henry's skill in marriage politics gave England ties with Scotland and Spain. He arranged the marriage of his daughter, Margaret Tudor, to James IV of Scotland and the marriage of his sons, Arthur and (after Arthur's death) Henry, to Catherine of Aragon, daughter of the Spanish rulers Ferdinand and Isabella.

The English monarchy of the late fifteenth century was not a new departure. The success of Henry VII was based on several factors: the absence of powerful opponents; lowered taxation, the result of twenty-five years of peace under Henry VII; and the desire, shared by ruler and ruled alike, for an orderly realm built on the assured succession of a single dynasty.

Italy

Compared to France and England, fourteenth- and fifteenth-century Italy was a land of cities. In northern Europe a town of over 20,000 or 30,000 people was unusual. The 100,000 or more people who lived in London or Paris in the fourteenth century made these capitals unlike any other cities north of the Alps. Yet at one time or another in the late Middle Ages, Milan, Venice, Florence, and Naples all had populations near or exceeding 100,000, and countless other Italian towns boasted populations of over 20,000. In comparison to northern Europe, however, the Italian peninsula seemed a power vacuum. The northern and central provinces largely belonged to the kingdom of Italy and thus were part of the Holy Roman Empire. Most of central Italy was part of the Papal States. Actual power, however, was most often located in Italy's flourishing towns. Political life revolved around the twin issues of who should dominate town governments and how could they learn to coexist peacefully.

By the late thirteenth century, political power in most Italian towns was divided among three major groups. The first was an old urban nobility that could trace its wealth back to grants of property and rights from kings, emperors, and bishops in the tenth and eleventh centuries. They were joined by a second group, the merchant families who enriched themselves in the twelfth and thirteenth centuries as Italians led the European economic expansion into the Mediterranean. These old urban groups were challenged in the first decades of the thirteenth century by modest artisans and merchants who had organized trade, neighborhood, or militia groups and referred to themselves as the *popolo*, that is, "the people" (see page 335). In many towns they elected a virtual parallel government headed by their own small council of elders, or *Anziani*. As early as 1198, the popolo of Milan had elected their own Captain of the People—an officer who served much as did the podestà, except in the interest of the people. The rise of the popolo brought little peace, however. "War and hatred have so multiplied among the Italians," observed one Florentine, "that in every town there is a division and enmity between two parties of citizens." It was not simply a fight divided along class lines. Townsmen gathered themselves together in factions based on wealth, family, profession, neighborhood, and even systems of clientage that reached back into the villages from which many of the townsmen had come. In times of unrest, urban nobles who held fortresses and even whole districts in the countryside often called on their peasants to form a band that might rival the town's own militia.

Riven with factions, townsmen would often turn control of their governments over to a *signor*, that is a "lord," or "tyrant," often a local noble with a private army. In 1264, for example, Obizzo d'Este took control of the town of Ferrara. In a carefully managed assembly of the people of Ferrara, Obizzo was proclaimed to be "Governor and Ruler and General and permanent Lord of the City of Ferrara." The rise of the Este lords of Ferrara seemed peaceful, but the force on which the transformation rested was clearer in Mantua. "[Pinamonte Bonacolsi (d. 1293)] usurped the lordship of his city and expelled his fellow-citizens and occupied their property," according to a chronicler. "And he was feared like the devil."[9] Once firmly in power, tyrants often allowed the town's government to continue to function as it had, requiring only that they should control all major political appointments.

The great republics of Venice and Florence escaped domination by signori, but only by undertaking significant constitutional change. In both republics political life was disrupted by large numbers of new citizens—immigrants drawn by the relatively greater economic opportunities in the towns and recently enriched merchants and speculators who demanded a voice in government. In 1297, reacting to increased competition for influence, the Venetian government enacted the so-called Closing of the Grand Council. The act guaranteed the political rights of the patriciate, the families who had held office during the late thirteenth century. Although the act initially enlarged to about 1100 the number of families eligible for public office, its ultimate effect was to freeze out subsequent arrivals. The Venetian patriciate became a closed urban nobility. Political tensions were hidden beneath a veneer of serenity as Venetians developed a myth of public-spirited patricians who governed in the interests of all the peoples, leaving others free to enrich themselves in trade and manufacture.

In Florence, by contrast, political life was convulsed by the issue of citizenship. Violent noble families, immigrants, and artisans of modest backgrounds found themselves cut off from civic participation by the passage of a series of reforms that culminated in the Ordinances of Justice of 1293–1295. These reforms, largely promoted by wealthy guildsmen, restricted political participation in Florence to members in good standing of certain merchant and artisan guilds. Further, members of violence-prone families were defined as "Magnate" (literally "the powerful") and therefore disqualified from holding public office. The Florentine system guaranteed that real political power remained concentrated in the hands of the great families, whose wealth was based primarily on banking and mercantile investments. Political power increasingly passed to individuals who used their family, neighbors, and political clients to dominate public life. After a political and diplomatic crisis in 1434 brought on by war and high taxes, virtual control of Florentine politics fell into the hands of Cosimo de' Medici, the wealthiest banker in the city. From 1434 to 1494, Cosimo; his son, Piero; his grandson, Lorenzo; and Lorenzo's son dominated the government in Florence. Al-

The Journey of the Magi The story of the journey of the Magi to Bethlehem to find the baby Jesus seemed a perfect image of the power and wisdom of rulers. This painting of the Magi was commissioned for the private chapel of Cosimo de' Medici, the de facto ruler of Florence. *(Palazzo Medici Riccardi, Florence/Art Resource, NY)*

ways careful to appease Florentine republican traditions, Medici control was virtually as complete as that of the lords of towns like Ferrara or Milan.

In the fifteenth century, the great towns of Italy dominated their lesser neighbors. The aristocratic Visconti family had taken control of Milan by the early fourteenth century and secured the title of duke. In the late fourteenth and fifteenth centuries the Viscontis and later their Sforza successors made marriage alliances with the French crown and created a splendid court culture in Milan. In a series of wars between the 1370s and 1450s, the dukes of Milan expanded their political control throughout most of Lombardy, Liguria, and, temporarily, Tuscany—the environs of Florence itself. It seemed to many that the Milanese were poised to unify all Italy under their control.

Republican Florence and Venice followed similar policies in dealing with warfare and competition with other states. Although Florentines maintained that they were protecting Florentine and Tuscan "liberty" against the Milanese invaders, their interests went beyond simple defense. Relations among Milan, Venice, Florence, Rome, and Naples were stabilized by the Peace of Lodi and the creation of the Italian League in 1454. In response to endemic warfare in Italy and the looming threat of the Ottoman Turks in the eastern Mediterranean (see page 423), the five powers agreed to the creation of spheres of influence that would prevent any one of them from expanding at the expense of the others. Despite several short wars, the league managed to avoid large-scale territorial changes from 1454 until 1494. Venice, Milan, and Florence were thus free to integrate much of northern and central Italy into what would become the Venetian republic and the duchies of Lombardy and Tuscany.

The limits of these territorial states of Italy became clear when King Charles VIII of France invaded Italy in 1494. French kings had hereditary claims to the duchy of Milan and to the kingdom of Naples, but an invitation from Ludovico Sforza of Milan finally enticed Charles to claim Naples.

The French invasion devastated Italy by touching off a series of wars called the Habsburg-Valois Wars. French control was immediately challenged by the Spanish, who themselves made claims on the south and much of Lombardy. The cost of warfare kept almost all governments in a state of crisis. Unrest brought on by the invasion allowed Pope Alexander VI (r. 1492–1503) to attempt to create a state for his son, Cesare Borgia (1475–1507), in central Italy.

In Florence, the wars destroyed the old Medici-dominated republic and brought in a new republican constitution. Fearing the French invaders, Piero de' Medici illegally surrendered key fortresses to Charles's army. Angry Florentines considered Piero's acts treasonous. Piero had little choice but to leave in order to avoid prosecution.

Anti-Medici republicans realized that their previous government had been a sham, with elections manipulated by the Medicis and their party. Reformers were initially led by the popular Dominican preacher Girolamo Savonarola (1452–1498). In the constitutional debates after 1494, Savonarola argued that true republican reform required a thoroughgoing religious reform of society. Gangs of youth flocked to his cause, attacking prostitutes and homosexuals. Many of his followers held "bonfires of vanities," burning wigs, silks, and other luxuries. In 1498, when his followers had lost influence in the government, Savonarola was arrested, tortured, and executed.

In spite of reforms, new fortresses, and a citizen militia, the Florentine government was unable to save itself from papal and imperial opposition. In 1512 the Medicis returned under papal and imperial protection. First treated as the leading citizens of Florence and as the emperor's allies in central Italy, the Medicis were later named dukes and then grand dukes of Tuscany. The grand duchy of Tuscany remained an independent, integrated, and well-governed state until the French Revolution of 1789. Venice also managed to maintain its republican form of government and its territorial state until the French Revolution; but, like the dukes of Tuscany, the governors of Venice were no longer able to act independently of the larger European powers.

The Habsburg-Valois Wars continued for over a half-century, ending with the Treaty of Cateau-Cambrésis in 1559, which left the Spanish kings in control of Milan, Naples, Sardinia, and Sicily. Thus, war and the political integration of the fifteenth century destroyed the tiny city-republics and left the remaining territorial states in a position where they could no longer act independently of foreign powers.

Germany and Switzerland

The issue of central versus local control played a key role in German affairs as well. The kingdom of Germany, or the Holy Roman Empire, of the late Middle Ages was dramatically different from the empire of the early thirteenth century (see pages 356–359). Emperors were unable to make claims to lands and jurisdictions outside Germany. And within Germany, power shifted to the east. Imperial power had previously rested on lands and castles in southwestern Germany. These strongholds melted away as emperors willingly pawned and sold the traditional crown lands in order to build up the holdings of their own families. Emperor Henry VII (r. 1308–1313) and his grandson, Charles IV (r. 1347–1378), for example, pawned and sold imperial lands west of the Rhine in order to secure the house of Luxemburg's claims to the crown of Bohemia and other lands in the east. The Habsburgs in Austria, the Wittelsbachs in Bavaria, and a host of lesser families staked out claims to power and influence in separate parts of the empire. As a result, Germany was becoming a loose collection of territories.

The local power of regional authorities in the empire was further cemented by the so-called Golden Bull of 1356, the most important constitutional document of late medieval German history. In it, Emperor Charles IV declared that henceforth the archbishops of Cologne, Mainz, and Trier plus the secular rulers of the Rhenish Palatinate, Saxony, Brandenburg, and Bohemia would be the seven electors responsible for the choice of a new emperor. The proclamation recognized the major political powers and defined a procedure for election. But it did not solve the inherent weakness of an electoral monarchy. Between the election of Rudolph of Habsburg in 1273 and 1519, there were fourteen emperors from six different dynasties, and only once, in 1378, did a son follow his father. The contrast between Germany and the monarchies of Iberia, France, and England is striking. By 1350, Germany had no hereditary monarchy, no common legal system, no common coinage, and no representative assembly. Political power rested in the hands of the territorial princes.

Territorial integration was least effective in what is now Switzerland, where a league of towns, provincial knights, and peasant villages successfully resisted a territorial prince. The Swiss Confederation began modestly enough in 1291 as a voluntary association to promote regional peace. In 1386 forces of the confederation defeated and killed Duke Leopold of Austria, who had claimed jurisdiction over the area governed by the confederation. By 1410, the confederation had conquered most of the traditionally Habsburg lands in the Swiss areas. By the 1470s the Swiss had invented the myth of William Tell, the fearless woodsman who refused to bow his head to a Habsburg official, as a justification for their independent and anti-aristocratic traditions. Their expansion culminated with the Battle of Nancy in Lorraine in 1477, when the Swiss infantry defeated a Burgundian army and killed Charles the Bold, the duke of Burgundy. From then on, the Swiss maintained their independence, and "Turning Swiss" became a battle cry for German towns and individuals who hoped to slow territorial integration.

Scandinavia and Eastern Europe

As in the rest of Europe, public authority in Scandinavia and eastern Europe depended to a large extent on relations among kings, their wealthy elites, and their powerful neighbors. In the fifteenth century, the Scandinavian kingdoms of Denmark, Sweden, and Norway—like the Swiss Confederation—lay open to economic and political influences from Germany. German merchants traded throughout the area, and German nobles sought to influence political life in the kingdoms. The Scandinavian aristocracy, however, especially in Denmark, remained wary of German interests. Scandinavian elites tended to intermarry and arrange themselves against the Germans.

In Denmark, rulers sought accommodations with the nobles and powerful cities of northern Germany. In Sweden and Norway, the situation was complicated by the fact that there was no nobility in the feudal sense of a class of vassals bound to a lord by an oath of homage. Aristocrats were merely leading landowners. Both they and the peasantry were traditionally represented in the Riksdag in Sweden and the Storting in Norway, popular assemblies that had the right to elect kings, authorize taxes, and make laws. The elites of Scandinavia spoke similar Germanic languages and had close social and economic ties with each other. Thus, it is not surprising that the crowns of the three kingdoms were joined during short periods of crisis. In 1397, the dowager Queen Margaret of Denmark was able to unite the Scandinavian crowns by the Union of Kalmar, which would nominally endure until 1523.

The political fluidity of Scandinavia was also typical of the Slavic East. German Teutonic knights controlled Prussia and, under the pretext of converting their pagan neighbors to Christianity, sought to expand eastward against the kingdom of Poland and the Lithuanian state. The conversion of the Lithuanian rulers to Christianity slowed and finally halted the German advance to the east. More serious for the knights was their defeat in 1410 at Tannenberg Forest in Prussia by a Polish-Lithuanian army led by Prince Vytautus (r. 1392–1439) of Lithuania. The reign of Prince Vytautus represented the high point of Lithuanian dominion. He ruled much of modern Poland and western Russia as well as modern Lithuania.

During the fifteenth century, Lithuania faced a formidable new opponent, the grand duchy of Moscow. Since the Mongol invasions in the thirteenth century, various Russian towns and principalities had been part of a Mongolian sphere of influence. With the waning of Mongol control, however, the Muscovites annexed other Russian territories. By 1478, Ivan III (r. 1462–1505), called "the Great," had taken control of the famed trading center of Novgorod. Two years later he was powerful enough to renounce Mongol overlordship and refuse further payments of tribute. After marriage to an émigré Byzantine princess living in Rome, Ivan began to call himself "Tsar" (Russian for "Caesar"), implying that in the wake of the Muslim conquest of Constantinople, Moscow had become the new Rome.

The stability resulting from the rise of Moscow enabled itinerant Russian warriors called *boyars* to transform themselves into landed aristocrats. The boyars came to play a dominant political, institutional, and legal role in provincial society through their control of provincial assemblies, or dumas. They used their political power to dominate the countryside and force formerly free peasants into a harsh serfdom from which the Russian peasantry would not emerge until the nineteenth century. It is too early to speak of a Russian national state, yet by 1500 the seeds of Russian dominion were clearly sown.

By 1500 it did seem that the French king's lawyer's claim that all within the kingdom belonged to the king was finally accepted. With the exception of Italy and Germany, central monarchies emerged from the wars of the fourteenth and fifteenth centuries much stronger. The Hundred Years' War and the resulting disorganization and unrest in France and England seemed to strike at the heart of the monarchies. But through the foundation of standing armies and the careful consolidation of power in the royal court, both countries seemed stronger and more able to defend themselves after the war. And as the Italians learned

in the wars following the French invasion of 1494, small regional states were no match for the monarchies. In part, Italians found that the economic and social changes of the late Middle Ages favored northern Europe rather than the regional governments of Italy.

ECONOMY AND SOCIETY

After nearly three centuries of dramatic growth, European society in 1300 was overpopulated and threatened by drastic economic and social problems. Estimates of Europe's population in 1300 have ranged from about 80 million to as high as 100 million. Levels would not be this high again for over two hundred years. Opportunities dwindled because of overpopulation, war, and epidemics. These shocks brought changes in trade and commerce. Lowered population, deflation, and transformed patterns of consumption also altered the nature of agriculture, which was still the foundation of the European economy. Changes brought on by wars, plagues, and religious controversy affected the structure and dynamics of families, the organization of work, and the culture in many parts of Europe.

The Black Death and Demographic Crisis

People in many parts of Europe were living on the edge of disaster in 1300. Given the low level of agricultural technology and the limited resources available, it became increasingly difficult for the towns and countryside to feed and support the growing population. The nature of the problem varied from place to place. There is evidence of a crisis of both births and deaths.

Growing numbers of people competed for land to farm and for jobs. Farm size declined throughout Europe as parents divided their land among their children. Rents for farmland increased as landlords found they could play one land-hungry farmer off against another. Competition for jobs kept wages low, and when taxes were added to high rents and low wages, many peasants and artisans found it difficult to marry and raise families. Thus, because of reduced opportunities brought on by overpopulation, poor townsmen and peasants tended to marry late and have small families.

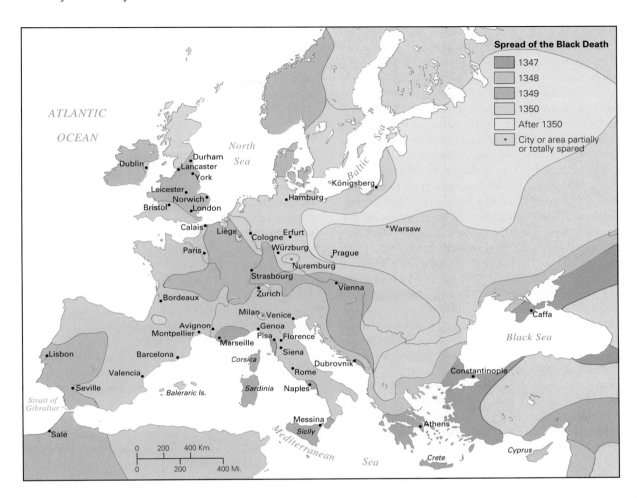

Map 11.2 The Progress of the Black Death The Black Death did not advance evenly across Europe; rather, as is clear from the dates at which it struck various regions, it followed the main lines of trade and communication.

More dramatic than this crisis of births were the famines that occurred in years of bad harvests. The great famine of 1315–1322 marks a turning point in the economic history of Europe. Wet and cold weather ruined crops in much of northern Europe. Food stocks were quickly exhausted, and mass starvation followed. People died so quickly, English chroniclers reported, that no one could keep up with the burials. At Ypres, in Flanders, 2800 people (about 10 percent of the population) died in just six months. And shortages continued. Seven other severe famines were reported in the south of France during the fourteenth century.

If Europe's problem had merely been one of famine brought on by overpopulation, recovery

should have been possible. But, because of the return of a deadly epidemic disease, the economy did not recover. In 1348 bubonic plague returned to western Europe for the first time in six hundred years. Genoese traders contracted the plague in Caffa on the Black Sea coast. Infected sailors carried the disease south into Egypt and west to Sicily and then on to Genoa and Venice. From there it followed established trade routes first into central Italy and later to the south of France, the Low Countries, England, and finally through the North and Baltic Seas into Germany and the Slavic lands to the east (Map 11.2).

The bacillus that caused "the great Mortality," as contemporaries called it, was *Yersinia pestis*. In its bubonic form, the plague attacks the lymphatic system, bringing painful, discolored swelling under the armpits and in the groin or lower abdomen. Some who survived the first days of high fever and internal hemorrhaging caused by the swellings recovered from the bubonic plague. No one, however, survived the rarer pneumonic or septicemic forms of the plague, which attacked the lungs and circulatory system. Mortality rates varied, but generally 60 percent or more of those infected died. In the initial infestation of 1348–1351, from 25 to 35 percent of Europe's population may have died. In some of Europe's larger cities the figures may have risen to as high as 60 percent. In Florence, the population probably declined from about 90,000 to 50,000 or even less. (See the box, "The Black Death.") And the nearby town of Siena likely fared even worse, with a total mortality of 55 percent in the town and its suburbs.

After the initial outbreak, the plague returned again in 1363, and then for three centuries thereafter almost no generation could avoid it. Less is known about the plague in Muslim lands and in the eastern Mediterranean, but the situation seems to be similar to the European experience. Because the plague tended to carry off the young, the almost generational return of the disease accounts for the depressed population levels found in many parts of Europe and western Asia until the late seventeenth or eighteenth century.

Lacking an understanding of either contagion or infection, fourteenth-century doctors depended on traditional theories inherited from the Greeks, especially the work of Galen. In Galenic medicine good health was a condition that depended on the proper balance of hot and cold, moist and dry bodily fluids, or humors. It was believed that this balance could be upset by corrupt air, the movements of planets, and even violent shifts in emotions. Without a clear understanding of the biological nature of the disease and lacking modern antibiotics, Europeans were unable to treat plague effectively. Yet in the fifteenth and sixteenth centuries, as the rhythms of the plague infestations became clearer, towns and, later, territorial governments perceived the contagious nature of the disease. Officials instituted increasingly effective quarantines and embargoes to restrict the movement of goods and people from areas where the plague was raging.

Alongside medical theory, however, another class of explanations developed. Taking a lead from miracle stories in which Jesus linked illness and sin, many Christians considered the "great Mortality" a signal of the end of the world or at least a sign of the severe judgment of God on a sinful world. A traditional religious response was to urge various moral reforms or penitential acts—charitable gifts, special prayers, processions. (See the feature, "Weighing the Evidence: A Painting of the Plague," on pages 434–435.) Women were often thought to be a source of moral pollution and hence one of the causes of God's wrath. In Muslim Egypt women were ordered off the streets; in Christian Europe prostitutes were driven out of towns.

A movement of penitents called "flagellants" arose in Hungary and spread quickly into Germany and across France and the Low Countries. These men and women moved from town to town urging repentance and social and political reconciliation. In an imitation of Christ's life and sufferings, they ritually beat ("flagellated") themselves between the shoulders with metal-tipped whips. The flagellants, in their quest for a purer, truly Christian society, brought suspicion on all those who were not Christian or were otherwise suspect.

In some parts of Europe there were murderous attacks on outsiders, especially lepers and Jews, who were suspected of spreading the contagion in an attempt to bring down Latin Christian civilization. Like many of the anti-Semitic myths, the stories of Jewish poisoners seemed to arise in the south of France and spread in their most virulent forms to German towns along the Rhine. In many Rhineland towns, the entire Jewish population was put to the sword. In Strasbourg, attacks on Jews even preceded the arrival of plague. Except in a few districts, officials opposed attacks on Jews, lepers, and heretics. After a few months of violence, the flagellants and the leaders of the religious riots were driven from towns.

It was a commonplace among contemporary chroniclers that "so many did die that everyone thought it was the end of the world." Yet it was the young, the elderly, and the poor—those least likely to pay taxes, own shops, or produce new children—who were the most common victims. Even in towns like Florence, however, where mortality rates were so high, recovery was rapid. Government offices were closed at most for only a few

The Black Death

The plague of 1348 in Florence dominates the popular tales that form the bulk of the **Decameron**. *Giovanni Boccaccio (1313–1375) probably described the plague to emphasize how unusual and irresponsible his protagonists—young men and women who fled Florence, abandoning family and friends—really were. If so, Boccaccio failed miserably. Readers celebrate the fresh and lively irony of the tales. Moreover, Boccaccio's description fits with everything scholars have since discovered about the first infestation of the plague in Italy. Boccaccio's descriptions make clear not just what happened, but how the events affected the sensibilities of the people.*

This pestilence was so powerful that it was transmitted to the healthy by contact with the sick, the way a fire close to dry or oily things will set them aflame. And the evil of the plague went even further: not only did talking to or being around the sick bring infection and a common death, but also touching the clothes of the sick or anything touched or used by them seemed to communicate this very disease to the person involved. . . . There came about such fear and such fantastic notions among those who remained alive that almost all of them took a very cruel attitude in the matter; that is, they completely avoided the sick and their possessions; and in so doing, each one believed that he was protecting his good health.

There were some people who thought that living moderately and avoiding any excess might help a great deal in resisting this disease, so they gathered in small groups and lived entirely apart from everyone else. . . . Others thought the opposite: they believed that drinking excessively, enjoying life, going about singing and celebrating, and satisfying in every way the appetites as best one could, laughing, and making light of everything that happened was the best medicine for such a disease. . . . And in this great affliction and misery of our city the revered authority of the laws, both divine and human, had fallen and almost completely disappeared, for like other men, the ministers and executors of the laws were either dead or sick or so short of help that it was impossible for them to fulfill their duties. . . .

Others were of a crueler opinion (though it was, perhaps, a safer one): they maintained that there was no better medicine against the plague than to flee from it. . . . This disaster had struck such fear into the hearts of men and women that brother abandoned brother, uncle abandoned nephew, sister left brother, and very often wife abandoned husband and—even worse, almost unbelievable—fathers and mothers neglected to tend and care for their children as if they were not their own. . . . And since the sick were abandoned by their neighbors, their parents, and their friends and there was a scarcity of servants, a practice almost unheard of before spread through the city: when a woman fell sick, . . . she did not mind having a manservant (whoever he might be, no matter how young or old he was), and she had no shame whatsoever in revealing any part of her body to him. . . .

Source: Giovanni Boccaccio, *The Decameron*, trans. Mark Musa and Peter Bondanella (New York: New American Library, 1982), pp. 6–10.

weeks; markets reopened as soon as the death rate began to decline. And within two years tax receipts were back at preplague levels. Below the surface, however, plague, population decline, and religious unrest fueled the economic and social transformations of the late Middle Ages.

Patterns of Economic Change

In the aftermath of plague, the economy of Europe changed in a number of profound ways. As we will see, Italy's domination of the European economy was challenged by the growth of trade and manufacturing in many parts of Europe. Further, Italian bankers came to face competition from equally astute local bankers. These changes in the structure of economic life were accompanied by other economic disruptions brought on by plague and population decline.

Discussions of the economy must begin with Italy. It was the fulcrum of the international economy in 1300. Italian merchants sold woolens produced in Flanders and Italy to Arab traders in North Africa, who sold them along the African coast and as far south as the Niger Delta. The Italians used the gold that they collected in payment to buy spices and raw materials in the East, which they resold at the regional fairs of northern Europe.

Because of their expertise in moving bullion and goods and their ready sources of capital, Italian merchants like the Ricciardis of Lucca were ideal bankers and financial advisers to the papacy and European kings, who often needed immediate sources of capital. Kings normally were expected to live off their own estates or a series of traditional tolls and duties. They had few cash reserves. In time of war, when they needed money quickly, they tended to trade the rights to various revenues to Italian bankers, who had cash at hand.

Merchants from Cremona, Genoa, Florence, and Siena also forged commercial agreements with the kings of France, Aragon, and Castile and with the papacy. The great merchant-banking houses consisted of loose associations with agents in most of the cities of Europe. In the course of their operations they developed a network of couriers to move business mail, as well as bookkeeping procedures and techniques for the quick transfer of funds over long distances.

The most powerful bank in fifteenth-century Europe was the Medici bank of Florence. Founded in 1397 by Giovanni de' Medici (1360–1429), the bank grew quickly because of its role as papal banker. Medici agents transferred papal revenues from all parts of Europe to Rome and managed papal alum mines, which provided an essential mineral to the growing cloth industry. Cosimo de' Medici (1389–1464), son and successor of Giovanni, formed his bank as a series of bilateral partnerships with easily controlled junior partners in other parts of Europe.

The dramatic career of the Frenchman Jacques Coeur (1395?–1456) demonstrated that by the mid-fifteenth century, Italian merchants were not the only ones who understood international trade. Af-

The Feast of Saint John the Baptist John the Baptist was the patron saint of Florence. Each year a procession in his honor included government officials, the great associations and guilds in the city, and representatives from surrounding villages. *(Scala/Art Resource, NY)*

ter making a fortune trading in southern France, Coeur managed the French royal mint and became the financial adviser of King Charles VII (r. 1422–1461). He put the French monarchy back on a solid financial footing after the Hundred Years' War, becoming in the process the wealthiest individual in France. Unsurprisingly, his wealth and influence earned him jealous enemies: He was accused of murdering the king's mistress, trading with Muslims, and stealing royal funds. In 1451 his property was confiscated, and he was jailed for a short time. He later led a papal expedition against the Turks in the Aegean, where he died.

International trade flourished in other areas besides Italy and France. By the end of the fifteenth century, Italians faced increased competition from local merchants and never managed to penetrate beyond the Rhine in Germany. Italian expertise was least influential in those regions of Europe touching the North and Baltic Seas, areas most noted for fishing (a critical source of protein for much of Europe), salt, grain, and furs. The Hanseatic League, an association of over a hundred trading cities centered on the German city of Lübeck, dominated northern commerce. By 1358 it was referred to as a "League of German Cities," and individual merchants could participate only if they were citizens of one of the member towns. In the late fourteenth and early fifteenth centuries the Hansa towns controlled grain shipments from eastern Europe to England and Scandinavia. The league's domination waned in the second half of the fifteenth century, however, as trade diversified. Dutch, English, and even south German merchants took shares of the wool, grain, and fur trades. Towns in the eastern Baltic found that their interests no longer coincided with those of the Rhineland towns that made up the Hanseatic League. Wroclaw (in modern Poland) signaled the nature of the change when it resigned from the league in 1474 to expand trade connections with the south German towns.

In contrast to Hanseatic merchants, south Germans adopted Italian techniques of trade, manufacture, and finance to expand their influence throughout central Europe. Their favored trade routes ran through Nuremberg and farther east to Wroclaw and into Lithuania and were as important as the northern routes controlled by the Hanseatic League. German merchants regularly bought spices in the markets of Venice and distrib-

uted them in central and eastern Europe. By the fifteenth century, the townsmen of south Germany also produced linen and cotton cloth, which found ready markets in central and eastern Europe.

The Fugger family of Augsburg in southern Germany, the most prosperous of the German commercial families, exemplifies this economic transformation. Hans Fugger (1348–1409) moved to Augsburg from a nearby village in the 1360s and quickly established himself as a weaver and wool merchant. By the 1470s, Hans's grandson, Jacob Fugger (1459–1525), was a dominant figure in the spice trade and also participated in a number of unusually large loans to a succession of German princes. They became leaders in the Tyrolean silver-mining industry, which expanded dramatically in the late fifteenth century. And in the early sixteenth century they handled all transfers of money from Germany to the papacy. Jacob Fugger's wealth increased fourfold between 1470 and 1500. The Fuggers were indispensable allies of the German emperors. Jacob himself ensured the election of Charles V as Holy Roman emperor in 1519, making a series of loans that allowed Charles to buy the influence that he needed to win election.

As wealthy as the great merchants were, in most parts of Europe, prosperity was still tied to agriculture and the production of food grains. In northern and western Europe, foodstuffs were produced on the manorial estates of great churchmen and nobles. These estates were worked by a combination of serfs who owed a variety of labor services and day laborers who were hired during planting and harvesting. In the aftermath of plague and population decline, landlords and employers found themselves competing for the reduced number of laborers who had survived the plague. In 1351 the English crown issued the Statute of Laborers, which pegged wages and the prices of commodities at preplague levels. According to the statute, regulation was necessary because laborers "withdrew themselves from serving great men and others unless they have living [in food] and wages double or treble of what they were [before the plague]." Government attempts to stabilize prices and control wages had little effect, however. Many large landowners gave up direct farming of their estates and instead leased out lands to independent peasant farmers, who, for the most part, worked their lands with family labor. In southwest Germany some landowners reforested their lands, hoping to take advantage of rising prices for timber and charcoal. In both cases, landlords reduced their dependence on laborers.

Cloth manufacture, not agriculture, was the part of the European economy that changed most dramatically in the late Middle Ages. First in Flanders, then later in Italy, England, and the rest of Europe, production shifted from urban workshops to the countryside. Industries in rural areas tended to be free of controls on quality or techniques. As a result, the production of light, cheap woolens, for which there was a significant demand, moved out of the cities and into the countryside. Rural production, whether in Flanders, Lombardy, or England, became the most dynamic part of the industry.

Rural cloth production, especially in southwest Germany and parts of England, was organized through the putting-out system. Merchants who owned the raw wool contracted with various artisans in the city, suburbs, or countryside—wherever the work could be done most cheaply—to process the wool into cloth. Rural manufacture was least expensive because it could be done as occasional or part-time labor by farmers, their wives, or children during slack times of the day or season. Because production was likely to be finished in the countryside (beyond guild supervision), the merchant was free to move the cloth to wherever it could most easily and profitably be sold; guild masters had no control over price or quality.

Two other developments also changed the woolen trade of the fifteenth century: the rise of Spain as an exporter of unprocessed wool and the emergence of England, long recognized as a source of prime wool, as a significant producer of finished cloth. Spain was an ideal region for the pasturing of livestock. Flocks of sheep regularly moved from mountainous summer pastures onto the plain in the late fall and winter. By the fifteenth century, highly prized Spanish wool from merino sheep was regularly exported to Italy, Flanders, and England. By 1500 there were over 3 million sheep in Castile alone, and revenues from duties on wool formed the backbone of royal finance.

In England, in contrast, economic transformation was tied to cloth production. Over the course of the late fourteenth and fifteenth centuries, wool exports declined as cloth exports rose. In 1350 the English exported just over 5000 bolts of cloth. By the 1470s exports had risen to 63,000 bolts, and

they doubled again by the 1520s. The growth of cloth exports contributed to the expansion of London. Located on the Thames River and easily reached by sea, the city was ideally placed to serve as both a political and an economic capital. During the fourteenth and fifteenth centuries, English commerce became increasingly controlled by London merchant-adventurers. Soon after 1500, over 80 percent of the cloth for export passed through the hands of the Londoners. This development, coupled with the rise of London as a center of administration and consumption, laid the foundation for the economic and demographic growth that would make London the largest and most prosperous city in western Europe by the eighteenth century.

All these patterns of economic change in the fifteenth century challenged customs and institutions by allowing new entrepreneurs into the marketplace. Patricians in many European towns, however, acted to dampen competition and preserve traditional values. Great banking families like the Medicis of Florence tended to avoid competition and concentrations of capital, because the leaders of rival banks were political and social peers. Not even the Medicis used political influence to create advantages for their own businesses. In northern Europe, governments in towns like Leiden restricted the concentration of resources in the hands of the town's leading cloth merchants. Their aim was to ensure full employment for the town's laborers, political power for the guild masters, and social stability in the town.

Full employment was the goal for men only, however. Opportunities for women declined significantly in the fifteenth century. Although men had controlled the guilds and most crafts in the thirteenth and early fourteenth centuries, women in England and many other parts of northern Europe had been actively involved in the local economy. Unlike southern Europe, where women had no public roles, some northern towns apparently even had women's guilds to protect their members' activities as artisans and even peddlers. Because they often worked before marriage, townswomen in northern Europe tended to marry at a later age than did women in Italy. Many women even earned their own marriage dowries. Since they had their own sources of income and often managed the shop of a deceased husband, women could be surprisingly independent. They were un-

Women at Work Although guild records tended to ignore the contributions of women, many women worked in their husband's shop. In this miniature, a woman is selling jewelry. Widows often managed the shops they inherited. *(Bibliothèque Nationale)*

der less pressure to remarry at the death of a spouse. Although their economic circumstances varied considerably, up to a quarter of the households in northern towns like Bern or Zurich were headed by women—almost entirely independent widows.

The fifteenth century brought new restrictions into women's lives. In England, for example, brewing ale had been a highly profitable part-time activity that women often combined with the running of a household. Ale was usually produced in small batches for household use and whatever went unconsumed would be sold. The introduction of beer changed matters. Because hops were added to beer as a preservative, it was easier to produce, store, and transport in large batches. Beer brewing became a highly profitable full-time trade, reducing the demand for the alewife's product and providing work for men as beer-makers.

At the same time the rights of women to work in urban crafts and industries were reduced. Wealthy fathers became less inclined to allow wives and daughters to work outside the home. Guilds banned the use of female laborers in many trades and severely limited the right of a widow to supervise her spouse's shop. For reasons that are not entirely clear, journeymen objected to working alongside women—perhaps because they now saw their status as employees as permanent instead of temporary. By the early sixteenth century, journeymen in Germany considered it "dishonorable" for a woman to work in a shop, even the daughter or wife of the master.

Despite the narrowing of economic opportunities for women, the overall economic prospects of peasants and laborers improved. Lowered rents and increased wages in the wake of plague meant a higher standard of living for small farmers and laborers. Before the plague struck in 1348, when grain prices were high and wages relatively low, most poor Europeans had subsisted on bread or grain-based gruel, consuming meat, fish, and cheese only a few times a week. A well-off peasant in England had lived on a daily ration of about two pounds of bread and a cup or two of oatmeal porridge washed down with three or four pints of ale; poorer peasants generally drank water except on very special occasions. After the plague, laborers were more prosperous. Adults in parts of Germany may have consumed nearly a liter of wine and a third of a pound of meat along with a pound or more of bread each day. Elsewhere people could substitute an equivalent portion of beer, ale, or cider for the wine. Hard times for landlords were good times for peasants and day laborers.

Landlords in England responded to their economic difficulties by converting their lands to grazing in order to produce for the growing woolen market and to reduce their need for labor. In parts of Italy, they invested in canals, irrigation, and new crops in order to increase profits. In eastern Europe, where landlords were able to take advantage of political and social unrest to force tenants into semi-free servile status, there was increased emphasis on commercial grain farming. This so-called second serfdom created an impoverished work force whose primary economic activity was in the lord's fields. Increasingly in the second half of the century, grains raised in Poland and Prussia found their way to markets in England and the Low Countries. Europe east of the Elbe River became a major producer of grain, but at a heavy social cost.

The loss of perhaps a third of the urban population due to the plague had serious consequences in the towns of Europe. Because of lower birthrates and higher death rates, late medieval towns needed a constant influx of immigrants in order to expand or even to maintain their population. Citizenship in most towns was restricted to masters in the most important guilds, and it was they who controlled government. In many towns, citizens constructed a system of taxation that worked to their own economic advantage and fell heavily on artisans and peasants. It was the masters of the most important guilds who were able to define working conditions in the industrialized trades, fields like metalworking and cloth production. Unskilled laborers and members of craft guilds depended for their economic well-being on personal relationships with powerful citizens who controlled the government and the markets. Peace and order in towns and in the countryside depended on a delicate balance of the interests of the well-to-do and the more humble—a balance easily destroyed by war, plague, and economic depression.

The Popular Revolts

The balance first broke in the 1330s, unleashing a wave of violence across Europe radically different from the violence of previous centuries. Private wars, vendettas, and popular outbursts had erupted in other times, but the violence, drama, and impact of the risings of the fourteenth century remain unique. Some of the revolts seemed directed at the remnants of the old feudal and manorial elites. In that respect they were, as some historians have maintained, merely "a high point in the struggle between landlords and tenants that had been going on at a local and uncoordinated level for at least two hundred years."[10] Urban revolts, however, often seemed to be popular revolutions against exploitation by the patricians and guild masters who dominated local politics and controlled the local economy. In nearly all cases, the popular risings against authorities seem to have been triggered by the breakdown of the traditional bonds that had been holding society together.

The first disturbances occurred in the industrial towns of Flanders during the 1330s. Flemish wealth was based on the manufacture of woolen cloth, which was dominated by the weavers of the towns of Ghent, Bruges, and Ypres. In 1338, just as the first battles of the Hundred Years' War were being waged, James van Artevelde was elected "captain," or emergency leader, of Ghent through the support of laborers and artisans who feared the weavers. Faced with the opposition of the local count, hostility from the other towns, and rising discontent in Ghent itself, van Artevelde found himself increasingly isolated. He was assassinated in July 1345 by local faction leaders, in an act that was as much a personal vendetta as a political statement. Politics in Ghent quickly reverted to its traditional pattern: The well-to-do were again in control.

In the aftermath of war and plague, urban and rural risings also broke out in France. Following the French disaster at Poitiers in 1356, Étienne Marcel, provost or director of the merchants of Paris, mobilized a protest movement. He advocated ordinances that resembled a French Magna Carta, providing that royal officials should be subject to the Estates General and that the Estates should control taxation. This revolution seemed too radical to conservative townsmen in the provinces. Marcel's only allies were bands of rebellious countrymen roaming the region around Paris. The rural movement, or *jacquerie* (the name comes from *jacque,* French for the "jacket" typically worn by peasants), began in response to long-standing economic and political grievances in the countryside that had been worsened by warfare. The rebels and eventually Marcel himself were isolated and then defeated by aristocratic armies.

Two decades after the defeat of the French rebels, Europe again experienced insurrections. But the risings of the 1370s and 1380s differed from the previous revolts in several significant ways. Political unrest now was much more broadly based than it had been. There were political revolutions in many German towns as members of lowly artisan guilds claimed the right to sit alongside patricians in urban governments.

In 1378 a dramatic revolt occurred in central Italy. In reaction to a costly Florentine war with the papacy, the Ciompi, unskilled workers in the woolen industry, led a popular revolution hoping to expand participation in government and limit the authority of the guild masters over semiskilled artisans and day laborers. Barely six weeks after the Ciompi risings, however, wealthy conservatives quashed the new guilds and exiled or executed the leaders of the movement, leaving political and economic power even more firmly in the hands of the patricians.

Not long after the destruction of the Ciompi, England was rocked by the Rising of 1381, often called the Peasants' Revolt despite the fact that townsmen as well as peasants participated. England seethed with unrest as a result of plague, landlord claims for traditional dues, and finally a poll tax that placed a heavy burden on the common people. To most, it seemed that England's fiscal and political problems were the responsibility of the king's evil advisers, who the poor believed supported the ambitions of the wealthy. The heart of the uprising was a revolt by rural peasants and artisans in the southeast, primarily in Kent and Essex. Popular armies led by Wat Tyler (d. 1381), who may have had some military experience, converged on London in June 1381. Tyler was murdered during a dramatic meeting with Richard II outside London, and a reaction against the rebels quickly ensued. (See the box, "The Rising of 1381.")

Most of the revolts had few lasting consequences, for the elites quickly regained control. A series of revolts in Spain, however, had long-lasting and unfortunate effects on Iberian society. In 1391 an attack on the Jews of Seville led to murders, forced conversions, and suppression of synagogues throughout Spain. In the aftermath large portions of the urban Jewish population either converted to Christianity or moved into villages away from the large commercial cities. The Jewish population in Castile may have declined by a fourth. Although the anti-Jewish feelings were expressed in religious terms, the underlying cause was anger over the economic prominence of some Jewish or *converso* (recently converted Jewish-Christian) families. After 1391, anti-Jewish feeling increasingly became racial. As one rebel said, "The converso remains a Jew and therefore should be barred from public office."[11] Antagonism against Jews and conversos continued to build until the expulsion of the Jews from Spain in 1492 (see page 429).

FORMATION OF THE OTTOMAN AND SPANISH EMPIRES

In both Iberia and the eastern Mediterranean, political integration in the fifteenth century occurred because of political changes undreamed in previous centuries. The rise of the Ottoman Empire and the unification of Spain created the two powers around which politics and diplomacy would revolve in sixteenth-century Europe.

The Ottoman Turks

In 1453, the Muslim Ottoman Turks breached the walls of Constantinople, killed Emperor Constantine XI (r. 1448–1453), and destroyed the last vestiges of the Byzantine Empire and the Roman imperial tradition that reached back to the emperor

The Rising of 1381

The author of this chronicle—probably the most complete account of the English revolt of 1381—seems to have been an eyewitness to the dramatic events in London. Like most literate writers, the chronicler seems more at home with the attitudes and opinions of civil officials and landlords than with the concerns of the "rabble."

Wherefore the commons rose against [the royal] commissioner sent to investigate [rebellious acts in the region] and came before him to tell him that he was a traitor to the king and the kingdom and was maliciously proposing to undo them by the use of false inquests taken before him. Accordingly they made him swear on the Bible that never again would he hold such sessions nor act as a justice in such inquests. . . . They proposed to kill all the lawyers, jurors and royal servants they could find. . . .

[The rebels came to London, where they executed several royal servants. They, and possibly their leader, Wat Tyler, forced the king to agree to allow them to deal "with all the traitors against him."] And they required that henceforth no man should be a serf nor make homage or any type of service to any lord, but should give four pence for an acre of land. They asked also that no one should serve any man except at his own will and by means of a regular covenant. . . .

[In a confused melee during meeting with King Richard, Tyler was stabbed.] Wat spurred his horse, crying to the commons to avenge him, and the horse carried him some four score paces and then he fell to the ground half dead. And when the commons saw him fall, and did not know for certain how it happened, they began to bend their bows and to shoot. Therefore the king himself spurred his horse, and rode out to them, commanding them that they should all come before him at the field of St. John of Clerkenwell [a few hundred yards from where Tyler was wounded]. . . .

Afterwards, when the king had reached the open fields, he made the commons array themselves on the west side. . . . [The mayor of London had Wat Tyler] carried out to the middle of Smithfield [a market area on the edge of town] . . . and had him beheaded. . . . And so ended his wretched life. But the mayor had his head set on a pole and carried before him to the king, who still remained on the field. . . . And when the commons saw that their chieftain, Wat Tyler, was dead in such a manner, they fell to the ground there among the corn, like beaten men, imploring the king for mercy for their misdeeds. And the king benevolently granted them mercy.

Source: The Anonimalle Chronicle, in R. B. Dobson, *The Peasant's Revolt of 1381* (New York: St. Martin's Press, 1970), pp. 123, 125, 128, 161, 166–167.

Augustus. The sack of Constantinople sent shock waves through Christian Europe and brought forth calls for new crusades to liberate the East from the evils of Islam. It also stirred anti-Christian feelings among the Turks. The leader of the Turkish army, Sultan Mehmed II the Conqueror (r. 1451–1481), was acclaimed the greatest of all *ghazi*—that is, a crusading warrior who was, according to a Turkish poet, "the instrument of Allah, a servant of God, who purifies the earth from the filth of polytheism [i.e., the Christian Trinity]." The rise of the Ottoman Turks led to a profound clash between Christian and Muslim civilizations.

Turks had been invited into the Balkans as allies of the Byzantine emperors. Early in the fifteenth century, they were only one, and perhaps

The Siege of Constantinople
The siege of Constantinople by the Turks required the attackers to isolate the city both by sea and by land. This miniature from the fifteenth century shows the Turkish camps, as well as the movements of Turkish boats, completing the isolation of the city. *(Bibliothèque Nationale)*

not even the greatest, of the Balkan issues that concerned Christian Europe (Map 11.3). As the power of the Turks advanced, it became clear that a variety of other factors were at play. Hungarians, Venetians, and Germans also threatened the independence of local rulers. In the 1420s, for example, as the Turks and the Hungarians fought for control of

Serbia, the Serbian king moved easily from alliance with one to alliance with the other. By changing religion, rulers often retained their political and economic influence. The Christian aristocracy of late-fifteenth-century Bosnia, for example, was welcomed into Islam and instantly created a cohesive elite fighting force for the Turks. Conversely,

Map 11.3 Turkey and Eastern Europe With the conquest of Constantinople, Syria, and Palestine, the Ottoman Turks controlled the eastern Mediterranean and dominated Europe below the Danube River. The Holy Roman emperors, rulers of Italy, and kings of Spain had to be concerned about potential invasions by land or by sea.

as Turkish power in Albania grew, one noble, George Castriota (d. 1467), known by his Turkish name Skanderbeg, reconverted to Christianity and became a leading figure in the resistance to the Turks. Only after his death were the Turks able to fully integrate Albania into their empire.

The defeat of a Christian crusading army at Varna on the Black Sea coast in 1444 virtually sealed the fate of Constantinople. It was only a matter of time before the Turks took the city. When Mehmed II finally turned his attention to Constantinople in 1453, the siege of the city took only fifty-three days. Turkish artillery breached the walls before a Venetian navy or a Hungarian army could come to the city's defense.

After the fall of Constantinople, the Turks worked to consolidate their new conquests. Ana-

tolia was the heart of the Ottoman Empire. Through alliance and conquest, Ottoman domination extended through Syria and Palestine and by 1517 to Egypt. Even the Muslim powers of North Africa were nominally under Turkish control. To the west and north of Constantinople, the Turks dominated Croatia, Bosnia, Dalmatia, Albania, eastern Hungary, Moldava, Bulgaria, and Greece. Turkish strength was based on a number of factors. The first was the loyalty and efficiency of the sultan's crack troops, the Janissaries. These troops were young boys forcibly taken from the subject Christian populations, trained in Turkish language and customs, and converted to Islam. Although they functioned as special protectors of the Christian community from which they were drawn, they were separated from it by their new faith. Because the Turkish population viewed them as outsiders, they were particularly loyal to the sultan.

The situation of the Janissaries underlines a secondary explanation for Ottoman strength: the unusually tolerant attitudes of Mehmed, who saw himself not only as the greatest of the ghazi but also as emperor, heir to Byzantine and ancient imperial traditions. Immediately after the conquest of Constantinople, he repopulated the city with Greeks, Armenians, Jews, and Muslims. Religious groups lived in separate districts centered on a church or synagogue, but each religious community retained the right to select its own leaders. Mehmed transferred the capital of the Turkish state to Constantinople. And by building mosques, hospitals, hostels, and bridges, he breathed new life into the city, which he referred to as Istanbul—that is, "the city." In the fifty years following the conquest, the population of the city grew an extraordinary 500 percent, from about 40,000 to over 200,000, making it the largest city in Europe, as it had been in antiquity. (See the box, "Encounters with the West: A European View of Constantinople.")

At a time when Christian Europe seemed less and less willing to deal with non-Christian minorities, the Ottoman Empire was truly exceptional. Christians and Jews were tolerated as long as they paid a special poll tax and accepted some Turkish supervision. Christian and Jewish leaders supervised the internal affairs of their respective communities. Muslims and non-Muslims belonged to the same trade associations and traveled throughout the empire. Mehmed quickly made trade agreements with the Italian powers in an attempt to consolidate his power. And in Serbia, Bulgaria, Macedonia, and Albania, he left in place previous social and political institutions, requiring only loyalty to his new empire.

Mehmed had to tread carefully because the Turks had a number of powerful enemies. The problems that the Ottoman Empire faced were most clear during the reign of Mehmed's son, Bayazid (r. 1481–1512). Following Turkish tradition, Mehmed had not chosen a successor but let his sons fight for control. Normally, the successful claimant achieved the throne by doing away with his closest relatives. Bayazid's brother, Jem, however, fled into the protective custody of Christian powers, where he spent the rest of his life. In times of crisis, kings and popes would threaten to fo-

ment rebellion in Ottoman lands by releasing him. Bayazid also had to worry about the Mamluk Turks, who controlled Egypt and Syria, and the new Safavid dynasty in Persia. Although both were Muslim, they were willing to join with various Christian states to reduce the power of the Ottomans. Only in the second decade of the sixteenth century, after Bayazid's son, Selim (r. 1512–1520), had defeated the Persians and the Mamluks, were the Ottomans finally safe from attack from the east or south.

The Union of Crowns in Spain

While expanding across the Mediterranean, the Turks came in contact with the other new state of the fifteenth century, the newly unified kingdom of Spain. In 1469, Ferdinand, heir to the kingdom of Aragon and Catalonia, married Isabella, daughter of the king of Castile. Five years later Isabella became queen of Castile, and in 1479, Ferdinand took control of the kingdom of Aragon (see Map 10.1 on page 354). This union of crowns would lead to the creation of a united Spain.

The permanence of the union was surprising because the two kingdoms were so different. Castile was a much larger and more populous state. It had taken the lead in the fight to reconquer Iberia and end Muslim rule (see page 332). As a result, economic power within Castile was divided among those groups most responsible for the Reconquista: military orders and nobles. The military orders of Calatrava, Santiago, and Alcantara were militias formed by men who had taken a religious vow similar to the vow taken by a monk, with an added vow to fight against the enemies of Christianity. In the course of the Reconquista the military orders assumed control of vast districts. Lay nobles who aided in the Reconquista also held large tracts of land and were very proud of their independence.

Castile's power stemmed from its agrarian wealth. During the Reconquista, Castilians took control of large regions and turned them into ranges for grazing merino sheep, producers of the prized merino wool exported to the woolen markets of Flanders and Italy. To maximize the profits from wool production, the kings authorized the creation of the Mesta, a brotherhood of sheep producers. The pastoral economy grew to the point that by the early sixteenth century there were

∾ ENCOUNTERS WITH THE WEST ∾

A European View of Constantinople

In the late fifteenth century, Italian governments began to send permanent ambassadors to foreign courts. They were the first governments to do so. Venetian ambassadors quickly earned an international reputation as careful observers of the countries to which they had been assigned. The following evaluation of the Ottoman Empire was written in 1585 by the Venetian ambassador Gianfrancesco Morosini. It is a combination of shrewd observation and praise of an alien civilization that was meant to highlight the limits of European values.

[The Turks] were organized as military squadrons or commando units until 1300 A.D., when one of their number, named Ottoman, a man of low birth, began to build a reputation as a strong and spirited leader. Shrewd and clever, he took advantage of rivalries among his people, attracted many of them to him, and led them in war and conquest, making himself master of various towns and provinces of both the Turks and their neighbors. . . .

They succeed to the throne without any kind of ceremony of election or coronation. According to Turkish law of succession, which resembles most countries' laws in this respect, the oldest son should succeed to the throne as soon as the father dies. But in fact, whichever of the sons can first enter the royal compound in Constantinople is called the sultan and is obeyed by the people and by the army. Since he has control of his father's treasure he can easily gain the favor of the janissaries and with their help the rest of the army and the civilians. . . .

The security of the empire depends more than anything else on the large numbers of land and sea forces which the Turks keep continually under arms. These are what make them feared throughout the world. The sultan always has about 280,000 well-paid men in his service. . . . These include roughly 16,000 janissaries who form the Grand Signor's advanced guard. . . .

The whole empire is inhabited by three groups of people: Turks, Moors [non-Turkish Muslims], and Christians. In Asia and Africa the Moors are more numerous than the Turks, while in Europe the largest number are Christians, almost all of whom practice the Greek rite. There are also many Jews since that is really their homeland, even though they live in it like strangers rather than natives.

In appearance they are very pious adherents of their false religion. . . . They are very regular in observing the hours of prayer and they always have the name of God on their lips, but never blaspheme. Every wealthy Turk builds a mosque, making it as splendid as he can, and provides a rich endowment for its upkeep. As a result, the mosques are kept so clean and orderly that they put us Christians to shame. . . . In addition to the mosques they also build asylums more pleasing than their own houses, and in many of these they will give food for three days to anyone who asks for it—not only Turks, but also Christians and Jews.

Source: J. C. Davis, *Pursuit of Power: Venetian Ambassadors' Reports on Spain, Turkey, and France in the Age of Philip II, 1560–1600* (New York: Harper & Row, 1970), pp. 126, 127, 129, 134–135.

nearly 3.5 million sheep in Castile. So great were the profits accruing to the Crown from the exporting of wool that all other aspects of the economy were sacrificed to the needs of the Mesta. Farmers who lived along the routes by which the vast flocks moved from mountains to the plains often lost their crops to the hungry animals. The agricultural economy was virtually extinguished in some areas.

Economic power in Castile lay with the nobility, but political power rested with the monarch. Because the nobility was largely exempt from taxation, nobles ignored the cortes, the popular assembly, which could do little more than approve royal demands. The towns of Castile were important only as fortresses and staging points for militias rather than as centers of trade and commerce. No force was capable of opposing the will of the monarch. As John II of Castile (r. 1406–1454) explained,

All my vassals, subjects, and people, whatever their estate, . . . are, according to all divine, human, . . . and even natural law, compelled and bound . . . to my word and deed. . . . The king holds this position not from men but from God, whose place he holds in temporal matters.[12]

The kingdom of Aragon was dramatically different. The center of the kingdom was Barcelona, an important trading center in the Mediterranean. In the fourteenth and fifteenth centuries the kings of Aragon concentrated their efforts on expanding their influence in the Mediterranean, south of France and Italy. By the middle of the fifteenth century the Aragonese empire included the kingdom of Naples, Sicily, the Balearic Islands, and Sardinia.

The power of the Aragonese king, in sharp contrast to the Castilian monarchy, was limited because the Crown was not unified. The ruler was king in Aragon and Navarre but was count in Catalonia. Aragon, Catalonia, and Valencia each maintained its own cortes. In each area the traditional nobility and the towns had a great deal more influence than they had in Castile. The power of the cortes is clear in the coronation oath taken by the Aragonese nobility: "We who are as good as you and together are more powerful than you, make you our king and lord, provided that you observe our laws and liberties, and if not, not."[13] The distinction with Castile could not be stronger.

The union of the crowns of Aragon and Castile did little to unify the two monarchies. By 1474, Castile and Aragon already had a long history of warfare and mutual distrust. Nobles fought over disputed boundaries, and Castilian nobles felt exploited by Aragonese merchants. Trade duties and internal boundaries continued to separate the two. The two realms even lacked a treaty to allow for the extradition of criminals from one kingdom to the other. Castilians never accepted Ferdinand as more than their queen's consort. After the death of Isabella in 1504, he ruled in Castile only as regent for his infant grand-

THE UNION OF CROWNS IN SPAIN

1469	Ferdinand of Aragon marries Isabella of Castile
1474	Isabella becomes queen of Castile
1478	Spanish Inquisition is established
1479	Ferdinand becomes king of Aragon
1492	Conquest of Granada; Columbus's first voyage; expulsion of Jews from Spain
1496	Joanna of Castile marries Philip of Habsburg
1501	Catherine of Aragon marries Arthur Tudor of England
1504	Expulsion of Muslims from Spain; death of Isabella; Ferdinand rules Castile as regent for his grandson, Charles I

son, Charles I (r. 1516–1556). "Spain" would not emerge in an institutional sense until the late sixteenth century.

Nonetheless, the reign of Isabella and Ferdinand marked a profound change in politics and society in the Iberian kingdoms. The monarchs visited all parts of their realm, reorganized municipal governments, took control of the powerful military orders, strengthened the power of royal law courts, and extended the international influence of the monarchies. Many of their actions were designed to advance the interests of Aragon in the Mediterranean. Ferdinand and Isabella married their daughter, Joanna, to Philip of Habsburg in 1496 to draw the Holy Roman Empire into the Italian wars brought on by the French invasion (see page 412). The marriage of their daughter, Catherine of Aragon, to Prince Arthur of England in 1501 was designed to obtain yet another ally against the French. Those two marriages would have momentous consequences for European history in the sixteenth century.

The reign of Ferdinand and Isabella is especially memorable because of the events of 1492. In January of that year, a crusading army conquered Granada, the last Muslim stronghold in Iberia. In March, Ferdinand and Isabella ordered the Jews of Castile and Aragon to convert or leave the kingdom within four months. In April, Isabella issued

Ferdinand and Isabella Interrogating a Jew Jews in Spain and many other parts of Europe were considered to be under the specific jurisdiction of local rulers. Jews and their converso relatives turned to the king and queen in 1492 when Jews faced the order to convert or leave the kingdom. *(Museo de Zaragoza)*

perhaps 2 percent of the population of Iberia was Jewish, and the Muslim population may have been as high as 50 percent. The various groups were inextricably mixed. The statutes of the Jewish community in Barcelona were written in Catalan rather than Hebrew. *Maranos,* Jewish converts to Christianity, and *moriscos*, Muslim converts, mixed continuously with Christians and with members of their former religions. It was difficult at times to know which religion these converts, or conversos, actually practiced. One surprised northern visitor to Spain remarked that one noble's circle was filled with "Christians, Moors, and Jews and he lets them live in peace in their faith."

This tolerant mingling of Christians, Muslims, and Jews came under attack by 1400, however. Complaints arose from a variety of sources. Many of the most important financiers and courtiers were Jews or conversos, which increased tensions among the communities. The most conservative Christians desired a community free of non-Christian influences. All three religious communities thought that there should be distinct dress and behavior that would identify each group. Christians seemed concerned that many of the conversos were likely to reconvert to Judaism, and the fear of reconversion, or "judaizing," led many to advocate the institution of the Spanish Inquisition.

Inquisitions were well known in many parts of Europe, but the Spanish Inquisition was unique because in 1478 Pope Sixtus IV placed the grand inquisitor under the direct control of the monarchs. Like most Christian rulers, Ferdinand and Isabella believed that uniform Christian orthodoxy was the only firm basis for a strong kingdom. Inquisitors attacked those aspects of converso tradition that seemed to make the conversos less than fully Christian. They were concerned that many conversos and maranos had converted falsely and were continuing to follow Jewish or Muslim ritual. The "New Christians" tended to live near their Muslim or Jewish relatives, eat the foods enjoyed in their former communities, and observe holy days, such as Yom Kippur, the Jewish day of atonement. Over four thousand converso families fled from Andalusia in southern Spain in the wake of the arrival of an inquisitor in 1490.

Because its administration, finances, and appointments were in Spanish hands, the Spanish Inquisition quickly became an important instrument for the expansion of state power. Many inquisitors

her commission authorizing Christopher Columbus "to discover and acquire islands and mainland in the Ocean Sea" (see page 487).

The conquest of Granada and the expulsion of the Jews represented a radical shift in the Spanish mentality. Until the beginning of the fifteenth century, Spain maintained a level of religious tolerance unusual in Christendom. In the fourteenth century, used their offices to attack wealthy or politically important converso families both to drive them from public life and to fill the royal treasury, which was where the estates of those judged guilty wound up. "This inquisition is as much to take the conversos' estates as to exalt the faith," was the despairing conclusion of one conversa woman.[14]

Ferdinand and Isabella seem to have concluded that the only way to protect the "New Christians" was to order all Jews who would not convert to leave the kingdom within four months. The order was signed on March 31, 1492, and published in late April after an unsuccessful attempt by converso and Jewish leaders to persuade the monarchs not to implement it.

Many Jews could not dispose of their possessions in the four months allowed and so chose to convert and remain. But it is estimated that about ten thousand Jews left Aragon and that even more left Castile. Many moved to Portugal and then to North Africa. Some went east to Constantinople or north to the Low Countries. In 1504, the expulsion order was extended to include all Muslims.

The economic and social costs of the expulsion were profound. Not every Muslim or Jew was wealthy and cultured, but the exiles did include many doctors, bankers, and merchants. Spanish culture, which had been open to influences from Muslim and Jewish sources, became less so in later centuries. After the expulsion, there opened a chasm of distrust between the "Old Christians" and the "New." As early as the first decades of the fifteenth century, some religious orders had refused to accept "New Christians." They required that their members demonstrate *limpieza de sangre,* a purity of blood. By 1500 the same tests of blood purity were extended to a majority of religious and public offices. Thus, by the end of the fifteenth century, the Iberian kingdoms had created more powerful, unified governments, but at a terrible cost to the only area in Christendom that had ever practiced religious tolerance.

SUMMARY

Europe in 1500 was profoundly different from the Europe of two centuries earlier. The economy had grown more complex in the wake of plague and demographic change. New patterns of trade and banking and new manufacturing techniques spread throughout Europe. Along with economic recovery came increased social and political consciousness, manifested in the urban and rural uprisings of the fourteenth century.

The kings of France and England, the princes and despots in Germany and Italy, and the papacy managed to overcome political and cultural crises. After the Hundred Years' War and challenges from aristocrats, townsmen, and peasants, governments grew stronger as kings, princes, and town patricians used royal courts and patronage to extend their control. Military advances in the fifteenth century, such as the institution of standing armies, gave advantages to larger governments, but the experiences of the Italian and German states demonstrated that regional powers, under certain circumstances, could remain virtually independent of royal control. Yet the strength of regional and local powers was largely overshadowed by the rise of the Turkish and Spanish empires. It was they who would dominate politics and diplomacy in the next century.

In the aftermath of schism and conciliar reform, the church also was transformed. Because of conciliar challenges to papal authority, popes had to deal much more carefully with the governments of Europe. The popes who returned to Rome from Avignon in the fifteenth century were adept at using art and literary culture to explain and magnify their court and their place in Christian history and society. Art and literature played an important role in the reform and expression of public life. It is to the role of culture that we turn in the next chapter.

NOTES

1. Quoted in Guillaume Mollat, *The Popes at Avignon, 1305–1378* (London: Thomas Nelson, 1963), p. 112.
2. Quoted in Mary Aston, *Lollards and Reformers: Images and Literacy in Late Medieval Religion* (Ronceverte, W.V.: 1984), p. 60.
3. Quoted in Francis Oakley, *The Western Church in the Later Middle Ages* (Ithaca, N.Y.: Cornell University Press, 1979), pp. 65–66.
4. Quoted in Charles T. Wood, *Joan of Arc and Richard III* (New York: Oxford University Press, 1988), pp. 56–57.
5. Quoted in Michael T. Clanchy, "Law, Government, and Society in Medieval England," *History* 59 (1974): 75.
6. A. Buchon, *Choix des Chroniques* (Paris, 1875), p. 565, as quoted in John Gillingham and J. C. Holt, eds.,

War and Government in the Middle Ages (Totowa, N.J.: Barnes & Noble, 1984), p. 85.

7. Quoted in Peter Shervey Lewis, *Later Medieval France: The Polity* (New York: Macmillan, 1968), p. 15.

8. Quoted in Jeffrey Richards, "The Riddle of Richard III," *History Today* 33 (August 1983): 20.

9. Salimbene de Adam, quoted in John Larner, *Italy in the Age of Dante and Petrarch, 1215–1380* (New York: Longman, 1980), p. 141.

10. Rodney Hilton in *The English Rising of 1381,* ed. R. H. Hilton and T. H. Aston (Cambridge, England: Cambridge University Press, 1984), p. 3.

11. Quoted in Angus MacKay, "Popular Movements and Pogroms, in Fifteenth-Century Spain," *Past & Present* 55 (1972): 52.

12. Quoted in Angus MacKay, *Spain in the Middle Ages: From Frontier to Empire, 1000–1500* (London: Macmillan, 1977), p. 137.

13. Ibid., p. 105.

14. Haim Beinart, ed., *Records of the Trials of the Spanish Inquisition in Ciudad Real,* vol. 1 (Jerusalem: The Israel Academy of Sciences and Humanities, 1974), p. 391. Trans. Duane Osheim.

SUGGESTED READING

General Surveys

Brady, Thomas A., Jr., Heiko A. Oberman, and James D. Tracy. *Handbook of European History, 1400–1600.* 2 vols. 1994–1996. An excellent collection of studies by leading scholars in Europe and North America on all aspects of the period.

Hay, Denys. *Europe in the Fourteenth and Fifteenth Centuries.* 1966. A well-written introductory survey of politics and society in Europe between 1300 and 1500; includes coverage of Scandinavia and the Slavic lands as well as the central areas of northwestern Europe.

War and Government

Allmand, Christopher. *The Hundred Years' War: England and France at War, 1300–1450.* 1988. A single-volume summary of the war and its impact on late medieval politics, government, military institutions, literature, and nationalism.

Du Boulay, F. R. H. *Germany in the Later Middle Ages.* 1983. This survey of German history designed for students emphasizes the growth of territorial governments at the expense of the central authorities.

Duby, G. *France in the Middle Ages, 987–1460.* Translated by Juliet Vale. 1991. In this general survey, France's most distinguished medievalist concentrates on social and cultural life. Includes excellent pictures, maps, and diagrams.

Goodman, A. *The New Monarchy: England, 1471–1534.* 1988. A short introduction to the changed nature of monarchy after the Wars of the Roses.

Guenée, B. *States and Rulers in Later Medieval Europe.* Trans. by Juliet Vale. 1985. The best general introduction to the nature of government in the late Middle Ages. It introduces recent trends in historical research.

Keen, Maurice H. *English Society in the Later Middle Ages, 1348–1500.* 1990. A recent general introduction to late medieval England that covers culture and religion as well as politics.

Larner, John. *Italy in the Age of Dante and Petrarch, 1215–1380.* 1980. A short introduction to the general developments in fourteenth-century Italy, treating but not concentrating on Florence and Venice.

Sumption, Jonathon. *The Hundred Years' War.* 1990. A projected multivolume history of the war. Vol. 1, *Trial by Battle,* is an excellent narrative of the background diplomacy and the first decades of the war.

Warner, Marina. *Joan of Arc: The Image of Female Heroism.* 1981. An excellent and quite readable book emphasizing the conflicting religious and political opinions about "the Maid."

Christianity and the Papacy

Cohen, J. *The Friars and the Jews: The Evolution of Medieval Anti-Judaism.* 1982. In a complex, closely argued study, Cohen describes the changed attitudes toward Jews in the thirteenth and fourteenth centuries.

Oakley, Francis. *The Western Church in the Later Middle Ages.* 1979. The best general history of the church in the late Middle Ages. Oakley gives superior treatments of the Great Schism and conciliarism.

Partner, Peter. *The Lands of St. Peter.* 1972. A thorough account of the political and diplomatic initiatives in the Papal States—the area that was the key to the practical power of the papacy.

Swanson, Ronald N. *Religion and Devotion in Europe, c. 1215–c. 1515.* 1995. A general introduction to the place of the church in social life in the late Middle Ages, with special attention to the connection of social and religious history.

Plague and Society

Abulafia, D. "Asia, Africa and the Trade of Medieval Europe." In *Cambridge Economic History.* 1987. A thorough introductory discussion of international trade in the late Middle Ages.

Carmichael, Ann G. *Plague and the Poor in Renaissance Florence.* 1985. A work directed at scholars that investigates the plague in a specific town, emphasizing the way in which the social and economic conditions that preceded the plague conditioned responses to the epidemic.

De Roover, R. A. *The Rise and Decline of the Medici Bank, 1397–1494.* 1966. Based largely on the family's business correspondence, this is a clear discussion of the business practices of this fifteenth-century bank.

Dyer, C. *Standards of Living in the Later Middle Ages: Social Change in England, c. 1200–1500.* 1989. An account that includes a sophisticated discussion of dietary changes in the wake of population decline and changed commodity prices in fifteenth-century England.

Hanawalt, Barbara, ed. *Women and Work in Pre-Industrial Europe.* 1986. Sophisticated case studies of the changing status of women's work in the late Middle Ages in England, France, and Germany.

Hatcher, J. *Plague, Population, and the English Economy, 1348–1530.* 1977. A clear discussion of the effect of declining population on the economy of England. This short introduction is designed for students.

Herlihy, David. *Women, Family and Society in Medieval Europe: Historical Essays, 1978–1991.* 1995. A collection of essays on late medieval European society. Extremely thoughtful and well written.

Howell, M. C. *Women, Production and Patriarchy in Late Medieval Cities.* 1986. After thoroughly reconstructing guild life in the Low Countries, the author argues that women were frozen out of the cloth industry. A difficult but important work.

Klapisch-Zuber, Christiane. *Women, Family, and Ritual in Renaissance Italy.* 1987. A collection of essays that make clear the contradictory pressures placed on women in late medieval Italy. Not always easy reading, but very rewarding.

Miskimin, Harry A. *The Economy of Early Renaissance Europe, 1300–1460.* 1975. An excellent, readable survey of how the economies of various parts of Europe responded to economic decline and plague.

Mollat, Michel, and Philippe Wolff. *The Popular Revolutions of the Late Middle Ages.* 1973. The best survey of the major revolutions of the fourteenth century, emphasizing the local political conditions that brought on the revolutions.

Ziegler, Philip. *The Black Death.* 1971. Although superseded on many specific points, this remains the best single volume on the plague in the fourteenth century.

The Ottoman and Spanish Empires

Holt, P. M., Ann Katharine Swynford Lambton, and Bernard Lewis, eds. *The Cambridge History of Islam.* 1970. The essays in this volume provide a general introduction for nonspecialists.

Housley, N. *The Later Crusades: From Lyons to Alcazar, 1274–1580.* 1992. This comprehensive account of crusading history includes an especially good consideration of Christian and Muslim relations in Iberia and the Balkans.

Inalcik, H. *The Ottoman Empire: The Classical Age, 1300–1600.* 1973. A general discussion of the growth of the Ottoman state by Turkey's best medieval historian.

Kamen, H. A. F. *The Spanish Inquisition.* 1966. This passionate introduction to Spain's most controversial institution demonstrates the truth of Lord Acton's observation that "Absolute power corrupts absolutely." Kamen gives an especially clear discussion of court procedures.

MacKay, A. *Spain in the Middle Ages: From Frontier to Empire, 1000–1500.* 1977. This short general introduction to Spain emphasizes the institutional changes that occurred in the late fourteenth and fifteenth centuries.

A PAINTING OF THE PLAGUE

Writers who survived the coming of bubonic plague in 1348 described a world of terror in which things seemed changed forever. Look at this painting, *St. Sebastian Interceding for the Plague-Stricken,* created by the Flemish artist Josse Lieferinxe between 1497 and 1499. One dying man seems to be falling terrified to the ground while a female bystander in the background screams in alarm. Images of Christ, Saint Sebastian (pierced by arrows), a devil, and a priest seem to indicate that something terrifying and undreamed-of is happening. But what exactly was the terror and what had changed?

The art of the later Middle Ages is an extremely valuable source for understanding social and religious values. As you look at *St. Sebastian Interceding for the Plague-Stricken,* the first step is to understand what men and women in the fourteenth and fifteenth centuries thought about death. After 1400, European Christians often depicted the universality of death in paintings showing the Dance of Death. The motif varies, but typically Death grasps the hands of men and women, rich and poor, noble and peasant, and leads them away. Deathbed scenes were another popular motif. In the late Middle Ages most people believed that at death the good and evil acts committed by an individual were tallied in the Book of Life and the person was granted either eternal life in Purgatory and then Paradise or consigned to eternal suffering in Hell. Judgment scenes often depict the Virgin Mary or another saint pleading before God or contending with the Devil or demons over the souls of the dying.

It was essential for people to prepare for a good death. Individuals studied the *artes moriendi,* the arts of dying. A lingering, painful illness was often interpreted as an opportunity for penitential suffering that would be good for the soul. At the point of death, the dying person could confess and receive both absolution for sins and the last sacraments of the church. From that moment on, he or she needed to maintain a calm faith, free from fear. Salvation and eternal life depended on avoiding further sin, especially the questioning of God's forgiveness and mercy. Death was a public event. Clergy, family, religious societies, even neighbors helped the dying person to keep hope. The person might pray, "Virgin Mary, Mother of God, I have placed my hope in you. Free my soul from care, and from Hell, and bitter death."[*]

The concept of a good death is critical to understanding the European response to bubonic plague. To be sure, individuals rarely look forward to death, now or in the Middle Ages. Boccaccio and numerous chroniclers remarked on the suddenness of death and on the lack of priests to hear confession. (See the box, "The Black Death" on page 417.) Individuals who were healthy in the morning might be dead by nightfall. The suddenness, the lack of preparation for a good death, heightened the dread that accompanied the onset of illness and death.

Medieval Christians turned to patron saints who could represent them before God at the point of death and to stop the onslaught of the plague. Three patron saints were especially popular. The Virgin Mary was often shown using her cloak to shelter towns and individuals from arrows carrying pestilence. Saint Roch, himself a victim of plague, was thought to intercede and protect those who prayed in his name. And Saint Sebastian, an early Christian martyr shot with arrows (later understood as symbols of death by plague), was thought to be an especially effective patron during epidemics. In times of plague, people went on pilgrimages to local shrines dedicated to these or local saints, carried images of the saints in processions, and built churches and chapels dedicated to the saints in thanks for deliverance from plague.

*Quoted in Philippe Ariès, *The Hour of Our Death* (New York: Knopf, 1981), p. 108.

Lieferinxe: St. Sebastian Interceding for the Plague-Stricken *(Walters Art Gallery, Baltimore)*

With these issues in mind, what do we see in Lieferinxe's painting? The painting portrays an outbreak of plague. We note first the body of the dead person, carefully shrouded. Ideally the dead, like the body in the foreground, were taken to a church and then given a Christian burial. But chroniclers often remarked that so many died, and died so quickly, that no one could be found to bury them properly. In many towns the dead were gathered on carts and hauled to large common graves outside the town. We can see one such cart leaving the castle in the background. In a series of images, then, Lieferinxe shows what mattered most to people. In the foreground is the shrouded body attended by a priest and by other clerics bearing a cross. This person experienced a good death. In contrast, the man who has fallen behind the body is suffering a bad death, one that caught him unawares. He is the object of the concern and grief of those near him. In the sky just above the castle walls, a white-robed angel and a horned, ax-wielding demon contend over the souls of the dead and dying. At the top of the painting, Christ listens to the prayers of Saint Sebastian. The painting thus portrays the impact and horror of plague and also shows the way in which the epidemic might be ended.

Returning to our original question, we find that the terror of epidemic plague was not entirely like a modern panic. Medieval people understood the horror and panic as well as the solutions to the epidemic in terms of traditional religious values: The terror was to be caught unawares. ✒

CHAPTER 12

The Renaissance

I talians of the fourteenth and fifteenth centuries believed that the world needed to be dramatically reformed, and they were sure they knew why. "As the city of Rome had perished at the hands of perverse and tyrannical Emperors, so did Latin studies and literature undergo similar ruin and diminution. . . . And Italy was invaded by Goths and Lombards, barbarous, uncouth peoples, who practically extinguished all knowledge of literature."[1] This extinction of knowledge, according to Leonardo Bruni, a writer and later chancelor in fifteenth-century Florence, was responsible for the moral and political decay he feared had weakened Italian public life. The only answer, he was sure, was to change the way Italians were educated and how they thought about their past.

Bruni's feelings were common among artists and writers. Paolo Ucello's painting of the Battle of San Romano is an example of what had changed. The vivid colors and the realistic use of perspective to arrange the figures make it seem that we are present at the battle itself. This was a new kind of painting. Renaissance Italians wrote of themselves and their contemporaries as having "revived" arts, "rescued" painting, and "rediscovered" classical authors. They even coined the phrases "Dark Ages" and "Middle Ages" to describe the period that separated classical antiquity from the culture of their own times. In the sixteenth century the painter and art historian Giorgio Vasari described the revival as a *rinascità*, an Italian word meaning "rebirth." And to this day we use the French translation of that word, *renaissance,* to describe the period between 1300 and 1600.

We also use *renaissance* to describe any time of intense creativity and change that differs dramatically from what has gone before. This particular

Ucello's *The Battle of San Romano* (detail), ca. 1450, showing a complex, realistic scene—a Renaissance innovation.

437

definition of the word comes to us primarily from the work of the Swiss historian Jacob Burckhardt. In his book *The Civilization of the Renaissance in Italy* (1860), Burckhardt argued that the creativity and cultural brilliance of the period resulted when Italians suddenly found themselves freed from the medieval restraints of religion, guild, community, and family. Renaissance Italians, he believed, were the first individuals to recognize the state as an autonomous moral structure free from the strictures of religious or philosophical traditions. During the time of the Renaissance, an individual's success or failure in all matters depended on personal qualities of creative brilliance rather than on status in a family, religion, or guild. What Burckhardt thought he saw in Renaissance Italy were the first signs of the romantic individualism and the nationalism that characterized his own society.

Both Leonardo Bruni and Jacob Burckhardt misunderstood the relationship between the Renaissance and the period that preceded it. There was no "Dark Age." The culture of Renaissance Europe was in no way superior to the religious, philosophical, and literary culture that preceded or followed it. Although the culture of Renaissance Europe was in many aspects new and innovative, it had close ties both to the ideas of the High Middle Ages and to traditional Christian values.

We cannot answer aesthetic questions of whether Renaissance architecture, literature, and philosophy were actually superior to the culture out of which they grew. We can, however, describe the Renaissance in Europe as an important cultural movement that aimed to reform and renew by making art, education, religion, and political life congruent with the reformers' conception of classical and early Christian traditions. As we will see, Italians, and then other Europeans, came to believe that the social and moral values as well as the literature of classical Rome offered the best chance to change their own society for the better. This enthusiasm for a past culture became the measure for changes in literature, education, and art that established cultural standards that were to hold for the next five hundred years. Renaissance men and women misunderstood important aspects of classical culture; nevertheless, their attempts at reform had a profound effect on the development of European culture.

HUMANISM AND CULTURE IN ITALY, 1300–1500

Logic and Scholastic philosophy (see page 380) dominated university education in northern Europe in the fourteenth and fifteenth centuries, but had less influence in Italy, where education focused on the practical issues of town life rather than on theological speculation. Educated Italians of this period were interested in the *studia humanitatis*, which we now call humanism. By *humanism*, Italians meant rhetoric and literature—the arts of persuasion—not an ideological or a moral program based on philosophical arguments or religious assumptions about human nature. Poetry, history, letter writing, and oratory based on forms and aesthetic values consciously borrowed from ancient Greece and Rome formed the center of intellectual life.

Humanistic thought in the Renaissance was very much a product of the urban milieu of fourteenth- and fifteenth-century Italy. Italians turned to models from classical antiquity in an attempt to deal with current issues of cultural, political, and educational reform. The humanistic movement began as a belief in the superiority of the literature and history of the past. As humanists discovered more about ancient culture, they were able to understand more clearly the historical context in which Roman and Greek writers and thinkers lived. And by the early sixteenth century, their debates on learning, civic duty, and the classical legacy had led them to a new vision of the past and a new appreciation of the nature of politics.

The Emergence of Humanism

Humanism initially held greater appeal in Italy than elsewhere in Europe because the culture in central and northern Italy was significantly more secular and more urban than the culture of much of the rest of Europe. Members of the clergy were not likely to dominate government and education in Italy. Quite the reverse: Boards dominated by laymen had built and were administering the great urban churches of Italy. Religious hospitals and charities were often reorganized and centralized under government control. In 1300, four cities in Italy had populations of about 100,000 (Milan, Venice, Florence, and Naples), and countless others had populations of 40,000 or more. By contrast, London, which may have had a population of 100,000, was the only city in England with more than 40,000 inhabitants. Even the powerful Italian aristocracy tended to live at least part of the year in towns and conform to urban social and legal practices.

Differences between Italy and northern Europe are apparent in the structure of local education. In northern Europe, education was organized to provide clergy for local churches. In the towns of Italy, education was much more likely to be supervised by town governments to provide training in accounting, arithmetic, and the composition of business letters. In Italy it was common for town governments to hire lay grammar masters to teach in free public schools. They competed with numerous private masters and individual tutors who were prepared to teach all subjects. Giovanni Villani, a fourteenth-century merchant and historian, described Florence in 1338 as a city of about 100,000 people in which perhaps as many as 10,000 young girls and boys completed elementary education and 1000 continued their studies to prepare for careers in commerce. Compared to education in the towns of northern Europe, education in Villani's Florence seems broad based and practical. This may have been typical of education in the commercial towns of central and northern Italy.

Italian towns were also the focus of theorizing about towns as moral, religious, and political communities. Writers wanted to define the nature of the commune—the town government. Moralists often used "the common good" and "the good of the commune" as synonyms. By 1300 it was usual for towns to celebrate the feast day of their patron saint as a major political as well as religious festival. And town governments often supervised the construction and expansion of cathedrals, churches, and hospitals as a sign of their wealth and prestige. Literature of the early fourteenth century tended to emphasize the culture of towns. Italian historians chose to write the histories of their hometowns. Most, like Giovanni Villani of Florence, were convinced that their towns could rival ancient Rome. The majority of educated Italians in the early fourteenth century, however, were not captivated by thoughts of ancient Rome. Theirs was a practical world in which most intellectuals were men trained in notarial arts—the everyday skills of oratory, letter writing, and the recording of legal documents.

Vernacular Literatures

The humanistic movement, however, was not simply a continuation of practical and literary movements. The extent of its innovation will be clearer if we look briefly at the vernacular literatures (that is, written in native languages, rather than Latin) of the fourteenth and fifteenth centuries. Vernacular literatures continued to treat traditional Christian moral and ethical concerns with reference to traditional values and ideas. Even the most famous and most innovative work of the fourteenth century, *The Decameron* by Giovanni Boccaccio (1313–1375), was, in certain respects, traditional. Boccaccio hoped the lively and irreverent descriptions of contemporary Italians, which make his *Decameron* a classic of European literature, would also lead individuals to understand both what it is that makes them human and the folly of human desires. The tale describes a group of privileged young people who abandon friends and family during the plague of 1348 (see pages 414–417) to go into the country, where on successive days they mix feasting, dancing, and song with one hundred tales of love, intrigue, and gaiety. With its mix of traditional and contemporary images, Boccaccio's book spawned numerous imitators in Italy and elsewhere. But the point too often missed by Boccaccio's imitators was, as he himself said, that "to have compassion for those who suffer is a human quality which everyone should possess. . . ."

Boccaccio's work influenced another vernacular writer, Geoffrey Chaucer (ca. 1343–1400), the son of a London burgher, who served as a diplomat, courtier, and member of Parliament. In addition to the pervasive French influence, Chaucer read and studied Boccaccio. Chaucer's most well-known work, *The Canterbury Tales*, consists of stories told by a group of thirty pilgrims who left the London suburbs on a pilgrimage to the shrine of Saint Thomas à Becket at Canterbury. The narrators and the stories themselves allow Chaucer to describe a variety of moral and social types, creating an acute, sometimes bitter, portrait of English life. The Wife of Bath is typical of Chaucer's pilgrims: "She was a worthy woman all her life, husbands at the churchdoor she had five." After describing her own five marriages, she makes the point that marriage is a proper way to achieve moral perfection, but it can be so only if the woman is master.

Although Chaucer's characters have an ironic view of the good and evil that abound in society, Chaucer's contemporary, William Langland (ca. 1330–ca. 1400), takes a decidedly more serious view of the ills of English life. Whereas Dante, Boccaccio, and Chaucer all told realistic tales about life as it really seemed to be, Langland used the traditional allegorical language (that is, symbolic language where a place or person represents an idea) of medieval Europe. In *Piers Plowman* he writes of people caught between the "Valley of Death" and the "Tower of Truth." In his visions Langland describes the seven deadly sins that threaten all of society and follows with an exhortation to do better. Both Chaucer and Langland expected their audience to immediately recognize commonly held ideas and values.

Women and Culture Christine de Pizan objected to male denigration of the moral and cultural value of women. This illumination from her *City of the Ladies* shows her ideal society, a place where women, like men, are allowed to study and create. *(Bibliothèque Nationale)*

Despite the persistence of old forms of literature, new vernacular styles arose, although they still dealt with traditional values and ideas. Throughout Europe many writers directly addressed their cares and concerns. Some collected letters or wrote short works of piety, like *The Mirror for Simple Souls* of Marguerite of Porete (d. 1310). Though Marguerite was ultimately executed as a heretic, her work continued to circulate anonymously. Her frank description of love and God's love for humans inspired many other writers in the fourteenth and fifteenth centuries. Less erotic but equally riveting is the memoir of Margery Kempe, an alewife from England. She describes how she left her husband and family, dressed in white (symbolic of virginity), and joined with other pilgrims on trips to Spain, Italy, and Jerusalem.

One of the most unusual of the new vernacular writers was Christine de Pizan (1369–1430), the daughter of an Italian physician at the court of Charles V of France. Her father and later her husband had encouraged her to learn languages and to write. When the deaths of both of these men left her with responsibility for her children and little money, she turned to writing. From 1389 until her death, she lived and wrote at the French court. She composed a short life of Joan of Arc and an instructional book for the education of the crown prince, but she is perhaps best known for *The Book of the City of the Ladies* (1405). In it she added her own voice to what is known as the *querelle des femmes*, the "argument over women." Christine wrote to counter the many writings that characterized women as inferior to men and incapable of moral judgments. She argued that the problem was education: "If it were customary to send daughters to school like sons, and if they were then taught the natural sciences, they would learn as thoroughly and understand the subtleties of all the arts and sciences as well as sons." Christine described in her book an ideal city of ladies in which prudence, justice, and reason would protect women from ignorant male critics.

All these vernacular writings built on popular tales and sayings as well as traditional moral and religious writings. Unlike the early humanists, the vernacular writers saw little need for new cultural and intellectual models. The humanists' need for new models seems to have developed out of particular Italian political and social needs.

Early Humanism

The first Italians who looked back consciously to the literary and historical examples of ancient Rome were a group of northern Italian lawyers and notaries who imitated Roman authors. These practical men found Roman history and literature more stimulating and useful than medieval philosophy. Writers like Albertino Mussato of Padua (1262–1329) adopted classical styles in their poetry and histories. Albertino used his play *The Ecerinis* (1315) to tell of the fall of Can Grande della Scala, the tyrannical ruler of Verona (d. 1329) and to warn his neighbors of the dangers of tyranny. He celebrated the independent city-states and urged a renewal of republican values in the cities of the Po Valley. "The rule of justice lasts forever," Albertino concluded. "Virtue soars to heavenly joys."[2] From its earliest, the classical revival in Italy was tied to issues of moral and political reform.

This largely emotional fascination for the ancient world was transformed into a literary movement for reform by Francesco Petrarch (1304–1374), who popularized the idea of mixing classical moral and literary ideas with the concerns of the fourteenth century. Petrarch was the son of an exiled Florentine notary living at the papal court in Avignon. His father sent him to study law at the University of Bologna, but Petrarch had little interest in the law. After his father's death he quickly abandoned law for literature. Repelled by the urban violence and wars he had experienced, Petrarch was highly critical of his contemporaries: "I never liked this age," he once confessed. He criticized the "Babylonian Captivity" of the papacy in Avignon, as he named it (see page 397); he supported an attempt to resurrect a republican government in Rome; and he believed that imitation of the actions, values, and culture of the ancient Romans was the only way to reform his world.

Petrarch believed that an age of darkness—he coined the expression "Dark Ages"—separated the Roman world from his own time and that the separation could be overcome only through a study and reconstruction of classical values: "Once the darkness has been broken, our descendants will perhaps be able to return to the pure, pristine radiance."[3] A brilliant poet and linguist and a tireless self-promoter, he lived his entire life as an example of the way in which classical values could serve as a vehicle for moral and intellectual reform. Petrarch's program, and in many respects the entire Renaissance, involved first of all a reconstruction of classical culture, then a careful study and imitation of the classical heritage, and finally a series of moral and cultural changes that went beyond the mere copying of ancient values and styles.

Petrarch labored throughout his life to reconstruct the history and literature of Rome. He learned to read and write classical Latin. While still in his twenties, he discovered fragments of Livy's *Roman History*, an important source for the history of Republican Rome. He annotated and reorganized the fragments in an attempt to reconstruct the form Livy himself had intended. His work on Livy was merely the first step. In the 1330s he discovered a number of classical works, including orations by Cicero, the great philosopher, statesman, and opponent of Julius Caesar (see page 185). In 1345 he found the collection of letters that Cicero, while in exile, had written to his friend Atticus. These letters, filled with gossip, questions about politics in Rome, and complaints about his forced withdrawal from public life, created the portrait of an individual who was much more complex than the austere philosopher of medieval legend.

Petrarch was and remained a committed Christian. He recognized the tension between the Christian present and pagan antiquity. "My wishes fluctuate and my desires conflict, and in their struggle they tear me apart," he said.[4] Yet he prized the beauty and moral value of ancient learning. He wrote *The Lives of Illustrious Men*, biographies of men from antiquity whose lives he thought were worthy of emulation. He composed an epic Latin poem, *Africa*, about the Roman patrician Scipio Africanus. To spread humanistic values, he issued collections of his letters, written in classically inspired Latin, and his Italian poems. He believed that study and memorization of the writings of classical authors could lead to the internalization of the ideas and values expressed in those works, just as a honeybee drinks nectar to create honey. He argued that the ancient moral philosophers were superior to the Scholastic philosophers, whose work ended with the determination of truth, or correct responses. "The true moral philosophers and useful teachers of the virtues," he concluded, "are those whose first and last intention is to make hearer and reader good, those who do not merely teach what virtue and vice are but sow into our hearts love of the best . . . and hatred of the worst."[5] (See the box, "Petrarch Responds to His Critics.")

Humanistic Studies

Petrarch's belief in humanism inspired a broad-based transformation of Italian intellectual life that affected discussions of politics, education, literature, and philosophy. Wherever he traveled in Italy, numerous young scholars flocked to him. His style of historical and literary investigation of the past became the basis for a new appreciation of the present.

Petrarch's program of humanistic studies became especially popular with the wealthy oligarchy that dominated political life in Florence. The Florentine chancellor Coluccio Salutati (1331–1406) and a generation of young intellectuals who formed his circle evolved an ideology of civic humanism. Civic humanists wrote letters, orations, and histories praising their city's classical virtues and history. In the process they gave a practical and public meaning to the Petrarchan program. Civic humanists argued, like Cicero himself, that there was a moral and ethical value intrinsic to public life. In a letter to a friend, Coluccio Salutati wrote that public life is "something holy and holier than idleness in [religious] solitude." To another he added, "The active life you flee is to be followed both as an exercise in virtue and because of the necessity of brotherly love."[6]

More than Petrarch himself, civic humanists viewed their task as the creation of men of virtue who could take the lead in government and protect their fellow citizens from lawlessness and tyranny. In the early years of the fifteenth century, civic humanists praised Florence for remaining a republic of free citizens rather than falling under the control of a lord, like the people of Milan, whose government was dominated by the Viscontis (see page 411). In his *Panegyric on the City of Florence* (ca. 1400), Leonardo Bruni (ca. 1370–1444) recalled the history of the Roman Republic and suggested that Florence could recreate the virtues of the Roman state. To civic humanists, the study of Rome and its virtues was the key to the continued prosperity of Florence and similar Italian republics.

One of Petrarch's most enthusiastic followers was Guarino of Verona (1374–1460), who became the leading advocate of educational reform in Renaissance Italy. After spending five years in Constantinople learning Greek and collecting classical manuscripts, he became the most successful teacher and translator of Greek literature in Italy. There had been previously a widespread interest in Greek literature—Petrarch owned a copy of the *Iliad*, though he never managed to learn to read it—and Greek studies had been advanced by Manuel Chrysoloras (1350–1415), who, after his arrival from Constantinople in 1397, taught Greek for three years in Florence. Chrysoloras was later joined by other Greek intellectuals, especially after the fall of Constantinople to the Turks in 1453. Throughout the fifteenth century there was enthusiasm for Greek philosophy and theology. Guarino built on this interest.

Guarino emphasized careful study of grammar and memorization of large bodies of classical history and poetry. He coached students to write orations in the style of Cicero. Guarino believed that through a profound understanding of Greek and Latin literature and a careful imitation of the style of the great authors, a person could come to exhibit the moral and ethical values for which Cicero, Seneca, and Plutarch were justly famous. Although it is unclear that Guarino's style of education delivered the moral training he advocated, it did provide a thorough education in literature and oratory. In an age that admired the ability to speak and write persuasively, the new style of humanistic education pioneered by Guarino spread quickly throughout Europe. The elegy spoken at Guarino's funeral sums up Italian views of humanistic education as well as the contribution of Guarino himself: "No one was considered noble, as leading a blameless life, unless he had followed Guarino's courses."

Guarino's authority spread quickly. One of his early students, Vittorino da Feltre (1378–1446), was appointed tutor to the Gonzaga dukes of Mantua. Like Guarino, he emphasized close literary study and careful imitation of classical authors. But the school he founded, the Villa Giocosa, was innovative because he advocated games and exercises as well as formal study. In addition, Vittorino required that bright young boys from poor families be included among the seventy students normally resident in his school. Vittorino

Petrarch Responds to His Critics

Many traditional philosophers and theologians criticized humanists as "pagans" because of their lack of interest in discovering logical and theological truths and their love of non-Christian writers. In this excerpt from "On My Own Ignorance and That of Many Others," a letter written to defend humanistic studies, Petrarch discusses Cicero and explains the value of his work to Christians.

[Cicero] points out the miraculously coherent structure and disposition of the body, sense and limbs, and finally reason and sedulous activity. . . . And all this he does merely to lead us to this conclusion: whatever we behold with our eyes or perceive with our intellect is made by God for the well-being of man and governed by divine providence and counsel. . . . [In response to his critics who argued for the superiority of philosophy he adds] I have read all of Aristotle's moral books. . . . Sometimes I have become more learned through them when I went home, but not better, not so good as I ought to be; and I often complained to myself, occasionally to others too, that by no facts was the promise fulfilled which the philosopher makes at the beginning of the first book of his *Ethics*, namely, that "we learn this part of philosophy not with the purpose of gaining knowledge but of becoming better." . . . However, what is the use of knowing what virtue is if it is not loved when known? What is the use of knowing sin if it is not abhorred when it is known? However, everyone who has become thoroughly familiar with our Latin authors knows that they stamp and drive deep into the heart the sharpest and most ardent stings of speech by which . . . those who stick to the ground [are] lifted up to the highest thoughts and to honest desire. . . .

Cicero, read with a pious and modest attitude, . . . was profitable to everybody, so far as eloquence is concerned, to many others as regards living. This was especially true in [Saint] Augustine's case. . . . I confess, I admire Cicero as much or even more than all whoever wrote a line in any nation. . . . If to admire Cicero means to be a Ciceronian, I am a Ciceronian. I admire him so much that I wonder at people who do not admire him. . . . However, when we come to think or speak of religion, that is, of supreme truth and true happiness, and of eternal salvation, then I am certainly not a Ciceronian, or a Platonist, but a Christian. I even feel sure that Cicero himself would have been a Christian if he had been able to see Christ and to comprehend His doctrine.

Source: Petrarch, "On His Own Ignorance and That of Many Others," in *The Renaissance Philosophy of Man,* ed. Ernst Cassirer, Paul Oskar Kristeller, and John H. Randall (Chicago: University of Chicago Press, 1948), pp. 86, 103, 104, 114, 115.

was so renowned that noblemen from across Italy sent their sons to be educated at the Villa Giocosa.

Humanistic education had its limits, however. Leonardo Bruni of Florence once composed a curriculum for a young woman to follow. He urged her to learn literature and moral philosophy as well as to read religious writers. But, he suggested, there was no reason to study rhetoric: "For why should the subtleties of . . . rhetorical conundrums consume the powers of a woman, who never sees the forum? . . . The contests of the forum, like those of warfare and battle, are the sphere of men."[7] To what extent did women participate in the cultural and artistic movements of the fourteenth and fifteenth centuries? Was the position of women better than it had been previously? The current of misogyny, the assumption that women were intellectually and morally weaker than men, continued during the Renaissance, but it was not unopposed.

Isabella d'Este As part of the program to revive ancient Roman practices, Italian rulers had medals struck containing their own images. This image of Isabella was meant to celebrate the woman herself and the fact that her husband held the imperial office of duke. *(Kunsthistorisches Museum, Vienna)*

During the fifteenth century many women did learn to read and even to write. Religious women and wives of merchants read educational and spiritual literature. Some women needed to write in order to manage the economic and political interests of the family. Alessandra Macinghi-Strozzi of Florence (1407–1471), for example, wrote numerous letters to her sons in exile describing her efforts to find spouses for her children and to influence the government to end their exile. Yet many men were suspicious of literate women. Just how suspicious is evident in the career of Isotta Nogarola (b. 1418) of Verona, one of a number of fifteenth- and sixteenth-century Italian women whose literary abilities equaled those of male humanists. Isotta quickly became known as a gifted writer, but men's response to her work was mixed. One anonymous critic suggested that it was unnatural for a woman to have such scholarly interests and accused her of equally unnatural sexual interests. Guarino of Verona himself wrote to her saying that if she was truly to be edu-

cated she must put off female sensibilities and find "a man within the woman."[8]

The problem for humanistically educated women was that there was no acceptable role for them. A noblewoman like Isabella d'Este (see page 464), wife of the duke of Mantua, might gather humanists and painters around her at court, but it was not generally believed that women could create literary works of true merit. When women tried, they were usually rebuffed and urged to reject the values of civic humanism and to hold instead to traditional Christian virtues of rejection of the world. A woman who had literary or cultural interests was expected to enter a convent. Isotta Nogarola was given this advice when she informed a male humanist friend that she was contemplating marriage. It was wrong, he said, "that a virgin should consider marriage, or even think about that liberty of lascivious morals."[9] Throughout the fifteenth and early sixteenth centuries some women in Italy and the rest of Europe learned classical languages and philosophy, but they became rarer as time passed. The virtues of humanism were public virtues, and Europeans of the Renaissance remained uncomfortable with the idea that women might act directly and publicly. (See the box, "Cassandra Fedele Defends Liberal Arts for Women.")

The Transformation of Humanism

The fascination with education based on ancient authorities was heightened by the discovery in 1416 in the Monastery of Saint Gall in Switzerland of a complete manuscript of Quintilian's *Institutes of Oratory*, a first-century treatise on the proper education for a young Roman patrician. It was found by Poggio Bracciolini (1380–1459), who had been part of the humanist circle in Florence. The discovery was hardly accidental. Like Petrarch himself, the humanists of the fifteenth century scoured Europe looking for ancient texts to read and study. In searching out the knowledge of the past, these fifteenth-century humanists made a series of discoveries that changed their understanding of language, philosophy, and religion. Their desire to imitate led to a profound transformation of knowledge.

A Florentine antiquary, Niccolò Niccoli, coordinated and paid for much of the search for new manuscripts. A wealthy bachelor, Niccolò (1364–1437) spent the fortune he had inherited from his

Cassandra Fedele Defends Liberal Arts for Women

Cassandra Fedele (1465–1558) by the age of 12 had learned Latin and later learned Greek, rhetoric, and history. The Venetian senate praised her as an ornament of learning in the city, but there was no place for an educated woman. She eventually married a provincial physician and was unable to maintain her early prominence, although she occasionally wrote letters and orations. In this oration, which is in the form of a typical defense of liberal studies, she adds her own plea for education for women.

Aware of the weakness of my sex and the paucity of my talent, blushing, I decided to honor and obey [those who have urged me to consider how women could profit from assiduous study] . . . in order that the common crowd may be ashamed of itself and stop being offensive to me, devoted as I am to the liberal arts. . . . What woman, I ask, has such force and ability of mind and speech that she could adequately meet the standard of the greatness of letters or your learned ears? Thus daunted by the difficulty of the task and conscious of my weakness, I might easily have shirked this opportunity to speak, if your well-known kindness and clemency had not urged me to it. For I am not unaware that you are not in the habit of demanding or expecting from anyone more than the nature of the subject itself allows, or the person's own strength can promise of them.

Even an ignorant man—not only a philosopher—sees and admits that man is rightly distinguished from a beast above all by [the capacity of] reason. For what else so greatly delights, enriches and honors both of them than the teaching and understanding of letters and the liberal arts? . . . Moreover, simple men, ignorant of literature, even if they have by nature this potential seed of genius and reason, leave it alone and uncultivated throughout their whole lives, stifle it with neglect and sloth, and render themselves unfit for greatness. . . . But learned men, filled with a rich knowledge of divine and human things, turn all their thoughts and motions of the mind toward the goal of reason and thus free the mind, [otherwise] subject to so many anxieties, from all infirmity. . . . States and princes, moreover, who favor and cultivate these studies become much more humane, pleasing, and noble, and purely [through liberal studies] win for themselves a sweet reputation for humanity. . . . For this reason the ancients rightfully judged all leaders deficient in letters, however skillful in military affairs, to be crude and ignorant. As for the utility of letters, enough said. . . . Of these fruits I myself have tasted a little and [have esteemed myself in that enterprise] more than abject and hopeless; and armed with distaff and needle—woman's weapons—I march forth [to defend] the belief that even though the study of letters promises and offers no reward for women and no dignity, every woman ought to seek and embrace these studies for that pleasure and delight alone that [comes] from them.

Source: M. L. King and A. Rabil, *Her Immaculate Hand: Selected Works by and About the Women Humanists of Quattrocento Italy* (Binghamton, N.Y.: Center for Medieval and Early Renaissance Studies, State University of New York, 1983), pp. 74–77.

father by collecting ancient statuary, reliefs, and, most of all, books. When he died, his collection of more than eight hundred volumes of Latin and Greek texts was taken over by Cosimo de' Medici. It became the foundation of the humanist library housed in the Monastery of San Marco in Florence. Niccolò specified that all his books "should be accessible to everyone," and humanists from across Italy and the rest of Europe came to Florence to study his collection. It would be difficult to overemphasize the importance of the ancient texts collected and copied in Florence. Niccolò's library prompted Pope Nicholas V (r. 1447–1455) to begin the collection that is now the Apostolic Library of the Vatican in Rome. The Vatican library became a lending library, serving the humanist community in Rome. Similar collections were made in Venice, Milan, and Urbino. The Greek and Latin sources collected in these libraries allowed humanists to study classical languages in a way not possible before.

The career of Lorenzo Valla (1407–1457) illustrates the transformation that took place in the fifteenth century. Valla was born near Rome and received a traditional humanistic education in Greek and Latin studies. He spent the rest of his life at universities and courts lecturing on philosophy and literature. Valla was convinced that the key to philosophical and legal problems lay in historical-textual research. Valla's studies had led him to understand that language changes—that it, too, has a life and a history. In 1440 he published a work called *On the Donation of Constantine*. The *Donation of Constantine* purported to record the gift by the emperor Constantine (r. 311–337) of jurisdiction over Rome to the pope when the capital of the empire was moved to Constantinople (see page 283). In the high and late Middle Ages, the papacy used the document to defend its right to political dominion in central Italy. The donation had long been criticized by legal theorists, who argued that Constantine had no right to make it. Valla attacked the legitimacy of the document itself. Because of its language and form, he argued, it could not have been written at the time of Constantine:

Through his [the writer's] babbling, he reveals his most impudent forgery himself. . . . Where he deals with the gifts he says "a diadem . . . made of pure gold and precious jewels." The ignoramus did not know that the diadem was made of cloth, probably silk. . . . He thinks it had to be made of gold, since nowadays kings usually wear a circle of gold set with jewels.[10]

Valla was correct. The *Donation* was a forgery written in the eighth century.

Valla later turned his attention to the New Testament. Jerome (331–420) had put together the Vulgate edition of the Bible in an attempt to create a single accepted Latin version of the Old and New Testaments (see page 258). In 1444 Valla published his *Annotations on the New Testament*. In this

work he used his training in classical languages to correct the standard Latin text and to show numerous examples of mistranslations by Jerome and his contemporaries. Valla believed that true understanding of Christian theology depended on clear knowledge of the past. His annotations on the New Testament were of critical importance to humanists outside Italy and were highly influential during the Protestant Reformation.

The transformation of humanism exemplified by Valla was fully expected by some Florentines. They anticipated that literary studies would lead eventually to philosophy. In 1456, a young Florentine began studying Greek with just such a change in mind. Supported by the Medici rulers of Florence, Marsilio Ficino (1433–1499) began a project to translate the works of Plato into Latin and to interpret Plato in the light of Christian tradition. Between 1463 and 1469 he translated all of the Platonic dialogues. He was at the center of a circle of humanists who were interested in Platonism and its role in art and society. In 1469 he published the first versions of his *Platonic Theology*.

Ficino believed that Platonism, like Christianity, demonstrated the dignity of humanity. He wrote that everything was connected along a hierarchy ranging from the lowliest matter to the person of God. The human soul was located at the midpoint of this hierarchy and was a bridge between matter and God. True wisdom, and especially experience of the divine, could be gained only through contemplation and love. According to Ficino, logic and scientific observation did not lead to true understanding, for humans know logically only that which they can define in human language; they can, however, love things, such as God, that they are not fully able to comprehend.

Ficino's belief in the dignity of man was shared by Giovanni Pico della Mirandola (1463–1494), who proposed to debate with other philosophers nine hundred theses dealing with the nature of man, the origins of knowledge, and the uses of philosophy. Pico extended Ficino's idea of the hierarchy of being, arguing that humans surpassed even the angels in dignity. Angels held a fixed position in the hierarchy, just below God. In contrast, humans could either move up or move down in the hierarchy, depending on the extent to which they embraced spiritual or worldly interests. Pico further believed that he had proved that there was truth in all philosophies. He was one of the first

～ ENCOUNTERS WITH THE WEST ～

Rabbi Mordecai Dato Criticizes the Humanists

Until the Renaissance, Europeans exhibited little interest in Jewish learning. But beginning with Giovanni Pico della Mirandola, many Christian humanists became convinced that the Jewish Cabala shared an original wisdom with Egyptian magic, Greek mystical philosophy, and Christianity. And they enthusiastically studied Jewish literature in order to combine it with other traditions. Jews, however, worried that knowledge of their philosophy and theology would be used in an attempt to convert them. In this selection, Rabbi Mordecai Dato (1525–ca. 1591), who lived in northern Italy, protests to a Jewish colleague that in trying to combine so many traditions, humanists misunderstand them.

Let me inform you of two things: first . . . that whatever is said by one of the sages of the *Safed* [the original Cabala mystics] . . . in the introduction to the works of Truth and Justice [i.e., Cabala] is based upon the words of the Book of Splendor [Zahor, a thirteenth-century book of mysticism]; their words are its words; they emerge from its radiance, and without them no man might raise his hands or feet . . . in learning or in criticism, to speak about this wisdom, for they fear the great fire which consumes that man who makes things up from his heart, who has not heard [them] from his teacher as required in the Book of Splendor. . . . They ought not to rely upon their understanding or their dialectics, [though] they are very great, save in the interpretation of some few sayings of the Book of Splendor which seem to contradict one another . . . and even this only under certain conditions stated in the book itself. Secondly, that the words of the Book of

Splendor are based upon tradition, and that one may not question them.

Everything which is probable ought to be accepted graciously—and that which is without reason ought to be confirmed by reason. [However], one is not obligated to find a rational explanation of the kind which I have mentioned for all the words of the Book of Wisdom, for many have fallen [in the attempt]. Go and see how one of the sages of the [gentile] nations, Johannes Reuchlin, made himself wise in one work which he made, which I saw many years ago, bringing selection after selection, at random . . . to find words of favor and natural philosophic reason in the words of the Book of Wisdom. And in his many clever words, albeit he avoided corporealization, he compared the Creator to his form, and the servant to his master [that is, he made critical logical errors] . . . heaven forbid.

Dato's letter is partially translated in Robert Bonfil, *Rabbis and Jewish Communities in Renaissance Italy* (Oxford and New York: Oxford University Press for The Littman Library, 1990), pp. 295–296.

humanists to learn Hebrew and to argue that divine wisdom could be found in Jewish mystical literature. Along with others, he studied the Jewish Cabala, a collection of mystical and occult writings that humanists believed dated from the time of Moses. Pico's adoption of the Hebrew mystical writings was often controversial in the Jewish community as well as among Christians.

(See the box, "Encounters with the West: Rabbi Mordecai Dato Criticizes the Humanists.")

Pico's ideas were shared by other humanists, who argued that there was an original divine illumination—a "Pristine Theology," they called it—that preceded both Moses and Plato. These humanists found theological truth in what they believed was ancient Egyptian, Greek, and Jewish magic. Ficino himself popularized the *Corpus Hermeticum* (the Hermetic collection), an amalgam of magical texts of the first century A.D. that was mistakenly assumed to date from the age of Moses and Pythagoras. Like the writings of Plato and his followers, Hermetic texts explained how the mind could influence and be influenced by the material and celestial worlds.

Along with Hermetic magic many humanists of the fifteenth and sixteenth centuries investigated astrology and alchemy. Hermetic magic, astrology, and alchemy posit the existence of a direct, reciprocal connection between the cosmos and the natural world. In the late medieval and Renaissance world, astrological and alchemical theories seemed reasonable. By the late fifteenth century many humanists assumed that personality as well as the ability to respond to certain crises was profoundly affected by the stars. It was not by accident that for a century or more after 1500, astrologers were official or unofficial members of most European courts. Belief in astrology was not universal, however. Some humanists, like Pico, opposed it because it seemed to deny that humans had free will.

Interest in alchemy was equally widespread though more controversial. Alchemists believed that everything was made of a primary material and that it was possible to transmute one substance into another. The most popular version, and the most open to hucksters and frauds, was the belief that base metals could be turned into gold. The hopes of most alchemists, however, were more profound. They were convinced that they could unlock the explanation of the properties of the whole cosmos. On a personal and religious level as well as on a material level, practitioners hoped to take the impure and make it pure. The interest in understanding and manipulating nature that lay at the heart of Hermetic magic, astrology, and alchemy was an important stimulus to scientific investigations and, ultimately, to the rise of modern scientific thought.

Humanism and Political Thought

The humanists' plan to rediscover classical sources fit well with their political interests. "One can say," observed Leonardo Bruni, "that letters and the study of the Latin language went hand in hand

with the condition of the Roman republic." Petrarch and the civic humanists believed that rulers, whether in a republic or a principality, should exhibit all the classical and Christian virtues of faith, hope, love, prudence, temperance, fortitude, and justice. Those qualities were the key to good government and good law. A virtuous ruler would be loved and obeyed. Those virtues were also the key to the preservation of government. The civic humanists viewed governments and laws as essentially unchanging and static. They believed that when change did occur, it most likely happened by chance—that is, because of fortune (the Roman goddess Fortuna). Humanists believed that the only protection against chance was true virtue, for the virtuous would never be dominated by fortune. Thus, beginning with Petrarch, humanists advised rulers to love their subjects, to be magnanimous with their possessions, and to maintain the rule of law. Humanistic tracts of the fourteenth and fifteenth centuries were full of classical and Christian examples of virtuous actions by moral rulers.

The French invasions of Italy in 1494 (see page 412) and the warfare that followed called into question many of the humanists' assumptions about the lessons and virtues of classical civilization. Francesco Guicciardini (1483–1540), a Florentine patrician who had served in papal armies, suggested that history held no clear lessons. Unless the causes of two different events were identical down to the smallest detail, he said, the results could be radically different. An even more thorough critique was offered by Guicciardini's friend and fellow Florentine, Niccolò Machiavelli (1469–1527). After a humanistic education and service from 1494 to 1512 in the anti-Medicean republican government of Florence, Machiavelli was forced by the Medici to abandon public life and leave Florence. While living on his farm outside Florence, Machiavelli developed in a series of writings what he believed was a new science of politics. He wrote *Discourses on Livy*, a treatise on military organization, a history of Florence, and even a Renaissance play entitled *The Mandrake Root*. He is best remembered, however, for *The Prince* (1513), a small tract numbering less than a hundred pages.

Machiavelli felt that his contemporaries paid too little heed to the lessons to be learned from history. Thus, in his discourses on Livy he comments on Roman government, the role of religion, and the nature of political virtue, emphasizing the sophisticated Roman analysis of political and military situations. A shortcoming more serious than ignorance of history, Machiavelli believed, was his contemporaries' ignorance of the true motivations for people's actions. His play *The Mandrake Root* is a comedy about the ruses used to seduce a young woman. In truth, however, none of the characters is fooled. All of them, from the young woman being seduced to her husband, realize what is happening but use the seduction to their own advantage. In the play Machiavelli implicitly challenges the humanistic assumption that educated individuals will naturally choose virtue over vice. He explicitly criticizes these same assumptions in *The Prince*. He rejects the humanistic belief that human nature is essentially good and that individuals, given an opportunity, will naturally be helpful and honorable. Machiavelli holds the contrary view, that individuals are much more likely to respond to fear and that power rather than the arts of rhetoric makes for good government.

Machiavelli's use of the Italian word *virtù* led him to be vilified as amoral. Machiavelli deliberately chose a word that meant both "manliness" or "ability" and "virtue as a moral quality." Earlier humanists had restricted *virtù* to the second meaning, using the word to refer to virtues like prudence, magnanimity, and love. Machiavelli tried to show that in some situations these "virtues" could have violent, even evil, consequences. If, for example, a prince was so magnanimous in giving away his wealth that he was forced to raise taxes, his subjects might come to hate him. Conversely, a prince who, through cruelty to the enemies of his state, brought peace and stability to his subjects might be obeyed and perhaps even loved by them. A virtuous ruler must be mindful of the goals to be achieved—that is what Machiavelli really meant by the phrase often translated as "the ends justify the means."

Machiavelli expected his readers to be aware of the ambiguous nature of virtue—whether understood as ability or as moral behavior. "One will discover," he concludes, "that something which appears to be a virtue, if pursued, will end in his destruction; while some other thing which seems to be a vice, if pursued, will result in his safety and his well-being."[11]

Like Guicciardini, Machiavelli rejected earlier humanistic assumptions that one needed merely

Machiavelli In this portrait Machiavelli is dressed as a government official. He wrote to a friend during his exile that each night when he returned from the fields he dressed again in his curial robes and pondered the behavior of governments and princes. *(Scala/Art Resource, NY)*

to imitate the great leaders of the past. Governing is a process that requires different skills at different times, he warned: "The man who adapts his course of action to the nature of the times will succeed and, likewise, the man who sets his course of action out of tune with the times will come to grief."[12] The abilities that allow a prince to gain power may not be the abilities that will allow him to maintain it.

With the writings of Machiavelli, humanistic ideas of intellectual, moral, and political reform came to maturation. Petrarch and the early humanists believed fully in the powers of classical wisdom to transform society. Machiavelli and his contemporaries admitted the importance of classical wisdom but also recognized the ambiguity of any application of classical learning to contemporary life.

THE ARTS IN ITALY, 1250–1550

Townsmen and artists in Renaissance Italy shared the humanists' perception of the importance of classical antiquity. Filippo Villani (d. 1405), a wealthy Florentine from an important business family, wrote that artists had recently "reawakened a lifeless and almost extinct art." In the middle of the fifteenth century the sculptor Lorenzo Ghiberti concluded that with the rise of Christianity "not only statues and paintings [were destroyed], but the books and commentaries and handbooks and rules on which men relied for their training." Italian writers and painters themselves recognized that the literary recovery of past practices was essential. The Renaissance of the arts can be divided into three periods. In the early Renaissance artists first imitated nature. In the middle period artists rediscovered classical ideas of proportion. In the High Renaissance, artists were "superior to nature but also to the artists of the ancient world," according to the artist and architect Giorgio Vasari (1511–1574), who wrote a famous history of the eminent artists of his day.

The Artistic Renaissance

The first stirrings of the new styles can be found in the late thirteenth century. The greatest innovator of the era was Giotto di Bondone of Florence (ca. 1266–1337). Although Giotto had a modest background, his fellow citizens, popes, and patrons

Giotto's Naturalism Later painters praised the naturalistic emotion of Giotto's painting. In this detail from the Arena Chapel, Giotto portrays the kiss of Judas, one of the most dramatic moments in Christian history. *(Scala/Art Resource, NY)*

throughout Italy quickly recognized his skill. He traveled as far south as Rome and as far north as Padua painting churches and chapels. According to later artists and commentators, Giotto broke with the prevailing stiff, highly symbolic style and introduced lifelike portrayals of living persons. He produced paintings of dramatic situations, showing events located in a specific time and place. The frescoes of the Arena Chapel in Padua (1304–1314), for example, recount episodes in the life of Christ. In a series of scenes leading from Christ's birth to his crucifixion, Giotto situates his actors in towns and countryside in what appears to be actual space. More significantly, Giotto manages to capture the drama of key events, like Judas's kiss of betrayal in the Garden of Gethsemane. Even Michelangelo, the master of the High Renaissance, studied Giotto's painting. Giotto was in such demand throughout Italy that his native Florence gave him a public appointment so that he would be required by law to remain in the city.

Early in the fifteenth century, Florentine artists devised new ways to represent nature that surpassed even the innovations of Giotto. The revolutionary nature of these artistic developments is evident from the careers of Lorenzo Ghiberti (1378–1455), Filippo Brunelleschi (1377–1446), and Masaccio (born Tomasso di ser Giovanni di Mone, 1401–ca. 1428). Their sculpture, architecture, and painting began an ongoing series of experiments with the representation of space through linear perspective. Perspective is a system for representing three-dimensional objects on a two-dimensional plane. It is based on two observations: (1) As parallel lines recede into the distance, they seem to converge; and (2) there is a geometrical relationship that regulates the relative size of objects at various distances from the viewer. Painters of the Renaissance literally found themselves looking at their world from a new perspective.

In 1401 Ghiberti won a commission to design door panels for the baptistery of San Giovanni in Florence. He was to spend the rest of his life working on two sets of bronze doors. The reliefs he created told the stories of the New Testament (the north doors) and the Old Testament (the east doors). In the commissions for the Old Testament scenes, Ghiberti used the new techniques of linear perspective to create a sense of space into which he placed his classically inspired figures. His work made him instantly famous throughout Italy. Later

The Doors of Paradise Ghiberti worked on panels for the baptistery from 1403 to 1453. In his representations of scenes from the Old Testament he combined a love of ancient statuary with the new Florentine interest in linear perspective. (*Alinari/Art Resource, NY*)

in the sixteenth century Michelangelo remarked that the east doors were worthy to be the "Doors of Paradise," and so they have since been known.

In the competition for the baptistery commission, Ghiberti had beaten the young Filippo Brunelleschi, who, as a result, gave up sculpture for architecture and later left Florence to study in Rome. While in Rome he is said to have visited and measured surviving examples of classical architecture—the artistic equivalent of humanistic literary research. When he returned to Florence, he had a firm sense of the nature of Roman architecture and how its forms could be adapted for Florentine life. According to Vasari, he was capable of "visualizing Rome as it was before the fall." Brunelleschi's debt to Rome is evident in his masterpiece, Florence's foundling hospital. Built as a

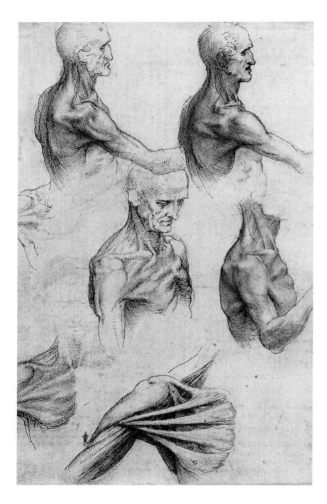

Leonardo da Vinci's Anatomical Drawings Leonardo studied carefully to record as accurately as possible the appearance of the human body. He was convinced that his keen observations made him the equal of any humanist. *(The Royal Collection © Her Majesty Queen Elizabeth II)*

of Santa Maria Novella. Masaccio built on experiments in linear perspective to create a painting in which a flat wall seems to become a recessed chapel. The space created is filled with the images of Christ crucified, the Father, and the Holy Spirit.

In the middle years of the fifteenth century, artists came to terms with the innovations of the earlier period. In the second half of the fifteenth century, however, artists like the Florentine Sandro Botticelli (1445–1510) added a profound understanding of classical symbolism to the technical interests of Masaccio and Brunelleschi. Botticelli's famous *Birth of Venus* and *Primavera* (*Spring*, 1478), both painted for Medici houses, are filled with Neo-Platonic symbolism concerning truth, beauty, and the virtues of humanity. (See the feature, "Weighing the Evidence: The Art of Renaissance Florence," on pages 470–471.)

The high point in the development of Renaissance art came at the beginning of the sixteenth century in the work of several artists throughout Italy. Artists in Venice learned perspective from the Florentines and added their own tradition of subtle coloring in oils. Raphael Sanzio (1483–1520), who arrived in Rome from his native Urbino in 1508, demonstrated that artistic brilliance was not simply a Florentine monopoly. His decorations of the Vatican palaces in Rome included his *School of Athens*, a painting that literally shows the debt of the Renaissance to past learning by portraying the great philosophers of the past as well as contemporary artists. It is in effect the synthesis of the classical learning and artistic innovation for which the Renaissance is famous.

The work of two Florentines, Leonardo da Vinci (1452–1519) and Michelangelo Buonarroti (1475–1564), best exemplifies the sophisticated heights that art achieved early in the sixteenth century. Leonardo, the bastard son of a notary, was raised in the village of Vinci outside of Florence. Cut off from the humanistic milieu of the city, he desired above all else to prove that his artistry was the equal of the formal learning of his social superiors. In his notebooks he confessed, "I am fully conscious that, not being a literary man, certain presumptuous persons will think they may reasonably blame me, alleging that I am not a man of letters."[13] But he defended his lack of classical education by arguing that all the best writing, like the best painting and invention, is based on the close observation of nature. Close

combination of hemispheres and cubes and resembling a Greek stoa or an arcaded Roman basilica, the long, low structure is an example of how profoundly different Renaissance architecture was from the towering Gothic of the Middle Ages.

In the first decade of the fifteenth century, many commentators believed that painting would never be as innovative as either sculpture or architecture. They knew of no classical models that had survived for imitation. Yet the possibilities in painting became apparent in 1427 with the unveiling of Masaccio's *Trinity* in the Florentine church observation and scientific analysis made Leonardo's work uniquely creative in all these fields. Leonardo is famous for his plans for bridges, airships, submarines, and fortresses. There seemed to be no branch of learning in which he was not interested. In painting he developed chiaroscuro, a technique for showing aerial perspective. He painted horizons as shaded zones rather than as sharp lines. "I know," he said, "that the greater or less quantity of air that lies between the eye and the object makes the outlines of that object more or less distinct."[14] It was his analytical observation that made Leonardo so influential on his contemporaries.

Michelangelo, however, was widely hailed as the capstone of Renaissance art. In the words of a contemporary, "He alone has triumphed over ancient artists, modern artists and over Nature itself." In his career we can follow the rise of Renaissance artists from the ranks of mere craftsmen to honored creators, courtiers who were the equals of the humanists—in fact, Michelangelo shared Petrarch's concern for reform and renewal in Italian society. We can also discern the synthesis of the artistic and intellectual transformations of the Renaissance with a profound religious sensitivity.

The importance of Michelangelo's contribution is obvious in two of his most important works: the statue *David* in Florence and his commissions in the Sistine Chapel of the Vatican in Rome. From his youth Michelangelo had studied and imitated antique sculpture, to the point that some of his creations were thought by many actually to be antique. He used his understanding of classical art in *David* (1501). Artists and citizens of Florence alike hailed the mammoth statue as a masterpiece. Citizens recalled David's defeat of the giant Goliath, saving Israel from almost certain conquest by the Philistines. *David* thus became a symbol of the youthful Florentine republic struggling to maintain its freedom against great odds. The statue was moved to a place of honor before the Palazzo Vecchio, Florence's city hall, signifying, as Vasari noted, that "just as David had protected his people and governed them justly, so whoever ruled Florence should vigorously defend the city and govern it with justice."[15]

Michelangelo was a committed republican and Florentine, but he spent much of his life working in Rome on a series of papal commissions. In 1508 he was called to Rome to work on the ceiling of the Sistine Chapel. Michelangelo spent four years decorating the ceiling with hundreds of figures and with nine scenes from the book of Genesis, including the famous *Creation of Adam*. In the late 1530s, he completed painting *The Last Judgment* on the wall above the altar. In that painting the techniques of perspective and the conscious recognition of debts to classical culture recede into the background as the artist surrounds Christ in judgment with saints and sinners, including in the hollow, empty skin of Saint Bartholomew a psychological self-portrait of an artist increasingly concerned with his own spiritual shortcomings.

Michelangelo's self-portrait reminds us that the intellectual content of the artist's work is one of its most enduring traits. He was a Platonist who believed that the form and beauty of a statue were contained in the stone itself. The artist's job was to peel away excess material and reveal the beauty within. As he noted in one of his poems, it was a process like that of religious salvation:

Just as by carving . . . we set
Into hard mountain rock
A living figure
Which grows most where the stone is most removed;
In like manner, some good works . . .
Are concealed by the excess of my very flesh.[16]

Art and Patronage

The religious passion of Michelangelo's poetry indicates one of the reasons that art was so popular in Renaissance Italy. Art, like poetry, provided symbols and images through which Italians could reason about the most important issues of their communities. Italians willingly spent vast sums on art because of its ability to communicate social, political, and spiritual values.

Italy in the fourteenth and fifteenth centuries was unusually wealthy relative to the towns and principalities of northern Europe. Despite the population decline caused by plague and the accompanying economic dislocations, per person wealth in Italy remained quite high. Because of banking, international trade, and even service as mercenaries, Italians, and particularly Florentines, had money to spend on arts and luxuries. Thus, the Italians of the Renaissance, whether as public or private patrons, could afford to use consumption of art as a form of competition for social and

The Sistine Chapel Painted from 1508 to 1512, the ceiling of the Sistine Chapel is Michelangelo's most famous work. Powerfully summarizing Renaissance faith in the unity of Christian faith and pagan wisdom, Michelangelo illustrated God's giving life to Adam (among other biblical scenes), while around the ceiling's border he placed *sibyls*, classical symbols of knowledge. *(Vatican Museums. Photo: A. Bracchetti/P. Zigrossi)*

political status. Increasingly in the fourteenth and fifteenth centuries there was a market for luxuries, including art, and there were numerous shops in which artists could be trained.

Artists in the modern world are accustomed to standing outside society as critics of commonly held ideas. In the late Middle Ages and Renaissance, artists were not alienated commentators. In 1300 most art was religious in subject and was created to be displayed in public. Throughout Europe art fulfilled a devotional function. Painted crucifixes, altar paintings, and banners were often endowed as devotional or penitential objects. The Arena Chapel in Padua, with its frescoes by Giotto, was built and endowed by a merchant anxious to pay for some of his sins.

In the late Middle Ages and Renaissance, numerous paintings and statues throughout Italy (and much of the rest of Europe) were revered for

their miraculous powers. During plague, drought, and times of war, people had recourse to the sacred power of the saints represented in these works of art. (See the feature, "Weighing the Evidence: A Painting of the Plague," on pages 434–435.) The construction of the great churches of the period was often a community project that lasted for decades, even centuries. These gigantic structures were mixtures of piety, civic pride, and religious patronage. The city council of Siena, for example, voted to rebuild its Gothic cathedral of Saint Mary, saying that the blessed Virgin "was, is and will be in the future the head of this city" and that through veneration of her "Siena may be protected from harm." Accordingly, it is clear that although the subject of art was primarily religious, the message was bound up in the civic values and ideas of the fourteenth and fifteenth centuries.

The first burst of artistic creativity in the fourteenth century was paid for by public institutions. Communal governments built and redecorated city halls to house government and to promote civic pride. These buildings contained the jail, the mint, law courts, assembly rooms, and even living quarters for administrators. Towns also reorganized streets, public squares, and the myriad hospitals and lodgings for travelers that dotted the city. In most towns there was a remarkable emphasis on the beauty of the work. Civic officials often named special commissions to consult with a variety of artists and architects before approving building projects. Governments, with an eye to the appearance of public areas, legislated the width of streets, height limits, and even the style of façades on houses.

The series of paintings called the *Good Government of Siena* illustrates how Italians used art to communicate political ideas. Painted in the first half of the fourteenth century by Ambrogio Lorenzetti (ca. 1300–1348), *Good Government* combined allegorical representations of Wisdom and the cardinal virtues on one wall with realistic street scenes of a well-ordered Siena on an adjacent wall. Across from the scenes of good government are its opposite, graphic representations of murder, rape, and general injustice and disorder. In this work the government sent a clear political message in a realistic painting that reminded viewers of specific events, times, places, and people. The popular preacher San Bernardino of Siena (1380–1444) made clear the message of Lorenzetti's painting: "To see Peace depicted is a delight and so it is a shame to see War painted on the other wall." And Bernardino's sermon reminded listeners of the conclusions they should draw: "Oh my brothers and fathers, love and embrace each other . . . give your aid to this toil which I have undertaken so gladly, to bring about love and peace among you."[17]

In Florence public art was often organized and paid for by various guild organizations. Guild membership was a prerequisite for citizenship, so guildsmen set the tone in politics as well as in the commercial life of the city. Most major guilds commissioned sculpture for the Chapel of Or San Michele, a famous shrine in the grain market (its painting of the Virgin was popularly thought to have wonder-working powers) and seat of the Guelf party, the city's most powerful political organization. Guilds took responsibility for the building and maintenance of other structures in the city as well. The guild of the cloth merchants paid for the frescoes in the baptistery of Saint John the Baptist (the city's patron saint) and commissioned the bronze doors by Lorenzo Ghiberti. The guild of the silk merchants oversaw the selection of Filippo Brunelleschi to design the foundling hospital. Guildsmen took pride in the creation of a beautiful environment, but as the cloth makers made clear in their decision to supervise the baptistery, the work reflected not only on the city and its patron saint but also on the power and influence of the guild itself.

The princes who ruled outside the republics of Italy often had similarly precise messages that they wished to communicate. Renaissance popes embarked on a quite specific ideological program in the late fifteenth century to assert their role as both spiritual leaders of Christendom and temporal lords of a central Italian state (see page 466). Rulers like the Este dukes of Ferrara and the Sforza dukes of Milan constructed castles within their cities or hunting lodges and villas in the countryside and decorated them with pictures of the hunt or knights in combat, scenes that emphasized their noble virtues and their natural right to rule.

By the mid-fifteenth century, patrons of art works in Florence and most other regions of Italy were more and more likely to be wealthy individuals. Republics, where all families were in principle equal, initially displayed a great suspicion of elaborate city palaces and rural villas. By the middle of the fifteenth century, however, such reserve was found in none but the most conservative republics, like Venice or Lucca.

Palaces, gardens, and villas became the settings in which the wealthy could entertain their peers, receive clients, and debate the political issues of the day. The public rooms of these palaces were decorated with portraits, gem collections, books, ceramics, and statuary. Many villas and palaces included private chapels. In the Medici palace in Florence, for example, the chapel is the setting for a painting of the Magi (the three Wise Men who came to worship the infant Jesus) in which the artist, Benozzo Gozzoli (1420–1498), used faces of members of the Medici family for the portraits of the Wise Men and their entourage. The Magi, known to be wise and virtuous rulers, were an apt symbol for the family that had come to dominate the city.

Artists at princely courts were expected to work for the glory of their lord. Often the genre of choice was the portrait. Perhaps the most successful portraitists of the sixteenth century were Sofonisba Anguissola (1532–1625) and her five sisters, all of whom were well-known painters. Anguissola won renown as a prodigy; one of her paintings was sent to Michelangelo, who forwarded it to the Medici in Florence. Later she was called to the Spanish court, where she produced portraits of the king, queen, and their daughter. She continued to paint after her marriage and return to Italy. Even in her nineties, painters from all parts of Europe visited her to talk about techniques of portraiture.

THE SPREAD OF THE RENAISSANCE, 1350–1536

By 1500, the Renaissance had spread from Italy to the rest of Europe. Even in the Slavic East, beyond the borders of the old Roman Empire, in Prague and Wroclaw one could find a renewed interest in classical ideas about art and literature. As ideas about the past and its relevance to contemporary life spread, however, the message was transformed in several important ways. Outside of Italy, Rome and its history did not play the dominant role they played in Italy. Humanists were interested more in religious than in political reform, and they responded to a number of important local interests. Yet the Renaissance idea of renewal based on a deep understanding and imitation of the past remained at the center of the movement. The key to the spread of humanistic culture was the rise of printing, which allowed for the distribution of texts that previously had been available only in Italy.

The Impact of Printing

In the fifteenth century the desire to have and to read complete texts of classical works was widespread, but the number of copies was severely limited by the time and expense of hand-copying, collating, and checking manuscripts. Poggio Bracciolini's letters are punctuated with remarks about the time and expense of reproducing the various

classical manuscripts he had discovered. One copy he had commissioned was so inaccurate and illegible as to be nearly unusable. Traveling to repositories and libraries was often easier than creating a personal library. It was rarely possible for someone who read a manuscript once to keep a complete copy to compare with other works.

The invention of printing with movable lead type changed things dramatically. Although block printing had long been known in China and was a popular way to produce playing cards and small woodcuts in Europe, only with the creation of movable type in the 1450s did printing become a practical way to produce books. Johann Gutenberg (d. 1468) in the German city of Mainz produced between 180 and 200 copies of the so-called Gutenberg Bible in 1452–1453. It was followed shortly by editions of the Psalms. German printers spread their techniques rapidly. As early as 1460, there were printing presses in Rome and Venice, and by 1470 the technique had spread to the Low Countries, France, and England. It has been estimated that by 1500 there were a thousand presses in 265 towns (Map 12.1). The output of the early presses in the first century of their existence was extremely varied. Gutenberg's first mass printing, for example, was of a thousand copies of a letter of indulgence, a remission of penance, for participation in a crusade. Early printers also produced highly popular and profitable small devotional books, abridged collections of saints' lives, and other popular literature, as well as the complete editions of classical authors and their humanistic and theological texts.

There has been a long and complex debate over the impact of printing, but there is general agreement on a number of points. An unexpected aspect of print culture was the rise of the printshop as a center of culture and communication. The printers Aldus Manutius (1450–1515) in Venice and Johannes Froben (d. 1527) in Basel were humanists. Both invited humanists to work in their shops as they edited their texts and corrected the proofs before printing. Printshops became a natural gathering place for clerics and laymen. Thus, they were natural sources of humanist ideas and later, in the sixteenth century, of Protestant religious programs. Printing allowed for the creation of agreed-upon standard editions of works in law, theology, philosophy, and science. Scholars in various parts of the

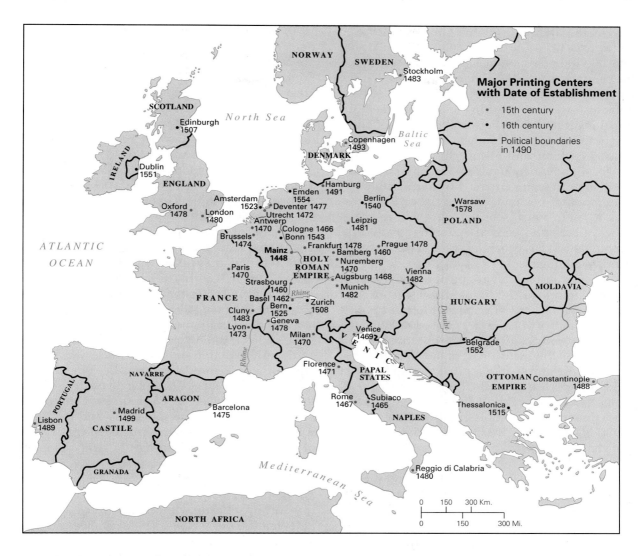

Map 12.1 The Spread of Printing Printing technology moved rapidly along major trade routes to the most populous and prosperous areas of Europe. The technology was rapidly adopted in highly literate centers such as the Low Countries, the Rhine Valley, and northern Italy.

world could feel fairly confident that they and their colleagues were analyzing identical texts. Similarly, producing accurate medical and herbal diagrams, maps, and even reproductions of art and architecture was easier. Multiple copies of texts also made possible the study of rare and esoteric literary, philosophical, and scientific texts in all parts of the world. Scholars studied standard editions of important texts like the Bible thoroughly and systematically.

Humanism Outside Italy

As the influence of the humanist movement extended beyond Italy, the interests of the humanists changed. Although there was a strong religious strain in Italian humanism, public life lay at the center of Italian programs of education and reform. Outside Italy, however, moral and religious reform formed the heart of the movement. Northern humanists wanted to reform and renew Christian life. In the aftermath of the Great Schism (see pages 398–401), Christians continued to desire reform within the church. Critics complained that the clergy was wealthy and ignorant and that the laity was uneducated and superstitious. Northern humanists were involved in the building of educational institutions, in the search for and publication of texts by Church Fathers, and in the writing of local customs and history. In the work of the two best-known humanists, Thomas More and Desiderius Erasmus, there is a sharp critique of contemporary behavior and, in the case of Erasmus, a call to a new sense of piety. The religious views of Erasmus were so influential that northern humanism has generally come to be known as "Christian humanism."

The intellectual environment of the northern Europe into which humanism spread had changed significantly since the thirteenth century. The universities of Paris and Oxford retained the status they had acquired earlier but found themselves competing with a host of new foundations. Most of these universities aspired, as the charter of Heidelburg (1386) noted, "to imitate Paris in all things." Like Paris, almost all had theological faculties dominated by scholastically trained theologians. Nevertheless, the new foundations often had chairs of rhetoric, or "eloquence," which left considerable scope for those who advocated humanistic learning. These new universities, from Bratislava in Slovokia (1465) to Uppsala in Sweden (1477), also reflected the increased national feeling in various regions of Europe. The earliest university in German-speaking lands, the Charles University in Prague (1348), was founded at the request of Emperor Charles IV of Luxembourg, whose court was in Prague. Vienna (1365), Aix (1409), Louvain (1425), and numerous other universities owed their foundation to the pride and ambition of local rulers.

Humanists on faculties of law in French universities practiced the historical study of jurisprudence. Like Lorenzo Valla, they believed that historical and linguistic studies were the best way to learn the law. Italian-trained French lawyers introduced what came to be called the "Gallican style" of jurisprudence. Because legal ideas, like language, changed over time, they argued that Roman law had to be studied as a historically created system and not as an abstract and unchanging structure. Humanists like Guillaume Budé (1468–

1540) moved from the study of law to considerations of Roman coinage, religion, and economic life in order to better understand the formation of Roman law. The desire to understand the law led other humanist-legists to add the study of society in ancient Gaul to their work on Rome and then the law of other societies as well.

The new universities often became centers of linguistic studies. Humanistic interest in language inspired the foundation of "trilingual" colleges in Spain, France, and the Low Countries to foster serious study of Hebrew, Greek, and Latin. Like Italian humanists, other humanists believed that knowledge of languages would allow students to understand more clearly the truths of Christianity. Typical of this movement was the archbishop of Toledo, Francisco Jiménez de Cisneros (1436–1517), who founded the University of Alcalá in 1508 with chairs of Latin, Greek, and Hebrew. He began the publication of a vast new edition of the Bible, called the "Polyglot Bible" (1522) because it had parallel columns in Latin, Greek, and, where appropriate, Hebrew. Unlike Valla, Jiménez did not intend to challenge the Vulgate (see page 446). Rather, he expected to clear up any confusion about its meaning. The university and the Bible were part of an effort to complete the conversion of Muslims and Jews and reform religious practices among the old Christians.

To the northern humanists, the discovery and publication of early Christian authors seemed critical to any reform within the church. Jacques Lefèvre d'Étaples (1455–1529) of France was one of the most famous of these humanistic editors of early Christian texts. He initially gained fame for his textual work on Aristotle. But after 1500 he concentrated on the edition of texts by the early Church Fathers. The true spirit of Christianity, he believed, would be most clear in the works and lives of those who lived closest to the age of the apostles. Christian humanists inspired by Lefèvre became key players in the later Reformation movements in France. Lefèvre's faith in the value of classical languages was shared by John Colet (1467–1519) of England, founder of St. Paul's School in London. He instituted a thorough program of teaching Latin and Greek aimed at creating scholars who would have access to the earliest Christian writings.

Tensions between the humanists and the advocates of Scholastic methods broke out over the cultural and linguistic studies that formed the heart of the humanist program. Humanists like Pico della Mirandola (see page 446) believed that there were universal moral and spiritual truths in other philosophies and religions. Following Pico's lead, Johannes Reuchlin (1455–1522) of Württemberg embarked on a study of the Cabala. Johannes Pfefferkorn, a Dominican priest and recent convert from Judaism, attacked Reuchlin's use of Jewish traditions in the study of Christian theology. Sides were quickly drawn. The theological faculties of the German universities generally supported the Dominican. The humanists supported Reuchlin. In his own defense Reuchlin issued *The Letters of Illustrious Men*, a volume of letters that he had received in support of his position. This work gave rise to one of the great satires of the Renaissance, *The Letters of Obscure Men* (1516), written by anonymous authors and purporting to be letters from various narrow-minded Scholastics in defense of the Dominican. Although the debate arose over the validity of Hebraic studies for Christian theology and not over humanistic ideas of reform or wisdom, it indicates the tension and divisions between the humanists and much of the Scholastic community. The early controversies of the Protestant Reformation were initially misunderstood by many as a continuation of the conflicts between humanists and Scholastic theologians over the uses of Hebrew learning.

Thomas More and Desiderius Erasmus

The careers of two humanists exemplified both the strength and the limits of the humanistic movement outside Italy: Sir Thomas More (1478–1535) of London and Desiderius Erasmus (1466–1536) of Rotterdam. After becoming close friends during one of Erasmus's visits to England, the two developed their careers along very different paths. More had been educated at St. Anthony's school in London and became a lawyer. A friend of John Colet, he translated Lucan and wrote a humanistic history of Richard III while pursuing his public career. He is most famous for his work *Utopia* (1516), the description of an ideal society located on the island of Utopia (literally "nowhere") in the newly explored oceans. This powerful and contradictory work is written in two books. Book I is a debate over the moral value of public service between Morus, a well-intentioned but practical politician, and

Hythloday, a widely traveled idealist. Morus tries to make the bureaucrat's argument about working for change from within the system. Hythloday rejects the argument out of hand. Thomas More himself seems to have been unsure at that time about the virtues of public service. He was of two minds, and the debate between Morus and Hythloday reflects his indecision. As part of his critique of justice and politics in Europe, Hythloday describes in Book II the commonwealth of Utopia, in which there is no private property but strict equality of possessions, and, as a result, harmony, tolerance, and little or no violence.

Since the publication of *Utopia*, debates have raged about whether More, or we, could ever really hope to live in such a society. Some scholars have questioned how seriously More took this work—he seems to have written the initial sections merely to amuse friends. Yet whatever More's intentions, Utopia's society of equality, cooperation, and tolerance continues to inspire social commentators.

Ironically, More himself, like his creation Morus, soon found himself trying to work for justice within precisely the sort of autocratic court that Hythloday criticized. Not long after the completion of *Utopia*, More entered the service of King Henry VIII (r. 1509–1547), eventually serving as chancellor of England. As a staunch Catholic and royal official, More never acted on utopian principles of peace and toleration. He was, in fact, responsible for persecution of English Protestants in the years before Henry VIII's break with Rome (see pages 527–529). More's opposition to Henry's break with the papacy and divorce and his refusal to acknowledge Henry as the head of the English church led him to resign his offices. He was eventually imprisoned and executed. More's writing was a stinging critique of political values. He implied that society could be reformed, yet in the period after 1521, his humanism and the ideas of Utopia had no influence on his own public life.

Unlike More, who was drawn to the power of king and pope, Erasmus always avoided working for authorities. Often called the "Prince of Humanists," he was easily the best-known humanist of the early sixteenth century. He was born the illegitimate son of a priest in the Low Countries. Forced by relatives into a monastery, he disliked the conservative piety and authoritarian discipline of traditional monastic life. Once allowed out of the monastery to serve as an episcopal secretary, he never returned. He lived and taught in France, England, Italy, and Switzerland. Of all the humanists it was Erasmus who most benefited from the printing revolution. The printer Aldus Manutius invited him to live and work in Venice, and he spent the last productive years of his life at Johannes Froben's press in Basel. He left the city only when Protestant reformers took control of the city government.

Over a long career Erasmus brought out repeated editions of works designed to educate Christians. His *Adages*, first published in 1500, was a collection of proverbs from Greek and Roman sources. The work was immensely popular, and Erasmus repeatedly brought out expanded edi-

Van Eyck: The Arnolfini Wedding Careful observation of people and places was typical of the new art of both the north and the south. Van Eyck seems to have recreated this scene to the smallest detail. His own image appears in the mirror on the wall. *(Reproduced by Courtesy of the Trustees, The National Gallery, London)*

tions. He tried to present Greek and Roman wisdom that would illuminate everyday problems. *The Colloquies* was a collection of popular stories, designed as primers for students, that taught moral lessons even as they served as examples of good language. His ironic *Praise of Folly* (1511) was dedicated to Thomas More. An oration by Folly in praise of folly, it was satire of a type unknown since antiquity. Folly's catalog of vices includes everyone from the ignoramus to the scholar. But more seriously, Erasmus believed, as Saint Paul had said, that Christians must be "fools for Christ." In effect, human existence is folly. Erasmus's Folly first made an observation that Shakespeare would refine and make famous: "Now the whole life of mortal men, what is it but a sort of play in which . . . [each person] plays his own part until the director gives him his cue to leave the stage."[18]

Erasmus's greatest contributions to European intellectual life were his edition of and commentaries on the New Testament. After finding and publishing in 1505 Lorenzo Valla's *Annotations on the New Testament*, Erasmus embarked on creating a critical edition of the Greek text and a Latin translation independent of the fourth-century Latin Vulgate of Jerome. Like Valla, and unlike Jiménez, Erasmus corrected parts of the Vulgate. He rejected the authority of tradition, saying, "The sin of corruption is greater, and the need for careful revision by scholars is greater also, where the source of corruption was ignorance."[19] What was revolutionary in his edition was his commentary, which emphasized the literal and historical recounting of human experiences. This edition was the basis of later vernacular translations of the Bible during the Reformation.

Underlying Erasmus's scholarly output was what he called his "Philosophy of Christ." Erasmus was convinced that the true essence of Christianity was to be found in the life and actions of Christ. Reasonable, self-reliant, truly Christian people did not need superstitious rituals or magic. In his *Colloquies* he gives the example of a terrified priest who during a shipwreck promised everything to the Virgin Mary in order to be saved from drowning. But, Erasmus observed, it would have been more practical to start swimming!

Erasmus believed that classical and Christian wisdom could wipe away violence, superstition, and ignorance. Unlike More, Erasmus never abandoned the humanistic program. Yet his philosophy of Christ, based on faith in the goodness and educability of the individual, was swamped in the 1520s and 1530s by the sectarian claims of both Protestants and Catholics. Although Erasmus's New Testament was influential in the Reformation, his calls for reforms based on tolerance and reason were not.

Renaissance Art in the North

In the early fifteenth century, while Brunelleschi and Masaccio were revolutionizing the ways in which Italian artists viewed their world, artists north of the Alps, especially in Flanders, were making equally striking advances in the way they painted and sculpted. Artistic innovation in the North began with changes tied closely to the world of northern courts; only later did artists take up the styles of the Italian Renaissance. Northerners took Italian Renaissance art and fit it to a new environment.

   Northern art of the late fourteenth and fifteenth centuries changed in two significant ways. In sculpture, the long, austere, unbroken vertical lines typical of Gothic sculpture gave way to a much more complex and emotional sculpture. In painting, Flemish artists moved from ornate, vividly colored paintings to experiments with ways to create a sense of depth. Artists strove to paint and sculpt works that more faithfully represented reality. The sculptures of Claus Sluter (1350–1406), created for a family chapel of the Burgundian dukes at Champmol, held a lifelike drama unlike the previous Gothic sculpture. Court painters like Jan van Eyck (c. 1390–1441) in miniatures, portraits, and altar paintings also moved away from a highly formalized style to a careful representation of specific places. In Van Eyck's portrait of the Italian banker and courtier Giovanni Arnolfini and his bride, the image of the painter is reflected in a small mirror behind the couple, and above the mirror is written, "Jan van Eyck was here, 1434." Where Italians of the early fifteenth century tried to recreate space through linear perspective, the Flemish used aerial perspective, softening colors and tones to create the illusion of depth.

   The influence of Renaissance styles in the north of Europe dates from the reign of the French king Francis I (r. 1515–1547), when Italian artists in

Portrait of a Black Man Albrect Dürer sketched this portrait in the early sixteenth century, most likely in a commercial center such as Venice or Nuremberg. By that time it was common to show one of the Three Wise Men as black, but such depictions, unlike Dürer's drawing here, were rarely based on portrait studies. (*Graphische Sammlung, Albertina*)

significant numbers traveled north. Francis invited Italian artists to his court—most notably Leonardo da Vinci, who spent the last years of his life in France. The most influential of the Italian-style creations in France was doubtless Francis's château Fontainebleau, whose decorations contained mythologies, histories, and allegories of the kind found in the Italian courts. Throughout the sixteenth century, Italianate buildings and paintings sprang up throughout Europe.

   Perhaps the most famous artist who traveled to Italy, learned Italian techniques, and then transformed them to fit the environment of northern Europe was Albrecht Dürer of Nuremberg (1471–1528). Son of a well-known goldsmith,

Dürer became a painter and traveled first through France and Flanders learning the techniques popular in northern Europe. Then in 1494 he left Nuremberg on the first of two trips to Italy, during which he sketched Italian landscapes and studied the work of Italian artists, especially in Venice. What he learned in Italy, combined with the friendship of some of Germany's leading humanists, formed the basis of Dürer's works, which combined northern humanistic interests with the Italian techniques of composition and linear perspective. Dürer worked in charcoal, watercolors, and paints, but his influence was most widely spread through the numerous woodcuts that he produced on classical and contemporary themes. His woodcut *Whore of Babylon*, prepared in the context of the debate over the reform of the church, is based on sketches of Venetian prostitutes completed during his first visit to Italy.

Numerous other artists and engravers traveled south to see the great works of Italian artists. The engravings they produced and distributed back home made the innovations of the Italians available to those who were unable to travel to the south. In fact, some now lost or destroyed creations are known only through the engravings produced by northern artists eager to learn about Italian techniques.

THE RENAISSANCE AND COURT SOCIETY

The educational programs of the humanists and innovations in the arts between 1300 and 1550 provided an opportunity for rulers and popes alike to use culture to define and celebrate their power. Art, literature, and politics merged in the brilliant life of the Renaissance Italian courts, both secular and papal. To understand fully the Renaissance and its importance in the history of Europe, we need to examine the uses of culture by governments, specifically investigating the transformation of European ideas about service at court during the fourteenth and fifteenth centuries. We will take as a model the politics and cultural life at one noble court: the court of the Gonzaga family of Mantua. We will also discuss the development of the idea of the Renaissance gentleman and courtier made famous by Baldassare Castiglione, who was reared at the Gonzaga court. Finally, we will see how the Renaissance papacy melded the

secular and religious aspects of art, culture, and politics in its glittering court in Rome.

The Elaboration of the Court

The courts of northern Italy interested themselves in the cultural and artistic innovations of the Renaissance artists and humanists inspired by classical civilization, and they closely imitated many of the values and new styles that were developing in the courts of northern Europe, such as the court of Burgundy. Throughout Europe, attendance at court became increasingly important to members of the nobility as a source of revenue and influence. Kings and the great territorial lords were equally interested in drawing people to their courts as a way to influence and control the noble and the powerful.

Rulers in most parts of Europe instituted monarchical orders of knighthood to reward allies and followers. The most famous in the English-speaking world was the Order of the Garter, founded in 1349 by King Edward III. The orders were but one of the innovations in the organization of the court during the fourteenth and fifteenth centuries. The numbers of cooks, servants, huntsmen, musicians, and artists employed at court jumped dramatically in the late Middle Ages. In this the papal court itself was a model for the rest of Europe. The popes at Avignon in the fourteenth century already had a household of nearly six hundred persons. If one included all the bureaucrats, merchants, local officials, and visitors who continually swarmed around the elaborate papal court, the number grew even larger.

Courts were becoming theaters built around a series of widely understood signs and images that the ruler could manipulate. Culture was meant to reflect the image of the ruler. On important political or personal occasions, rulers organized jousts or tournaments around themes drawn from mythology. The dukes of Milan indicated the relative status of courtiers by inviting them to participate in particular hunts or jousts. They similarly organized their courtiers during feasts or elaborate entries into the towns and cities of their realms.

The late fourteenth and fifteenth centuries were periods of growth in the political and bureaucratic power of European rulers. The increasingly elaborate and sumptuous courts were one of the tools that rulers used to create a unified culture and ideology. At the court of the Gonzagas in Mantua, one of the most widely known of the fifteenth-century courts, the manipulation of Renaissance culture for political purposes was most complete. Aristocratic values, humanism, and art all played a part in the creation of the Gonzaga reputation.

The Court of Mantua

The city of Mantua, with perhaps 25,000 inhabitants in 1500, was small in comparison with Milan or Venice—the two cities with which it was most commonly allied. Located in a rich farming region along the Po River, Mantua did not have a large merchant or manufacturing class. Most Mantuans were involved in agriculture and regional trade in foodstuffs. The town had been a typical medieval Italian city-state until its government was overthrown by the noble Bonacolsi family in the thirteenth century. Members of the family took control of most of the important communal offices, and friends of the Bonacolsis filled the representative assemblies. The Bonacolsis, in turn, were ousted from the city in 1328 by their erstwhile comrades, the Gonzagas, who ruled the city until 1627.

The Gonzagas faced a problem typical of many of the families who took control of towns in northern Italy. The state they were creating was relatively small, their right to rule was not very widely recognized, and their control over the area was weak. The first step for the Gonzagas was the creation of fortresses and fortified towns that could withstand foreign enemies. The second step was to gain recognition of their right to rule. They had, after all, taken power in a palace revolution. In 1329 they were named imperial vicars, or representatives in the region. Later, in 1432, they bought the title "marquis" from Emperor Sigismund for the relatively low price of £12,000—equivalent to a year's pay for their courtiers. By 1500 they had exchanged that title for "duke."

Merely buying the title, however, did little to improve the status of the family. The family's reputation was enhanced by Gianfrancesco (d. 1444) and Lodovico (d. 1478), who brought the Renaissance and the new court style to Mantua. Located in a strategic area between the Milanese and Venetian states, the Gonzagas maintained themselves through astute diplomatic connections with other Italian and European courts and through

service as well-paid mercenaries in the Italian wars of the fifteenth and sixteenth centuries. Lodovico served the Venetians, the Milanese, the Florentines, and even the far-off Neapolitans. With considerable understatement Lodovico concluded, "We have worn armor for a long time."

The creation of a brilliant court was an essential part of the Gonzaga program. By 1500 there may have been eight hundred or more nobles, cooks, maids, and horsemen gathered in the court. Critics called them idlers "who have no other function but to cater to the tastes of the Duke." Early in the Renaissance the Gonzagas involved themselves in the cultural movement of humanism. It was under the tutelage of the Gonzagas that Vittorino da Feltre created his educational experiment in Villa Giocosa, which drew noble pupils from throughout Italy. It would be hard to overestimate the value for the Gonzagas of a school that attracted sons of the dukes of Urbino, Ferrara, and Milan and numerous lesser nobles. The family also called numerous artists to Mantua. Lodovico invited Antonio Pisano, called Pisanello (ca. 1415–ca. 1456), probably the most famous court artist of the fifteenth century. Pisanello created a series of frescoes on Arthurian themes for the Gonzaga palace. In these frescoes Lodovico is portrayed as a hero of King Arthur's roundtable.

Although the Gonzagas never lost interest in the chivalric values of Arthurian romances, they are much better known for their patronage of art with classical themes. Leon Battista Alberti redesigned the façade of the church of Sant'Andrea for the Gonzagas in the form of a Roman triumphal arch. The church, which long had been associated with the family, became a monument to the Gonzaga court just as the Arch of Constantine celebrated imperial power. In the 1460s Lodovico invited Andrea Mantegna (1441–1506) to his court. Trained in Padua and Venice, Mantegna was at that time the leading painter in northern Italy. His masterwork is the *Camera degli Sposi* (literally, the "room of the spouses"), completed in 1474. It features family portraits of Lodovico Gonzaga and his family framed in imitation of Roman imperial portrait medallions. One scene shows Lodovico welcoming his son, a newly appointed cardinal, back from Rome—proof to all of the new status of the Gonzagas.

The Gonzaga court, like most other courts, was both public and private. Finances for the city,

appointments to public offices, and important political decisions were made by the men who dominated the court. On the other hand, as the prince's
domestic setting, it was both a place where women
were expected to be seen and a place where they
had influence. Women were actively involved in
creating the ideology of the court. Through the
patronage of classical paintings, often with moral
and political messages, wives of princes helped
make the court better known and more widely accepted throughout Italy and Europe.

The arrival of Isabella d'Este (1494–1539) at
court as the wife of Franceso Gonzaga marked the
high point of the Renaissance in Mantua. Isabella
had been classically educated at Ferrara by the son
of Guarino of Verona. She maintained an interest
in art, architecture, and music. As a patron of the
arts, she knew what she wanted. In one commission she specified the themes and the balance of
the work and told the artist to "add nothing." (See
the box, "Isabella d'Este Orders Art.") Isabella was
also an accomplished musician, playing a variety
of string and keyboard instruments. She and others of the Gonzaga family recruited musicians
from Flanders as well as Italians to their court. By
the end of the sixteenth century, Mantua was the
most important musical center of Europe. One festival brought 12,000 visitors to the city. It was in
Mantua that Claudio Monteverdi (1567–1643)
wrote works that established the genre of opera.

In the fourteenth century Petrarch had complained that however enjoyable feasting in Mantua might be, the place was dusty, plagued by
mosquitoes, and overrun with frogs. By the end of
the fifteenth century, the Gonzagas had secured
for themselves a prominent place on the Italian,
and the European, stage.

Castiglione and the European Gentleman

Renaissance ideas did not just spread in intellectual circles. They also were part of the transformation of the medieval knight into the early modern
"gentleman." In 1528, Baldassare Castiglione
(1478–1529) published *The Book of the Courtier*, a
work in which he distilled what he had learned in
his years at the various courts of Italy. Castiglione
was born in Mantua, distantly related to the ruling
Gonzaga family. He grew up at court and was sent
to the Sforza court in Milan to finish his education.
He returned home in 1499 to begin a career that

would include service in Mantua, Urbino, and
Rome. During his career Castiglione met the
greatest lights of the Renaissance. While he was in
Rome, he became friends with Michelangelo and
Raphael as well as with numerous humanistic
writers. He died in Spain while on a mission for
Pope Clement VII. When informed of his death,
the emperor Charles V remarked, "One of the
greatest knights in the world has died!" In his life
and in his book Castiglione summed up the great
changes that had transformed the nature of late
medieval chivalry.

The Book of the Courtier reports a series of fic-
tional discussions at the court of Urbino held over
the course of four nights in March 1507. Among
the participants are the duchess of Urbino, Elizabeth Gonzaga; her lady-in-waiting; and a group of
humanists, men of action, and courtiers. In four
evenings, members of the circle try to describe the
perfect gentleman of court. In the process they debate the nature of nobility, humor, women, and
love.

It was in many respects a typical gathering at
court and it reflects contemporary views of relations between men and women. The wives of
princes were expected to be organizers of life at
court, but still paragons of domestic virtues. The
women organize the discussion, which is carried
on by men. They direct and influence the talk by
jokes and short intervention but cannot afford to
dominate discussion. "[Women] must be more cir-
cumspect, and more careful not to give occasion
for evil being said of them . . . for a woman has not
so many ways of defending herself against false
calumnies as a man has."[20]

The topics were not randomly chosen. Castiglione explained that he wished "to describe the
form of courtiership most appropriate for a gentleman living at the courts of princes." Castiglione's
popularity was based on his deliberate joining of
humanistic ideas and traditional chivalric values.
Although his topic was the court with all its trappings, Castiglione tells his readers that his models
for the discussion are Greek and Latin dialogues,
especially those of Cicero and Plato. He was a Platonist. He believed that there was an inborn quality of "grace" that all truly noble gentlemen had. It
had to be brought out, however, just as Michelangelo freed his figures from stone. Castiglione held
that all moral and courtly virtues existed in tension
with their opposites: "no magnanimity without

Isabella d'Este Orders Art

In addition to her literary and musical interests, Isabella d'Este, the marchioness of Mantua, managed to create one of the foremost collections of Renaissance art in sixteenth-century Italy. In her quest to get representative works by the leading artists of the period, she has left an unparalleled collection of letters. In the following letter to Pietro Perugino she describes what she expects from a painting she had asked him to complete.

Master Perugino, painter, [shall] make a painting on canvas 2½ braccia high and 3 braccia wide, and the said Pietro, the contractor, is obliged to paint on it a certain work of Lasciviousness and Modesty (in conflict) with these and many other embellishments, transmitted in this instruction to the said Pietro by the said Marchioness of Mantua, the copy of which is as follows:

Our poetic invention, which we greatly want to see painted by you, is the battle of Chastity against Lasciviousness, that is to say, Pallas and Diana fighting vigorously against Venus and Cupid. And Pallas should seem almost to have vanquished Cupid, having broken his golden arrow and cast his silver bow underfoot; with one hand she is holding him by the bandage which the blind boy has before his eyes, and with the other she is lifting her lance and about to kill him. . . . And to give more expression and decoration to the picture, beside Pallas I want to have the olive tree sacred to her, with a shield leaning against it bearing the head of Medusa, and with the owl, the bird peculiar to Pallas, perched among the branches. And beside Venus I want her favorite tree, the myrtle, to be placed, but to enhance the beauty of the fount of water mist be included, such as a river or the sea, where fauns, satyrs and more cupids will be seen, hastening to the help of Cupid, some swimming through the river, some flying, and some riding upon white swans, coming to join such an amorous battle. . . .

I am sending you all these details in a small drawing so that with both the written description and the drawing you will be able to consider my wishes in this matter. But if you think that perhaps there are too many figures in this for one picture, it is left to you to reduce them as you please, provided that you do not remove the principal basis, which consists of the four figures of Pallas, Diana, Venus and Cupid. If no inconvenience occurs I shall consider myself well satisfied; you are free to reduce them, but not to add anything else. Please be content with this arrangement.

Source: David S. Chambers, *Patrons and Artists in the Italian Renaissance* (London and New York: Macmillan, 1970), pp. 136–138.

pusillanimity." With numerous examples of good and bad in the world, wisdom could be revealed only through careful imitation, for like the classical authors favored by humanists, Castiglione advises that "He who lacks wisdom and knowledge will have nothing to say or do."[21]

But what Castiglione's readers recalled most clearly was his advice about behavior. Francesco Guicciardini of Florence once remarked that "When I was young, I used to scoff at knowing how to play, dance, and sing, and other such frivolities. . . . I have nevertheless seen from experience that these ornaments and accomplishments lend dignity and reputation even to men of good rank."[22] Guicciardini's comment underlines the value that readers found in Castiglione's work. Grace may be inbred, but it needed to be brought to the attention of those who controlled the court. Courtiers should first of all study the military arts. They had to fight, but only in situations where their prowess would be noticed. Castiglione adds practical advice about how to dress, talk, and participate in music and dancing: Never leap about wildly when dancing as peasants might, but dance only with an air of dignity and decorum. Castiglione further urges the courtier to be careful in dress: The French are "overdressed"; the Italians too quickly adopt the most recent and colorful styles. Reflecting political as well as social realities, Castiglione advises black or dark colors, which "reflect the sobriety of the Spaniards, since external appearances often bear witness to what is within."

The courtier always must be at pains "to earn that universal regard which everyone covets." Too much imitation and obvious study, however, lead to affectation. Castiglione counseled courtiers to carry themselves with a certain diffidence or unstudied naturalness (*sprezzatura*) covering their artifice. If courtiers are successful, they will exhibit "that graceful and nonchalant spontaneity (as it is often called) . . . so that those who are watching them imagine that they couldn't and wouldn't even know how to make a mistake." Thus, Castiglione's courtier walked a fine line between clearly imitated and apparently natural grace.

Castiglione's book was an immediate success and widely followed even by those who claimed to have rejected it. By 1561 it was available in Spanish, French, and English translations. The reasons are not difficult to find. It was critical for the courtier "to win for himself the mind and favour of the prince." And even those who disliked music, dancing, and light conversation learned Castiglione's arts "to open the way to the favour of princes." Many of the court arts that Castiglione preached had been traditional for centuries. Yet Castiglione's humanistic explanations and emphasis on form, control, and fashion had never seemed so essential as they did to the cultured gentlemen of the courts of the Renaissance and early modern Europe. (See the box, "Giovanni della Casa on the Perfect Gentleman.")

The Renaissance Papacy

The issues of power and how it is displayed had religious as well as secular dimensions. After its fourteenth- and fifteenth-century struggles over jurisdiction, the Renaissance papacy found itself in need of a political and ideological counterweight to the centrifugal forces of conciliarism, reform, and local feeling. Popes needed to defend

their primacy within the church from conciliarists who had argued that all Christians, including the pope, were bound to obey the commands of general councils. The ideological focus of the revived papacy was Rome.

The first step in the creation of a new Rome was taken by Pope Nicholas V (r. 1446–1455), a cleric who had spent many years in the cultural environment of Renaissance Florence. Hoping to restore Rome and its church to their former glory, Nicholas and his successors patronized the arts, established a lively court culture, and sponsored numerous building projects. Nicholas was an avid collector of ancient manuscripts that seemed to demonstrate the intellectual and religious primacy of Rome. He invited numerous artists and intellectuals to the papal court, including the Florentine architect and writer Leon Battista Alberti (1404–1472). On the basis of his research in topography and reading done in Rome, Alberti wrote his treatise *On Architecture* (1452), the most important work on architecture produced during the Renaissance. It was probably under Alberti's influence that Nicholas embarked on a series of ambitious urban renewal projects in Rome, which included the construction of bridges, rebuilding of roads, and even plans for the rebuilding of Saint Peter's Basilica.

The transformation of Rome had an ideological purpose. As one orator proclaimed, "Illuminated by the light of faith and Christian truth, [Rome] is destined to be the firmament of religion . . . , the secure haven for Christians."[23] Thus, the papal response to critics was to note that Rome and its government were central to political and religious life in Christendom. By reviving the style and organization of classical antiquity, the church sought to link papal Rome to an imperial tradition reaching back to Augustus and even to Alexander the Great. Papal restorers rebuilt the earliest Christian churches of the city, emphasizing the literal continuity of imperial authority and apostolic tradition. To papal supporters, there could be only one authority in the church. Early tradition and the continuity of the city itself, they assumed, demonstrated papal primacy.

One particular monument in Rome captures especially vividly the cultural, religious, and ideological program of the papacy: the Sistine Chapel in the Vatican Palace. The chapel is best known for the decoration of the ceiling by the Florentine

Giovanni della Casa on the Perfect Gentleman

Giovanni della Casa (1503–1556), bishop of Benevento and a papal bureaucrat, wrote a book about how to get on at court. Il Galateo (Sir Galahad) *was a practical book of manners, concluding that the courtier should adopt not the most virtuous customs but the customs typical of the court.*

You must understand it behooves you to frame and order your manners and doings . . . to please those with whom you live. . . . For you must not only refrain from such things as being foul, filthy, loathsome, and nasty, but we must not so much as name them. . . . It is an ill-favoured fashion that some men use, openly to thrust their hands in what part of their body they like.

Likewise, I like it ill to see a gentleman settle himself to do the needs of nature in the presence of men, and after he had done to truss himself again before them. Neither would I have him (if I may give him counsel), when he comes from such an occupation, so much as wash his hands in the sight of honest company, for that the cause of his washing puts them in mind of some filthy matter that has been done apart. . . .

Besides, let not a man sit so that he turn his tail to him that sits next to him, nor lie tottering with one leg so high above the other that a man may see all bare that his clothes would cover. For such parts be never [dis]played but amongst those to whom a man need use no reverence. It is very true that if a gentleman should use such fashions before his servants, or in the presence of some friend of meaner condition than himself, it would betoken no pride, but a love and familiarity. . . .

We say that those be good manners and fashions which bring a delight or at least offend not their senses, their minds and conceits with whom we live. . . . It is not enough for a man to do things that be good, but he must also have a care he does them with a good grace. And good grace is nothing else but such a manner of light (as I may call it) as shines in the aptness of things. . . . Without which even proportion and measure, even that which is good is not fair.

Source: James Bruce Ross and Mary Martin McLaughlin, eds., *The Portable Renaissance Reader* (New York: Viking, 1953), pp. 340–347, from the 1576 translation by Robert Peterson.

artist Michelangelo (see page 452) and for the striking images of his painting of the Last Judgment. The chapel, however, was begun by Pope Sixtus IV in 1475. It was to be an audience chamber in which an enthroned pope could meet the representatives of other states. In addition it was thought that the college of cardinals would gather in the chapel for the election of new popes.

The decorations done before Michelangelo painted the ceiling reflect the intellectual and ideological values that Sixtus hoped to transmit to the churches and governments of Christendom. Along the lower sidewalls of the chapel are portraits of earlier popes, a feature typical of early Roman churches. More significant are two cycles of paintings of the lives of Moses and Christ, drawing parallels between them. To execute the scenes, Sixtus called to Rome some of the greatest artists of the late fifteenth century: Sandro Botticelli, Domenico Ghirlandaio, Luca Signorelli, and Pietro Perugino. The works illustrate the continuity of the Old Testament and New Testament and emphasize the importance of obedience to the authority of God. The meaning is most obvious in Perugino's painting of Saint Peter receiving the keys to the Kingdom of Heaven from Christ. The allusion is to Matthew 16:18: "Thou art Peter and upon this rock I shall build my church." The keys are the symbol of the

Giving of the Keys to Saint Peter Pietro Perugino's painting of Saint Peter's receiving from Christ the keys to "bind and loose" on earth and in heaven illustrates the basis of papal claims to authority within the Christian church. This is the central message of the decorative plan of the Sistine Chapel. *(Scala/Art Resource, NY)*

claim of the pope, as successor of Saint Peter, to have the power to bind and loose sinners and their punishments.

Directly across from Perugino's painting is Botticelli's *The Judgment of Corah*, which portrays the story of Corah, who challenged the leadership of Moses and Aaron while the Israelites wandered in the wilderness. Corah and his supporters, according to Numbers 16:33, were carried live into Hell. Various popes had cited the implications of the judgment of Corah. Eugenius IV (r. 1431–1437), for example, recalled the fate of Corah when he refused to acknowledge the power of the councils. The pope was bound to oppose the council, he argued, "to save the people entrusted to his care, lest together with those who hold the power of the council above that of the papacy they suffer a punishment even more dire than that which befell Corah."[24]

The effects of Renaissance revival were profound. Rome grew from a modest population of about 17,000 in 1400 to 35,000 in 1450. By 1517 the city had a population of over 85,000, five times its population at the end of the Great Schism. The papal program was a success. Rome was transformed from a provincial town to a major European capital, perhaps the most important artistic and cultural center of the sixteenth century. Visitors to the Sistine Chapel, like visitors to the papal city itself, were expected to leave with a more profound sense of the antiquity of the papal office and of the continuity of papal exercise of religious

authority. Because the building and decorating were being completed as the Protestant Reformation was beginning in Germany, some historians have criticized the expense of the political and cultural program undertaken by the Renaissance popes. But to contemporaries on the scene the work was a logical and necessary attempt to strengthen the church's standing in Christendom.

SUMMARY

Neither the world of Petrarch nor the world of courts described by Castiglione brought the beginning of modern individualism or a culture radically different from the medieval past. Between 1300 and 1600, however, Europe experienced profound cultural innovation in literature, political and social thought, and art. The attitudes toward the past and ideas about education formed in this period became the model of European cultural life for the next two hundred years. The cultural values of modern Europe were those inherited from the Renaissance.

The impulse for change arose from the belief, shared by thinkers from Petrarch to Machiavelli, that there was a great deal to be learned from study of the Roman past. This was the basis for humanistic innovations in language, history, and politics. Even revolutionary thinkers like Lorenzo Valla and Niccolò Machiavelli began with the study of classical literature and history. The same transformation is evident among the artists. Early in the fifteenth century, Florentines who experimented with perspective were intent on recovering lost Roman knowledge, and Michelangelo was praised not only for mastering but for going beyond Roman norms.

Issues of reform and renewal were less tied to public life in the monarchies of northern Europe. Moral and spiritual issues were more important. Yet the same movement from imitation to transformation is evident. Erasmus and Dürer assimilated the best of the new art and culture from Italy, but in the *Praise of Folly* and in Dürer's woodcuts, the use of past ideas and models was neither simple nor direct.

The integration of art, literature, and public life was most evident in the ways that art was used by governments. The Gonzaga court and the papacy clearly recognized the value of artistic and literary works as a way to explain and justify power and influence. The beauty of Mantegna's painting or the power of Michelangelo's vision does not obscure the message about power and authority.

Innovation depended on the study of the past. As humanists came to know more fully the art and history of Greece and Rome, they recognized the extent to which classical culture represented only one source of legal, historical, or moral understanding. Europeans' recognition of other, often competing, traditions would be tested in the sixteenth century, when they came face to face with a previously unknown world. It is to the geographic discoveries and European expansion that we now turn.

NOTES

1. Quoted in Federico Chabod, *Machiavelli and the Renaissance* (New York: Harper & Row, 1958), p. 153.
2. Albertino Mussato, *The Ecerinis*, trans. Joseph R. Berrigan. As quoted in Berrigan, "A Tale of Two Cities: Verona and Padua in the Late Middle Ages," in *Art and Politics in Late Medieval and Renaissance Italy, 1250–1500*, ed. Charles M. Rosenberg (Notre Dame, Ind.: University of Notre Dame Press, 1990), p. 77.
3. Quoted in J. B. Trapp, ed., *Background to the English Renaissance* (London: Gray-Mills Publishing, 1974), p. 11.
4. Quoted in N. Mann, *Petrarch* (Oxford: Oxford University Press), p. 67.
5. Petrarch, "On His Own Ignorance and That of Many Others," in *The Renaissance Philosophy of Man*, ed. Ernst Cassirer, Paul Oskar Kristeller, and John H. Randall (Chicago: University of Chicago Press, 1948), p. 105.
6. Quoted in Benjamin G. Kohl and Ronald G. Witt, *The Earthly Republic* (Philadelphia: University of Pennsylvania Press, 1978), p. 11.
7. Quoted in M. L. King, *Women of the Renaissance* (Chicago: University of Chicago Press, 1991), p. 194.
8. Quoted ibid., p. 222.
9. Quoted ibid., p. 198.
10. K. R. Bartlett, *The Civilization of the Italian Renaissance* (Lexington, Mass.: D. C. Heath, 1992), p. 314.
11. Quoted in *The Portable Machiavelli*, ed. and trans. Peter Bondanella and Mark Musa (New York: Penguin Books, 1979), p. 128.
12. Quoted ibid., p. 160.
13. Quoted in *The Notebooks of Leonardo da Vinci*, ed. J. P. Richter, vol. 1 (New York: Dover, 1883 and 1970), p. 14.
14. Quoted ibid., p. 129.
15. Giorgio Vasari, *The Lives of the Artists*, trans. George Bull (Baltimore: Penguin, 1965), p. 338.
16. Julia Bondanella and Mark Musa, eds., *The Italian Renaissance Reader* (New York: Meridian Books, 1987), p. 377.
17. I. Origo, *The Merchant of Prato: Francesco di Marco Datini*, 1335–1410 (New York: Knopf, 1957), pp. 155–156.
18. Quoted in A. Rabil, Jr., *Renaissance Humanism: Foundations, Forms, and Legacy*, vol. 2 (Philadelphia: University of Pennsylvania Press, 1988), p. 236.
19. Quoted ibid., p. 229.
20. Quoted in R. M. San Juan, "The Court Lady's Dilemma: Isabella d'Este and Art Collecting in the Renaissance," *Oxford Art Journal* 14 (1991): 71.
21. Unless otherwise noted, quotes of Castiglione are from Baldassare Castiglione, *The Book of the Courtier*, trans. George Bull (Baltimore: Penguin Books, 1967).
22. Quoted in R. W. Hanning and D. Rosand, eds., *Castiglione: The Ideal and the Real in Renaissance Culture* (New Haven, Conn.: Yale University Press, 1983), p. 17.
23. Raffaele Brandolini, as quoted in Charles L. Stinger, *The Renaissance in Rome* (Bloomington: Indiana University Press, 1985), p. 156.
24. Quoted in Leopold D. Ettlinger, *The Sistine Chapel Before Michelangelo* (Oxford: Oxford University Press, 1965), p. 105.

SUGGESTED READING

General Surveys

Brown, Alison. *The Renaissance.* 1988. An excellent short introduction to Renaissance art and culture designed for those with little or no background in the field.

(continued on page 472)

*W*eighing the Evidence

THE ART OF RENAISSANCE FLORENCE

In 1478 or shortly thereafter a member of the Medici family probably commissioned Sandro Botticelli to create the painting *Primavera (Spring)*. Since its completion, critics have been fascinated by its composition and lyrical qualities. Notice the figures who make up the picture. At the center is Venus, goddess of love. The group to Venus's left tells the classical myth of the return of spring. Zephyrus, the west wind, who brings the fertility and growth of springtime, pursues Chloris, a goddess of fertility. Flowers flow from Chloris's mouth as Zephyrus changes her into Flora, the flower-covered goddess of spring, who stands to her right. These figures are balanced by the group to Venus's right—the three Graces, who are dancing beside the figure of Mercury, the messenger and in this context the god of May. We can easily agree with the critics and connoisseurs who praise the grace and enchantment of Botticelli's mysterious wood filled with dark trees loaded with oranges and his meadow covered with flowers. The work demonstrates Botticelli's great artistic skill and the sophisticated knowledge of classical mythology current in Florence in the last quarter of the fifteenth century. But, you might ask, how much more can it tell us about the culture of Renaissance Florence?

Historians and art historians have struggled to find the best way to use art as a tool in historical studies. In the late nineteenth and early twentieth centuries, art connoisseurs carefully studied brush strokes and coloring so that they could understand and immediately recognize the techniques of the great masters. They believed that knowledge of an artist's technique would allow them to understand why the works of that artist were so widely popular. Modern historians, however, usually approach a work of art in other ways. We can ask, "What did the artist mean to paint?" Or we can ask, "How does Botticelli's *Primavera* compare to other great works of art, such as Pablo Picasso's *Guernica*?" But the most fruitful

inquiry is, "What might Botticelli's contemporaries have noticed in the work?"

To consider what that last question implies, it becomes important to know the social and artistic conventions that might illuminate the meanings in the work, where the work was intended to be displayed, and, finally, how the work comments on the social and cultural interests of the people whom the artist expected to view it.

Contemporaries valued Botticelli's brush stroke—that is, his artistic touch. But, surprisingly, they valued just as highly the materials in which he worked. One of the few contracts we have for a work by Botticelli notes carefully the cost and quantities of gold foil and aquamarine blue paint (an expensive and precious color). From this we can see that Botticelli's contemporaries were very aware of color. As Leon Battista Alberti observed critically of fifteenth-century Italians, most people associate gold leaf and deep blue colors with sumptuousness and majesty. Florentines were also very aware of the writings of contemporary humanists—and especially of the humanist belief that classical and Christian wisdom were basically one. Imbuing classical images with contemporary meanings did not seem odd to them. Botticelli's great popularity in Florence actually rested in part on his sophisticated use of classically inspired figures to comment on contemporary issues.

Primavera was meant to decorate the palace of a relative of Lorenzo de' Medici. It was probably designed to be seen by Lorenzo "the Magnificent" himself, who not only held a position of political and economic importance in the city but was a gifted poet and leader of a *brigata*, or company of poets and humanists. The brigata, in fact, was the primary audience for Botticelli's work. Lorenzo and the poets of his circle were actively combining what they believed was the best of their Tuscan culture with the classical philosophy and literature revived by the humanists. Lorenzo once wore on his armor the motto *Le Tems revient*, which

470

Botticelli: Primavera *(Art Resource, NY)*

loosely translated means "The ages shall be renewed." As we have seen, this renewal was an idea popular among the artists and humanists of Renaissance Italy. In *Primavera* Botticelli uses a number of symbols meant to remind viewers of Lorenzo de' Medici and his cultural interests. Look at the oranges in the trees, for example. They resemble the three balls on the Medici crest. The coming of spring in the person of Flora is precisely the sort of image with which Lorenzo wanted to be associated.

But what of the three Graces? How do they fit into a picture meant to celebrate the merging of old and new in Medicean Florence? For Lorenzo's contemporaries, they may have been the best possible image of the marriage of classical and Tuscan traditions. Lorenzo and his friends knew of the Graces and their association with spring from a variety of classical sources. These particular Graces, however, are Tuscan. The cut of their gowns and their dance would have been recognizable to Lorenzo's friends as typically Florentine. Lorenzo himself had earlier composed a dance, "A Simple Dance Called Venus," which could easily be the dance that they are doing. Next to them stands Venus, the goddess of love. But here she represents spring, flowering (Flora is, after all, the root of the name Florence), and renewal. Her arm is raised in a gesture of invitation. She is inviting us, or, more accurately, the Florentines of Lorenzo's time, to join in a dance of celebration and renewal.

What do we finally see in Botticelli's *Primavera*? It is not simply an imitation of either a classical text or any known classical figure. It seems instead that Botticelli created a sort of visual poem that incorporated numerous themes of classical learning and cultural renewal that were, by the late 1460s and 1470s, widely associated with Lorenzo de' Medici, the cultural and political master of Florentine life. The historian finds in the art of the Renaissance works of great beauty that convey through their materials, composition, and symbols a sense of the values and ideas that animated contemporary politics and culture.

Hale, John R. *The Civilization of Europe in the Renaissance.* 1994. A beautifully written survey of the culture of Europe from the fifteenth to the seventeenth century.

Kelly, Joan. *Women, History & Theory.* 1984. Includes Kelly's famous "Did Women Have a Renaissance?" as well as an essay on the *querelle des femmes.*

King, M. L. *Women of the Renaissance.* 1991. A survey of the social, economic, and cultural experience of women during the Renaissance.

Nauert, Charles G., Jr. *Humanism and the Culture of Renaissance Europe.* 1995. An excellent short survey of European thought in the Renaissance.

Rabil, Albert, Jr. *Renaissance Humanism: Foundations, Forms and Legacy.* 3 vols. 1988. An excellent and quite accessible introduction to Renaissance humanism.

Humanism

Kohn, Benjamin, and Ronald Witt, eds. *The Earthly Republic.* 1978. An important anthology of writings by fourteenth- and fifteenth-century civic humanists. The general introduction is an especially clear discussion of the rise of civic humanism.

Mann, N. *Petrarch.* 1984. An excellent introduction to Petrarch's life and thought, designed for readers with little prior experience with Renaissance thought.

Skinner, Q. *The Foundations of Modern Political Thought.* Vol. 1. *The Renaissance.* 1978. A survey of political thought that attempts to place thinkers in their social and political context.

Woodward, W. H., ed. *Vittorino da Feltre and Other Humanist Educators: Essays and Versions. An Introduction to the History of Classical Education.* 1897. A volume of essays and documents that are excellent introductions to the Renaissance educational program.

Art and Society in Renaissance Italy

Baxendall, Michael. *Painting and Experience in Fifteenth-Century Italy.* 1972. A volume that helps the reader see the art of the Renaissance as it would have been seen in the period.

Dempsey, Charles. *The Portrayal of Love: Botticelli's Primavera and Humanist Culture at the time of Lorenzo the Magnificent.* 1992. A complex but rewarding demonstration of how artistic and literary culture are combined in a single work. Essential for our discussion of Botticelli's *Primavera.*

Goldthwaite, Richard. *Wealth and the Demand for Art in Italy, 1300–1600.* 1993. A thoughtful essay about the social and economic influences on the creation and patronage of art.

Hartt, F. *History of Italian Renaissance Art: Painting, Sculpture, Architecture.* 1987. A comprehensive and lavishly illustrated survey of Renaissance art that is sensitive to the social and political milieu in which artists worked.

Letts, R. M. *The Renaissance.* 1992. An excellent introductory essay on the art of Renaissance Italy. Especially good on the innovations of the early fifteenth century.

Panofsky, E. *Renaissance and Renascences in Western Art.* 1969. A difficult but important essay on the concept of Renaissance and on the nature of the differences between the Renaissance and previous periods of creative innovation.

Humanism and Culture Outside Italy

Eisenstein, E. L. *The Printing Press as an Agent of Change: Communications and Cultural Transformations in Early Modern Europe.* 1979. A discussion of the ways in which print culture changed social and intellectual life, rather than of the technology of print itself.

Goodman, A., and A. Mackay, eds. *The Impact of Humanism.* 1990. A volume of basic surveys of the arrival of Italian humanistic ideas in the various lands of Europe.

Marius, R. *Thomas More: A Biography.* 1984. A beautifully written biography that questions More's humanistic interests and looks particularly at his divided feelings about religion and the state.

Murray, Linda. *The Late Renaissance and Mannerism.* 1967. An introductory survey that traces Renaissance themes as they move out of Italy, especially through France, Germany, and Flanders.

Panofsky, E. *Albrecht Dürer.* 1948. The best study of the life and work of Germany's greatest Renaissance artist.

Courts and Castiglione

Burke, Peter. *The Fortunes of the Courtier: The European Reception of Castiglione's Cortegiano.* 1995. A well-written survey of the influence of Castiglione's ideas.

Dickens, A. G., ed. *The Courts of Europe.* 1977. A well-illustrated collection of essays for the general reader on courts from the Middle Ages to the eighteenth century.

Elias, N. *The Civilizing Process.* 1978. A classic discussion of the transformation of manners and behavior at the courts of Renaissance Europe. Contains difficult analysis but lively descriptions.

Ettlinger, Leopold. *The Sistine Chapel before Michelangelo.* 1965. A scholarly discussion of the images and papal ideology discussed in this chapter.

Keen, Maurice. *Chivalry.* 1984. A well-written survey of chivalry that includes discussion on its transformation at the end of the Middle Ages.

Stinger, Charles L. *The Renaissance in Rome.* 1985. An engaging survey of the vibrant cultural life at the papal court and in the city during the Renaissance.

Woods-Marsden, J. *The Gonzaga of Mantua and Pisanello's Arthurian Frescoes.* 1988. A broad and well-illustrated discussion of how the artistic interests of the Gonzagas served their social and political needs.

CHAPTER 13

Europe, the Old World and the New

I n the spring of 1493, Christopher Columbus wrote to a friend and supporter at the court of Ferdinand and Isabella, reporting the glorious discoveries he had recently made during his successful trip to the Indies. "I found very many islands filled with people innumerable, and of them all I have taken possession for their Highnesses, by proclamation made and with the royal standard unfurled, and no opposition was offered to me."[1] His actions, as reported in the letter, seemed to establish beyond question Spanish claims to these new lands. Columbus went on to enumerate the wealth, rivers, natural resources, and marvels to be found in this new world. He concluded by promising he could send the monarchs "as much gold as they need" and "a thousand other things of value." This letter, rather than a more sober report sent to the monarchs themselves, was almost instantly printed and reprinted throughout Europe.

Columbus soon arrived at the Spanish court himself, accompanied by seven natives from the Caribbean and countless green parrots. His initial enthusiasm—and awards—were great, but neither lasted particularly long. Columbus's voyage was both a capstone of previous contacts with non-European societies and a prelude to dramatic, often tragic encounters between Europe and the rest of the world. As we shall see, Europeans tended to respond to the challenges of this new world according to their view of themselves and the old world they had known.

Columbus's adventure was part of a series of voyages begun in the last decade of the fifteenth century that eventually carried Europeans to most parts of the world, unifying the "Old World" continents of Asia, Africa,

French map of
the New World,
ca. 1550.

and Europe with a "New World": the Americas and the islands of the Pacific. The story of the first navigators, their technological advances, and the colonies they established may seem straightforward, but scholars interested in the discoveries and expansion that occurred during the late fifteenth and sixteenth centuries have viewed these events in vastly different ways. Accounts of the meeting of the Old World and the New, perhaps more than any other episode of Western history, have been shaded by the perspectives of both the writer and the reader.

Those who wanted to focus on the transfer of European religion and culture to new lands have viewed Christopher Columbus and the other early explorers as important symbols of the creation of a New World with new values. Those who sought the origins of modern scientific rationalism have believed that Columbus's voyage across the Atlantic Ocean proves that he was a "Renaissance man" who saw through the myths and superstitions of the Middle Ages. However, the descendants of the native peoples who greeted the newly arriving Europeans—the Amerindians, Aborigines, Maori, and Polynesians who lived in North and South America, Australia, New Zealand, and the islands of the Pacific—remind us that the outsiders brought slavery, modern warfare, and epidemic diseases that virtually destroyed indigenous cultures.

Spain commissioned Columbus to sail west because the Portuguese already controlled eastern routes to Asia around the African coast and because certain technological innovations made long open-sea voyages possible. Thus, as those who celebrate Columbus's achievements have said, the story includes national competition, the development of navigational techniques, and strategic choices. Another aspect of the story, however, is the political, cultural, and military clash that took place in the Atlantic, the Caribbean, and Central and South America. The Europeans overthrew the great empires of the Aztecs and Incas, but the transfer of European culture was never as complete as the Europeans thought or expected. The language and customs of the conquered peoples, blanketed by European language and law, survived, though the lands colonized by the Europeans would never again be as they had been before their encounter with the Old World.

THE EUROPEAN BACKGROUND, 1250–1492

Over the course of the late Middle Ages, Europeans developed the desire and the ability to reach distant lands in Africa and Asia. Three critical factors for the exploratory voyages of the fifteenth and early sixteenth centuries were technology, curiosity and interest, and geographic knowledge. A series of technological innovations made sailing far out into the ocean less risky and more predictable than it had been. The writings of classical geographers, myths and traditional tales, and merchants' accounts of their travels fueled popular interest in the East and made ocean routes to the East seem safe and reasonable alternatives to overland travel.

Navigational Innovations

The invention of several navigational aids in the fourteenth and fifteenth centuries made sailing in open waters easier and more predictable. Especially important was the fly compass, consisting of a magnetic needle attached to a paper disk (or "fly"). The simple compass had been invented in China and was known in Europe by the late twelfth century, but it was not initially marked off in degrees so was only a rudimentary aid to navigation. By 1500, astrolabes and other devices enabling sailors to use the position of the sun and stars to assist in navigation were also available. An astrolabe allowed sailors to measure the altitude of the polestar in the sky and thereby calculate the latitude, or distance from the equator, at which their ship was sailing. Still, until the general adoption of charts marked with degrees of latitude, most navigators relied on the compass, experience, and instinct.

The most common Mediterranean ship of the late Middle Ages was a galley powered by a combination of sails and oars; such a vessel was able to travel quickly and easily along the coast. Because of limited space and the need for a large crew of rowers, galleys were not ideal for long-distance travel or transport of bulky materials. Throughout the Mediterranean, shipbuilders experimented with new designs, and during the fifteenth century the Portuguese and Spanish perfected the caravel. Large, square sails efficiently caught the wind and propelled the caravel forward, and smaller triangular sails (lateens) allowed the caravel to tack diagonally across a headwind, virtually sailing into the wind. The caravel was larger and needed a smaller crew than the galley, and it was more maneuverable than ships with only square sails.

By the 1490s the Portuguese and Spanish had developed the ships and techniques that would make long open-sea voyages possible. What remained was for Europeans, especially the Portuguese and Spanish, to conclude that such voyages were both possible and profitable.

Lands Beyond Christendom

The Greeks and Romans had contacts with the civilizations of Asia and Africa, and in the Middle Ages interest in the lands beyond Christendom had never been lost. In the thirteenth and fourteenth centuries, European economic and cultural contacts with these lands greatly increased. The rising volume of trade between Europe and North Africa brought with it information about the wealthy African kingdoms of the Niger Delta. The Mongols in the thirteenth century allowed European merchants and missionaries to travel along trade routes extending all the way to China, opening regions formerly closed to them by hostile Muslim governments.

Trade in the Mediterranean also kept Christians and Muslims, Europeans and North Africans in close contact. Europeans sold textiles to Arab traders, who carried them across the Sahara to Timbuktu, where they were sold for gold bullion from the ancient African kingdoms of Ghana and Mali located just above the Niger River. European chroniclers recorded the pilgrimage to Mecca of Mansa Musa, the fabulously wealthy fourteenth-century emperor of Mali. Italian merchants tried unsuccessfully to trade directly with the African kingdoms, but Muslim merchants prevented any permanent contact.

Europeans enjoyed more successful trade connections farther east. The discovery in London of a brass shard inscribed with a Japanese character attests to the breadth of connections in the early fourteenth century. After the rise of the Mongols, Italian merchants regularly traveled east through Constantinople and on to India and China. By the fourteenth century, they knew how long travel to China might take and the probable expenses along the way.

European intellectuals also maintained an interest in the lands beyond Christendom. They had

The World Beyond Christendom
Medieval Christians believed that wondrous peoples lived beyond the borders of Christendom. Images of headless or one-legged men were usually included in travel accounts. This picture from Marco Polo's *Travels* shows what many Europeans expected to find when they traveled. (*Bibliothèque Nationale*)

read the late classical and early medieval authors who described Africa, the Indies, and China. The work of the greatest of the classical geographers, Ptolemy of Alexandria (ca. A.D. 127–145), was known only indirectly until the early fifteenth century, but medieval thinkers read avidly and speculated endlessly about the information contained in the works of authors from Late Antiquity, such as Martianus Capella, who lived in the fifth century A.D. Martianus preserved fantastic myths and tales along with geographic observations that he had gathered from the writings of Ptolemy and others. He reported, for example, that there were snakes in Calabria, in isolated southern Italy, that sucked milk from cows and men who became wolves—the earliest mention of werewolves. Martianus assumed that a person who traveled to the south and east of Europe was more and more likely to find wonders. Moreover, it seemed to early geographers that the heat at the equator must be so intense that it would be impossible for life to exist there. By the twelfth century, fictitious reports circulated widely in the West of a wealthy Christian country in the East or possibly in Africa. The fictitious kingdom of Prester John was often associated with the Christian groups living near the shrine of Saint Thomas in India or the kingdom of Ethiopia. In the fifteenth century, European Christians looked to Prester John and eventually to the Christians of Ethiopia for aid against the Muslims.

Tales of geographic marvels are epitomized by the *Travels of Sir John Mandeville*, a book probably written in France but purporting to be the observations of a knight from St. Albans, just north of London. Mandeville says that he left England in 1322 or 1323 and traveled to Constantinople, Jerusalem, Egypt, India, China, Persia, and Turkey. In the first half of the book he describes what seems to be a typical pilgrimage to the Holy Land. As the author's travels continue eastward, however, the narrative shifts dramatically. Sir John describes the islands of wonders, inhabited by dog-headed men, one-eyed giants, headless men, and hermaphrodites. Not only does he describe his discovery of the lost tribes of Israel but he also records the location of Paradise. Less fantastically, Mandeville reports that the world could be, and in fact has been, circumnavigated. He adds that the lands south of the equator, the Antipodes, are habitable.

Mandeville's *Travels* and similar fantastic tales kept alive geographic speculation. They also raised expectations in travelers who actually did venture to the East. Thirteenth-century visitors to central Asia carefully asked their Mongol hosts about the exact locations of these wonders. Columbus, in his dispatches, included reports he had received of an island of Amazons in the Caribbean, and he believed that he had found the rivers flowing from Paradise along the coast of Venezuela.

More reliable information became available in the thirteenth century largely because of the arrival of the Mongols. Jenghiz Khan and his descendants created an empire that reached from eastern Hungary to China (see page 368). This *pax Mongolica*, or area of Mongol-enforced peace, was a region tolerant of racial and cultural differences. In the 1240s and 1250s a series of papal representatives traveled to the Mongol capital at Karakorum near Lake Baikal in Siberia. The letters of these papal ambassadors, who worked extensively to gain converts and allies for a crusade against the Turks, were widely read and greatly increased accurate knowledge about Asia. Other missionaries and diplomats journeyed to the Mongol court and some continued farther east to India and China. By the early fourteenth century, the church had established a bishop in Beijing.

Italian merchants followed closely on the heels of the churchmen and diplomats. The pax Mongolica offered the chance to trade directly in Asia and the adventure of visiting lands known only from travel literature. In 1262, Niccolò and Maffeo Polo left on their first trip to China. On a later journey the two Venetians took Niccolò's son, Marco (1255–1324), who remained in China for sixteen or seventeen years. Marco dictated an account of his travels to a Pisan as they both sat as prisoners of war in a Genoese jail in 1298. It is difficult to know how much of the text really represents Marco's own observations and how much is chivalric invention by the Pisan. Some even suggest that Marco himself never traveled to China. His contemporaries, however, seem to have had few doubts. The book was widely known. Columbus himself owned and extensively annotated a copy of Marco Polo's *Travels*.

In his account Marco claims that he was an influential official in China; and he may, in fact, be the "Po-Lo" mentioned in Chinese sources as a low-level imperial bureaucrat of the emperor

Pegalotti on Travel to the East

In his Handbook for Merchants, *Francesco Pegalotti describes travel to Asia and the commercial customs of the area, demonstrating how usual such travel had become by 1340, when his work was published.*

First [of all] it is advisable for him [the traveler] to let his beard grow long and not shave. And at Tana [on the Black Sea coast] he should furnish himself with guide-interpreters, and he should not try to save by hiring a poor one instead of a good one. . . . And besides interpreters he ought to take along at least two good manservants who know the Cumanic [Mongol] tongue well. And if the merchant wishes to take along from Tana any woman with him, he may do so— and if he does not wish to take one, there is no obligation; yet if he takes one, he will be regarded as a man of higher condition than if he does not take one. . . . And [for the stretch] from Tana to Astrakhan he ought to furnish himself with food for twenty-five days—that is with flour and salt and fish, for you find meat in sufficiency in every locality along the road. . . . The road leading from Tana to Cathay is quite safe both by day and by night, according to what the merchants report who have used it—except that if he should die along the road, when going or returning, everything would go to the lord of the country where the merchant dies. . . .

All silver which the merchants carry with them when going to Cathay, the lord of Cathay causes to be withdrawn and placed in his treasury; and to the merchants who bring it he gives paper money, that is, yellow paper stamped with the seal of the said lord, that money being called *balisci*. And with the said money you may and can purchase silk and any other merchandise or foods you may wish to buy. And all the people of the country are bound to accept it, and yet people do not pay more for merchandise although it is paper money.

Source: R. S. Lopez and I. Raymond, eds., *Medieval Trade in the Mediterranean World* (New York: Columbia University Press, 1955), pp. 356, 357, 358.

Kublai Khan. Marco describes the long, difficult trip to China, his equally arduous return, and the cities and industries he found. He was most impressed by the trade of Ch'nan (modern Hangzhou on the central coast of China)—one hundred times greater, he thought, than the trade of Alexandria in Egypt, a renowned port on the Mediterranean. Marco also visited modern Sri Lanka, Java, and Sumatra. His tales mix a merchant's observations of ports, markets, and trade with myths and marvels—tales of dog-headed men and the kingdom of Prester John.

By 1300 there seems to have been a modest community of Italians in China. By the late thirteenth and fourteenth centuries, Italian traders were traveling directly to the East in search of Asian silks, spices, pearls, and ivory. They and other European merchants could consult the *Handbook for Merchants* (1340) by the Florentine Francesco Pegalotti, which described the best roads, likely stopping points, and the appropriate freight animals for a trip to the East. (See the box, "Pegalotti on Travel to the East.") These merchants found that they had cheap access to spices, silks, and even porcelains, which they shipped back to the West. Fragmentary reports of Europeans in the Spice Islands (also known as the Moluccas), Japan, and India indicate that many Europeans in addition to merchants traveled simply for the adventure of visiting new lands.

The Revolution in Geography

The situation changed significantly over the course of the fourteenth century. With the conversion of the Mongols to Islam, the breakdown of

Mongol unity, and the subsequent rise of the Ottoman Turks in the fourteenth century, the highly integrated and unusually open trade network fell apart. The caravan routes across southern Russia, Persia, and Afghanistan were closed to Europeans. Western merchants once again became dependent on Muslim middlemen.

The reports of travelers, however, continued to circulate long after the closing of the trade routes. This new information was avidly followed by Western geographers anxious to assimilate it. Marco Polo's *Travels* and the classical geographic theories of Ptolemy contributed to a veritable revolution in geography in the decades before the Portuguese and Spanish voyages.

In 1375, Abraham Cresques, a Jewish mathematician from the Mediterranean island of Majorca, produced what has come to be known as the *Catalan World Atlas*. He combined the traditional medieval *mappamundi* (or world map) with a Mediterranean portolan. The mappamundi attempted to show both spatial and theological relationships. It often followed the O-T form—that is, a circle divided into three parts (①) representing Europe, Africa, and Asia, the lands of the descendants of Noah. Jerusalem—the symbolic center of the Christian religion—is always at the center of the map. The portolan, in contrast, was entirely practical. From the late thirteenth century, mariners had been developing atlases that included sailing instructions and accurate portrayals of ports, islands, and shallows along with general compass readings. The *Catalan World Atlas* largely holds to the portolan tradition but has more accurate representations of the lands surrounding the Mediterranean.

In the fifteenth century, following Ptolemy's suggestions, mapmakers began to divide their maps into squares marking lines of longitude and latitude. This format made it possible to accurately show the contours of various lands and the relationship of one landmass to another. Numerous maps of the world were produced in this period. The culmination of this cartography was a globe constructed for the city of Nuremberg in 1492, the very year Columbus set sail. From these increasingly accurate maps, it has become possible to document the first exploration of the Azores, the Cape Verde Islands, and the western coast of Africa.

The Florentine mathematician Paolo Toscanelli, in a letter of 1474 to the king of Portugal, included a map demonstrating, he believed, the short distance to be covered if one were to sail straight west first to Japan and then on to China. Columbus knew the letter and some think he may have corresponded with the Florentine. Not surprisingly, Columbus, after his voyages, observed that maps had been of no use to him. True enough. But without the accumulation of knowledge by travelers and the mingling of that knowledge with classical ideas about geography, it is doubtful whether Columbus or the Portuguese Vasco da Gama would have undertaken or could have found governments willing to support the voyages that so dramatically changed the relations between Europe and the rest of the world.

PORTUGUESE VOYAGES OF DISCOVERY, 1350–1515

Portugal, a tiny country on the edge of Europe, for a short time led the European expansion. Portuguese sailors were the first Europeans to perfect the complex techniques of using the winds and currents of the south Atlantic, especially along the western coast of Africa (Map 13.1). Portugal's experience gives a good indication of the options open to the Europeans as they extended their influence into new areas. As the Portuguese moved down the African coast and later as they tried to compete commercially in Asia, they found that they could not automatically transfer European economic and commercial traditions into new environments. In each new location, they faced new challenges. Solutions varied from place to place. In some areas the Portuguese created a network of relatively isolated naval and trading stations to control the movement of goods. In other areas they attempted to create large, dominant Portuguese colonies. In still other areas they used plantation slavery to create commercial products for the international market. The other European states would use these same strategies in Asia and in the New World as they too extended their economic and political interests beyond continental Europe.

The Early Voyages

Portugal, like other late medieval European states, hoped that exploration and expansion would lead to "gold and Christians." The search for Christians

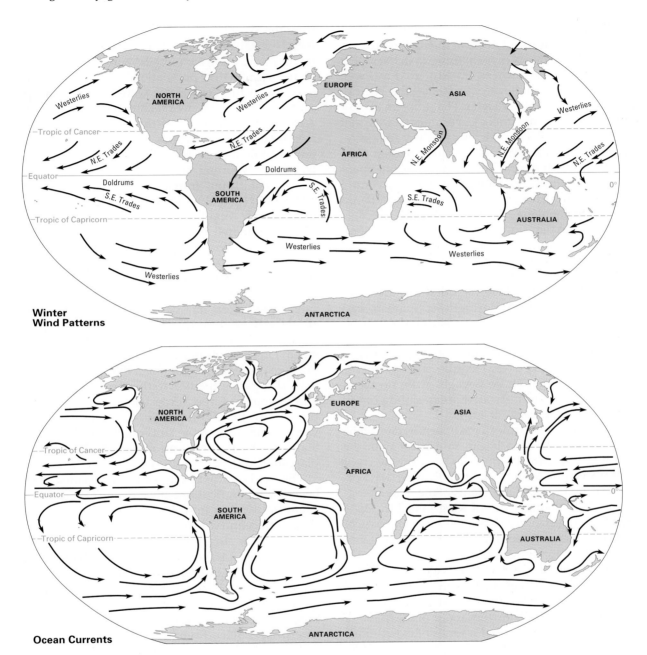

**Winter
Wind Patterns**

Ocean Currents

Map 13.1 Winds and Currents Winds and ocean currents move in giant clockwise and counterclockwise circles that limit the directions in which ships can sail efficiently. It was impossible, for example, for the explorers to sail directly south along the entire western coast of Africa.

was accelerated in the fifteenth century by the growing power of the Ottoman Turks. After the conquest of Constantinople in 1453 (see page 426), Turkish expansion into Syria and Palestine, and Turkish raids reaching into Austria and northeastern Italy, Europeans increasingly hoped for an alliance with the mythical Christian kingdoms of the East to open a second front against the Turks.

For the Portuguese, facing the Atlantic and insulated from the direct Turkish threat, the promise of gold was no doubt more alluring than the search for Christians. The nearest source of gold was well known to late medieval Christians: the African kingdoms of the Niger Delta. The problem for European traders and their governments was that commercial contacts with this wealthy region remained controlled by the Muslim Berber merchants of North Africa. The Portuguese and Spanish hoped to break the monopoly by taking control of the North African coast or by means of a flanking movement along the western coast of Africa.

Actual exploration of the Atlantic had begun long before Europeans recognized the extent of the Turkish threat. By 1350, the Madeiras and the Canaries, groups of islands off the western coast of Africa, regularly were included on European maps. By about 1365, Portuguese, Spanish, and probably French sailors were visiting the Canary Islands. By 1400, the Azores, one-third of the way across the Atlantic, were known and from early in the fifteenth century were regular ports of call for Portuguese ships. These voyages were no mean feat, calling for sophisticated ocean sailing out of sight of land for weeks at a time.

In the second decade of the fifteenth century the Portuguese expansion began in earnest with the capture of the Muslim port of Ceuta on the coast of Morocco (see Map 13.2). From then on, the Portuguese, led by Prince Henry "the Navigator" (1394–1460), younger son of King John I (r. 1385–1433), moved steadily down the western coast of Africa. Contemporaries reported that Prince Henry was intent on reaching the "River of Gold"—that is, the Gold Coast of Africa and the Niger Delta. To accomplish this, he directed efforts to colonize the Canaries (which eventually were lost to the Spanish), the Azores, and Madeira, the largest of the Madeira Islands. He also sponsored a series of expeditions down the African coast, reaching Senegal and the Cape Verde Islands by 1444. The Portuguese quickly established trading stations in the region and soon were exporting gold and slaves to Lisbon.

Prince Henry is often credited with creating a virtual school of seamanship in his court at Sagres on the coast of Portugal, but his efforts at colonization may have had more importance for Portuguese expansion. The islands off the coast of Africa were uninhabited, except for the Canaries, which the Portuguese tried unsuccessfully to wrest

from the Spanish. Thus, the Portuguese could not merely establish trading communities within a larger population, for on the Azores and Madeira there was no native population. As a result, by the early 1440s the Portuguese were bringing sheep, seed, and peasants to the hitherto uninhabited Azores and Madeira, and the Crown was forced to grant extensive lordships to nobles to encourage immigration to the Azores. The islanders survived largely by exporting sheep and grain to Iberia.

A significant transformation occurred on Madeira in the 1440s, when the Portuguese introduced sugar cane to the island. Within a decade sugar dominated the island's economy. By 1452, there was a water mill for processing the cane, and in the 1470s sugar revenues from Madeira constituted nearly 2 percent of the Crown's total income.

Sugar production was capital- and labor-intensive. A great many workers were needed to cut the cane, and expensive mills and lengthy processing were needed to extract and to produce sugar. On Madeira most of the work was done by Portuguese peasants. But when the Portuguese extended sugar cultivation to the newly discovered and colonized Cape Verde Islands in the 1460s, they found that Portuguese peasants would not work voluntarily in the sultry equatorial climate. Soon the Portuguese introduced a slave-based plantation system to produce sugar.

Slaves imported from the Black Sea areas had been used in agriculture since the introduction of sugar cultivation into the Mediterranean in the thirteenth century. The Portuguese had been trading in slaves along the western coast of Africa since the late 1440s—the date from which black slaves appear in Lisbon. African slaves along with slaves from the East could be found in Italy and throughout the Mediterranean in the fifteenth century, most often as domestics or laborers in small enterprises. Since Roman times, however, there had been no slave-based industries on the scale of the Portuguese sugar plantations. Sugar production in the New World would be modeled on the slave-based plantation system perfected by the Portuguese in their island colonies in the Atlantic.

The Search for a Sea Route to Asia

Until the middle of the fifteenth century, the Niger Delta remained the focus of Portuguese interest. Only after securing control of the western coast of

Africa through the extension of sugar cultivation to Madeira and the Cape Verdes, developing the gold and slave trade in Senegal, and constructing a fortress to control the Volta River (in modern Ghana) and secure access to most gold-producing areas of West Africa did the Portuguese look seriously at sailing around Africa and discovering a sea route to Asia.

The fifteenth-century sailors who first tried to sail down the coast of Africa faced enormous difficulties. Water and wind currents tend to move in clockwise and counterclockwise circles against which it is difficult for a sail-powered ship to make progress (see Map 13.1). Winds near the equator generally blow from the east, and farther to the north and south the westerlies prevail. In some zones and at certain times there are pockets of stillness with few breezes to propel ships. A navigator had to find winds and currents moving in the direction he wished to travel. Sailing directly to and from a port was virtually impossible.

By the second half of the fifteenth century, Portuguese sailors had learned to tack along a course, searching for favorable winds and currents. Knowledge of winds and currents allowed Bartholomeu Dias (1450?–1500) in 1487 to explore the coast of southern Africa (Map 13.2). He followed the traditional Portuguese routes until southeasterly winds forced him to sail south and west, almost to the Brazilian and Argentine coasts. Then he was able to ride the westerlies well past the southern tip of Africa, where he turned north. On his return he sighted what he called "the Cape of Storms," later renamed "the Cape of Good Hope" by the Portuguese king. Dias had perfected the techniques for searching out currents in the Southern Hemisphere and opened the way to India.

A decade after Dias's return from the Cape of Good Hope, Vasco da Gama (1460?–1524) set sail on a voyage that would take him to Calicut on the western coast of India. Using the information gathered from countless navigators and travelers, da Gama set sail in 1497 with four square-rigged, armed caravels and over 170 men. He had been provided with maps and reports that indicated what he might expect to find along the eastern coast of Africa. He also carried textiles and metal utensils, merchandise of the type usually traded along the western coast of Africa. This was a trade mission and not really a voyage exploring the unknown.

Da Gama followed established routes beyond the Cape of Good Hope and into the Indian Ocean. He traveled up the coast until he reached Malindi in Mozambique, where he hired an Arab pilot who taught him the route to Calicut. Although the goods the Portuguese traders presented were not appropriate for the sophisticated Asian market, da Gama did manage to collect a cargo of Indian spices, which he brought back to Portugal, arriving in 1499. From 1500 until the Portuguese lost their last colonies in the twentieth century (Goa, 1961; Mozambique, 1975), Portugal remained a presence in the Indian Ocean.

The Portuguese in Asia

Trade in the Indian Ocean was nominally controlled by Muslims, but in fact a mixture of ethnic and religious groups—including Muslims, Hindus, and Nestorian Christians—participated in the movement of cottons, silks, and spices throughout the region. The mixture of trade reflected the political situation. Vasco da Gama's arrival coincided with the rise of the Moguls, Muslim descendants of Jenghiz Khan. By 1530, they had gained control of most of northern India and during the sixteenth century, Mogul influence increased in the south. Throughout the sixteenth century the Moguls remained tolerant of the religious, cultural, and economic diversity found in India. Neither Muslim nor Hindu powers initially recognized the threat the Portuguese represented.

The Portuguese probably encountered some hostility, but there is no reason to believe that they could not have joined this complex mixture of traders. Local rulers collected taxes and ensured political control but otherwise left the various ethnic and religious communities to manage their own trade and manufacture. The problem for the Portuguese was that the products they brought from Europe had little value in sophisticated, highly developed Asian markets. In response to this difficult situation, they created a "Trading-Post Empire," an empire based on control of trade rather than on colonization.

Portugal's commercial empire in the East was based on fortified, strategically placed naval bases. As early as Vasco da Gama's second expedition in 1502, Portuguese bombarded Calicut and defeated an Arab fleet off the coast of India. This encounter set the stage for Portugal's most

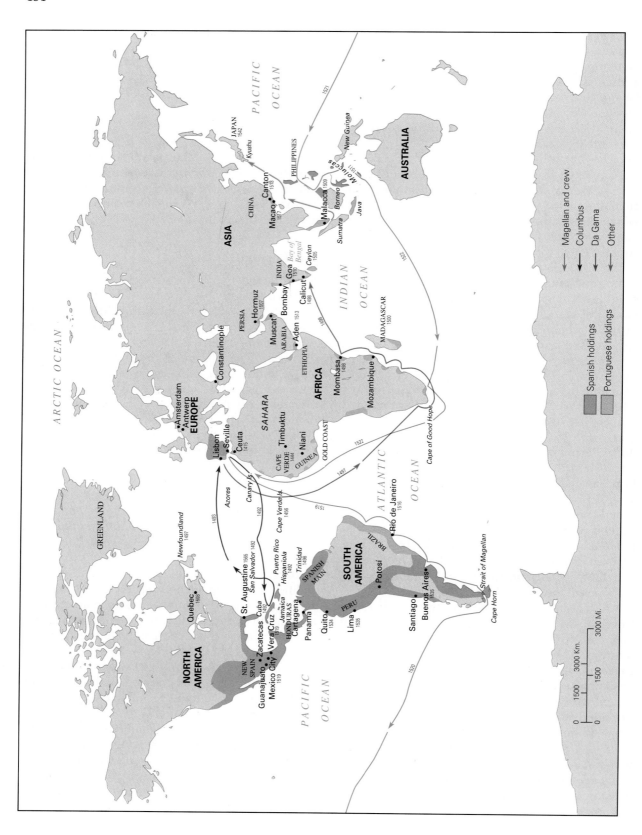

ARCTIC OCEAN

GREENLAND

Newfoundland 1497

Quebec 1608

NORTH AMERICA

NEW SPAIN 1519

Guanajuato • Zacatecas • Vera Cruz 1519
Mexico City

HONDURAS
Cartagena
Panama
St. Augustine 1565
San Salvador 1492
Cuba 1492
Jamaica
Puerto Rico 1492
Hispaniola 1492
Trinidad 1498

PACIFIC OCEAN

Azores
Canary Is. 1492
Cape Verde Is. 1456

SPANISH MAIN

Quito 1534
Lima 1535
PERU

SOUTH AMERICA

Potosi
Santiago
Buenos Aires 1535

BRAZIL

Rio de Janeiro 1516

Strait of Magellan

Cape Horn

ATLANTIC OCEAN

EUROPE
Lisbon
Seville
Amsterdam
Antwerp
Ceuta 1415

SAHARA

Timbuktu
Niani
CAPE VERDE 1444
GUINEA
GOLD COAST

AFRICA

ETHIOPIA

Mombasa 1498
Mozambique

MADAGASCAR 1500

Cape of Good Hope

Constantinople

PERSIA
Hormuz 1507
ARABIA
Muscat
Aden 1513

INDIA
Bombay
Goa 1510
Calicut 1498
Ceylon 1505

Bay of Bengal

INDIAN OCEAN

ASIA

CHINA
Canton
Macao 1557

JAPAN 1542
Kyushu

PHILIPPINES

Malacca 1509
Borneo
Sumatra
Java

Moluccas 1511
New Guinea

AUSTRALIA

PACIFIC OCEAN

Magellan and crew
Columbus
Da Gama
Other

Spanish holdings
Portuguese holdings

3000 Mi.
3000 Km.
1500
1500
0
0

Albuquerque Defends the Portuguese Empire

In this letter of 1512 to the king of Portugal, Alfonso d' Albuquerque, the governor-general of Portugal's colonies in India, informs the king of conditions in the East, explains his strategy, and defends himself against his critics.

The first time the Muslims entered Goa, we killed one of their captains. They were greatly grieved by the [Portuguese] capture of Goa and there is great fear of Your Highness among them. You must reduce the power of [the Muslim] rulers, take their coastal territories from them and build good fortresses in their principal places. Otherwise you will not be able to set India on the right path and you will always have to have a large body of troops there to keep it pacified. Any alliance which you may agree with one or other Indian king or lord must be secured, Sire, because otherwise you may be certain that, the moment your back is turned, they will at once become your enemies.

What I am describing has now become quite usual among them. In India there is not the same punctiliousness as in Portugal about keeping truth, friendship and trust, for nobody here has any of these qualities. Therefore, Sire, put your faith in good fortresses and order them to be built; gain control over India in time and do not place any confidence in the friendship of the kings and lords of this region because you did not arrive here with a just cause to gain domination of their trade with blandishments and peace treaties. Do not let anybody in Portugal make you think that this is a very hard thing to achieve and that, once achieved, it will place you under great obligation. I tell you this, Sire, because I am still in India and I would like people to sell their property and take part in this enterprise that is so much to your advantage, so great, so lucrative and so valuable. . . .

In a place where there is merchandise to be had and the Muslim traders will not let us have precious stones or spices by fair dealing, and we want to take these foods by force, then we must fight the Muslims for them. . . . If, on the other hand, they see us with a large body of troops, they do us honor, and no thought of deceit or trickery enters their heads. They exchange their goods for ours without fighting and they will abandon the delusion that they will expel us from India.

Source: T. F. Earle and J. Villiers, eds., *Albuquerque: Caesar of the East* (Warminster, England: Aris and Phillips, 1990), p. 109.

important strategist of empire, Alfonso d'Albuquerque (1453–1515), governor-general of Portuguese colonies in India. He convinced the monarchy that the key to dominance in the region was the creation of fortified naval bases designed to permit the Portuguese to dominate the Bay of Bengal and thereby control access to the spices in the Spice Islands. (See the box, "Albuquerque Defends the Portuguese Empire.") By 1510, Albuquerque had captured Goa (on the Indian coast south of Bombay) and Hormuz (controlling access to the Persian Gulf). Later he conquered the sultanate of Malacca on the Malay Peninsula, winning control of the straits that run from the Bay of Bengal to the Spice Islands. By 1600, the Portuguese had created a network of naval bases that reached from Mozambique and Mombasa on the eastern coast of Africa to Goa on the western coast of India and to the island of Macao off the southeastern coast of China (see Map 13.2).

The Portuguese established a royal trading firm, the Casa da India, to control the trade in

Map 13.2 World Exploration The voyages of Columbus, da Gama, and Magellan charted the major sea-lanes that became essential for communication, trade, and warfare for the next three hundred years.

Portuguese in India This watercolor by a Portuguese traveler shows the varied people and customs and the great wealth to be found in India. Europeans were fascinated by all that seemed different from their own world. *(Biblioteca Casanatense)*

cinnamon, ginger, cloves, mace, and a variety of peppers. Although their control was far from total, the Portuguese did become significant exporters of spices to Europe. More significant was the creation of the Portuguese Estado da India, or India office, to control Portuguese naval forces, administer ports, and regulate maritime trade. Under the Portuguese system all merchants were expected to acquire export licenses and to ship products through Portuguese ports.

Both the casa and the estado depended on naval power for their influence. Local boats were no match for the well-built Portuguese ships armed with cannon. Although the Portuguese navy was too small to enforce a complete blockade of clandestine trade, the Portuguese did manage to change the patterns of commerce in the area. Many Asians found it convenient to pay for export licenses and to trade through Portuguese ports. They even found it convenient to ship in European-style vessels and to use Portuguese as the language of commerce.

SPANISH VOYAGES OF DISCOVERY, 1492–1522

As early as 1479 the Spanish kingdoms had agreed to leave the exploration and colonization of the African coast to the Portuguese, yet they watched nervously as the Portuguese expanded their African contacts. The Castilians concentrated their efforts on what came to be called the "Enterprise of the Indies."

The sailing and exploration necessary to compete with the Portuguese produced critical information about winds and currents around the world and facilitated later voyages. They also established the basic approaches that the Spanish would follow in their exploration, conquest, and colonization of the lands to which they came.

The Role of Columbus

The story of the enterprise begins with Christopher Columbus (1451–1506), a brilliant seaman, courtier, and self-promoter who has become a symbol of European expansion. During the nineteenth century, patriots of the newly created United States of America celebrated Columbus as proof that the discovery and development of North America was not dependent on the British. By the early twentieth century, Italian immigrants to North America regarded him as a symbol of Italy's important role in the history of the Americas. And finally, modern historians have celebrated Columbus as one of the great men of the Renaissance who managed to break with medieval myth and superstition. The voyages of Columbus, they have argued, shattered the isolation and parochial vision of the Europeans. Columbus, however, was not a "Renaissance man" of vision, the harbinger of a new, more rational world. And he certainly was not a bold pioneer who fearlessly did what no others could conceive of doing.

Columbus was born into a modest family in Genoa and spent his early years in travel and in the service of the Castilian and Portuguese crowns. He apparently first put his plans to sail west to Asia before King John II (r. 1481–1495) of Portugal. Only after Portuguese rejection did he approach the Spanish monarchs, Ferdinand and Isabella. His vision seems to have been thoroughly traditional and medieval. Studying information in *Imago Mundi* (*Image of the World*, 1410), by the French philosopher Pierre d'Ailly (1350–1420), he convinced himself that the distance between the coast of Europe and Asia was much less than it actually is. Pierre d'Ailly had estimated that water covered only about one-quarter of the globe. This estimate put the east coast of Asia within easy reach of the western edge of Europe. "This sea is navigable in a few days if the wind is favorable," was d'Ailly's conclusion.

D'Ailly's theories seemed to be confirmed by the work of the Florentine mathematician Paolo Toscanelli (see page 480). Columbus knew of Toscanelli's calculations and even revised them downward. From his own reading of an apocryphal book of the Bible (Esdras 6:42) that reported that only one-seventh of the world was covered with water, Columbus concluded that the distance from the west coast of Europe to the east coast of Asia was about 5000 miles instead of the actual 12,000. Columbus's reading of traditional sources put Japan in the approximate location of the Virgin Islands. (It is not surprising that Columbus remained convinced that the Bahamas were islands just off the coast of Asia.)

Like Marco Polo before him, Columbus expected to find the marvels reported in the classical sources. In his own journals he recorded reports of islands where women avoided domestic responsibilities and instead hunted with bow and arrow. And he interpreted what he was told in the context of his assumptions. When Amerindians told him of Cuba, he concluded that it "must be Japan according to the indications that these people give of its size and wealth."[2] And on the basis of first-century descriptions, he assured Spanish authori-

OVERSEAS EXPLORATION AND CONQUEST

ca. 1350	The Madeira and Canary Islands are charted
ca. 1400	The Azores are charted
1444	Cape Verde Islands are discovered by Prince Henry the Navigator
1487	Dias is the first European to sail around the Cape of Good Hope
1492	Columbus sails from Spain and discovers the New World
1494	Treaty of Tordesillas
1497	Da Gama sails around the Cape of Good Hope and arrives in India; Cabot sights Newfoundland
1501	Vespucci sails along the coast of Brazil and concludes that Columbus had discovered a new continent
1507	Waldseemüller issues the first map showing "America"
1510	Portuguese capture Goa
1513	Balboa crosses the Isthmus of Panama and is the first European to see the Pacific Ocean
1519–1522	Magellan's expedition sails around the world from east to west
1519–1523	Cortés lands in Mexico, conquers the Aztecs, and destroys Tenochtitlán
1533	Pizarro conquers Cuzco, the Incas' capital
1534	Cartier discovers the St. Lawrence River
1542	Charles V issues the New Laws
1545	The Spanish discover the silver mines at Potosí

ties that King Solomon's mines were only a short distance west of his newly discovered islands. In addition to finding the gold of Solomon, Columbus also expected that by sailing west he could fulfill a series of medieval prophecies that would lead to the conversion of the whole world to Christianity. This conversion, he believed, would shortly precede the second coming of Christ. In Columbus's own view, then, his voyages were epochal not because they were ushering in a newer, more empirical world but because they signaled the completion of the long history of the creation and redemption.

Columbus's enthusiasm for the venture was only partially shared by Ferdinand and Isabella. Vasco da Gama was well supplied with large ships and a crew of over 170 men, but Columbus sailed in 1492 with three small ships and a crew of 90. Da Gama carried extra supplies and materials for trade and letters for the rulers he knew he would meet. Columbus had nothing similar. His commission did authorize him as "Admiral of Spain" to take possession of all he should find, but royal expectations do not seem to have been great.

After a stop in the Canary Islands, the small fleet sailed west. Columbus assumed that he would find the islands of Japan after sailing about 3000 miles. On October 12, about ten days later than he had calculated, he reached landfall on what he believed were small islands in the Japanese chain. He had actually landed in the Bahamas

(see Map 13.2). Because Columbus announced to the world he had arrived in the Indies, the indigenous populations have since been called "Indians" and the islands are called the "West Indies." (See the box, "Christopher Columbus Describes His Discoveries.")

Columbus returned to the New World three more times—in 1493, 1498, and 1502—exploring extensively in the Bahamas and along the coast of Panama and Venezuela, 800 miles to the south and east of the island of Hispaniola. The enthusiasm his discoveries raised was evident on his second voyage. He oversaw a fleet of seventeen ships with 1500 sailors, churchmen, and adventurers. And Columbus's initial rewards were great. He was granted a hereditary title, a governorship of the new lands, and one-tenth of all the wealth he had discovered.

Columbus reported to the Spanish monarchs that the "Indians" on the islands were friendly and open to the new arrivals. He described simple, naked people, eager, he believed, to learn of Christianity and European ways. The Taínos, or Arawaks, whom he had misidentified, did live

Cosa's Columbian Map Juan de la Cosa traveled with Columbus. His map of 1500 shows what was known of the New World and how it was connected to the Old. The western portions seem to be as accurate as he could make them; the east still holds traditional images such as the three kings. (*Museo Naval de Madrid*)

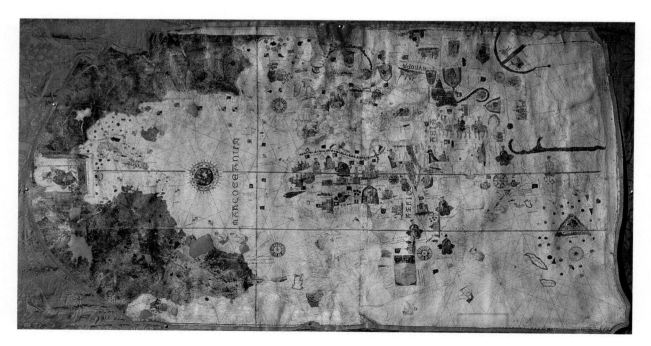

Christopher Columbus Describes His Discoveries

Columbus's hopes for wealth and titles for himself depended on getting and maintaining the goodwill of Ferdinand and Isabella. After each of his voyages he emphasized his accomplishments and their potential to enrich the Spanish monarchs. Columbus wrote this letter toward the conclusion of the first voyage, which he believed might secure his rights to lordship over all the new territories he found. He took pains to make clear that what he had found was what one would expect to find on the edge of Asia. In that respect this document deserves to be compared to the later observations of Friar Bernardino de Sahagún on page 503.

In conclusion, to speak only of what has been accomplished on this voyage, which was so hasty, their highnesses can see that I give them as much gold as they may need, if their highnesses will render me very slight assistance; moreover, spice and cotton, as much as their highnesses shall command; and mastic [yellow resin necessary for various adhesives], as much as they shall order to be shipped and which, up to now, has been found only in Greece, in the island of Chios, and the Seignory [of Venice] sells it for what it pleases; and also wood, as much as they shall order to be shipped, and slaves, as many as they shall order to be shipped and who will be from the idolaters. And I believe that I have found rhubarb and cinnamon [both were considered essential for medicine], and I shall find a thousand other things of value, which people I have left here will have discovered, for I have not delayed at any point . . . and in truth I shall have done more, if the ships had served me as reason demanded.

Source: C. Columbus, A. Bernáldez, et al., eds., *The Voyages of Christopher Columbus*, part 1 (London: Argonaut Press, 1930), p. 16.

---

simple, uncomplicated lives. The islands easily produced sweet potatoes, maize, beans, and squash, which along with fish provided an abundant diet. Initially these peoples shared their food and knowledge with the newcomers, who they seem to have thought were sky-visitors.

The Spanish, for their part, praised this smiling and happy people. Visitors commonly believed they had discovered a simple, virtuous people who, if converted, would be exemplars of Christian virtues to the Europeans. Columbus himself observed that

they are very gentle and do not know what evil is; nor do they kill others, nor steal; and they are without weapons. . . . They say very quickly any prayer that we tell them to say, and they make the sign of the cross, †. So your Highnesses ought to resolve to make them Christians.[3]

The Spanish authorities changed their opinion quickly. The settlers Columbus left at his fortress set an unfortunate example. They seized foodstocks, kidnapped women, and embarked on a frenzied search for gold. Those who did not kill one another were killed by the Taínos.

During succeeding voyages, Columbus struggled to make his discoveries the financial windfall he had promised the monarchs. He was unable to administer this vast new land. He quickly lost control of the colonists and was forced to allow the vicious exploitation of the island population. He and other Spanish settlers claimed larger and larger portions of the land and required the Indians to work it. Islands that easily supported a population of perhaps a million natives could not support those indigenous peoples and the Spanish newcomers and still provide exports to Spain. Largely because of diseases (see page 501), scholars have estimated that the native population of the islands may have fallen to little more than 30,000 by 1520. By the middle of the sixteenth century, the native population had virtually disappeared.

Columbus remained convinced that he would find vast fortunes just over the horizon. But he found neither the great quantities of gold he promised nor a sea passage to Asia. Even in the face of mounting evidence to the contrary, Columbus maintained that Asia must be just beyond the lands he was exploring. With the islands in revolt and his explorations seemingly going nowhere, the Spanish monarchs stripped Columbus of his titles and commands. Once he was returned to Spain in chains. After his final trip he maintained that he had finally found either the Ganges River of India or one of the rivers that flow out of the earthly paradise. Although Columbus died in 1506, rich and honored for his discoveries, he never gained all the power and wealth he had expected. He remained frustrated and embittered by the Crown's refusal to support one more voyage during which he expected to find the mainland of Asia.

In 1501, after sailing along the coast of Brazil, the Florentine geographer Amerigo Vespucci (1451–1512) drew the obvious conclusion from the information collected by Columbus's explorations. He argued that Columbus had discovered a new continent unknown to the classical world. These claims were accepted by the German mapmaker Martin Waldseemüller, who in 1507 honored Amerigo's claim by publishing the first map showing "America."

Columbus's Successors

Columbus's discoveries set off a debate over which nations had the right to be involved in trade and exploration. Portuguese claims were based on a papal bull of 1481, issued by Pope Sixtus IV (r. 1471–1484), that granted Portugal rights to discoveries south of the Canaries and west of Africa. After Columbus's return, the Spaniards lobbied one of Sixtus's successors, Alexander VI (r. 1492–1503), whose family, the Borgias, was from the kingdom of Aragon. In a series of bulls, Pope Alexander allowed the Spanish to claim all lands lying 400 miles or more west of the Azores. Finally, in the Treaty of Tordesillas (1494), Spain and Portugal agreed that the line of demarcation between their two areas should be drawn 1480 miles west of the Azores. The treaty was signed just six years before Petro Alvares Cabral (1467–1520) discovered the coast of Brazil. Thus the Spanish unwittingly granted the Portuguese rights to Brazil.

Adventurers and explorers worried little about the legality of exploration. Even as Columbus lay dying in 1506, others, some without royal permission, sailed up and down the eastern coasts of North and South America. Amerigo Vespucci traveled on Spanish vessels as far as Argentina, while Spanish explorers sailed among the islands of the Caribbean and along the coast of the Yucatán Peninsula. Vasco Nuñez de Balboa crossed the Isthmus of Panama in 1513 and found the Pacific Ocean where the natives living in the region said it would be.

The most important of the explorations that Columbus inspired was the voyage undertaken by Ferdinand Magellan in 1519 (see Map 13.2). Although his motives are unclear, Magellan (1480?–1521) may have planned to complete Columbus's dream of sailing to the Indies. By the 1510s mariners and others understood that the Americas were a new and hitherto unknown land, but they did not know what lay beyond them or what the distance was from the Americas to the Spice Islands of Asia. After sailing along the well-known coastal regions of South America, Magellan continued south, charting currents and looking for a passage into the Pacific. Early in 1520 he made the passage through the dangerous straits (now the Strait of Magellan) separating Tierra del Fuego from the mainland. The turbulent waters of the straits marked the boundary of the Atlantic and the Pacific Oceans. Once into the Pacific, Magellan sailed north and west to escape the cold and to find winds and currents that would allow him to continue to Asia. It took almost four months to travel from the straits to the Philippines. During that time, a crew member reported, "We ate biscuit, which was no longer biscuit, but powder of biscuit swarming with worms, for they had eaten the good."[4] The crew suffered greatly from scurvy and a shortage of water and at times had to eat the rats aboard ship to survive. Nevertheless, Magellan managed to reach the Philippines by March 1521. A month later, he was killed by natives.

Spanish survivors in two remaining ships continued west, reaching the Moluccas, where they traded merchandise that they had carried along for a small cargo of cloves. The Portuguese captured one of the ships as it tried to return to the Americas. The other proceeded on through the Indian Ocean, avoiding Portuguese patrols. It continued around Africa and back to Spain, landing with a crew of 15 at Cádiz in September 1522 after a voyage of three years and the loss of four ships and 245 men. No cargo of spices could have been worth the sacrifices. But the significance of the voyage was not the spices but the route established from South America to the Spice Islands. Further, Magellan completed and confirmed the knowledge of wind and ocean currents that European sailors had been accumulating. One of his sailors wrote of him: "More accurately than any man in the world did he understand sea charts and navigation."[5] The way was open for the vast movement of Europeans and European culture into all parts of the world.

Spanish adventurers were not the only ones to follow in Columbus's wake. The French and the English, however, concentrated their explorations further to the north. Building on a tradition of fishing off the coast of Newfoundland, English sailors under the command of John Cabot (1450?–1499?) sighted Newfoundland in 1497, and later voyages explored the coast as far south as New England. Cabot initiated an intense period of English exploration that would lead to an unsuccessful attempt to found a colony on Roanoke Island in 1587 and eventually to permanent settlement at Jamestown in 1607. French explorers followed Cabot to the north. In 1534, Jacques Cartier (1491–1557) received a royal commission to look for a passage to the East. He discovered the St. Lawrence River and began the process of exploration and trading that would lead to permanent settlements in Canada beginning in the early seventeenth century. But British and French settlements in the New World came later. The sixteenth century belonged to the Spanish.

Spanish penetration of the New World was not simply built on the model of the Portuguese in Asia. The Spaniards established no complex network of trade and commerce, and no strong states opposed their interests. A "Trading-Post Empire" could not have worked in the New World. To succeed, the Spaniards needed to colonize and reorganize the lands they had discovered.

SPAIN'S COLONIAL EMPIRE, 1492–1600

Between 1492 and 1600, almost 200,000 Spaniards immigrated to the New World. New Spain, as they called these newly claimed lands, was neither the old society transported across the ocean nor Amerindian society with a thin patina of Spanish and European culture. To understand the history of New Spain, we will discuss the two major civilizations the Spaniards overthrew, the conquests themselves, and the institutions the Spaniards created in the wake of conquest. We will also discuss the attempts by many of the Spanish to secure fair treatment of the indigenous peoples who had been made part of the Spanish Empire.

The Americas Before the European Invasion

The Spaniards and later their European peers entered a world vastly different from their own. It was a world formed by two momentous events. The first was the creation of the continents of North and South America. North and South America, along with Africa and the Eurasian landmass, were once part of a single supercontinent. The breakup of this supercontinent left the Americas, Africa, and Eurasia free to evolve in dramatically different ways. From one continent to another, the differences in plants and animals were so dramatic that one eighteenth-century naturalist confessed, "I was seized with terror at the thought of ranging to many new and unknown parts of natural history."[6] The continental breakup occurred millions of years ago, long before the appearance of human beings and many other forms of mammalian life.

The second momentous event was the temporary rejoining of the Americas to the Eurasian landmass by land and ice bridges that allowed Asians to cross over the Bering Strait to the Americas in the period between 30,000 and 10,000 B.C. Their arrival and its timing were important for two reasons. These hunter-gatherers seem to have played a significant role in the extinction of several large mammals—mastodons, mammoths, giant buffalo, and even early camels and horses. No easily domesticable large animals remained on the continent. These peoples also arrived in the Americas long before the beginnings of the Neolithic agricultural revolution, which involved the domestication of numerous plants and animals. The agricultural revolution in the Americas occurred around 3000 B.C., perhaps six thousand years after similar developments in the Old World (see page 7). The peoples of the Americas created complex societies, but those societies lacked large domesticated meat or pack animals (the llama was the largest), iron and other hard metals, and the wheel.

By the time of Columbus's arrival, relatively populous societies were living throughout North and South America. Population estimates for the two continents range from 30 million to 100 million—the lower figure is probably more correct. There were complex mound-builder societies in eastern North America and along the Mississippi River and pueblo societies in the deserts of the American Southwest, but the greatest centers of Amerindian civilization were in central and coastal Mexico and in the mountains of Peru.

In the late fifteenth century the two most powerful centers were the empires of the Aztecs and the Incas. When the collection of tribes now known as the "Aztec" (or Mexican) peoples appeared in central Mexico in the early fourteenth century, they found a flourishing civilization centered on the

cities and towns dotting the Valley of Mexico. Through conquest, the Aztecs united the many Nahuatl-speaking groups living in the valley into a confederation centered on the Aztec capital of Tenochtitlán, a city of perhaps 200,000 people built on an island in Lake Texcoco (Map 13.3). In early-sixteenth-century Europe, only London, Constantinople, and Naples would have been as large as the Aztec capital. The Spanish conqueror Hernán Cortés (see pages 494–497) described Aztec cities "that seemed like an enchanted vision" and that literally rose out of the water of Lake Texcoco. Only Venice could have equaled the sight. The whole valley supported an unusually high population of about a million, fed by farmers who raised a wide variety of crops on farms carefully formed beside canals and in the marshes on the edge of Lake Texcoco. Using canals along the edge of the lake and other canals in Tenochtitlán itself, mer-

Tenochtitlán The Aztec capital was built on an island. Its central temples and markets were connected to the rest of the city and the suburbs on the lake shore by numerous canals. The city and its surrounding market gardens seemed to the Spanish to be floating on water. *(The Newberry Library, Chicago)*

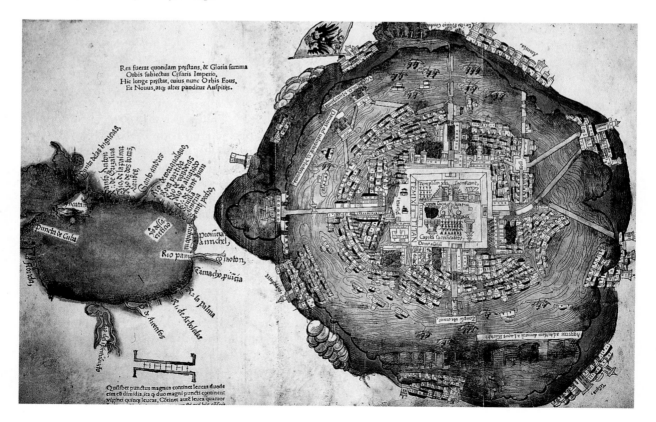

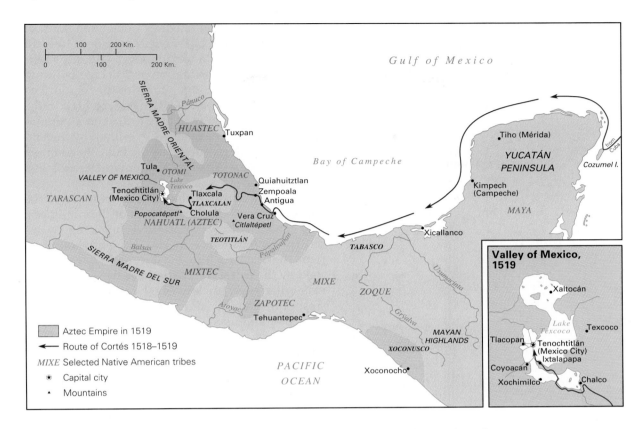

Map 13.3 Mexico and Central America The Valley of Mexico was a populous region of scattered towns, most of which were part of the Aztec Empire. As Cortés marched inland from Vera Cruz toward the valley, he passed through lands that had been in an almost constant state of war with the Aztecs.

chants easily moved food, textiles, gold and silver ornaments, jewels, and ceremonial feathered capes into the city markets. Spaniards later estimated that 50,000 or more people shopped in the city on market days.

Religion was integral to the Aztecs' understanding of their empire. They believed that the world was finite and that they lived in the last of five empires. It was only continued human sacrifice to Huitzilopochtli that allowed the world to continue. The Aztecs believed that the hearts of sacrificial victims were necessary to sustain their god, to ensure that the sun would rise again each morning. Thus, the Aztecs believed that their continued sacrifice to their god was essential for the continuation of life.

Tenochtitlán was the center of an imperial culture based on tribute. Towns and villages under Aztec control paid tribute in food and precious

metals. To emphasize that Aztec power and dominance were complete, the Aztecs not only collected vast quantities of maize, beans, squash, and textiles but demanded tribute in everything down to centipedes and snakes. The most chilling tribute, however, was in humans for sacrifice. When there were no longer wars of expansion to provide prisoners, the Aztecs and their neighbors fought "flower wars"—highly ritualized battles to provide prisoners to be sacrificed. Five thousand victims were sacrificed at the coronation of Moctezuma II (r. 1502–1520) in 1502. Even more, reportedly twenty thousand, were sacrificed at the dedication of the great temple of Huitzilopochtli in Tenochtitlán.

Aztec society was a warrior society that maintained a perpetual state of war with the peoples beyond the mountains that ringed the Valley of Mexico—especially the people along the Caribbean

Map 13.4 Peru and Central America The Inca Empire was accessible to the Spaniards only by sea. Spanish exploration and domination brought the destruction of Inca mountain citadels and the transfer of administrative power to the new Spanish city of Lima on the coast.

coast. Given this state of war, plus the heavy burdens in tribute placed on the nearby subject cities, it is no small wonder that the Aztecs were obsessed by the contingencies of life. At the end of each calendar cycle of fifty-two years, all fires in the empire were extinguished until fire-priests ascertained that the world would continue. And the Aztec world did continue until August 1523 (see page 497).

The other great Amerindian empire of the fifteenth century, the empire of the Incas, was also of recent origin. During the fifteenth century the Incas formed efficient armies and expanded their control beyond the central highlands of Peru. Fifteen thousand miles of road and a sophisticated administrative system allowed the Incas to create a state that extended from Ecuador to Chile (Map

13.4). As they expanded, they demanded political control and tribute but seem to have been tolerant of local traditions and language. The Incas perfected systems of irrigation and bridge-building initiated by earlier inhabitants of the region. The empire, centered on the city of Cuzco high in the mountains of Peru, was able to sustain a population that may have reached 10 million by the end of the fifteenth century. (See the box, "Encounters with the West: An Inca Nobleman Defends His Civilization.")

Human sacrifice, though not unknown to the Incas, was not an essential part of their religious life. Their state was unsettled, however, by increasingly harsh tax exactions. Under the Inca system, the title Paca Inca, or "Great Inca," was inherited by the eldest son of the ruler's principal wife. The ruler's wealth, however, was retained by the rest of his family, who maintained the court as if the ruler still lived. Thus, each new ruler needed money to finance the creation of an entirely new court, and taxes were not only high but continuously increasing.

Both great Amerindian empires, despite their brilliance, rested on uneasy conquests. Subject groups would be willing allies for any invader.

The Spanish Conquests

Hernán Cortés (1485–1546) was ambitious to make something of himself in the New World. Of a poor but aristocratic background from the Extremadura region of southwest Spain, he had gone to the West Indies in 1504 to seek his fortune in the service of the governor of Cuba. The governor gave him a commission to lead an expeditionary force to investigate reports of a wealthy and prosperous Indian civilization. From the very beginning, Spanish authorities seem to have distrusted his aims. He was forced to depart hastily from Cuba to evade formal notification that the governor of Cuba had revoked his commission because of insubordination.

Cortés landed in Mexico at the site of the city he would name Vera Cruz ("True Cross") early in 1519 with a tiny command of 500 men, 16 horses, 11 ships, and some artillery. Aided by a devastating outbreak of smallpox and Amerindian peoples happy to overthrow Aztec control, Cortés and his troops managed to destroy the network of city-states dominated by the Aztecs of Tenochtitlán in

~ **ENCOUNTERS WITH THE WEST** ~

An Inca Nobleman Defends His Civilization

Huamán Poma was born into a noble Inca family with a long history of service first to the Inca kings and later to the Spanish administrators. Although Huamán Poma became a Christian and adapted to Spanish rule, he wrote this letter to the king of Spain in 1613 explaining the great merits of the Inca civilization that he feared would be lost. In the excerpt included here, he describes the Inca understanding of the origins of the world. His "traditional world" is, however, one heavily influenced by his new Christian faith.

The first white people in the world were brought by God to this country. They were descended from those who survived the flood in Noah's Ark. It is said that they were born in pairs, male and female, and therefore they multiplied rapidly.

These people were incapable of useful work. They could not make proper clothes so they wore garments of leaves and straw. Not knowing how to build houses, they lived in caves and under rocks. They worshipped God with a constant outpouring of sound like the twitter of birds, saying: "Lord how long shall I cry and not be heard?" . . .

In their turn these first people were succeeded by the two castes: the great lords, who were the ancestors of our Incas, and the common people, who were descended from bastards and multiplied rapidly in number.

However barbarous they may have been, our ancestors had some glimmer of understanding of God. Even the mere saying of [God's name] is a sign of faith and an important step forward. Christians have much to learn from our people's good way of life. . . .

Their usual diet consisted of maize, potatoes and other tubers; cress, sorrel, and lupin; pond-weed, laver and a grass with yellow flowers; leaves for chewing; mushrooms, edible grubs, shells, shrimps, crab and various sorts of fish. . . . The burial of the dead was conducted with dignity, but without undue ceremony in vaults constructed for the purpose. There were separate vaults, which were whitewashed and painted, for people of high rank. The Indians believed that after death they would have to endure hard labor, torture, hunger, thirst and fire. Thus they had their own conception of Hell, which they called the place under the earth or the abode of demons.

Source: Huamán Poma, *Letter to a King: A Picture History of the Inca Civilization* (New York: E. P. Dutton, 1978), pp. 24–25, 30.

two years and lay claim to the Valley of Mexico for the king of Spain. The manner in which Cortés explained and justified his mission can serve as a model against which to measure the adventures of other sixteenth-century Europeans in the Americas.

Cortés, like Machiavelli, believed in the power of truly able leaders (men of virtú) to overcome chance through bold acts. Even so, an attempt to capture a city of 200,000 with an army of 500 seems more foolhardy than bold. Cortés seems to have attempted it simply because he found himself with very little choice. With his commission revoked by the governor of Cuba, Cortés arrived on the mainland as a rebel against both the governor of Cuba and the king of Spain. Much of what he did and said concerning the great Aztec Empire was an attempt to justify his initial act of insubordination and win back royal support. Cortés burned his ships so that his troops were forced to go with him. Then he founded the city of Vera Cruz, whose town government, which was his own creation, offered him a new commission to proceed inland to

veyotlipan.

Cortés and Doña Marina
Doña Marina was the critical mediator in gathering Amerindian allies and negotiating with local leaders. In this illustration from a sixteenth-century codex, Cortés—shown with Doña Marina and his army, which includes Amerindian allies—is greeted by local leaders during the march to Tenochtitlán. *(Trans. no. V/C 31(2). Courtesy Department of Library Sciences, American Museum of Natural History)*

Tenochtitlán. He quickly found allies among native groups that for their own reasons wished to see the Aztec Empire destroyed. The allied forces moved toward Tenochtitlán.

Cortés was greatly aided by fortune in the form of Malintzin, a Mexican woman who after her conversion called herself Doña Marina (ca. 1501–1550). Malintzin was Cortés's interpreter and, later, his mistress. Without her, one of Cortés's followers recalled, "We could not have understood the language of New Spain and Mexico." Her story illustrates many of the complex interactions at play in sixteenth-century Mexico. Born an Aztec, she was given away, ending up in the hands of Mayans, who gave her, along with twenty other women, to Cortés. Knowing the languages of the Mayans and Mexicans, and quickly learning Spanish, she was the one person who could mediate between Spaniard and native. She became Christian and after bearing Cortés a son, she finished her life in Spain as the wife of a Span-

ish gentleman. Like many of the natives who felt no affection for the Aztecs of Tenochtitlán, she did not find it difficult to aid the Spaniard.

Despite the help of Malintzin and Spaniards who had previously lived with the natives, the meeting of Aztecs and Spaniards demonstrated the breadth of the chasm separating the Old World and the New as well as the difficulty the one had in understanding the other. At first the Aztec king Moctezuma was unconcerned about the coming of the Spaniards. Later he seems to have attempted to buy them off. And finally he and his successors fought desperately to drive them out of Tenochtitlán. The Aztecs' indecision was caused in large part by the fact that in neither words nor gestures did the two groups speak the same language. Hearing that the Spaniards were marching toward Tenochtitlán, Moctezuma sent ambassadors bearing gold, silver, and other costly gifts, which they presented in a most humble fashion to the Spaniards. To a modern ear the gifts sound like (and have often been interpreted to be) desperate attempts to buy off the invaders. To Cortés, or any European or Asian resident of the Old World, such gifts were a sign of submission. But to Moctezuma and most Amerindians, the giving of gifts with great humility by otherwise powerful and proud people could be a sign of wealth and status. Seen in that light, Moctezuma's lavish gifts and apparent humility probably demonstrated to the Aztecs' own satisfaction the superiority of their civilization, and Cortés's acceptance of the gifts seemed to indicate his recognition of his own inferior status.

Spaniards later claimed that Moctezuma was confounded by the sudden appearance of these peoples from the East. Cortés reported to the king of Spain that when he first met Moctezuma, the Aztec leader said, "We have always held that those who descended from [the god Quetzalcoatl] would come and conquer this land and take us as his vassals." Later Spaniards explained that the Aztecs believed that Quetzalcoatl, the serpent-god symbolically conquered by Huitzilopochtli, had traveled to the East, promising one day to return and reclaim his lands, thus ending Aztec rule. The Spaniards believed that Moctezuma had been so ambivalent toward them because of his belief in that myth.

There seems, however, to be little truth in either of those stories. Cortés was simply attempting to justify his conquest. There is no surviving pre-conquest source for Moctezuma's supposed confession, and the myth of the return of Quetzalcoatl was first recorded in Spanish, not Indian, sources long after the conquest. In truth, neither Cortés nor historians can satisfactorily explain in Western terms Moctezuma's initial response to the Spaniards. Cortés took the Aztec leader captive in 1521 and began what would be a two-year battle to take control of the city and its empire. Although weakened by the arrival of virulent Old World diseases, the Aztecs continued to fight even as more and more of the subject peoples joined the Spanish forces. The Spaniards cut off food and water to the capital, but still the Aztecs fought.

Different understandings of the rules of war, different traditions of diplomacy, and different cultures prevented the Aztecs and Cortés from reaching any understanding. The peoples of the Valley of Mexico tried to take captives to be sacrificed in temples. The Spaniards, to Aztec eyes, killed indiscriminately and needlessly on the bat-

tlefield. Cortés later complained of the Aztecs' refusal to negotiate: "We showed them more signs of peace than have ever been shown to a vanquished people." Thus, to end a war that neither side could resolve in any other way, in August 1523 Cortés and his allies completely destroyed Tenochtitlán.

Cortés's insubordination was a model for other adventurers. His own lieutenants later rebelled against his control and attempted to create their own governments as they searched for riches and Eldorado, a mythical city of gold. Later adventurers marched throughout the North American Southwest and Central and South America following rumors of hidden riches. Using private armies and torturing native peoples, veterans of Cortés's army and newly arrived speculators hoped to find wealth that would allow them to live like nobles on their return to Spain. Like

Aztec Warrior This watercolor, by a Mexican artist who was trained in European painting, depicts a pre-Aztec ruler. But the dress and the stone-edged sword would have been typical of the Aztecs, too. *(Bibliothèque Nationale)*

Cortés, they claimed that they were acting for the monarchy and for Christianity, but in fact they expected that success would justify their most vicious acts.

Francisco Pizarro (1470–1541) was the most successful of the private adventurers. Poor, illegitimate at birth, he arrived in the Americas ambitious for riches and power. After serving in Balboa's army, participating in several slaving expeditions, and helping to found Panama City, Pizarro was prosperous but still not wealthy. Rumors of Inca wealth filtered through to Central America. Pizarro and a partner resolved in 1530 to lead an expedition down the west coast of South America in search of the Inca capital. Benefiting from disorganization caused by a smallpox epidemic and ensuing civil war, Pizarro was able to find local allies. Like Cortés, he used numerous Indian allies in his most important battles. Aided by Amerindians eager to throw off Inca domination, he captured and executed the Paca Inca and conquered the capital of Cuzco by 1533. He later built a new capital on the coast at Lima (see Map 13.4) from where he worked to extend his control over all of the old Inca Empire. Pizarro and his Spanish partners seized vast amounts of gold and silver from the Incas. The Spanish eventually discovered silver mines at Potosí, which would be a critical source of revenue for the Spanish monarchy. Resistance to Spanish rule continued into the 1570s, when the last of the independent Inca strongholds was finally destroyed.

Colonial Organization

The Spanish crown needed to create a colonial government that could control the actions of the numerous adventurers and create an orderly economy. Although the Spaniards proclaimed that they would "give to those strange lands the form of our own [land]," the resulting political and economic organization of the new Spanish possessions was a curious mixture of the Old World and the New.

The head of the administration was the monarchy. As early as the reigns of Ferdinand and Isabella, Spanish monarchs had tried to curb the excesses of the explorers and conquerors who traveled in their name. Isabella initially opposed the enslavement of Amerindians and any slave trade in the new lands. Further, they promoted a broad-

based debate about the rights of Amerindians and the nature of religious conversion. Royal influence, however, was limited by the sheer distance between the court and the new provinces. It could easily take two years for a royal response to a question to arrive at its destination. Things moved so slowly that as one viceroy ruefully noted, "If death came from Madrid, we should all live to a very old age." Given the difficulties of communication, the powers of local administrators had to be very broad.

By 1535, Spanish colonial administration was firmly established in the form it would retain for the next two hundred years. The king created a Council of the Indies located at court, eventually in Madrid, which saw to all legal and administrative issues pertaining to the new possessions. The new territories themselves were eventually divided into the viceroyalty of Mexico (primarily Central America and part of Venezuela) and the viceroyalty of Peru.

In Spain, Castilian conquerors completely dominated newly won lands, but in New Spain, royal administrators created Indian municipalities, or districts, in which Spaniards had no formal right to live or work. Government in these municipalities remained largely in the hands of preconquest native elites. Throughout the sixteenth century, official documents in these communities continued to be written in Nahuatl, the Aztec language. As long as taxes or tribute was paid and missionaries were allowed to circulate, the Spanish government tolerated considerable autonomy in the Indian municipalities.

The problem that most plagued the government was the conquerors' desire for laborers to work on the lands and in the mines that they had seized. From Columbus's first visit, the Spanish adopted a system of forced labor developed in Spain. A colonist called an *encomendero* was offered a grant, or *encomienda*, of a certain number of people or tribes who were required to work under his direction. In theory, the encomendero was to be a protector of the conquered peoples, someone who would Christianize and civilize them. In theory, Indians who voluntarily agreed to listen to missionaries or to convert to Christianity could not be put under the control of an encomendero. If they refused, however, the Spaniards believed they had the right of conquest. In fact, the conquerors assumed that they were entitled to encomiendas. Cortés himself claimed 115,000 people in Mexico, and Pizarro claimed 20,000 in Peru. In many areas encomenderos simply collected the traditional payments that the pre-conquest elites had claimed. In cases where the subject peoples were forced into mining districts, however, the conditions were brutal.

The pressures exerted by the encomenderos were worsened by the precipitous fall in the indigenous population. Old World diseases such as smallpox and measles swept through populations with no previous exposure to them (see page 501). In central Mexico, where we know most about population movements, the pre-conquest population was at least 10 or 12 million and may have been twice that. By the mid-sixteenth century, the native population may have fallen to just over 6 million, and it probably declined to less than 1 million early in the seventeenth century before beginning to grow again.

A large population was essential to the Spanish and the Portuguese when they introduced the Old World plantation system to the New World. The Caribbean islands and Brazil were ideal for the production of sugar—a commercial crop in great demand throughout Europe. At first, plantations and mines were worked by Amerindians, but when their numbers declined, the Spanish and Portuguese imported large numbers of slaves from Africa.

Africans had participated in the initial stages of the conquest. Some had lived in Spain and become Christian; indeed, Amerindians called them "black whitemen." Most Africans, however, were enslaved laborers. African slaves were in Cuba by 1518; they labored in the mines of Honduras by the 1540s. After the 1560s the Portuguese began importing large numbers of African slaves into Brazil to work on the sugar plantations. It has been estimated that 62,500 slaves were imported into Spanish America and 50,000 into Brazil during the sixteenth century. By 1810, when the movement to abolish the slave trade began to grow, almost 10 million Africans had been involuntarily transported to the New World.

The conquerors had hoped to find vast quantities of wealth that they could take back to the Old World. In the viceroyalty of Mexico the search for Eldorado remained unsuccessful. The discovery in 1545 of the silver mines at Potosí in Peru, however, fulfilled the Spaniards' wildest dreams.

Between 1550 and 1650, the Spanish probably sent back to Spain 181 tons of gold and 16,000 tons of silver, one-fifth of which was paid directly into the royal treasury. The tonnage of precious metals seemed so great to the French scholar Jean Bodin (see page 581) that he held this infusion of wealth responsible for the great inflation that was disrupting the European economy in the late sixteenth century. Bodin overestimated the European-wide impact of the precious metals, but they did represent one-quarter of the income of King Philip II of Spain in the 1560s and made him the richest monarch in Europe.

The Debate over Indian Rights

To most conquerors the opportunities for wealth and power need little justification, but the more thoughtful among the Spaniards were uneasy. "Tell me," demanded Friar Antonio Montesinos in 1511, "by what right or justice do you hold these Indians in such cruel and horrible slavery? By what right do you wage such detestable wars on these people who lived idly and peacefully in their own lands?"[7]

Initially the conquerors claimed the right to wage a just war of conquest if Amerindians refused to allow missionaries to live and work among them. Later, based on reports of human sacrifice and cannibalism written by Columbus and other early explorers, Europeans concluded that the inhabitants of the New World rejected basic natural laws. Juan Ginés de Sepulveda, chaplain of Holy Roman Emperor Charles V, argued in 1544 that the idolatry and cannibalism of the Indians made them, in Aristotle's terms, natural slaves—"barbarous and inhuman peoples abhorring all civil life, customs and virtue" was how he put it. People lacking "civil life" and "virtue" clearly could not be allowed self-government. Other writers commented that nakedness and cannibalism were both signs of the lack of "civility" among the Amerindians. Sepulveda implied that Indians were merely "humanlike," not necessarily human.

Franciscan and Dominican missionaries were especially vocal opponents of views like Sepulveda's. To these missionaries, the Indians initially seemed innocent and ideal subjects for conversion to the simple piety of Christ and his first apostles. In their eyes, Indians were like children who could be converted and led by example and, where

Crusade for Justice The criticisms of Bartolomé de Las Casas were published widely and accompanied by woodcuts like this one showing the cruelty of the conquerors toward the Amerindians. In response to Las Casas, Charles V passed laws protecting the rights of the indigenous peoples. (*The John Carter Brown Library at Brown University, Providence*)

necessary, by stern discipline. These mendicants saw themselves as advocates for Indians; they desired to protect the natives from the depredations of the Spanish conquerors and the corruptions of European civilization. The most eloquent defender of Indian rights was Bartolomé de Las Casas (1474–1566), a former encomendero who became a Dominican missionary and eventually bishop of Chiapas in southern Mexico. Las Casas passionately condemned the violence and brutality of the Spanish conquests. As part of a famous debate with Sepulveda, Las Casas rejected the "humanlike" argument. "All races of the world are men," he declared. All are evolving along a historical continuum. It was wrong, he added, to dismiss any culture or society as outside of natural law. Like all other peoples, Indians had reason. That being the case, even the most brutal could be civilized and Christianized. There was, in the view of Las Casas, no argument for natural slavery.

Charles V (who was king of Spain as well as Holy Roman emperor) accepted Las Casas's criticisms of the colonial administration. In 1542 he issued "New Laws" aimed at ending the virtual independence of the most adventurous of the encomenderos. He further abolished Indian slavery and greatly restricted the transfer of encomiendas. At first the European conquerors in Mexico and Peru rejected royal attempts to restrict their rights in the New World, but from the 1540s Indians were protected from the most extreme exploitation.

We should have no illusion, however, that these measures reflected some acceptance of cultural pluralism. The very mendicants who protected Indians assumed that Westernization and Christianization would quickly follow. And in some cases when it did not, as during revolts in the 1560s, the mendicants themselves reacted with a puzzled sense of anger, frustration, and betrayal.

THE COLUMBIAN EXCHANGE

The conquerors, adventurers, and traders who followed in the wake of Christopher Columbus and Vasco da Gama profoundly altered the Old World and the New. Before 1492 there had been a system of world trade, but now, as the Spanish proclaimed, Europe and especially Spain were at the center of economic and political life. As the Spanish and other Europeans moved throughout the world, they carried with them religions, ideas, diseases, people, plants, and animals—forever uniting the Old World and the New. This amalgamation of culture is known as the "Columbian Exchange."

Disease

Columbus and those who followed him brought not only people to the New World but also numerous Old World diseases. "Virgin-soil" epidemics—that is, epidemics of previously unknown diseases—are invariably fierce. Although the New World may have passed syphilis to Spain, from which it quickly spread throughout the Old World, diseases transferred from the Old World to the New were much more virulent than syphilis. Smallpox spread from Cuba to Mexico as early as 1519. It was soon followed by diphtheria, measles, trachoma, whooping cough, chickenpox, bubonic plague, malaria, typhoid fever, cholera, yellow fever, scarlet fever, amoebic dysentery, influenza, and some varieties of tuberculosis. Disease served as the silent ally of the conquerors. During critical points in the conquest of Tenochtitlán, smallpox was raging in the Aztec population. The disease later moved along traditional trade networks. An epidemic shortly before Pizarro's expedition to Peru carried off the Paca Inca and may have contributed to the unrest and civil war that worked to the advantage of the invaders.

Lacking sources, historians cannot trace accurately the movement of epidemic disease or its effect on the New World populations, yet many archaeologists and historians remain convinced that Old World diseases moved north from Mexico and ravaged and disrupted Amerindian populations in eastern North America long before the arrival of European immigrants. In most of the New World, 90 percent or more of the native population was destroyed by wave after wave of previously unknown diseases. Explorers and colonists did not so much enter an empty land as an "emptied" one.

It was at least partially because of disease that both the Spanish and the Portuguese needed to import large numbers of African slaves to work their plantations and mines (see page 499). With the settlement of southeastern North America, plantation agriculture was extended to include the production of tobacco and later cotton. As a result of the needs of plantation economies and the labor shortage caused by disease, African slaves were

brought in large numbers. In the Caribbean and along the coasts of Central and South America the Africans created an African-Caribbean or African American culture that amalgamated African, European, and American civilizations.

Plants and Animals

It became increasingly clear to the Spaniards that the New World had been completely isolated from the Old. (See the box, "The New World and the

Old World in the New This painting of "traditional" Amerindian culture shows animals brought by the Spaniards to the New World. The lives of the Amerindians were changed forever by the introduction of horses, sheep, chickens, and cows, as well as apples, peaches, wheat, and oats. *(From Martínez Compañon, Trujillo del Peru, vol. II, plate 77. Courtesy, Harvard College Library)*

Old.") The impact of Old World peoples on native populations was immediately evident to all. But scholars have recently argued that the importation of plants and animals had an even more profound effect than the arrival of Europeans. The changes that began in 1492 created "Neo-Europes" in what are now Canada, the United States, Mexico, Argentina, Australia, and New Zealand. The flora and fauna of the Old World, accustomed to a relatively harsh, competitive environment, found ideal conditions in the new lands. Like the rabbits carried to the Canary Islands and to Australia, plants and animals alike multiplied.

The most important meat and dairy animals in the New World—cattle, sheep, goats, and pigs—are imports from the Old World. Sailors initially brought pigs or goats aboard ship because they were easily transportable sources of protein. When let loose on the Caribbean islands, they quickly took over. The spread of horses through what is now Mexico, Brazil, Argentina, the United States, and Canada was equally dramatic. To the list of domesticated animals can be added donkeys, dogs, cats, and chickens. The changes these animals brought were profound. Cattle, pigs, and chickens quickly became staples of the New World diet. Horses enabled Amerindians and Europeans to travel across and settle on the vast plains of both North and South America.

The flora of the New World was equally changed. Even contemporaries noted how Old World plants flourished in the New. Because Old World plants came from a more hostile, more competitive environment, they were able to drive out their New World competitors. By 1555, European clover was widely distributed in Mexico—Aztecs called it "Castilian grass." Other Old World grasses, as well as weeds like dandelion, quickly followed. Domesticated plants like apples, peaches, and artichokes spread rapidly and naturally in the new environment. Early in the twentieth century it was estimated that only one-quarter of the grasses found on the broad prairies of the Argentine pampas were native before the arrival of Columbus. Studies of plant life in California, Australia, and New Zealand offer much the same results. The Old World also provided new and widely grown small grains like oats, barley, and wheat.

The exchange went both ways. Crops from the New World also had an effect on the Old World.

By the seventeenth century, maize (or American corn), potatoes, and sweet potatoes had significantly altered the diets of Europe and Asia. It was the addition of maize and potatoes that supported the dramatic population growth in areas like Italy, Ireland, and Scandinavia. With the addition of the tomato in the nineteenth century, much of the modern European diet became dependent on New World foods.

The new plants and new animals, as well as the social and political changes initiated by the Europeans, pulled the Old World and the New more closely together.

Culture

One reason for the accommodation between the Old World and the New was that the Europeans and Amerindians tended to interpret conquest and cultural transformation in the same way. The peoples living in the Valley of Mexico believed that their conquest was fated by the gods and would bring in new gods. The Spaniards' beliefs were strikingly similar, based on the revelation of divine will and the omnipotence of the Christian God. Cortés, by whitewashing former Aztec temples and converting native priests into white-clad Christian priests, was in a way fulfilling the Aztecs' expectations about their conqueror.

Acculturation was also facilitated by the Spanish tendency to place churches and shrines at the sites of former Aztec temples. The shrine of the Virgin of Guadalupe (north of modern Mexico City), for example, was located on the site of the temple of the goddess Tonantzin, an Aztec fertility-goddess of childbirth and midwives. (See the feature, "Weighing the Evidence: A Mexican Shrine," on pages 506–507.) Early missionaries reported that Indians quickly took to Christianity, although investigations later in the sixteenth century raised questions about the depth of their belief. Nonetheless, Christianity quickly became the dominant religion of the peoples of the New World.

The colonists tended to view their domination of the New World as a divine vindication of their own culture and civilization. During the sixteenth century, they set about remaking the world they had found. In the century after the conquest of Mexico, Spaniards founded 190 new cities in the Americas. Lima, Bogotá, and many others were

The New World and the Old

In an effort to understand the New World, the Spanish friar Bernardino de Sahagún (1499?–1590) interviewed Mexicans about their way of life before the arrival of the Europeans. The resulting volume, called the **Florentine Codex** *because it now reposes in Florence, is a valuable source on life and religion in Mexico before the Spanish conquests. In this excerpt from the* **Codex,** *the friar reflects on the relation of the New World and the Old.*

It occurred to me to write here that in the diversity of foods there are scarcely any which resemble ours. It seems that this people had never been discovered until these times, because, of the foods which we enjoy and are enjoying in the regions whence we came, we find none here. We do not even find here the domesticated animals which those of us who came from Spain and all Europe use, from which it appears that [the people] did not come from those regions. Nor had men from those regions come to discover this land, for if they had come from there, they would have come to make them known in other times; from them we would find wheat, barley, or rye, or chicken from there, or horses, or bulls, or donkeys, or sheep, or goats, or other domesticated animals which we utilize, whence it appears that only in these times have these lands been discovered and not before.

As to the preaching of the Gospel in these regions, there has been much doubt as to whether or not it has been preached before now. . . . Two trusted religious assured me that in Oaxaca, . . . they have some very ancient paintings, painted on deerskin, which contained many things alluded to in the preaching of the Gospel. Among others was one where there were three women dressed as Indian women. . . . And on the ground before them was a naked man, legs and arms stretched on a cross, arms and legs tied to the cross with cords. This seems to me to allude to Our Lady [the Virgin Mary] and her two sisters and to our crucified Redeemer, which they must have derived from ancient sermons.

So in conclusion I say it is possible that they were preached to and that they completely lost the Faith which was preached to them and returned to the ancient idolatries. And now it seems to me that our Lord God . . . has desired to give [them] the Spanish nation to be as a fountain from which flows the doctrine of the Catholic Faith.

Source: Reprinted by permission from B. de Sahagún, *The Florentine Codex: General History of the Things of New Spain,* part 1, ed. and trans. Arthur J. O. Anderson and Charles E. Dibble (Santa Fe, N.M.: School of American Research, 1950), pp. 96–97. Copyright 1982 by the School of American Research, Santa Fe, and the University of Utah.

proudly modeled on and compared to the cities of Spain. In 1573, King Philip II (r. 1556–1598) established ordinances requiring all new cities to be based on a uniform grid with a main plaza, market, and religious center. The new cities became hubs of social and political life in the colonies. In these cities, religious orders founded colleges for basic education much like the universities they had organized in the Old World. And by mid-century, the Crown had authorized the foundation of universities in Mexico City and Lima modeled after the great Spanish university of Salamanca.

Colonists attempted to recreate in all essentials the society of Spain.

The experience of the Spanish and the Portuguese in the sixteenth century seemed confirmed by the later experiences of the French and English in the seventeenth century. In seventeenth-century New England, the English Puritan John Winthrop concluded, "For the natives, they are nearly all dead of smallpox, so as the Lord hath cleared our title to what we possess."[8] A seventeenth-century French observer came to a similar conclusion: "Touching these savages, there is a thing that I cannot omit to remark to you, it is that it appears visibly that God wishes that they yield their place to new peoples."[9] Political philosophers believed that if there was no evidence that a land was being cultivated by the indigenous people, the rights to that land passed to those who would use and improve it. Thus, colonists believed that they had divine and legal sanction to take and to remake these new lands in a European image.

SUMMARY

Modern historians considering decolonization, economic revolutions in many parts of Asia, and multiculturalism have been changing their ways of thinking about European expansion in the fifteenth century. The expansion of Europe was not the movement of highly developed commercial economies into underdeveloped areas. In Asia, the Portuguese and later the Dutch and English were a military presence long before they were an economic one. In the New World, even as the Spanish conquered people and changed their language, government, and religion, many aspects of Amerindian culture survived in the local Indian municipalities.

The economic, political, and cultural changes brought about by the conquest created a hybrid culture. It is impossible to say whether the economic and technical benefits of the amalgamation of the Old World and the New outweigh the costs. But even those who celebrate the transformation of the New World would probably agree with the conclusions of a native American in the Pacific Northwest: "I am not sorry the missionaries came. But I wish they had known how to let their news change people's lives from the inside, without imposing their culture over our ways."[10] Tolerance, however, was not yet a hallmark of Western societies. Europeans were incapable of allowing others to change "from the inside." The inability to understand and tolerate others was to be a key to the strife created by the other great event of the sixteenth century, the movement to reform church and society.

NOTES

1. Quoted in John H. Parry and Robert G. Keith, eds., *The New Iberian World: A Documentary History of the Discovery and Settlement of Latin America to the Early Seventeenth Century*, vol. 2 (New York: Times Books, 1984), p. 59.
2. Quoted in William D. Phillips, Jr., and Carla Rahn Phillips, *The Worlds of Christopher Columbus* (Cambridge, England: Cambridge University Press, 1992), p. 163.
3. Quoted ibid., p. 166.
4. Quoted in J. H. Parry, ed., *The European Reconnaissance: Selected Documents* (New York: Harper & Row, 1968), p. 242.
5. Quoted in Alfred W. Crosby, *Ecological Imperialism: The Biological Expansion of Europe, 900–1900* (Cambridge, England: Cambridge University Press, 1986), p. 125.
6. Quoted ibid., p. 11.
7. Quoted in Mark A. Burkholder and Lyman L. Johnson, *Colonial Latin America* (Oxford: Oxford University Press, 1990), p. 29.
8. Quoted in Crosby, p. 208.
9. Quoted ibid., p. 215.
10. Quoted in Maria Parker Pascua, "Ozette: A Makah Village in 1491," *National Geographic* (October 1991), p. 53.

SUGGESTED READING

General Surveys
Bethell, Leslie, ed., *The Cambridge History of Latin America*. Vol 1. 1984. A standard work with excellent discussions of America before the conquest as well as discussions of colonial life.
Crosby, Alfred W. *The Columbian Voyages, the Columbian Exchange, and Their Historians*. 1988. A short pamphlet about historical writing on Columbus and the expansion of Europeans; an excellent place for a beginning student to start.
Curtin, P. *The Tropical Atlantic in the Age of the Slave Trade*. 1991. An introductory pamphlet that is an excellent first work for students interested in the history of slavery and the movement of peoples from Africa to the New World.
Levenson, J. A., ed. *Circa 1492: Art in the Age of Exploration*. 1991. A museum catalog showing art from Asia, Africa, America, and Europe at the time of Columbus; it includes essays on politics and culture aimed at a general audience.
Parry, J. H. *The Age of Reconnaissance*. 1981. A classic introductory survey of Portuguese, Spanish, English,

and French exploration and conquest to the end of the seventeenth century.

Scammell, Geoffrey. *The First Imperial Age: European Overseas Expansion, 1400–1715*. 1989. As the title implies, this is an introductory survey of European colonial interests through the early eighteenth century. The author puts the Spanish and Portuguese explorations in the context of later French and English experiences.

The European Background

Campbell, Mary B. *The Witness and the Other World: Exotic European Travel Writing, 400–1600*. 1988. A literary study of the narratives written by or about travelers, emphasizing especially the interest Columbus had in the reports of previous travelers.

Fernandez-Armesto, Felipe. *Before Columbus: Exploration and Colonization from the Mediterranean to the Atlantic, 1229–1492*. 1987. A well-written and accessible political and institutional narrative, especially valuable on the early Portuguese voyages.

Phillips, J. R. S. *The Medieval Expansion of Europe*. 1988. The best survey of European interest in and knowledge of the world beyond Christendom; especially good on European travelers to the East in the thirteenth century.

Exploration and Empire

Boxer, C. R. *The Portuguese Seaborne Empire, 1415–1825*. 1977. A classic political and institutional narrative of the Portuguese empire; detailed but accessible even to those with little background.

Burkholder, Mark A., and Lyman L. Johnson. *Colonial Latin America*. 1990. A thorough introduction to the conquest and colonization of Central and South America by the Spanish and Portuguese.

Clendinnen, Inga. *Ambivalent Conquests: Maya and Spaniard in Yucatan, 1517–1570*. 1987. A skillful, ironic study of the attempts of Maya and Spaniard to understand each other. It concentrates on the way in which Mayans transform European Christianity, including many of their pre-conquest beliefs and practices.

———. *Aztecs: An Interpretation*. 1991. A dramatic, beautifully written essay on the Aztecs that shows how daily life, religion, and imperialism were linked.

Elliott, John H. *The Old World and the New, 1492–1650*. 1970. Besides supplying the title for this chapter, these essays are excellent considerations of the reciprocal relations between the colonies and the kingdoms of Spain.

———. *Spain and Its World, 1500–1700: Selected Essays*. 1989. Essays by the greatest living historian of Spain and the New World. The essay on the mental world of Cortés is especially important.

Fuentes, Carlos. *The Buried Mirror: Reflections on Spain and the New World*. 1992. An essay with numerous illustrations, many in color, on the melding of the cultures of Spain and the New World, by one of Mexico's greatest writers. The author's reflections on the merging of Christianity and indigenous religions are particularly valuable.

Hale, John R. *Renaissance Exploration*. 1968. A broad-based introductory survey that emphasizes the technological and geographic innovations that were part of the early voyages.

Moseley, M. E. *The Incas and Their Ancestors: The Archaeology of Peru*. 1992. This general introduction to the Incas includes excellent maps and illustrations.

Phillips, W. D., Jr., and C. R. Phillips. *The Worlds of Christopher Columbus*. 1992. Though written for a popular audience, this is an excellent survey of Columbus and his voyages and an up-to-date summary of recent work on Columbus, maritime technology, and Spanish colonial interests.

Cultural Exchange

Crosby, A. W. *Ecological Imperialism: The Biological Expansion of Europe, 900–1900*. 1986. A discussion of how migrating peoples carried with them plants, animals, and diseases; has an excellent collection of maps and illustrations.

Hanke, L. *Aristotle and the American Indians: A Study in Race Prejudice in the Modern World*. 1959. The most general of Hanke's books about race and prejudice in the Old and New Worlds. Hanke states clearly the philosophical basis of debates over equality from classical Greece to the nineteenth century.

Pagden, Anthony. *The Fall of Natural Man: The American Indian and the Origin of Comparative Ethnology*. 1982. A brilliant, difficult, and rewarding book on the debate over Indians' rights in the sixteenth century.

Smithsonian Institution. *Seeds of Change*. 1991. This museum catalog has excellent illustrations and introductory essays on the transfer of diseases and plants between the Old World and the New. There is an especially good chapter on religion in the period before the arrival of the Spaniards.

A MEXICAN SHRINE

The shrine of the Virgin of Guadalupe lies on a slight hill on the edge of Mexico City, a bare three miles from the center of what was the Aztec city of Tenochtitlán. It is likely the holiest shrine in the Americas, visited by perhaps 15,000 pilgrims and tourists daily. Singing and prayer begin as pilgrims come in sight of the shrine; people fall to their knees in penance and devotion as they approach the church; and the pious hang homemade and commercially purchased *ex votos* (votive medals) along the walls. Pilgrim groups often break into traditional chants praising God for the dawn and concluding, "God bless you, Mary."*

The image the pilgrims venerate is a painting of a dark-skinned woman. We see her standing in

The Virgin of Guadalupe *(Enrique Franco-Torrijos)*

the shimmering light of the moon seeming to combine Aztec and Spanish elements. According to later chronicles, the painting was found in 1531 by Juan Diego, an Aztec convert to Christianity, whose story was first told in Nahuatl, the Aztec language, rather than in Spanish. The pious Indian reported meeting a dark-skinned woman who identified herself as Mary, the Mother of God. She told him where to find the image and required that a shrine be built in her honor because she was the merciful mother of this land. Juan Diego eventually presented the painting of the Virgin carefully wrapped in his cloak to the bishop of Mexico City.

First a simple chapel and by the eighteenth century the magnificent church we see here, this shrine quickly became the most popular Mexican shrine and a symbol of Indian integration into the Christian world. The historian, however, wishes to know how such a shrine developed and how it came to possess such powerful associations for the people of Mexico. Who were the original worshipers? What was the connection of the Spanish to the shrine? And finally, what can this shrine tell us about the colonial experience in Mexico?

The shrine had a complex history during Mexico's colonial period—it was not simply a Christian center of Amerindian devotion. The shrine itself is located on the site of the pre-conquest shrine of Tonantzin, an Aztec fertility-goddess. Spanish priests who troubled to learn Nahuatl reported that Tonantzin's shrine was popular throughout the region. By the middle of the sixteenth century, Franciscan missionaries had managed to substitute the veneration of the Virgin Mary, whom they called "the good little grandmother,"** for worship of Tonantzin, "Our Mother." The adoption of Guadalupe by all Mexicans was not, however, a simple process.

*Quoted from a 1940 report in Victor and Edith Turner, *Image and Pilgrimage in Christian Culture, Anthropological Perspectives* (New York: Columbia University Press, 1978), p. 96.
**Quoted in William B. Taylor, "The Virgin of Guadalupe in New Spain: An Inquiry into the Social History of Marian Devotion," *American Ethnologist* 14 (1987): 11.

Pilgrims Approaching the Shrine of the Virgin of Guadalupe *(Alyx Kellington/DDB Stock Photo)*

As historians quickly learn, narratives may not necessarily be composed when they claim they were. Although the shrine to the Virgin is known to have existed in the sixteenth century, the story of Juan Diego's discovery of the painting cannot be shown to have circulated before the seventeenth century, perhaps not before the 1660s. This time sequence is very significant since it is Juan Diego who clearly identifies Guadalupe as a special Indian shrine. And that identification raises a further question: If Guadalupe appealed only to local Indians, who popularized the shrine? The answer seems to be that Guadalupe was most popular with the residents of Mexico City and with priests and clergy who were creole (people of mixed Spanish and Indian parentage)—individuals who did not fit easily in either the Spanish or the Indian communities. By the mid-sixteenth century, the shrine had come to mark the edge of Mexico City. An Englishman remarked that Spaniards could not pass the shrine without stopping and praying for protection from evil. If the shrine was primarily of interest to creoles and to residents of Mexico City, how did it come to represent all of Mexico, especially the Indian population of Mexico?

The Virgin of Guadalupe seems to have become popular with the Indians of Mexico only over the course of the late seventeenth and the eighteenth centuries. Veneration of her expanded as part of a general social and cultural transformation. The spread of the cult seems to have been the work of creole priests who celebrated the Feast of the Apparition, when the Virgin appeared to the humble Indian convert. There were reports of miracles by the Virgin of Guadalupe in various parts of Mexico. And by the late eighteenth century, an English traveler reported:

If you travel through the *ranchos* of the entire kingdom you will find that two things are rarely lacking: an image of Nuestra Señora de Guadalupe and a poor school master who teaches reading and Christian doctrine.[†]

Mexicans seem to have embraced the cult of the Virgin for a variety of reasons. To many she was the "little grandmother," the mediator between humble people and the authorities. Yet in some cases, when the bonds between the authorities and the more humble people were broken, the Indians often took comfort in their belief that "Most Holy Mary is praying for us." And finally, during the revolutions of the ninteenth century, for those who understood themselves to be Mexican, separated from the Spanish government, the Virgin became a powerful symbol of independence and justice for Indians and common people.

What can historians learn from such a shrine? First, that symbols have many meanings. Depending on time and place, the Virgin of Guadalupe appealed to the religious and social concerns of Spaniards, creoles, and Indians. Second, and perhaps as important, the history of the shrine of Guadalupe shows us that religious symbols, ideas, and traditions may evolve over time. ✸

[†]Ibid., p. 15.

CHAPTER 14

The Age of the Reformation

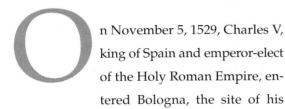

On November 5, 1529, Charles V, king of Spain and emperor-elect of the Holy Roman Empire, entered Bologna, the site of his coronation. He was met by twenty cardinals, four hundred papal guards, and a host of other papal and imperial soldiers. As he moved through the city, Charles's heralds tossed eight thousand ducats of gold and silver into the waiting crowds. Gates and streets were decorated with medallions of emperors and statues of patricians recalling ancient virtues and reminding the emperor-elect of his duties to preserve the law and defend Christendom.

Charles and his advisers believed that God had selected him to reestablish the power of the empire and to cement the special relationship between emperor and pope. But by the end of Charles's reign in 1556, less than thirty years after his triumphant entry into Bologna, just the opposite had occurred. The empire had become little more than a German state. And the coronation of Charles by Pope Leo X in Bologna was, in fact, the last papal coronation of an emperor.

This dramatic reversal resulted from a series of political, diplomatic, and religious crises that changed forever the face of Europe. The key issue was the sixteenth-century movement known as the Reformation, an ever widening controversy over the nature of Christianity, the relationship between the individual and God, and the role of government in society. The struggle began as an apparently minor theological controversy in Germany—a "quarrel between monks," as the papacy saw it. Debates about salvation quickly widened into arguments about the sacraments—that is, the means by which individuals receive God's grace. By the middle of the century, disagreements had expanded to the point that both the

Charles V and Clement VII entering Bologna, 1530.

Christian religion and politics were changed for-ever. As the controversy continued, issues spread from questions of theology to those of ecclesiastical and political organization. In the heat of this religious crisis the modern Christian churches, both Protestant and Catholic, were formed.

The Roman Catholic, Lutheran, Calvinist, and Anglican churches all came into being in the sixteenth century. But to speak of "Lutheran" or "Roman Catholic" during the first decades of the Reformation is to ignore the fluidity of the situation in which Europeans found themselves. At first, no one foresaw that the result of the controversies would be separate churches. The reformers of the first half of the sixteenth century shared many characteristics. Most had been influenced by the cultural and literary interests of the humanists. Many had received a humanistic education, with its emphasis on literary studies and the study of Latin, Greek, and Hebrew. Although most reformers eventually rejected the general humanistic assumption of the dignity and essential goodness of individuals, they shared with the humanists a faith in linguistic studies of Christian traditions, especially of the Bible. Almost all emphasized the Bible as the unique source of religious authority and rejected the medieval church's complex view of salvation. Initially, they all rejected any claim of special status or authority for the priesthood. And because of increasingly violent debates over theology and church government, the idea of a single Christendom did not survive the century.

The debates over religion and the power and authority of the church that raged during this period did not occur in a political vacuum. Supporters of the church, like Emperor Charles V, would gladly have used force to suppress the new theology, but events conspired to make such a response unrealistic. In Germany, the emperor faced hostile towns and princes as well as French and Turkish military threats—all of which made action against religious dissidents impossible. In England and Scandinavia, in contrast, monarchs viewed the church as an illegitimate political power and a threat to strong royal government, and reformers soon found themselves with royal patrons. Elsewhere, especially in eastern Europe, there was no strong central government to enforce religious unity, and a variety of Christian traditions coexisted.

By the second half of the sixteenth century it was clear that there would never again be a single Christian church in western Europe. Political and religious powers concentrated their energies on a process of theological definition and institutionalization that historians call the "Second Reformation," or "Confessionalization." With the changes of the late sixteenth century it becomes appropriate to speak of Roman Catholic, Anglican, and Lutheran as clearly defined confessions, or systems of religious beliefs and practices.

In Protestant and Catholic churches the changes in religion increased the importance of the moral control exercised by religious authorities. Far from freeing the individual, the Christian churches of the late sixteenth century all emphasized correct doctrine and orderliness in personal behavior. The early Protestants may have rejected a sacramental system that they thought oppressed the individual, but the institutions that replaced the old church developed their own traditions of control. The increased moral control by churches accompanied and even fostered the growth in state power that would characterize the late sixteenth and seventeenth centuries.

THE REFORMATION MOVEMENTS, CA. 1517–1545

In 1517 a little-known professor of theology at the University of Wittenberg in Saxony began a protest against practices in the late medieval church. Martin Luther had no carefully worked-out idea about the nature of the church and salvation, but his theology struck a responsive chord with many of his contemporaries. Although the various protests resulted in the creation of separate and well-defined religious traditions, the differences among the reformers were not initially as clear as they became in the second half of the sixteenth century. Thus, it is appropriate to speak of "reformation movements" because all the reformers, even the most radical, shared with Luther a sense that the essential sacramental and priestly powers claimed by the medieval church were illegitimate.

"Protestant" is the label we now use to describe the churches that arose in opposition to the medieval Christian church. It is important to understand, however, that the word *Protestant* was originally a political term used to describe German princes who opposed imperial attempts to end a truce between supporters and opponents of the religious reformers in the 1530s. Only later was *Protestant* applied to the resulting churches. The reformers tended to think of themselves as "evangelical reformed Christians." They were evangelical in the sense that they believed that authority derived from the Word of God, the Bible. They were reformed Christians because their aim was merely to restore Christianity to the form they believed it exhibited in the first centuries of its existence.

The Late Medieval Context

Questions of an individual's salvation and personal relationship to God and to the Christian community remained at the heart of religious practice and theological speculation in the sixteenth as in previous centuries. Nominalist theologians, the leading thinkers of the late Middle Ages, rejected the key assumption of previous Scholastics —that there were universal ideas and generally applicable rules of order for moral life (see page 380). In the words of William of Ockham (ca. 1285–1347), "No universal really exists outside the mind." Truth was to be found in daily experience or in revealed scripture, not in complex logical systems. At the heart is Ockham's method— known as Ockham's razor—that what can be explained with only a few logical speculations "is vainly explained by assuming more."

Nominalist theologians rejected vast logical systems, but they held on to the traditional rituals and beliefs that tied together the Christian community. They believed in a holy covenant in which God would save those Christians who, by means of the church's sacraments and through penitential acts, were partners in their own salvation. Foremost among the penitential acts was the feeding of "Christ's Poor," especially on important feast days. The pious constructed and supported hospices for travelers and hospitals for the sick. Christians went on pilgrimages to shrines like the tomb of Saint Thomas à Becket in Canterbury or the church of Saint James of Compostela in Spain. They also built small chapels, called chantry chapels, for the sake of their own souls. To moralists, work itself was in some sense a penitential and ennobling act.

The most common religious practice of the late Middle Ages was participation in religious brotherhoods. Members vowed to attend monthly meetings, to participate in processions on feast days, and to maintain peaceful and charitable relations with fellow members. Religious brotherhoods often played a political role as well. In the south of France, for example, city governments often met in the chapels of the Brotherhoods of the Holy Spirit.

The most typical religious feast was that of *Corpus Christi* (the "Body of Christ"). The feast celebrated and venerated the sacrament of the mass and the ritual by which the bread offered to the laity became the actual body of Christ. Corpus Christi was popular with the church hierarchy because it emphasized the role of the priest in the central ritual of Christianity. The laity, however, equated Corpus Christi with the body of citizens who made up the civic community.

Kingdoms, provinces, and towns all had patron saints who, believers thought, offered protection from natural as well as political disasters. There were royal saints like Edward of England, Louis of France, and Olaf of Norway. Festivals in honor of the saints were a major event in the town or kingdom. The most revered saint in the late Middle Ages was the Virgin Mary, the mother of Jesus. The most popular new pilgrimage shrines in the north of Europe were dedicated to the Virgin. It was she, the Sienese maintained, who protected them from their Florentine rivals. As the veneration of the Virgin Mary shows, in the late Middle Ages it was not possible to distinguish between religion and society, church and state.

Women played a prominent role in late medieval religious life. Holy women who claimed any sort of moral standing often did so because of visions or prophetic gifts such as knowledge of future events or of the status of souls in Purgatory. Reputations for sanctity provided a profound moral authority. The Italian Blessed Angela of Foligno (ca. 1248–1309) had several visions and became the object of a large circle of devoted followers. She was typical of a number of late medieval female religious figures who on the death of a spouse turned to religion. Like Angela, these women tended to gather "families" around them, people whom they described as their spiritual "fathers" or "children." They offered moral counsel and warned businessmen and politicians of the dangers of lying and sharp dealings. "Oh my sons, fathers, and brothers," counseled Angela, "see that you love one another amongst your-selves . . . [and] likewise unto all people."[1]

In the late Middle Ages religious houses for women probably outnumbered those for men. For unmarried or unmarriageable (because of disabilities) daughters, convents were an economical, safe, and controlled environment. Moralists denounced the dumping of women in convents: "They give [unmarriageable daughters] to a convent, as if they were the scum and vomit of the world," was the conclusion of Saint Bernardino of Siena (1380–1444). The general public, however, believed that well-run communities of women promoted the spiritual and physical health of the community. In a society in which women were not allowed to control their own property and in which women outside the nobility lacked a visible role in political and intellectual life, a religious vocation may have appealed to women because it allowed them to define their own religious and social relationships. A religious vocation offered other advantages, too. Well-to-do or aristocratic parents appreciated the fact that the traditional gift that accompanied a daughter entering a religious house was much smaller than a dowry.

Some women declined to join convents, which required vows of chastity and obedience to a rule and close male supervision. Margery Kempe (ca. 1373–1439) of Lynn, England, traveled throughout Christendom on a variety of pilgrimages. She left her husband and family, dressed in white (symbolic of virginity), and joined with other pilgrims on trips to Spain, Italy, and Jerusalem. Many other women chose to live as anchoresses, or recluses, in closed cells beside churches and hospitals or in rooms in private houses. Men and women traveled from all parts of England seeking the counsel of the Blessed Julian of Norwich (d. after 1413), who lived in a tiny cell built into the wall of a parish church.

The most controversial group of religious women were the Beguines, who lived in communities without taking formal vows and often with minimal connections to the local church hierarchy (see page 376). By the early fifteenth century, Beguines were suspect because clerics believed that these independent women rejected traditional religious cloistering and the moral leadership of male clergy and were particularly susceptible to heresy. Critics maintained that unsupervised Beguines held to what was called the "Heresy of the Free Spirit," a belief that one who had achieved spiritual perfection was no longer capable of sin. Rumors of sexual orgies, spread by fearful clerical critics, quickly brought suspect women before local inquisitors. Although some Beguines may have held such a belief in spiritual perfection, the majority certainly did not. But they were feared by an ecclesiastical hierarchy that distrusted independence.

A more conservative movement for renewal in the church was the Brothers and Sisters of the Common Life founded by the Dutchman Geert Groote (1340–1384). A popular preacher and reformer, Groote gathered male and female followers into quasi-monastic communities at Deventer in the Low Countries. Eventually a community of Augustinian canons was added at Windesheim. Brothers and Sisters of the Common Life supported themselves as book-copyists and teachers in small religious schools in the Low Countries. Members of these communities followed a strict, conservative spirituality that has come to be known as the *devotio moderna,* or "modern devotion." Although they called themselves "modern," their piety was traditional. Their ideas are encapsulated in *The Imitation of Christ,* a popular work advocating a traditional sort of monastic spirituality written by Thomas à Kempis (ca. 1380–1471), a canon of Windesheim. They advocated the contrary ideals of fourteenth-century religious life: broader participation by the laity and strict control by clerical authorities.

Religious life in the late medieval period was broadly based and vigorous. Theologians, lay women and men, and popular preachers could take heart they were furthering their own salvation and that of their neighbors. Thus, if reform was to be radically new, it would have to involve more than simple moral change.

Martin Luther and the New Theology

Martin Luther (1483–1546) eventually challenged many of the assumptions of late medieval Christians. He seemed to burst onto the scene in 1517, when he objected to the way in which papal indulgences—that is, the remission of penalties owed for sins—were being bought and sold in the bishopric of Brandenburg. Luther's father, a miner from the small town of Mansfeld, had hoped that his son would take a degree in law and become a wealthy and prestigious lawyer. Luther chose in-

Cranach: The True Church and the False This woodcut was designed to make clear the distinction between the evangelical church and the papacy. On one side Christ and his sacrifice are clearly at the center; on the other the pope and innumerable church officials are caught in the flames of Hell. *(Staatliche Kunstsammlungen Dresden)*

stead to enter a monastery and eventually become a priest.

Throughout his life, Martin Luther seems to have been troubled by a sense of his own sinfulness and unworthiness. According to late medieval theology, the life of a Christian was a continuing cycle of sin, confession, contrition, and penance, and the only way to achieve salvation was to have confessed all one's sins and at least begun a cycle of penance at the time of one's death. Christians lived in fear of dying suddenly without having any chance to confess. The purchase of indulgences, membership in penitential brotherhoods, ritualized charity, and veneration of popular saints were seen as ways to acquire merit and salvation in the eyes of God.

Luther came to believe that the church's requirement that believers achieve salvation by means of confession, contrition, and penance made too great a demand on the faithful. Instead, Luther said, citing the New Testament, salvation (or justification) was God's gift to the faithful. Luther's belief is known as "justification by faith." Acts of charity were important products of God's love, but in Luther's opinion, they were not necessary for salvation. Late in his life, Luther explained how he came by these ideas:

Though I lived as a monk without reproach, I felt that I was a sinner before God with an extremely disturbed conscience. I could not believe that he was placated by my [acts of penance]. I did not love, yes, I hated the righteous God who punishes sinners. . . . At last, by the mercy of God, . . . I gave context to the words, namely, "In it the righteousness of God is revealed, as it is written, 'He who through faith is righteous shall live.'" There I began to understand that . . . the righteous lives by a gift of God, namely by faith. . . . Here I felt that I was altogether born again and had entered paradise itself through open gates.[2]

Although Luther recalled a sudden, dramatic revelation, it now seems clear that his insight developed slowly over the course of his academic career and during his defense of his teachings. Nonetheless, his recollection conveys a sense of the novelty of his theology and the reasons why his attack on the late medieval church proved to be so much more devastating than the complaints of earlier critics.

Other critics had complained of impious priests, an unresponsive bureaucracy, and a church too much involved in matters of government, but the theology that Luther developed struck at the very structure of the church itself. Luther separated justification from acts of sanctification—from the good works or charity expected of all Christians. In Luther's theology the acts of piety so typical of the medieval church were quite unnecessary for salvation, because Christ's sacrifice had brought justification once and for all. Justification came entirely from God and was independent of human acts. Luther argued that the Christian was at the same time sinner and saved, so the penitential cycle and careful preparation for a "good death" were, in his opinion, unnecessary.

Luther also attacked the place of the priesthood in the sacramental life of the church. The church taught that, through the actions of ordained priests, Christ was really present in the bread and wine of the sacrament of Holy Communion. Luther agreed that the sacrament transformed the bread and wine into the body and blood of Christ, but he denied that priests had a role in the transformation. Priests distributed only the bread to the laity, reserving the consecrated wine for themselves—further emphasizing their own special status. Priests, in Luther's view, were not mediators between God and individual Christians. John Wyclif and John Hus (see page 400) had argued against the spiritual authority of unworthy priests. Luther, however, directly challenged the role of the clergy and the institutional church in the attainment of salvation. Thus he argued for a "priesthood of all believers."

In the years before 1517, Luther's views on salvation and his reservations about the traditional ways of teaching theology attracted little interest outside his own university. Matters changed, however, when he challenged the sale of indulgences. Indulgences were often granted because of pilgrimages, or great acts of charity or sacrifice. The papacy frequently authorized the sale of indulgences to pay various expenses. Unscrupulous

priests often left the impression that purchase of an indulgence freed a soul from purgatory. After getting no response to his initial complaints, Luther made public his "Ninety-five Theses." Luther probably posted these theses on indulgences on the door of the Wittenberg Castle church, the usual way to announce topics for theological discussion about the interpretation of the Scriptures and the nature of penance. Luther's text created a firestorm when it was quickly translated and printed throughout German-speaking lands. His complaints about the sale of indulgences encapsulated German feelings about unworthy priests and economic abuses by the clergy. Luther was acclaimed as the spokesman of the German people.

In a debate with a papal representative in Leipzig in 1519, Luther was forced to admit that in some of his positions he agreed with the Czech heretic John Hus. In the Leipzig debate and in the following year Luther responded to his critics and tried to explain more fully the nature of the changes he advocated. Three tracts were especially important. In *Address to the Christian Nobility of the German Nation,* Luther urged the princes to reject papal claims of temporal and spiritual authority. (See the box, "Martin Luther's Address to the Christian Nobility of the German Nation.") In *On the Babylonian Captivity of the Church,* he argued for the principle of *sola scriptura*—that is, authority in the church had to be based on teachings found in the Bible. In *On Christian Freedom,* he explained clearly his understanding of salvation: "A Christian has all he needs in faith and needs no works to justify him." Luther was speaking of spiritual freedom from unnecessary ritual, not social or political freedom. This distinction would later be crucial to Luther's opposition to political and economic protests by peasants and artisans.

In 1520, Pope Leo X (r. 1513–1521) condemned Luther's teachings and gave him sixty days to recant. Luther refused to do so and publically burned the papal letter. In 1521, Emperor Charles V called an imperial diet, or parliament, at Worms to deal with the religious crisis. Charles demanded that Luther submit to papal authority. Luther, however, explained that religious decisions must be based on personal experience and conscience:

Unless I am convicted by the testimony of Scripture or by clear reason, for I do not trust either in the Pope or in

Martin Luther's Address to the Christian Nobility of the German Nation

Luther wrote this tract to the rulers of Germany to explain the nature of his conflict with the church over ecclesiastical authority. In this excerpt, he makes clear his disagreements with the system of clerical status and immunities that had grown throughout the Middle Ages. Compare his statements with those in the box, "Ignatius Loyola's Spiritual Exercises" on page 537.

The Romanists have very cleverly built three walls around themselves. In the first place, when pressed by the temporal power, they have made decrees and declared that the temporal power had no jurisdiction over them, but that on the contrary, the spiritual power is above the temporal. In the second place, when the attempt is made to reprove them with the Scriptures, they raise the objection that only the pope may interpret the Scriptures. In the third place if threatened with a council, their story is that no one may summon a council but the Pope.

Let us begin by attacking the first wall. It is pure invention that the Pope, bishops, priests, and monks are called the spiritual estate while princes, lords, craftsmen, and peasants are the temporal estate. This is indeed a piece of deceit and hypocrisy: . . . all Christians are truly of the spiritual estate. . . . The Pope or bishop anoints, shaves heads, ordains, consecrates, and prescribes garb different from that of the laity, but he can never make a man into a Christian or into a spiritual man by so doing. He might well make a man into a hypo-crite or a humbug and a blockhead, but never a Christian or a spiritual man. . . . Therefore a priest in Christendom is nothing else but an officeholder. As long as he holds his office, he takes precedence; where he is deposed, he is a peasant or a townsman like anybody else. . . .

The second wall is still more loosely built and less substantial. The Romanists want to be the only masters of Holy Scripture, although they never learn a thing from the Bible their life long. . . . Besides, if we are all priests, . . . and all have one faith, one gospel, one sacrament, why should we not also have the power to test and judge what is right or wrong in matters of faith?

The third wall falls of itself, when the first two are down. When the Pope acts contrary to the Scriptures, it is our duty to stand by the Scriptures and to reprove him and to constrain him, according to the word of Christ. . . . The Romanists have no basis in Scripture for their claim that the Pope alone was right to call or to confirm a council. This is just their own ruling, and it is only valid so long as it is not harmful to Christendom or contrary to the laws of God.

Source: Martin Luther, *Three Treatises,* in *The American Edition of Luther's Works* (Philadelphia: Fortress Press, 1970), pp. 10–22.

councils alone, since it is well known that they have often erred and contradicted themselves, . . . I cannot and will not retract anything, for it is neither safe nor right to go against conscience. I cannot do otherwise, here I stand, may God help me. Amen.[3]

The emperor and his allies, however, stayed firmly in the papal camp. The excommunicated Luther was placed under an imperial ban—that is, declared an outlaw. As Luther left the Diet of Worms, friendly princes took him to Wartburg Castle in Saxony, where they could protect him. During a year of isolation at Wartburg, Luther used Erasmus's edition of the Greek New Testament as the basis of a translation into German of the New Testament, which became an influential literary as well as religious work.

THE REFORMATION AND COUNTER-REFORMATION

1513–1517	Fifth Lateran Council meets to consider reform of the Catholic church
1517	Luther makes public his "Ninety-five Theses"
1518	Zwingli is appointed people's priest of Zurich
1520	Pope Leo X condemns Luther's teachings
1521	Luther appears at the Diet of Worms
1524–1525	Peasant revolts in Germany
1527	Imperial troops sack Rome
1530	Melanchthon composes the Augsburg Confession summarizing Lutheran belief
1534	Calvin flees from Paris; Loyola founds the Society of Jesus
1535	The Anabaptist community of Münster is destroyed
1536	Calvin arrives in Geneva and publishes the first edition of *Institutes of the Christian Religion*
1545–1563	Council of Trent meets to reform the Catholic church
1555	Emperor Charles V accepts the Peace of Augsburg

The Reformation of the Communities

Luther challenged the authority of the clerical hierarchy and called on lay people to take responsibility for their own salvation. His ideas spread rapidly in the towns and countryside of Germany because he and his followers took advantage of the new technology of printing. (See the feature, "Weighing the Evidence: A Reformation Woodcut," on pages 542–543.) Perhaps 300,000 copies of his early tracts were published in the first years of the protest. Luther's claim that the Scriptures must be the basis of all life and his appeal to the

judgment of the laity seem to have struck a responsive chord in towns and villages, where councils of local people were accustomed to making decisions based on ideas of the common good. It is also true that townsmen and villagers saw religious and civic life as being inextricably interconnected. For them, there was no such thing as a religiously neutral act.

The impact of Luther's ideas quickly became evident. If the active intercession of the clergy was not necessary for the salvation of individuals, then, according to Luther's followers, there was no reason for the clergy to remain unmarried and celibate, and there was no reason for men or women to cloister themselves in monasteries or convents. Also, maintained Luther's partisans, there was no need to restrict the laity's participation in the sacrament of the Eucharist. Thus, the priest must distribute wine to the laity along with the bread. With the spread of Luther's ideas came the end of a very visual part of the clerical monopoly. Because Luther's followers believed that penitential acts were not prerequisites for salvation, they tended to set aside the veneration of saints and not to make pilgrimages to the shrines and holy places all over Europe.

Many historians have referred to the spread of these reform ideas as "the Reformation of the Common Man." In Strasbourg, Nuremberg, Zurich, and other towns, ideas about the primacy of the Bible and attacks on clerical privilege were spread by "people's priests," preachers hired by the town government to see to preaching and the care of souls in the community. Many of the most famous reformers initially gained a following through preaching. The message then seems to have spread especially quickly among artisan and mercantile groups, which put pressure on town governments to press for reform. Agitation was often riotous. One resident of Augsburg exposed himself during a church service to protest what he believed was an evil and idolatrous service.

To quell disturbances and to arrive at a consensus within the community, cautious town councils often set up debates between reformers and church representatives. Because the church hierarchy rarely approved of such debates, traditional views were often poorly represented, giving a great advantage to the reformers. The two sides argued over the authority of the church hierarchy, the nature of salvation, and whether papal authority and the seven sacraments could be demonstrated in the Bible. At the conclusion of such a debate, many town governments ordered that preaching and practice in the town should be according to the "Word of God"—a code for reformed practice. In reformed towns, the city council became a council of elders for the church. Thus, civil government came to play an important role in the local organization of the church.

The case of Zurich is instructive. In 1519 the people's priest of Zurich was Huldrych Zwingli (1484–1531), son of a rural official from a nearby village. After a university education, he became a typical late medieval country priest, right down to his numerous mistresses. Yet after experiences as a military chaplain and an acquaintance with the humanist writings of Erasmus, Zwingli began to preach strongly biblical sermons. In 1522 he defended a group of laymen who broke a required Lenten fast to show their disapproval of what they saw as useless ritual. Later in the same year he requested episcopal permission to marry. Early in 1523, he led a group of reformers in a public debate over the nature of the church. The city council declared in favor of the reformers, and Zurich became, in effect, a Protestant city.

Unlike Luther, Zwingli believed that reform should be a communal movement—that town governments should take the lead in bringing reform to the community. Zwingli explained that moral regeneration of individuals was an essential precondition for God's gift of grace. In the years following 1523, the reformers restructured church services, abolishing mass; they also removed religious images from churches and suppressed monastic institutions. Zwingli further disagreed with Luther about the nature of the sacrament of Holy Communion. Whereas Luther, like Catholic theologians, accepted that Christ was truly present in the bread and wine, Zwingli argued that Christ's presence was merely spiritual—the bread and wine merely signified Christ. This disagreement created within the movement for reform a division that made a common response to papal or imperial pressure difficult (Map 14.1).

The reform message spread from towns into the countryside, but often with effects that the reformers did not expect or desire. Luther thought his message was a spiritual and theological one.

Many peasants and modest artisans, however, believed Luther's message of biblical freedom carried material as well as theological meaning.

In many parts of Germany villagers and peasants found themselves under increasing pressure from landlords and territorial princes. Taking advantage of changed economic and political conditions, these lords were intent on regaining claims to ancient manorial rights, on suppressing peasant claims to use common lands, and on imposing new taxes and tithes. Like townsmen, peasants saw religious and material life as closely connected. They argued that new tithes and taxes did not just go against tradition but violated the Word of God. Using Luther's argument that authority should be based on the Scriptures, peasants from the district of Zurich, for example, petitioned the town council in 1523–1524, claiming that they

Peasant Freedom The German peasants believed Luther's call for individual freedom of conscience included economic and political freedom. Their revolt of 1524–1525 struck terror in the hearts of German rulers. As this woodcut indicates, the peasant army was lightly armed. Many carried only tools, pitchforks, flails, and scythes. (*Title page of an anonymous pamphlet from the Peasants' War, 1525*)

- Signatories to initial Protestation
- Cities where reform movement failed or was suppressed
- Other cities and towns of the Reformation
- Boundary of the Holy Roman Empire

SWEDEN
DENMARK
Baltic Sea
Stralsund
Rostock
Greifswald
Lübeck
Wismar
Hamburg
Stettin
Lüneburg
Bremen
BRANDENBURG
POLAND
Celle
Hanover
Braunschweig
Magdeburg
Paderborn
Einbeck
Goslar
Wittenberg
Göttingen
NETHERLANDS
Nordhausen
Torgau
Mühlhausen
Frankenhausen
Leipzig
Cologne
Eisenach
Erfurt
SILESIA
Gotha
Weimar
Zwickau
H O L Y R O M A N E M P I R E
LUXEMBOURG
Frankfurt
Schweinfurt
Mainz
Würzburg
Bamberg
Prague
Worms
Kitzingen
BOHEMIA
Windsheim
Rothenburg
Nuremberg
Schwäbisch-Hall
Heilbronn
Weissenburg
Schwäbisch-Gmünd
Regensburg
Strasbourg
Esslingen
Nördlingen
Reutlingen
Rottweil
Ulm
Augsburg
Freiburg-im-Breisgau
Biberach
Munich
Mulhouse
Ravensburg
Memmingen
Waldshut
Kaufbeuren
Constance
Kempton
Isny
Lindau
AUSTRIA
SWISS CONFED.
TYROL
HUNGARY
FRANCE

0   50   100 Km.
0   50   100 Mi.

Map 14.1 Reform in Germany The pattern of religious reform in Germany was complex. Although some territorial princes, such as the dukes of Bavaria, rejected the reform, most free towns, particularly those in the southwest, adopted it.

should not be required to pay tithes on their produce because there was no biblical justification for doing so. Townsmen rejected the peasants' demand, noting that the Bible did not forbid such payments and saying that the peasants should make them out of love.

Demands that landlords and magistrates give up human ordinances and follow "Godly Law" soon turned to violence. Peasants, miners, and villagers in 1524 and 1525 participated in a series of uprisings that began on the borderlands between Switzerland and Germany and spread throughout southwest Germany, upper Austria, and even into northern Italy. Bands of peasants and villagers, perhaps a total of 300,000 in the empire, revolted against their seigneurial lords or even their territorial overlords.

Luther initially counseled landlords and princes to redress the just grievances. As reports of riots and increased violence continued to reach Wittenberg, however, Luther condemned the rebels as "mad dogs" and urged that they be destroyed. Territorial princes and large cities quickly raised armies to meet the threat. The peasants were defeated and destroyed in a series of battles in April 1525. It seems likely that, in response to these rebellions, lords lived in fear of another re-volt and were careful not to overburden their tenants. But when it became clear that the reformers were unwilling to follow the implications of their own theology, villagers and peasants lost interest in the progress of the reform. As a townsman of Zurich commented, "Many came to a great hatred of the preachers, where before they would have bitten off their feet for the Gospel."[4]

John Calvin and the Reformed Tradition

The revolts of 1524 and 1525 demonstrated the mixed messages traveling under the rubric "true, or biblical religion." In the 1530s, the theological arguments of the reformers began to take on a greater clarity, mostly because of the Franco-Swiss reformer John Calvin (1509–1564). Calvin had a humanistic education in Paris and became a lawyer before coming under the influence of reform-minded thinkers in France. In 1534 he fled from Paris as royal pressures against reformers increased. He arrived in Geneva in 1536, where he would remain, except for a short exile, until the end of his life.

Because of the central location of Geneva and the power of Calvin's theology, Geneva quickly replaced Wittenberg as the source of Protestant thought and became a haven for many of Europe's religious refugees. Calvin's ideas about salvation and the godly community rapidly spread to France, the Low Countries, Scotland, and England. Until the end of his life, Calvin was a magnet drawing people interested in reform.

The heart of Calvin's appeal lay in his formal theological writings. In 1536 he published the first of many editions of *Institutes of the Christian Religion*, which was to become the summa of reform theology. In it Calvin laid out a doctrine of the absolute power of God and the complete depravity and powerlessness of humanity.

Calvin believed in predestination, that "the word of God takes root and grows only in those whom the Lord, by his eternal election, has predestined to be his children." Like Luther, Calvin viewed salvation as a mysterious gift of God.

Calvin believed that from the beginning of time God had elected those to be saved and those to be damned and that human actions play no part in the divine plan. The elect—that is, the people to whom God graciously grants salvation—freely do

John Calvin This image of Calvin in his study is similar to countless pictures of Saint Jerome and Erasmus at work and reminds viewers of Calvin's humanistic education and the role of Christian and classical learning in his theology. *(Lauros/Giraudon/Art Resource, NY)*

good works in response to "God's benevolence." Further, Calvin suggested, the elect would benefit from "signs of divine benevolence," an idea that would have a profound impact on the Calvinist understanding of the relationship of wealth to spiritual life. Calvin believed that good works and a well-ordered society were the result of God's grace. By the seventeenth century, followers of Calvin widely believed that the elect had a duty to work in the secular world and that wealth accumulated in business was a sign of God's favor. It was an idea nicely adapted to the increasingly wealthy world of early modern Europe.

That connection between salvation and material life, however, lay in the future. The aspect of election that most interested Calvin was the creation of a truly Christian community by the elect. To accomplish this, Calvinist Christians, later to be known as members of the Reformed church, purged their churches of any manifestation of "superstition." Like Zwingli they rejected the idea that Christ was really present in the sacrament of Holy Communion. They rejected the role of saints. They removed from their churches and destroyed paintings and statuary that they believed were indications of idolatry.

Public officials were to be "vicars of God." They had the power to lead and correct both the faithful and the unregenerate sinners who lived in Christian communities. In his years in Geneva, Calvin tried to create a "Christian Commonwealth," but Geneva was far from a theocracy. Calvin's initial attempts to create a Christian community by requiring public confession and allowing church leaders to discipline sinners were rejected by Geneva's city council, which exiled Calvin in 1538.

On his return in 1541 he sought to institute church reforms modeled on those he had observed in the Protestant city of Strasbourg. Calvin's Reformed church hierarchy was made up of four offices: preachers, teachers, deacons, and elders. Preachers and teachers saw to the care and education of the faithful. Deacons, as in the early church, were charged with attending to the material needs of the congregation. The elders—the true leaders of the Genevan church—were selected from the patriciate that dominated the civil government of the city. Thus, it makes as much sense to speak of a church governed by the town as a town dominated by the church. The elders actively intervened in education, charity, and attempts to regulate prostitution. Consistories, or church courts, made up of community elders who enforced community moral and religious values, became one of the most important characteristics of Reformed (Calvinist) communities.

Reformed churchmen reacted promptly and harshly to events that seemed to threaten either church or state. The most famous event was the capture, trial, and execution of Michael Servetus (1511–1553), a Spanish physician and radical theologian who rejected generally accepted doctrines like the Trinity and specifically criticized many of Calvin's teachings in the *Institutes*. After corresponding with Servetus for a time, Calvin remarked that if Servetus were in Geneva, "I would not suffer him to get out alive." After living in various parts of Europe, Servetus eventually did anonymously come to Geneva. He was recognized

and arrested. Calvin was as good as his word. After a public debate and trial, Servetus was burned at the stake for blaspheming the Trinity and the Christian religion. Calvin's condemnation of Servetus was all too typical of Christians in the sixteenth century. Lutherans, Calvinists, and Catholics all believed that protection of true religion required harsh measures. All too few could have said, as the humanist reformer Sebastion Castellio did, "To burn a heretic is not to defend a doctrine, but to burn a man."[5]

The Radical Reform of the Anabaptists

Michael Servetus was but one of a number of extremists who claimed to be carrying out the full reform implied in the teachings of Luther, Zwingli, and Calvin. Called "Anabaptists" (or "rebaptizers" because of their rejection of infant baptism), or simply "radicals," they tended to take biblical commands more literally than the mainline reformers. They rejected infant baptism as unbiblical, and they refused to take civil oaths or hold public office, for to do so would be to compromise with unreformed civil society.

The earliest of the radicals allied themselves with the rebels of 1525. Thomas Müntzer (1490–1525) was an influential preacher who believed in divine revelation through visions and dreams. His own visions told him that the poor were the true elect and that the end of the world was at hand. An active participant in the revolts of 1525, Müntzer called on the elect to drive out the ungodly. After the defeat of the rebels, he was captured and executed by the German princes.

Other radicals, such as the revolutionaries who took control of the north German city of Münster, rejected infant baptism, adopted polygamy, and proclaimed a new "Kingdom of Righteousness." The reformers of Münster instituted the new kingdom in the city by rebaptizing those who joined their cause and driving out those who opposed them. They abolished private property rights in Münster and instituted new laws concerning morality and behavior. Leadership in the city eventually passed to a tailor, Jan of Leiden (d. 1535), who proclaimed himself the new messiah and lord of the world. The Anabaptists were opposed by the prince-bishop of Münster, the political and religious lord of the city. After a sixteen-month siege, the bishop and his allies recaptured

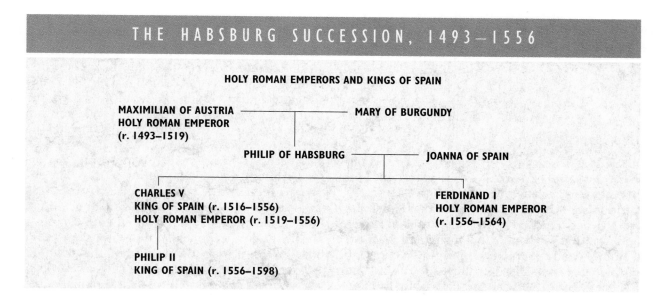

THE HABSBURG SUCCESSION, 1493–1556

HOLY ROMAN EMPERORS AND KINGS OF SPAIN

MAXIMILIAN OF AUSTRIA ——————— MARY OF BURGUNDY
HOLY ROMAN EMPEROR
(r. 1493–1519)

PHILIP OF HABSBURG ——————— JOANNA OF SPAIN

CHARLES V   FERDINAND I
KING OF SPAIN (r. 1516–1556)   HOLY ROMAN EMPEROR
HOLY ROMAN EMPEROR (r. 1519–1556)   (r. 1556–1564)

PHILIP II
KING OF SPAIN (r. 1556–1598)

the city from the Anabaptists in 1535. Besieging forces massacred men, women, and children. Jan of Leiden was captured and executed by mutilation with red-hot tongs.

With the destruction of the Münster revolutionaries in 1535, the Anabaptist movement turned inward. Under leaders like Menno Simons (1495–1561), who founded the Mennonites, and Jakob Hutter (d. 1536), who founded the Moravian Societies, the radicals rejected the violent establishment of truly holy cities. To varying degrees they also rejected connections with civil society, military service, even civil courts. They did, however, believe that their own communities were communities of the elect. They tended to close themselves off from outsiders and enforce a strict discipline over their members. The elders of these communities were empowered to excommunicate or "shun" those who violated the community's precepts. Anabaptist communities have proved unusually durable. Moravian and Mennonite communities continue to exist in western Europe, North America, and even in parts of what used to be the Soviet Union.

Like Luther, all of the early reformers appealed to the authority of the Bible in their attacks on church tradition. Yet in the villages and towns of Germany and Switzerland, many radicals were prepared to move far beyond the positions Luther had advocated. When they did so, Luther found

himself in the odd position of appealing for vigorous action to the very imperial authorities whose inaction had allowed his own protest to survive.

THE EMPIRE OF CHARLES V (r. 1519–1556)

Luther believed that secular authorities should be benevolently neutral in religious matters. In his eyes, the success of the early Reformation was simply God's will:

I simply taught, preached and wrote God's Word; otherwise I did nothing. And while I slept or drank Wittenberg beer with my friends . . . , the Word so greatly weakened the Papacy that no prince or emperor ever inflicted such losses on it. I did nothing; the Word did everything.[6]

As great as the word of God was, Luther must have known that even as he drank his beer, the Holy Roman emperor could have crushed the reform movement if he had chosen to enforce imperial decrees. But attempts to resolve religious conflict became entangled with attempts to hold together the family lands of the Habsburg emperor and with political rivalries among the various German princes. The eventual religious settlement required a constitutional compromise that preserved the virtual autonomy of the great princes of Germany. The political realities of sixteenth-century Europe were that political leaders were afraid of the emperor even when he tried to preserve the essential unity of the Christian church.

Imperial Challenges

Emperor Charles V (r. 1519–1556) was the beneficiary of a series of marriages that, in the words of his courtiers, seemed to re-create the empire of Charlemagne. From his father, Philip of Habsburg, he inherited claims to Austria, the imperial crown, and Burgundian lands that included the Low Countries and the county of Burgundy. Through his mother, Joanna, the daughter of Ferdinand and Isabella of Spain, Charles became heir to the kingdoms of Castile, Aragon, Sicily, Naples, and Spanish America. During the Italian wars of the early sixteenth century, Charles's holdings in Italy expanded to include the duchy of Milan and most of the rest of Lombardy. By 1506 he was duke in the Burgundian lands; in 1516 he became king of Aragon and Castile; and in 1519 he was elected Holy Roman emperor. Every government in Europe had to deal with one part or another of Charles's empire. His chancellor enthused, "[God] has set you on the way towards a world monarchy, towards the gathering of all Christendom under a single shepherd."

Charles seems to have sincerely desired such a world monarchy, but each of the areas under his control challenged his authority. In Castile, for example, grandees, townsmen, and peasants felt they had grounds for complaint. They objected that taxes were too heavy and that Charles disregarded the Cortes and his natural advisers, the old nobility. But most of all they complained that too many of his officials were foreigners whom he had brought with him from his home in Flanders. Protests festered in the towns and villages of Castile and finally broke out into a revolt called the Comunero (townsmen's or citizens') movement. Between 1517 and 1522, when religious reform was making dramatic advances in Germany, many of the most important towns of Spain were in open rebellion against the Crown. Charles's forces eventually took control of the situation, and by 1522 he had crushed the Comuneros. Between

1522 and 1530, he was careful to spend much of his time in his Spanish kingdoms.

Charles's claims in Italy, as well as his claims to lands in the Pyrenees and in the Low Countries, brought him into direct conflict with the Valois kings of France. Again in the critical 1520s, the Habsburgs and the Valois fought a series of wars (see page 412). Charles dramatically defeated the French at Pavia in northern Italy in 1525, sacked and occupied Rome in 1527, and became the virtual arbitrator of Italian politics. In the course of the struggle, the Catholic Francis I of France, whose title was "the Most Christian king," found it to his advantage to ally himself with Charles's most serious opponents, the Protestants and the Turks. Francis demonstrated the truth of Machiavelli's dictum that private virtues very often play a small role in political and diplomatic life. The Habsburg-Valois Wars dragged on until, in exhaustion, the French king Henry II (r. 1547–1559) and the Spanish king Philip II (r. 1556–1598) signed the Treaty of Cateau-Cambrésis in 1559.

Charles was not the only ruler to claim the title "emperor" and a succession reaching back to the Roman Empire. After the conquest of Constantinople in 1453, the sultan of the Ottoman Turks began to refer to himself as "the Emperor." After consolidating control of Constantinople and the Balkans, Turkish armies under the command of Emperor Suleiman (r. 1520–1566), known as "the Magnificent," resumed their expansion to the north and west. After capturing Belgrade, Turkish forces soundly defeated a Hungarian army at the Battle of Mohács in 1526. Charles appealed for unity within Christendom against the threat. Even Martin Luther agreed that Christians should unite during invasion.

Suleiman's army besieged Vienna in 1529 before being forced to retreat. Turks also created a navy in the Mediterranean and, with French encouragement, began a series of raids along the coasts of Italy and Spain. The Turkish fleet remained a threat throughout the sixteenth century. The reign of Suleiman in many respects marked the permanent entry of Turkey into the European military and diplomatic system. Turkish pressure was yet another reason why Charles was unable to deal with German Protestants in a direct and uncompromising way. (See the box, "Encounters

The Capture of Belgrade During the sixteenth century Ottoman Turks dominated the Balkans militarily and were a significant force in European diplomacy. They were masters of coordinated attacks combining artillery and infantry. *(Österreichische Nationalbibliothek)*

with the West: Duels Among Europeans and Turks.")

German Politics

The political configuration of Germany had an on-going influence on the course of the religious re-form. In 1500, Germany was much less centralized than France or England. Since 1495, seven elec-toral princes (three archbishops and four lay princes) and a larger circle of imperial princes had claimed the right to representation in the imperial council, and nearly three hundred other towns or principalities demanded various exemptions from imperial control. The emperor's claims in most ar-eas amounted to the right to collect modest taxes on households and individuals, a court of high justice, and the right to proclaim imperial truces. Yet the empire lacked a unified legal system, and the emperor himself had only one vote on the im-perial council. In many respects political central-

ization and innovation were characteristics of in-dividual territories, not of the empire as a whole. The power of the emperor depended on his rela-tions with the towns and princes of Germany.

In the first years after Luther issued his "Ninety-five Theses," he was defended by the elector Frederick of Saxony, who held a key vote in Charles's quest for election as Holy Roman em-peror. As long as Frederick protected Luther, im-perial officials had to proceed against him with caution. When Luther was outlawed by the impe-rial Diet of Worms in 1521, Frederick and many other princes and towns refused to enforce the edict against him and his followers unless their own grievances with the emperor and their com-plaints about the church were taken up at the same time. In 1522 and 1526 the emperor again tried to enforce the ban, but imperial officials were bluntly informed that the towns were unable to conform. At the Diet of Speyer in 1526, delegates passed a resolution empowering princes and

Duels Among Europeans and Turks

A Flemish diplomat in the service of Ferdinand I of Austria (who became Emperor Ferdinand I after the abdication of Charles V), Augier Ghislain De Busbecq (1522–1592) was twice sent to Constantinople as ambassador. Understanding the Turks and their interests was critical for the Germans as attacks by the Turks in eastern Europe prevented the empire from either suppressing the German Protestants or pressing German claims against the French. The following selection is part of a letter written from Constantinople in 1560. In it, Busbecq discusses violence among the Turks and contrasts it with Europeans' behavior.

The mention I made a while ago of matters in the confines of Hungary, gives me occasion to tell you, what the Turks think of duels, which among Christians are accounted a singular badge of personal valor. There was one Arstambey, a sanjack [district official], who lived on the frontier of Hungary, who was very much famed as a robust person [Arsta signifies a lion in Turkey]. He was an expert with the bow; no man brandished his sword with more strength; none was more terrible to his enemy. Not far from his district there also dwelt one Ulybey, also a sanjack, who was jealous of the same praise. And this jealousy (initiated perhaps by other occasions) at length occasioned hatred and many bloody combats between them. It happened thus, Ulybey was sent for to Constantinople, upon what occasion I know not. When he arrived there, the Pashas [governors] had asked many questions of him in the Divan [court] concerning other matters. At last they demanded how it was that he and Arstambey came to fall out? . . . To put his own cause in the best light, he said that once Arstambey had laid an ambush and wounded him treacherously.

Which he said, Arstambey need not have done, if he would have shown himself worthy of the name he bears because Ulybey often challenged him to fight hand to hand and never refused to meet him on the field. The Pashas, taking great offense, replied, "How dare you challenge a fellow soldier to a duel? What? Was there no Christian to fight with? Do both of you eat your emperor's bread? And yet, you attempt to take one another's life? What precedent did you have for this? Don't you know that whichever of you had died, the emperor would have lost a subject?" Whereupon, by their command, he was carried off to prison where he lay pining for many months. And at last, with difficulty, he was released, but with the loss of his reputation.

It is quite different among us Christians. Our people will draw their swords many times against each other before they ever come in sight of a public enemy, and unfortunately, they count it a brave and honorable thing to do. What should one do in such a case? Vice has usurped the seat of virtue and that which is worthy of punishment is counted noble and glorious.

Source: The Four Epistles of A. G. Busbequius Concerning His Embassy to Turkey (London: J. Taylor & J. Wyat, 1694), pp. 196–198.

towns to settle religious matters in their territories as they saw fit. In effect, this resolution legitimated the reform in territories where authorities chose to follow the new teachings and presaged the eventual shape of the final religious settlement in Germany.

German princes took advantage of the emperor's relative powerlessness and made choices reflecting a complex of religious, political, and diplomatic issues. Electoral Saxony and ducal Saxony, the two parts of the province of Saxony, split over the issue of reform. Electoral Saxony, Luther's homeland, was Lutheran. Ducal Saxony was strongly Catholic. Especially in the autonomous towns, many decisions about religion were often made with an eye on the choices made by neighbors and competitors.

Some rulers made decisions that were even more consciously cynical. The Grand Master of the religious order of the Teutonic Knights, Albrecht von Hohenzollern (1490–1568), who controlled the duchy of Prussia, renounced his monastic vows. Then, at the urging of Luther and other reformers, he secularized the order's estates (that is, he transferred them from church to private ownership), which then became East Prussia, hereditary lands of the Hohenzollern family. In other territories, rulers managed to claim the properties of suppressed religious orders. Even when, as in the case of Count Philip of Hesse (1504–1567), much of the revenue from secularization was used to create

hospitals and an organized system of charity, the reforming prince was still enriched.

Some rulers found their personal reservations about Luther reinforced by their fears of popular unrest. Luther's call for decisions based on personal conscience seemed to the dukes of Bavaria, for example, to be a call for attacks on princely authority and even anarchy. In the confused and fluid situation of the 1520s and 1530s, imperial interests were never the primary issue.

The Religious Settlement

With the fading of the Turkish threat on Vienna in 1529, Charles V renewed his pressure on the German principalities at a meeting of the imperial diet at Augsburg in 1530. It was for this diet that Philip Melanchthon (1497–1560), Luther's closest adviser, prepared the Augsburg Confession, which would

The Augsburg Confession In this woodcut of the Augsburg Confession being read to Charles V, the artist has included in the background text and images of the Lutheran teachings on the sacraments and the nature of salvation. In contrast are the images on the left of a papal ceremony and court hierarchy in which, the artist implies, Christ is not present. *(Kunstsammlung Veste Coburg)*

526

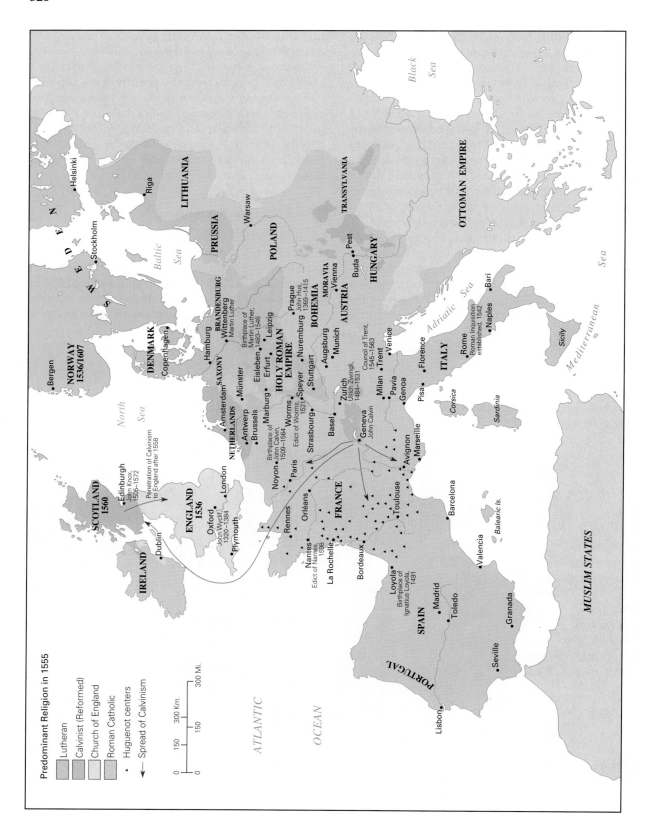

Predominant Religion in 1555

- Lutheran
- Calvinist (Reformed)
- Church of England
- Roman Catholic
- ◂ Huguenot centers
- → Spread of Calvinism

0   150   300 Km.
0   150   300 Mi.

become the basic statement of the Lutheran faith. Melanchthon hoped that the document would form the basis of compromise with Catholic powers, but the possibility was rejected out of hand by the imperial party. Charles aimed to affirm his strength in Germany by forcing the princes to end the reform movement and enforce the papal and imperial bans on Luther's teachings.

The Protestant princes responded by forming the League of Schmalkalden. At first, the founders of the league claimed that they were interested in protecting Reformed preaching, but the league quickly developed as a center of opposition to imperial influence in general. Eventually Charles and a group of allied princes managed to defeat the league at the Battle of Mühlberg in 1547. The emperor was unable to continue pressure on the Protestants, however, because he had depended on the support of some Protestant princes in his battles with the league. As a result, even after military defeat the Protestant princes were able to maintain religious autonomy. In the Religious Peace of Augsburg of 1555 the emperor formally acknowledged the principle that sovereign princes could choose the religion to be practiced in their territories, *cuius regio, eius religio* ("whose territory, his religion"). There were limits, however, for leaders could only remain under papal authority or adopt the Augsburg Confession outlined by Melanchthon. Reformed churches associated with Zwingli or Calvin were not legally recognized (Map 14.2).

Shortly after the settlement, Charles abdicated his Spanish and imperial titles. Exhausted by years of political and religious struggle, he ceded the imperial crown to his brother, Ferdinand (r. 1556–1564). His possessions in the Low Countries, Spain, Italy, and the New World he ceded to his son, Philip II (r. 1556–1598). Charles had believed his courtiers who compared his empire to that of the ancient Romans. He had believed that his duty as emperor was to unite Christendom under one

law and one church. But in no part of his empire did he ever command the authority that would have allowed him to unite his lands politically, let alone to re-establish religious unity. Following his abdication, Charles retired to a monastery in Spain, where he died in 1558.

THE ENGLISH REFORMATION, 1520–1603

England was closely tied to Germany. Since the twelfth century, large numbers of German merchants had lived and traded in England, and there was a major English community in Cologne. Anglo-German connections became especially significant during the Reformation. Reformers from Wittenberg and other Protestant towns had contact with English merchants from London who traded and traveled on the Continent. One reformer, William Tyndale (ca. 1494–1536), served as a bridge between the Continent and England. He had a humanistic education in classical languages and began working on a translation of the Bible in the 1520s. Forced to flee London by the church hierarchy, he visited Luther in Wittenberg before settling in Antwerp, where he completed his translation of the New Testament. By 1526, copies of his translation and his religious tracts flooded into England. By the 1520s, Lutheran influence was noticeable in London and Cambridge. To some extent the ground may have been prepared for the reformers by the few surviving Lollards, the followers of Wyclif, who had argued for church reform in the late fourteenth and fifteenth centuries (see page 400). Lollards, who tended to be literate, were an ideal market for Tyndale's English Bible and his numerous tracts.

As in Germany, institutional change in the church followed from both secular issues and reform ideas. In England, an initially hostile monarch began to tolerate reform ideas when he perceived the papacy as an unbiblical, tyrannical force blocking essential state policy.

Map 14.2 Protestants and Catholics in 1555
Christendom in western Europe was divided into three major groups. Lutheran influence was largely confined to parts of Germany and Scandinavia, while Calvinist influence spread from Switzerland into Scotland, the Low Countries, and parts of France. Most of the West, however, remained within the Roman Church.

Henry VIII and the Monarchical Reformation

Henry VIII (r. 1509–1547) began his reign as a popular and powerful king. Handsome, athletic, and artistic, he seemed to be the ideal ruler. Henry took an interest in theology and humanistic culture. At first, he was quite hostile to Luther's reform ideas and wrote *Defense of the Seven Sacraments*, which earned him the title "Defender of the Faith" from a grateful Pope Leo X. Throughout his life Henry remained suspicious of many Protestant ideas, but he led the initial phase of the break between the English church and the papacy because of his political problems with the highly orthodox Holy Roman emperor Charles V. The first phase of the English Reformation was thus a monarchical reformation.

Henry VII had initiated closer relations with Spain when he married his eldest son, Arthur, prince of Wales, to Ferdinand of Aragon's daughter, Catherine. After Arthur's death the future Henry VIII was married to Catherine in 1509. Henry VIII later tried to further the Anglo-imperial alliance when he arranged a treaty by which the emperor Charles V, who was Catherine of Aragon's nephew, agreed to marry Henry's daughter, Mary Tudor. But by the late 1520s the Anglo-imperial alliance fell apart when Charles, responding to Spanish pressures, renounced the proposed marriage and instead married a Portuguese princess.

Henry's relations with Charles were further weakened by what the English called "The King's Great Matter," that is, his determination to divorce Catherine of Aragon. Recalling the unrest of the Wars of the Roses, Henry believed that he needed a son to ensure that the Tudors could maintain control of the English crown. By 1527, Henry and Catherine had a daughter, Mary, but no living sons. Henry became convinced that he remained without a male heir because, by biblical standards, he had committed incest by marrying his brother's widow. As Leviticus 20:21 says, "If a man takes his brother's wife, it is impurity; . . . they shall remain childless." Henry desired an annulment. Unfortunately for him, Leo X's successor, Pope Clement VII (r. 1523–1534), was a virtual prisoner of imperial troops who had recently sacked Rome and taken control of most of Italy. As long as Charles supported Catherine of Aragon and his forces occupied Rome, there would be no possibility of a papally sanctioned annulment of the marriage.

The king's advisers quickly divided into two camps. Sir Thomas More, the royal chancellor and a staunch Catholic, urged the king to continue his policy of negotiation with the papacy and his efforts to destroy the growing Protestant party. Until his resignation in 1532, More led royal authorities in a vigorous campaign against the dissemination of the newly translated Tyndale Bible and against the spread of Protestant ideas. More was opposed and eventually ousted by a radical party of Protestants led by Thomas Cranmer (1489–1556) and Thomas Cromwell (1485?–1540), who saw in the king's desire for a divorce an effective wedge to pry Henry out of the papal camp. Cromwell, who eventually replaced More as chancellor, advised the king that the marriage problem could be solved by the English clergy without papal interference.

Between 1532 and 1535, Henry and Parliament took a number of steps that effectively left the king in control of the English church. Early in 1533, Cranmer was named archbishop of Canterbury. Later in the year Parliament ruled that appeals of cases concerning wills, marriages, and ecclesiastical grants had to be heard in England. In May an English court annulled the king's marriage to Catherine. Four months later, Henry's new queen, Anne Boleyn, gave birth to a daughter, Elizabeth.

Even before Cromwell became chancellor, Henry had attacked absentee clergy, restricted church courts, and prohibited the payment of certain papal taxes. After the split began, the king started to seize church properties. Parliamentary action culminated in the passage of the Act of Supremacy in 1534, which declared the king to be "the Protector and only Supreme Head of the Church and the Clergy of England." (See the box, "The Act of Supremacy.") Henry meant to enforce his control by requiring a public oath supporting the act. Sir Thomas More refused to take the oath and was arrested, tried, and executed for treason. In some respects, Parliament had acted as an instrument of reform, much like the town councils of the German and Swiss towns that moderated debates over the reform of the church. In England, however, Parliament and perhaps a majority of the laity perceived this reformation primarily as a political issue.

Cromwell and Cranmer had hoped to use the "King's Great Matter" as a way to begin a Lutheran-style reform of the church. But, though separated from the papal party, Henry remained suspicious of religious changes. Although he continued to object to the parts of the older tradition that he called "idolatry and other evil and naughty ceremonies," he rejected the Protestant under-

The Act of Supremacy

The Act of Supremacy makes clear what issues Henry VIII considered essential in the correction of the English church. Issued in 1534, it is the constitutional basis for the subsequent development of the Church of England. As befits a document dealing with the "King's Great Matter," the Act of Supremacy is entirely practical. This excerpt makes an interesting comparison with Luther's discussion of clerical authority in his "Address to the Christian Nobility" (see the box on page 515).

Albeit the King's Majesty justly and rightfully is and ought to be the supreme head of the Church of England, and so is recognized by the clergy of this realm in their Convocations; yet nevertheless for the corroboration and confirmation thereof, and for the increase of virtue in Christ's religion within this realm of England, and to repress and extirpate all errors, heresies and other enormities and abuses heretofore used in the same, Be it enacted by the authority of this present Parliament that the King our sovereign lord, his heirs and successor kings of this realm, shall be taken, accepted, and reputed the only supreme head in earth of the Church of England. . . . And that our said sovereign lord, his heirs, and successor kings of this realm, shall have full power and authority from time to time to visit, repress, redress, reform, order, correct, restrain and amend all such errors, heresies, abuses, offenses, contempts and enormities, whatsoever they be, which by any manner spiritual authority or jurisdiction ought or may lawfully be reformed, repressed, ordered . . . most to the pleasure of Almighty God, the increase of virtue in Christ's religion, and for the conservation of the peace, unity and tranquillity of this realm.

Source: David Englander, Diana Norman, Rosemary O'Day, and W. R. Owens, eds., *Culture and Belief in Europe, 1450–1600: An Anthology of Sources* (Oxford, England: Basil Blackwell in association with the Open University, 1990), pp. 442–443.

standing of justification and what anti-Protestant critics called "bibliolatry." He complained of radicals who "do wrest and interpret and so untruly allege [novel understandings of Scripture] to subvert and overturn as well the sacraments of Holy Church as the power and authority of princes and magistrates." Between 1534 and Henry's death in 1547, neither the Protestant nor the Catholic party was able to gain the upper hand at court or in the English church. Substantive changes in the English church would be made by Henry's children.

Reform and Counter-Reform Under Edward and Mary

Prince Edward, Henry's only surviving son in 1547, was born to Henry's third wife, Jane Seymour. He was only 10 years old at his father's death. By chance, Edward Seymour, who was Prince Edward's uncle, and the Protestant faction were in favor at the time of Henry's death. Seymour was named duke of Somerset and Lord Protector of the young king Edward VI (r. 1547–1553). Under Somerset, the Protestants were able to make significant changes in religious life in England. The Protestant party quickly changed the nature of the Eucharist, allowing the laity to take both bread and wine in the Protestant manner. The process of confiscating properties belonging to chapels and shrines was completed under Edward. In an act of great symbolic meaning, priests were legally allowed to marry; many had already done so. Finally, Archbishop Cranmer introduced the first edition of the English *Book of Common Prayer* in 1549. The book updated some late medieval English prayers and combined them with liturgical and theological ideas taken from Luther, Zwingli, and Calvin. In its beautifully expressive English, it provided the laity with a primer on how to combine English religious traditions with reform theology. Later, continental Protestants were named to teach theology at Oxford and Cambridge. If Edward had not died of tuberculosis in 1553, England's reform would have looked very much like the changes that occurred in Switzerland and southern Germany.

Protestant reformers attempted to prevent Mary Tudor (r. 1553–1558), Henry's Catholic daughter, from claiming the throne, but Mary and the Catholic party quickly moved into control of the court and the church. Mary immediately

The Queen in Parliament This image was meant to show the willingness of the Commons to support the queen, a key element of the Elizabethan Settlement. *(Bibliothèque Nationale)*

declared previous reform decrees to be void. Cardinal Reginald Pole (1500–1558), who had advocated reform within the Catholic church, became the center of the Catholic restoration party in Mary's England. Pole rooted out Protestants within the church. More than eight hundred gentlemen, clerics, and students fled England for the Protestant parts of the Continent. Three hundred mostly humble artisans and laborers were tried and executed by church courts, earning the queen her nickname, "Bloody Mary."

The policies of the queen brought about an abrupt return of the English church to papal authority. Most of the English quickly and easily returned to traditional religious practices. Statues were removed from hiding and restored to places of honor in churches and chapels. Although there is no conclusive evidence, the queen's initial successes may indicate that the Reformation was not broadly supported by the people. In fact, the restoration of Catholicism by Mary might have worked if the queen had not died after little more than six years on the throne. At her death there was still no clear indication of what the final settlement of the reform would be in England.

The Elizabethan Settlement

Queen Elizabeth (r. 1558–1603), daughter of Anne Boleyn, succeeded to the throne at the death of her half-sister. The reign of Elizabeth was one of the most enigmatic and successful of English history. She managed to gain control of the various political and religious factions in the country and play off a variety of international powers against each other. She seems to have understood well the necessity of striking a balance between opposing forces.

Her first great problem was a religious settlement. Early in her reign she twice left church services at the elevation of the bread by the priest. Since in Catholic thought it was the action of the priest that made Christ present in the bread, she was indicating symbolically her opposition to a purely Catholic understanding of the sacraments. In the next few years she continued to work for the restoration of many features of her father's and her half-brother's reforms. In 1559 the new Act of Supremacy and an Act of Uniformity reinstituted royal control of the English church and reestablished uniform liturgical and doctrinal standards. The *Book of Common Prayer* composed by

Cranmer was brought back, and final changes were made in the liturgy of the church.

Protestants had hoped for a complete victory, but the "Elizabethan Settlement" was considerably less than that. Although figures are lacking, it is likely that a large portion of the English population did not support a return to Henry's and Edward's reforms. After making clear her significant differences with Rome, Elizabeth confounded her most fervent Protestant supporters by offering a number of concessions to Anglo-Catholics. She herself remained celibate, and she ordered the Anglican clergy to do the same—although there was little she could do to prevent clerical marriage. More important, she and her closest advisers allowed a great variety of customs and practices favored by Anglo-Catholics. These matters, the queen's supporters argued, were not essential to salvation, and thus individuals could be allowed to choose. Many of the prayers in the *Book of Common Prayer*, for example, seemed "papist" to the most radical Protestants. Similarly, many of the traditional clerical vestments and altar furnishings remained unchanged. Elizabeth probably knew that the Protestants had no alternative to supporting her and thus felt free to win back the support of the Anglo-Catholics.

In fact, from the 1570s Elizabeth seems to have been especially concerned to regain control of insubordinate clerics. In these years the main outlines of her religious settlement became clear. She created a reformed liturgy that seemed acceptable to both Protestants and Catholics. At the same time she retained the parish and diocesan structure of the medieval church. She seems to have been most careful to restrict theological debate to the universities.

Toward the end of Elizabeth's reign, Richard Hooker (1554–1600) published his *Laws of Ecclesiastical Polity*, which provides an excellent description of the Anglican (English) church born of the Elizabethan Settlement. England, Hooker maintains, has its own way of handling religious affairs. Theologically it represents a middle way between the traditions cultivated by the Roman church and the more radically biblical religion favored by the Lutherans of Germany and the Calvinists of Switzerland. The Church of England moderated Luther's and Calvin's absolute reliance on Scriptures with history and tradition. In areas where tradition was strong, processions and other pre-Reformation traditions continued to animate village life. In other areas, more austere reformed practices were likely to predominate.

REFORM IN OTHER STATES, 1523–1560

In England and in the empire of Charles V the success of the new religious ideas depended greatly on the political situation. It would be naive to conclude, as Luther claimed, that "the Word did everything." Yet this complex religious reform movement cannot be reduced to the politics of kings and princes. The issues will be clearer if we survey politics and reform in the rest of Europe, noting whether and to what extent the new ideas took root. In France, for example, the widespread, popular support of the old religion limited the options of the country's political leaders. Similarly, in northern Europe religious reform was an issue both of popular feeling and of royal politics.

France

Luther's work, and later the ideas of the urban reformers of southwestern Germany and Switzerland, passed quickly and easily into France. Geneva is in a French-speaking area close to the French border. It, like Strasbourg, was easy for French Protestants to reach. Perhaps because of France's proximity to the Calvinists in French-speaking Switzerland or because of the clarity and power of Calvin's *Institutes*, French Protestants, known as Huguenots, were tied more closely to the Calvinists of Geneva than to the Lutherans of Germany.

It is difficult, however, to know how many French Christians were Protestants. At the height of the Reformation's popularity, Protestants probably represented no more than 10 percent of the total population of France. It has been estimated that there were about 2100 Protestant congregations in the 1560s—in a country that had perhaps 32,000 traditional parish congregations. Protestants seem to have been a diverse mix that included two of the three most important noble families at court: the Bourbon and the Montmorency families. Clerics interested in moral reform and artisans who worked at new trades, like the printing industry, also made up a significant portion of the converts. As a group Protestants tended to be of higher-than-average literacy even if they were not necessarily among the most prestigious lords in French society. The Protestant population was spread throughout the country. Protestants were well represented in towns; they were probably a numerical majority in the southern and western towns of La Rochelle, Montpellier, and Nîmes. Paris was the one part of the realm in which they had little influence, and their absence in the capital may have been their undoing.

The conservative theologians of the Sorbonne in Paris were some of Luther's earliest opponents. They complained that many masters at the University of Paris were "Lutheran." As early as 1523, Parisian authorities seized and burned books said to be by Luther. But as in Germany, there was no clear understanding of who or what a Lutheran was. The Sorbonne theologians were suspicious of a number of "pre-reformers," including Jacques Lefèvre d'Étaples (1450–1537), who late in life had come to an understanding of justification quite like Luther's. Others were clerics who were intent on religious reform within the traditional structures. Unlike Luther and the French Protestants, these pre-reformers did not challenge the priests' relationship to the sacraments. They were interested in the piety and behavior of churchmen. They never challenged the role of the clergy in salvation. King Francis's own sister, Margaret of Angoulême (1492–1549), gathered a group of religious persons at her court, even including several reformers. (See the box, "The Conversion of Jeanne d'Albret.") But Margaret herself urged that theology be left to scholars; she believed that the laity should stick to simple pieties. Like Margaret, most French Christians had no clear sense that Protestant teachings required a complete break with medieval Christian traditions.

Like previous French kings, Francis I (r. 1515–1547) hoped to extend royal jurisdictions in France and make France an international power. Engaged in the seemingly intractable wars with the Habsburgs, Francis generally ignored religious questions. In 1525, he was taken captive in the wake of a military disaster at Pavia in Lombardy. He was held prisoner for nearly a year, during which time conservatives at the Sorbonne and in Paris moved actively against suspected Protestants. Francis was not initially opposed to what seemed to be moral reform within the church. His own view was that

the king's duty was to preserve order and prevent scandal, and at first carrying out that duty meant protecting reformers whom the conservative militants persecuted. The king feared disorder more than he feared religious reform.

On October 18, 1534, however, Francis's attitude changed when he and all Paris awoke to find the city covered with anti-Catholic placards containing, in the words of the writers, "true articles on the horrible, great and insufferable abuses of the Papal Mass." The response of the Parisians was immediate and hostile. They attacked foreigners, especially those who by dress or speech seemed "Lutheran"—that is, German or Flemish. Several months later Francis himself led a religious procession through Paris in honor of the Blessed Sacrament. The "Affair of the Placards" changed Francis's ideas about the sources of disorder. Opposition to traditional religious practices became more difficult and more dangerous. John Calvin himself was forced to leave Paris and eventually France because he feared persecution. Between 1534 and 1560, some ten thousand Protestants fled France, many joining Calvin in Geneva.

By the middle of the sixteenth century it was clear that neither Protestant nor Catholic factions would be able to control religious and political life in France. Francis I died in 1547, and the stage was set for a series of destructive factional struggles over religion and political power that would continue for the rest of the century. In Chapter 15 we will examine this struggle known as the "French Religious Wars."

Eastern Europe

In some respects, a political vacuum in eastern Europe allowed for the expansion of Protestantism. The church hierarchy was not in a position to enforce orthodoxy. Some rulers were indifferent to religious debates, as were the Muslim Ottoman Turks, who controlled much of eastern Hungary and what is now Romania. Other rulers offered toleration because they could ill afford to alienate any portion of their subject populations.

Protestant ideas initially passed through the German communities of Poland and the trading towns along the Baltic coast. But in the 1540s, Calvinist ideas spread quickly among the Polish nobles, especially those at the royal court. Given

The Conversion of Jeanne d'Albret

Jeanne d'Albret was the niece of King Francis I and mother of Henry of Navarre, the future Henry IV. In this letter, written in 1555 to Viscount Gourdon, a Huguenot supporter, she explains the pressures to remain Catholic and why she chose to become Protestant. After her conversion, her court became a center of the Huguenot movement.

I am writing to tell you that up to now I have followed in the footsteps of the deceased Queen, my most honored mother—whom God forgive—in the matter of hesitation between the two religions. The said Queen [was] warned by her late brother the King, François I of good and glorious memory, my much honored uncle, not to get new doctrines in her head so that from then on she confined herself to amusing stories. . . . Besides, I well remember how long ago, the late King, my most honored father . . . surprised the said Queen when she was praying in her rooms with the ministers Roussel and Farel, and how with great annoyance he slapped her right cheek and forbade her sharply to meddle in matters of doctrine. He shook a stick at me which cost me many bitter tears and has kept me fearful and compliant until after they had both died. Now that I am freed by the death of my said father two months ago . . . a reform seems so right and so necessary that, for my part, I consider that it would be disloyalty and cowardice to God, to my conscience and to my people to remain any longer in a state of suspense and indecision. . . . It is necessary for sincere persons to take counsel together to decide how to proceed, both now and in the future. Knowing that you are noble and courageous and that you have learned persons about you, I beg you to meet me.

Source: Nancy L. Roelker, trans., *Queen of Navarre: Jeanne d'Albret, 1528–1572* (Cambridge, Mass.: Harvard University Press, 1968), p. 127 (slightly adapted).

the power and influence of some of the noble families, Catholics were unable to suppress the various secret Calvinist congregations. During the first half of the sixteenth century, Protestantism became so well established in Poland that it could not be rooted out. Throughout the sixteenth century, Protestantism remained one of the rallying points for those opposed to the expansion of royal power.

The situation was much the same in Hungary and Romania. Among German colonists, Magyars, and ethnic Romanians there were numerous individuals who were interested first in Luther's message and later in Calvinist revisions of the reformed theology. Because no one could hope to enforce uniformity, some cities adopted a moderate Lutheran theology, and others followed a Calvinist confession. By the 1560s the Estates (representative assemblies) of Transylvania had decreed that both religions were to be tolerated. Further, when various radical groups migrated from the west in search of toleration, they too were able to create their own communities in Slavic and Magyar areas.

The Reformation was to have virtually no influence farther to the east, in Russia. The Orthodox church in Russia was much more firmly under control than was the church in the West. The Russian church followed the traditions of the Greek church, and Western arguments over justification made little sense in Orthodox churches. Given the historic suspicion of the Orthodox for Rome, the Russians were more tolerant of contacts with the Protestants of northern Europe. But there would be no theological innovation or reform in Russia.

Scandinavia

All of Scandinavia became Lutheran. Initial influences drifted north from Germany, carried by Hanseatic merchants and students who had studied at the universities of northern Germany. Yet the reform in Sweden and Denmark even more than in England was a monarchical reformation. In both Scandinavian kingdoms the kings began with an attack on the temporal rights and properties of the church. Changes in liturgy and practice came later as reformers gained the protection of the kings.

Since 1397 all Scandinavia had been united in theory in the Union of Kalmar (see page 413). But early in the sixteenth century the last pretenses of unity were shattered. Christian I of Denmark (r. 1513–1523) invaded Sweden and captured Stockholm, the capital. So great was his brutality that within a few years Gustav Vasa, a leading noble, was able to secure the loyalty of most of the Swedes and in 1523 was elected king of Sweden. Gustav's motto was "All power is of God." Like Henry VIII of England, Gustav (r. 1523–1560) moved carefully in an attempt to retain the loyalty of as many groups as possible. Although he never formally adopted a national confession of faith, the church and Swedish state gradually took on a more Lutheran character. In an effort to secure royal finances, the Riksdag, or parliament, passed the Västerås Ordinances, which secularized ecclesiastical lands and authorized the preaching of the "Pure Word of God." Olaus Petri (1493–1552), Sweden's principal reform preacher, was installed by royal order in the cathedral of Stockholm.

In Denmark the reformers also moved cautiously. Frederick I (r. 1523–1533) and his son, Christian III (r. 1534–1559), continued the policy of secularization and control that Christian I had initiated. Danish kings seemed interested in reform as a diplomatic means of attack on the Roman church. It seems that in Denmark the old religion simply suffered from a sort of royal indifference. The kings tended to support reformers as a way to attack the political power of the bishops. The Danes finally accepted the Augsburg Confession, which was becoming the most widely accepted explanation of Lutheran belief, in 1538. The transformation of practice proceeded slowly over the next decades.

In the frontier regions of Scandinavia—Finland, Iceland, and Norway—the reform was undertaken as a matter of royal policy. Initially there were only a few local reformers to introduce the new theology and practice. In many regions resistance to the Reformation continued for several generations. One valley hidden in the mountains of western Norway continued to follow the old religion for three centuries after its contacts with Rome had been severed.

THE LATE REFORMATION, CA. 1545–1600

In the first half of the sixteenth century, the term *Lutheran* applied to anyone who was anticlerical. As Francesco Guicciardini (1483–1540), a papal governor in central Italy, remarked:

I know of no one who loathes the ambition, the avarice, and the sensuality of the clergy more than I. . . . In spite of all this, the positions I have held under several popes have forced me, for my own good, to further their interests. Were it not for that, I should have loved Martin Luther as much as myself—not so that I might be free of the laws based on Christian religion as it is generally interpreted and understood; but to see this bunch of rascals get their just deserts, that is, to be without vices or without authority.[7]

Guicciardini's remarks catch both the frustration many Christians felt with the traditional church and also the very real confusion over just what it was that Luther had said. In parts of Germany by the late 1520s and across Europe by the 1550s, political and religious leaders attempted to make clearer to the peoples of Europe just what *Lutheran, Calvinist,* and *Catholic* had come to mean. Historians term the process of defining and explaining what each group believed, or confessed, the "Second Reformation," or "Confessionalization." After the middle of the sixteenth century, it was true that along with theological and political changes, the Reformation represented a broad cultural movement.

The profound changes that began in the sixteenth century continued into the seventeenth. People began to sort out what it meant to belong to one church instead of to another. Central governments supported religious authorities who desired religious uniformity and control over individual Christians. In all parts of Europe, religious behavior changed. Both Protestants and Catholics became more concerned with the personal rather than the communal aspects of Christianity. After the sixteenth century, the nature of Christianity and its place in public life, whether in Protestant or in Catholic countries, differed profoundly from what it had been in the Middle Ages.

Catholic Reform

Historians commonly speak of both a movement for traditional reform and renewal within the Catholic church and a "Counter-Reformation," which was a direct response to and rejection of the theological positions championed by the Protestants. It is certainly true that one can categorize certain acts as clearly challenging the Protestants, but to do so is to miss the point that the energetic actions of the Roman church during the sixteenth century both affirmed traditional teachings and created new institutions better fitted to the early modern world.

The idea of purer, earlier church practices to which the "modern" church should return had been a commonplace for centuries. The great ecumenical Council of Constance early in the fifteenth century had called for "reform in head and members" (see page 400). In 1512, five years before Luther made his public protests, Pope Julius II (r. 1503–1513) convened another ecumenical council, the Fifth Lateran Council (1513–1517), which was expected to look into the problems of nonresident clergy, multiple benefices, and a host of other issues. This tradition of moral reform was especially strong in Spain, Portugal, and Italy, lands where political rulers were either indifferent or opposed to Protestant reforms.

The desire for reform along traditional lines was deeply felt within the church. In the wake of the sack of Rome by imperial troops in 1527, one Roman cardinal, Bishop Gian Matteo Giberti of Verona (1495–1543), returned to his diocese and began a thoroughgoing reform. He conducted visitations of the churches and other religious institutions in Verona, preached tirelessly, worked hard to raise the educational level of his clergy, and required that priests live within their parishes. Giberti believed that morally rigorous traditional reform and renewal could counter the malaise he perceived. Other reforming bishops could be found throughout Catholic Europe.

New religious foundations sprang up to renew the church. The Spanish mystic Teresa of Avila (1515–1582) reflected the thinking of many

A Counter-Reformation Saint Saint Teresa of Avila came from a converso family. She believed that renewal within the Christian church would come through mysticism, prayer, and a return to traditional religious practices. She founded a reformed Carmelite order of nuns to further religious renewal in Spain. *(MAS Barcelona)*

when she complained, "No wonder the Church is as it is, when the religious live as they do." Members of the new orders set out to change the church through example. The Florentine Filippo Neri (1515–1595) founded the Oratorian order, so named because of the monks' habit of leading the laity in prayer services. Filippo was joined in his work by Giovanni Palestrina (ca. 1525–1594), who composed music for the modest but moving prayer gatherings in Rome. Palestrina's music combined medieval plainchants with newer styles of polyphony, creating complex harmonies without obscuring the words and meaning of the text. The popularity of the Oratorians and their services can be measured in part by the fact that oratories, small chapels modeled on those favored by Filippo, remain to this day important centers of the musical life in the city of Rome.

The Catholic reform of the sixteenth century, however, was better known for its mystical theology than for its music. In Italy and France, but especially in Spain, a profusion of reformers chose to reform the church through austere prayer and contemplation. Teresa of Avila, who belonged to a wealthy converso family, led a movement to reform the lax practices within the religious houses of Spain. Famed for her rigorous religious life, her trances, and her raptures, Teresa animated a movement to reform the order of Carmelite nuns in Spain. Because of her writings about her mystical experiences she was named a "Doctor of the Church," a title reserved for the greatest of the church's theologians.

The most important of the new religious orders was the Society of Jesus, or Jesuits, founded in 1534 by Ignatius Loyola (1491–1556). A conservative Spanish nobleman, Loyola was wounded and nearly killed in battle. During a long and painful rehabilitation, he continuously read accounts of lives of the saints. After recovering, he went on a pilgrimage and experienced a profound conversion.

Loyola initially meant to organize a missionary order directed at the Muslims. The structure of his order reflected his military experience. It had a well-defined chain of command leading to the general of the order and then to the pope. To educate and discipline the members, Loyola composed *Spiritual Exercises,* emphasizing the importance of obedience. (See the box, "Ignatius Loyola's Spiritual Exercises.") He prohibited Jesuits from holding any ecclesiastical office that might compromise their autonomy. After papal approval of the order in 1540, the Jesuits directed their activities primarily to education in Catholic areas and reconversion of Protestants.

Throughout Europe, Jesuits gained fame for their work as educators of the laity and as spiritual advisers to the political leaders of Catholic Europe. In the late sixteenth and early seventeenth centuries they were responsible for a number of famous conversions, including that of Christina (1626–1689), the Lutheran queen of Sweden, who abdicated her throne in 1654 and spent the rest of her life in Rome. Jesuits were especially successful in bringing many parts of the Holy Roman Empire back into communion with the papacy. They have rightly been called the vanguard of the Catholic reform movement.

Catholic reformers were convinced that one of the reasons for the success of the Protestants was that faithful Christians had no clear guide about

what were and what were not orthodox teachings. The first Catholic response to the reformers was to try to separate ideas they held to be correct from those they held to be incorrect. Successive popes made public lists of books and ideas that they considered to be in error. The lists were combined into the *Index of Prohibited Books* in 1559. The climate of suspicion was such that the works of humanists like Erasmus were prohibited alongside the works of Protestants like Martin Luther. The *Index* continued to be revised into the twentieth century. It was finally suppressed in 1966.

During the first half of the sixteenth century, Catholics joined Protestants in calls for an ecumenical council that all believed would solve the problems dogging the Christian church. But in the unsettled political and diplomatic atmosphere that lasted into the 1540s, it was impossible to find any agreement about where or when a universal council should meet. Finally, in 1545, at a time when the hostilities between the Valois and Habsburgs had cooled, Pope Paul III (r. 1534–1549) was able to open an ecumenical council in the city of Trent, a German imperial city located on the Italian side of the Alps.

It is difficult to overemphasize the importance of the Council of Trent. It marked and defined the Roman Catholic church for the next four hundred years. Reformers within the Catholic church hoped that it would be possible to create a broadly based reform party within the church and that the council would define theological positions acceptable to the Protestants, making reunion possible. Unfortunately for the reformers, conservatives quickly took over the Italian-controlled council.

The Council of Trent sat in three sessions between 1545 and 1563. The initial debates were clearly meant to mark the boundaries between Protestant heresy and the orthodox positions of the Catholic church. In response to the Protestant emphasis on the Scriptures, the council said that the church always recognized the validity of traditional teaching and understanding. Delegates rejected the humanists' work on the text of the Bible, declaring that the Latin Vulgate edition compiled by Jerome was the authorized text. In response to the widely held Protestant belief that salvation came through faith alone, the council declared that good works were not merely the outcome of faith but were prerequisites to salvation. The council rejected Protes-

Ignatius Loyola's Spiritual Exercises

Loyola intended the spiritual exercises to be a tool for meditation and prayer by which members of the Society of Jesus would grow in faith, understanding, and obedience. Loyola sets out a series of meditations that are to continue over the course of a month, which reflect his views on the relations of individual Jesuits to the Catholic church.

The following rules are to be observed in order that we might hold the opinions we should hold in the Church militant.

We should put away completely our own opinion and keep our minds ready and eager to give our entire obedience to our holy Mother the hierarchical Church, Christ our Lord's undoubted spouse.

We should speak with approval of confession to a priest, of the reception of Holy Communion once a year, still more once a month, most of all once a week, the requisite conditions being duly fulfilled.

We should openly approve of the frequent hearing of Mass, and also of hymns, psalms and lengthy prayers, both inside and outside the church. . . .

We should speak with approval of religious orders, and the states of virginity and celibacy, not rating matrimony as high as any of these.

We should approve of relics of the saints, showing reverence for them and praying to the saints themselves. . . .

We should approve of the laws of fasting and abstinence in Lent . . . as well as mortifications both interior and exterior.

We should praise church decoration and architecture, as well as statues, which we should venerate in view of what they portray.

Finally, all the Church's commandments should be spoken of favorably, our minds always being eager to find arguments in her defense, never in criticism.

We should be inclined to approve and speak well of the regulations and instructions as well as the personal conduct of our superiors. It may well be that these are not or have not been always praiseworthy; but to criticize them, whether in public utterances or in dealings with ordinary people, is likely to give rise to complaint and scandal rather than to do good. . . .

To arrive at complete certainty, this is the attitude of mind we should maintain: I will believe that the white object I see is black if that should be the decision of the hierarchical Church, for I believe that between Christ our Lord the Bridegroom and His Bride the Church, there is one and the same Spirit, ruling and guiding us for our soul's good. For our Holy Mother the Church is guided and ruled by the same Spirit, the Lord who gave the Ten Commandments.

Source: David Englander, Diana Norman, Rosemary O'Day, and W. R. Owens, eds., *Culture and Belief in Europe, 1450–1600: An Anthology of Sources* (Oxford, England: Basil Blackwell in association with the Open University, 1990), pp. 241–242.

tant positions on the sacraments, the giving of wine to the laity during Holy Communion, the marriage of clergy, and the granting of indulgences.

Protestant critics often list these positions and conclude that the work of the council was merely negative. To do so, however, is to ignore the many ways in which the decrees of the council were an essential part of the creation of the Roman Catholic church that would function for the next four centuries. The delegates at Trent generally felt that the real cause of the Protestant movement was the lack of leadership and supervision within the church. Many of the acts of the council dealt with that issue. First, the council affirmed apostolic succession—

the idea that the authority of a bishop is transmitted through a succession of bishops, ultimately leading back through the popes to Saint Peter. Thus, the council underlined the ultimate authority of the pope in administrative as well as theological matters. The council ordered that local bishops should reside in their dioceses, that they should establish seminaries to see to the education of parish clergy, and that, through regular visitation and supervision, they should make certain that the laity participated in the sacramental life of the church. At the final sessions of the council the nature of the Roman Catholic church was summed up in the Creed of Pius IV, which like the Lutheran Augsburg Confession summarized the basic position of the church.

Confessionalization

The labors of the Jesuits and the deliberations of the Council of Trent at midcentury made clear that reconciliation between the Protestant reformers and the Catholic church was not possible. Signs of the recognition of the permanence of the separation include the flight of several important Protestant religious leaders from Italy in the late 1540s and the wholesale migration of Protestant communities from Modena, Lucca, and other Italian towns to Switzerland. These actions signify the beginnings of the theological, political, and social separation of "Protestant" and "Catholic" in European society.

The theological separation was marked in a number of visual and symbolic ways. Churches in which both bread and wine were distributed to the laity during the sacrament of Holy Communion passed from Catholic to Protestant. Churches in which the altar was moved forward to face the congregation but the statuary was retained were likely to be Lutheran. Churches in which statues were destroyed and all other forms of art were removed were likely to be Reformed (Calvinist), for Calvin had advised that "only those things are to be sculpted or painted which the eye is capable of seeing; let not God's majesty, which is far above the perception of the eyes, be debased through unseemly representations."[8] Even matters like singing differentiated the churches. Although the Calvinist tradition tended to believe that music,

like art, drew the Christian away from consideration of the word, Luther believed that "next to the Word of God, music deserves the highest praise." Lutherans emphasized congregational singing and the use of music within the worship service. Countless pastors in the sixteenth and seventeenth centuries followed Luther in composing hymns and even theoretical tracts on music. This tradition would reach its zenith in the church music of Johann Sebastian Bach (1685–1750), most of whose choral works were composed to be part of the normal worship service.

Music had played an important role in Catholic services since well before the Reformation; it was really architecture that distinguished Catholic churches from Protestant churches in the late sixteenth and seventeenth centuries. In Rome, the great religious orders built new churches in the baroque style (see page 582). Baroque artists and architects absorbed all the classical lessons of the Renaissance and then went beyond them, sometimes deliberately violating them. Baroque art celebrates the supernatural, the ways in which God is not bound by the laws of nature. Where Renaissance art was meant to depict nature, baroque paintings and sculpture seemed to defy gravity. The work celebrated the supernatural power and splendor of the papacy. This drama and power are clear in the construction of the Jesuit Church of the Jesù in Rome and especially in Gianlorenzo Bernini's (1598–1680) throne of Saint Peter made for the church of St. Peter in the Vatican. The construction of baroque churches, first in Spain and Italy but especially in the Catholic parts of Germany, created yet another boundary between an austere Protestantism and a visual and mystical Catholicism.

The Regulation of Religious Life

Because of the continuing religious confusion and political disorder brought on by the reforms, churchmen, like state officials, were intent on enforcing what they understood to be true Christianity. Yet this true religion was much less a public and communal religion than medieval Christianity had been. Medieval Christians had worried greatly about public sins that complicated life in a community. In the age of confessionalization, the-

The Jesù in Rome This church is the center of the Jesuit Order and the burial place of Saint Ignatius Loyola. Its baroque architecture set the tone for many later buildings in Rome and for many new Catholic churches elsewhere. *(Scala/Art Resource, NY)*

ologians—both Protestant and Catholic—worried about the moral status and interior life of individuals. Sexual sins and gluttony now seemed more dangerous than economic sins like avarice or usury. Even penance was understood as less a "restitution" that would reintegrate one into the Christian community than a process of coming to feel a true sense of contrition for sins.

The changed attitude toward penance made the sense of Christian community less important and left individuals isolated and more subject to the influence of the church authorities. In all parts of Europe officials became preoccupied with the control and supervision of the laity.

All of the major religious groups in the late sixteenth century emphasized education, right doctrine, and social control. In Catholic areas there was renewed emphasis on private confession by the laity to ensure a proper understanding of doctrine. During this period Charles Borromeo, archbishop of Milan (1538–1584), introduced the private confessional box, which isolated priest and penitent from the prying ears of the community. This allowed confessors time and opportunity to carefully instruct individual consciences. As early as the 1520s some Lutheran princes had begun visitations to ensure that the laity understood basic doctrine. Churchmen in both Protestant and Catholic areas used catechisms, handbooks containing instruction for the laity. The first and most famous was by Luther himself. Luther's *Small Catechism* includes the Lord's Prayer, Ten Commandments, and Apostles' Creed along with simple, clear explanations of what they mean. More than Catholic rulers, Protestant rulers used church courts to enforce discipline within the community.

Churchmen began to criticize semireligious popular celebrations such as May Day, harvest feasts, and the Feast of Fools, whose origins lay in popular myths and practices that preceded Christianity, because they seemed to encourage superstition and because they mocked the social and political order with, for example, parodies of fat or ignorant clergy and foolish magistrates.

Religious authorities also were concerned by what seemed to be out-of-control mysticism and dangerous religious practices, especially among women. The impact of the Reformation on the status of women has often been debated. The Protestant position is that the Reformation freed women from the cloistered control of traditional convents. Further, the Protestant attack on state-controlled prostitution reduced one of the basest forms of exploitation. To the realists who argued that young, unmarried men would always need sexual outlets, Luther replied that one cannot merely substitute one evil practice for another. Critics of the Reformation counter that a convent was one of very few organizations that a woman could administer and direct. Women who took religious vows, Catholics point out, could engage in intellectual and religious pursuits similar to those enjoyed by men. The destruction of religious houses for women, Catholics argued, destroyed one of the few alternatives that women had to life in an authoritarian, patriarchal society.

In fact, in the late sixteenth and early seventeenth centuries, both Protestant and Catholic authorities viewed with suspicion any signs of religious independence by women. In the first years of the Reformation, some women did leave convents, eager to participate in the reform of the church. Early in the 1520s some women wrote tracts concerning the morality of the clergy. And there was for a time a tradition of women deacons in some Calvinist churches. Yet like the female witches discussed in Chapter 15, these religious women seemed to be dangerous. Lutheran and Calvinist theologians argued that a woman's religious vocation should be in the Christian care and education of her family. And even the most famous of the sixteenth- and seventeenth-century female Catholic mystics were greeted with suspicion and some hostility. Religious women in Catholic convents were required to subordinate their mysticism to the guidance they received from male spiritual advisers. Calvinist theologians exhibited similar suspicions toward the theological and spiritual insights of Protestant women. For the laity in general and for women in particular, the late Reformation brought increased control by religious authorities.

SUMMARY

During the age of the Reformation, Europe experienced a number of profound shocks. The medieval assumption that there was a unified Christendom in the West was shattered. No longer could Europeans assume that at heart they held similar views of the world and the place of individuals in it. Charles V had begun his reign with the hope that there would be one law and one empire. He ended it by dividing his empire and retiring to a monastery.

The Protestant challenge did not simply attack the institutional structure or the moral lapses as previous heretical movements had done. The early Protestant reformers rejected the very nature of the medieval church. Peasants and artisans argued that Luther's message of Christian freedom liberated them from both economic and spiritual oppression. Both Protestant and peasant rejected the traditions of the late Middle Ages.

Monarchies and republics throughout Europe came to view religious institutions and religious choices as matters of state. When faced by theological challenges and cries for moral reform, governments reacted in ways that offered religious change and bolstered the claims of secular government. In England and Sweden, calls for reform resulted in the secularization of church property, which put vast new sources of wealth in the hands of the kings. In the towns of Germany and Switzerland, governments redoubled their efforts to regulate religion and moral life. Thus, both Reformation and Counter-Reformation brought about a significant strengthening of religious and secular authorities.

Ironically, the reforms that Luther and other Protestants advocated on the basis of clear, incontrovertible religious truths eventually led to the suspicion that no truths could be known with certainty. Religious strife led some to conclude that in matters of religion toleration was the only appropriate option. Others concluded that if the truth could not be known, the state must be allowed to make the big decisions. And the states of the seventeenth century were quite willing to do so.

NOTES

1. Angela of Foligno, *The Book of Divine Consolation of the Blessed Angel of Foligno,* trans. Mary G. Steegmann (New York: Cooper Square Publishers, 1966), p. 260.
2. Martin Luther, *Works,* vol. 34 (Philadelphia: Fortress Press, 1955; St. Louis: Concordia Publishing House, 1986), pp. 336–337.
3. Quoted in Steven Ozment, *The Age of Reform, 1250–1550* (New Haven: Yale University Press, 1980), p. 245.
4. Quoted in Robert W. Scribner, *The German Reformation* (London: Macmillan, 1986), p. 32.
5. Quoted in Carter Lindberg, *The European Reformations* (New York: Blackwell Publishers, 1996), p. 269.
6. Quoted in Euan Cameron, *The European Reformation* (Oxford, England: Clarendon Press, 1991), pp. 106–107.
7. Francesco Guicciardini, *Maxims and Reflections (Ricordi),* trans. Mario Domandi (Philadelphia: University of Pennsylvania Press, 1965), p. 48.
8. Quoted in Lindberg, *European Reformations,* p. 375.

SUGGESTED READING

General Surveys

Bossy, John. *Christianity in the West, 1400–1700.* 1985. A subtle, important essay arguing that the Reformation ended communal Christianity and created in its place a more personal religion emphasizing individual self-control.

Cameron, Euan. *The European Reformation.* 1991. The best recent history of the Reformation, emphasizing the common principles of the major reformers.

Chatellier, Louis. *The Europe of the Devout: The Catholic Reformation and the Formation of a New Society.* 1989. An important study of the reconstruction of Catholic Christianity in the late sixteenth century.

Chaunu, Pierre, ed. *The Reformation.* 1989. A colorfully illustrated general history of the Reformation containing essays on the major events.

Davidson, Nicholas S. *The Counter Reformation.* 1987. A short introduction emphasizing how the accomplishments of the Council of Trent laid the basis for a Catholic revival.

Dickens, Arthur G., and John Tonkin. *The Reformation in Historical Thought.* 1985. A comprehensive survey of debates over the meanings of the Reformation, beginning with the earliest historians and continuing into the twentieth century.

Eisenstein, Elizabeth. *The Printing Revolution in Early Modern Europe.* 1983. A general study of the printing revolution that includes a chapter on the importance of printing in the spread of reform.

Englander, David, Diana Norman, Rosemary O'Day, and W. R. Owens, eds. *Culture and Belief in Europe, 1450–1600: An Anthology of Sources.* 1990. A collection of documents illustrating religious and social values and giving an excellent overview of popular reform.

Lindberg, Carter. *The European Reformations.* 1996. A very balanced introduction that tries to give serious coverage to northern and eastern Europe.

Oberman, Heiko, Thomas Brady, and James Tracy, eds. *Handbook of European History, 1400–1600: Late Middle Ages, Renaissance, and Reformation.* 1994–1995. A collection of excellent introductory studies of political, religious, and social life.

O'Connell, Marvin R. *The Counter Reformation, 1559–1610.* 1974. A very good general introduction to the theology and politics of reform in Catholic Europe.

Ozment, Steven. *The Age of Reform, 1250–1550.* 1980. A clear, well-written introduction to late medieval and Reformation religious ideas, emphasizing the ways in which reformers transformed medieval theological debates.

Schilling, Heinz, ed. *Religion, Political Culture, and the Emergence of Early Modern Society.* 1992. A demanding collection of essays on the organization and regulation of Protestant churches in Germany and the Netherlands, making clear the way in which the new churches disciplined their members.

The Reformers

Bainton, Roland H. *Here I Stand: A Life of Martin Luther.* 1978. First published in 1950 but still an excellent introduction to the life of the reformer.

Bouwsma, William. *John Calvin: A Sixteenth-Century Portrait.* 1987. An important but demanding book on Calvin, emphasizing his debt to the humanist movements of the fifteenth and sixteenth centuries.

Dillenberger, John, ed. *Martin Luther: Selections from His Writings.* 1961. An excellent collection of writings that allows readers to follow the evolution of Luther's thought.

McGrath, Alister E. *A Life of John Calvin: A Study in the Shaping of Western Culture.* 1990. An excellent biography emphasizing the definitive role of Calvin's religious thought.

Oberman, Heiko. *Luther: Man Between God and the Devil.* 1989. A brilliant, beautifully written essay connecting Luther to prevailing late medieval ideas about sin, death, and the devil.

(continued on page 544)

A REFORMATION WOODCUT

Erhard Schön's 1533 woodcut "There Is No Greater Treasure Here on Earth Than an Obedient Wife Who Desires Honor" and other broadsheets like it informed and amused Europeans of all walks of life in the late fifteenth and sixteenth centuries. Schön's image of a henpecked husband and his wife followed by others would have been instantly recognizable to most people. Accompanying texts made clear the message implied in the woodcut itself. But how may we, centuries later, "read" this message? How does the modern historian analyze Schön's broadsheet to investigate popular ideas about social roles, religion, and politics? What do it and similar broadsheets tell us about popular responses to the social and religious tumults of the sixteenth century?

Look at the simple and clear lines of the woodcut. They give a clue about the popularity of broadsheets. They were cheap and easy to produce and were printed on inexpensive paper. Artists would sketch an image that an artisan would later carve onto a block. A printer could produce a thousand or more copies from a single block. Even famous artists like Albrecht Dürer (see page 461) sold highly profitable prints on religious, political, and cultural themes.

Almost anyone could afford broadsheets. Laborers and modest merchants decorated their houses with pictures on popular themes. In the middle of the fifteenth century, before the Reformation, most images were of saints. It was widely believed, for example, that anyone who looked at an image of Saint Christopher would not die on that day.

During the political and religious unrest of the sixteenth century, artists increasingly produced images that referred to the debates over religion. Schön himself made his living in Nuremberg producing and selling woodcuts. He and other artists in the city were closely tuned to the attitudes of the local population. One popular image was entitled "The Roman Clergy's Procession into Hell."

Schön's image reproduced here reflected a worry shared by both Protestants and Catholics: the rebellious nature of women. Evidence suggests that women in the late fifteenth and sixteenth centuries may have been marrying at a later age and thus were likely to be more independent-minded than their younger sisters. The ranks of single women were swollen by widows and by former nuns who had left convents and liberated themselves from male supervision. Thus, it was not difficult for men in the sixteenth century to spot women who seemed unnecessarily independent of male control.

Let us turn again to the woodcut, to see what worried villagers and townsmen and how Schön visualized their fears. Notice the henpecked husband. He is harnessed to a cart carrying laundry. Both the harness and the laundry were popular images associated with women's duties. During popular festivals, German villagers often harnessed unmarried women to a plow to signify that they were shirking their duty by not marrying and raising children. Doing the laundry was popularly thought to be the first duty that a powerful wife would force on her weak-kneed husband. Countless other images show women, whip in hand, supervising foolish husbands as they pound diapers with a laundry flail. "Woe is me," says the poor man, all this because "I took a wife." As if the message were not clear enough, look at what the woman carries in her left hand: his purse, his sword, and his pants. (The question "Who wears the pants in the family?" was as familiar then as now.) But the woman responds that he is in this position not because of marriage but because he has been carousing: "If you will not work to support me, then you must wash, spin, and draw the cart."*

*Keith Moxey, *Peasants, Warriors and Wives: Popular Imagery in the Reformation* (Chicago: University of Chicago Press, 1989), pp. 108–109; includes a translation of portions of the texts in the broadsheet.

Schön: There Is No Greater Treasure Here on Earth Than an Obedient Wife Who Desires Honor *(Gotha, Schlossmuseum)*

The figures following the cart are commenting on the situation. The young journeyman is asking the young maiden at his side, "What do you say about this?" She responds, "I have no desire for such power." The woman dressed as a fool counsels the young man never to marry and thus to avoid anxiety and suffering. But an old man, identified as "the wise man," closes the procession and ends the debate over marriage. "Do not listen to this foolish woman," he counsels. "God determines how your life together will be, so stay with her in love and suffering and always be patient."

If we think about this woodcut's images and texts, we can understand the contrary hopes and fears in sixteenth-century Germany. Like the young woman, the Christian wife was expected to avoid claiming power either inside or outside the home. Martin Luther concluded that "the husband is the head of the wife even as Christ is head of the Church. . . . Therefore as the Church is subject to Christ, so let wives be subject to their husbands in everything."** Authority was to be in the hands of husbands and fathers. But if the good wife was required to avoid power, the good husband was also expected to follow Luther's precepts for the Christian family. As the wise old man observes, the husband must be a loving and forgiving master.

Schön's woodcut and others similar to it should remind you of the "argument over women" discussed in Chapter 12 (see page 440). The words of the wise man and the young maid bring to mind Christine de Pizan's *City of the Ladies* when they urge love and understanding, but their hopefulness is undercut by the power and immediacy of the image. As the broadsheet makes clear, suspicion of women characterized even the most simple literature of Reformation Europe. ✎

**Ephesians 5:23–24.

Potter, George R., and Mark Greengrass, eds. *John Calvin.* 1983. Selections from Calvin's most important works, along with short introductions.

Reformation in Specific Countries

Brady, Thomas A. *Turning Swiss: Cities and Empire, 1450–1550.* 1985. A masterful history of the political and ideological concerns of the townsmen of southwestern Germany.

Collinson, Patrick. *The Birthpangs of Protestant England: Religious and Cultural Change in the Sixteenth and Seventeenth Centuries.* 1988. A series of lectures describing the process by which the Protestant religion was established in England.

Dickens, Arthur G. *The English Reformation.* 1964. A classic, clear discussion of English religion, emphasizing the popular enthusiasm for reform, which Dickens believes is connected to the earlier Lollard movements.

Fenlon, Dermot. *Heresy and Obedience in Tridentine Italy: Cardinal Pole and the Counter Reformation.* 1972. A complex book that argues that there was a strong interest in church reform in papal circles until the middle of the sixteenth century.

Greengrass, Mark. *The French Reformation.* 1987. A short pamphlet to introduce students to the political and religious development of the Reformation in France.

Haigh, Christopher, ed. *The English Reformation Revised.* 1987. A collection of essays criticizing Dickens's thesis on the popular basis of reform in England; the introduction is especially useful for following what is still an important debate over reform.

Hsia, R. Po-Chia, ed. *German People and the Reformation.* 1988. A collection of essays that introduce and comment on the various currents of research on the German Reformation.

Moeller, Bernt. *Imperial Cities and the Reformation.* 1972. Three classic essays on why townsmen responded so enthusiastically to the reform message.

Monter, E. William. *Calvin's Geneva.* 1967. A fascinating introduction to life in Geneva during the Reformation, emphasizing that the city was not a theocracy controlled by Calvin.

Moxey, Keith. *Peasants, Warriors, and Wives: Popular Imagery in the Reformation.* 1989. A study of social and religious ideas spread throughout Germany by means of woodcuts; it contains numerous illustrations.

Roper, Lyndal. *The Holy Household: Women and Morals in Reformation Augsburg.* 1990. A study of domestic values in a Protestant city, demonstrating the ways in which reform ideas limited women's religious role to instruction within the family.

Scarisbrick, J. J. *The Reformation and the English People.* 1984. An excellent, clearly written survey of religious practice in England, emphasizing the vitality and popularity of the church on the eve of the Reformation.

Scribner, Robert W. *The German Reformation.* 1986. A short introduction for students to the reform in Germany; it has excellent summaries of social and political issues in Germany.

———. *For the Sake of Simple Folk: Popular Propaganda for the German Reformation.* 1981. A study, illustrated with contemporary woodcuts, that shows how reformers used the new technology of printing to spread popular ideas about reform.

CHAPTER 15

Europe in the Age of Religious War, 1555–1648

In the early hours of a sultry summer morning—August 24, 1572—armed noblemen accompanied by the personal guard of the king of France hunted out about one hundred other nobles, asleep in their lodgings in and around the royal palace in Paris, and murdered them in cold blood. The attackers were Catholic, their victims were Protestant—but all were French nobles, many of them related to one another. The king and his counselors had planned the murders as a preemptive political strike because they feared that other Protestant noblemen were gathering an army outside of Paris. But the calculated strike became a general massacre when ordinary Parisians learned that their king had authorized the murders of Protestant leaders. Believing they were acting in the king's name, these Parisians, who were overwhelmingly Catholic, turned on their neighbors. About three thousand Protestants were murdered in Paris over the next three days.

This massacre came to be called the Saint Bartholomew's Day Massacre for the Catholic saint on whose feast day it fell. Though particularly horrible in its scope (indeed, thousands more people were murdered in the French provinces as word of events in Paris spread), the massacres were not unusual in the deadly combination of religious and political antagonisms they reflected. Throughout Europe ordinary people took religious conflict into their own hands as rulers, for their part, tried to enforce religious uniformity, or at least religious peace. Religious conflicts were by definition intractable political conflicts, since virtually every religious group felt that all others were heretics who must not be tolerated, and rulers of all stripes looked to religious authority and institutions to uphold their own power.

The Saint Bartholomew's
Day Massacre.

In addition, existing political tensions contributed to instability and violence, especially when reinforced by religious difference. Royal governments continued to consolidate authority, but resistance to royal power by provinces, nobles, or towns accustomed to independence now might have religious sanction. Tensions everywhere were also worsened by the rise of prices and unemployment as the sixteenth century wore on. Economic stress was heightened because changes in military technology and tactics made warfare itself more destructive than ever before.

A period of tension, even extraordinary violence, in political and social life, the late sixteenth and early seventeenth centuries were also distinguished by great creativity in some areas of cultural and intellectual life. The plays of Shakespeare, for example, mirrored the passions but also reflected on the tensions of the day and helped to analyze Europeans' circumstances with a new degree of sophistication.

SOCIETY AND THE STATE

Religious strife, warfare, and economic change disrupted the lives of whole communities as well as individuals in the late sixteenth and early seventeenth centuries. The sixteenth century, especially, saw profound economic transformation that, by the end of the century, altered power relations in cities, in the countryside, and in the relationship of both to central governments.

The most obvious economic change was a steady rise in prices, which resulted in the concentration of wealth in fewer hands. Economic change by itself, however, did not spawn all of this era's social and political change. States made war for religious and dynastic reasons more than for calculated economic advantage. Nevertheless, together, the movements of the economy and the policies of governments created notable shifts in centers of wealth and power.

Economic Transformation and the New Elites

Sixteenth-century observers attributed rising prices to the inflationary effects of the influx of precious metals from Spanish territories in the New World. Historians now believe that there were also European causes for this "price revolution." Steady population growth caused a relative shortage of goods, particularly food, and the result was a rise in prices. Both the amount and the effect of price changes were highly localized, depending on factors such as the structure of local economies and the success of harvests. Between 1550 and 1600, however, the price of grain may have risen between 50 and 100 percent, and sometimes more, in cities throughout Europe—including eastern Europe, the breadbasket for growing urban areas to the west. Where we have data about wages, we can estimate that wages lost between one-tenth and one-fourth of their value by the end of the century. The political and religious struggles of the era thus took place against a background of increasing want, and economic distress was often expressed in both political and religious terms.

These economic changes affected the wealthy as well as the poor. During this period, monarchs were making new accommodations with the hereditary aristocracy—with the Crown usually emerging stronger, if only through concessions to aristocrats' economic interests. Underlying this new symbiosis of monarchy and traditional warrior-nobles were the effects of economic changes that would eventually blur lines between these noble families and new elites and simplify power relationships within the state. Conditions in the countryside, where there were fewer resources to feed more mouths, grew less favorable. But at the same time more capital became available to wealthy urban or landholding families to invest in the countryside, by buying land outright on which to live like gentry or by making loans to desperate peasants. This capital came from profits from expanded production and trade and was also an effect of the scarcity of land as population and prices rose. Enterprising landholders raised ground rents wherever they could, or they converted land to the production of wool, grain, and other cash crops destined for distant markets.

As a result, a stratum of wealthy, educated, and socially ambitious "new gentry," as these families were called in England, began growing and solidifying. Many of the men of these families were royal officeholders, and they held on to their offices, confident of their wealth and the leisure it made possible. Where the practice existed, many bought titles outright or were granted nobility as a benefit of their offices. They often lent money to royal governments. The monumental expense of wars made becoming a lender to government, as well as to individuals, an attractive way to live off one's capital.

No one would have confused these up-and-coming families with warrior-aristocrats from old families, but the social distinctions between them are less important (to us) than what they had in common: legal privilege, the security of landownership, a cooperative relationship with the monarchy. Monarchs deliberately favored the new gentry as counterweights to independent aristocrats.

City governments also changed character as wealth accumulated in the hands of formerly commercial families. By the beginning of the seventeenth century, traditional guild control of government had been subverted in many places. Town councils became dominated by successive generations of privileged families, now more likely to live from landed than from commercial wealth. Towns became more closely tied to royal interests by means of the mutual interests of Crown and town elites. The long medieval tradition of towns serving as independent corporate bodies had come to an end.

Economic Change and the Common People

The growth of markets around Europe and in Spanish possessions overseas had a profound effect on urban producers in western Europe. Production of cloth on a large scale for export, for example, now required huge amounts of capital—much more than a typical guild craftsman could amass. In many regions, guild members lost political power in towns as the relative importance of their limited scale of production declined, and the guild structure itself began to break down. The decline in market size for traditional artisans meant that fewer and fewer apprentices and journeymen could expect to become master artisans. The masters began to treat apprentices virtually as wage laborers, at times letting them go when there was not enough work. The household mode of production, in which apprentices and journeymen had worked and lived side by side with the master's family, also began to break down, with profound economic, social, and political consequences.

Effects on women workers were particularly dramatic. One of the first reflections of the dire circumstances faced by artisans was an attempt to lessen competition at the expense of the artisans' own mothers, sisters, daughters, and sons. Increasingly, widows were forbidden to continue practicing their husband's trade, though they headed from 10 to 15 percent of households in many trades. Women had traditionally learned and practiced many trades but rarely followed the formal progress from apprenticeship to master status. A woman usually combined work of this kind with household production, with selling her products and those of her husband, and with bearing and nursing children. Outright exclusion of women from guild organization appears as early as the thirteenth century but now began regularly to appear in guild statutes. In addition, town governments tried to restrict women's participation in work such as selling in markets, which they had long dominated. Even midwives had to defend their practices, even though as part of housewifery women were expected to know about herbal remedies and practical medicine. (See the box, "A Woman Defends Her Right to Practice Healing.") Working women thus began to have difficulty supporting themselves if single or widowed and difficulty supporting their children. In the changing position of such women, we can see the distress of the entire stratum of society that they represent.

Many women worked in cloth production, for spinning was a life skill that women learned as a matter of course. Cloth production was changing, too; it became increasingly controlled by new investor-producers with large amounts of capital and access to distant markets. These entrepreneurs bought up large amounts of wool and hired it out to be cleaned, spun into thread, and woven into cloth by wage laborers in urban workshops or by pieceworkers in their homes. Thousands of women and men in the countryside helped to support themselves and families in this way.

Wealth in the countryside was also becoming more stratified, creating more families that could not adequately support themselves on the land. In western Europe, the most dramatic impact came from the investment in land by wealthy elites. Countless peasants lost their lands to these "rentiers," who lent them money and reclaimed the land when the money was not repaid. Other peasants were unable to rent land as rents rose, or they were unable to make a secure living because of the higher cost of land. To survive, some sought work

A Woman Defends Her Right to Practice Healing

In this document, Katharine Carberiner testifies to the city council of Munich that she does not deliberately compete with male doctors but has skills that might lead other women to choose her rather than male medical practitioners.

I use my feminine skills, given by the grace of God, only when someone entreats me earnestly, and never advertise myself, but only when someone has been left for lost. . . . I do whatever I can possibly do . . . using only simple and allowable means that should not be forbidden or proscribed in the least. Not one person who has come under my care has a complaint or grievance against me. If the doctors, apothecaries or barber-surgeons have claimed this, it is solely out of spite.

At all times, as is natural, women have more trust in other women to discover their secrets, problems and illnesses, than they have in men—but perhaps this jealousy came from that. Undoubtedly as well, husbands who love and cherish their wives will seek any help and assistance they can, even that from women, if the wives have been given up (by the doctors) or otherwise come into great danger.

Because I know that I can help in my own small way, I will do all I can, even, as according to the Gospel, we should help pull an ox out of a well it has fallen into on Sunday.

Source: Merry Wiesner, "Women's Defense of Their Public Role," in Mary Beth Rose, ed., *Women in the Middle Ages and the Renaissance* (Syracuse: Syracuse University Press, 1986), p. 9.

as day laborers on the land of rich landlords or more prosperous farmers. But with the demise of so many opportunities for farming, there was not enough work. Many found their way to cities, where they swelled the ranks of the poor. Others, like some of their urban counterparts, coped by becoming part of the newly expanding network of cloth production, combining spinning and weaving with subsistence farming. However, one bad harvest might send them out on the roads begging or odd-jobbing; many did not long survive such a life.

In eastern Europe, peasants faced other dilemmas, for their lands had a different relationship to the wider European economy. The more densely urbanized western Europe, whose wealth controlled the patterns of trade, sought bulk goods, particularly grain, from eastern Germany, Poland, and Lithuania. Thus, there was an economic incentive for landowners in eastern Europe to bind peasants to the land just as the desire of their rulers for greater cooperation had granted the landlords more power. Serfdom now spread in eastern Europe when precisely the opposite conditions prevailed in the West.

Coping with Poverty and Violence

The common people of Europe did not submit passively either to economic difficulties or to the religious and political crises of their day. The townspeople of France and the Netherlands, for example, played a significant role in the establishment and defense of their "reformed" as well as Catholic religions. Whether Catholic or Protestant, common people took the initiative in attacking members of the other faith to rid their communities of them. At the community level, heretics were considered to be spiritual pollution that might provoke God's wrath. Thus, ordinary citizens believed that they had to eliminate heretics if the state failed to do so. Both elites and common people were responsible for the violence that sometimes occurred in the name of religion.

Ordinary people fought in wars from conviction but also from the need for self-defense. Indeed, although nobles remained military leaders, armies consisted mostly of infantry made up of common people, not mounted knights. It was ordinary people who defended the walls of towns, dug siege works, and manned artillery batteries. Women were part of armies, too. Much of the day-to-day work of finding food and firewood, cleaning guns, and endlessly repairing inadequate clothing was handled individually by women looking after their husbands and lovers among the troops.

Many men joined the armies and navies of their rulers because the military seemed a reasonable way of life, given their options. Landless farm hands, day laborers, and out-of-work artisans found the prospect of employment in the army attractive enough to outweigh the dangers of military life. Desertion was common, since joining up represented a choice, even if a choice among evils. Nothing more than the rumor that a soldier's home village was threatened might prompt a man to abandon his post. Battle-hardened troops could threaten their commanders not only with desertion but with mutiny. A mutiny of Spanish troops in 1574 was a well-organized affair, some-

what like a strike. Whole units of the army mutinied together and found ways to defend themselves while they negotiated with the Spanish command. Occasionally, mutinies were brutally suppressed; more often, they were successful and troops received some of their back wages.

Townspeople and countrypeople participated in riots and rebellions to protest their circumstances when the situation was particularly dire or when other means of action had failed. The devastation of civil war in France, for example, led to a number of peasant rebellions and urban uprisings. Former soldiers, prosperous farmers, or even noble landlords whose economic fortunes were tied to peasant profits might lead rural revolts. If they succeeded, it would be only to relieve a local problem, such as a local tax burden. Urban protests could begin spontaneously when new grievances worsened existing problems. In a town in central France in 1594, for example, the execution for thievery of a servant whose master was believed to be a thief became the occasion for a demonstration to protest the privilege of the well-to-do. In Naples, in 1585, food riots were provoked not

Food and Clothing Distributed by Government Officials In this rendering, a poor woman receives bread and a destitute man, clothing. Wealthy citizens' wills began to reflect the new definition of charity: Bequests to institutions increased and personal donations to the poor dwindled. *(The British Library)*

simply by a shortage of grain but by a government decision to raise the price of bread during the shortage. The property of the privileged was sometimes seized, and city leaders were sometimes killed, but these protests rarely generated lasting political change and were usually brutally quashed.

Governments at all levels tried to cope with the increasing problem of poverty by changing the administration and scale of poor relief. In both Catholic and Protestant Europe, caring for the poor became more institutionalized and systematic and more removed from religious impulses. In traditional Catholic doctrine, charity had been considered one of the many random ways by which an individual could merit grace and move toward eternal life. Such ideas were anathema to Protestant doctrine, but, interestingly, official Catholic practice concerning charity began to change early in the sixteenth century, before the pressure of Protestantism. Official Protestant attitudes toward charity, when they later came into being, closely resembled Catholic ones.

In the second half of the sixteenth century, public almshouses and poorhouses to distribute food or to care for orphans or the destitute sprang up in towns throughout Catholic and Protestant Europe. In certain ways, these institutions reflected an optimistic vision, drawn from humanism, of an ideal Christian community attentive to material want. But by the end of the century, the distribution of food was accompanied by attempts to distinguish "deserving" from "undeserving" poor, by an insistence that the poor be forced to work to receive their ration of food, and even by an effort to compel the poor to live in almshouses and poorhouses.

These efforts were not uniformly successful. Begging was outlawed by Catholic and Protestant city governments alike, but never thoroughly suppressed. Catholic religious orders and parishes often resisted efforts at rationalizing their charitable work imposed from above—even by Catholic governments. Nonetheless, the trend was clear. From viewing the poor as a fact of life and as an occasional lesson in Christian humility, European elites were beginning to view them collectively as a social problem and individual poor people as problems too, in need of collective control and institutional discipline. The establishment of centralized poor relief thus reflected a vision of Christian community in which the relationship between religious belief and community order, at least for elites, became increasingly direct.

The Hunt for Witches and the Illusion of Order

Between approximately 1550 and 1650, Europe saw a dramatic increase in the persecution of women and men for alleged witchcraft. Approximately one hundred thousand people were tried and about sixty thousand executed. The surge in witch-hunting was closely linked to the aftermath of the Protestant Reformation.

Certain kinds of witchcraft had long existed in Europe. So-called black magic of various kinds—one peasant casting a spell on another peasant's cow—had been common since the Middle Ages and continued to be a routine and favored means of coping with personal difficulty. What began to make black magic seem menacing to magistrates, judges, and other authorities were theories linking black magic to Devil worship. Catholic leaders and legal scholars first began to advance such theories in the fifteenth century. By the late sixteenth century, both Catholic and Protestant elites viewed a witch not only as someone who might cast harmful spells but also as a heretic. Persecution for witchcraft rose dramatically after the initial phases of the Reformation ended, reflecting a continuation of reforming zeal directed at the traditional forms of folk religion and magic.

As far as we can tell, no proof that an accused person ever attended a Devil-worshiping "black" Sabbath was ever produced in any witch trial. Nevertheless, authorities were certain that Devil worship occurred, so convinced were they that Satan was in their midst and that the folkways of common people were somehow threatening.

Contemporary legal procedures allowed the use of torture to extract confessions. Torture or the threat of torture led most of those accused of witchcraft to "confess." Probably willing to say what they thought their captors wanted to hear, many named accomplices or others who were also "witches." In this way, a single initial accusation could lead to dozens of prosecutions. In regions where procedures for appealing convictions and sentences were fragile or nonexistent, prosecutions were pursued with zeal. They were widespread, for example, in the small principalities and imperial cities of the Holy Roman Empire, which were virtually independent of all higher authority.

Prosecutions also numbered in the thousands in Switzerland, Poland, France, and Scotland. The majority—perhaps 80 percent—of those convicted and executed in all areas of Europe were women. Lacking legal, social, and political resources, women may have been more likely than men to use black magic for self-protection or advancement and hence were accused more often than men by their neighbors. Community fear and guilt may account for the fact that many of the accused women were poor. The marked increase in poverty during the late sixteenth and early seventeenth centuries made poor women particularly vulnerable to accusations of witchcraft. It was easier to find such a person menacing—and to accuse her of something—than to feel guilty because of her evident need. The modern stereotype that depicts the witch as an ugly old crone dates from this period.

Christian dogma and classically inspired humanistic writing portrayed women as morally weaker than men and thus as more susceptible to the Devil's enticements. Devil worship was described in sexual terms, and the prosecution of witches had a voyeuristic, sexual dimension. The bodies of accused witches were searched for the "Devil's mark"—a blemish thought to be the imprint of the Devil. Both Protestantism and Catholicism taught that sexual lust was evil. One theory is that women accused of being witches were victims of the guilt that elite men felt because of the latter's own sexual longings, which they believed were sinful and might be evidence of damnation. These men sought to lay blame elsewhere.

The witch-hunts virtually ended by the late seventeenth century, as intellectual energies shifted from religious to scientific thought. (See Chapter 17.) Reflecting religious fear, guilt, and class divisions, the witch-hunts are central to understanding European life in this period. They are both the last chapter in the history of the Reformation and a first chapter in the history of the modern state.

IMPERIAL SPAIN AND THE LIMITS OF POWER

To contemporary observers, no political fact of the late sixteenth century was more obvious than the ascendancy of Spain. Philip II (r. 1556–1598) even-

tually ruled Portugal as well as Spain, plus the Netherlands, parts of Italy, and Spanish territories in the Americas (Map 15.1). Yet imperial Spain did not escape the political, social, and religious turmoil of the era. Explosive combinations of religious dissent and political disaffection led to revolt against Spain in the Netherlands. This conflict highlights the tensions of sixteenth-century political life: towns, provinces, and nobles trying to safeguard medieval liberties against efforts at greater centralization, with the added complications of economic strain and religious division. The revolt also demonstrated the material limits of royal power, since even with gold and silver from the American colonies pouring in, Philip could at times barely afford to keep armies in the field. As American resources dwindled in the seventeenth century, Philip's successors faced severe financial and political strains even in their Spanish homelands.

The Revolt of the Netherlands

Philip II's power stemmed in part from the far-flung territories he inherited from his father, the Habsburg Holy Roman emperor Charles V: Spain, the Low Countries (the Netherlands), the duchy of Milan, the kingdom of Naples, and the conquered lands in the Americas. (Control of Charles's Austrian lands had passed to his brother, Philip's uncle.) Treasure fleets bearing precious metals from the New World began to reach Spain regularly during Philip's reign. In addition, Spain now belonged to an expanding trading economy unlike any that had existed in Europe before. To supply its colonies, Spain needed timber and other shipbuilding materials from the hinterlands of the Baltic Sea. Grain from the Baltic fed the urban populations of Spain (where wool was the principal cash crop) and the Netherlands, while the Netherlands, in turn, was a source of finished goods, such as cloth. The major exchange point for all of these goods was the city of Antwerp in the Netherlands, the leading trading center of all of Europe.

Thus, Spain's expanding trading network necessitated tight links with the Netherlands, the real jewel among Philip's European possessions. These seventeen provinces (constituting mostly the modern nations of Belgium and the Netherlands) had been centers of trade and manufacture since the twelfth century and, in the fourteenth

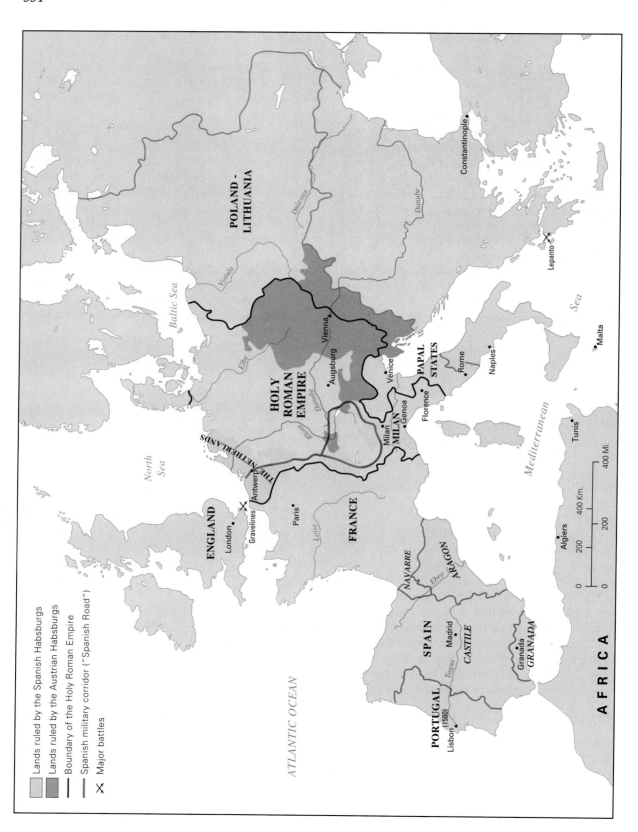

554

POLAND - LITHUANIA

Dniester

Danube

Constantinople •

Lepanto ✗

Baltic Sea

Sea

Vistula

Vienna •

Elbe

Augsburg •

Danube

HOLY ROMAN EMPIRE

Venice •

PAPAL STATES

Rome •

Naples •

Malta •

Rhine

Milan • MILAN • Genoa

Florence •

Mediterranean

Tunis •

THE NETHERLANDS

North Sea

Antwerp •

✗ Gravelines

Paris •

FRANCE

Loire

ENGLAND

London •

NAVARRE

ARAGON

Ebro

400 Mi.

400 Km.

200

200

0

0

Algiers •

ATLANTIC OCEAN

SPAIN

Madrid •

CASTILE

Tagus

Granada • *GRANADA*

PORTUGAL

(1580)

Lisbon •

A F R I C A

Lands ruled by the Spanish Habsburgs

Lands ruled by the Austrian Habsburgs

Boundary of the Holy Roman Empire

Spanish military corridor ("Spanish Road")

✗ Major battles

The City of Antwerp Antwerp, in the southern Netherlands, was the point of sale for Portuguese spices brought from around Africa, the selling and transshipping center for Baltic goods, including timber, fur, and grain, and the source for manufactured goods such as cloth. *(Musées royaux des Beaux-Arts de Belgique)*

and fifteenth centuries, had enjoyed political importance and a period of cultural innovation under the control of the dukes of Burgundy. By the time Philip inherited the provinces from his father, a sort of federal system of government had evolved to accommodate the various regional centers of power there. Each province had a representative assembly (Estates) that controlled taxation, but each also acknowledged a central administrative authority in the form of a governing council sitting in Brussels. Heading the principal council of state was a governor-general, typically, like Philip, a member of the Habsburg family.

Map 15.1 The Spanish Habsburgs and Europe Philip II's control of territories in northern Italy permitted the overland access of Spanish troops to the Netherlands and heightened the Spanish threat to France. Lands bordering the western Mediterranean made the sea a natural sphere of Spanish influence as well. Habsburg lands in central Europe were controlled after 1556 by Charles V's brother Ferdinand and his descendants.

Yet the revolt in the Netherlands that began early in Philip's reign clearly showed the limits to dynastic rule in such diverse territories (Map 15.2). Political power, here and elsewhere, was still highly decentralized, and Philip, like other rulers, could rule effectively only with the cooperation of local elites. Clumsy efforts to adjust this distribution of power in his favor caused Philip to push his subjects in the Netherlands into revolt.

Economic, political, and religious tensions began to strain the relationship between Philip and his subjects in the Netherlands early in his reign. Tensions arose partly over taxation and partly over Spanish insistence on maintaining tight control. Although taxes paid, in effect, to Spain were always resented, bad harvests and commercial disruptions occasioned by wars in the Baltic region in the 1560s depressed the Netherlands' economy and made it difficult for the provinces to afford higher taxes. When the Peace of Cateau-Cambrésis of 1559 brought an end to the long struggle over territory between the Habsburgs

Map 15.2 The Netherlands, 1559–1609 The seventeen provinces of the Netherlands were strikingly diverse politically, economically, and culturally. Like his father, Philip was, technically, the ruler of each province separately: He was count of Flanders, duke of Brabant, and so forth.

and the Valois kings of France, the people of the Netherlands had reason to hope for lower tax burdens and reduced levels of Spanish control.

Philip, born and raised in Spain, had little real familiarity with the densely populated, linguistically diverse Netherlands and never visited there after 1559. To assist the governor-general, his half-sister, Margaret of Parma, he left in place a council composed of ministers and secretaries who either were Spanish themselves or had close ties to the Spanish court. These arrangements affronted local nobles who had fought for Philip and his father before 1559 and who were accustomed to positions of influence in the council of state.

To economic and political tensions were added severe religious problems created by the policies of Philip II. These policies addressed both heresy and ecclesiastical administration. Unlike his father, Philip directed the hunt for heretics not just at lower-class dissenters but also at well-to-do Calvinists—followers of the French Protestant religious reformer John Calvin—who now existed in increasing numbers. Punishment for heresy now included confiscation of family property as well as execution of the individual.

To ensure a high degree of religious control, Philip proposed in 1561 to add fourteen new bishoprics to the Netherlands' traditional four. Local nobles feared their family members would be passed over for appointment to these new church offices in favor of Spaniards or locals sympathetic to Spain. Moreover, each new bishopric was to have inquisitors to root out heretics. By 1565, municipal councils in the Netherlands routinely refused to enforce Philip's religious policies, believing that urban prosperity—as well as their personal security—depended on relative restraint in the prosecution of heresy. Leading nobles stopped enforcing the policies on their estates.

During the spring and summer of 1566, religious dissension in the Netherlands grew dramatically. Encouraged by greater tolerance, Protestants began to hold open-air meetings, and in many towns ordinary people began to embrace Protestantism for the first time. In a series of actions called the "iconoclastic fury," townsfolk stripped Catholic churches of the relics and statues deemed idolatrous by Calvinist doctrine. Reflecting the economic strain of these years, food riots also occurred. Both Spanish authorities and local elites feared the outbreak of general unrest. (See the box, "Elite Fears of Popular Religious Unrest in the Netherlands.")

By early 1567 Calvinist insurgents had seized two towns in the southern Netherlands by force of arms in hopes of stirring a general revolt that would secure freedom of worship. Nobles in various areas also supported a widening rebellion, for their own religious and political reasons. Margaret of Parma successfully quelled the uprisings by rallying city governments and loyal nobles, now alarmed for their own power and property. But she then learned that far away in Spain a decision had been made to send in the Spanish duke of Alba with an army of ten thousand men.

Alba arrived in August 1567 and, to bolster his own shaky standing at the Spanish court, acted more like a conqueror than a peacemaker. He bil-

Elite Fears of Popular Religious Unrest in the Netherlands

In 1566, Calvinists in the Netherlands, urged to action by their preachers, plundered Catholic churches and defied local authorities by holding large public worship services. In document (a), a government agent in a small city reports on the iconoclasm he has witnessed. In document (b), a member of Margaret of Parma's government, writing to a friend in Spain, describes his fears about the effects of the Calvinists' activities.

(a)

The audacity of the Calvinist preachers in this area has grown so great that in their sermons they admonish the people that it is not enough to remove all idolatry from their hearts; they must also remove it from their sight. Little by little, it seems, they are trying to impress upon their hearers the need to pillage the churches and abolish all images.

(b)

The town of Ypres, among others, is in turmoil on account of the daring of the populace inside and outside who go to the open-air services in the thousands, armed and defended as if they were going off to perform some great exploit of war. It is to be feared that the first blow will fall on the monasteries and clergy and that the fire, once lit, will spread, and that, since trade is beginning to cease on account of these troubles, several working folk—constrained by hunger—will join in, waiting for the opportunity to acquire a share of the property of the rich.

Source: Geoffrey Parker, *The Dutch Revolt* (London: Penguin, 1985), pp. 75–76.

leted troops in friendly cities, established new courts to try rebels, arrested thousands of people, executed about a thousand rebels (including Catholics as well as prominent Protestants), and imposed onerous taxes to support his own army. Thus, Alba repeated every mistake of Spanish policy that had triggered rebellion in the first place.

Margaret of Parma resigned in disgust and left the Netherlands. Protestants from rebellious towns escaped into exile and were joined by nobles who had been declared treasonous for minor lapses of loyalty. The most important of these was William of Nassau, prince of Orange (1533–1584), whose lands outside of the Netherlands, in France and the empire, lay out of Spanish reach and so could be used to finance continued warfare against Spain. Thus, a significant community with military capability began to grow in exile.

In 1572, ships of exiled Calvinist privateers known as the "Sea Beggars" captured some fifty towns in the northern provinces. The towns' impoverished inhabitants—eager to strike a blow at expensive Spanish rule—welcomed the exiles. Shortly thereafter, noble armies led by William of Orange invaded the southern provinces but were forced by Alba to withdraw when promised French help did not arrive. For the rest of the century, the northern provinces became increasingly Calvinist strongholds and were the center of opposition to the Spanish, who concentrated their efforts against rebellion in the wealthier southern provinces. Occasionally the French and English lent aid to the rebels.

The Spanish never had the resources to crush the rebellion. The war in the Netherlands exemplifies many of the tensions of the era—such as ones arising from aristocratic privilege, dynastic right, regionalism, and religion. The revolt was also a stage for the destructive and costly technology of warfare in this period. In an attempt to supply the

Netherlands with seasoned veterans and materiel from Spain and Spanish territories in Italy, the Spanish developed the "Spanish Road," an innovative string of supply depots where provisions could be gathered in advance of troops sent along the "Road" to the Netherlands (see Map 15.1).

Spanish supply efforts came partly in response to improved fortifications in the Netherlands' cities, some of which were equipped with new defensive works known as "bastions"; such cities could not be taken by storm but had to be besieged for long periods. Military campaigns in the Netherlands now consisted of grueling sieges, skirmishes in a city's surrounding area for control of villages' supplies, and occasional pitched battles between besiegers and forces attempting to break the siege. Vast numbers of men were required both for an effective besieging force and for garrisoning the fortresses that controlled farmlands and defended major towns. Inevitably, the army put a great strain on the countryside, and both soldiers and civilians suffered great privations. On occasion, Spanish troops reacted violently to difficult conditions and to delayed pay (American treasure dwindled badly between 1572 and 1578). In 1576, Spanish troops sacked the hitherto loyal southern city of Antwerp and massacred about eight thousand people. This event was remembered in the Netherlands as the "Spanish Fury."

Angered by the massacre, leaders in the southern provinces now raised money for citizen armies to protect themselves against the Spanish. In late 1576 the southern leaders concluded the Pacification of Ghent, an alliance with William of Orange and the northern rebels. The terms of the agreement called for nonbelligerence on religious grounds and cooperation to drive the Spanish out. This treaty might have initiated a self-governing United Netherlands were it not for old divisions and Spanish recovery.

The northern and southern provinces were increasingly divided by religion. When Calvinist artisans now seized control of several cities in the southern provinces, city leaders and nobles there grew frightened on political and religious grounds at the same time. Philip's new commander in the Netherlands, Margaret's son Alexander, duke of Parma, was skilled as both a negotiator and a soldier, and by 1578 had renewed shipments of American treasure to help him. He wooed the Catholic elites of the southern provinces back into

REVOLT OF THE NETHERLANDS

1559	Peace of Cateau-Cambrésis
1561	Philip II attempts to place fourteen new bishoprics in the Netherlands
1564	Netherlands city councils and nobility ignore Philip's law against heresy
1566	Calvinist "iconoclastic fury" begins
1567	Duke of Alba arrives in the Netherlands; Margaret of Parma resigns her duties as governor-general
1572	"Second Revolt" of the Netherlands, led by William of Orange, begins
1573	Alba is relieved of his command
1576	Sack of Antwerp Pacification of Ghent
1579	Union of Utrecht
1609	Truce is declared between Spain and the Netherlands

loyalty to Philip, in return for promises to respect their provincial liberties and to safeguard their property from troops.

By 1579 the northern provinces concluded a defensive alliance, the Union of Utrecht, against the increasingly unified south. Parma could not cope with the geographic barrier of four rivers that bisect the Low Countries (see Map 15.2), and he faced declining resources as Spain diverted money to conflicts with England in 1588 and in France after 1589. In 1609 a truce was finally concluded between Spain and the northern provinces. This truce did not formally recognize the "United Provinces" as an independent entity, though in fact they were. The modern nations of Belgium and the Netherlands are the distant result of this truce.

The independent United Provinces (usually called, simply, the Netherlands) was a fragile state, an accident of warfare at first. But commercial prosperity had begun to emerge as its greatest strength. Much of the economic activity of Antwerp had shifted north to Amsterdam in the province of Holland because of fighting in the south and a naval

The Bastion Seen here in an example from an Italian fortress, the bastion was the triangular projection from the fortress wall. It enabled defenders to fire on the flanks of besieging forces; lower than medieval fortress walls and reinforced with earth, walls built in this manner were also less vulnerable to artillery blasts. *(Universitäts und Stadtbibliothek Cologne)*

blockade of Antwerp by rebel ships. Philip's policies had created a new enemy nation and had enriched it at his expense.

The Failure of the Invincible Armada

The political and economic importance of the Netherlands lured Spain into wider strategic involvement, most notably against England. England and Spain had long maintained cordial relations. They had a common foe in France and common economic interests. Philip's marriage to Mary Tudor, the Catholic queen of England (r. 1553–1558), had been a logical step in that relationship, though the opportunity to return England to Catholicism was an added inducement to maintaining close ties. Even after the accession of the Protestant queen Elizabeth (r. 1558-1603), Spanish-English relations initially remained cordial.

Relations started to sour, however, when Elizabeth began tolerating the use of English ports by the rebel Sea Beggars and authorizing English attacks on Spanish treasure fleets. In response, Spain supported Catholic resistance to Elizabeth within England, including a series of plots to replace Elizabeth on the throne with Mary, Queen of Scots. Greater Spanish success in the Netherlands, raids

by the Spanish and English on each other's shipping, and Elizabeth's execution of Mary in 1587 prompted Philip to order an invasion of England. A fleet (*armada*) of Spanish warships sailed in 1588.

"The enterprise of England," as the plan was called in Spain, represented an astounding logistical effort. The Spanish Armada was supposed to clear the English Channel of English ships in order to permit an invading force—troops under Parma in the Netherlands—to cross the Channel on barges. The fleet of about 130 ships also carried troops from Spain to supplement Parma's force, as well as large quantities of supplies for the invasion. The sheer number of ships required for the undertaking meant that some, inevitably, were slower supply ships, or naval vessels designed for the more protected waters of the Mediterranean. The fleet as a whole was slower and less maneuverable than the English force it faced. The English also had the advantage in arms, since they had better long-range artillery and better-trained gunners.

When the Armada entered the Channel on July 29, the English fleet fell in behind them, with the westerly wind and current in their favor. They could harass the Spanish with artillery from a distance without sustaining much damage themselves. The logistical problems of the Spanish plan, given the technologies of the day, then became apparent: Parma could not get his men readied on their barges quickly enough once the fleet's presence in the Channel had been confirmed by messenger. Nor could the fleet protect itself while waiting offshore, since no friendly harbor was available. On the night of August 7, the English launched eight fireships into the anchored Spanish fleet; at dawn on August 8, they attacked the disorganized enemy off Gravelines, and their advantage in arms was decisive (see Map 15.1).

The Battle at Gravelines was the first major gun battle by sailing ships and helped set the future course of naval warfare. For the Spanish, it was a disaster. Many ships were sunk at Gravelines. Many more sank in bad weather, or were forced into hostile harbors, as the Spanish rounded the northern tip of the British Isles and sailed for home along the west coast of Ireland. Fifteen thousand sailors and soldiers—half of all on board—died in battle or on the return journey. Less than half of Philip's great fleet made it back to Spain.

Successes at Home and Around the Mediterranean

Many of Philip's interests still centered on the Mediterranean, despite the new overseas empire and his preoccupation with the Netherlands. Spain and the kingdom of Naples had exchanged trade for centuries. Newer ties had been forged with the duchy of Milan and the city-state of Genoa, whose bankers were financiers to the Spanish monarchy. Charles V had tried to secure the western Mediterranean against the Turks and their client states along the African coast, but it was under Philip that the Turkish threat in the western Mediterranean receded.

The years of the greatest Turkish threat coincided with the beginning of the Netherlands' revolt. To Philip and his advisers, the Turks represented a potential internal threat to Spain as well. Philip thus inaugurated a new wave of persecution of his Muslim subjects, eventually provoking a major rebellion in Granada between 1568 and 1571. After this revolt was crushed, the Muslim inhabitants of Granada were forcibly exiled farther north in Spain. The Spanish allied temporarily with the papacy and Venice—both were concerned with the Turkish advances in the Mediter-

ranean—and their combined navies inflicted a massive defeat on the Turkish navy at Lepanto, off the coast of Greece, in October 1571 (see Map 15.1). The Turks remained a power in the eastern Mediterranean, but their ability to threaten Spain and Spanish possessions in the west was over.

Philip's powers in each of his Spanish kingdoms were circumscribed by the traditional privileges of towns, nobility, and clergy. In Aragon, for example, he could raise revenues only by appealing to local assemblies, the Cortes. In Castile, the arid kingdom in the center of the Iberian Peninsula, the king was able to levy taxes with greater ease but only because of concessions that allowed nobles undisputed authority over their peasants. Philip established his permanent capital, Madrid, and his principal residence, the Escorial, there. The Spanish Empire became more and more Castilian as the reign progressed, with royal advisers and counselors increasingly drawn only from the Castilian elite. Yet the rural economy of Castile was stunted by the dual oppression of landholders and royal tax collectors.

Philip made significant inroads into Aragonese independence by the end of his reign. Noble feuds and peasant rebellions had combined to create virtual anarchy in some areas of Aragon by the 1580s, and in 1591 Philip sent in veteran troops from the Netherlands campaigns to establish firmer royal control. Philip was successful in the long run in Aragon because he used adequate force but tempered it afterward with constitutional changes that were cleverly moderate. Finally, he cemented the peace by doing what he had failed to do in the Netherlands. He appeared in Aragon in person, in the words of a contemporary, "like a rainbow at the end of a storm."[1]

Philip also invaded and successfully annexed Portugal in 1580, thus completing the unification of the Iberian Peninsula. The annexation was ensured by armed force but had been preceded by careful negotiation to guarantee that Philip's claim to the throne—through his mother—would find some support within the country. This was old-fashioned dynastic politics at its best. When Philip died in 1598, he was old and ill, a man for whom daily life had become a painful burden. His Armada had been crushed; he had never quelled the Netherlands' revolt. Yet he had been more successful, by his own standards, in other regions that he ruled.

Spain in Decline

Spain steadily lost ground economically and strategically after the turn of the century. Imports of silver declined. The American mines were exhausted and the natives forced to work in them were decimated by European diseases and brutal treatment. Spain's economic health was further threatened by the very success of its colonies: Local industries in the Americas began to produce goods formerly obtained from Spain. The increasing presence of English, French, and Dutch shipping in the Americas provided colonists with rival sources for the goods they needed. Often, these competitors could offer their goods more cheaply than Spaniards could, for Spanish productivity was low and prices were high because of the inflationary effects of the influx of precious metals.

Spain renewed hostilities with the United Provinces in 1621, after the truce of 1609 had expired. Philip IV (r. 1621–1645) also aided his Habsburg cousins in the Thirty Years' War in the Holy Roman Empire (see page 571). Squeezed for troops and revenue for these commitments, other Spanish territories revolted. The uprisings reflected both economic distress and unresolved issues of regional autonomy. The government of Spain was Castilian, and Castile bore the brunt of the financial support of the state. The chief minister to Philip IV, Gaspar de Guzmán, Count Olivares (1587–1645), was an energetic Castilian aristocrat determined to distribute the burdens of government more equitably among the various regions of Spain. His policies provoked rebellions in Catalonia and Portugal.

In Catalonia, a province of the kingdom of Aragon, the revolt began as a popular uprising against the billeting of troops. At one point Catalan leaders invited French troops south to defend them and solemnly transferred their loyalty to the French king in the hope that he would respect their autonomy. Spain resumed control only in 1652, after years of military struggle and promises to respect Catalan liberties.

In Portugal, a war of independence began in 1640, also with a popular revolt. The Spanish government tried to restore order with troops under the command of a leading Portuguese prince, John, duke of Braganza. The duke, however, was the nearest living relative to the last king of Portugal, and he seized this opportunity to claim the

Philip II in 1583 Dressed in the austere black in fashion at the Spanish court, Philip holds a rosary and wears the Order of the Golden Fleece, an order of knighthood, around his neck. At age 56 Philip has outlived four wives and most of his children. *(Museo del Prado, Madrid)*

crown of Portugal for himself and lead a fight for independence. Although war dragged on until 1668, the Portuguese under John IV (r. 1640–1656) succeeded in winning independence from Spain.

As a result of these uprisings, Count Olivares resigned in disgrace in 1643. In 1647 there would also be upheaval in Spain's Italian possessions of Sicily and Naples. By midcentury, Spain had lost its position as the preeminent state in Europe.

RELIGIOUS AND POLITICAL CRISIS IN FRANCE AND ENGLAND

Civil war wracked France from 1562 until 1598. As in the Netherlands, the conflicts in France had religious and political origins as well as international implications, and political and religious questions became entangled in ways that made the conflicts almost impossible to resolve. Though a temporary resolution was achieved by 1598, religious division still existed, and conflict over the legitimate nature and extent of royal power remained. England, in contrast, was spared dramatic political and religious upheaval in the second half of the sixteenth century, in part because of the talents—and long life—of its ruler. But in the seventeenth century, constitutional and religious dissent began to reinforce each other in new and dramatic ways and threaten the stability of the realm.

The French Religious Wars

The king of France, Henry II (r. 1547–1559), had concluded the Peace of Cateau-Cambrésis with Philip II in 1559, ending the Habsburg-Valois Wars, but had died in July of that year from wounds suffered at a tournament held to celebrate the new treaty. His death was a political disaster. Great noble families vied for influence over his 15-year-old son, Francis II (r. 1559–1560). Two brothers of the house of Guise were related to the young king by marriage and succeeded in dominating him. But the Guises faced continual challenges from members of the Bourbon family, who claimed the right to influence the king because they were princes of royal blood and stood next in line to the throne after Henry II's sons.

The queen mother, Catherine de' Medici (1519–1589), worked carefully and intelligently to balance the nobles' interests. She gained greater authority when, in late 1560, the sickly Francis died and was succeeded by his brother, Charles IX—a 10-year-old for whom Catherine was officially the regent. But keeping the conflicts among the great courtiers from boiling over into civil war proved impossible.

In France, as elsewhere, noble conflict invariably had a violent component. Noble men went about armed and accompanied by armed entourages. Although they relied on patronage and army commands from the Crown, the Crown depended on their services. Provincial landholdings afforded enough resources to support private warfare, and the nobles assumed a right to wage it.

In addition, religious tension was rising throughout France. (Henry II had welcomed the 1559 treaty in part because he wanted to turn his attention to "heresy.") Public preaching by, and secret meetings of, Protestants (known as "Huguenots" in France) were causing unrest in towns. At court, members of the Bourbon family and other leading nobles had converted to Protestantism and worshiped openly in their rooms in the palace. In 1561 Catherine convened a national religious council, known as the Colloquy of Poissy, to reconcile the two faiths. When it failed, she decided that the only practical course was at least provisional religious toleration, so she issued a limited edict of toleration in the name of the king in January 1562.

The edict, however, led only to further unrest. Ignoring its restrictions, Protestants armed themselves, while townspeople of both faiths insulted and attacked one another at worship sites and religious festivals. Then in March 1562, at Vassy, the duke of Guise's men killed a few dozen Protestants gathered in worship near one of the duke's estates.

The killing at Vassy began the first of six civil wars because it brought together the military power of the nobility with the broader problem of religious division. In some ways, the initial conflict was decisive. The Protestant army lost the principal pitched battle of the war, near Dreux, west of Paris, in December. This defeat ultimately checked the growth of the Protestant movement. It reduced the appeal of the movement to nobles, and the limited rights granted to Protestants in the Crown's peace edict made it difficult for Protestant townspeople to worship, particularly in areas where they were not a majority. But if the Protestants were not powerful enough to win, neither could the Crown decisively beat them.

The turning point most obvious to contemporaries came a decade later. The Protestant faction was still well represented at court by the Bourbon princes and by the very able and influential nobleman Gaspard de Coligny, related to the Bourbons by marriage. Coligny pressed for a war against Spain in aid of Protestant rebels in the Netherlands. Alarmed by this pressure and by rumors of Protestant armies outside of Paris, Charles IX (r. 1560–1574) and his mother authorized royal guards to murder Coligny and other Protestant leaders on August 24, 1572—Saint Bartholomew's Day. Coligny's murder touched off a massacre of

THE FRENCH SUCCESSION, 1515–1715

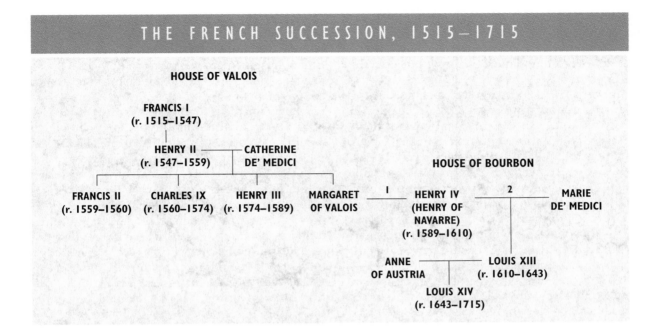

HOUSE OF VALOIS

FRANCIS I
(r. 1515–1547)

HENRY II — **CATHERINE DE' MEDICI**
(r. 1547–1559)

HOUSE OF BOURBON

FRANCIS II (r. 1559–1560)   **CHARLES IX** (r. 1560–1574)   **HENRY III** (r. 1574–1589)   **MARGARET OF VALOIS** — 1 — **HENRY IV (HENRY OF NAVARRE)** (r. 1589–1610) — 2 — **MARIE DE' MEDICI**

ANNE OF AUSTRIA — **LOUIS XIII** (r. 1610–1643)

LOUIS XIV (r. 1643–1715)

Protestants throughout Paris and, once news from Paris had spread, throughout the kingdom.

The Saint Bartholomew's Day Massacre revealed the degree to which religious differences had strained the fabric of community life. Neighbor murdered neighbor, in an effort to rid the community of heretical pollution; bodies of the dead, including Coligny's, were torn apart, mutilated. Gathered in the south of France, the remaining Huguenot forces vowed "never [to] trust those who have so often and so treacherously broken faith and the public peace."[2] Many Catholics also renounced reconciliation. When further war produced the inevitable truces and limited toleration, some noblemen formed a Catholic league to fight in place of the vacillating monarchy.

Another impetus to the breakdown of royal authority by the 1580s was the accession to the throne of Charles's brother, Henry III (r. 1574–1589), another king of limited abilities. Middle-aged, Henry had no children. The heir to his throne was the Protestant Henry of Navarre, and the assumption of the throne by a Protestant was unimaginable to the zealous Catholic faction at court and to thousands of ordinary Catholics besides. By the end of Henry III's reign, the king had almost no royal authority left to wield. He was forced to cooperate with first one of the warring parties and then with

another. In December 1588, he resorted to murdering two members of the Guise family who led the ultra-Catholic faction, and, in turn, he was murdered by a priest in early 1589.

Henry of Navarre, who became Henry IV (r. 1589–1610), had to fight for his throne. Facing him were Catholic armies now subsidized by Philip II of Spain, an extremist Catholic city government in Paris, a kingdom of subjects who were tired of war but mainly Catholic, and only meager support from Protestants abroad. Given these obstacles, Henry was able to force acceptance of his rule only after agreeing to return to Catholicism himself.

After his conversion in 1593, the wars continued for a time, but, after thirty years of civil war, many of his subjects realized that only rallying to the monarchy could save France from chaos. Catholic nobility and townspeople fought among themselves over the direction to take. The nobility favored acceptance of Henry IV and imposed its will on the citizens of Paris and other cities.

The civil wars had demonstrated the power of the warrior-nobility to disrupt the state. But now nobles grew increasingly disposed, for both psychological and practical reasons, to cooperate with the Crown. Service to a successful king could be a source of glory, and Henry was personally esteemed because he was a talented general and brave, gregarious, and charming. The civil war period thus proved to be an important phase in the continual accommodation of the nobility to the power of the state.

In April 1598 Henry granted toleration for the Huguenot minority in a royal edict proclaimed in the city of Nantes. The Edict of Nantes was primarily a repetition of provisions from the most generous edicts that had ended the various civil wars. Nobles were allowed to practice the Protestant faith on their estates; townspeople were granted more limited rights to worship in selected towns in each region. Protestants were guaranteed access to schools, hospitals, royal appointments, and separate judicial institutions to ensure fair treatment. They were also guaranteed rights of self-defense—specifically, the right to maintain garrisons in about two hundred towns. About half of these garrisons would be paid for by the Crown.

The problem was that the Edict of Nantes, like any royal edict, could be revoked by the king at any time. Moreover, the provision allowing Protestants to keep garrisoned towns reflected concessions to powerful nobles who could support their followers by paid garrison duty. These concessions also meant that living peacefully with religious diversity was not yet thought to be possible. Thus, although Henry IV successfully ended the French religious wars, the problem of religious and political division within France had not been solved.

The Consolidation of Royal Authority in France, 1610–1643

During Henry IV's reign, France recovered from the long years of civil war. Population and productivity began to grow; the Crown encouraged internal improvements to facilitate commerce. Henry's chief minister, Maximilien de Béthune, duke of Sully (1560–1641), increased royal revenue by nibbling away at traditional local self-government and control of taxation. He succeeded in creating a budget surplus and in extending mechanisms of centralized government.

Yet Henry's regime was stable only in comparison with the preceding years of civil war. The power of the great nobility had not been definitively broken. Several leading nobles plotted with foreign powers, including Spain, to influence French policy and gain materially themselves.

Moreover, the king had agreed to a provision, known as the *paulette* (named for the functionary who first administered it), that allowed royal officeholders not merely to own their offices but also to bequeath those offices to their heirs in return for the payment of an annual fee. It was, primarily, a financial expedient to raise revenue after decades of civil war. In addition, the paulette helped cement the loyalty of royal bureaucrats at a critical time, particularly that of the royal judges of the supreme law court, the Parlement of Paris, who had recently agreed to register the Edict of Nantes only under duress. However, that privileged position made royal officeholders largely immune from royal control since a position in the royal bureaucracy now became property, like the landed property of the traditional nobility.

A fanatical Catholic assassinated Henry IV in 1610. Henry's death left his son, Louis XIII (r. 1610–1643), only 9 years old, to face the challenges of governing as well as a return of religious conflict. Louis's mother, Marie de' Medici, acted ably as regent, but was temporarily disgraced when her unpopular leading minister was assassinated in 1617. This courtier was an Italian, and hence doubly resented for being a foreigner as well as for his crass ambition. His rise and fall was typical of the volatile court life of the period, as great aristocrats vied to control and profit from royal policies.

Soon after Louis took control of government from his mother, he faced a major rebellion by his Huguenot subjects in southwestern France. Huguenots felt threatened by the recent marriage of the king to a Spanish princess and by Louis's reintroduction of Catholic institutions in nearby Navarre (see Map 15.1). Louis's ancestors had themselves established Protestantism in this small kingdom bordering Spain, now united to the French crown. Certain Huguenot nobles, afraid that royal support of toleration was wavering, initiated fighting in 1621 as a show of force against the king.

These religious wars persisted, on and off, until 1629. They reflected not only the continuing power of great nobles to wield independent military might, but also the importance of fortifications in warfare: The Crown had difficulty successfully besieging even small fortress towns. The course of the wars also reflected the ascendancy of the western port city of La Rochelle—well-fortified, Protestant-controlled, and wealthy from mounting overseas and European trade. Not until the king took the city, after a siege lasting more than a year and costing thousands of lives, did the Protestants accept a peace on royal terms.

The Peace of Alais (1629) was a political triumph for the Crown because it broke the connection between religious dissent and political upheaval. The treaty reaffirmed the policy of religious toleration but rescinded the Protestants' military and political privileges. It thus deprived French Protestants of the means for further rebellion while reinforcing their dependence on the Crown for religious toleration. Most of the remaining great noble leaders began to convert to Catholicism.

The Peace of Alais was also a personal triumph for the king's leading minister, who crafted the treaty and who had directed the bloody siege that made it possible: Armand-Jean du Plessis (1585–1642), Cardinal Richelieu. From a provincial noble family, Richelieu had risen in the service of the queen mother. His enormous intelligence was apparent to everyone at court; he was admired and feared for his skill in the political game of seeking and bestowing patronage—a crucial skill in an age when elites received offices and honor through carefully cultivated links with the court. His control of many lucrative church offices gave him the resources to build up a large network of clients. He and the king—whose sensitive temperament Richelieu handled adeptly—formed a lasting partnership from this point on that had a decisive impact not only on French policy but also on the entire shape of the French state. (See the box, "Richelieu Supports the Authority of the State.")

Richelieu favored an aggressive foreign policy to counter what he believed still to be the greatest threat to the French crown: the Spanish Habsburgs. War had resumed between the Netherlands and Spain when their truce expired in 1621 (see page 561); since then, Richelieu had used his growing power to direct limited military campaigns against Spanish power in Italy. After 1630, with the king's full confidence, he superintended large-scale fighting against Spain in the Netherlands itself, as well as in Italy, and subsidized armies fighting the Spanish and Austrian Habsburgs in Germany.

Richelieu's policies were opposed by many people, who saw taxes double, then triple, in just a few years. Many courtiers and provincial elites had favored the tenuous peace with a fellow Catholic state and objected to alliances with German Protestants. They were alarmed by the increasing taxes and by the famine, disease, and, above all, the revolts that accompanied the peasants' distress. Their own power was also directly threatened by Richelieu's monopoly of royal patronage and by his creation of new mechanisms of government to manage his policies, which bypassed their offices. In 1632, for example, Richelieu created the office of *intendant*. Intendants had wide powers for defense and administration in the provinces that overrode the established bureaucracy.

By 1640 Richelieu's ambitious foreign policy seemed to be bearing fruit. The French had won territory along their northern and eastern borders by their successes against Habsburg forces. But when Richelieu and Louis XIII died within five months of each other, in December 1642 and May 1643, Richelieu's legacy was tested. Louis XIII was succeeded by his 5-year-old son, and the warrior-nobility as well as royal bureaucrats would dramatically challenge the Crown's new authority.

England: Precarious Stability, 1558–1603

England experienced no civil wars during the second half of the sixteenth century, but religious dissent challenged the stability of the monarchy. In Elizabeth I (r. 1558–1603), England—in stark contrast to France—possessed an able and long-lived ruler. Elizabeth was well educated in the humanistic tradition and was already an astute politician at the age of 25, when she acceded to the throne. Religious, political, and constitutional disputes existed in England as elsewhere, but they would not provoke violence on anything like the continental scale.

Elizabeth came to the throne at the death of her Catholic half-sister, Mary Tudor (r. 1553–1558), wife of Philip II. Elizabeth faced the urgent problem of reaching a policy of consensus in religious matters—a consensus that could embrace the two extremes of the Catholic-like doctrine and practice of Anglicanism, which had prevailed under her father, Henry VIII (r. 1509–1547), and Calvinist-inspired Protestantism, which had developed under her half-brother, Edward VI (r. 1547–1553). True Catholicism, such as Mary had tried to reimpose, was out of the question. The Roman church had never recognized Henry VIII's self-made di-

Richelieu Supports the Authority of the State

In this excerpt from his **Political Testament** *(assembled from his notes after his death by loyal secretaries), Richelieu justifies methods for ensuring obedience to the Crown. Notice his pessimistic view of human rationality; rewards (such as patronage) but also severity are both necessary to ensure obedience.*

It is a common but nevertheless true saying which has long been repeated by intelligent men that punishments and rewards are the two most important instruments of government in a realm. It is certain that whatever else one may do in governing states, one must be inflexible in punishing those who fail to obey, and religiously scrupulous in rewarding those who perform notable services. In other words, one would not govern badly if guided by this precept since most people can be held to their duty through either fear or hope. I rate punishments, I must say, higher than rewards, because if it were necessary to dispense with one of these, it would be better to give up the latter than the former. The good ought to be adhered to for its own sake, and in all justice no one should be rewarded for this. But there is no crime which does not violate those precepts men are obligated to obey, so that punishment to be expected for disobedience of this sort is therefore justified, and this obligation is so direct in many cases that to let the act go unpunished is to commit further error.

I speak here of things which injure the state and which have been premeditated, and not of those lesser offenses which result from chance or misfortune, toward which princes may and should often show indulgence. But while in matters of this sort it can be praise-worthy to pardon, it is a criminal omission not to punish breaches which open the door to licentious abandon. Both theologians and political experts agree that on special occasions it would be an error not to pardon certain individuals, but it would be inexcusable for those charged with public responsibilities to substitute indulgence for severe punishment. Experience teaches those who have had long practice in this world that men easily lose the memory of rewards and, when they are heaped with them, they expect even more, and become both ambitious and ungrateful at the same time. This teaches us to realize that punishments are a surer means of holding a person to his duty, since people are less likely to forget what has made an impression on their emotions. This is more persuasive for most men than reason, which has little power over many minds.

To be severe in dealing with private individuals who glory in disobeying the laws and orders of the state makes a good impression on the people, and one can commit no greater crime against the public interest than to be indulgent toward those who violate them. In thinking over the many cabals, factions, and plottings which have occurred in this realm in my time, I can recall none in which leniency induced any person with evil inclinations to rectify the error of his ways.

Source: Henry Bertram Hill, ed. and trans., *The Political Testament of Cardinal Richelieu* (Madison: University of Wisconsin Press, 1965), pp. 84–86.

vorce and thus regarded Elizabeth as a bastard with no right to the throne.

Most important to Elizabeth was a new Act of Supremacy (1559), intended to restore the monarch as head of the Church of England. Elizabeth and most of her ministers were willing to accept some room for maneuver between liturgical practice and personal belief for the sake of defeating the common enemy, Roman Catholicism. For example, a new prayer book, the *Book of Common Prayer,* incorporated, side by side, elements of both traditional and radical interpretations of

Elizabeth I: The Armada Portrait Both serene and resolute, Elizabeth is flanked by "before" and "after" glimpses of the Spanish fleet; her hand rests on the globe in a gesture of dominion that also memorializes the circumnavigation of the globe by her famous captain, Sir Francis Drake, some years before. *(By kind permission of Marquess of Tavistock and Trustees of Bedford Estate)*

communion. Church liturgy, clerical vestments, and, above all, the hierarchical structure of the clergy closely resembled Catholicism, however. Elizabeth firmly handled resistance to the Act of Supremacy. She simply arrested bishops and lords whose votes would have blocked its passage by Parliament.

The problem of religious dissent, however, was not definitively solved. Catholicism continued to be practiced. Loyal nobility and gentry in the north of England practiced it with discretion. But priests returning from exile beginning in the 1570s, most newly imbued with the proselytizing zeal of the Counter-Reformation (the Catholic response to the Protestant Reformation), practiced it more visibly. In the last twenty years of Elizabeth's reign, approximately 180 Catholics were executed for treason; two-thirds of them were priests. (By 1585, being a priest in itself was a crime.)

In the long run, however, the greater threat to the English crown came from growing tensions with the most radical Protestants in the realm, known (by their enemies initially) as Puritans. Puritanism was a broad movement for reform of church practice along familiar Protestant lines: emphasis on Bible reading, preaching, private scrutiny of conscience, and a de-emphasis on institutional ritual and clerical authority. Most Puritans had accepted Elizabeth's religious compromise for practical reasons but grew increasingly alienated by her insistence on clerical authority. A significant Presbyterian underground movement began to form among them. Presbyterians wanted to dismantle the episcopacy, the hierarchy of priests and bishops, and govern the church instead with councils, called "presbyterys," that included lay members of the congregation. Laws were passed late in the reign to enable the Crown more easily to prosecute, and even to force into exile, anyone who attended "nonconformist" (non-Anglican) services.

The greatest challenge Elizabeth faced from Puritans came in Parliament, where they were well represented by many literate gentry. Parliament met only when called by the monarch, and in theory could merely voice opinions and complaints; it could not initiate legislation or demand changes in royal policy. However, only Parliament could vote taxes, and, since its authority had, in effect, helped constitute royal authority by means of the Acts of Supremacy, Parliament's supposedly consultative role had been expanded by the monarchy itself. During Elizabeth's reign, Puritans used meetings of Parliament to press their cause of further religious reform. In 1586, they went so far as to introduce bills calling for an end to the episcopacy and the Anglican prayer book. Elizabeth had to resort to imprisoning one Puritan leader to end debate on the issue and on Parliament's right to address it.

Elizabeth's reign saw the beginnings of English expansion overseas, but great interest in overseas possessions lay in the future; Elizabeth, like all her forebears, felt her interests tightly linked to affairs on the European continent. Her prime interest lay in safeguarding the independence of the Netherlands. Philip II's policy in the Netherlands increasingly alarmed her, especially in view of France's weakness. She began to send small sums of money to the rebels and allowed their ships access to southern English ports, from which they could raid Spanish-held towns on the Netherlands' coast. In 1585, in the wake of the duke of Parma's successes against the rebellions, she committed troops to help the rebels.

Her decision was a reaction not only to the threat of a single continental power dominating the Netherlands but also to the threat of Catholicism. Spain had threatened her interests, and even her throne, in other ways. From 1579 to 1583, the Spanish had helped the Irish fight English domination and were involved in several plots to replace Elizabeth with her Catholic cousin, Mary, Queen of Scots. These threats occurred at the height of the return of Catholic exiles to England.

Eventually, in 1588, the English faced the Spanish Armada and the threat of invasion that it brought. The defeat of the Armada was by no means certain for the English. They did not know, for example, how poorly prepared Parma actually was to cross the Channel. Thus, in the wake of victory, a mythology quickly built that portrayed Spain as an aggressive Goliath confronting the tiny David of England. The victory over the Spanish fleet was quite rightly celebrated, for it ended any Catholic threat to Elizabeth's rule.

The success against the Armada has tended to overshadow other aims and outcomes of Elizabeth's foreign policy. In the case of Ireland, England was Goliath to Ireland's David. Since the twelfth century, an Anglo-Irish state dominated by great princely families had been loosely supervised from England, but most of Ireland remained under the control of Gaelic chieftains. Just as Charles V and Philip II attempted to tighten their governing mechanisms in the Netherlands, so in England did Henry VIII's minister, Thomas Cromwell, streamline control of outlying areas such as Wales and Anglo-Ireland. Cromwell proposed that the whole of Ireland be brought under English control partly by the established mechanism of feudal ties: The Irish chieftains were to do homage as vassals to the king of England.

Under Elizabeth, this legalistic approach gave way to virtual conquest. Elizabeth's governor, Sir Henry Sidney, appointed in 1565, inaugurated a policy whereby Gaelic lords, by means of various technicalities, could be entirely dispossessed of their land. Any Englishman capable of raising a private force could help enforce these dispossessions and settle his conquered lands as he saw fit. This policy provoked stiff Irish resistance, which was viewed as rebellion and provided the excuse for further military action, more confiscations of land, and more new English settlers. Eventually, the Irish, with Spanish assistance, mounted a major rebellion, consciously Catholic and aimed against the "heretic" queen. The rebellion gave the English an excuse for brutal suppression and massive transfers of land to English control. The political domination of the Irish was complete with the defeat, in 1601, of the able Gaelic chieftain Hugh O'Neill, lord of Tyrone, who controlled most of the northern quarter of the island. Although the English were unable to impose their Protestantism on the conquered Irish, to Elizabeth and her English subjects the conquests in Ireland seemed as successful as the victory over the Spanish Armada.

The English enjoyed remarkable peace at home during Elizabeth's reign. However, her reign ended on a note of strain. The foreign involvements, particularly in Ireland, had been very expensive. Taxation granted by Parliament more than doubled during her reign, and local taxes further burdened the people. Price inflation caused by government spending, social problems caused by returned, unemployed soldiers, and a series of bad harvests heightened popular resentment against taxation. Despite her achievements, therefore, Elizabeth passed two potential problems on to her successors: unresolved religious tensions and financial instability. Elizabeth's successors would also find in Parliament an increasing focus of opposition to their policies.

Rising Tensions in England, 1603–1642

In 1603 Queen Elizabeth died and James VI of Scotland acceded to the English throne as James I (r. 1603–1625). Religious tensions between Anglicans and Puritans were temporarily quieted under James because of a plot, in 1605, by Catholic dissenters. The Gunpowder Plot, as it was called, was a conspiracy to blow up the palace housing both king and Parliament at Westminster. The attention of Protestants of all stripes once again became focused not on their differences but on their common enemy, Catholicism.

Financial problems were James's most pressing concern. Court life became more elaborate and an increasing drain on the monarchy's resources. James's own leanings toward extravagance were partly to blame for his financial problems, but so were pressures for patronage from elites. There were considerable debts left from the Irish conflicts and wars with Spain. Moreover, as the reign progressed, James was forced into further foreign involvement. His daughter and her husband, a German prince, were trying to defend their claim to rule Bohemia against the powerful Austrian Habsburgs (see page 573).

To raise revenue without Parliament's consent, James, like Elizabeth, relied on sources of revenue that the Crown had enjoyed since medieval times: customs duties granted to the monarch for life, wardship (the right to manage and liberally borrow from the estates of minor nobles), and the sale of monopolies, which conveyed the right to be sole agent for a particular kind of goods. James increased the number of monopolies sold and added other measures, such as the sale of Crown lands and of noble titles, to increase royal revenue.

These expanded financial expedients were resented: Merchants opposed monopolies' arbitrary restriction of production and trade; common people found that the prices of certain ordinary commodities, like soap, rose prohibitively. Resentments among the nobility were sharpened, and general criticism of the court heightened, by James's favoritism of certain courtiers and their families. The chief beneficiary of patronage and the most influential adviser to the king was George

Villiers (1592–1628), duke of Buckingham, a powerful but corrupt and inadequate first minister.

When James summoned Parliament for funds in 1621, Parliament used the occasion to protest court corruption and the king's financial expedients. The members impeached and removed from office two royal ministers. In 1624, still faced with expensive commitments to Protestants abroad and in failing health, James again called Parliament, which voted new taxes but also openly debated the king's foreign policy.

Under James's son, Charles I (r. 1625–1649), tensions between Crown and Parliament rose. One reason was the growing financial strain of foreign policy as well as the policies themselves. Retaining the unpopular duke of Buckingham as chief courtier and adviser, Charles declared war on Spain and pursued an indecisive but costly foreign policy in France in support of the Huguenot rebels there. Many wealthy merchants opposed this aggressive foreign policy, which disrupted trading relationships. In 1626, Parliament was dissolved without granting any monies in order to stifle its objections to royal policies. The Crown's reliance on unpopular financial expedients thus of necessity continued and reached a new level of coercion. In 1627, Charles imprisoned certain gentry who refused to lend money to the government.

Above all, Charles's religious policies were a source of controversy. Charles was personally inclined toward "high church" practices: an emphasis on ceremony and sacrament reminiscent of Catholic ritual. He also was a believer in Arminianism, a school of thought that justified the emphasis on sacrament and ritual by denying the Calvinist notion that God's grace cannot be earned. These emphases highlighted the authority of clerics instead of lay control over religion. Charles was intent on fashioning an official religion that would better reflect and justify royal claims to power but found himself on a collision course with gentry and aristocrats who leaned toward Puritanism.

Charles's views were supported by William Laud (1573–1645), archbishop of Canterbury from 1633 and thus leader of the Church of England. He tried to impose ritual changes in worship, spread Arminian ideas, and censor opposing views. He also challenged the redistribution of church property, which had occurred in the Reformation of the sixteenth century, and thereby alienated the gentry on economic as well as religious grounds.

Charles's style of rule worsened religious, political, and economic tensions. Cold and intensely private, he was not a man to build confidence or smooth over tensions with charm or dexterous political maneuvering. His court was ruled by formal protocol, and access to the king himself was highly restricted—a serious problem in an age when personal access to the monarch was the guarantee of political power.

Struggle over issues of revenue and religion dominated debate in the Parliament of 1628–1629, which Charles had called, once again, to get funds for his foreign policy. In 1628 the members of Parliament presented the king with a document called the Petition of Right, which protested his financial policies as well as arbitrary imprisonment. (Seventeen of Parliament's members had been imprisoned for refusing loans to the Crown.) Though couched conservatively as a restatement of customary practice, the petition was in fact a bold claim to a tradition of parliamentary participation in the government of the realm. It reflected Parliament's growing determination to check arbitrary royal actions. Charles dissolved the Parliament in March 1629, having decided that the money he might extract was not worth the risk.

For eleven years, Charles ruled without Parliament. When he was forced to call Parliament again, in 1640, not only were royal finances in desperate straits but political tension had risen markedly on many fronts. In the intervening eleven years, Archbishop Laud's religious policies had raised concern and opposition among a wide spectrum of elites, not just radical Puritans, as well as among ordinary citizens of London, where his clerical influence was greatest. Moreover, Charles had pressed collection of revenues far beyond traditional bounds. In 1634, for example, he revived annual collection of "ship money"—a medieval tax levied on coastal districts to help support the navy during war. England, however, was not at war, and the tax was levied not only on seaports but on inland areas, too. Resistance to the collection of various customs duties and taxes grew; some gentry refused outright to pay them.

In addition, Charles also faced a rebellion by his Scottish subjects, which had occasioned his now desperate need for money. Like Philip II in the Netherlands, Charles tried to rule in Scotland through a small council of men who did not represent the local elite. He also tried to force the Scots, most of whom practiced Presbyterianism, to adopt Anglican liturgy and ritual. In 1639, Charles had started a war against them but, lacking men and money, was forced to agree to a peace treaty. Intent on renewing the war, he was forced to summon Parliament to obtain funds.

Thus, in the spring of 1640, Charles faced Parliament further weakened by military failure. His political skills were far too limited for him to reestablish a workable relationship with Parliament under the circumstances; indeed, he compounded his own difficulties. Charles dissolved this body, which is now known as the "Short Parliament," after just three weeks, when members questioned the war with the Scots and other royal policies. More politically risky even than dissolving the Parliament at this juncture was the lack of respect Charles had shown the members: A number of them were harassed or arrested. Mistrust fo-

Criticism of Monopolies Holders of royally granted monopolies were bitterly resented by English consumers and tradespeople alike, as this contemporary print reveals. The greedy beast pictured here controls even ordinary commodities such as pins, soap, and butter. *(Courtesy of the Trustees of the British Museum)*

mented by the eleven years in which Charles had ruled without Parliament thus increased.

Another humiliating and decisive defeat at the hands of the Scots later in 1640 made summoning another Parliament imperative. Members of Parliament could now exploit the king's predicament. This Parliament is known as the "Long Parliament" because it sat from 1640 to 1653. Charles was forced to agree not to dissolve or adjourn Parliament without the members' own consent and to summon Parliament at least every three years. Parliament abolished many of his unorthodox and traditional sources of revenue and impeached and removed from office his leading ministers, including Archbishop Laud. The royal commander deemed responsible for the Scottish fiasco, Thomas Wentworth, earl of Strafford, was executed without trial in May 1641.

The execution of Strafford shocked many aristocrats in the House of Lords as well as some moderate members of the House of Commons. Meanwhile, Parliament began debating the perennially thorny religious question. A bare majority of members favored abolition of Anglican bishops as a first step in thoroughgoing religious reform. Working people in London, kept apprised of the issues by the regular publication of parliamentary debates, demonstrated in support of that majority. Moderate members of Parliament, in contrast, favored checking the king's power but not upsetting the Elizabethan religious compromise.

An event that unified public and parliamentary opinion at a crucial time—a revolt against English rule in Ireland in October 1641—temporarily eclipsed these divisions and once again focused suspicion on the king. The broad consensus of anti-Catholicism once again became the temporary driving force in politics. Few trusted the king with the troops necessary to quash the rebellion, however. It was even widely rumored that Charles would use Irish soldiers against his English subjects. Parliament demanded control of the army to put down the rebellion, and in November the Puritan majority introduced a document known as the "Grand Remonstrance," an appeal to the people and a long catalog of parliamentary grievances against the king. By a narrow margin it was passed, further setting public opinion in London against Charles. The king's remaining support in Parliament eroded in January 1642, when he attempted to arrest five leading members on charges of treason. The five escaped, but the attempt set the stage for wider violence. The king withdrew from London, unsure he could defend himself there, and began to raise an army. In mid-1642 the kingdom stood at the brink of civil war.

THE HOLY ROMAN EMPIRE AND THE THIRTY YEARS' WAR

The Holy Roman Empire enjoyed a period of comparative quiet after the Peace of Augsburg halted religious and political wars in 1555. By the early seventeenth century, however, fresh causes of instability brought about renewed fighting. Especially destabilizing was the drive by the Habsburgs, as emperors and territorial princes, to reverse the successes of Protestantism both in their own lands and in the empire at large and to consolidate their rule in their diverse personal territories.

In the Thirty Years' War (1618–1648), as it is now called, we can see the continuation of conflicts from the sixteenth century—religious tensions, regionalism versus centralizing forces, dynastic and strategic rivalries between rulers. The war was particularly destructive because of the size of the armies, the burden they imposed on civilian populations, and the degree to which army commanders evaded control by the states for which they fought. Some areas of the empire suffered catastrophic losses in population and productive capacity. As a result of the war, the empire was eclipsed as a political unit by the regional powers within it.

Peace Through Diversity, 1555–ca. 1618

Through most of the second half of the sixteenth century, the Holy Roman Empire enjoyed an uneasy peace. The Peace of Augsburg (1555) permitted rulers of the various states to impose either Lutheranism or Catholicism in their lands and, for a time, proved to be a workable enough solution to the problem of religious division. Complicating matters, however, was the rise of Calvinism, for which no provision had been necessary in 1555. A number of rulers adopted this newest religion, but the impact of their choices was felt more directly outside the empire than within it because they chose to support French Huguenots and the Dutch

THE THIRTY YEARS' WAR, 1618–1648

1618	Bohemian revolt against Habsburg rule Defenestration of Prague
1619	Ferdinand II is elected Holy Roman emperor
	Frederick, elector of the Palatinate, is elected king of Bohemia
1620	Catholic victory at Battle of White Mountain
1621	Truce between Spain and the Netherlands expires; war between Spain and the Netherlands begins
1626	Imperial forces defeat armies of Christian IV of Denmark
1629	Peace of Lübeck
1631	Swedes under Gustav Adolf defeat imperial forces at Breitenfeld
	Catholic forces sack Magdeburg
1632	Death of Gustav Adolf
1635	Peace of Prague
1643	French defeat Spanish in the Netherlands
1648	Peace of Westphalia

rebels but not to disturb the peace within the empire. For the most part, there was not a second wave of reforming zeal among the population.

The Habsburgs ruled over a diverse group of territories. Most lay within the boundaries of the empire, but many were not German (Map 15.3). Though largely contiguous, the territories comprised independent duchies and kingdoms, each with its own institutional structure. Habsburg lands included speakers of Italian, German, and Czech, as well as other languages. The non-German lands of Bohemia and Hungary had been distinct kingdoms since the High Middle Ages. Most of Hungary was now under Ottoman domination, but Bohemia, with its rich capital, Prague, was a wealthy center of population and culture in central Europe.

Unlike the Netherlands, these linguistically and culturally diverse lands were still governed by highly decentralized institutions. The Habsburg family often divided rule of the various territories among themselves. For example, during the lifetime of Holy Roman Emperor Charles V, his brother Ferdinand (d. 1564) was more active than he in governing these family lands. At Ferdinand's death, as he wished, rule of the various provinces and kingdoms was split among his three sons. One member of the family was routinely elected Holy Roman emperor.

Moreover, the Habsburgs, unlike most of their contemporaries, made no attempt to impose religious uniformity in this period. Ferdinand was firmly Catholic but tolerant of diverse reform efforts within the church, including clerical marriage and allowing the laity to receive both wine and bread at communion. His son, Emperor Maximilian II (r. 1564–1576), granted limited rights of worship to Protestant subjects within his lands and kept his distance from policies pursued by Catholic rulers elsewhere—most notably, those of his cousin, Philip II, in the Netherlands. During Maximilian's reign, partly because of his positive leadership and partly because of a lack of persecution, a variety of faiths flourished side by side in Habsburg lands. In this tolerant atmosphere, education, printing, and humanistic intellectual life flourished.

But, given the course of events elsewhere in Europe, this late Renaissance was unlikely to last. The balance began to shift under Maximilian's son, Rudolf II (r. 1576–1612). Rudolf shared the religious style of his father and grandfather. He was an energetic patron of the arts and sponsored the work of scientists. Yet he was virtually a recluse at his court, pursuing an eccentric intellectual life, and he did not attend carefully to the routine problems of governing.

In any case, the religious balance began to shift on its own in the second half of the century in the wake of the appearance of resurgent Catholicism. Members of the Jesuit order began to appear in Habsburg lands in the reign of Maximilian. Tough-minded and well trained, they established Catholic schools and became confessors and preachers to the upper classes. Self-confident Catholicism emerged as one form of cultural identity among the German-speaking ruling classes and thus as a religious impetus to further political consolidation of all these Habsburg territories. Ferdinand II (r. 1619–1637) was raised in the atmosphere of reformed Catholicism. He was committed both to tighter rule and to uniformity in matters of relig-

Map 15.3 Territories of the Austrian Habsburgs In addition to the lands constituting modern Austria, Austrian Habsburg lands comprised the Tyrol (modern west Austria and northeast Italy), Carniola (modern Slovenia), part of Croatia, Bohemia (the core of the modern Czech Republic and southern Poland), and Hungary. Most of Hungary had been in Ottoman hands since the Battle of Mohács in 1527.

ion. Like the English under Elizabeth, Habsburg subjects had enjoyed a period of relative peace in political and religious matters. Now, as in England, the stage was set for conflict of both kinds.

The Thirty Years' War, 1618–1648

Both political and religious problems surfaced early in the seventeenth century. In one incident, in 1606, the aggressively Catholic prince of Bavaria seized an imperial free city in north central Germany, in the wake of religious in-fighting there—a city theoretically subject to no one but the emperor himself. Tensions between Catholic and

Protestant states (and among Protestants, for Calvinists and Lutherans were not necessarily allies) were further heightened by a succession crisis. The childless emperor Rudolf II was aging, and factions of the Habsburg family sought allies among the German states to promote their various candidates for the imperial crown.

In 1618 a revolt against Habsburg rule in the kingdom of Bohemia touched off widespread warfare. Bohemia (the core of the modern Czech Republic) was populous and prosperous and had a large Protestant population. Rudolf II had used Prague, its bustling capital, as an imperial capital. Although Catholicism was reclaiming lost ground,

574

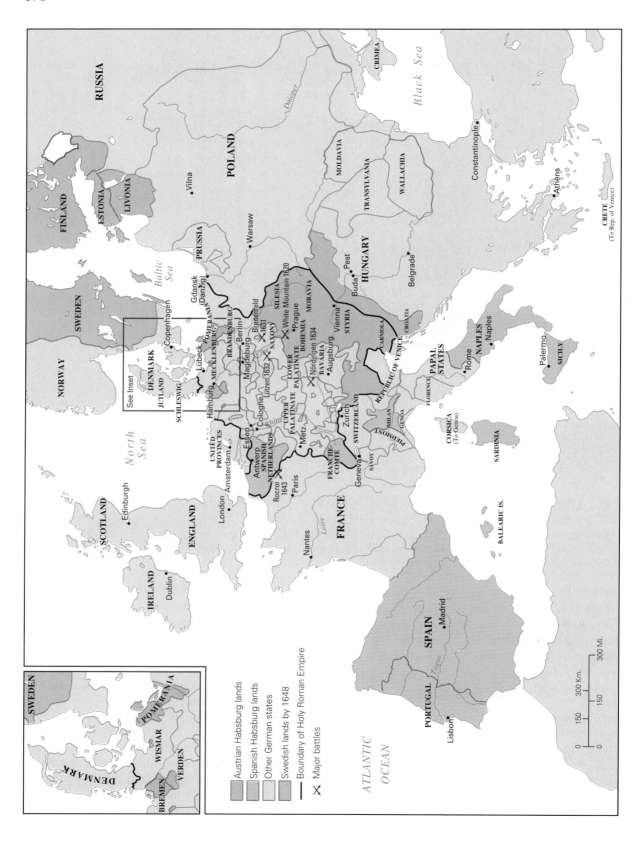

Protestants had been confirmed in their rights to worship in the early seventeenth century both by Rudolf and by his younger brother, Matthias, who hoped to succeed Rudolf as king of Bohemia and as Holy Roman emperor. The crown of Bohemia was bestowed by election, so rival claimants to this wealthy throne needed the acquiescence of the ruling elites, both Protestant and Catholic, of the kingdom.

When Matthias did become king of Bohemia and Holy Roman emperor (r. 1612–1619), he reneged on his promise to the Protestants. The Habsburg succession to the Bohemian throne seemed secure, and concessions to Protestant elites seemed less necessary. As in the Netherlands, there was in Bohemia a delicate balance between regional integrity and Bohemia's expectation of sharing its ruler with other regions. As Philip II had done, Matthias appointed a council of regents that enforced unpopular policies, particularly with regard to religion. The right to build new Protestant churches was denied. Bohemian crown lands were given to the Catholic church.

On May 23, 1618, delegates to a Protestant assembly that had unsuccessfully petitioned Matthias to end these policies marched to the palace in Prague where the hated royal officials met. After a confrontation over their demands, the delegates "tried" the officials on the spot for treason and, literally, threw them out the window of the palace. The incident became known as the Defenestration of Prague (from the Latin, *fenestra*, "window"). (The officials' lives were saved only because they fell into a pile of manure.) The rebels proceeded to set up their own government.

The new Bohemian government deposed Matthias's successor as king, his Catholic cousin, Ferdinand, and elected a new king in 1619. Ferdinand, however, ruled as Holy Roman emperor until 1637. The direct challenge to Habsburg control in Bohemia had implications for the empire as a whole because the new king of Bohemia was a Protestant, Frederick, elector of the Palatinate. Frederick was a Calvinist prince. His territories in

Map 15.4 Europe in the Thirty Years' War The Thirty Years' War was fought largely within the borders of the Holy Roman Empire. It was the result of conflicts within the empire as well as the meddling of neighbors for their own strategic advantage.

west central Germany (called the Lower Palatinate and the Upper Palatinate) carried with them the right to be one of the seven electors who chose the emperor.

Encouraged by these events, Protestant subjects in other Habsburg lands asked for guarantees of freedom of worship like those enjoyed by Protestants in Bohemia. This new Protestant success seemed to threaten the religious balance of power in the empire. Other princes saw their chance to make political gains. Rival claimants to Habsburg rule in Hungary took up arms. The Protestant king of Denmark, Christian IV (r. 1588-1648), who was also duke of Holstein in northern Germany, sought to take advantage of the situation and conquer more German territory.

Foreign powers were also interested in these events. England practiced a pro-Protestant foreign policy, and the English king, James I, was Frederick's father-in-law. Spain's supply routes north from Italy to the Netherlands passed next to Frederick's lands in western Germany. France's first interest was its rivalry with Spain; thus, France kept its eye on the border principalities that were strategically important to Spain. In addition, it was in France's interest, much to the disgust of the devout Catholic faction at the French court, to keep Protestant as well as Catholic rulers in the empire strong enough to thwart Austrian Habsburg ambitions.

The revolt in Bohemia thus triggered a widespread war because it challenged Habsburg control in a direct and undeniable fashion and because other princes felt their interests to be involved. From the outset, the war was not only a conflict over the Habsburgs' power in their own lands but also a conflict over the balance of power in the empire and in Europe (Map 15.4).

By the fall of 1620 a Catholic army was closing in on Bohemia; the army was supported by the duke of Bavaria, who had been offered the Palatinate as a victory prize. On November 8, on a hillside west of Prague, the Catholic force faced a Bohemian army that had not garnered much concrete aid from Protestant allies. The resulting Battle of White Mountain was a complete Catholic victory.

Fighting then became more widespread. The truce between Spain and the Netherlands, established in 1609, expired in 1621, and the nearby Lower Palatinate, now in Catholic hands, offered a staging point for Spanish forces. At this point,

Christian IV, the Protestant king of Denmark, decided to seize more territory, both to give himself greater control over profitable German Baltic seaports and to defend himself against any Catholic attempt to seize northern German territory. Christian received little help from Protestant allies, however; the Dutch were busy with Spain, the English were still wary of continental entanglements, and Denmark's regional rivals, the Swedish, were uninterested in furthering Danish ambitions in the Baltic.

The confusing blend of politics and religion that motivated the Protestant rulers was also evident on the Catholic side. Imperial forces defeated Christian's armies in 1626. Alarmed at the possibility of greater imperial control in northern Germany, Catholic princes led by the duke of Bavaria arranged a truce that led to the Peace of Lübeck in 1629—and to Denmark's withdrawal from the fighting on relatively generous terms.

Christian's rival, Gustav Adolf, king of Sweden (r. 1611–1632), immediately assumed the role of Protestant champion. A brilliant and innovative military leader, Gustav Adolf hoped to gain territory along the Baltic seacoast, but personal aggrandizement also was one of his goals. His campaigns were capped by a victory over an imperial army at Breitenfeld in Saxony in 1631. The tide turned in the favor of imperial forces, however, after Gustav Adolf was killed at the Battle of Lützen in late 1632. A decisive imperial victory over a combined Swedish and German Protestant army, at Nördlingen in 1634, led to a general peace treaty favorable to the Catholics: the Peace of Prague (1635).

The Peace of Prague brought only a temporary peace, however, because French involvement increased, now that other anti-Habsburg forces had been eclipsed. France tried to seize imperial territory along its own eastern border and generously subsidized continued fighting within the empire by channeling monies to Protestant mercenaries there. Fighting dragged on. The Swedes reentered the war, hoping to obtain territory on the northern coast. In the south, rivals to the Habsburgs in Hungary tried to seize territory. By the end of the war, order had disintegrated so completely in the wake of the marauding armies that both staunchly Catholic rulers and firmly Protestant ones made alliances with religious enemies to safeguard their states.

A comprehensive peace treaty did not become possible until France withdrew its sponsorship of continued fighting. There were domestic reasons for France's withdrawal. Louis XIII (r. 1610–1643), the king of France, had died, leaving a minor child to rule and to face the burden of war debt. France wanted only a workable balance of power in the empire; more important to France was the continued rivalry with the Spanish Habsburgs for control of territory along France's eastern and northern borders and in Italy. A defeat by France in the Spanish Netherlands in 1643 had convinced Spain to concentrate on that rivalry too, and fighting between them continued until 1659.

The Effects of the War

The Thirty Years' War caused economic devastation and population decline in many parts of the empire and had long-term political consequences for the empire as a whole. One reason for the war's devastation was a further step in the application of firepower to warfare that increased both the size of armies and their deadly force in battle. This was the use of volley fire, the arrangement of foot soldiers in parallel lines so that one line of men could fire while another reloaded. This tactic, pioneered in the Netherlands around the turn of the century, was further refined by Gustav Adolf of Sweden. Gustav Adolf amassed large numbers of troops and increased the rate of fire so that a virtually continuous barrage was maintained; he also used maneuverable field artillery to protect the massed troops from cavalry charges.

Following Gustav Adolf's lead, armies of all the major states adopted these tactics. Despite these new offensive tactics, defensive tactics—such as holding fortresses—remained important, and pitched battles, such as at Nördlingen in 1634, still tended to be part of sieges. The costs in resources and human life of this kind of warfare reached unheard-of dimensions. Popular printed literature and court drama both condemned the seeming irrationality of the war.

Where fighting had been concentrated, such as in parts of Saxony, between a third and half of the inhabitants of rural villages and major towns may have disappeared. Many starved, were caught in the fighting, or were killed by marauding soldiers. The most notorious atrocity occurred

Gustav Adolf at the Battle of Lützen In this detail of Jan Asselyn's *Charge by the Swedish Cavalry*, the Swedish king (in the plumed hat with raised sword) leads a successful cavalry charge, a tactic he had helped to refine. Leading advancing infantry later in the battle, Gustav Adolf was shot and killed. *(Herzog Anton Ulrich—Museum Braunschweig)*

in the aftermath of the siege of Magdeburg in 1631. After the city surrendered to besieging Catholic forces, long-deprived soldiers ate and drank themselves into a frenzy, raped and killed indiscriminately, and set fires that destroyed the town (killing some of their own ranks in the process). Some victims of war migrated to other regions in search of peaceful conditions and work. Some joined the armies in order to survive. Others formed their own armed bands to fight off the soldiers or to steal back enough goods to live on.

Compounding these effects of war were the actions of armies hired by enterprising mercenary generals for whom loyalty to the princes who paid them took a back seat to personal advancement. They contracted to provide, supply, and lead troops and thus were more willing than the princes would have been to allow troops to live "economically" on plunder. All states and commanders strained to pay and supply their troops, but mercenary armies, and their generals, were especially difficult to control.

A series of treaties known as the Peace of Westphalia (1648) finally ended fighting in the empire. The treaties recognized Calvinism as a tolerated religion within the empire. The requirement that

all subjects must follow their rulers' faith was retained, but some leeway was allowed for those who now found themselves under new rulers. The property of those who decided to move elsewhere for religious reasons was protected. In its recognition of religious plurality, the Peace of Westphalia effectively put an end to religious war in the empire. The rights of states, however, were still enforced over the desires of individuals.

In political matters, the treaties reflected some of the recent successes of the Swedish by granting them Baltic coast territory. France gained the important towns of Metz, Toul, and Verdun on its eastern border. Most of the major Catholic and Protestant rulers in the empire, such as the dukes of Bavaria and Saxony, extended their territories at the expense of smaller principalities and cities. The son of Frederick, king of Bohemia, was given the smaller of the two Palatine territories that his father had held. The Upper Palatinate—as well as the right to be a new elector of the emperor—was given to the powerful duke of Bavaria.

The most important political outcomes of the war were not explicitly mentioned in the peace treaties because no one needed to have them spelled out. One outcome was that the states within the empire would henceforth be virtually autonomous. From this point forward, each major state of the empire would conduct its own foreign policy; the Holy Roman Empire was no longer a meaningful political entity. Another outcome was that the Habsburgs, though weakened as emperors, were strengthened as rulers of their own hereditary lands on the eastern fringes of the empire. They moved their capital from Prague to Vienna, and the government of Habsburg lands gained in importance as administration of the empire waned.

SOCIETY AND CULTURE

Both imaginative literature and speculative writing, such as political theory, bear the stamp of their times. In the late sixteenth and early seventeenth centuries, political speculation often concerned questions of the legitimacy of rulers and of the relationship of political power to divine authority—urgent problems in an age when religious division threatened the very foundations of political order. The form as well as the content of thought reflected its context. Authors and rulers alike often relied on still-prevalent oral modes of communication. Indeed, some of the greatest literature of the period and some of the most effective political statements were presented as drama and not conveyed in print. Nevertheless, literacy continued to spread and led to greater opportunities for knowledge and reflection. The medium of print became increasingly important to political life. In the visual arts, the dramatic impulse was wedded to religious purposes to create works that conveyed both power and emotion.

Literacy and Literature

Traditional oral culture changed slowly under the impact of the spread of printing, education, and literacy. (See the feature, "Weighing the Evidence: Signatures," on pages 586–587.) Works of literature from the late sixteenth and early seventeenth century incorporate material from traditional folktales, consciously reflecting the coexistence of oral and literature culture. In *Don Quixote*, by Spain's Miguel de Cervantes (1547–1616), the title character and his companion, Sancho Panza, have a long discussion about the subject. The squire Panza

speaks in the style that was customary in oral culture—a rather roundabout and repetitive style, by our standards, that enabled the speaker and listener to remember what was said. Much of the richness of *Don Quixote* is due to the interweaving of prose styles and topical concerns from throughout Cervantes' culture—from the oral world of peasants to the refined world of court life. The detachment that enabled Cervantes to accomplish this rich portrayal came about from highly developed literacy and the awareness of language that literacy made possible.

The spread of education and literacy in the late sixteenth century had a dramatic impact on attitudes toward literature and on literature itself. The value of education—particularly of the continuing humanist recovery of ancient wisdom—was reflected in much literature of the period. Writers found in humanistic education a vision of what it meant to be cultivated and disciplined men of the world. This vision provided the beginnings of a new self-image for members of the warrior class.

Certain elite women who were able to secure a humanistic education were moved to reflect on their own situation in society. The French poet Louise Labé (1526–1566), writing in 1555, described the benefits of education for women but exaggerated its availability:

Since the time has come . . . when the severe laws of men no longer prevent women from applying themselves to the sciences and other disciplines, it seems to me that those of us who can should use this long-craved freedom to study and let men see how greatly they wronged us when depriving us of its honor and advantages. . . . Apart from the good name our sex will acquire thereby, we shall have caused men to devote more time and effort in the public good to virtuous studies.[3]

It is customary to regard the French author Michel de Montaigne (1533–1592) as the epitome of the reflective and—most important—*self*-reflective gentleman. Montaigne had trained for the law and became a judge in the Parlement of Bordeaux; he resigned from the court in 1570, however, and retired to his small chateau, where he wrote his *Essais* (from which we derive the word *essays*), a collection of short reflections that were revolutionary in both form and content. Montaigne invented writing in the form of a sketch, a "try" (the literal meaning of *essai*), which enabled him to combine self-reflection with formal analysis.

∼ ENCOUNTERS WITH THE WEST ∼

Montaigne Discusses Barbarity in the New World and the Old

In one of his most famous essays, Michel de Montaigne ironically compares the customs of Native Americans, about whom he has heard, with the customs of his own society.

They have their wars with [other] nations, to which they go quite naked, with no other arms than bows or wooden spears. . . . It is astonishing that firmness they show in their combats, which never end but in slaughter and bloodshed; for, as to routs and terror, they know nothing of either.

Each man brings back as his trophy the head of the enemy he has killed. . . . After they have treated their prisoners well for a long time with all the hospitality they can think of . . . they kill him with their swords. This done, they roast him and eat him in common and send some pieces to their absent friends.

I am not sorry that we notice the barbarous horror of such acts, but am heartily sorry that . . . we should be so blind to our own. I think there is more barbarity . . . in tearing by tortures and the rack a body still full of feeling, in roasting a man bit by bit, having him bitten and mangled by dogs (as we have not only read but seen within fresh memory . . . among neighbors and fellow citizens, and what is worse, on the pretext of piety and religion).

Three of these men (were brought to France) . . . and [someone] wanted to know what they had found most amazing. . . . They said that in the first place they thought it very strange that so many grown men, bearded, strong and armed who were around the king . . . should submit to obey a child. . . . Second (they have a way in their language of speaking of men as halves of one another), they had noticed that there were among us men full and gorged with all sorts of good things, and that their other halves were beggars at their doors, emaciated with hunger and poverty; and they thought it strange that these needy halves could endure such injustice.

Source: Donald M. Frame, trans., *The Complete Essays of Montaigne* (Stanford, Calif.: Stanford University Press, 1948), pp. 153, 155–159.

Montaigne's reflections ranged from the destructiveness of the French civil wars to the consequences of European exploration of the New World. Toward all of these events and circumstances, Montaigne was able to achieve an analytic detachment remarkable for his day. For example, he noted an irony in Europeans labeling New World peoples "savage," given Europeans' seemingly endless and wanton violence against those "savages" and against each other. (See the box, "Encounters with the West: Montaigne Discusses Barbarity in the New World and the Old.") He deflated pretensions to superiority in his own class of Frenchmen by noting "however high the chair, one is still sitting on one's own behind."

Montaigne's greatest achievement was the deep exploration of his own private moral and intellectual life, detached from any vocation or social role (though not detached, of course, from the leisure that his status made possible). Owing to the spread of printing and literacy, Montaigne had—in addition to his own effort and the resources of leisure—a virtually unparalleled opportunity to reflect on the world through reading the wide variety of printed texts available to him. For the first time, it was possible for the leisured lay reader to juxtapose different events, values, and cultures. Montaigne's writings thus reflect a distancing from his own society and a tolerance of others.

His essays also reveal a distancing from himself, and this distancing is another result of literacy—not simply the ability to read and write but the ability to put literacy to use so that one might enjoy long periods of solitude and reflection in the company of other solitary voices contained in books. Montaigne's works mark the beginning of what we know as the "invention" of private life, in which an individual is known more by internal character and personality traits than by social role and past behavior.

Dramatists, poets, and prose writers like Montaigne generally ask profound and in some ways timeless questions about the meaning of human experience; however, the kinds of questions thought important change as society changes. The works of the great English poet and playwright William Shakespeare (1564–1616) are still compelling to us because of the profundity of the questions he asked about love, honor, and political legitimacy, but he asked these questions in terms appropriate to his own day. One of his favorite themes—evident in *Hamlet* and *Macbeth*—is the legitimacy of rulers. He was at his most skilled, perhaps, when exploring the contradictions in values between the growing commercial world he saw around him and the older, seemingly more stable world of feudal society. Subtle political commentary distinguishes Shakespeare's later plays, written near and shortly after the death of Queen Elizabeth in 1603, when political and economic problems were becoming increasingly visible. Shakespeare explored not only the duties of rulers but also the rights of their subjects. In *Coriolanus,* he portrays commoners as poor but as neither ignorant nor wretched; they are in fact fully rational and capable of analyzing their situation—perhaps more capable, Shakespeare hints, than their ruler is. The play is safely set in ancient Rome, but the social and political tensions it depicts clearly referred to the Elizabethan present.

Shakespeare, Cervantes, and other writers of their day were also representatives of what were starting to be self-consciously distinct national literatures. The spread of humanism added a historical dimension to their awareness of their own languages and to their subject matter: their own society and its past. This kind of self-consciousness is evident in Shakespeare's play *Richard II.* The playwright depicts the kingdom of England, which King Richard is destroying, in terms that reflect the Elizabethan sense of England as a separate and self-contained nation:

This royal throne of kings, this sceptred isle,
This earth of majesty, this seat of Mars,
This other Eden, demi-paradise,
This fortress built by Nature for herself
Against infection and the hand of war,
This happy breed of men, this little world,
This precious stone set in the silver sea,
Which serves it in the office of a wall,
Or as [a] moat defensive to a house,
Against the envy of less happier lands;
This blessed plot, this earth, this realm, this England . . .
(*Richard II,* act 2, sc. 1, lines 40–50)[4]

The Great Age of Theater

Shakespeare's career was possible because his life coincided with the rise of professional theater. In the capitals of both England and Spain, professional theaters first opened in the 1570s. Some drama was produced at court or in aristocratic households, but most public theaters drew large and very mixed audiences, including the poorest city dwellers. Playwrights, including Shakespeare, often wrote in teams under great pressure to keep acting companies supplied with material. The best-known dramatist in Spain in this period, Lope de Vega (1562–1635), wrote more than fifteen hundred works with a wide range of topics. Although religious themes remained popular in Spanish theater, as an echo of medieval drama, most plays in England and Spain treated secular subjects and, as in *Coriolanus,* safely disguised political commentary.

Over time, theater became increasingly restricted to aristocratic circles. In England, Puritan criticism of the "immorality" of public performance drove actors and playwrights to seek royal patronage. The first professional theater to open in Paris, in 1629, as political and religious turmoil quieted, quickly became dependent on Cardinal Richelieu's patronage. Inevitably, as court patronage grew in importance, the wide range of subject matter treated in plays began to narrow to those of aristocratic concern, such as family honor and martial glory. These themes were depicted in the work of the Spaniard Pedro Calderón (1600–1681), who wrote for his enthusiastic patron, Philip IV, and in that of the Frenchman Pierre Corneille (1606–1684), whose great tragedy of aristocratic life, *Le Cid*, was one of the early successes of the seventeenth-century French theater.

That drama was one of the most important art forms of the late sixteenth and early seventeenth centuries is reflected in its impact on the development of music: The opera, which weds drama to music, was invented in Italy in the early seventeenth century. The first great work in this genre is generally acknowledged to be *Orfeo* (*Orpheus,* 1607) by Claudio Monteverdi (1567–1643). Opera, like drama, reflected the influence of humanism in its secular themes as well as a desire more precisely to emulate Greek drama, which had used both words and music. The practice of music itself changed under the dramatic impulse. Monteverdi was the first master of a new musical style known as monody, which emphasized the progression of chords. Monodic music was inherently dramatic, creating a sense of forward movement, expectation, and resolution.

Sovereignty in Ceremony, Image, and Word

Whether produced formally on a stage or in some less structured setting, drama was a favored method of communication in this era because people responded to and made extensive use of oral communication. Dramatic gesture and storytelling to get a message across were commonplace and were important components of politics.

What we might call "street drama" was an ordinary occurrence: When great noble governors entered major towns, such as when Margaret of Parma entered Brussels, a solemn yet ostentatious formal "entry" was often staged. The dignitary would ride into the town through its main gate, usually beneath a canopy made of luxurious cloth. The event might include staged tableaux in the town's streets, with costumed townspeople acting in brief symbolic dramas such as David and Goliath, and it might end in an elaborate banquet. A remnant of these proceedings survives today in the ceremony by which distinguished visitors are given "the keys to the city," which, in the sixteenth century, really were useful.

Royalty made deliberate and careful use of dramatic ceremony. Royal entries into towns took on an added weight, as did royal funerals and other occasions. These dramas reinforced political and constitutional assumptions in the minds of witnesses and participants. Thus, over time, we can see changes in the representations of royal power. In France, for example, the ritual entry of the king into Paris had originally stressed the participation of elites such as the leading guilds, judges, and administrators and had symbolized their active part in governing the city and the kingdom. But in the last half of the sixteenth century, the procession began to glorify the king alone.

The very fact that rulers experimented self-consciously with self-representation suggests that issues pertaining to the nature and extent of royal power were profoundly important and far from settled. Queen Elizabeth had the particular burden of assuming the throne in a period of great instability. Hence, she paid a great deal of attention to the image of herself that she fashioned in words and authorized to be fashioned in painting. Elizabeth styled herself variously as mother to her people and as a warrior-queen (drawing on ancient myths of Amazon women). She made artful use of the image of her virginity to buttress each of these images—as the wholly devoted, self-sacrificing mother (which, of course, had religious tradition behind it) or as an androgynous ruler, woman but doing the bodily work of man. (See the box, "Elizabeth I Addresses Her Troops.")

More formal speculation about constitutional matters also resulted from the tumult of the sixteenth and seventeenth centuries. The civil wars in France provided the impetus for energetic reconsideration of the principles and theories underlying royal government. The Huguenot party advanced an elaborate argument for the limitation of royal power, particularly after the Saint Bartholomew's Day Massacre. The best-known Huguenot tract (probably authored by the well-educated nobleman Philippe Duplessis-Mornay), *Defense of Liberty Against Tyrants* (1579), advanced the notion of a contract between the king and the people. Under the terms of this contract, obedience to the king was conditional, dependent on his acting for the common good—above all, maintaining and protecting God's true church.

Alternative theories enhancing royal authority were offered, principally in support of the Catholic position though also simply to buttress the beleaguered monarchy itself. The most famous of these appeared in *The Six Books of the Republic* (1576), by the legal scholar Jean Bodin (1530–1596). Bodin was a Catholic but offered a fundamentally secular perspective on the purposes and source of power

Elizabeth I Addresses Her Troops

The day after English ships dispersed the Spanish Armada in 1588, Elizabeth addressed a contingent of her troops. She used the opportunity to fashion an image of herself as a warrior above all but also as the beloved familiar of her people, unafraid of potential plots against her.

My loving people, we have been persuaded by some that are careful of our safety, to take heed how we commit ourselves to armed multitudes, for fear of treachery. But I assure you, I do not desire to live to distrust my faithful and loving people. Let tyrants fear. I have always so behaved myself that, under God, I have placed my chiefest strength in the loyal hearts and good will of my subjects; and therefore I am come amongst you, as you see, at this time, not for my reaction or disport, but being resolved, in the midst and heat of the battle, to live or die amongst you all, to lay down for my God, and for my kingdom, and for my people, my honor and my blood, even in the dust. I know I have the body of a weak and feeble woman, but I have the heart and the stomach of a king, and of a king of England too, and think foul scorn that Parma or Spain, or any prince of Europe should dare to invade the borders of my realm; to which, rather than any dishonor shall grow by me, I myself will take up arms, I myself will be your general, judge, and rewarder of every one of your virtues in the field.

Source: J. E. Neale, *Queen Elizabeth I* (New York: Anchor, 1957), pp. 308–309.

within a state. His special contribution was a vision of a truly sovereign monarch. Bodin offered theoretical understanding that is essential to states today and is the ground on which people can claim rights and protection from the state—namely, that there is a final sovereign authority. For Bodin that authority was the king. He recognized that in practice there were limitations to royal power, but it was the theoretical grounding for royal authority that interested Bodin.

French contract theory legitimized resistance to the Catholic monarchy but had to be abandoned when Henry IV granted toleration in 1598. In England, theoretical justification of resistance to Charles I was initially limited to invoking tradition and precedent; contract theory as well as other sweeping claims regarding subjects' rights would be more fully developed later in the century.

Bodin's theory of sovereignty, however, was immediately echoed in other theoretical works, most notably that of Hugo Grotius (1583–1645). A Dutch jurist and diplomat, Grotius developed the first principles of modern international law. He accepted the existence of sovereign states who owed no loyalty to higher authority (such as the papacy) and thus needed new principles to govern their interactions. His major work, *De Jure Belli ac Pacis (On the Law of War and Peace)* (1625), was written in response to the turmoil of the Thirty Years' War. Grotius argued that relations between states could be based on respect for treaties voluntarily reached between them. In perhaps his boldest move he argued that war must be justified and developed criteria to distinguish just wars.

Baroque Art and Architecture

Speculation about and celebration of power, as well as of dramatic emotion, also occurred in the visual arts—most notably in painting and architecture, in the style now known as "baroque." The word *baroque* comes from the Portuguese *barroco*, used to describe irregularly shaped pearls; the term as applied to the arts was initially derogatory, describing illogic and irregularity. Baroque architecture modified the precision, symmetry, and orderliness of Renaissance architecture to produce a sense of greater dynamism in space. Façades and

interiors were both massive and, through clever use of architectural and decorative components, suggestive of movement. Hence baroque churches, for example, were impressively grand and emotionally engaging at the same time. Baroque techniques were pioneered in Italy, first in church design, in the late sixteenth century and spread slowly, with many regional variations, especially throughout Catholic Europe, during the seventeenth century.

One of the primary purposes of baroque architecture and painting was to encourage piety that was emotionally involved but also capable of inspiring awe. Italian baroque painting made use of the realism developed in Renaissance art but added dynamism and emotional energy—such as by painting throngs of people or by using light to create direction and energy in the scene portrayed. Dramatic illusion was also a common device, such as painting a chapel ceiling with receding figures apparently ascending to heaven.

The most influential baroque painter in northern Europe was Peter Paul Rubens (1577–1640), a native of Flanders in the southern Netherlands.

His early career in Italy, from 1600 to 1608, was profoundly important both in shaping him as an artist and in establishing his secondary career as a diplomat, trusted by his princely patrons. Throughout his life, he undertook diplomatic missions, on behalf of the viceroys in the Spanish Netherlands, to Spain, France, and England, where he also gained artistic commissions. He simultaneously maintained a large studio in Antwerp where he could train students. Rubens's subject matter varied widely. It included church design and decoration as well as portraiture and landscapes. His technique was distinguished by the brilliant use of color and by the dynamic energy of his figures, often executed on a very large scale.

SUMMARY

The late sixteenth and early seventeenth centuries were an era of intense struggle over political and religious authority. Rulers everywhere, through a variety of expedients, tried to buttress and expand royal power. They were resisted by traditional centers of power, such as independent-minded nobles. But they were also resisted by the novel challenge of religious dissent, which empowered subjects both to claim a greater right to question authority and to risk more in their attempts to oppose it. In some areas of Europe, such as the Holy Roman Empire, the struggles reached some resolution. In other areas, such as England, decades of bloody conflict still lay ahead.

On the whole, these conflicts did not result in victories for ordinary people, since for the most part it was victorious elites who decided matters of religion and governance in their own interests. In addition, the difficult economic circumstances of these decades meant that working people, desperate for a secure livelihood, rioted or took up arms out of economic as well as religious concern.

Yet however grim the circumstances people faced, the technology of print and the spread of literacy helped spur speculative and creative works by providing the means for reflection and the audiences to receive it. Ironically, the increased importance of court life, although a cause of political strain, was also a source of patronage for art, literature, and drama. Some of the works we still value, such as Rubens's paintings, portray the splendor and power of court life. Other works, such as Shakespeare's plays, both reflect and re-

flect on the tensions and contradictions in the society of the day: for example, the importance of the stability provided by royal authority and the dignity and wisdom of ordinary people, who had no claim to power at all.

NOTES

1. Quoted in A. W. Lovett, *Early Habsburg Spain, 1517–1598* (Oxford, England: Oxford University Press, 1986), p. 212.
2. Quoted in R. J. Knecht, *The French Wars of Religion, 1559–1598* (London: Longman, 1989), p. 109.
3. Quoted in Ann Rosalind Jones, "City Women and Their Audiences: Louise Labé and Veronica Franco," in Margaret W. Ferguson et al., *Rewriting the Renaissance: The Discourses of Sexual Difference in Early Modern Europe* (Chicago: University of Chicago Press, 1986), p. 307.
4. From *The Riverside Shakespeare*, 2d ed. (Boston: Houghton Mifflin, 1997), p. 855.

SUGGESTED READING

General Surveys

Bonney, Richard. *The European Dynastic States, 1494–1660.* 1991. A recent, rich survey of the period. Good on eastern as well as western Europe but written from an English point of view; thus, it does not consider England as part of Europe.

Elliott, J. H. *Europe Divided, 1559–1598.* 1968. An older but still reliable and readable survey by a leading scholar of Spanish history.

Hale, J. R. *War and Society in Renaissance Europe.* 1985. An analysis of war as a function of government and as a part of social, economic, and intellectual life through the sixteenth century.

Parker, Geoffrey. *The Military Revolution.* 1988; and Black, Jeremy. *A Military Revolution?* 1991. Two works that disagree about the nature and extent of the changes in military practices and their significance for military, political, and social history. Black tries to refute claims for a dramatic military "revolution."

Society and Economy

Braudel, Fernand. *The Perspective of the World.* Vol. 3, *Civilization and Capitalism, 15th to 18th Century.* Translated by S. Reynolds. 1984. A particularly useful volume by this celebrated author of economic history concerning overall patterns in the European and international economies.

Gutman, Myron P. *Toward the Modern Economy.* 1988. An account of the development of cloth production and the decline of guild manufacture through the early modern period.

Huppert, George. *After the Black Death: A Social History of Early Modern Europe.* 1986. A survey of developments in social and economic history throughout Europe from the fifteenth through the seventeenth centuries. A brief but very usable bibliography will guide further reading.

Jütte, Robert. *Poverty and Deviance in Early Modern Europe.* 1994. Discusses poverty, poor relief, and peasant rebellion.

Klaits, Joseph. *Servants of Satan.* 1985.

Levack, Brian P. *The Witch-Hunt in Early Modern Europe.* 1987. Two surveys of witch-hunting in the sixteenth and seventeenth centuries. Levack synthesizes the work of various historians with particular care; Klaits's work is more interpretive.

Wiesner, Merry. *Women and Gender in Early Modern Europe.* 1993. Discusses all aspects of women's experience, including their working lives.

Spain and the Dutch

Elliott, J. H. *Imperial Spain, 1469–1716.* 1963.

Lynch, John. *Spain, 1516–1598: From Nation-State to World Empire.* 1991. Two excellent surveys.

Parker, Geoffrey. *The Army of Flanders and the Spanish Road.* 1972. A detailed study of Spanish innovations in supplying its armies during the Netherlands' revolt.

———. *The Dutch Revolt.* 2d ed. 1985. The best survey of the revolt available in English.

Wedgewood, C. V. *William the Silent.* 1968. A sympathetic biography of the aristocratic leader of the Dutch revolt, which portrays him as a man ahead of his time in his acceptance of religious diversity. Useful for capturing the flavor of the period, though not for its interpretation.

France and England

Bercé, Yves-Marie. *The Birth of Absolutism: A History of France, 1598–1661.* 1992. A readable recent interpretation of the foundations of absolutism in France.

Diefendorf, Barbara. *Beneath the Cross: Catholics and Huguenots in Sixteenth-Century Paris.* 1991. Traces the intersection of political and religious conflict in the French capital during the religious wars. Excellent bibliography.

Hirst, Derek. *Authority and Conflict: England, 1603–1658.* 1986. A thorough study of political and social conditions in England.

Holt, Mack P. *The French Wars of Religion, 1562–1629.* 1995. An up-to-date synthesis that evaluates social and political context while not slighting the importance of religion.

Mattingly, Garrett. *The Armada.* 1959. A well-crafted and gripping narrative of the sailing of the Armada and all the interrelated events in France, the Netherlands, England, and Spain, told from a decidedly English perspective.

Smith, A. G. R. *The Emergence of a Nation-State: The Commonwealth of England, 1529–1660.* 1984. A good place to start through the immense bibliography on the Elizabethan period.

The Thirty Years' War and Its Aftermath

Evans, R. J. W. *The Making of the Hapsburg Monarchy.* 1979. A thorough survey of the rise of the Austrian Habsburg state from the breakup of Charles V's empire, emphasizing the importance of the ideology and institutions of Catholicism in shaping the identity and guaranteeing the coherence of the Habsburg state.

Parker, Geoffrey. *The Thirty Years' War.* 2d ed. 1987. A readable general history by one of the best-known military historians.

Literacy, Literature, and Political Theory

Church, William F. *Constitutional Thought in Sixteenth-Century France.* 1969. A survey of sixteenth-century political theory in France.

Eagleton, Terry. *William Shakespeare.* 1986. A brief and highly readable interpretation of Shakespeare that emphasizes the tensions in the plays caused by language and by ideas from the new world of bourgeois, commercial life.

Giesey, Ralph E. *The Royal Funeral Ceremony in Renaissance France.* 1960. One of the earliest studies of royal ceremony in the period.

Greenblatt, Stephen. *Renaissance Self-Fashioning.* 1979. An interpretation of sixteenth-century literature and culture that emphasizes the "invention" of interior self-reflection and self-awareness.

Houston, R. A. *Literacy in Early Modern Europe.* 1988. A general introduction to the issues of the spread of education and the impact of literacy in Europe.

Kamen, Henry. *The Rise of Toleration.* 1967. This older and rather optimistic study chronicles the slow emergence of secularism and toleration during and after the Reformation.

Kelley, Donald R. *The Beginnings of Ideology: Consciousness and Society in the French Reformation.* 1981. A study of political thought, including but not limited to formal theory, as inspired by the experience of the wars of religion.

Ong, Walter J. *Orality and Literacy: The Technologizing of the Word.* 1982. A synthesis of scholarship that concentrates on the psychological and cultural impact of literacy.

Patterson, Annabel. *Shakespeare and the Popular Voice.* 1989. An interpretation of Shakespeare's work that emphasizes his connection to the complex political and social milieu of his day.

Regosin, J. *The Matter of My Book: Montaigne's "Essais" as the Book of the Self.* 1977. One of the leading scholarly treatments of Montaigne's work.

Weighing the Evidence

SIGNATURES

Right now you are staring at words printed on the page of a book. We are so dependent on written communication that we cannot imagine functioning without these symbols. The often-heard warning "Don't believe everything you read" reflects our habit of trusting written information. But what might it be like if words were only fleeting events—spoken and heard in moments of personal interaction—and not things, objects gazed at in silence, easily saved and retrieved?

Let us consider what evidence we have about the spread of literacy in the sixteenth century. Historians have gained a rough idea about what portion of the population was literate in the sixteenth century by counting the signatures on representative samples of legal documents such as wills and marriage contracts. The ability to sign one's name is a fairly reliable indication of literacy in the sixteenth century because then, unlike today, writing was taught in schools only *after* reading was already mastered. For this reason, however, the *lack* of a signature may mask considerable reading ability, for no special significance was attached to learning to write one's name. Sixteenth-century documents are filled with signatures like those reproduced here: the scissors, for a tailor; the arrow, for a fletcher (arrow-maker). Both of the men who made these marks may well have been able to read.

Where documentation is dense, such as in towns, and where the evidence of signatures has been collected, we have profiles of the literacy rates of selected communities. Literacy rates varied widely according to the location of a particular community (remote ones had fewer literate inhabitants) and its economy (certain trades favored literacy; poverty generally worked against it). Overall, men were more literate than women, and western and northern Europeans were more literate than southern and eastern Europeans. In prosperous regions of western Europe, where literacy rates were highest, there was nearly 100 percent literacy, as one might predict, among bureaucrats, officials, and well-to-do townsmen. Among artisans, the rate neared 50 percent. Among peasants, it could be 10 percent or lower.

If we suppose these figures to be accurate, what can we conclude about the impact of literacy on people's lives? Our own reliance on literacy once led us to assume that people in the past would naturally use these skills if they knew how and that literate knowledge—gleaned from books—would quickly replace folk traditions and knowledge communicated orally. But the "signatures" of the tailor, the fletcher, and thousands of others imply that many Europeans lived with partial literacy. And we now realize that the spread of literacy only slowly changed Europeans' reliance on oral communication. Reading and writing supplemented but initially did not replace traditional ways of learning and communicating.

Aristocrats, for example, usually learned to read and write and occasionally were highly educated. But they learned their most valued skills, such as estate management and military expertise, from their older peers, rather as artisan children learned their skills through apprenticeship. Nobles kept copious written records about their landed property but often relied on memory instead of documents to settle disputes. At all levels of society, most reading was done in a group. It was integrated into the common entertainment of storytelling, illustrated in the drawing reproduced here. An evening's storytelling in a household or tavern might include reading aloud but was not fundamentally changed by the inclusion of reading.

Signatures from English Court Depositions (*Adapted from David Cressy,* Literacy and the Social Order *[Cambridge, England: Cambridge University Press, 1980], p. 60.*)

Tailor   Fletcher

Joseph Anton Koch: Shepherds Around the Fire (*Staatliche Kunstsammlungen Dresden/Kupferstich-Kabinett*)

There is evidence that people who could read still trusted written material less than, or at least no more than, spoken information. A literate peasant would consult a farmer's almanac, but more for entertainment than for information. His first-hand knowledge of the local climate, crops, and animal husbandry seemed more reliable to him—and was likely to be more reliable—than any text that a distant publisher might provide. Nobles frequently wrote brief letters to each other in which they said little other than "Please trust X, the bearer of this letter." The real message was imparted orally. It was face-to-face communication, built on a personal relationship, that was trusted.

Some of the most dramatic evidence of the persistence of oral culture is in the use of language that is preserved in informal documents such as long letters or the relatively rare memoir. Most people still relied on the repetitive phrasing that is common when language is wholly oral. Thus, even when they wrote words down, they were "thinking" without literacy.

Although we have learned that evidence of literacy does not mean that sixteenth-century people relied on reading and writing the way we do, we are just beginning to understand what their limited reliance on it really meant for their lives and their society. Access to literacy and the use of documents were tools of power and control. Our tailor might be at a disadvantage in a transaction if he could not read the document he signed. But unlike us, he did not need documents to establish his identity. And with virtually none of his past recorded in writing, he and other sixteenth-century people were free in ways that we are not.

Consider also the tenacity of oral communication. Let us set aside our assumption that written information is superior and try to imagine how powerful oral communication can be. Look carefully at the evidence supplied in the drawing of shepherds gathered around a fire. It dates from the late eighteenth century, when literacy was increasingly widespread and when the persistent oral culture of lower-class people was beginning to be derided in the way that illiteracy is derided today. The cultural gap between literate and illiterate is reflected here in the somewhat derisive representations of the subjects: They are made to seem uncouth. Yet still captured is something of the power of speech and of hearing. Words are events here, and speaker and listeners are active in their parts. The speaker gestures while his companions lean forward attentively to hear and perhaps to argue with him.

In an oral culture, information always is accompanied by sensory input: the sights, smells, and sounds of the person conveying it. And you always know your source. Is it any wonder that common people resisted the "authority" of book learning? ✢

CHAPTER 16

Europe in the Age of Louis XIV, ca. 1610–1715

Toward the end of his reign, the subjects of Louis XIV of France began to grumble that he had lived too long. In fact, he outlived his own son and grandson and was followed on the throne by a great-grandson when he died in 1715. In his prime, Louis symbolized the success of royal power in surmounting the challenges of warrior-nobles, in suppressing religious dissent, in tapping the wealth of the nation's population, and in waging war. A period of cultural brilliance early in his reign and the spectacle of an elaborate court life crowned his achievements. By the end of his reign, however, France was struggling under economic distress brought on by the many wars fought for his glory. Although Louis outlived his welcome, he was then, and is for us now, a symbol of the age that ended with his death.

In England, by contrast, the Crown was not as successful in overcoming political and religious challenges to its authority. Resistance to the king, led by Parliament, resulted in a revolutionary overturning of royal authority that was temporary but had long-term consequences. In central and eastern Europe, a period of state building in the aftermath of the Thirty Years' War led to the dominance in the region of Austria, Brandenburg-Prussia, and Russia. The power of these states derived, in part, from the economic relationship of their lands to the wider European economy.

The seventeenth century also witnessed a dynamic phase of European overseas expansion, following on the successes of the Portuguese and the Spanish in the fifteenth and sixteenth centuries. Eager migrants settled in the Americas in ever increasing numbers, while forced migrants—enslaved Africans—were transported by the thousands to work on the

The king in martial glory: Louis XIV in Roman armor, by the contemporary painter Charles Le Brun.

profitable plantations of European colonizers. Aristocrats, merchants, and peasants back in Europe jockeyed to take advantage of—or to mitigate the effects of—the local political and economic impact of Europe's expansion.

FRANCE IN THE AGE OF ABSOLUTISM

Absolutism describes the extraordinary concentration of power in royal hands achieved by the kings of France, most notably Louis XIV (r. 1643–1715), in the seventeenth century. Louis continued the expansion of state power begun by his father's minister, Cardinal Richelieu (see page 565). The extension of royal power, under Louis as well as his predecessor, was accelerated by the desire to sustain an expensive and aggressive foreign policy. The policy itself was a traditional one: fighting the familiar Habsburg enemy and seeking military glory more generally. Louis XIV's successes in these undertakings made him both envied and emulated by other rulers; the French court became a model of culture and refinement. But increased royal authority was not accepted without protest either by common French people or by elites.

The Last Challenge to Absolutism

Louis came to the throne as a 5-year-old child in 1643. Acting as his regent, his mother, Anne of Austria (1601–1666), had to defuse a serious challenge to royal authority during her son's minority. Together with her chief minister and personal friend, Cardinal Jules Mazarin (1602–1666), she faced opposition from royal bureaucrats and the traditional nobility as well as the common people.

Revolts against the concentration of power in royal hands and against high taxation that had prevailed under Louis's father began immediately. In one province, a group of armed peasants cornered the intendant and forced him to agree to lower taxes; elsewhere, provincial parlements tried to abolish special ranks of officials created by Richelieu. In 1648, after several more years of foreign war and of financial expedients to sustain it, the most serious revolt began, led by the Parlement and the other sovereign law courts in Paris. The source of the Parlement's leverage over the monarchy was its traditional right to register laws

and edicts, which amounted to a right of judicial review. Now, the Parlement, as the legitimate guardian of royal authority, attempted to extend this power by debating and even initiating government policy: The courts sitting together drew up a reform program abolishing most of the machinery of government established under Richelieu and calling for consent to future taxation. The citizens of Paris rose to defend the courts when royal troops were sent against them in October. In the countryside, the machinery of government, particularly tax collection, virtually ceased to function.

Mazarin was forced to accept the proposed reform of government, at least in theory. He also had to avert challenges by great nobles for control of the young king's council. Civil war waxed and waned around France from 1648 until 1653. The main combatants were conventionally ambitious great nobles, but reform-minded urban dwellers often had to make common cause with them, to benefit from their military power. Meanwhile, middling nobles in the region around Paris began to meet on their own to plan a thoroughgoing reform program and to prepare for a meeting of the Estates General to enact it.

These revolts, begun in 1648, were derided with the name "Fronde," which was a children's game of the time. However, the Fronde was a serious challenge to the legacy of royal government as it had developed under Richelieu. It ended without a noteworthy impact on the growth of royal power for several reasons. First, Mazarin methodically regained control of the kingdom through armed force and by making concessions to win the loyalty of individual aristocrats, always eager for the fruits of royal service. Meanwhile, the Parlement of Paris, as well as many citizens of the capital, welcomed a return to royal authority when civil war caused starvation as well as political unrest.

Moreover, the Parlement of Paris was a law court, not a representative assembly. Its legitimacy derived from its role as upholder of royal law, and it could not, over time, challenge the king on the pretext of upholding royal tradition in his name. Parlementaires tended to see the Estates General as a rival institution and helped quash the proposed meeting of an Estates General. Above all, they did not want reforms to include measures like the abolition of the paulette, a fee guaranteeing the hereditary right to royal office (see page 564), which were against their own self-interest.

Unlike in England, there was in France no single institutional focus for resistance to royal power. A strong-willed and able ruler, such as Louis XIV proved to be, could eclipse challenges to royal power, particularly when he satisfied the ambitions of aristocrats and those bureaucrats who profited from the expansion of royal authority.

France Under Louis XIV, 1661–1715

Louis XIV fully assumed control of government at Mazarin's death in 1661. It was a propitious moment. The Peace of the Pyrenees in 1659 had ended in France's favor the wars with Spain that had dragged on since the end of the Thirty Years' War. As part of the peace agreement, Louis married a Spanish princess, Maria Theresa. Louis had been called *le Dieudonné,* "the gift of God," when he was born in 1638, twenty years after his parents' marriage. He was physically attractive and extremely vigorous; he had been carefully and lovingly coached in his duties by Mazarin and by his mother, Queen Anne. Louis XIV proved a diligent king. He put in hours a day at a desk while sustaining the ceremonial life of the court with its elaborate hunts, balls, and other public events.

In the first ten years of his active reign, Louis achieved a degree of control over the mechanisms of government unparalleled in the history of monarchy in France or anywhere else in Europe. He did not invent any new bureaucratic devices but rather used existing ranks of officials in new ways that increased government efficiency and the centralization of control. He radically reduced the number of men in his High Council, the advisory body closest to the king, to include only three or four great ministers of state affairs. This intimate group, with Louis's active participation, handled all policymaking. The ministers of state, war, and finance were chosen exclusively from men of modest backgrounds whose training and experience fitted them for such positions. Jean-Baptiste Colbert (1619–1683), perhaps the greatest of them, served as minister of finance and of most domestic policy from 1665 until his death; he was from a merchant family and had served for years under Mazarin.

Several dozen other officials, picked from the ranks of up-and-coming lawyers and administrators, drew up laws and regulations and passed them to the intendants for execution at the provincial level. These officials at the center were often sent to the provinces as short-term intendants on special supervisory missions. The effect of this system was largely to bypass many entrenched provincial officials, particularly many responsible for tax collecting. The money saved by the more efficient collection of taxes enabled the government to streamline the bureaucracy: Dozens of the offices created to bring cash to the Crown were bought back by the Crown from their owners.

The system still relied on the bonds of patronage and personal service, however. Officials rose through the ranks by means of service to the great, and family connection and personal loyalty still were essential. Of the seventeen different men who were part of Louis XIV's High Council during his reign, five were members of the Colbert family, for example. In the provinces, important local families vied for minor posts, which at least provided prestige and some income.

Some of the benefits of centralized administration can be seen in certain achievements of the early years of Louis's regime. Colbert actively encouraged France's economic development. He reduced internal tolls and customs barriers, relics of medieval decentralization. He encouraged industry with state subsidies and protective tariffs. He set up state-sponsored trading companies—the two most important being the East India Company and the West India Company, established in 1664.

Mercantilism, the philosophy behind Colbert's efforts, stressed self-sufficiency in manufactured goods, tight control of trade to foster the domestic economy, and the absolute value of bullion. Capital for development—bullion—was presumed to be limited in quantity. Protectionist policies were believed necessary to guarantee a favorable balance of payments.

This static model of national wealth did not wholly fit the facts of growing international trade in the seventeenth century. Nevertheless, mercantilist philosophy was helpful to France. France became self-sufficient in the all-important production of woolen cloth, and French industry expanded notably in other sectors. Colbert's greatest success was the deliberate expansion of the navy and merchant marine. By 1677 the size of the navy had increased almost six times, to 144 ships. By the end of Louis XIV's reign, the French navy was virtually the equal of the English navy.

A general determination to manage national resources distinguished Louis's regime. Colbert and the other ministers began to develop the kind of planned government policymaking that we now take for granted. Partly by means of their itinerant supervisory officials, they tried to formulate and execute policy based on carefully collected information. How many men of military age were available? How abundant was the harvest? Answers to such questions enabled not only the formulation of sound economic policy but the deliberate management of production and services to achieve certain goals, such as the recruitment and supply of the king's vast armies.

Beginning in 1673, Louis tried to bring the religious life of the realm more fully under royal control by claiming for himself some of the church revenues and powers of appointment in France that still remained to the pope. Partly to bolster his position with the pope, he also began to attack the Huguenot community in France. He offered financial inducements for conversions to Catholicism, then quartered troops in Huguenots' households to force them to convert. In 1685 he declared that there was no longer any Protestant community, and he officially revoked the Edict of Nantes. A hundred thousand Protestant subjects who refused even nominal conversion to Catholicism chose to emigrate.

Despite the achievement of unprecedented centralized control, Louis's regime is poorly described by the term *absolutism*, which historians often apply to it. By modern standards, the power of the Crown was still greatly limited. Neither Louis nor his chief apologists claimed that he was all-powerful, in the sense of being above the law. Louis's foremost apologist, Bishop Jacques Bossuet (1627–1704), asserted that although the king was guided only by fear of God and his own reason in his application and interpretation of law, he was obligated to act within the law. The "divine right" of kingship, effectively claimed by Louis, did not mean unlimited power to rule; rather it meant that hereditary monarchy was the divinely ordained form of government, best suited to human needs.

Absolutism meant not iron-fisted control of the realm but rather the successful focusing of energy and loyalties on the Crown, in the absence of alternative institutions. The government functioned well in the opening decades of Louis's reign because his role as the focal point of power and loyalty was both logical, after the preceding years of

unrest, and skillfully exploited. Much of the glue holding together the absolutist state lay in informal mechanisms such as patronage and court life, as well as in the traditional hunt for military glory—all of which Louis amply supplied.

The Life of the Court

An observer comparing the way prominent noble families in the mid-sixteenth and mid-seventeenth centuries lived would have noticed striking differences. By the second half of the seventeenth century, most sovereigns or territorial princes had the power to crush revolts, and the heirs of the feudal nobility had to accommodate themselves to the increased power of the Crown. The nobility relinquished its former independence but retained economic and social supremacy and, as a consequence, considerable political clout. Nobles also developed new ways to safeguard their privilege by means of cultural distinctions. This process was particularly dramatic in France as a strong Crown won out over an independent and powerful nobility.

A sign of Louis's success in marshaling the loyalty of the aristocracy was the brilliant court life that his regime sustained. No longer able to wield independent political power, aristocrats lived at court whenever they could, where they could participate in the endless jostling for patronage and prestige—for commands in the royal army and for offices and honorific positions at court itself. Both women and men struggled to secure royal favor for themselves, their relations, and their clients. (See the box, "Politics and Ritual at the Court of Louis XIV.") In this environment, new codes of behavior were used to ensure their political and social distinctiveness. Elaborate rules of courtesy and etiquette regulated court life. Instead of safeguarding one's status with a code of honor backed up by force of arms, the seventeenth-century courtier relied on elegant ceremonial, precise etiquette, and clever conversation. (See the feature, "Weighing the Evidence: Table Manners," on pages 622–623.)

As literacy became more widespread, and the power of educated bureaucrats of humble origin became more obvious, more and more nobles from the traditional aristocracy began to use reading and writing as a means to think critically about their behavior—in the case of men, to reimagine them-

Politics and Ritual at the Court of Louis XIV

This document is from the memoirs of Louis de Rouvroy, duke of Saint-Simon (1675–1755), a favored courtier but one critical of Louis's power over the nobility. Notice his descriptions of court ceremony focusing on the most private moments of the king—an example of Louis's deliberate and exaggerated use of tradition, in this case of personal familiarity among warriors.

The frequent fetes, the . . . promenades at Versailles, the journeys, were means on which the king seized in order to distinguish or mortify courtiers, and thus render them more assiduous in pleasing him. He felt that of real favors he had not enough to bestow. . . . He therefore unceasingly invented all sorts of ideal ones, little preferences and petty distinctions, which answered his purpose as well.

He was exceedingly jealous of the attention paid him. . . . He looked to the right and to the left, not only upon rising but upon going to bed, at his meals, in passing through his apartments, or his gardens of Versailles . . . ; not one escaped him, not even those who hoped to remain unnoticed. He marked well all absences from court. . . .

At eight o'clock [every morning] the chief valet . . . woke the king. At the quarter [hour] the grand chamberlain was called, and those who had what was called the *grandes entrées.* The chamberlain or chief gentleman drew back the [bed] curtains and presented holy water from the vase. . . . The same officer gave [the king] his dressing gown; immediately after, other privileged courtiers entered, and then everybody, in time to find the king putting on his shoes and stockings. . . . Every other day we saw him shave himself; . . . he often spoke of [hunting] and sometimes said a word to somebody.

Source: Bayle St. John, trans., *The Memoirs of the Duke of Saint-Simon on the Reign of Louis XIV and the Regency,* 8th ed. (London: George Allen, 1913); quoted in Merry Wiesner et al., eds., *Discovering the Western Past,* 3d ed., vol. 2 (Boston: Houghton Mifflin, 1997), pp. 37–38.

selves as gentlemen rather than primarily as warriors. Noble women and men alike began to reflect on their new roles by means of writing—in letters, memoirs, and the first novels. A prominent theme of these works is the increasing necessity for a truly private life of affection and trust, with which to counterbalance the public façade necessary to an aspiring courtier. The most influential early French novel was *The Princess of Cleves* by Marie-Madeleine Pioche de la Vergne (1634–1693), best known by her title, Madame de Lafayette. Mme. de Lafayette's novel treats the particular difficulties faced by aristocratic women who, without military careers to buttress their honor, were more vulnerable than men to gossip and slander at court.

Louis XIV's court is usually associated with the palace he built at Versailles, southwest of Paris.

Some of the greatest talent of the day worked on the design and construction of Versailles from 1670 through the 1680s. It became a masterpiece of luxurious but restrained baroque styling—a model for royal and aristocratic palaces throughout Europe for the next one hundred years.

Before Louis's court settled in at Versailles, it traveled among the king's several chateaux in the countryside and in Paris, and in this period of the reign, court life was actually at its most creative and productive. These early years of Louis's personal reign were the heyday of French drama. The comedian Jean-Baptiste Poquelin, known as Molière (1622–1673), impressed the young Louis with his productions in the late 1650s and was rewarded with the use of a theater in the main royal palace in Paris. Like Shakespeare earlier in the

Louis at Versailles Louis XIV (center, on horseback) is pictured among a throng of courtiers at a grotto in the gardens of Versailles. The symbol of the sun appeared throughout the palace; the image of Louis as the "Sun King" further enchanced his authority. *(Château de Versailles/Art Resource, NY)*

century, Molière explored the social and political tensions of his day. He satirized the pretensions of the aristocracy, the social climbing of the bourgeoisie, the self-righteous piety of clerics. Some of his plays were banned from performance, but most not only were tolerated but were extremely popular with the elite audiences they mocked—their popularity is testimony to the confidence of Louis's regime in its early days.

Also popular at court were the tragedies of Jean Racine (1639–1699), who was for French theater what Shakespeare was to the English: the master of the poetic use of language. His plays, which treated familiar classical stories, focused on the emotional and psychological life of the characters and tended to stress the limits that fate places even on royal persons. The pessimism in Racine foreshadowed the less successful second half of Louis's reign.

Louis XIV and a Half-Century of War

Wars initiated by Louis XIV dominated the attention of most European states in the second half of the seventeenth century. Louis's wars sprang from traditional causes: the importance of the glory and dynastic aggrandizement of the king and the preoccupation of the aristocracy with military life.

But if Louis's wars were spurred by familiar concerns about territorial and economic advantage, they were more demanding on state resources than any previous wars.

In France and elsewhere, the size of armies and the need for greater state management of them grew markedly. The new offensive tactics developed during the Thirty Years' War (see page 576) changed the character of armies and hence the demands on governments to provide for them. A higher proportion of soldiers became gunners, and their effectiveness lay in how well they operated as a unit. Armies began to train seriously off the field of battle because drill and discipline were vital to success. The numbers of men on the battlefield increased somewhat, but the total numbers of men in arms supported by the state at any time increased dramatically once the organization to support them was in place. Late in the century, France kept about 400,000 men in arms when at war (which was most of the time).

Ironically, battles were not necessarily made more decisive by the great augmentation in army size. Most wars were still won by destroying enemy resources and by wearing down enemy forces. States that tended to matters off the battlefield such as recruitment and supply were most likely to be successful. Louis XIV's victories in the second half of the century are partly traceable to his regime's attention to such concerns.

Louis's first war reflected the continuing French preoccupation with Spanish power. The goal was territory along France's eastern border to add to the land recently gained by the Peace of Westphalia (1648) and the Peace of the Pyrenees (1659). Louis invoked rather dubious dynastic claims to demand, from Spain, lands in the Spanish Netherlands and the large independent county on France's eastern border called the Franche-Comté (Map 16.1).

War began in 1667. French troops first seized a wedge of territory in the Spanish Netherlands without difficulty and then, in early 1668, occupied the Franche-Comté. But the French retained only some towns in the Spanish Netherlands by the Treaty of Aix-la-Chapelle, which ended the brief conflict later that year. Louis had already begun to negotiate with the Austrian Habsburgs over the eventual division of Spanish Habsburg lands, for it seemed likely that the Spanish king, Charles II (r. 1665–1700), would die without heirs. So, for the moment, Louis was content to return the Franche-Comté, confident that he would get it back, and much more, in the future.

Louis's focus then shifted from Spain to a new enemy: the Dutch. The Dutch had been allied with France since the beginning of their existence as provinces in rebellion against Spain. The French now turned against the Dutch for reasons that reflect the growth of the international trading economy—specifically, the Dutch dominance of seaborne trade. The French at first tried to lessen the Dutch advantage in trade with tariff barriers against Dutch goods. But, after the easy victories of 1667–1668, Louis's generals urged action against the vulnerable Dutch lands. "It is impossible that his Majesty should tolerate any longer the insolence and arrogance of that nation," added the pragmatic Colbert in 1670.[1]

The Dutch War began in 1672, with Louis personally leading one of the largest armies ever fielded in Europe—perhaps 120,000 men. At the same time, the Dutch were challenged at sea by England. The English had fought the Dutch over these same issues, such as trade, in the 1650s; now Louis secretly sent the English king a pension to ensure his alliance with the French.

At first, the French were spectacularly successful against the tiny Dutch army. Louis, however, presumptuously overrode a plan to move decisively on Amsterdam so that he could preside at the solemn reinstatement of Catholic worship in one of the Dutch provincial cathedrals. The Dutch opened dikes and flooded the countryside to protect their capital, and what had begun as a French rout became a stalemate. Moreover, the Dutch were beating combined English and French forces at sea and were gathering allies who felt threatened by Louis's aggression. The French soon faced German and Austrian forces along their frontier, and, by 1674, the English had joined the alliance against France as well.

Nonetheless, the French managed to hold their own, and the Peace of Nijmegen, in 1678, gave the illusion of a French victory. Not only had the French met the challenge of an alliance against them, but Spain ceded them further border areas in the Spanish Netherlands as well as control of the Franche-Comté.

Ensconced at Versailles since 1682, Louis seemed to be at the height of his powers. Yet the Dutch War had in fact cost him more than he had gained. Meeting the alliance against him had meant

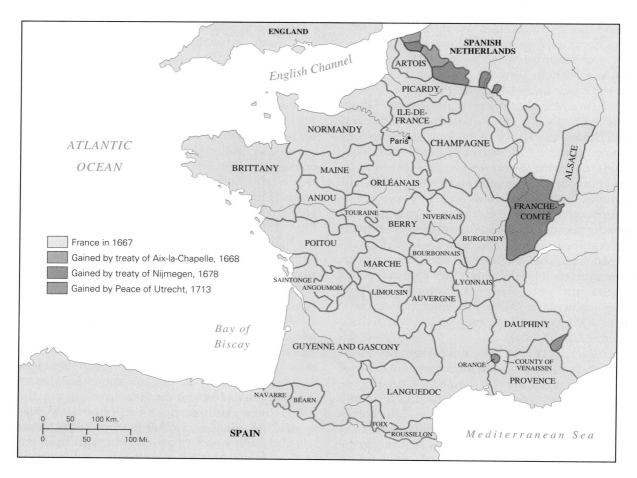

Map 16.1 Territorial Gains of Louis XIV, 1667–1715 Louis's wars, though enormously expensive for France, produced only modest gains of territory along France's eastern and northern frontiers.

fielding ever-increasing numbers of men—more than 200,000 in arms at one time. Internal reforms in government and finance ended under the pressure of paying for war, and old financial expedients of borrowing money and selling privileges were revived. Other government obligations, such as encouraging overseas trade, were neglected. Colbert's death in 1683 dramatically symbolized the end of an era of innovation in the French regime.

Louis's unforgiving Dutch opponent, William of Orange, king of England from 1689 to 1702, renewed former alliances against him. The war, now known as the Nine Years' War, or King William's War, was touched off late in 1688 by French aggression—an invasion of Germany to claim an in-

heritance there. In his ongoing dispute with the pope, Louis seized the papal territory of Avignon in southern France. Boldest of all, he helped the exiled Catholic claimant to the English crown mount an invasion to reclaim his throne.

A widespread war began with all the major powers—Spain, the Netherlands, England, Austria, the major German states—ranged against France. The French also carried the fighting abroad by seizing English territory in Canada. As with the Dutch War, the Nine Years' War was costly but had indecisive results on most fronts. And this time there was no illusion of victory for Louis. In the Treaty of Ryswick (1697), Louis had to give up most of the territories in Germany, the

Spanish Netherlands, and northern Spain that he managed to occupy by war's end. Avignon went back to the pope, and Louis gave up his contentious claim to papal revenues. The terrible burden of taxes to pay for the wars combined with crop failures in 1693 and 1694 caused widespread starvation in the countryside. French courtiers began to criticize Louis openly.

The final major war of Louis's reign, now called the War of Spanish Succession, broke out in 1702. In some ways it was a straightforward dynastic war in which France and its perennial Habsburg opponent had an equal interest. Both Louis and Holy Roman Emperor Leopold I (r. 1657–1705) hoped to claim for their heirs the throne of Spain, left open at the death in 1700 of the Spanish king, Charles II. A will of Charles II gave the throne to Louis's grandson, Philip of Anjou, who quickly proceeded to enter Spain and claim his new kingdom. War was made inevitable when Louis renounced one of the conditions of Charles's will by insisting that Philip's accession to the throne of Spain did not mean that he had abandoned his rights to the throne of France. This declaration was an act of sheer belligerence, for Philip was only third in line for the French throne. The Dutch and the English responded to the prospect of a Frenchman on the throne of Spain and the consequent disruption of the balance of power in Europe by joining the emperor in a formal Great Alliance in 1701. The Dutch and English also wanted to defend their colonial interests, since the French had already begun to profit from new trading opportunities with the Spanish colonies.

Again the French fought a major war on several fronts on land and at sea. Again the people of France felt the cost in crushing taxes worsened by harvest failures. Major revolts inside France forced Louis to divert troops from the war. For a time it seemed that the French would be soundly defeated, but they were saved by the superior organization of their forces and by dynastic accident: Unexpected deaths in the Habsburg family meant that the Austrian claimant to the Spanish throne suddenly was poised to inherit rule of Austria and the empire as well. The English, who were more afraid of a revival of unified Habsburg control of Spain and Austria than of French domination of Spain, began peace negotiations with France.

The Peace of Utrecht in 1713 resolved long-standing political conflicts and helped to set the agenda of European politics for the eighteenth century. Philip of Anjou became Philip V of Spain, but on the condition that the Spanish and French crowns would never be worn by the same monarch. To maintain the balance of power against French interests, the Spanish Netherlands and Spanish territories in Italy were ceded to Austria, which for many decades would be France's major continental rival. The Peace of Utrecht also marked the beginning of England's dominance of overseas trade and colonization. The French gave to England lands in Canada and the Caribbean and renounced any privileged relationship with Spanish colonies. England was allowed to control the highly profitable slave trade with Spanish colonies.

Louis XIV had added small amounts of strategically valuable territory along France's eastern border (see Map 16.1), and a Bourbon ruled in Spain. But the costs in human life and resources were great for the slim results achieved. Moreover, the army and navy had swallowed up capital for investment and trade; strategic opportunities overseas were lost, never to be regained. Louis's government had been innovative in its early years but remained constrained by traditional ways of imagining the interest of the state.

THE ENGLISH REVOLUTION

In England, unlike in France, a representative institution—Parliament—became an effective, permanent brake on royal authority. The process by which Parliament gained a secure role in governing the kingdom was neither easy nor peaceful, however. As we saw in Chapter 15, conflicts between the English crown and its subjects, focused in the Crown-Parliament conflict, concerned control over taxation and the direction of religious reform. Beginning in 1642, England was beset by civil war between royal and parliamentary forces. The king was eventually defeated and executed, and there followed a period when the monarchy was abolished altogether. The monarchy was restored in 1660, but Parliament retained a crucial role in governing the kingdom, a role that was confirmed when, in 1688, it again deposed a monarch whose fiscal and religious policies became unacceptable to its members.

Civil War and Revolution, 1642–1649

Fighting broke between Charles I and parliamentary armies in the late summer of 1642. The Long Parliament (see page 571) continued to represent a broad coalition of critics and opponents of the monarchy, ranging from aristocrats concerned primarily with the abuses of royal prerogative to radical Puritans eager for thorough religious reform and determined to defeat the king. Fighting was halfhearted, initially, and the tide of war at first favored Charles.

In 1643, however, the scope of the war broadened. Charles made peace with Irish rebels and brought Irish troops to England to help his cause. Parliament, in turn, sought military aid from the Scots in exchange for promises that Presbyterianism would become the religion of England. Meanwhile, Oliver Cromwell (1599–1658), a Puritan member of the Long Parliament and a cavalry officer, helped reorganize parliamentary forces in order to defeat the king's forces. The eleven-hundred-man cavalry trained by Cromwell and known as the "Ironsides" helped parliamentary and Scottish infantry defeat the king's troops at Marston Moor in July 1644. The victory made Cromwell famous.

Shortly afterward, Parliament reorganized its forces to create the New Model Army, rigorously trained like Cromwell's Ironsides. Sitting members of Parliament were barred from commanding troops, hence upper-class control of the army was reduced. This army played a decisive role not only in the war but also in the political settlement that followed the fighting.

The New Model Army won a convincing victory over royal forces at Naseby in 1645. In the spring of 1646, Charles surrendered to a Scottish army in the north. In January 1647, Parliament paid the Scots for their services in the war and took the king into custody. In the negotiations that followed, Charles tried to play his opponents off against each other, and, as he hoped, divisions among them widened.

Most members of Parliament were Presbyterians, Puritans who favored a strongly unified and controlled state church along Calvinist lines. They wanted peace with the king in return for acceptance of the new church structure and parliamentary control of standing militias for a specified pe-

riod. They did not favor expanding the right to vote or other dramatic constitutional or legal change. These men were increasingly alarmed by the rise of sectarian differences and the actual religious freedom that many ordinary people were claiming for themselves. With the weakening of royal authority and the disruption of civil war, censorship was relaxed and public preaching by ordinary women and men who felt a religious inspiration was becoming commonplace.

Above all, Presbyterian gentry in Parliament feared more radical groups in the army and in London that had supported them up to this point but favored more thoroughgoing reform. Most officers of the New Model Army, such as Cromwell, were Independents, Puritans who favored a decentralized church, a degree of religious toleration, and a wider sharing of political power among men of property, not just among the very wealthy gentry. In London, a well-organized artisans' movement known as the Levelers favored universal manhood suffrage, reform of law, and better access to education in addition to decentralized churches—in short, the separation of political power from wealth and virtual freedom of religion. Many of the rank and file of the army were deeply influenced by Leveler ideas.

In May 1647 the majority in Parliament voted to disband the New Model Army without first paying most of the soldiers' back wages and to offer terms to the king. This move provoked the first direct intervention by the army in politics. Representatives of the soldiers were chosen to present grievances to Parliament but, when this failed, the army seized the king and, in August, occupied Westminster, Parliament's meeting place. Independent and Leveler elements in the army debated the direction of possible reform to be imposed on Parliament. (See the box, "The Putney Debates.")

However, in November, Charles escaped from his captors and raised a new army among his erstwhile enemies, the Scots, who were also alarmed by the growing radicalism in England. Civil war began again early in 1648. Although it ended quickly with a victory by Cromwell and the New Model Army in August, the renewed war further hardened political divisions and enhanced the power of the army. The king was widely blamed for the renewed bloodshed, and the army did not

The Putney Debates

In October 1647, representatives of the Leveler movement in the army ranks confronted Independents—largely comprising the officer corps—in formally staged debates in a church at Putney, outside London. The debates reflected the importance of the army in deciding the shape of change. Reproduced here is one exchange between the Leveler representative, Thomas Rainsborough, advocating universal manhood suffrage, and Cromwell's fellow officer, Henry Ireton, who argues for a franchise more restricted to men of some means.

Rainsborough: . . . Really I think that the poorest he that is in England hath a life to live as the greatest he; and therefore truly, sir, I think it's clear, that every man that is to live under a government ought first by his own consent to put himself under that government; and I do think that the poorest man in England is not at all bound in a strict sense to that government that he hath not had a voice to put himself under; and I am confident that, when I have heard the reasons against it, that something will be said to answer those reasons, insomuch that I should doubt whether I was an Englishman or no, that should doubt of these things.

Ireton: That's this.

Give me leave to tell you, that if you make this the rule, I think you must fly for refuge to an absolute natural right, and you must deny all civil right; and I am sure it will come to that in the consequence. . . . I think that no person hath a right to an interest or share in the disposing of the affairs of the kingdom, and in determining or choosing those that shall determine what laws we shall be ruled by here, no person hath a right to this that hath not a permanent fixed interest in this kingdom, and those persons together are properly the represented of this kingdom, who taken together, and consequently are to make up the representers of this kingdom, are the representers, who taken together do comprehend whatsoever is of real or permanent interest in the kingdom, and I am sure there is otherwise (I cannot tell what), otherwise any man can say why a foreigner coming in amongst us, or as many as will be coming in amongst us, or by force or otherwise settling themselves here, or at least by our permission having a being here, why they should not as well lay claim to it as any other. We talk of birthright. Truly birthright there is thus much claim: men may justly have by birthright, by their very being born in England, that we should not seclude them out of England. That we should not refuse to give them air and place and ground, and the freedom of the highways and other things, to live amongst us, not any man that is born here, though he in birth, or by his birth there come nothing at all that is part of the permanent interest of this kingdom to him. That I think is due to a man by birth. But that by a man's being born here he shall have a share in that power that shall dispose of the lands here, and of all things here, I do not think it a sufficient ground, but I am sure if we look upon that which is the utmost, within man's view, of what was originally the constitution of this kingdom, upon that which is most radical and fundamental, and which if you take away, there is no man hath any land, any goods, you take away any civil interest, and that is this: that those that choose the representers for the making of laws by which this state and kingdom are to be governed, are the persons who taken together, do comprehend the local interest of this kingdom; that is, the persons in whom all land lies, and those in corporations in whom all trading lies. This is the most fundamental constitution of this kingdom, and which if you do not allow, you allow none at all.

Source: G. E. Aylmer, ed., *The Levellers in the English Revolution* (Ithaca: Cornell University Press, 1975), pp. 100–101.

trust him to keep any agreement he might now sign. When Parliament, still dominated by Presbyterians, once again voted to negotiate with the king, army troops under a Colonel Thomas Pride prevented members who favored Presbyterianism or the king from attending sessions. The "Rump" Parliament that remained after "Pride's Purge" voted to try the king. Charles I was executed for "treason, tyranny and bloodshed" against his people on January 30, 1649.

The Interregnum, 1649–1660

A Commonwealth—a republic—was declared. Executive power resided in a council of state. Legislative power resided in a one-chamber Parliament, the Rump Parliament (the House of Lords was abolished). Declaring a republic proved far easier than running one, however. The execution of the king shocked most English and Scots people and alienated many elites from the new regime.

The legitimacy of the Commonwealth government would always be in question.

The tasks of making and implementing policy were made difficult by the narrow political base on which the government now rested. Excluded were the majority of the reformist gentry who had been purged from Parliament. Also excluded were the more radical Levelers; Leveler leaders in London were arrested when they published tracts critical of the new government. Within a few years, many disillusioned Levelers would join a new religious movement called the Society of Friends, or Quakers, which espoused complete religious autonomy. Quakers refused all oaths or service to the state, and they refused to acknowledge social rank.

Above all, the new government was vulnerable to the power of the army, which had created it. In 1649 and 1650 Cromwell led expeditions to Ireland and Scotland, partly for sheer revenge and partly to put down resistance to the new English government. In Ireland, Cromwell's forces acted with great ruthlessness. English control there was

Popular Preaching in England Many women took advantage of the collapse of royal authority to preach in public—a radical activity for women at the time. This print satirizes the Quakers, a religious movement that attracted many women. *(Mary Evans Picture Library)*

furthered by more dispossession of Irish land-holders, which also served to pay off the army's wages. Meanwhile, Parliament could not agree on systematic reforms, particularly the one reform Independents in the army insisted on: more broadly based elections for a new Parliament. Fresh from his victories in the north, Cromwell led his armies to London and dissolved Parliament in the spring of 1652.

In 1653 some army officers drew up the "Instrument of Government," England's first and only written constitution. It provided for an executive, the Lord Protector, and a Parliament to be based on somewhat wider male suffrage. Cromwell was the natural choice for Lord Protector, and whatever success the government of the Protectorate had was largely due to him.

Cromwell was an extremely able leader who was not averse to compromise. Although he had used the army against Parliament in 1648, he had worked hard to reconcile the Rump Parliament and the army before marching on London in 1652. He believed in a state church, but one that allowed for control, including choice of minister, by local congregations. He also believed in toleration for other Protestant sects, as well as for Catholics and Jews, as long as no one disturbed the peace.

As Lord Protector, Cromwell oversaw impressive reforms in law that testify to his belief in the limits of governing authority. For example, contrary to the practice of his day, he opposed capital punishment for petty crimes. The government of the Protectorate, however, accomplished little because Parliament remained internally divided and opposed to Cromwell's initiatives. Cromwell was challenged by radical republicans in Parliament who thought the Protectorate represented a step backward, away from republican government. In the population at large, there were still royalist sympathizers, and a royalist uprising in 1655 forced the temporary division of England into military districts administered by generals.

In the end, the Protectorate could not survive the strains over policy and the challenges to its legitimacy. When Cromwell died of a sudden illness in September 1658, the Protectorate did not long survive him. In February 1660, the decisive action of one army general seeking a solution to the chaos enabled all the surviving members of the Long Parliament to rejoin the Rump. The Parliament summarily dissolved itself and called for new elections.

Oliver Cromwell Cromwell had seen his family's income decline under the weight of Charles I's exactions. Elected to Parliament in 1628 and again in 1640, he also brought a long-standing religious zeal to his public life. His opposition to the "tyranny and usurpation" of the Anglican church hierarchy first prompted him to criticize royal government. *(In the collection of the Duke of Buccleuch and Queensberry KT)*

The newly elected Parliament recalled Charles II, son of Charles I, from exile abroad and restored the monarchy. The chaos and radicalism of the late civil war and interregnum—the period between reigns, as the years from 1649 to 1660 came to be called—now spawned a conservative reaction.

The Restoration, 1660–1685

Charles II (r. 1660–1685) claimed his throne at the age of 30. He had learned from his years of uncertain exile and from the fate of his father. He did not seek retribution but rather offered a general pardon to all but a few rebels (mostly those who had signed his father's death warrant), and he suggested to Parliament a relatively tolerant religious settlement that would include Anglicans as well as

Presbyterians. He was far more politically adept than his father and far more willing to compromise.

That the re-established royal government was not more tolerant than it turned out to be was not Charles's doing but Parliament's. During the 1660s, the "Cavalier" Parliament, named for royalists in the civil war, passed harsh laws aimed at religious dissenters. Anglican orthodoxy was reimposed, including the re-establishment of bishops and the Anglican *Book of Common Prayer.* All officeholders and clergy were required to swear oaths of obedience to the king and to the established church. As a result, hundreds of them were forced out of office. Holding nonconformist religious services became illegal, and Parliament passed a "five-mile" act to prevent dissenting ministers from traveling near their former congregations. Property laws were strengthened and the criminal codes made more severe.

The king's behavior began to mimic prerevolutionary royalist positions. Charles II began to flirt with Catholicism, and his brother and heir, James, openly converted. Charles promulgated a declaration of tolerance that would have included Catholics as well as nonconformist Protestants, but Parliament would not accept it. When Parliament moved to exclude the Catholic James from succession to the throne, Charles dissolved it. A subsequent Parliament, cowed by fears of a new civil war, backed down. By the end of his reign, Charles was financially independent of Parliament thanks to increased revenue from overseas trade and to secret subsidies from France, his recent ally against Dutch trading rivals.

Underneath this seeming return to a prerevolutionary status quo were conditions that reflected the legacy of the revolution that had cost Charles I his head. First, despite the harsh laws, to silence all dissent was not possible. After two decades of religious pluralism and broadly based political activity it was impossible to reimpose conformity; there were well-established communities of various sects and a self-confidence that bred vigorous resistance. Also, anti-Catholic feeling still united all Protestants. In 1678 Charles's secret treaties with the French became known, and rumors of a Catholic plot to murder Charles and reimpose Catholicism became widespread. No evidence of any plot was ever unearthed, though thirty-five people were executed for alleged participation. Parliament focused its attention on anti-Catholicism, passing an act barring all but Anglicans from Parliament itself.

The clearest reflection of the regime's revolutionary background was the power of Parliament: It was able to assert its policies against the desires of the king. Nevertheless, financial independence and firm political tactics enabled Charles to retain a great deal of power. If he had been followed by an able successor, Parliament might have lost a good measure of its confidence and independence. But his brother James's reign and its aftermath further enhanced Parliament's power.

The Glorious Revolution, 1688

When James II (r. 1685–1689) succeeded Charles, Parliament's royalist leanings were at first evident. James was granted customs duties for life and was also given funds to suppress a rebellion by one of Charles's illegitimate sons. James did not try to impose Catholicism on England, but he did try to achieve toleration for Catholics in two declarations of indulgence in 1687 and 1688. His efforts were undermined by his heavy-handed tactics. When several leading Anglican bishops refused to read the declarations from their pulpits, he had them imprisoned and tried for seditious libel. The jury, however, acquitted them.

James also failed because of the coincidence of other events. In 1685, at the outset of James's reign, Louis XIV in France had revoked the Edict of Nantes. The possibility that subjects and monarchs in France and, by extension, elsewhere could be of different faiths seemed increasingly unlikely. Popular fears of James's Catholicism were thus heightened early in his reign, and his later declarations of tolerance, though benefiting Protestant dissenters, were viewed with suspicion. In 1688, not only were the Anglican bishops acquitted but the king's second wife, who was Catholic, gave birth to a son. The birth raised the specter of a Catholic succession.

In June 1688, to put pressure on James, leading members of Parliament invited William of Orange, husband of James's Protestant daughter, Mary, to come to England. William mounted an invasion that became a rout when James refused to defend his throne. James simply abandoned England and went to France. William called Parliament, which declared James to have abdicated and offered the throne to him and to Mary. James eventually invaded Ireland in 1690 with French support but was defeated by William at the Battle of Boyne that year.

The substitution of William (r. 1689–1702) and Mary (r. 1689–1694) for James, known as the "Glorious Revolution," was engineered by Parliament and confirmed its power. Parliament presented the new sovereigns with a Declaration of Rights upon their accession and, later that year, with a Bill of Rights that defended freedom of speech, called for frequent Parliaments, and required subsequent monarchs to be Protestant. The effectiveness of these documents was reinforced by Parliament's power of the purse. Parliament's role in the political process was ensured by William's interests in funding his ambitious military efforts, particularly to support the Netherlands' ongoing wars with France.

The issues that had faced the English since the beginning of the century were common to all European states: religious division and elite power, fiscal strains and resistance to taxation. Yet events in England had so far set it apart from the experience of other states in that the incremental assumption of authority by a well-established institution, Parliament, made challenge of the monarchy more legitimate and more effective. Political participation also developed more broadly in England than in other states. In the long run, the strength of Parliament would make easier the task of permanently broadening participation in government.

NEW POWERS IN CENTRAL AND EASTERN EUROPE

By the end of the seventeenth century, three states dominated central and eastern Europe: Austria, Brandenburg-Prussia, and Russia. After the Thirty Years' War, the Habsburgs' power as emperors waned, and their interest in the coherence of their own territories, which centered on Austria, grew. Brandenburg-Prussia, in northeastern Germany, grew to a position of power rivaling that of the Habsburg state. The rulers of Brandenburg-Prussia had gained lands in the Peace of Westphalia, and astute management transformed their relatively small and scattered holdings into one of the most powerful states in Europe. Russia's new stature in eastern Europe resulted in part from the weakness of its greatest rival, Poland, and the determination of one leader, Peter the Great, to as-

sume a major role in European affairs. Sweden controlled valuable Baltic territory through much of the century but by the end of the century was also eclipsed by Russia as a power in the region.

The development of and the competition among states in central and eastern Europe was closely linked to developments in western Europe. This was true politically and strategically as well as economically. One of the most important factors influencing the internal political development of these states was their relationship to the wider European economy: They were sources of grain and raw materials for the more densely urbanized west.

The Consolidation of Austria

The Thirty Years' War (see pages 571–577) weakened the Habsburgs as emperors but strengthened them in their own lands. The main Habsburg lands in 1648 were a collection of principalities comprising modern Austria, the kingdom of Hungary (largely in Turkish hands), and the kingdom of Bohemia (see Map 16.2). In 1713 the Peace of Utrecht ceded the Spanish Netherlands to Austria and renamed them the "Austrian Netherlands." Although language and ethnic differences prevented an absolutist state along French lines, Leopold I (r. 1657–1705) instituted political and institutional changes that enabled the Habsburg state to become one of the most powerful states in Europe through the eighteenth century.

Much of the coherence that already existed in Leopold's lands had been achieved by his predecessors in the wake of the Thirty Years' War. The lands of rebels in Bohemia had been confiscated and redistributed among loyal, mostly Austrian, families. In return for political and military support for the emperor, these families were given the right to exploit their newly acquired land and the peasants who worked it. The desire to recover population and productivity after the destruction of the Thirty Years' War gave landlords further incentive to curtail peasants' autonomy sharply, particularly in devastated Bohemia. Austrian landlords throughout the Habsburg domains provided grain and timber for the export market and grain and other foodstuffs for the Austrian armies, and elite families provided the army with officers. This political-economic arrangement provoked numerous serious peasant revolts, but the peasants were not able to force changes in a system that suited both the elites and the central authority.

Although Leopold had lost much influence within the empire itself, an imperial government made up of various councils, a war ministry, financial officials, and the like still functioned in his capital, Vienna. Leopold worked to extricate the government of his own lands from the apparatus of imperial institutions, which were staffed largely by Germans more loyal to imperial than to Habsburg interests. In addition, Leopold used the Catholic church as an institutional and ideological support for the Habsburg state.

Leopold's personal preoccupation was the reestablishment of zealous Catholicism throughout his territories. Acceptance of Catholicism became the litmus test of loyalty to the Habsburg regime,

Celebrating Habsburg Power Leopold I is depicted here trampling a Turkish soldier, wearing armor and a medieval order of knighthood around his neck—appropriate garb with which to represent a victory over "the Infidel." Compare this illustration with the painting of Louis XIV in Roman armor on page 588. (*Kunsthistorisches Museum, Vienna*)

and Protestantism vanished among elites. Leopold encouraged the work of Jesuit teachers and members of other Catholic orders. These men and women helped staff his government and administered religious life down to the most local levels.

Leopold's most dramatic success, as a Habsburg and as a religious leader, was his reconquest of the kingdom of Hungary from the Ottoman Empire. Since the mid-sixteenth century, the Habsburgs had controlled only a narrow strip of the kingdom. Preoccupied with countering Louis XIV's aggression, Leopold did not himself choose to begin a reconquest. His centralizing policies, however, alienated nobles and townspeople in the portion of Hungary he did control, as did his repression of Protestantism, which had flourished in Hungary. Hungarian nobles began a revolt, aided by the Turks, aiming for a reunited Hungary under Ottoman protection.

The Habsburgs emerged victorious in part because they received help from, among others, the talented Polish king, Jan Sobieski, whose own lands in Ukraine were threatened by the Turks. The Turks overreached their supply lines to besiege Vienna in 1683. After the siege failed, Habsburg armies slowly pressed east and south, recovering Buda, the capital of Hungary, in 1686 and Belgrade in 1688. The Danube basin lay once again in Christian hands.

Leopold gave land in the reclaimed kingdom to Austrian officers whom he believed were loyal to him. The traditions of Hungarian separatism, however, were strong, and the great magnates—whether they had defended the Habsburgs against Turkish encroachment or guarded the frontier for Turkish overlords—retained their independence. The peasantry, as elsewhere, suffered a decline in status as a result of the Crown's efforts to ensure the loyalty of elites. In the long run, Hungarian independence weakened the Habsburg state, but in the short run Leopold's victory over the Turks and the recovery of Hungary itself were momentous events, confirming the Habsburgs as the preeminent power in central Europe.

The Rise of Brandenburg-Prussia

Three German states, in addition to Austria, gained territory and stature after the Thirty Years' War: Bavaria, Saxony, and Brandenburg-Prussia. By the end of the seventeenth century, the strongest was

Brandenburg-Prussia, a conglomeration of small territories held, by dynastic accident, by the Hohenzollern family. The two principal territories were electoral Brandenburg, in northeastern Germany, with its capital, Berlin, and the duchy of Prussia, a fief of the Polish crown along the Baltic coast east of Poland proper (see Map 16.2). In addition there was a handful of small principalities near the Netherlands. The manipulation of resources and power that enabled these unpromising lands to become a powerful state was primarily the work of Frederick William, known as "the Great Elector" (r. 1640–1688).

Frederick William used the occasion of a war to effect a permanent change in the structure of government. He took advantage of a war between Poland and its rivals, Sweden and Russia (the First Great Northern War, described in the next section), to win independence for the duchy of Prussia from Polish overlordship. When his involvement in the war ended in 1657, he kept intact the general war commissariat, a combined civilian and military body that had efficiently directed the war effort; he thus bypassed traditional councils and representative bodies. He also used the standing army to force the payment of high taxes. Most significantly, he established a positive relationship with the *Junkers,* hereditary landholders, which assured him both revenue and loyalty. He agreed to allow the Junkers virtually total control of their own lands in return for their agreement to support his government—in short, to surrender their accustomed political independence.

Peasants and townspeople were taxed, but nobles were not. The freedom to control their estates led many nobles to invest in profitable agriculture for the export market. The peasants were serfs who received no benefits from the increased productivity of the land. Frederick William further enhanced his state's power by sponsoring state industries. These industries did not have to fear competition from urban producers because the towns had been frozen out of the political process and saddled with heavy taxes. Although an oppressive place for many Germans, Brandenburg-Prussia attracted many skilled refugees, such as Huguenot artisans fleeing Louis XIV.

Bavaria and Saxony, in contrast to Brandenburg-Prussia, had vibrant towns, largely free peasantries, and weaker aristocracies but were less powerful in international affairs. Power on the European stage depended on military force. Such power, whether in a large state like France or in a small one like Brandenburg-Prussia, usually came at the expense of the state's inhabitants.

Competition Around the Baltic: The Demise of the Polish State and the Zenith of Swedish Power

The rivers and port cities of the Baltic coast were conduits for the growing trade between the Baltic hinterland and the rest of Europe; tolls assessed on the passage of timber, grain, and naval stores were an important source of local income, and the commodities themselves brought profits to their producers. This trading system had profound social and political consequences for all of the states bordering the Baltic Sea in the seventeenth century.

First, it was a spur to war: Sweden and Denmark fought over control of the sea-lanes connecting the Baltic and North Seas. Sweden, Poland, and Russia fought for control of the eastern Baltic coastline in the sixteenth and seventeenth centuries. In the seventeenth century, Poland and Russia fought over grain- and timber-producing lands comprising modern Belarus, parts of modern Russia, and Ukraine. Second, profits from the production of grain for export in such volume reinforced the power of large landholders, particularly within Poland, where most of the grain was produced.

In 1600 a large portion of the Baltic hinterland lay under the control of Poland-Lithuania, a dual kingdom at the height of its power (Map 16.2). A marriage in 1386 had brought the duchy of Lithuania under a joint ruler with Poland; earlier in the fourteenth century, Lithuania had conquered Belarus and Ukraine. Poland-Lithuania commanded considerable resources, including the Vistula and Niemen Rivers and the ports of Gdansk and Riga on the Baltic coast. Like the neighboring Habsburg lands, it was a multi-ethnic state, particularly in the huge duchy of Lithuania, where Russian-speakers predominated. Poland was Catholic but had a large minority of Protestants and Jews. Owing to ties with Poland, Lithuanians themselves were mostly Catholic (and some were Protestant), but Russian-speakers were Orthodox. German-speaking families dominated trade in most coastal cities.

Internal strains and external challenges began to mount in Poland-Lithuania in the late sixteenth century. The economic power of Polish landlords

Map 16.2 New Powers in Central and Eastern Europe The balance of power in central and eastern Europe shifted with the strengthening of Austria, the rise of Brandenburg-Prussia, and the expansion of Russia at the expense of Poland and Sweden.

gave them considerable political clout; the king was forced to grant concessions that weakened urban freedoms and bound peasants to the nobles' estates. In 1572 the sudden death of the very able but childless king, Sigismund II (r. 1548–1572), only enhanced the nobles' power. Sigismund's successors would be elected, would have no voice in the succession, and would be closely supervised by noble counselors.

The spread of the Counter-Reformation, encouraged by the Crown, created tensions with both Protestant and Orthodox subjects in the diverse kingdom. In Ukraine, communities of Cossacks, nomadic farmer-warriors, grew as Polish and Lithuanian peasants fled harsh conditions to join them. The Cossacks had long been tolerated because they were a military buffer against the Ottoman Turks to the south, but now Polish landlords wanted to reincorporate the Cossacks into the profitable political-economic system that they controlled. Meanwhile, the Crown was involved in several wars. From 1609 to 1612 Polish armies tried but failed to impose a Polish king on the Russians during a dispute over the succession. While aiding Austria in the Thirty Years' War against the Turks, their common enemy, the Poles lost Livonia (modern Latvia) and other bits of northern territory to the aggressive Gustav Adolf of Sweden.

In 1648 the Polish crown faced revolt and invasion that it could not counter. The Cossacks, with the Crimean Tatars and their Ottoman overlords as allies, staged a major revolt, defeated Polish armies, and established an independent state. In 1654 the Cossacks transferred their allegiance to Moscow and became part of a Russian invasion of Poland that, by the next year, had engulfed much of the eastern half of the dual kingdom. At the same time, the Swedes seized central Poland and competed with the Russians for control elsewhere; the Swedes were helped by Polish and Lithuanian aristocrats acting like independent warlords.

Often called the First Great Northern War, this war is remembered in Poland as "the Deluge." Polish royal armies managed to recover much territory—most important, the western half of Ukraine. But the invasions and subsequent fighting were disastrous. The population of Poland may have declined by as much as 40 percent, and vital urban economies were in ruins. The Catholic identity of the Polish heartland had been a rallying point for resistance to the Protestant Swedes and the Ortho-

dox Russians, but the religious tolerance that had distinguished the Polish kingdom and had been mandated in its constitution was thereafter abandoned. In addition, much of its recovery of territory was only nominal. In parts of Lithuania inhabited by Russian-speaking peoples, the Russian presence during the wars had achieved local transfers of power from Lithuanian to Russian landlords loyal to Moscow.

The elective Polish crown passed in 1674 to the brilliant military commander Jan Sobieski (r. 1674–1696), known as "Vanquisher of the Turks" for his victory in raising the siege of Vienna. Given Poland's internal weakness, however, Sobieski's victories in the long run helped the Austrian and Russian rivals of the Turks more than they helped the Poles. His successor, Augustus II of Saxony (r. 1697–1704, 1709–1733), dragged Poland back into war, from which Russia would emerge the obvious winner in the power struggle in eastern Europe.

On the Baltic coast, however, Sweden remained the dominant power through most of the seventeenth century. Swedish efforts to control Baltic territory began in the sixteenth century, first to counter the power of its perennial rival, Denmark, in the western Baltic. It then competed with Poland to control Livonia, whose principal city, Riga, was an important trading center for goods from both Lithuania and Russia. By 1617, under Gustav Adolf, the Swedes gained the lands to the north surrounding the Gulf of Finland (the most direct outlet for Russian goods) and in 1621 displaced the Poles in Livonia itself. Swedish intervention in the Thirty Years' War came when imperial successes against Denmark both threatened the Baltic coast and created an opportunity to strike at Sweden's old enemy. The Treaty of Westphalia (1648) confirmed Sweden's earlier gains and added control of further coastal territory, mostly at Denmark's expense.

The port cities held by Sweden were indeed profitable but simply served to pay for the costly wars necessary to seize and defend them. All of these efforts to hold Baltic territory were driven by dynastic and strategic needs as much as economic rationales. The ruling dynasty struggled against Denmark's control of western Baltic territory in order to safeguard its independence from the Danes, who had ruled the combined kingdoms until 1523. Similarly, competition with Poland for the east Baltic was part of a dynastic struggle after

War for the Baltic Control of the Baltic littoral was hotly contested throughout the seventeenth century. While fighting in Poland during the First Great Northern War, the Swedes were attacked, in turn, by their longstanding rivals, the Danes. The Swedish king, Karl Gustav, marched his army over frozen sea lanes and beat the Danes at the Battle of Ifveros, depicted here, in the winter of 1658. *(National Museum of Stockholm)*

1592. Sigismund Vasa, son of the king of Sweden, had been elected king of Poland in 1587 but also inherited the Swedish throne in 1592. Other members of the ruling Swedish Vasa family fought him successfully to regain rule over Sweden and extricate Swedish interests from Poland's continental preoccupations. Sigismund ruled Poland until his death in 1632 but was replaced on the Swedish throne by an uncle in 1604.

The one permanent gain that Sweden realized from its aggression in the First Great Northern War was the renunciation of the Polish Vasa line to any claim to the Swedish crown. Owing to its earlier gains, Sweden remained the dominant power on the Baltic coast until the end of the century, when it was supplanted by the powerful Russian state.

The Expansion of Russia: From Ivan "the Terrible" Through Peter "the Great"

The Russian state expanded dramatically through the sixteenth century. Ivan IV (r. 1533–1584) was proclaimed "Tsar [Russian for "Caesar"] of All the Russias" in 1547. This act was the culmination of the accumulation of land and authority by the princes of Moscow through the late Middle Ages, when Moscow had vied for pre-eminence with other Russian principalities. Ivan IV's grandfather, Ivan III (r. 1462–1505), the first to use the title *tsar,* had absorbed neighboring Russian principalities and ended Moscow's subservience to Mongol overlords.

Ivan IV, also known as Ivan "the Terrible," was the first actually to be crowned tsar and routinely to use the title. His use of the title aptly reflected his imperial intentions, as he continued Moscow's push westward and, especially, eastward against the Mongol states of central Asia. Two of the three Mongol states to the east and south fell, and the Russians pushed eastward over the Ural Mountains to Siberia for the first time.

Within this expanding empire, Ivan IV ruled as an autocrat. Part of his authority stemmed from his own personality. He was willing—perhaps because of mental imbalance—to use ruthless methods, including the torture and murder of thousands of subjects, to enforce his will. The practice of gathering tribute for Mongol overlords had put many resources in the hands of Muscovite princes. Ivan IV was able to bypass noble participation and intensify the centralization of government by creating ranks of officials, known as the service gentry, loyal only to him. The name "the Terrible" comes from the Russian word *groznyi*, which is better translated as "awe-inspiring."

A period of disputed succession known as the Time of Troubles followed Ivan's death in 1584, not unlike similar crises in other European states, where jealous aristocrats vied for power during periods of royal weakness. In this case, aristocratic factions fought among themselves as well as against armies of Cossacks and other common people who disputed nobles' ambitions and wanted less oppressive government. Nonetheless, the foundations of the large and cohesive state laid by Ivan enabled Michael Romanov to rebuild autocratic government readily after being chosen tsar in 1613.

The Romanovs were an eminent aristocratic family related to Ivan's. Michael (r. 1613–1645) was chosen to rule by an assembly of aristocrats, gentry, and commoners who were more alarmed at the civil wars and recent Polish incursions than at the prospect of a return to strong tsarist rule. Michael was succeeded by his son, Alexis (r. 1645–1676), who presided over the extension of Russian control to Ukraine in 1654 and developed interest in further relationships with the West.

Shifting the balance of power in eastern Europe and the Baltic in Russia's favor was also the work of Alexis's son, Peter I, "the Great" (r. 1682–1725). Peter accomplished this by military successes against his enemies and by forcibly reorienting Russian government and society toward involvement with the rest of Europe.

Peter was almost literally larger than life. Nearly 7 feet tall, he towered over most of his contemporaries and had physical and mental energy to match his size. He set himself to learning trades and studied soldiering by rising in the ranks of the military like any common soldier. He traveled abroad to learn as much as he could about other states' economies and government. He wanted the revenue, manufacturing output, technology and trade, and, above all, the up-to-date army and navy that other rulers enjoyed. In short, Peter sought for Russia a more evolved state system because of the strength it would give him.

Peter initiated a bold and even brutal series of changes in Russian society upon his accession to power. Peasants already were bearing the brunt of taxation, but their tax burden worsened when they were assessed arbitrarily by head and not by output of the land. Peter noticed that European monarchs coexisted with a privileged but educated aristocracy and that a brilliant court life symbolized and reinforced the rulers' authority.

Peter the Great This portrait by a Dutch artist shows Peter in military dress according to European fashions of the day. (*Rijksmuseum-Stichting, Amsterdam*)

Peter the Great Changes Russia

Peter the Great's reforms included not only monumental building and a new relationship with elites but also practical changes in education, technology, and administration. Writing about a hundred years after the end of Peter's reign, the Russian historian Mikhail Pogodin (1800–1875) reflected on all the changes Peter had introduced, perhaps exaggerating only the respect Peter earned in foreign eyes in his lifetime.

Yes, Peter the Great did much for Russia. . . . One keeps adding and one cannot reach the sum. We cannot open our eyes, cannot make a move, cannot turn in any direction without encountering him everywhere, at home, in the streets, in church, in school, in court, in the regiment. . . .

We wake up. What day is it today? . . . Peter ordered us to count the years from the birth of Christ; Peter ordered us to count the months from January.

It is time to dress—our clothing is made according to the fashion established by Peter the First, our uniform according to his model. The cloth is woven in a factory which he created. . . .

Newspapers are brought in—Peter the Great introduced them.

You must buy different things—they all, from the silk neckerchief to the sole of your shoe, will remind you of Peter. . . . Some were ordered by him . . . or improved by him, carried on his ships, into his harbors, on his canals, on his roads.

Let us go to the university—the first secular school was founded by Peter the Great.

You decide to travel abroad—following [his] example; you will be received well—Peter the Great placed Russia among the European states and began to instill respect for her; and so on and so on.

Source: Nicholas V. Riasanovsky, *A History of Russia*, 2d ed. (London: Oxford University Press, 1969), pp. 266–267.

So he set out to refashion Russian society in what amounted to an enforced cultural revolution. (See the box, "Peter the Great Changes Russia.") He provoked a direct confrontation with Russia's traditional aristocracy over everything from education to matters of dress. He elevated numerous new families to the ranks of gentry and created an official ranking system for the nobility to encourage and reward service to his government.

Peter's effort to reorient his nation culturally, economically, and politically toward Europe was most apparent in the construction of the city of St. Petersburg on the Gulf of Finland, which provided access to the Baltic Sea (see Map 16.2). In stark contrast to Moscow, dominated by the medieval fortress of the Kremlin and churches in the traditional Russian style, St. Petersburg was a modern European city with wide avenues and palaces designed for a sophisticated court life.

But although Peter was highly intelligent, practical, and determined to create a more productive and better governed society, he was also cruel, ruthless, and authoritarian. The building of St. Petersburg cost staggering sums in money and in workers' lives. Peter's entire reform system was carried out autocratically; resistance was brutally suppressed. Victims of Peter's oppression included his son, Alexis, who died after torture while awaiting execution for questioning his father's policies.

Peter faced elite as well as populist rebellions against the exactions and the cultural changes of his regime. The most serious challenge, in 1707, was a revolt of Cossacks of the Don River region against the regime's tightened controls. The primary reason for the high cost of Peter's government to the Russian people was not the tsar's determination to increase his internal power but rather his ambition for territorial gain—hence Peter's emphasis on an improved, and costly, army and navy. Working side by side with workers and technicians, many of whom he had recruited while abroad, Peter created the Russian navy from scratch. At first, ships were built in the south to contest Turkish control of the Black Sea; later, they were built in the north to contest the Baltic. Peter also modernized the Russian army by employing tactics, training, and discipline he had observed in the West. He introduced military conscription. By 1709, Russia was able to manufacture most of the up-to-date firearms its army needed.

Russia waged war virtually throughout Peter's reign. Initially with some success, he struck at the Ottomans and their client state in the Crimea. Later phases of these conflicts brought reverses, however. Peter was spectacularly successful against his northern competitor, Sweden, for control of the weakened Polish state and the Baltic Sea. The conflicts between Sweden and Russia, known as the Second Great Northern War, raged from 1700 to 1709 and, in a less intense phase, lasted until 1721. By the Treaty of Nystadt in 1721, Russia gained the territory in the Gulf of Finland near St. Petersburg that it now has, plus Livonia and Estonia. These acquisitions gave Russia a secure window on the Baltic and, in combination with its gains of Lithuanian territory earlier in the century, made Russia the pre-eminent Baltic power at Sweden's and Poland's expense.

THE RISE OF OVERSEAS TRADE

By the beginning of the seventeenth century, competition from the Dutch, French, and English was disrupting the Spanish and Portuguese trading empires in Asia and the New World. During the seventeenth century, European trade and colonization expanded and changed dramatically. The Dutch not only became masters of the spice trade but led the expansion of that trade to include many other commodities. In the Americas, a new trading system linking Europe, Africa, and the New World came into being with the expansion of sugar and tobacco production. French and English colonists began settling in North America in increasing numbers. By the end of the century, trading and colonial outposts around the world figured regularly as bargaining chips in disagreements between European states. More importantly, overseas trade had a dramatic impact on life within Europe: on patterns of production and consumption, on social stratification, and the distribution of wealth.

The Growth of Trading Empires: The Success of the Dutch

By the end of the sixteenth century, the Dutch and the English were trying to make incursions into the Portuguese-controlled spice trade with areas of India, Ceylon, and the East Indies. Spain had annexed Portugal in 1580, but the drain on Spain's resources from its wars with the Dutch and French prevented Spain from adequately defending its enlarged trading empire in Asia. The Dutch and, to a lesser degree, the English rapidly supplanted Portuguese control of this lucrative trade (Map 16.3).

The Dutch were particularly well placed to be successful competitors in overseas trade. They already dominated seaborne trade within Europe, including the most important long-distance trade, which linked Spain and Portugal—with their wine and salt, as well as spices, hides, and gold from abroad—with the Baltic seacoast, where these products were sold for grain and timber produced in Germany, Poland-Lithuania, and Scandinavia. The geographic position of the Netherlands and the fact that the Dutch consumed more Baltic grain than any other area, because of their densely urbanized economy, help to explain their dominance of this trade. In addition, the Dutch had improved the design of their merchant ships to enhance their profits. By 1600 they were building the *fluitschip* (flyship) to transport cargo economically; it was a vessel with a long, flat hull and simple rigging and made from cheap materials.

The Dutch were successful in Asia because of institutional as well as technological innovations. In 1602 the Dutch East India Company was formed. The company combined the government management of trade, typical of the period, with both public and private investment. In the past, groups of investors had funded single voyages or small numbers of ships on a one-time basis. The formation of the Dutch East India Company created a permanent pool of capital to sustain trade. After 1612 investments in the company were negotiable as stock. The enlarged pool of capital meant the risks and delays of longer voyages

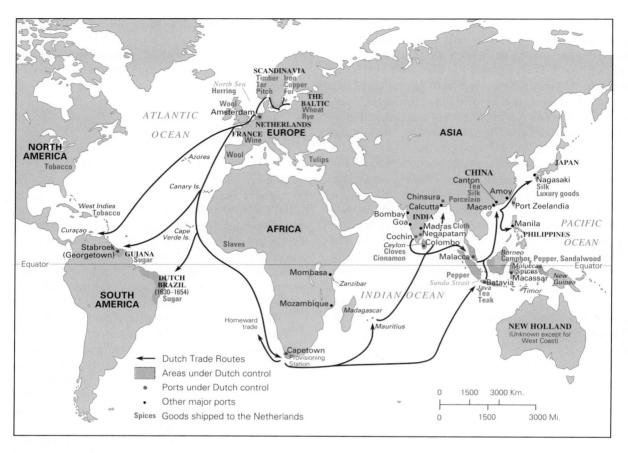

Map 16.3 Dutch Commerce in the Seventeenth Century The Dutch supplanted Portuguese control of trade with Asia and dominated seaborne trade within Europe.

could be spread among larger numbers of investors. In addition, more money was available for warehouses, docks, and ships. The English East India Company, founded in 1607, also supported trade, but more modestly. It had one-tenth the capital of the Dutch company and did not use the same system of permanent capital held as stock by investors until 1657. The Bank of Amsterdam, founded in 1609, became the depository for the bullion that flowed into the Netherlands with trade. The bank established currency-exchange rates and issued paper money and instruments of credit to facilitate commerce.

A dramatic expansion of trade with Asia resulted from the Dutch innovations, so much so that by 1650 the European market for spices was glutted, and traders' profits had begun to fall. To control the supply of spices, the Dutch seized some of the areas where they were produced.

Control of supply helped prop up prices, but these gains were somewhat offset by greater military and administrative costs.

The Dutch and English further responded to the oversupply of spices by diversifying their trade. The proportion of spices in cargoes from the East fell from about 70 percent at midcentury to just over 20 percent by the century's end. New consumer goods such as tea, coffee, silks, and cotton fabrics took their place. The demand of ordinary people for inexpensive yet serviceable Indian cottons grew steadily. Eventually, the Dutch and the English diversified their trade in Asia even more by entering the local carrying trade among Asian states. Doing so enabled them to make profits without purchasing goods, and it slowed the drain of hard currency from Europe—currency in increasingly short supply as silver mines in the Americas were worked out. (See the box, "En-

The Grain Market in Amsterdam Though the Dutch had spectacular success overseas in the seventeenth century, dominance of the carrying trade within Europe, particularly with the Baltic, remained a foundation of its prosperity. Grain exported from the Baltic was the single most important commodity traded in Amsterdam. (*British Library*)

counters with the West: Agents of the Dutch East India Company Confront Asian Powers.")

The "Golden Age" of the Netherlands

The prosperity occasioned by the Netherlands' "mother trade" within Europe and its burgeoning overseas commerce helped to foster social and political conditions unique within Europe. The concentration of trade and shipping sustained a large merchant oligarchy but also an extensive and prosperous artisanal sector. Disparities of wealth were smaller here than anywhere else in Europe. The shipbuilding and fishing trades, among others, supported large numbers of workers with a high standard of living for the age.

Political decentralization in the Netherlands persisted: Each of the seven provinces retained considerable autonomy. However, merchant oligarchs in the Estates of the province of Holland in fact constituted the government for the whole for long periods because of Holland's economic dominance. The head of government was the pensionary (executive secretary) of Holland's Estates. An Estates General existed but had no independent powers of taxation.

The only competition in the running of affairs came from the House of Orange, aristocratic leaders of the revolt against Spain (see pages 553–558). They exercised what control they had by means of the office of *stadholder*— a kind of military governorship—to which they were elected in individual provinces. Their principal interest was the traditional one of military glory and self-promotion. Therein lay a portion of their influence, for they continued to lead the defense of the Netherlands against Spanish attempts at reconquest until the Peace of Westphalia in 1648. Their power also came from the fact that they represented the only possible counterweight within the Netherlands to the dominance of Amsterdam merchant interests. Small towns dependent on land-based trade or rural areas dominated by farmers and gentry looked to the stadholders of the Orange family to defend their interests.

As elsewhere, religion was a source of political conflict. The stadholders and the leading families of Holland, known as regents, vied for control of the state church; the pensionaries and regents of Holland generally favored less rigid and austere Calvinism than the stadholders' faction. This view reflected the needs of the diverse mercantile com-

≈ **ENCOUNTERS WITH THE WEST** ≈

Agents of the Dutch East India Company Confront Asian Powers

This 1655 letter from a local agent of the Dutch East India Company to its board of directors (the "Seventeen") shows that the Dutch had to maintain good working relationships with local powers in Asia, in this case, with the king of Siam (modern Thailand). The letter discusses the Dutch blockade of Tennasserim, a major port under Siamese control, and the promises of help the Dutch, via their local agents, had made the king for some of his military ventures.

It appears that the merchant Hendrich Craijer Zalr had promised, so they [the Siamese] say, 20 ships, which was a very rash proceeding on his part, and thereupon they made the above-mentioned expedition, which they said, if our support did not appear, would be obliged to return unsuccessful and with shame and dishonor to the crown, as was actually the case. Moreover, it happened that a writing had come unexpectedly from the governor of Tennasserim that two Dutch ships had held the harbor there for 2 months, and had prevented the entrance and departure of foreign traders, which caused great annoyance in Siam, especially at Court, and embittered everyone against us. This gave the [English] Companies very favorable opportunity to blacken us and to make us odious to everyone, and to change the King's feeble opposition into open enmity, the more so since the news has from time to time been confirmed and assured, and no one there doubts it any longer.

Wherefore the resident Westerwolt, who was convinced of the contrary, since he would certainly have been informed before any such action was taken, finally found himself obliged to ask that certain persons, on the King's behalf and on his own, should be deputed and sent overland to Tennasserim, in order to discover on the spot the truth of the case, which request was granted by the King, and on our behalf the junior merchant, Hugo van Crujlenburgh was sent.

Meanwhile the aforementioned resident Westerwolt had on various occasions made complaint of the bad and unreasonable treatment received, . . . so that the resident was in very great embarrassment and did not know whether even his life was any longer safe. These questions were for the most part on the subject of the help asked for against Singgora, the Siamese professing to have gone to war with the Spanish on our account, and to have suffered much damage in the same, and that we now refused to assist his Majesty against the rebels with ships and men; whereas the beforementioned merchant, Hendrich Craijer, had definitely made him such promises.

Source: Records of the Relations Between Siam and Foreign Countries in the Seventeenth Century (Bangkok: Council of theVajiranana National Library, 1916), vol. 2. Quoted in Alfred J. Andrea and James H. Overfield, *The Human Record: Sources of Global History*, 2d ed., vol. 2: *Since 1500* (Boston: Houghton Mifflin, 1994), pp. 134–135.

munities of Holland, where thousands of Jews as well as Catholics and various kinds of Protestants lived. Foreign policy also turned on Holland's desire for peace in order to foster commerce versus the stadholder's greater willingness to engage in warfare for territory and dynastic advantage.

These differences notwithstanding, Dutch commercial dominance involved them in costly wars throughout the second half of the century. Between 1657 and 1660 the Dutch defended Denmark against Swedish ambitions in order to safeguard the sea-lanes and port cities of the Baltic.

Other, more costly, conflicts arose simply because of rivalry with other states, notably England and France. Under Cromwell, the English attempted to close their ports to the Dutch carrying trade. In 1672 the English under Charles II allied with the French, assuming that together they could destroy Dutch power and perhaps even divide the Netherlands' territory between them. The Dutch navy, rebuilt since Cromwell's challenge, soon forced England out of the alliance.

Owing largely to the land war with France, the Estates in Holland lost control of policy to William of Nassau (d. 1702), prince of Orange after 1672. William drew the Netherlands into his family's long-standing close relationship with England. Like other members of his family before him, William had married into the English royal family: His wife was Mary, daughter of James II.

Ironically, after he and Mary assumed the English throne in 1689 (see page 602), Dutch commerce suffered more in alliance with England than in its previous rivalry. William used Dutch re-

sources for the land war against Louis XIV and reserved for the English navy the fight at sea. Dutch maritime strength was being eclipsed by English seapower by the end of the century.

The Netherlands was controlled by a privileged few for most of the seventeenth century and was virtually a monarchy led from abroad by the end of the century. Nevertheless, the Netherlands appeared to contemporaries to be an astonishing exception to the normal structures of politics. In France and most other states in Europe, political life was dominated by a court where aristocrats and ministers mingled and conspired and an elaborate ritual of honor and deference glorified the king. The princes of Orange surrounded themselves with splendid trappings, but their court was not the sole focus of political life in the Netherlands. The portraits of the Dutch painter Rembrandt van Rijn (1606–1667) portray the austerity of the merchant oligarchs; theirs was a novel kind of power that could be symbolized with ostentatious simplicity.

Rembrandt: The Syndics of the Cloth Drapers' Guild (1662) In this painting, the last group portrait of his career, Rembrandt depicts the guild members with artful, stylized simplicity. It was Rembrandt's genius also to be able to convey a sense of personality and drama in such commissioned portraits. *(Rijksmuseum-Stichting, Amsterdam)*

The Growth of Atlantic Colonies and Commerce

In the seventeenth century, the Dutch, the English, and the French joined the Spanish as colonial and commercial powers in the Americas. The Spanish colonial empire, in theory a trading system closed to outsiders, was in fact vulnerable to incursion by other European traders. Spanish treasure fleets themselves were an attraction. In 1628, for example, a Dutch captain seized the entire fleet. But by then Spain's goals and those of its competitors had begun to shift; the limits of an economy based on the extraction of wealth rather than on the production of wealth became clear with the declining output of the Spanish silver mines during the 1620s. In response, the Spanish and their Dutch, French, and English competitors expanded the production of the cash crops of sugar and tobacco.

The European demand for sugar and tobacco, both addictive substances, grew steadily in the seventeenth century. The plantation system—the use of forced labor to work large tracts of land—had been developed on Mediterranean islands in the Middle Ages by European entrepreneurs who used slaves from the Black Sea region as well as local labor. Sugar production by this system was established on Atlantic Islands, using African labor, and then in the Americas by the Spanish and Portuguese. The French, English, and Dutch followed their lead and established sugar plantations on the Caribbean islands they held. Sugar production in the New World grew from about 20,000 tons in 1600 to about 200,000 tons by 1770.

While the Dutch were exploiting Portuguese weakness in the eastern spice trade, they were also seizing sugar regions in Brazil and replacing the Portuguese in slaving ports in Africa. The Portuguese were able to retake some of their Brazilian territory, but because the Dutch monopolized the carrying trade, they were able to become the official supplier of slaves to Spanish plantations in the New World and the chief supplier to most other regions. The Dutch were able to make handsome profits until the end of the seventeenth century, when they were supplanted by the British.

Aware of the great Spanish territorial advantage in the New World, and hoping for treasures such as the Spanish had found, the English, French, and Dutch were also ambitious to explore and settle North America. From the early six-teenth century, French, Dutch, English, and Portuguese seamen had fished and traded off Newfoundland. By 1630, small French and Scottish settlements in Acadia (near modern Nova Scotia) and on the St. Lawrence River and English settlements in Newfoundland were established to systematically exploit the timber, fish, and fur of the north Atlantic coasts.

In England population growth and consequent unemployment, as well as religious discontent, created a large pool of potential colonists. The first of the English settlements to endure in what was to become the United States was established at Jamestown, named for James I, in Virginia in 1607. ("Virginia," named for Elizabeth I, the "virgin" queen, was an extremely vague designation for the Atlantic coast of North America and its hinterland.)

The Crown encouraged colonization, but a private company similar to the companies that financed long-distance trade was established actually to organize the enterprise. The directors of the Virginia Company were London businessmen. Investors and would-be colonists purchased shares. Shareholders among the colonists could participate in a colonial assembly, though the governor appointed by the company was the final authority.

The colonists arrived in Virginia with ambitious and optimistic instructions. They were to open mines, establish profitable cultivation, and search for sea routes to Asia. However, the colonists struggled at first merely to survive. (See the box, "The Disappointments of the Virginia Colony.") The indigenous peoples in Virginia, unlike those in Spanish-held territory, were not organized in urbanized, rigidly hierarchical societies that, after conquest, could provide the invaders with a labor force. Indeed, the native Americans in this region were quickly wiped out by European diseases. The introduction of tobacco as a cash crop a few years later saved the colonists economically—though the Virginia Company had already gone bankrupt and the Crown had assumed control of the colony. With the cultivation of tobacco, the Virginia colony, like the Caribbean islands, became dependent on forced, eventually slave, labor.

Among the Virginia colonists were impoverished men and women who came as servants indentured to those who had paid their passage. Colonies established to the north, in what was called "New England," also drew people from the

The Disappointments of the Virginia Colony

In this letter sent to the Virginia Company in 1608, Captain John Smith (1580–1631) explains some-what angrily that the colony cannot produce the profits that the investors were hoping for. He notes the folly of carrying boats west over the fall line of the Virginia rivers—where, it had been assumed, they might sight the Pacific Ocean as the Spaniards had done in Panama. He reports no sign of the colony of Sir Walter Raleigh, which vanished after settlement in North Carolina in 1587. He also notes the difficulties of extracting wealth and the difficulties of mere survival.

I have received your letter, wherein you write that . . . we feed you but with ifs and ands and hopes, and some few proofs . . . and that we must expressly follow your instructions sent by Captain Newport [the commander of the sup-ply ship], the charge of whose voyage . . . we cannot defray.

For the quartered boat to be borne by the soldiers over the falls, Newport had 120 of the best men. . . . If he had burned her to ashes, one might have carried her in a bag, but as she is, five hundred cannot, to a navigable place above the falls. And for him, at that time to find in the South Sea a mine of gold, or any of them sent by Sir Walter Raleigh, at our consultation I told them was as likely as the rest. . . . In their absence I followed the new begun works of pitch and tar, glass, [potash, and lumber], whereof some small quantities we have sent you. But if you rightly consider, what an infinite toil it is in Russia and [Sweden], where the woods are proper for naught else [and where] there be the help of both man and beast . . . yet thousands of those poor people can scarce get necessaries to live. . . .

From your ship we had not provision in victuals worth twenty pound, and we are more than two hundred to live upon this. . . . Though there be fish in the sea, fowls in the air, and beasts in the woods . . . they are so wild and we so weak and ignorant, we cannot much trouble them.

Source: Philip L. Barbour, ed., *The Complete Works of Captain John Smith (1580–1631)*, vol. 2 (Chapel Hill: University of North Carolina Press, 1986), pp. 187–189.

margins of English society: Early settlers there were religious dissidents. The first to arrive were the Pilgrims, who arrived at New Plymouth (modern Massachusetts) in 1620. They were a community of religious separatists who had origi-nally immigrated to the Netherlands from Eng-land for freedom of conscience.

Following the Pilgrims came Puritans escap-ing escalating persecution under Charles I. The first, in 1629, settled under the auspices of another royally chartered company, the Massachusetts Bay Company. Among their number were many pros-perous Puritan merchants and landholders. Inde-pendence from investors in London allowed them an unprecedented degree of self-government once the Massachusetts Bay colony was established.

Nevertheless, the colonies in North America were disappointments to England because they generated much less wealth than expected. Ship-ping timber back to Europe proved too expensive, though New England timber did supply some of the Caribbean colonists' needs. The fur trade be-came less lucrative as English settlement pushed westward the native Americans who did most of the trapping and as French trappers to the north encroached on the trade. Certain colonists profited enormously from the tobacco economy, but the mother country did so only moderately because the demand in Europe for tobacco never grew as quickly as the demand for sugar.

The colonies' greatest strength, from the Eng-lish viewpoint, was that the settlements continued

Map 16.4 British and French in North America, ca. 1700 By 1700 a veritable ring of French-claimed territory encircled the coastal colonies of England. English-claimed areas, however, were more densely settled and more economically viable.

to attract migrants. By 1640 Massachusetts had some 14,000 European inhabitants. Through most of the next century, the growth of colonial populations in North America would result in an English advantage over the French in control of territory. In the long run, however, the size of the colonial communities, their degree of routine political independence from the mother country, and their loose economic ties to England led them to seek independence.

The French began their settlement of North America at the same time as the English, in the same push to compensate for their mutual weakness vis-à-vis the Spanish (Map 16.4). The French efforts, however, had very different results, owing

partly to the sites of their settlements but mostly to the relationship between the mother country and the colonies. The French hold on territory was always tenuous because of the scant number of colonists from France. There seems to have been less economic impetus for colonization from France than from England. And, after the French crown took over the colonies, there was no religious impetus, for only Catholics were allowed to settle in New France. Moreover, control by the Crown forced a traditional hierarchical political organization on the French colonies. There was a royal governor, and large tracts of land were set aside for privileged investors. Thus, there was little in North America to tempt people of modest means who were seeking a better life.

The first successful French colony was established in Acadia in 1605. This settlement was an exception among the French efforts because it was founded by Huguenots, not by Catholics. A few years later, the intrepid explorer Samuel de Champlain (1567?–1635) navigated the St. Lawrence River and founded Quebec City. He convinced the royal government, emerging from its preoccupations with religious wars at home, to promote the development of the colony. French explorers went on to establish Montreal, farther inland on the St. Lawrence (1642), and to explore the Great Lakes and the Mississippi River basin (see Map 16.4).

Such investment as the French crown was able to attract went into profitable trade, mainly in furs, and not into the difficult business of colonization. French trappers and traders who ventured into wilderness areas were renowned for their hardiness and adaptability, but it was not their business to establish European-style communities. Quebec remained more of a trading station, dependent on shipments of food from France, than a growing urban community. Much of the energy of French colonization was expended by men and women of religious orders bringing their zeal to new frontiers. By the middle of the seventeenth century, all of New France had only about three thousand European inhabitants.

The seeming weakness of the French colonial effort in North America was not much noticed at the time. French and English fishermen, trappers, and traders competed intensely with each other, and there were outright battles between English and French settlements. But for both England and

France the major profits and strategic interests in the New World lay to the south, in the Caribbean. The Dutch experience in North America reveals the degree to which North America was of secondary importance, for all colonial powers, to the plantation profits farther south. In 1624 the Dutch founded a trading center, New Amsterdam, at the site of modern New York City. In 1674 they relinquished it to the English in return for recognition of the Dutch claims to sugar-producing Guiana (modern Suriname) in South America. Consequently, by far the largest group of migrants to European-held territories in the Americas were forced migrants: African men and women sold into slavery and transported across the Atlantic. A conservative estimate is that approximately 1,350,000 Africans were forcibly transported as slave labor to the New World during the seventeenth century.

The Beginning of the End of Traditional Society

Within Europe, the economic impact of overseas trade was profound. Merchants and investors in a few of Europe's largest cities reaped great profits. Mediterranean trading centers such as Venice and Genoa, once the heart of European trade, did not share in the profits generated by goods now being shipped to and from the New World. Atlantic ports such as Seville, through which most Spanish commerce with the New World flowed, and, above all, Amsterdam began to flourish. The population of Amsterdam increased from about 30,000 to 200,000 in the course of the seventeenth century.

All capital cities, however, not just seaports, grew substantially in the seventeenth century. Increasing numbers of government functionaries, courtiers and their hangers-on, and people involved in trade lived and worked in capital cities. These cities also grew indirectly from the demand such people generated for services and products, ranging from fashionable clothing to exotic foodstuffs. For the first time, cities employed vast numbers of country people. Perhaps as much as one-fifth of the population of England passed through London at one time or another, creating the mobile, volatile community so active in the English civil war and its aftermath.

The economy became more productive and flexible as it expanded, but social stratification in-

Marie de l'Incarnation, Colonial Settler Marie Guyart (1599–1672), as she was known in lay life, was an Ursuline nun who abandoned her own family in France to help found a convent and school for girls in Quebec, Canada. She welcomed both settlers' daughters and Native American girls to the school; she also learned several Amerindian languages during her life. *(Thomas Fisher Rare Book Library, University of Toronto)*

creased. Patterns of consumption in cities reflected the economic gulfs between residents. Most people could not afford to buy imported pepper or sugar. Poverty increased in cities, even in vibrant Amsterdam, because they attracted people fleeing rural unemployment. As growing central governments increased their tax burdens on peasants, many rural people were caught in a cycle of debt; they abandoned farming and made their way to cities.

Many such people on the margins of economic life were innovative in their efforts to survive, but they were increasingly vulnerable to both economic forces and state power. Thousands of rural people, particularly those close to thriving urban centers, supplemented their farm income by means of the putting-out system, or cottage industry. An entrepreneur loaned, or "put out," raw materials to rural workers, who processed them at home and returned a finished product to the entrepreneur. For example, the rural workers might receive wool to be spun and woven into cloth. The entrepreneur would pay the workers by the piece and then sell the finished product. In the long run, the putting-out system left workers open to economic vulnerability of a new, more modern, sort. A local harvest failure might still endanger them, and so might a foreign war or disaster at sea that affected the long-distance trade for their product.

Peasant rebellions occurred throughout the century as a result of depressed economic conditions and heavy taxation. Some of the revolts were extremely localized and involved limited direct action, such as seizing the tax collector's grain or stopping the movement of grain to the great cities. Urban demand for grain often caused severe shortages in rural areas in western Europe, despite the booming trade in grain with eastern Europe via the Baltic.

The typical peasant revolt in western Europe during the seventeenth century, however, was directed against escalating taxation. Tax rebellions often formed spontaneously, perhaps as tax officials passed through a village, but they were not mere chaotic gatherings of rabble. Countryfolk were accustomed to defending themselves as communities—against brigands and marauding soldiers, for example. Local gentry and even prosperous peasants might ordinarily fulfill the function of local constable or other lowly state office and generally be interested in maintaining order; yet they led such revolts from time to time, convinced that they represented the legitimate interests of the community against rapacious officials higher up. The scale of peasant violence meant that thousands of troops at times had to be diverted from a state's foreign wars; as a matter of routine, soldiers accompanied tax officials and enforced collection all over Europe. Thus, as the ambitions of rulers grew, so too did resistance of ordinary people to the exactions of the state.

SUMMARY

The beginning of the seventeenth century was marked by religious turmoil and by social and political upheaval. By the end of the century, the former had faded as a source of collective anxiety, and the latter was largely resolved. Nascent political configurations in the Low Countries, in the Holy Roman Empire, and on the frontiers of eastern Europe had evolved into new centers of power: the Netherlands, Brandenburg-Prussia, and the newly powerful Russia of Peter the Great. Most European states had moved from internal division—with independent provinces and aristocrats going their own way—to relative stability. This internal stability was both cause and consequence of rulers' desire to make war on an ever larger scale. By the end of the century, only those states able to field large armies were competitive on the European stage.

At the beginning of the century, overseas trade and colonization had been the near monopoly of Spain and Portugal; at the century's end, the English, French, and Dutch controlled much of the trade with Asia and were reaping many profits in the Americas. Beneath all these developments lay subtle but significant economic, social, and cultural shifts. One effect of the increased wealth generated by overseas trade and the increased power of governments to tax their subjects was a widening of the gulf between poor and rich. New styles of behavior and patterns of consumption highlighted differences between social classes. Long-term effects of overseas voyages on European attitudes, as well as fundamental change in viewing the world culminating in the development of modern science, would have revolutionary effects on Europeans and their cultures.

NOTES

1. Quoted in D. H. Pennington, *Europe in the Seventeenth Century,* 2d ed. (London: Longman, 1989), p. 508.

SUGGESTED READING

General Surveys

Howard, Michael. *War in European History.* 1976. A general study of warfare emphasizing the relationship between war making and state development.

Pennington, D. H. *Europe in the Seventeenth Century.* 2d ed. 1989; and Bonney, Richard. *The European Dynastic*

States, 1494–1660. 1991. Two general histories covering various portions of the century.

France

Beik, William. *Absolutism and Society in Seventeenth-Century France.* 1984. A case study focusing on a province in southern France but nevertheless an important interpretation of the nature and functioning of the absolutist state; has an extensive bibliography.

Collins, James B. *The State in Early Modern France.* 1995. An up-to-date synthesis by one of the leading scholars of French absolutism.

Goubert, Pierre. *The French Peasantry in the Seventeeth Century.* 1986.

———. *Louis XIV and Twenty Million Frenchmen.* 1970. Two works that consider political and social history from a broad analytic framework that includes long-term economic, demographic, and cultural data.

England

Aylmer, G. E. *Rebellion or Revolution? England from Civil War to Restoration.* 1987. A useful work that summarizes the important studies on each facet of the revolution; has an extensive bibliography.

Hill, Christopher. *A Century of Revolution, 1603–1714.* Rev. ed. 1980.

———. *The World Turned Upside Down.* 1972. The first work is a general history, the second an exploration of Levelers, Diggers, and other groups of lower-class participants in the English revolution.

Stone, Lawrence. *The Causes of the English Revolution, 1529–1642.* 1972. A brief and clear introduction.

Central and Eastern Europe

Bérenger, Jean. *A History of the Hapsburg Empire, 1273–1700.* 1990. A detailed and nuanced history of all the Habsburg domains and of the Habsburgs' relationship to Europe as a whole.

Kirby, David. *Northern Europe in the Early Modern Period, 1492–1772.* 1990.

Oakley, Stewart P. *War and Peace in the Baltic, 1560–1790.* 1992. Two excellent surveys of the Baltic region in the early modern period.

Riasanovsky, Nicolas V. *A History of Russia.* 2d ed. 1969. A reliable and readable survey of Russian history from medieval times; has an extensive bibliography of major works available in English.

Vierhaus, Rudolf. *Germany in the Age of Absolutism.* 1988. A concise survey of the development of German states from the end of the Thirty Years' War through the eighteenth century.

Wandycz, Piotr. *The Price of Freedom: A History of East Central Europe from the Middle Ages to the Present.* 1992.

A lively survey of the histories of Poland, Hungary, and Bohemia.

Early Modern Economy, Society, and Culture

Alpers, Svetlana. *The Art of Describing: Dutch Art in the Seventeenth Century.* 1983. An innovative approach to Dutch art, considering it in its social and broader cultural context.

Bercé, Yves-Marie. *Revolt and Revolution in Early Modern Europe.* Translated by Joseph Bergin. 1987.

———. *History of Peasant Revolts.* Translated by A. Whitmore. 1990. The first work is a general, comparative survey of revolts and revolutionary movements of all sorts across Europe between 1500 and 1800; the second is a more intensive study of French peasant movements.

Blum, Jerome. *Lord and Peasant in Russia.* 1961. A work that highlights the extension of serfdom in Russia fostered by Peter the Great and other tsars.

Boxer, C. R. *The Dutch Seaborne Empire.* 1965. The standard work detailing the development of the Dutch empire.

Curtin, Philip D. *The Rise and Fall of the Plantation Complex.* 1990. A good starting place for understanding the reasons behind and the significance of Europeans' establishment of plantation agriculture in the New World.

De Vries, Jan. *The Economy of Europe in an Age of Crisis, 1600–1750.* 1976. The single most important work on the development of the European economy in this period, integrating developments within and around Europe with the growth of overseas empires.

Parry, J. H. *The Establishment of European Hegemony, 1415–1715.* 1961. A brief introduction to the motives, means, and results of European expansion through the seventeenth century; somewhat dated in its overemphasis on the English in North America but nevertheless a useful overview.

Ritchie, Robert C. *Captain Kidd and the War Against the Pirates.* 1986. An interesting work on the communities of castoffs and adventurers that grew up in the Caribbean during European expansion and their place in the Atlantic economic and political worlds.

Sabean, David Warren. *Power in the Blood.* 1984. An innovative series of essays about life in German villages from the sixteenth through the eighteenth centuries; raises questions about the increasing efforts of the state to control village life and the resistance mounted by villagers to these efforts.

Wolf, Eric R. *Europe and the People Without History.* 1982. A survey of European contact with and conquest of peoples after 1400; includes extensive treatments of non-European societies and detailed explanation of the economic and political interests of the Europeans.

TABLE MANNERS

If you were to sit down in a fancy restaurant, order a juicy steak, and then eat it with your bare hands, other diners would undoubtedly stare and think what bad manners you have. It has not always been the case that table manners meant very much—were able to signal social status, for example. It was not always the case that table manners existed at all in the sense that we know them. How did they evolve? How did they come to have the importance that they do? And why should historians pay any attention to them?

Imagine that you have been invited to dinner at a noble estate in the year 1500. As you sit down, you notice that there are no knives, forks, and spoons at your place at the table, and no napkins either. A servant (a young girl from a neighboring village) sets a roast of meat in front of you and your fellow diners. The lords and ladies on either side of you hack off pieces of meat with the knives that they always carry with them, and then they eat the meat with their fingers. Hunks of bread on the table in front of them catch the dripping juices.

One hundred fifty years later, in 1650, dinner is a much more "civilized" meal. Notice the well-to-do women dining in this engraving by the French artist Abraham Bosse (1602–1676). The table setting, with tablecloths, napkins, plates, and silverware, is recognizable to us. The lady at the extreme right holds up her fork and napkin in a somewhat forced and obvious gesture. These diners have the utensils that we take for granted, but the artist does not take them for granted: They are intended to be noticed by Bosse's elite audience.

In the seventeenth century, aristocrats and gentry signaled their political and social privilege with behavior that distinguished them from the lower classes in ways their more powerful ancestors had felt no need for. Historians have called this the invention of civility. As we have seen, proper courtesy to one's superiors at court was considered essential. It marked the fact that rituals

of honor and deference were increasingly taking the place of armed conflict as the routine behavior of the upper classes. Also essential, however, were certain standards of physical privacy and delicacy. Something as seemingly trivial as the use of a fork became charged with symbolic significance. As the actual power of the aristocrats was circumscribed by the state, they found new expressions of status. Since the sixteenth century, new kinds of manners had been touted in handbooks, reflecting changes that already had occurred at Italian courts. During the seventeenth century, these practices became more widespread and opened up a gulf of behavior between upper and lower classes.

Some of the new behaviors concerned bodily privacy and discretion. A nobleman now used a handkerchief instead of his fingers or coat sleeve, and he did not urinate in public. The new "rules" about eating are particularly interesting. Why did eating with a fork seem refined and desirable to aristocrats trying to buttress their own self-image? As any 3-year-old knows, eating with a fork is remarkably inefficient.

Using a fork kept you at a distance—literal and symbolic—from the animal you were eating. Napkins wiped away all trace of bloody juices from your lips. Interestingly, as diners began to use utensils, other eating arrangements changed in parallel ways. Sideboards had been in use for a long time, but pieces of meat were now discreetly carved on the sideboard and presented to diners in individual portions. The carcass was brought to the sideboard cut into roasts instead of unmistakably whole, and it was often decorated—as it is today—to further disguise it.

The new aristocrat was increasingly separated from the world of brute physical force, both in daily life and on the battlefield. In warfare, brute force was no longer adequate. Training, discipline, and tactical knowledge were more important and heightened the significance of rank,

Table Manners of the Upper Class in the Seventeenth Century *(Courtesy of the Trustees of the British Museum)*

which separated officers from the vast numbers of common soldiers (see page 595). Aristocrats now lived in a privileged world where violence was no longer a fact of life. Their new behavior codes signaled their new invulnerability to others. Above all, they worked to transform a loss—of the independence that had gone hand in hand with a more violent life—into a gain: a privileged immunity to violence.

Specific manners became important, then, because they were symbols of power. The symbolic distance between the powerful and the humble was reinforced by other changes in habits and behavior. A sixteenth-century warrior customarily traveled on horseback and often went from place to place within a city on foot, attended by his ret-inue. A seventeenth-century aristocrat was more likely to travel in a horsedrawn carriage. The presence of special commodities from abroad—such as sugar—in the seventeenth century created further possibilities for signaling status.

It is interesting to note that other personal habits still diverged dramatically from what we would consider acceptable today. Notice the large, stately bed in the same room as the dining table in Bosse's engraving. Interior space was still undifferentiated by our standards, and it was common for eating, talking, sleeping, and estate management all to go on in a single room. The grand bed is in the picture because, like the fork, it is a mark of status. Like virtually everything else, what is "proper" varies with historical circumstance. ✤

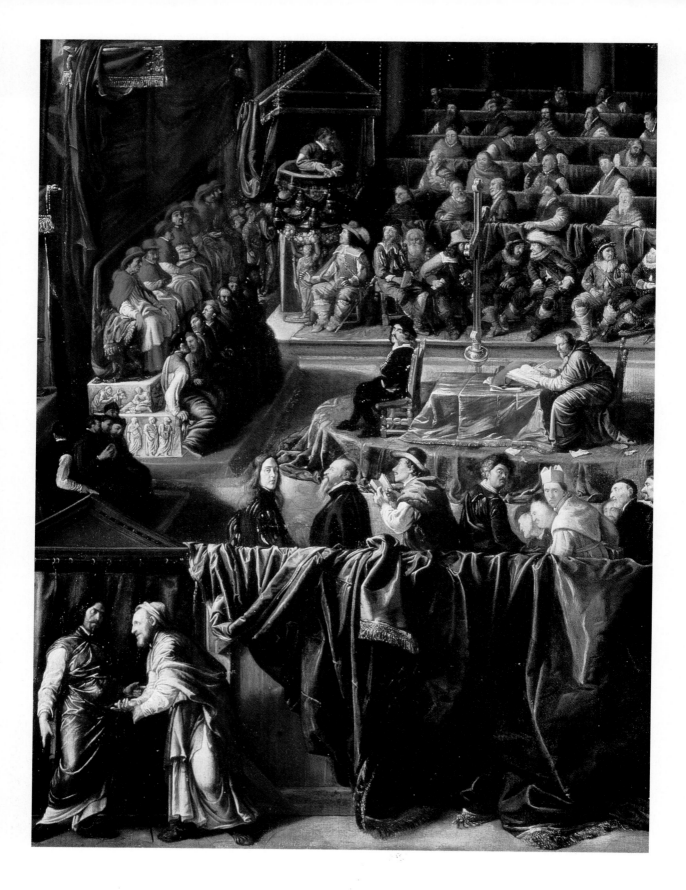

CHAPTER 17

A Revolution in World-View

As famous as the confrontation between the religious rebel Martin Luther and Holy Roman Emperor Charles V at Worms in 1521 is the confrontation between the astronomer Galileo and the judges of the papal inquisition that ended on June 22, 1633. On that day, Galileo knelt before the seven cardinals who represented the inquisition to renounce his errors and to receive his punishment. His "errors" included publishing scientific propositions that disagreed with views accepted by the church—particularly the view that the earth is stationary and does not spin on its axis and orbit the sun. As Galileo left the cardinals' presence, he is supposed to have muttered, "Eppur si muove" ("But it *does* move").

This seems a wonderful moment of historical drama, but we should be suspicious of it because it oversimplifies historical circumstances. The changes that we know as "the Reformation" and "the Scientific Revolution" were far more complex than the actions of a few individuals whose deeds now seem heroic and larger than life. Galileo, in fact, never made the defiant statement he is credited with.

Moreover, just as we cannot simply credit "heroes" with causing a revolution in scientific understanding, we cannot treat their new scientific views simply as truth finally overcoming ignorance and error. The history of scientific thought is not merely a history of discovery about the world; it is also a history of explanations of the world. From its beginnings the Scientific Revolution was a broad cultural movement. Copernicus, Galileo, and others contributed important new data to the pool of knowledge, but even more important was their collective contribution to a fundamentally

Trial of Galileo before
the inquisition, 1633.
(Anonymous, 17th century.)

new view of the universe and of the place of the earth and human beings in it.

By the end of the seventeenth century, a vision of an infinite but orderly cosmos appealing to human reason had largely replaced the medieval vision of a closed universe centered on earth and suffused with Christian purpose. Religion became an increasingly subordinate ally of science as confidence in an open-ended, experimental approach to knowledge came to be as strongly held as religious conviction. It is because of this larger shift in world-view, not because of particular scientific discoveries, that the seventeenth century may be labeled the era of the scientific *revolution*.

THE REVOLUTION IN ASTRONOMY

Because the Scientific Revolution was a revolution within science itself as well as a revolution in intellectual life more generally, we must seek its causes within the history of science as well as in the broader historical context. Many of the causes are familiar. They include the intellectual achievements of the Renaissance, the challenges that were posed by the discovery of the New World, the expansion of trade and production, the spread of literacy and access to books, and the increasing power of princes and monarchs.

The scientific origins of the seventeenth-century revolution in thought lie, for the most part, in developments in astronomy. Various advances in astronomy spurred dramatic intellectual transformation because of astronomy's role in the explanations of the world and of human life that had been devised by ancient and medieval scientists and philosophers. By the early part of the seventeenth century, fundamental astronomical tenets were successfully challenged. The consequence was the undermining of both the material explanation of the world (physics) and the philosophical explanation of the world (metaphysics) that had been standing for centuries.

The Inherited World-View and the Sixteenth-Century Context

Ancient and medieval astronomy accepted the perspective on the universe that unaided human senses support—namely, that the earth is at the center of the universe, and the celestial bodies ro-

tate around the earth. The intellectual and psychological journey from the notion of a closed world centered on the earth to an infinitely large universe of undifferentiated matter with no apparent place for humans was an immense process with complex causes.

The regular movements of heavenly bodies and the obvious importance of the sun for life on earth made astronomy a vital undertaking for both scientific and religious purposes in many ancient societies. Astronomers in ancient Greece carefully observed the heavens and learned to calculate and to predict the seemingly circular motion of the stars and the sun about the earth. The orbits of the planets were more difficult to explain, for the planets seemed to travel both east and west across the sky at various times and with no regularity that could be mathematically understood. Indeed, the very word *planet* comes from a Greek word meaning "wanderer."

We now know that all the planets simultaneously orbit the sun at different speeds and are at different distances from the sun. The relative positions of the planets thus constantly change; sometimes other planets are "ahead" of the earth and sometimes "behind." In the second century A.D. the Greek astronomer Ptolemy attempted to explain the planets' occasional "backward" motion by attributing it to "epicycles"—small circular orbits within the larger orbit. Ptolemy's mathematical explanations of the imagined epicycles were extremely complex, but neither Ptolemy nor medieval mathematicians and astronomers were ever able fully to account for planetary motion.

Ancient physics, most notably the work of Aristotle (384–322 B.C.), explained the fact that some objects (such as cannonballs) fall to earth but others (stars and planets) seem weightless relative to the earth by presuming that objects are made up of different sorts of matter. Aristotle thought that different kinds of matter had different inherent tendencies and properties. In this view, all earthbound matter (like cannonballs) falls because it is naturally attracted to earth—heaviness being a property of earthbound things.

In the Christian era, the Aristotelian explanation of the universe was infused with Christian meaning and purpose. The heavens were said to be made of different, pure matter because they were the abode of the angels. Both earth and the humans who inhabited it were changeable and

The Traditional Universe In this print from around 1600, heavenly bodies are depicted orbiting the earth in perfectly circular paths. In fact, the ancient astronomer Ptolemy believed that the planets followed complex orbits-within-orbits, known as *epicycles*, moving around the stationary earth. *(Hulton-Getty/Tony Stone Images)*

corruptible. Yet God had given human beings a unique and special place in the universe. The universe was thought to be literally a closed world with the stationary earth at the center. Revolving around the earth in circular orbits were the sun, the moon, the stars, and the planets. The motion of all lesser bodies was caused by the rotation of all the stars together in the crystal-like sphere in which they were embedded.

A few ancient astronomers theorized that the earth moved about the sun. Some medieval philosophers also adopted this heliocentric thesis (*helios* is the Greek word for "sun"), but it remained a minority view because it seemed to contradict both common sense and observed data. The sun and stars *appeared* to move around the earth with great regularity. Moreover, how could objects fall to earth if the earth was moving beneath them? Also, astronomers detected no difference in angles from which observers on earth viewed the stars at different times. Such differences would exist, they thought, if the earth changed positions by moving around the sun. It was inconceivable that the universe could be so large and the stars so distant that the earth's movement would produce no measurable change in the earth's position with respect to the stars.

Several conditions of intellectual life in the sixteenth century encouraged new work in astronomy and led to revision of the earth-centered world-view. The most important was the humanists' recovery of and commentary on ancient texts. Now able to work with new Greek versions of Ptolemy, mathematicians and astronomers noted that his explanations for the motions of the planets were imperfect and not simply inadequately transmitted, as they had long believed. Also, the discovery of the New World dramatically undercut the assumption that ancient knowledge was superior and specifically undermined Ptolemy's authority once again, for it disproved many of his assertions about geography.

The desire to explain heavenly motions better was still loaded with religious significance in the sixteenth century and was heightened by the immediate need for reform of the Julian calendar (named for Julius Caesar). Ancient observations of the movement of the sun, though remarkably accurate, could not measure the precise length of the solar year. By the sixteenth century, the cumulative error of this calendar had resulted in a change of ten days: The spring equinox fell on March 11 instead of March 21. An accurate and uniform system of dating was necessary for all rulers and their tax collectors and recordkeepers but was the particular project of the church, because the calculation of the date of Easter was at stake.

Impetus for new and better astronomical observations and calculations arose from other features of the intellectual and political landscape as well. Increasingly as the century went on, princely courts became important sources of patronage for and sites of scientific activity. Rulers eager to buttress their own power by symbolically linking it to dominion over nature sponsored investigations of the world, as Ferdinand and Isabella had so successfully done, and displayed the marvels of nature at their courts. Sponsoring scientific inquiry also yielded practical benefits: better mapping of the ruler's domains and better technology for mining, gunnery, and navigation.

Finally, schools of thought fashionable at the time, encouraged by the humanists' critique of Scholastic tradition, hinted at the possibilities of alternative physical and metaphysical systems. The first was Paracelsianism, named for the Swiss physician Philippus von Hohenheim (1493–1541), known as Paracelsus. Paracelsus offered an alternative to the theory, put forth by the ancient master, Galen (ca. 131–ca. 201), that the imbalance of bodily "humors" caused illness. He substituted a theory of chemical imbalance.

Neo-Platonism, the second school of thought, had a more systematic and far-reaching impact. Neo-Platonism, a revival primarily in Italian humanist circles of certain aspects of Plato's thought, contributed directly to innovation in science because it emphasized the abstract nature of true knowledge and thus encouraged mathematical investigation. This provided a spur to astronomical studies, which, since ancient times, had been concerned more with mathematical analysis of heavenly movements than with physical explanations for them. Also, like Paracelsianism, Neo-Platonism had a mystical dimension that encouraged creative speculation about the nature of matter and the organization of the universe. Neo-Platonists were particularly fascinated by the sun as a symbol of the one divine mind or soul at the heart of all creation.

The Copernican Challenge

Nicolaus Copernicus (1473–1543), son of a prosperous Polish merchant, pursued wide-ranging university studies in philosophy, law, astronomy, and mathematics—first in Cracow in Poland and then in Bologna and Padua in Italy. In Italy he was exposed to Neo-Platonic ideas. He took a degree in canon law in 1503 and became a cathedral canon in the city of Frauenburg in East Prussia (modern Poland), where he pursued his own interests in astronomy while carrying out administrative duties for the cathedral. When the pope asked Copernicus to assist with the reform of the Julian calendar, he replied that reform of the calendar required reform in astronomy. His major work, *De Revolutionibus Orbium Caelestium* (*On the Revolution of Heavenly Bodies*, 1543), was dedicated to the pope in the hopes that it would help with the task of calendar reform—as indeed it did. The Gregorian calendar, issued in 1582 during the pontificate of Gregory XIII (r. 1572–1585), was based on Copernicus's calculations.

Copernicus postulated that the earth and all the other planets orbit the sun. He did not assert that the earth does in fact move around the sun but offered the heliocentric system as a mathematical construct, useful for predicting the movements of planets, stars, and the sun. However, he walked a thin line between making claims for mathematical and physical reality. He had searched in ancient sources for thinkers who believed the earth did move. Other astronomers familiar with his work and reputation urged him to publish the results of his calculations. But not until 1542, twelve years after finishing the work, did he send *De Revolutionibus* to be published; he received a copy just before his death the next year. (See the box, "Copernicus's Preface to *On the Revolution of Heavenly Bodies*.")

Copernicus's colleagues were right: His work was immediately useful. Copernicus's schema

Copernicus's Preface to *On the Revolution of Heavenly Bodies*

In this dedicatory letter to the pope, Copernicus explains his desire to assist with calendar reform. Principally, however, he seeks to justify his novel conclusions. He not only cites ancient authority for the movement of the earth but also stresses the mathematical nature of the problem and of his solution.

To the Most Holy Lord, Pope Paul III

I may well presume, most Holy Father, that certain people, as soon as they hear that in this book about the Revolutions of the Spheres of the Universe I ascribe movement to the earthly globe, will cry out that, holding such views, I should at once be hissed off the stage. . . . How I came to dare to conceive such motion of the Earth, contrary to the received opinion of the Mathematicians and indeed contrary to the impression of the senses, is what your Holiness will rather expect to hear. So I should like your Holiness to know that I was induced to think of a method of computing the motions of the spheres by nothing else than the knowledge that the Mathematicians are inconsistent in these investigations. . . . Mathemati-

cians are so unsure of the movements of the Sun and the Moon that they cannot even explain . . . the constant length of the seasonal year.

. . . I pondered long upon this uncertainty of mathematical tradition. I . . . read again the works of all the philosophers on whom I could lay a hand to seek out whether any of them had ever supposed that the motions of the spheres were other[wise]. I found first in Cicero that Hicetas [of Syracuse, fifth century B.C.] had realized that the earth moved. . . . Mathematics are for mathematicians, and they, if I be not wholly deceived, will hold that my labors contribute somewhat . . . to the Church. . . . For under Leo X, the question of correcting the ecclesiastical calendar was . . . left undecided.

Source: Thomas S. Kuhn, *The Copernican Revolution* (Cambridge, Mass.: Harvard University Press, 1985), pp. 137–143.

made possible a simpler explanation of all planetary motion. For example, he accounted for most backward motion without resorting to epicycles. But Copernicus still assumed that the planets traveled in circular orbits, so he retained some epicycles to account for the circular motion.

By positing the earth's movement around the sun but also retaining features of the old system, such as circular orbits, Copernicus faced burdens of explanation not faced by Ptolemy. In general, however, the Copernican account of planetary motion was simpler than the Ptolemaic account. It appealed to other astronomers of the age because it was useful and because it highlighted the harmony of heavenly motion, which remained a fundamental physical and metaphysical principle. Accessible only to other astronomers, Copernicus's work only slowly led to conceptual revolu-

tion, as astronomers worked with his calculations and assembled other evidence to support the heliocentric theory.

The most important reason that Copernican theory only gradually led to fundamental conceptual change was that Copernicus did not resolve the physical problems his theory raised. If Copernicus were right, the earth would have to be made of the same stuff as other planets. How, then, would Copernicus explain the motion of objects on earth—the fact that they fall to the earth—if it was not in their nature to fall toward the heavy, stationary earth? In Copernicus's system, the movement of the earth caused the *apparent* motion of the stars. But if the stars did not rotate in their crystalline sphere, what made all other heavenly bodies move?

Copernicus was not as troubled by these questions as we might expect him to be. Since ancient

MILESTONES OF THE SCIENTIFIC REVOLUTION

1543	Copernicus, *On the Revolution of Heavenly Bodies*
	Vesalius, *On the Fabric of the Human Body*
1576	Construction of Brahe's observatory begins
1591	Galileo's law of falling bodies
1609	Kepler's third law of motion
1610	Galileo, *The Starry Messenger*
1620	Bacon, *Novum Organum*
1628	Harvey, *On the Motion of the Heart*
1632	Galileo, *Dialogue on the Two Chief Systems of the World*
1637	Descartes, *Discourse on Method*
1660	Boyle, *New Experiments Physico-Mechanical*
1668	Cavendish, *Grounds of Natural Philosophy*
1687	Newton, *Principia*

times, mathematical astronomy—the science of measuring and predicting the movement of heavenly bodies—had been far more important than, and had proceeded independently of, physical explanations for observed motion. Nevertheless, as Copernicus's own efforts to buttress his notion that the earth moves reveal, his theories directly contradicted many of the supposed laws of motion. The usefulness of his theories to other astronomers meant that the contradictions between mathematical and physical models for the universe would have to be resolved. Copernicus himself might be best understood as the last Ptolemaic astronomer, working within inherited questions and with known tools. His work itself did not constitute a revolution, but it did initiate one.

The First Copernican Astronomers

In the first generation of astronomers after the publication of *De Revolutionibus* in 1543 we can see the effects of Copernicus's work. His impressive computations rapidly won converts among fellow astronomers. Several particularly gifted astronomers

continued to develop the Copernican system. Thus, by the second quarter of the seventeenth century, they and many others accepted the heliocentric theory as a reality and not just as a useful mathematical fiction. The three most important astronomers to build on Copernican assumptions, and on the work of each other, were the Dane Tycho Brahe (1546–1601), the German Johannes Kepler (1571–1630), and the Italian Galileo Galilei (1564–1642).

Like generations of observers before him, Tycho Brahe had been stirred by the majesty of the regular movements of heavenly bodies. After witnessing a partial eclipse of the sun, he abandoned a career in government and became an astronomer. Brahe was the first truly post-Ptolemaic astronomer because he was the first to improve on the data that the ancients and all subsequent astronomers had used. Ironically, *no* theory of planetary motion or mathematics to explain it could have reconciled the data that Copernicus had used: They were simply too inaccurate, based as they were on naked-eye observations, even when errors of translation and copying, accumulated over centuries, had been corrected.

In 1576 the king of Denmark showered Brahe with properties and pensions enabling him to build an observatory, Uraniborg, on an island near Copenhagen. At Uraniborg, Brahe improved on ancient observations with large and very finely calibrated instruments that permitted precise measurements of celestial movements by the naked eye. His attention to precision and frequency of observation produced results that were twice as accurate as any previous data had been.

As a result of his observations, Brahe agreed with Copernicus that the various planets did rotate around the sun, not around the earth. He still could not be persuaded that the earth itself moved, for none of his data supported such a notion. Brahe's lasting and crucial contribution was his astronomical data. They would become obsolete as soon as data from use of the telescope were accumulated about a century later. But in the meantime, they were used by Johannes Kepler to further develop Copernicus's model and arrive at a more accurate heliocentric theory.

Kepler was young enough to be exposed to Copernican ideas from the outset of his training, and he quickly recognized in Brahe's data the means of resolving the problems in Copernican analysis. Though trained in his native Germany,

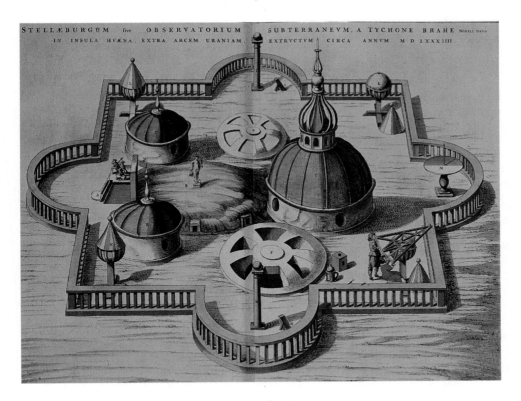

STELLÆBURGUM five OBSERVATORIUM SUBTERRANEVM, A TYCHONE BRAHE Nobili Dano
IN INSULA HVÆNA, EXTRA ARCEM URANIAM, EXTRVCTVM CIRCA ANNVM M D LXXXIIII.

Tycho Brahe's Observatory Brahe's fame was initially established by his observation and measurement of a new star in 1572, but his enduring contribution to astronomy was the meticulous collection of data by means of the instruments assembled at Uraniborg. *(The Fotomas Index)*

Kepler went to Prague, where Brahe spent the last years of his life after a quarrel with the Danish king, and became something of an apprentice to Brahe. After Brahe's death in 1601, Kepler kept his mentor's records of astronomical observation and continued to work at the imperial court as Rudolf II's court mathematician.

Kepler's contribution to the new astronomy, like that of Copernicus, was fundamentally mathematical. In it, we can see the stamp of the Neo-Platonic conviction about the purity of mathematical explanation. Kepler spent ten years working to apply Brahe's data to the most intricate of all the celestial motions—the movement of the planet Mars—as a key to explaining all planetary motion. Mars is close to the earth but farther from the sun than is the earth. This combination produces very puzzling and dramatic variations in the apparent movement of Mars to an earthly observer.

The result of Kepler's work was laws of planetary motion that, in the main, are still in use.

First, Kepler eliminated the need for epicycles by correctly asserting that planets follow elliptical and not circular orbits. Elliptical orbits could account, both mathematically and visually, for the motions of the planets when combined with Kepler's second law, which described the *rate* of a planet's motion around its orbital path. Kepler noted that the speed of a planet in its orbit slows proportionally as the planet's distance from the sun increases. A third law demonstrated that the distance of each planet from the sun and the time it takes each planet to orbit the sun are in a constant ratio.

Kepler's work was a breakthrough because it mathematically confirmed the Copernican heliocentric hypothesis. In so doing, the work directly challenged the ancient world-view, in which heavenly bodies constantly moved in circular orbits around a stationary earth. Hence, Kepler's laws invited speculation about the properties and motion of heavenly and terrestrial bodies alike. A new physics would be required to explain the novel motions that Kepler had posited. Kepler himself, in Neo-Platonic fashion, attributed planetary motion to the sun:

[The sun] is a fountain of light, rich in fruitful heat, most fair, limpid and pure . . . called king of the planets for his motion, heart of the world for his power. . . . Who would hesitate to confer the votes of the celestial motions on him who has been administering all other movements and changes by the benefit of the light which is entirely his possession?[1]

Galileo and the Triumph of Copernicanism

Galileo Galilei holds a pre-eminent position in the development of astronomy for several reasons. He provided compelling new evidence to support Copernican theory, and he contributed to the development of a new physics—or, more precisely, mechanics—that could account for the movement of bodies in new terms. Just as important, his efforts to publicize his findings and his condemnation by the church spurred popular debate about Copernican ideas in literate society and helped to determine the course science would take.

Born to a minor Florentine noble family, Galileo studied medicine and mathematics at the University of Pisa and became professor of mathematics there in 1589 at the age of 25. He had already completed important work on mechanics and within three years was given a chair at the University of Padua, where Copernicus had once studied. He continued work in mechanics during the 1590s but did not publish the results of his experiments until much later. Instead, he became famous for the results of his astronomical observations, which he began in 1609 and first published the next year. *Sidereus Nuncius* (*The Starry Messenger,* 1610) described in lay language the results of his scrutiny of the heavens with a telescope that he had built.

Galileo was the first person that we know who used a telescope to look at the sky. In *The Starry Messenger,* he documented sighting new (previously invisible) stars, another blow to the authority of ancient descriptions of the universe. He also noted craters and other "imperfections" on the surface of the moon as well as the existence of moons orbiting the planet Jupiter. Three years later he published his observations of sunspots in *Letters on Sunspots.* Sunspots are regions of relatively cool

gaseous material that appear as dark spots on the sun's surface. For Galileo the sunspots and the craters of the moon constituted proof that the heavens were not perfect and changeless but rather were like the supposedly "corrupt" and changeable earth. His telescopic observations also provided further support for Copernican heliocentrism because they revealed that each heavenly body rotated on its axis: Sunspots, for example, could be tracked across the visible surface of the sun as the sun rotated.

Galileo's principal contribution to mechanics lay in his working out of an early theory of inertia. As a result of a number of experiments with falling bodies (balls rolling on carefully constructed inclines—not free-falling objects that, according to myth, he dropped from the Leaning Tower of Pisa), Galileo ventured a new view of what is "natural" to bodies. Galileo's view was that uniform motion is as natural as a state of rest. In the ancient and medieval universe, all motion needed a cause, and all motion could be explained in terms of purpose. "I hold," Galileo countered, "that there exists nothing in external bodies . . . but size, shape, quantity and motion."[2] Galileo retained the old assumption that motion was somehow naturally circular. Nevertheless, his theory was a crucial step in explaining motion according to new principles and in fashioning a world-view that accepted a mechanical universe devoid of metaphysical purpose. These theories were published only toward the end of his life. His astronomical theories were more influential at the time.

Galileo's works were widely read, and his work became common currency in the scientific societies already flourishing in his lifetime and in courtly circles where science was encouraged. In 1610 Galileo became court mathematician to Cosimo de' Medici, the grand duke of Tuscany (r. 1609–1620), as a result of the fame brought by *The Starry Messenger.* Soon after his arrival, however, rumors that "Galileists" were openly promulgating heliocentrism led to an investigation and, in 1616, the official condemnation of Copernicus's works by the inquisition in Rome. This condemnation allowed room for maneuver. After meeting personally with the pope, Galileo was assured that he could continue to use Copernican theory, but only as a theory.

In 1632 Galileo issued a bold response to that limitation. *Dialogue on the Two Chief Systems of*

Galileo Confronts the Church

*His work increasingly under attack after the publication of **Letters on Sunspots** (1613), Galileo defended himself by criticizing the claim that biblical authority could decide matters of astronomy. This dangerous line of argument not only argued for a separation of theology and science but also presumed to evaluate the work of theologians and even offered an interpretation of biblical passages. In this document, from a 1615 essay couched as a letter to his patron Christina of Lorraine, Galileo broaches these ideas.*

But I do not feel obliged to believe that . . . God who has endowed us with senses, reason and intellect has intended to forgo their use and by some other means to give us knowledge which we can attain by them. . . . This must be especially true in those sciences of which but the faintest trace . . . is to be found in the Bible. Of astronomy, for instance, so little is found that none of the planets except Venus are so much as mentioned. . . .

Now, if the Holy Spirit has purposely neglected to teach us propositions of this sort as irrelevant to the highest goal (that is, to our salvation), how can anyone affirm that it is obligatory to take sides on them, and that one belief is required by faith, while another side is erroneous? . . . I would assert here something that was heard from [a respected cleric]: . . . "the intention of the Holy Ghost is to teach us how to go to heaven, not how heaven goes."

Moreover, we are unable to affirm that all interpreters of the Bible speak with divine inspiration, for if that were so there would exist no differences between them about the sense of a given passage. Hence [it would be wise] not to permit anyone to usurp scriptural texts and force them in some way to maintain any physical conclusion to be true, when at some future time the senses . . . may show the contrary. Who . . . will set bounds to human ingenuity? Who will assert that everything in the universe capable of being perceived is already . . . known?

Source: Stillman Drake, *The Discoveries and Opinions of Galileo* (New York: Doubleday, 1957), pp. 183–187.

the World was perhaps the most important single source for the popularization of Copernican theory. The work consists of a dialogue among three characters supposedly debating the merits of Copernican theory. Simplicio, the character representing the old world-view, was, as his name suggests, an example of ignorance, not wisdom. In this work, Galileo expresses his supreme confidence—bordering on arrogance—in his own powers and in human power generally to use the senses and reason to understand the physical world.

By publishing the *Dialogue,* Galileo was defying the papal ban on advocating Copernicanism. In an earlier work, *Letter to the Grand Duchess Christina* (1615), Galileo had also been impolitic. In the *Letter,* he had trespassed on the church's authority to interpret the Scriptures. (See the box, "Galileo Confronts the Church.") He was tried for heresy and forced to condemn his "errors" in 1633, though Pope Urban VIII (r. 1623–1644) intervened to give him the light sentence of house arrest at his villa in Tuscany. There, until his death in 1642, Galileo continued his investigations of mechanics.

THE SCIENTIFIC REVOLUTION GENERALIZED

Galileo's work found such a willing audience because Galileo, like Kepler and Brahe, was not working alone. Dozens of other scientists were working energetically on old problems from the fresh perspective offered by the breakthroughs in astronomy. Some were analyzing the nature of matter, now that it was supposed that all matter in the universe was somehow the same despite its varying appearances. Many of these thinkers addressed the metaphysical issues that their investigations inevitably raised.

The Promise of the New Science

No less a man than Francis Bacon (1561–1626), lord chancellor of England during the reign of James I, wrote a utopian essay extolling the benefits of science for a peaceful society and for human happiness. In *New Atlantis,* published one year after his death, Bacon argued that science would produce "things of use and practice for man's life."[3] In *New Atlantis* and in *Novum Organum* (1620), Bacon revealed his faith in science by advocating patient, systematic observation and experimentation to accumulate knowledge about the world. He argued that the proper method of investigation "derives axioms from . . . particulars, rising by gradual and unbroken ascent, so that it arrives at the most general axioms of all. This is the true way but untried."[4]

Bacon himself did not undertake experiments, though his widely read works were influential in encouraging both the empirical method (relying on observation and experimentation) and inductive reasoning (deriving general principles from particular facts). Indeed, Bacon was a visionary. Given the early date of his writings, it might even seem difficult to account for his enthusiasm and confidence. In fact, Bacon's writings reflect the widespread interest and confidence in science within his elite milieu, an interest actively encouraged by the state. In another of his writings he argued that a successful state should concentrate on effective "rule in religion *and nature,* as well as civil administration."[5]

Bacon's writing reflected the fact that an interest in exploring nature's secrets and exercising "dominion over nature" had become an indispensable part of princely rule. Princely courts were the main source of financial support for science and a primary site of scientific work during Bacon's lifetime. Part of the impetus for this development had come from the civic humanism of the Italian Renaissance, which had celebrated the state and service to it and had provided models both for educated rulers and for cultivated courtiers. The specific turning of the rulers' attention to science

and to its benefits for the state also reflected the scope of princely resources and ambitions: the desire of rulers for technical expertise in armaments, fortification, building projects in general, navigation, and mapmaking. (See the feature, "Weighing the Evidence: Modern Maps," on pages 654–655.)

The promise of the New World and the drive for overseas trade and exploration especially encouraged princely support of scientific investigation. A renowned patron of geographic investigation, from mapmaking to navigation, was Henry, prince of Wales (d. 1612), son of James I. Prince Henry patronized technical experts such as experienced gunners and seamen as well as those with broader and more theoretical expertise. One geographer at his court worked on the vital problem of calculating longitude, sketched the moon after reading and emulating Galileo's work with the telescope, and—in a spirit of empiricism often associated with Bacon—compiled information about the new territory Virginia, including the first dictionary of any Native American language.

Science was an ideological as well as a practical tool for power. Most courts housed collections of marvels, specimens of exotic plants and animals, and mechanical contrivances. These demonstrated the ruler's interest in investigation of the world—his or her status, in other words, as an educated person. These collections and the work of court experts also enhanced the ruler's reputation as a patron and the image of the ruler's power. Galileo was playing off such expectations when he named some of his newly discovered bodies "Medician Stars."

Exploring the secrets of nature became a tool for rulers and an honorable activity for scholars and courtiers. By the beginning of the seventeenth century, private salons and academies where investigators might meet on their own were another major site of scientific investigation. These, too, had their roots in the humanist culture of Italy, where circles of scholars without university affiliations had formed. They were an important alternative to princely patronage, since a ruler's funds might wax and wane according to his or her other commitments. Also, private organizations could avoid the hierarchical distinctions that were inevitable at court.

The earliest academy dedicated to scientific study was the Accadèmia Segreta (Secret Academy) founded in Naples in the 1540s. The members pur-

A Collection of Naturalia Displays of exotica, such as these specimens in Naples, symbolized the ruler's authority by suggesting his or her power over nature. *(From Ferrante Imperato,* Dell' Historia Naturale *[Naples, 1599]. By permission of the Houghton Library, Harvard University)*

sued experiments together, in order, in the words of one member, "to make a true anatomy of the things and operations of nature itself."[6] During the remainder of the sixteenth century and on into the seventeenth, such academies sprang up in many cities. The most celebrated was the Accadèmia dei Lincei, founded in Rome by an aristocrat in 1603. Its most famous member, Galileo, joined in 1611. The name "Lincei," from *lynx*, was chosen because of the legendary keen sight of that animal, an appropriate mascot for "searchers of secrets."

Galileo's notoriety and the importance of his discoveries forced acceptance or rejection of Copernicanism on all communities. Throughout the seventeenth century, specific investigation of natural phenomena would continue in increasingly sophisticated institutional settings. The flowering of scientific thought in the seventeenth century occurred because of the specific innovations in astronomy and the general spread of scientific investigation that had been achieved by the end of Bacon's life.

Scientific Thought in France: Descartes and a New Cosmology

Philosophers, mathematicians, and educated elites engaged in lively debate and practical investigation throughout Europe in the first half of the seventeenth century, but in France questions about cosmic order were being posed at a time of political disorder. The years following the religious wars

René Descartes had been given the best of traditional educations. From the Jesuits he had learned not only scholastic logic and rhetoric but also, perhaps for purposes of debate, Galileo's new discoveries. *(Royal Museum of Fine Arts, Copenhagen)*

saw the murder of Henry IV, another regency, and further civil war in the 1620s (see pages 564–565). In this environment, questions about order in the universe and the possibilities of human knowledge took on particular urgency. It is not surprising that a Frenchman, René Descartes (1596–1650), created the first fully articulated alternative world-view.

Descartes's work emerged in dialogue with a circle of other French thinkers. His work became more influential among philosophers and lay people than the work of some of his equally talented contemporaries because of its thoroughness and rigor, grounded in Descartes's mathematical expertise, and because of its graceful, readable French. His system was fully presented in his *Discours de la méthode* (*Discourse on Method*, 1637). This work was intended to be the centerpiece of a series of scien-

tific treatises, including works on optics and geometry. Descartes described some of his intellectual crises in *Meditations* (1641).

Descartes accepted Galileo's conclusion that the heavens and the earth are made of the same elements. In his theorizing about the composition of matter, he drew on ancient atomic models that previously had not been generally accepted. His theory that all matter is made up of identical bits, which he named "corpuscles," is a forerunner of modern atomic and quantum theories. Descartes believed that all the different appearances and behaviors of matter (for example, why stone is always hard and water is always wet) could be explained solely by the size, shape, and motion of these "corpuscles." Descartes's was an extremely mechanistic explanation of the universe. It nevertheless permitted new, more specific observations and hypotheses and greater understanding of inertia. For example, because he reimagined the universe as being filled with "corpuscles" free to move in any direction, "natural" motion no longer seemed either circular (Galileo's idea) or toward the center of the earth (Aristotle's idea). The new understanding of motion would be crucial to Isaac Newton's formulations later in the century.

In his various works, Descartes depicts and then firmly resolves the crisis of confidence that the new discoveries about the universe had produced. The collapse of the old explanations about the world made Descartes and other investigators doubt not only what they knew but also their capacity to know anything at all. Their physical senses—which denied that the earth moved, for example—had been proved untrustworthy. Descartes's solution was to re-envision the human rational capacity, the mind, as completely distinct from the world—that is, as distinct from the human body—and the betraying sense data it offers. In a leap of faith, Descartes presumed that he could count on the fact that God would not have given humans a mind if that mind were to betray them. For Descartes, God became the guarantor of human reasoning capacity, and humans, in Descartes's view, were distinguished by that capacity. This is the significance of his famous claim "I think, therefore I am."

Descartes thus achieved a resolution of the terrifying doubt about the world, a resolution that exalted the role of the human knower. The Cartesian universe was one of mechanical motion, not purpose or mystical meaning, and the Cartesian human being was pre-eminently a mind that could apprehend that universe. In what came to be known as "Cartesian dualism," Descartes was proposing that humans are detached from the world yet at the same time can be objective observers of the world.

Important implications followed from Descartes's ambitious view of human reason. One was the emphasis on deductive reasoning (a process of reasoning in which the conclusion follows necessarily from the stated premises), which naturally followed from his philosophical rejection of sense data. In actuality, Descartes did rely on sense data; he did experiments and urged his readers to keep careful records of their thoughts, observations, and conclusions. But, like the mathematician he was, he urged that science "[keep] the right order for one thing to be deduced from that which precedes it."[7] In the short run, Descartes's embrace of absolute certainty proved very useful to the advancement of knowledge because with a positive sense of purpose—even within the limits of deductive reasoning—natural philosophers could tolerate enormous uncertainty and speculate fruitfully about specific problems.

Descartes's vision of the enhanced position of the individual knower, and of the power of the knower's reason, was attractive to philosophers. (Galileo's self-confidence comes to mind.) His views were also attractive to educated lay people who sought in science an affirmation of their own status in the world, which could now be expressed in terms of intellectual power and power over nature, rather than only as political power. Descartes was careful not to advocate the "madness" of applying reason to changing the state. The state alone had made humans civilized, he maintained; and although he and other thinkers had to rebuild knowledge of the universe from its foundations, he believed it was "unreasonable for an individual to conceive the plan of reforming a state by changing everything from the foundations."[8]

Similar possibilities for human perception were being suggested in other areas of creative endeavor. Renaissance painters, who utilized the principles of linear perspective, presented views of the world as detached still life—more distant and distinct than the world ever was in real life. A similar detachment was evident in the memoirs and essays of writers such as Michel de Mon-

taigne (1533–1592; see page 578). Descartes's view of rationality, however, was the most radical detachment of all, for Descartes claimed objectivity for his perspective.

Though much of Cartesian physics would be surpassed by Newton at the end of the century, Descartes's assumption about the objectivity of the observer would become an enduring part of scientific practice. The sense of detachment from the world also fostered a belief in humans' ability to control nature. In our own time, we have become aware of the possible limits of our ability to control nature, as well as the arbitrariness of Descartes's distinction of mind and body. In Descartes's day, the most radical aspect of his thought was the reduction of God from being an active presence in the world to the position of guarantor of knowledge. Later generations of scientists would be fearful of Descartes's system because it seemed to encourage "atheism." In fact, a profound faith in God was necessary for Descartes's creativity in imagining his new world system—but the system did work without God. Although Descartes would have been surprised and offended by charges of atheism, he knew that his work would antagonize the church. He had moved to the Netherlands to study in 1628, and his *Discourse* was first published there.

A contemporary of Descartes, Blaise Pascal (1623–1662), drew attention in his writings and in his life to the limits of scientific knowledge. Son of a royal official, Pascal was perhaps the most brilliant mind of his generation. A mathematician like Descartes, he stressed the importance of mathematical representations of phenomena, built one of the first calculating machines, and invented probability theory. He also carried out experiments to investigate air pressure, the behavior of liquids, and the existence of vacuums.

Pascal's career alternated between periods of intense scientific work and religious retreat. Today he is well known for his writings that defended Jansenism, an austere strain of Catholicism, and explored the human soul and psyche. His *Pensées* (*Thoughts*, 1657) consists of the published fragments of his defense of Christian faith, which remained unfinished at the time of his early death. Pascal's appeal for generations after him may lie in his assumption that matters of faith and of feeling must also be open to investigation. His most famous statement, "The heart has its reasons which the reason knows not," can be read as a statement of the limits of the Cartesian world-view.

Science and Revolution in England

The new science had adherents and practitioners throughout Europe by 1650. Dutch scientists in the commercial milieu of the Netherlands, for example, had the freedom to pursue practical and experimental interests. The Dutch investigator Christiaan Huygens (1629–1695) worked on a great variety of problems, including air pressure and optics. He invented and patented the pendulum clock in 1657, the first device accurately to measure small units of time, essential for a variety of measurements.

England, however, because of the political revolution that occurred there, offered a unique environment for the development of science in the middle of the century. Religious and political struggle in England took place at a time when scientific questions were also to the fore. Thus, differing positions on science became part and parcel of differing positions on Puritanism, church hierarchy, and royal power. Scientific investigation and speculation were spurred by the urgency of religious and political agendas. Scientific, along with political and religious, debate was generally encouraged by the collapse of censorship beginning in the 1640s.

In the 1640s natural philosophers with Puritan leanings were encouraged in their investigations by dreams that science, of the practical Baconian sort, could be the means by which the perfection of life on earth could be brought about and the end of history, the reign of the saints preceding the return of Christ, accelerated. Their concerns ranged from improved production of gunpowder (for the armies fighting against Charles I) to surveying and mapmaking. Perhaps the best-known member of this group was Robert Boyle (1627–1691). In his career we can trace the evolution of English science through the second half of the seventeenth century.

Boyle and his colleagues were theoretically eclectic, drawing on Cartesian mechanics and even Paracelsian chemical theories. They attacked the university system, still under the sway of Aristotelianism, and proposed widespread reform of education. They were forced to moderate many of their positions, however, as the English revolution proceeded. Radical groups such as the Levelers used Hermeticism and the related Paracelsianism as part of their political and religious tenets. The ancient doctrine of Hermeticism, revived since the Renaissance, claimed that matter is universally imbued with divine (or magical) spirit. The Levelers and others believed that each person was capable of a godly life and divine knowledge without the coercive hierarchy of officials of church and state.

Boyle and his colleagues responded to these challenges. They gained institutional power, accepting positions at Oxford and Cambridge. They formed the core of the Royal Society of London, which they persuaded Charles II to recognize and charter on his accession to the throne in 1660. They worked to articulate a theoretical position that combined the orderliness of mechanism, a continued divine presence in the world, and a Baconian emphasis on scientific progress. This unwieldy set of notions was attractive to the educated elite of their day who wanted the certainties of science without losing all of the authoritarian aspects of the old Christian world-view.

Their most creative contribution, both to their own cause and to the advancement of science, was their emphasis on and refinement of experimental philosophy and practice. In 1660, Boyle published *New Experiments Physico-Mechanical*. The work described the results of his experiments with an air pump that he had designed, and it laid out general rules for experimental procedure. Descartes had accounted for motion by postulating that "corpuscles" of matter act on each other, thereby eliminating the possibility of a vacuum in nature. Recent experiments on air pressure suggested otherwise, however, and Boyle tried to confirm their findings with his air pump.

Boyle's efforts to demonstrate that a vacuum could exist—by evacuating a sealed chamber with his pump—were not successes by modern standards because they could not readily be replicated. Boyle tied the validity of experimental results to the agreement of witnesses to the experiment—a problematic solution, for only investigators sympathetic to his hypothesis and convinced of his credibility usually witnessed the results. In response to a Cambridge scholar who criticized his interpretation of one of his experiments, Boyle replied that he could not understand his critic's objections, ". . . the experiment having been tried both before our whole society [the Royal Society of London], and very critically, by its royal founder, his majesty himself."[9] Rather than debate differing interpretations, Boyle chose to fall back on the authority and prestige of the participants themselves. In English science in the mid-seventeenth century, the various aspects of the modern scientific profession—the agreement on principles, the acceptance of experimental procedures, and the authority of practitioners—were all being worked out simultaneously.

The Newtonian Synthesis:
The Copernican Revolution Completed

The Copernican revolution reached its high point with the work of the Englishman Isaac Newton (1642–1724), who was born the year Galileo died. Newton completed the new explanation for motion in the heavens and on earth that Copernicus's work had initiated and that Kepler, Galileo, and others had sought. In Newton's career, we can see how different was the climate for science by the second half of the seventeenth century. When Newton entered Cambridge University as a student in 1661, Copernicanism was studied, the benefits of scientific investigation were debated, and much attention was focused on the problems of Descartes's explanations of matter.

Like all the other natural philosophers before him, Newton was as concerned by questions of metaphysics as by physics. In the 1680s, he devoted himself primarily to the study of church history, theology, and alchemy. As a student at Cambridge he was strongly influenced by the work of a group of Neo-Platonists who were critical of Cartesian dualism, which posited God as a cause of all matter and motion but removed God as an explanation for the behavior of matter. Their concerns were both religious and scientific. As Newton says in some of his early writing while a student, "However we cast about we find almost no other reason for atheism than this [Cartesian] notion of bodies having . . . a complete, absolute and independent reality."[10] He reflected his mentors' concern to harmonize science with a securely Christian world-view following the "excesses" of the English revolution. Meanwhile, they were all uncertain how to account for motion in a world filled with matter, as Descartes had posited. The experiments of Robert Boyle in creating a vacuum shed further doubt on Descartes's schema.

Newton combined his scientific skepticism and his religious certainty to posit the existence of gravity—a mysterious force that accounts for the movement of heavenly bodies. Others had speculated about the existence of gravity, but Newton's extraordinary contribution was the mathematical computation of the laws of gravity and planetary motion, which he combined with a fully developed concept of inertia. The concept of inertia as so far elaborated by Galileo, Descartes, and others suggested the need for the concept of gravity. Otherwise, if a planet was "pushed" (say, in Kepler's view, by the "motive force" of the sun), it would

Isaac Newton Pictured here about fifteen years after the publication of the *Principia*, Newton was also one of the developers of calculus. The cumbersome mathematics he still relied on in the *Principia*, however, has led one scholar to ponder: "What manner of man he was who could use as a weapon what we can scarcely lift as a burden."[11] (*National Portrait Gallery, London*)

continue along that course forever unless "pulled back" by something else.

In 1687 Newton published *Philosophia Naturalis Principia Mathematica* (*Mathematical Principles of Natural Philosophy*). In this mathematical treatise—so intricate that it was inaccessible to lay people, even those able to read Latin—Newton lays out his laws of motion and expresses them as mathematical theorems that can be used to test future observations of moving bodies. Then he demonstrates that these laws also apply to the solar system, confirming the data already gathered about the planets and even predicting the existence of an as-yet-unseen planet. His supreme achievement was his law of gravitation, with which he could predict the discovery of the invisible planet. This law states that every body, indeed every bit of matter, in the universe exerts over every other body an attractive force proportional to the product of their masses and inversely proportional to the square of the distance between them. Newton not only accounted for motion but definitively united heaven and earth in a single scheme and created a convincing picture of an orderly nature.

Neither Newton nor anyone else claimed that his theorems resolved all questions about motion and matter. Exactly what gravity is and how it operates were not clear, as they still are not. Newton himself was troubled by his lack of understanding of gravity except in mathematical terms. He couched the *Principia* as a mathematical treatise rather than as a general treatise in philosophy because he felt he could make no systematic claims, as did Descartes, since the problem of gravity had not been solved. After its publication, he experienced periods of severe depression, leading to a nervous breakdown in 1693.

Newton's laws of motion are still taught because they still adequately account for most problems of motion. The fact that so fundamental a principle as gravity remains unexplained in no way diminishes Newton's achievement but is clear evidence about the nature of scientific understanding: Science provides explanatory schemas that account for many—but not all—observed phenomena. When a scientific explanation ceases to account satisfactorily for enough data, it collapses of its own weight. No schema explains everything, and each schema contains open door-

ways that lead to further discovery and blind alleys that lead to mistaken impressions. Newton, for example, also studied alchemy during his most productive years. He assumed that the spiritual forces that somehow accounted for gravity would mysteriously work on metals so that they might "quickly pass into gold."[12]

Other Branches of Science

The innovations in astronomy that led to the new mechanistic view of the behavior of matter did not automatically spill over to other branches of science. Developments in astronomy were very specific to that field; innovation came at the hands of skilled practitioners after the ancient and medieval inheritance had been fully assimilated and its errors made undeniable. Other branches of science followed their own paths, though all were strongly influenced by the mechanistic world-view.

In chemistry, the mechanistic assumption that all matter was composed of small, equivalent parts was crucial to understanding the properties and behavior of compounds (combinations of elements). But knowledge of these small units of matter was not yet detailed enough to be of much use in advancing chemistry conceptually. Nevertheless, the flawed conceptual schema did not hold back all chemical discovery and development. Lack of understanding of gases, and of the specific elements that make them up, for example, did not prevent the development and improvement of gunpowder. Indeed, unlike the innovations in astronomy, eventual conceptual innovation in chemistry and biology owed a great deal to the results of experiment and the slow accumulation of data.

A conceptual leap forward was made in biology in the sixteenth and seventeenth centuries. Because biological knowledge was mostly a byproduct of the practice of medicine, biological studies had been and remained very practical and experimental. But the discovery of *On Anatomical Procedures*, a treatise by Galen, encouraged dissection and other practical research. Andreas Vesalius (1514–1564), in particular, made important advances by following Galen's exhortation to anatomical research. Born in Brussels, Vesalius studied at the nearby University of Louvain, and then at Padua, where he was appointed professor of surgery. He ended his career as physician to Emperor Charles V and his son, Philip II of Spain. In his teaching at Padua he embodied newly discovered Galenic precepts by doing dissections himself rather than giving the work to technicians. In 1543 he published versions of his lectures as an illustrated compendium of anatomy, *De Humani Corporis Fabrica* (*On the Fabric of the Human Body*). The results of his dissections of human corpses, revealed in this work, demonstrated a number of errors in Galen's knowledge of human anatomy, much of which had been derived from dissection of animals. Neither Vesalius nor his immediate successors, however, questioned overall Galenic theory about the functioning of the human body, any more than Copernicus had utterly rejected Aristotelian physics.

The slow movement from new observation to changed explanation is clearly illustrated in the career of the Englishman William Harvey (1578–1657). Much like Vesalius, Harvey was educated first in his own land and then at Padua, where he benefited from the tradition of anatomical research. He also had a career as a practicing physician in London and at the courts of James I and Charles I.

Harvey postulated the circulation of the blood—postulated rather than discovered because, owing to the technology of the day, he could not observe the tiny capillaries where the movement of arterial blood into the veins occurs. After conducting on animals vivisectional experiments that revealed the actual functioning of the heart and lungs, he reasoned that circulation must occur. He carefully described his experiments and his conclusions in *Exercitatio Anatomica de Motu Cordis et Sanguinis in Animalibus* (1628), usually shortened to *De Motu Cordis* (*On the Motion of the Heart*).

Harvey's work challenged Galenic anatomy and, like Copernicus's discoveries, created new burdens of explanation. According to Galenic theory, the heart and the lungs helped each other to function. The heart sent nourishment to the lungs through the pulmonary artery, and the lungs provided raw material for the "vital spirit," which the heart gave to the blood to produce and sustain life. The lungs also helped the heart to sustain its "heat." Like "vital spirit," "heat" was considered necessary to living organisms. It was understood to be an innate property of organs, just as "heavi-ness," in traditional physics, was considered to be an innate property of earthbound objects. One chamber of the heart was supposedly reserved for the cleansing of waste products from venous blood—which was thought to be entirely separate from the "nourishing" blood pumped out by the heart.

From his observations, Harvey came to think of the heart in terms consonant with the new mechanistic notions about nature: as a pump to circulate the blood. But to Harvey the heart was never only that. Harvey did not leap to a new conceptualization of the body's function. Rather, he adjusted but did not abandon Galenic theories, for example, concerning how "heat" and "vital spirit" were made. The lungs had been thought to "ventilate" the heart by providing air to maintain "heat" (like bellows on a fire) and by drawing off heat to cool the heart as necessary. In light of his discovery of the pulmonary transit (that all of the blood is pumped through the lungs and back through the heart), Harvey suggested that the lungs carried out some of these functions for the blood, helping it to concoct the "vital spirit." Only in this context could the heart be thought of as a machine, circulating this life-giving material around the body.

Harvey's explanation of bodily functions in light of his new knowledge thus did not constitute a rupture with Galenic tradition. But by the end of his life, Harvey's own adjustments of Galenic theory were suggesting new conceptual possibilities. His work inspired additional research in physiology, chemistry, and physics. Robert Boyle's efforts to understand vacuums can be traced in part to questions Harvey raised about the function of the lungs and the properties of air.

SCIENCE AND SOCIETY

Scientists wrestled with questions about God, human capacity, and the possibilities of understanding the world every bit as intently as they attempted to find new explanations for the behavior of matter and the motion of the heavens. Eventually, the profound implications of the new scientific posture would affect thought and behavior throughout society. Once people no longer thought of the universe in hierarchical terms, questioning the hierarchical organization of society became easier. Once all matter was thought of as equal, thinking of all people as equal became easier. Once people questioned the authority of traditional knowledge about the universe, the way was clear for them to begin to question traditional views of the state and social order.

Such profound changes of perspective happened gradually. In the short term, Louis XIV and other rulers actually welcomed the new science for its practical value, and the practice of science remained wedded to religion. The advances in science did lead to revolutionary cultural change; but, until the end of the seventeenth century, traditional institutions and ideologies circumscribed this change.

The Rise of Scientific Professionalism

Institutions both old and new supported the new science developing in the sixteenth and seventeenth centuries. Some universities were the setting for scientific breakthroughs, but court patronage, a well-established institution, also sponsored scientific activity. The development of the Accadèmia dei Lincei (see page 635), to which Galileo belonged, and other academies was a step toward modern professional societies of scholars, although these new organizations depended on patronage.

In both England and France, royally sponsored scientific societies were founded in the third quarter of the century. The Royal Society of London, inaugurated in 1660, received royal recognition but no money and remained an informal institution sponsoring amateur scientific interests as well as specialized independent research. The Académie Royale des Sciences in France, established in 1666 by Jean-Baptiste Colbert, Louis XIV's minister of finance (see page 591), sponsored research and supported chosen scientists with pensions. These associations were extensions to science of traditional kinds of royal recognition and patronage. Thus, the French Académie was well funded but tightly controlled by the government of Louis XIV, and the Royal Society of London received little of Charles II's precious resources or his scarce political capital.

One important role of academies and patrons was to support the publication of scientific work.

The Accadèmia dei Lincei published two of Galileo's best-known works. The Royal Society of London published its fellows' work in *Philosophical Transactions of the Royal Society,* beginning in 1665.

The practice of seventeenth-century science took place in so many diverse institutions—academies, universities, royal courts—that neither *science* nor *scientist* was rigorously defined. Science as a discipline was not yet detached from broad metaphysical questions. Boyle, Newton, Pascal, and Descartes all concerned themselves with questions of religion, and all thought of themselves not as scientists but, like their medieval forebears, as natural philosophers. These natural philosophers were among the elite who met in aristocratic salons to discuss literature, politics, or science with equal ease and interest. Nevertheless, the beginning of the narrowing of the practice of science to a tightly defined, truly professional community is evident. Robert Boyle and his fellow advocates of experimentalism, for example, claimed that their procedures alone constituted true science.

The importance of court life and patronage to the new science had at first enabled women to be actively involved. Women ran important salons in France, aristocratic women everywhere were important sources of patronage for scientists, and women themselves were scientists, combining, as did men, science with other pursuits.

Noblewomen and daughters of gentry families had access to education in their homes, and a number of such women were active scientists—astronomers, mathematicians, and botanists. The astronomer Maria Cunitz (1610–1664), from Silesia (a Habsburg-controlled province, now in modern Poland), learned six languages with the support and encouragement of her father, who was a medical doctor. Later, she published a useful simplification of some of Kepler's mathematical calculations. Women from artisanal families might also receive useful training at home. Such was the case of the German entomologist Maria Sibylla Merian (1647–1717). Merian learned the techniques of illustration in the workshop of her father, an artist in Frankfurt. Later, she used her artistic training and her refined powers of observation to study and record the lives of insects and plants.

Margaret Cavendish, duchess of Newcastle (1623–1673), wrote several major philosophical

Maria Merian, Entomologist Merian's scientific drawings of insect life in Europe and South America (where she traveled with her daughter) were widely used and reproduced until the nineteenth century. Eleven insect and six plant species, which she discovered and recorded, are named for her. *(Oeffentliche Kunstsammlung Basel)*

works, including *Grounds of Natural Philosophy* (1668). She was a Cartesian but was influenced by Neo-Platonism. She believed matter to have "intelligence" and thus disagreed with Cartesian dualism, but she criticized English philosophers with whom she agreed on some matters because, like Descartes, she distrusted sense knowledge as a guide to philosophy.

Women were proposed as members of and were accepted in Italian academies regularly but they were excluded from formal membership in the academies in London and Paris, though they could use the academies' facilities and received prizes from the societies for their work. One reason for the exclusion of women was the limited amount of patronage available: Coveted positions automatically went to men. Moreover, the hierarchical distinction signified by gender made the ex-

clusion of women a useful way to define the academies as special and privileged.

Margaret Cavendish was aware of the degree to which her participation in scientific life depended on informal networks and on the resources available to her because of her aristocratic status. (See the box, "Margaret Cavendish Challenges Male Scientists.") Women scientists from more modest backgrounds, without Cavendish's resources, had to fight for the right to employment as public institutions gained importance as settings for the pursuit of science. The German astronomer Maria Winkelman (1670–1720), for example, tried to succeed her late husband in an official position in the Berlin Academy of Sciences in 1710. She had worked as her husband's unofficial partner during his tenure as astronomer to the academy and now sought to continue her work to

Astronomers Elisabetha and Johannes Hevelius were one of many collaborating couples among the scientists of the seventeenth century. Women were usually denied pensions and support for their research when they worked alone, however. *(From Hevelius,* Machinae coelestis. *By permission of the Houghton Library, Harvard University)*

support her four children. The academy would not extend an official position to Winkelman after her husband's death, however, despite her experience and accomplishments (she had discovered a new comet, for example, in 1702). The secretary of the academy stated:

That she be kept on in an official capacity to work on the calendar or to continue with observations simply will not do. Already during her husband's lifetime the society was burdened with ridicule because its calendar was prepared by a woman. If she were now to be kept on in such a capacity, mouths would gape even wider.[13]

Winkelman worked in private observatories, but was able to return to the Berlin Academy only as the unofficial assistant to her own son, whose training she herself had supervised.

Margaret Cavendish Challenges Male Scientists

In her preface to her earliest scientific work, **The Philosophical and Physical Opinions (1655),** *Cavendish addresses scholars at Oxford and Cambridge universities with deceptive humility. She implies that the seeming limitations of women's abilities are in fact the consequence of their exclusion from education and from participation in affairs.*

Most Famously Learned,

I here present to you this philosophical work, not that I can hope wise school-men and industrious laborious students should value it for any worth, but to receive it without scorn, for the good encouragement of our sex, lest in time we should grow irrational as idiots, by the dejectedness of our spirits, through the careless neglects and despisements of the masculine sex to the female, thinking it impossible we should have either learning or understanding, wit or judgment, as if we had not rational souls as well as men, and we out of a custom of dejectedness think so too, which makes us quit all industry towards profitable knowledge, being imployed only in low and petty imployments which take away not only our abilities towards arts but higher capacities in speculations, so that we are become like worms, that only live in the dull earth of ignorance, winding ourselves sometimes out by the help of some refreshing rain of good education, which seldom is given us, for we are kept like birds in cages, to hop up and down in our houses . . . ; thus by an opinion, which I hope is but an erroneous one in men, we are shut out of all power and authority by reason we are never employed either in civil or martial affairs, our counsels are despised and laughed at and the best of our actions are trodden down with scorn, by the over-weening conceit men have of themselves and through a despisement of us.

Source: Moira Ferguson, ed., *First Feminists: British Women Writers, 1578–1799* (Bloomington and New York: Indiana University Press and The Feminist Press, 1985), pp. 85–86.

The New Science and the Needs of the State

The new natural philosophy had implications for traditional notions about the state. The new world-view that all matter was alike and answerable to discernible natural laws gradually undermined political systems resting on a belief in the inherent inequality of persons and on royal prerogative. By the middle of the eighteenth century, a fully formed alternative political philosophy would argue for more "rational" government in keeping with the rational, natural order of things. But the change came slowly, and while it was coming, the state of Louis XIV and other rulers found much to admire and make use of in the new science.

New technological possibilities were very attractive to governments and members of ruling elites. Experiments with vacuum pumps had important applications in the mining industry. The astronomy professor at Gresham College in London was required to teach navigation, and other professors at Gresham worked with naval architects to improve the design of ships.

Governments also sponsored purely scientific research. The French Académie des Sciences sponsored the construction of an astronomical observatory in Paris. A naval expedition to Cayenne, in French Guiana, led to refinements of the pendulum clock but had as its main purpose progressive observations of the sun to permit the calculation of the earth's distance from the sun.

The sponsorship of pure science is evidence of both the adaptability of institutions and the complexity of change. Members of the elite, such as

Colbert in France, saw the opportunity not only for practical advances but also for prestige and, most important, confirmation of the orderliness of nature. It is hard to overestimate the psychological impact and intellectual power of this fundamental tenet of the new science—namely, that nature is an inanimate machine that reflects God's design not through its purposes but simply by its orderliness. Human beings could now hope to dominate nature in ways not possible before. Dominion, order, control—these were the goals of ambitious and powerful rulers in the seventeenth century.

Thus, in the short run, the new science supported a vision of order that was very pleasing to a monarch of absolutist pretensions. Louis XIV, among others, energetically sponsored scientific

investigation by the Académie des Sciences and reaped the benefits in improved ships, increasingly skillful military engineers, and new and improved industrial products.

Religion and the New Science

Because of Galileo's trial, the Catholic church is often seen as an opponent of scientific thought, and science and religion are often seen as antagonists. But this view is an oversimplification. Indeed, scientific thought remained closely tied to religion during the seventeenth century. Both religion and the Catholic church as an institution were involved with scientific advancement from the time of Copernicus. Copernicus himself was a cleric, as

Science and Royal Power This painting memorializes the founding of the French Académie des Sciences and the building of the royal observatory in Paris. This celebration of the institutions' openings reveals Louis XIV's belief in their importance, both symbolic and practical. (*Château de Versailles/Laurie Platt Winfrey, Inc.*)

were many philosophers and scientists active in the early seventeenth century. This is not surprising, for most research in the sciences to this point had occurred within universities sponsored and staffed by members of religious orders.

Moreover, religious and metaphysical concerns were central to the work of virtually every scientist. The entire Cartesian edifice of reasoning about the world, for example, was founded on Descartes's certainty about God. God's gift of the capacity to reason was the only certainty that Descartes claimed. Copernicus, Kepler, and other investigators perceived God's purpose in the mathematical regularity of nature. In addition, traditional Christian views of the operations and purpose of the universe were evident in the work of all scientists from Copernicus to Newton—from Galileo's acceptance of perfect circular motion to Newton's theological writings.

It is true that the new astronomy and mechanics challenged specific tenets of faith and the Catholic church's role in shaping and controlling matters of knowledge and faith. Adjusting to a new view of nature in which God was less immanently and obviously represented was not easy for the church, for several reasons. First of all, the church itself mirrored the hierarchy of the old view of the universe in its own hierarchy of believers, priests, bishops, popes, and saints. Moreover, in its sponsorship of institutions of higher learning, the church was the repository of the old view. In the inevitable scientific disagreements spawned by the new theories and discoveries, the church was both theoretically and literally invested in the old view.

Nevertheless, the church's condemnation of Galileo shocked many clerics, including a number of whom were scientists themselves, as well as three of Galileo's judges, who voted for leniency at his trial. Over the course of the centuries, several apparent conflicts between scientific arguments and sacred teachings had been resolved with great intelligence and flexibility. Many scientists who were also clerics continued to study and teach the new science when they could; for example, Copernicanism was taught by Catholic missionaries abroad. (See the box, "Encounters with the West: Jesuits and Astronomy in China.")

The rigid response of the church hierarchy to Galileo's challenge must be seen in the context of the Protestant Reformation, which, in the minds of the pope and others, had demonstrated the need for a firm response to any challenge. Galileo seemed threatening because he was well known, wrote for a wide audience, and, like the Protestants, presumed on the church's right to interpret the Scriptures.

The condemnation of Galileo had a chilling effect on scientific investigators in most Catholic regions of Europe. They could and did continue their research, but many could publish results only by smuggling manuscripts to Protestant lands. Descartes, as we have seen, left France for the more tolerant Netherlands, where his *Discourse on Method* was first published; he also sojourned at the Swedish court at the invitation of Queen Christina. Many of the most important empirical and theoretical innovations in science occurred in Protestant regions after the middle of the seventeenth century.

Protestant leaders, however, at first were not receptive to Copernican ideas because they defied scriptural authority as well as common sense. In 1549 one of Martin Luther's associates wrote:

The eyes are witnesses that the heavens revolve in the space of twenty-four hours. But certain men, either from love of novelty or to make a display of ingenuity, have concluded that the earth moves. . . . Now it is want of honesty and decency to assert such notions publicly and the example is pernicious. It is part of a good mind to accept the truth as revealed by God and to acquiesce in it.[14]

Protestant thinkers were also as troubled as Catholics by the metaphysical problems that the new theories seemed to raise. In 1611, one year after the publication of Galileo's *Starry Messenger*, the English poet John Donne (1573–1631) reflected in "An Anatomie of the World" on the confusion about human capacities and social relationships that Copernican astronomy caused:

[The] new Philosophy calls all in doubt,
The Element of fire is quite put out;
The Sun is lost, and th'earth, and no man's wit
Can well direct him where to look for it.
. . . .
Tis all in pieces, all coherence gone;
All just supply, and all Relation:
Prince, Subject, Father, Son, are things forgot,
For every man alone thinks he hath got
To be a Phoenix, and that then can be
None of that kinde, of which he is, but he.[15]

~ ENCOUNTERS WITH THE WEST ~

Jesuits and Astronomy in China

The Italian Matteo Ricci (1552–1610) was one of the first of a series of Jesuit missionaries to establish himself at the imperial court in China. He was appreciative as well as critical of Chinese science, but his remarks are more interesting to us because they reveal that Ricci himself regarded expertise in mathematics and astronomy as worthy of esteem. Ricci's own scientific knowledge was crucial to his acceptance at court; Jesuit missionaries who followed Ricci in the seventeenth century found their scientific expertise equally valued, and several openly taught Copernican theory there.

The Chinese have not only made considerable progress in moral philosophy but in astronomy and in many branches of mathematics as well. At one time they were quite proficient in arithmetic and geometry, but in the study and teaching of these branches of learning they labored with more or less confusion. They divide the heavens into constellations in a manner somewhat different from that which we employ. Their count of the stars outnumbers the calculations of our astronomers by fully four hundred, because they include in it many of the fainter stars which are not always visible. And yet with all this, the Chinese astronomers take no pains whatever to reduce the phenomena of celestial bodies to the discipline of mathematics. Much of their time is spent in determining the moment of eclipses and the mass of the planets and the stars, but here, too, their deductions are spoiled by innumerable errors. Finally they center their whole attention on that phase of astronomy which our scientists term astrology, which may be accounted for the fact that they believe that everything happening on this terrestrial globe of ours depends upon the stars.

Some knowledge of the science of mathematics was given to the Chinese by the Saracens [Mongols], who penetrated into their country from the West, but very little of this knowledge was based upon definite mathematical proofs. What the Saracens left them, for the most part, consisted of certain tables of rules by which the Chinese regulated their calendar and to which they reduced their calculations of planets and the movements of the heavenly bodies in general. The founder of the family which at present regulates the study of astrology prohibited anyone from indulging in the study of this science unless he were chosen for it by hereditary right. The prohibition was founded upon fear, lest he who should acquire a knowledge of the stars might become capable of disrupting the order of the empire and seek an opportunity to do so.

Source: Louis J. Gallagher, trans., *China in the Sixteenth Century: The Journals of Matthew Ricci: 1583–1610* (New York: Random House, 1953), pp. 30–31.

The dilemma of accounting in religious terms for the ideas of Copernicus and Descartes became more urgent for Protestants as the ideas acquired an anti-Catholic status after the trial of Galileo in 1633, and as they became common scientific currency by about 1640. The development of the new science in the mid-seventeenth century coincided with religious and political upheavals throughout Europe. Religious, political, and scientific view-points became inextricably mixed. A religious certainty about divine force that could account for the motion of bodies in a vacuum enabled Newton to develop his theories on motion and gravity. In short, religion did not merely remain in the scientists' panoply of explanations; it remained a fundamental building block of scientific thought, in the same way that it remained central to most scientists' lives.

The Mechanistic World Order and Human Affairs at the End of the Seventeenth Century

Traditional institutions and ideologies checked the potential effects of the new science for a time, but by the middle of the seventeenth century, political theory was beginning to show the impact of the mechanistic world-view. Political philosophers viewed neither the world nor human society as an organic whole in which each part was distinguished in nature and function from the rest. Thomas Hobbes, John Locke, and others reimagined the bonds that link citizens to each other and to their rulers.

Because of the political turmoil in England, Thomas Hobbes (1588–1679) spent much of his productive life on the Continent. After the beginnings of the parliamentary rebellion, he joined a group of royalist émigrés in France. He met Galileo and lived for extended periods in Paris, in contact with the circle of French thinkers that included Descartes. Like Descartes, he theorized about the nature and behavior of matter; he published a treatise on his views in 1655.

Hobbes is best known today for *Leviathan* (1651), his treatise on political philosophy. *Leviathan* applies to the world of human beings Hobbes's mostly Cartesian view of nature as composed of "self-motivated" atomlike structures. Hobbes viewed people as mechanistically as he viewed the rest of nature. In his view, people were made up of appetites of various sorts—the same kind of innate forces that drove all matter. The ideal state, concluded Hobbes, is one in which a strong sovereign controls the disorder that inevitably arises from the clash of desires. Unlike the medieval philosophers, Hobbes did not draw analogies between the state and the human body (the king as head, judges and magistrates as arms, and so forth). Instead, Hobbes compared the state to a machine that "ran" by means of laws and was kept in good working order by a skilled technician—the ruler.

Hobbes's pessimism about human behavior and his insistence on the need for order imposed from above reflect, like the work of Descartes, a concern for order in the wake of political turmoil. This concern was one reason he was welcomed into the community of French philosophers, who were naturally comfortable with royalty as a powerful guarantor of order. But Hobbes's work, like theirs, was a radical departure because it envisions citizens as potentially equal and constrained neither by morality nor by natural obedience to authority.

Another Englishman, John Locke (1632–1704), offered an entirely different vision of natural equality among people and of social order. Locke's major works, *Essay on Human Understanding* (1690) and *Two Treatises on Government* (1690), reflect the experimentalism of Robert Boyle, the systematizing rationality of Descartes, and other strands of the new scientific thought. In the *Essay*, Locke offers a view of human knowledge that is more pragmatic and utilitarian than the rigorous mathematical model of certainty used by many other philosophers. He argues that human knowledge is largely the product of experience. He agrees with Descartes that reason orders and explains human experience. But he thinks that reason does not necessarily perceive reality as it really is but rather perceives reality in a limited way that is nevertheless useful. Unlike Descartes, Locke thinks there are limits to what human reason can achieve, but Locke offers a more optimistic vision of the possible uses of human reason. Whereas Descartes was interested in mentally ordering and understanding the world, Locke was interested in humans' functioning in the world.

Locke's treatises on government reflect his notion of knowledge based on experience as well as his particular experiences as a member of elite circles in the aftermath of the English revolution. A trained physician, he served as personal physician and general political assistant to Anthony Ashley Cooper (1621–1683), Lord Shaftsbury, one of the members of Parliament most opposed to Charles II's pretensions to absolutist government. When James II acceded to the throne in 1685, Locke remained in the Netherlands, where he had fled to avoid prosecution for treason. He became an adviser to William of Orange and returned to England with William and Mary in 1688. Locke's view of the principles of good government, then, came to reflect the pro-parliamentary stance of his political milieu.

Unlike Hobbes, Locke argues that people are capable of restraint and mutual respect in their pursuit of self-interest. The state arises from a contract that individuals freely enter into to protect themselves, their property, and their happiness

Locke's View of the Purpose of Government

In this passage from the second of his treatises on government, Locke describes men as naturally free and willing to enter into communities only for the protection of property. Notice how Locke justifies private property as "natural" by linking it to an individual's labor.

Men being . . . by nature all free, equal, and independent, no one can be put out of this estate and subjected to the political power of another without his own consent. The only way whereby any one divests himself of his natural liberty and puts on the bonds of civil society is by agreeing with other men to join and unite into a community for their comfortable, safe, and peaceable living amongst one another, in a secure enjoyment of their properties and a greater security against any that are not of it. This any number of men may do, because it injures not the freedom of the rest; they are left as they were in the liberty of the state of nature. When any number of men have so consented to make one community or government, they are thereby presently incorporated and make one body politic wherein the majority have a right to act and conclude the rest. . . . And thus that which begins and acutally constitutes any political society is nothing but the consent of any number of freemen capable of a majority to unite and incorporate into such a society. And this is that, and that only, which did or could give beginning to any lawful government in the world.

    If man in the state of nature be so free . . . , and if he be absolute lord of his own person and possessions, equal to the greatest, and subject to nobody, why will he part with his freedom, why will he give up his empire and subject himself to the dominion and control of any other power?

    The great and chief end, therefore, of men's uniting into commonwealths and putting themselves under government is the preservation of their property. . . . Though the earth and all inferior creatures be common to all men, yet every man has a property in his own person; this nobody has any right to but himself. The labor of his body and the work of his hands, we may say, are properly his. Whatsoever then he removes out of the state that nature has provided and left it in, he has mixed his labor with, and joined to it something that is his own, and thereby makes it his property. It being by him removed from the common state nature has placed it in, it has by this labor something annexed to it that excludes the common right of other men. For this labor being the unquestionable property of the laborer, no man but he can have a right to what that is once joined to, at least where there is enough and as good left in common for others. . . . As much land as a man tills, plants, improves, cultivates, and can use the product of, so much is his property. He by his labor does, as it were, enclose it from the common.

Source: Second Treatise, in John Locke, *Two Treatises of Civil Government* (London: G. Routledge & Sons, 1884).

from possible aggression by others. They can invest the executive and legislative authority to carry out this protection in monarchy or any other governing institution, though Locke believed the English Parliament was the best available model. Because sovereignty resides with the people who enter into the contract, rebellion against abuse of power is justified. Thus, Locke frees people from arbitrary bonds of authority to the state and to each other.

    Locke's experience as a member of the elite of his society is apparent in his emphasis on private property, which he considers one of the fundamental human rights. (See the box, "Locke's View of the Purpose of Government.") Indeed, there is no place in his political vision for serious disagree-

Science Gains an Audience This illustration from Bernard de Fontenelle's major work popularized the new science. It reveals the audience for which the work was intended. A gentleman, sitting with a lady in a formal garden, gestures to a depiction of the solar system as it was now understood; the lady is presumed to understand and to be interested in the information. *(By permission of Houghton Library, Harvard University)*

ment about the nature of property. Locke even found a justification for slavery. He also did not consider women to be political beings in the same way as men. The family, he felt, was a separate domain from the state, not bound by the same contractual obligations.

Locke's dismissal of women from the realm of politics and of questions of power and justice from the family was not an accident. The ability of Locke and many other seventeenth-century thinkers to imagine a new physical or political order was constrained by the prevailing view of gender as a "nat-

ural" principle of order and hierarchy. Gender distinctions are in the main socially ascribed roles that are easily misinterpreted as "natural" differences between women and men. Although Margaret Cavendish (see the box on page 645) and other women disputed the validity of such distinctions, men frequently used them. Locke's use of gender as an arbitrary organizing principle gave his bold new political vision a claim to being "natural." The use of gender-specific vocabulary to describe nature itself had the effect of making the new objective attitude toward the world seem "natural."

Works by seventeenth-century scientists are filled with references to nature as a woman who must be "conquered," "subdued," or "penetrated."

Traditional gender distinctions limited and buttressed most facets of political thought, but in other areas, the fact of uncertainty and the need for tolerance was embraced. Another of Locke's influential works was the impassioned *Letter on Toleration* (1689). In it he argues that religious belief is fundamentally private and that only the most basic Christian principles need be accepted by everyone. Others went further than Locke by entirely removing traditional religion as a fundamental guarantor of morality and order. Fostering this climate of religious skepticism were religious pluralism in England and the irrationality of religious intolerance—demonstrated by Louis XIV's persecution of Protestants.

Pierre Bayle (1647–1706), a Frenchman of Protestant origins, argued that morality can be wholly detached from traditional religion. Bayle cited as an example of morality the philosopher Baruch Spinoza (1632–1677). Spinoza believed the state to have a moral purpose and human happiness to have spiritual roots. Yet he was not a Christian at all but a Dutch Jew who had been ejected from his local synagogue for supposed atheism. One need hardly be a Christian of any sort in order to be a moral being, Bayle concluded.

Bayle's skepticism toward traditional knowledge was more wide ranging than his views on religion. His best-known work, *Dictionnaire historique et critique* (*Historical and Critical Dictionary*, 1702), was a compendium of observations about and criticisms of virtually every thinker whose works were known at the time, including recent and lionized figures such as Descartes and Newton. Bayle was the first systematic skeptic, and he relentlessly exposed errors and shortcomings in all received knowledge. His works were very popular with elite lay readers.

Bayle's fellow countryman Bernard de Fontenelle (1657–1757), secretary to the Académie des Sciences from 1699 to 1741, was the greatest popularizer of the new science of his time. His *Entretiens sur la Pluralités des Mondes* (*Conversations on the Plurality of Worlds*, 1686) was, as the title implies, an informally presented description of the infinite universe of matter. It went through numerous editions and translations. As secretary to the Académie, Fontenelle continued his work as popularizer by publishing descriptions of the work of the Académie's scientists. He died one month short of his hundredth birthday. At his death in 1757 it was said that "the Philosophic spirit, today so much in evidence, owes its beginnings to Monsieur de Fontenelle."[16]

SUMMARY

Fontenelle is a fitting figure with whom to end a discussion of the Scientific Revolution because he represents, and worked to accomplish, the transference of the new natural philosophy into political and social philosophy—a movement we know as the "Enlightenment." The Scientific Revolution began, as innovation in scientific thinking often does, with a specific research problem whose answer led in unexpected directions. Copernicus's response to traditional astronomical problems led to scientific and philosophical innovation because of his solution and because of the context into which it was received.

Other scientists, following Copernicus, built on his theories, culminating in the work of Galileo, who supported Copernican theory with additional data and widely published his findings. The Frenchman Descartes was the first to fashion a systematic explanation for the operations of nature to replace the medieval view. The political and intellectual climate in England, meanwhile, encouraged the development of experimental science and inductive reasoning. Isaac Newton provided new theories to explain the behavior of matter and expressed them in mathematical terms that could apply to either the earth or the cosmos; with his work, traditional astronomy and physics were overturned.

Rulers made use of the new science for the practical results it offered despite the ideological challenge it presented to their power. By the end of the seventeenth century, the hierarchical Christian world-view grounded in the old science was being challenged on many fronts. A fully articulated secular world-view would be the product of the Enlightenment.

NOTES

1. Quoted in Thomas S. Kuhn, *The Copernican Revolution* (Cambridge, Mass.: Harvard University Press, 1985), p. 131.
2. Quoted in Margaret C. Jacob, *The Cultural Meaning of the Scientific Revolution* (Philadelphia: Temple, 1988), p. 18.
3. Quoted ibid., p. 33.
4. Quoted in Alan G. R. Smith, *Science and Society in the Sixteenth and Seventeenth Centuries* (New York: Science History Publications, 1972), p. 72.
5. Quoted in Jacob, *Cultural Meaning*, p. 32 (emphasis added).
6. Quoted in Bruce T. Moran, ed., *Patronage and Institutions: Science, Technology and Medicine at the European Court* (Rochester: The Boyden Press, 1991), p. 43.
7. Quoted in Jacob, *Cultural Meaning*, p. 59.
8. Quoted ibid., p. 58.
9. Quoted in Steven Shapin, *A Social History of Truth* (Chicago: University of Chicago Press, 1994), p. 298.
10. Quoted in Jacob, *Cultural Meaning*, p. 89.
11. Quoted in Smith, *Science and Society*, p. 130.
12. Quoted in Jacob, *Cultural Meaning*, p. 25.
13. Quoted in Londa Schiebinger, *The Mind Has No Sex?* (Cambridge, Mass.: Harvard University Press, 1989), p. 92.
14. Quoted in Kuhn, *The Copernican Revolution*, p. 191.
15. *Complete Poetry and Selected Prose of John Donne*, ed. John Hayward (Bloomsbury, England: Nonesuch Press, 1929), p. 365; quoted in Kuhn, *The Copernican Revolution*, p. 194.
16. Quoted in Paul Edwards, ed., *The Encyclopedia of Philosophy*, vol. 3 (New York: Macmillan, 1967), p. 209.

SUGGESTED READING

General Surveys

Debus, Allen G. *Man and Nature in the Renaissance.* 1978. A survey of developments in science and medicine during the two centuries leading up to the seventeenth-century revolution; its special contribution stems from Debus's emphasis on Paracelsianism and alchemy.

Hall, A. Rupert. *The Revolution in Science, 1500–1800.* 1983. A thorough introduction to all scientific disciplines that de-emphasizes the larger context of scientific development but explains many of the innovations in detail.

Kearney, Hugh. *Science and Change.* 1971. A readable general introduction to the Scientific Revolution.

Kuhn, Thomas. *The Copernican Revolution.* 1985. A readable treatment of the revolution in astronomy that also lucidly explains the Aristotelian world-view; important for setting Copernicus's work in the context of the history of astronomy; the first thing to read to understand the Copernican revolution.

———. *The Structure of Scientific Revolutions.* 1970. A path-breaking work that argues that all scientific schemas are systems of explanation and that science progresses by shifting from one general paradigm to another, not from error to "truth."

Lindberg, D. C., and R. S. Westman. *Reappraisals of the Scientific Revolution.* 1990. Essays re-evaluating classic interpretations of the Scientific Revolution. Includes a rich bibliography.

Mandrou, Robert. *From Humanism to Science.* 1978. A general intellectual history of the period 1450–1650 that sets the Scientific Revolution in the context of broader intellectual, social, and economic currents.

Merchant, Carolyn. *The Death of Nature: Women, Ecology and the Scientific Revolution.* 1980. An important corrective interpretation that focuses on the changing definition of nature—particularly how nature became something to be dominated and consumed—and the way in which this definition reinforced negative cultural views of women.

Thomas, Keith. *Religion and the Decline of Magic.* 1971. An exploration of the changing character of religious belief and "superstitious" practice; finds roots outside of science for changing, increasingly secular world-views.

Westfall, Richard S. *The Construction of Modern Science: Mechanisms and Mechanics.* 1977. A general treatment of the Scientific Revolution that emphasizes and explains the mechanistic world-view.

Individual Scientists

Bordo, Susan R. *The Flight to Objectivity: Essays on Cartesianism and Culture.* 1987. A collection that studies Descartes's work as a metaphysical and psychological crisis and discusses implications of Cartesian mind-body dualism.

Cohen, I. Bernard. *The Newtonian Revolution.* 1987. A brief introduction to Newton and the meaning of his discoveries; a good place to start on Newton.

Drake, Stillman. *Galileo at Work: His Scientific Biography.* 1978. A detailed chronological study that reveals Galileo's character and illuminates his scientific achievements.

Frank, Robert G., Jr. *Harvey and the Oxford Physiologists.* 1980. An explanation of Harvey's work in the context of traditional Galenic medicine and a discussion of the community of scholars who accepted and built on Harvey's innovations.

Redondi, Pietro. *Galileo Heretic.* 1987. A careful account of Galileo's confrontation with the church.

(continued on page 656)

MODERN MAPS

We take for granted that contemporary maps will provide accurate representations of geography and present information in standardized ways we can easily read. But how did these standards of clarity and accuracy come about?

Modern mapping was developed during the Scientific Revolution. Like most of the changes we have labeled the "Scientific Revolution," changes in mapping were the result of several influences: innovations in Renaissance art, knowledge gleaned from voyages of exploration, the impact of new astronomical discoveries, and the interest and support of princely patrons.

Let us look at Christopher Saxton's map of Somerset, a county in England. This map was printed in 1579 in one of the first atlases ever published. We might be struck by how different this map appears from contemporary maps; many of its features seem decorative or even quaint. Ships, not drawn to scale, ride at anchor or sail off the coast. Towns are represented not by dots of various sizes but by miniature town buildings. Relief

in the landscape is depicted with hills drawn, like the town buildings, from a side view inconsistent with the aerial perspective of the map as a whole. The large royal coat of arms that occupies the upper left quadrant of the map seems the most antiquated and irrelevant feature.

But is it irrelevant? Let us try to appreciate what a striking and powerful image this map must have been for its original viewers. Because the features are represented in ways that we consider decorative, it is easy for us to overlook the fact that this map illustrates a revolutionary method of depicting space. Saxton provides an aerial view of an entire county, with all locales arrayed in accurate spatial relationship to one another. This accurate rendering of space was, first, the result of the discovery of linear perspective by Renaissance artists. This discovery enabled space to be imagined from the perspective of a distanced observer. Saxton's maps—and the few others published at about the same time—represented the first time Europeans could take "visual possession" of the land they

Map of the County of Somerset, England, 1579
(British Library)

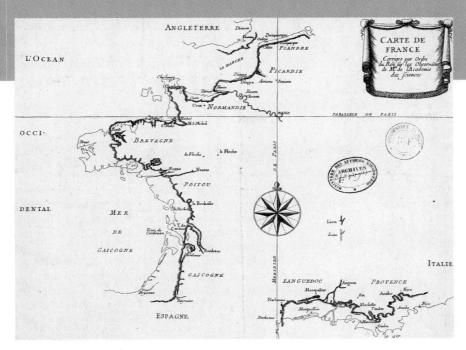

Map of the French Coastline, 1693 *(Bibliothèque Nationale)*

lived in, in the way we now take for granted whenever we buy a road map.[*]

Precise measurement of land forms—the location of hills in this map, for example—still relied on the established craft of systematic surveying. And here is where the royal coat of arms enters the picture, literally. Saxton's surveying and the production of his atlas were sponsored by the government of Queen Elizabeth. Thus, just as this map enabled contemporary observers to envision for the first time, in its entirety, the land they lived in, it simultaneously marked royal power over that land.

Now let us look at a 1693 map of the coastline of France. We immediately note that most decorative elements are gone: No ships sail the abundant seas, for example. The figure of a compass marks the Paris meridian—the site of the city, we are shown, has been precisely determined by means of its longitude and latitude. More accurate calculation of longitude had been made possible by the work of Kepler and Galileo, whose mapping of heavenly bodies provided known points in the night sky from which to calculate the longitude of the observer's position on earth. (Calculation of latitude had always been easier, since it involved

only determining the angle of the sun above the horizon, but it was also improved by better instrumentation in the seventeenth century.) After 1650, French cartographers, among others, systematically collected astronomical observations from around the world more precisely to map all known lands.

This map superimposes a corrected view of the coastline of France over an older rendering. The power of this coastline map, then, lies in the way it dramatically advertises the progress of mapmaking itself. Royal power remains connected to scientific effort: The title reads, "Map of France, corrected by order of the King by the observations of Messieurs of the Academy of Sciences."

Thus, both of these maps glorify royal power: one by linking it with a dramatically new visualization of the land it ruled, the other by presenting royalty as a patron and guarantor of knowledge. But in the second map, royal identity is no longer pictured along with the land it claims. Instead, the king is mentioned discreetly, in what is coming to be a standardized label.

Like all innovations of the Scientific Revolution, those in mapmaking had unintended consequences. Claims to royal power articulated on maps lost their force when placed next to the information the maps conveyed; royal power had many practical and ideological uses for the new science but, in the end, would be undermined by the world-view the new science made possible. ✎

[*]Richard Helgerson, "The Land Speaks: Cartography, Chorography, and Subversion in Renaissance England," *Representations* 16 (Fall 1986): 51. This discussion of Saxton's map and the evolution of mapmaking is drawn from Helgerson and from Norman J. W. Thrower, *Maps and Civilization* (Chicago: University of Chicago Press, 1996), chaps. 5 and 6.

Shapin, Steven, and Simon Schaffer. *Leviathan and the Air-Pump*. 1985. One of the most important studies of seventeenth-century science: traces the conflict between Cartesian science, as represented by Hobbes, and experimental science, in the work of Boyle; and shows the relationship of Hobbes and Boyle to their respective contexts as well as some of the political, cultural, and philosophical implications of each school of thought.

Thoren, Victor E. *The Lord of Uraniborg: A Biography of Tycho Brahe*. 1990. An up-to-date study of the life and work of the Danish astronomer.

Political, Social, and Cultural Contexts for Science

Biagioli, Mario. *Galileo, Courtier*. 1993. A new study that stresses the power of patronage relations to shape scientific process.

Hunter, Michael. *Science and Society in Restoration England*. 1981. A study that sets English science in its political and cultural contexts; critical of Webster's classic study (see below).

Jacob, Margaret C. *The Cultural Meaning of the Scientific Revolution*. 1988. An account that moves from the Scientific Revolution through the industrial transformation of the nineteenth century, sketching the relationship of developments in science, metaphysics, and technology to the political and social history of the various eras.

———. *The Newtonians and the English Revolution*. 1976. A work that links the development of Newtonian science to its political and social context and examines the simultaneous evolution of religion that could accept the new science yet maintain traditional perspectives.

Moran, Bruce T., ed. *Patronage and Institutions: Science, Technology and Medicine at the European Court*. 1991. A work that looks at royal courts as shaping and sustaining institutions for science from the early sixteenth century onward.

Schiebinger, Londa. *The Mind Has No Sex?* 1989. An examination of the participation of women in the practice of science and an explanation of how science began to reflect the exclusion of women in its values and objects of study—above all, in its claims about scientific "facts" about women themselves.

Webster, Charles. *The Great Instauration*. 1975. A classic study that links the development of the modern scientific attitude to the Puritan revolution in England.

VOLTAIRE.

CHAPTER 18

Europe on the Threshold of Modernity, ca. 1715–1789

Acustomer in one of the growing number of cafés in Paris on February 10, 1778, might have wondered if the king himself was entering the city, such was the commotion as Parisians turned out to welcome a former resident. Now 84, this old man had journeyed to the city to preside at the opening of his latest play, but everyone realized that this most likely would be his last visit, and he was given a hero's welcome. The king himself would not receive the visitor, but literary and political elites clamored to be admitted to audiences with him. Benjamin Franklin brought his grandson to receive the old man's blessing. Though he was treated like royalty, the man was not a ruler, but a political thinker and writer: the philosopher Voltaire.

A prolific writer, critic, and reformer in his own country of France, Voltaire was lionized by elites everywhere, including the rulers of several European states. Voltaire is an apt symbol for the age not only because of his personal influence, but also because he was simply the best known of dozens of thinkers and writers who made up the philosophical movement we know as the Enlightenment. The Enlightenment constituted a revolution in political philosophy, but it was also much more: The era witnessed the emergence of an informed body of public opinion, critical of the prevailing political system, that existed outside the corridors of power. The relationship between governments and the governed had begun to change: Subjects of monarchs were becoming citizens of nations.

Frederick the Great of Prussia, Catherine the Great of Russia, and other rulers self-consciously tried to use Enlightenment precepts to guide

Voltaire, by Houdon.
In the foyer of the
Théâtre Français, Paris.

their efforts at governing. They had mixed success, however. Powerful interests opposed their efforts at reform, and their own hereditary and autocratic power was incompatible with Enlightenment perspectives. Elites still sure of their power, as well as the traditional interests of states, dominated eighteenth-century politics.

Nevertheless, profound changes in economic, social, and political life began in this period. Economic growth spurred population growth, which in turn stimulated industry and trade. The increasing economic and strategic importance of overseas colonies made them important focal points of international conflict. The dramatic political and social changes that began as the century closed had their roots in the intellectual, economic, and social ferment of eighteenth-century life.

THE ENLIGHTENMENT

One of Isaac Newton's countrymen wrote the following epitaph for the English scientist:

Nature and Nature's Laws lay hid in Night.
God said, "Let Newton be," and all was Light.

The most important works of Enlightenment philosophy reflected the intellectual confidence that Newton's work generated. The poet's assertion that "all was Light," however, requires scrutiny.

The phrase evokes the determination and confidence of an intellectual elite that felt it held a new key to truth. In this sense, the Enlightenment was nothing less than the transfer into general philosophy, particularly political and social thought, of the intellectual revolution that had already taken place within the physical sciences. But, like the Scientific Revolution, the Enlightenment was not only sweeping in its impact but specific in its content. In this so-called Age of Reason, *reason* had specific meanings, and philosophers' speculations had particular goals.

Enlightenment philosophy occurred in the context of increasingly widespread publications and new opportunities in literary societies, clubs, and salons for the exchange of views. This context shaped the outline of Enlightenment thought, which was for the most part an elite set of preoccupations. It also determined the radicalism of the Enlightenment, by helping to ensure that an entire

level of society would share in attitudes that were fundamentally critical of that society.

Voltaire and the Enlightenment

The Enlightenment was not so much a body of thought as it was an intellectual and social movement. Originating in France, it consisted, first, of the application to political and social thought of the confidence in the intelligibility of natural law that theoretical science had recently achieved. Enlightenment thinkers combined confidence in the intelligibility of the world and its laws with confidence in the human capacity to discern and work in concert with those laws. The former confidence was Newton's legacy; the latter was the legacy of Descartes and Locke. The most dramatic effect of confidence was the desacralizing of social and political bonds—a new belief that society can be grounded on rational foundations to be determined by humans, not arbitrary foundations determined by God.

A wide range of thinkers participated in the Enlightenment; in France, they were known as *philosophes,* a term meaning not a formal philosopher but rather a thinker and critic. To most philosophes, the main agenda was clear. For too long, humans had been mired in ignorance. Rather than regarding themselves as thinkers, they thought of themselves as sinners. Arbitrary laws and institutions oppressed them. Lack of proper education and the tyranny of the church condemned them to ignorance. French thinkers singled out the Catholic church as the archenemy because of its opposition to their positive views of human nature and because it controlled much education and was still a force in political life.

The following passage from Voltaire's *Dictionnaire philosophique* (*Philosophical Dictionary,* 1764) is typical of his work in its casual format and biting wit and is also typical of the venomous Enlightenment view of the church. The dictionary entry for "authority" is not about authority in general but focuses on the arbitrary authority of the church:

A hundred times [you clerics] have been spoken to of the insolent absurdity with which you condemned Galileo, and I shall speak to you for the hundred and first. . . . I desire that there be engraved on the door of your holy office: Here seven cardinals assisted by minor brethren had the master of thought of Italy thrown into prison at the age of seventy, made him fast on bread and water, because he instructed the human race.

The life of Voltaire (1694–1778), the most famous of the philosophes, spanned the century. Born François-Marie Arouet to a middle-class family, he took the pen name Voltaire in 1718, after one of his early plays was a critical success. He was educated by the Jesuits, whom he despised but admired for their teaching methods. He produced a vast array of written work: plays, epic poems, novelettes—some of which have explicit philosophical or political content—as well as philosophical tracts. Voltaire moved in courtly circles. Mockery of the regent, the duke of Orléans, led to a year's imprisonment in 1717, and an exchange of insults with a leading courtier some years later led to enforced exile in Great Britain for two years.

After returning from Britain, Voltaire published his first major philosophical work. *Lettres philosophiques* (*Philosophical Letters*, 1734) revealed the influence of his British sojourn and helped to popularize Newton's achievement. The empirical tradition in British philosophy profoundly influenced Voltaire. To his confidence in the laws governing nature he added cautious confidence in humans' attempts to establish truth. From Locke's work (see pages 649–651) he drew confidence in human educability tempered by awareness of the finite nature of the human mind. These elements gave Voltaire's philosophy both its passionate conviction and its practicality.

Voltaire portrayed Great Britain as a more rational society than France. He was particularly impressed with the religious and intellectual toleration evident there. The British government had a more workable set of institutions and the economy was less crippled by the remnants of feudal privilege, and education was not in the hands of the church. (See the box, "Voltaire on Britain's Commercial Success.")

After the publication of his audacious *Lettres*, Voltaire was again forced into exile from Paris, and he resided for some years in the country home of a woman with whom he shared a remarkable intellectual and emotional relationship: Emilie, marquise du Châtelet (1706–1749). Châtelet was a mathematician and a scientist. She set to work on a French translation of Newton's *Principia* while Voltaire worked at his accustomed variety of writing, which also included a commen-

Etablissement de la nouvelle Philosophie. Notre Berceau fut un Caffé.

Café Society The caption under this contemporary illustration reads: "Establishment of the new philosophy; our cradle was the café." Cafés were one of the new settings where literate elites could discuss the new philosophy and explore its implications for social and political life. (*Carnavalet Museum, Paris*)

tary on Newton's work. Because of Châtelet's tutelage, Voltaire became more knowledgeable about the sciences and more serious in his efforts to apply scientific rationality to human affairs. He was devastated by her sudden death in 1749.

Shortly afterward, he accepted the invitation of the king of Prussia, Frederick II, to visit Berlin. His stay was stormy and brief because of disagreements with other court philosophers. He resided

Voltaire on Britain's Commercial Success

In this excerpt from **Philosophical Letters,** *Voltaire compares British trade and seapower with the commercial activities of the German and French elites, who scorn trade in order to engage in aristocratic pretentiousness and court politics. Voltaire's admiration for England and his penchant for criticizing irrationalities of all sorts are evident, as is his famed wit. Wit and irony were important tools, enabling Voltaire to advance trenchant criticism when seeming only to poke fun.*

Commerce, which has brought wealth to the citizenry of England, has helped to make them free, and freedom has developed commerce in its turn. By means of it the nation has grown great; it is commerce that little by little has strengthened the naval forces that make the English the masters of the seas. . . . Posterity may learn with some surprise that a little island with nothing of its own but a bit of lead, tin . . . and coarse wool became, by means of its commerce, powerful enough to send three fleets at one time to three different ends of the earth.

All this makes the English merchant justly proud; moreover, the younger brother of a peer of the realm does not scorn to enter into trade. . . . [In Germany], they are unable to imagine how [an aristocrat could enter trade since they have] as many as thirty Highnesses of the same name, with nothing to show for it but pride and a coat of arms.

In France anybody who wants to can [act the part of marquis] and whoever arrives in Paris with money to spend and a [plausible name] may indulge in such phrases as "a man of my rank and quality" and with sovereign eye look down upon a wholesaler. . . . Yet I don't know which is the more useful to a state, a well-powdered lord who knows precisely what time the king gets up in the morning . . . and who gives himself airs of grandeur while playing the role of slave in a minister's antechamber, or a great merchant who enriches his country.

Source: Ernest Dilworth, trans. and ed., *Voltaire: Philosophical Letters* (New York: Bobbs-Merrill, 1961), pp. 39–40.

for a time in Geneva, until his criticisms of the city's moral codes forced yet another exile on him. He spent most of the last twenty years of his life at his estates on the Franco-Swiss border, where he could be relatively free from interference by any government. These were productive years. He produced his best-known satirical novelette, *Candide,* in 1758. It criticized aristocratic privilege and the power of clerics as well as the naiveté of philosophers who took "natural law" to mean that the world was already operating as it should.

Voltaire's belief that one must struggle to overturn the accumulated habits of centuries is also reflected in his political activity. Voltaire became involved in several celebrated legal cases in which individuals were pitted against the authority of the church, which was still backed by the authority of the state. The most famous case was that of Jean Calas (1698–1762), a Protestant from southern France who was accused of murdering his son, allegedly to prevent him from converting to Catholicism. Calas maintained his innocence until his execution in 1762. Voltaire saw in this case the worst aspects of religious prejudice and injustice and worked tirelessly to establish Calas's innocence as a matter of principle and so that his family could inherit his property. In pursuit of justice in these cases and in criticism of his archenemy the church, Voltaire added a stream of straightforward political pamphlets to his literary output. He also worked closer to home, initiating agricultural reform on his estates and working to improve the status of peasants in the vicinity.

Voltaire died in Paris in May 1778, shortly after his triumphal return there. By then, he was no longer leader of the Enlightenment in strictly intellectual terms. Thinkers and writers more radical than he had earned prominence during his long life and had dismissed some of his beliefs, such as the notion that reform could be introduced by a monarch. But Voltaire had provided a crucial stimulus to French thought with his *Lettres philosophiques*. His importance lies also in his embodiment of the critical spirit of eighteenth-century rationalism: its confidence, its increasingly practical bent, its wit and sophistication. Until the end of his life, Voltaire remained a bridge between the increasingly diverse body of Enlightenment thought and the literate elite audience.

The Variety of Enlightenment Thought

Differences among philosophes grew as the century progressed. In the matter of religion, for example, there was virtual unanimity of opposition to the Catholic church among French thinkers, but no unanimity about God. Voltaire was a theist—believing firmly in God, creator of the universe, but not a specifically Christian God. To some later thinkers, God was irrelevant—the creator of the world, but a world that ran continuously according to established laws. Some philosophes were atheists, arguing that a universe that ran according to discoverable laws needs no higher purpose and no divine presence to explain, run, or justify it. In Protestant areas of Europe, in contrast to France, Enlightenment thought was often less hostile to Christianity.

Questions about social and political order, as well as about human rationality itself, were also pondered. Charles de Secondat (1689–1755), baron of Montesquieu, a French judge and legal philosopher, combined the belief that human institutions must be rational with Locke's assumption of human educability. Montesquieu's treatise *De L'Esprit des lois* (*The Spirit of the Laws*, 1748) was published in twenty-two printings within two years. In it Montesquieu maintained that laws were not meant to be arbitrary rules but derived naturally from human society: The more evolved a society was, the

MAJOR WORKS OF THE ENLIGHTENMENT	
1721	Montesquieu, *Persian Letters*
1734	Voltaire, *Philosophical Letters*
1748	Montesquieu, *The Spirit of the Laws* Hume, *Essay Concerning Human Understanding*
1758	Voltaire, *Candide*
1751–65	Diderot, *The Encyclopedia*
1762	Rousseau, *The Social Contract*
1764	Voltaire, *Philosophical Dictionary*
1776	Smith, *The Wealth of Nations*
1784	Kant, *What Is Enlightenment?*
1792	Wollstonecraft, *A Vindication of the Rights of Woman*
1795	Condorcet, *The Progress of the Human Mind*

more liberal were its laws. This notion provided a sense of the progress possible within society and government and deflated Europeans' pretensions in regard to other societies, for a variety of laws could equally be "rational" given differing conditions. Montesquieu is perhaps best known to Americans as the advocate of the separation of legislative, executive, and judicial powers that later became enshrined in the American Constitution. To Montesquieu, this scheme seemed to parallel in human government the balance of forces observable in nature and seemed best to guarantee liberty.

The "laws" of economic life were also investigated. In France, economic thinkers known as *physiocrats* proposed ending what they regarded as artificial control over land use in order to free productive capacity and permit the flow of produce to market. Their target was traditional forms of land tenure, including collective control of village lands by peasants and seigneurial rights over land and peasant labor by landlords. The freeing of restrictions on agriculture, manufacture, and trade was proposed by the Scotsman Adam Smith in his treatise *An Inquiry into the Nature and Causes of the Wealth of Nations* (1776).

Smith (1723–1790), a professor at the University of Glasgow, is best known in modern times as the originator of "laissez-faire" economics: the assumption that an economy will regulate itself without interference by government and, of more concern to Smith, without the monopolies and other economic privileges common in his day. Smith's schema for economic growth was not merely a rigid application to economics of faith in natural law. His ideas grew out of an optimistic view of human nature and human rationality that was heavily indebted to Locke. Humans, Smith believed, have drives and passions that they can direct and govern by means of reason and inherent sympathy for one another. Thus, Smith said, in seeking their own achievement and well-being, they are often "led by an invisible hand" to simultaneously benefit society as a whole.

Throughout the century, philosophers of various stripes disagreed about the nature and the limits of human reason. Smith's countryman and friend David Hume (1711–1776) was perhaps the most radical in his critique of the human capacity for knowing. He was the archskeptic, taking Locke's view of the limitations on pure reason to the point of doubting the efficacy of sense data. His major work in which he expounded these views, *Essay Concerning Human Understanding* (1748), led to important innovations later in the century in the work of the German philosopher Immanuel Kant but were, at the time, almost contrary to the prevailing spirit of confidence in empirical knowledge. Hume himself separated this work from his other efforts in moral, political, and economic philosophy, which were more in tune with the prevailing views of the day.

Mainstream confidence in empirical knowledge and in the intelligibility of the world is evident in the production of the *Encyclopédie* (*Encyclopedia*), a seventeen-volume compendium of knowledge, criticism, and philosophy assembled by leading philosophes in France and published there between 1751 and 1765. The volumes were designed to contain state-of-the-art knowledge about arts, sciences, technology, and philosophy. The guiding philosophy of the project, set forth by its chief editor, Denis Diderot (1713–1784), was a belief in the advance of human happiness through the advance of knowledge. The *Encyclopédie* was a kind of history of the advance of knowledge as

Diderot's Encyclopedia This illustration of typesetting at a newspaper printshop is one of many depicting industry and technology of the day in the multivolume *Encyclopedia*. Newspapers increased in size, number, and frequency of publication during the course of the eighteenth century. *(Division of Rare & Manuscript Collections, Cornell University Library)*

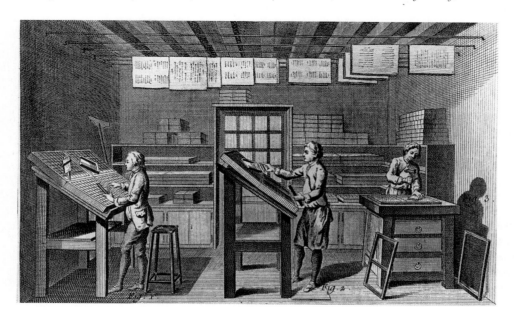

well as a compendium of known achievements. It was revolutionary in that it not only intrigued and inspired intellectuals but assisted thousands of government officials and professionals. Catherine the Great, empress of Russia, remarked in a letter that she consulted its pages to find guidance concerning one of her reform schemes.

The encyclopedia project illustrates the political context of Enlightenment thought as well as its philosophical premises. The Catholic church placed the work on the Index of prohibited books, and the French government might have barred its publication but for the fact that the official who would have made the decision was drawn to Enlightenment thinking. Many other officials, however, worked to suppress it. By the late 1750s, losses in wars overseas had made French officials highly sensitive to political challenges of any kind. Thus, like Voltaire, the major contributors to the *Encyclopédie* were lionized by certain segments of the elite and persecuted by others in their official functions.

The *Encyclopédie* reflects the complexities and limitations of Enlightenment thought on another score—the position of women. One might expect that the Enlightenment penchant for challenging received knowledge and traditional social and political hierarchies would lead to revised views of women's abilities and rights. Indeed, some contributors blamed women's inequality with men not on any deficiencies in women but rather on the customs and laws that had kept women from education and the development of their abilities. However, other contributors blamed women, and not society, for the inequality women suffered, or they argued that women had talents that fit them only for the domestic sphere.

Both positions were represented in Enlightenment thought as a whole. The assumption of the natural equality of all people provided a powerful ground for arguing the equality of women with men. Some thinkers, such as Mary Astell (1666–1731), challenged Locke's separation of family life from the public world of free, contractual relationships. (See the box, "An English Feminist Criticizes Unenlightened Views of Women.") Most advocated increased education for women, if only to make them more fit to raise enlightened children. By 1800 the most radical thinkers were advocating full citizenship rights for women and equal rights to property along with enhanced education.

The best-known proponent of those views was an English woman, Mary Wollstonecraft (1759–1797), who authored *A Vindication of the Rights of Woman* (1792). She assumed that most elite women would devote themselves to domestic duties, but she argued that without the responsibilities of citizenship, the leavening of education, and economic independence, women could be neither fully formed individuals nor worthy of their duties. Working women, she concluded, needed these rights simply to survive.

A more limited view of women's capacities was one element in the influential work of Jean-Jacques Rousseau (1712–1778). Like Locke, Rousseau could conceive of the free individual only as male, and he grounded his critique of the old order and his novel political ideas in an arbitrary division of gender roles. Rousseau's view of women was linked to a critique of the artificiality of elite, cosmopolitan society in which Enlightenment thought was then flourishing and in which aristocratic women were fully involved. Rousseau believed in the educability of men but was as concerned with issues of character and emotional life as with knowledge. Society—particularly the artificial courtly society—was corrupting. The true citizen had to cultivate virtue and sensibility, not manners, taste, or refinement. Rousseau designated women as guarantors of the "natural" virtues of children and as nurturers of the emotional life and character of men—but not as fully formed beings in their own right.

Rousseau's emphasis on the education and virtue of citizens was the underpinning of his larger political vision, set forth in *Du Contrat social* (*The Social Contract*, 1762). He imagined an egalitarian republic—possible particularly in small states such as his native Geneva—in which men would consent to be governed because the government would determine and act in accordance with the "general will" of the citizens. The "general will" was not majority opinion but rather what each citizen *would* want if he were fully informed and were acting in accordance with his highest nature. The "general will" became apparent whenever the citizens met as a body and made collective decisions, and it could be imposed on all inhabitants. (See the box, "Rousseau Discusses the Benefits of Submitting to the General Will.") This was a breathtaking vision of direct democracy—but one with ominous possibilities, for Rousseau

An English Feminist Criticizes Unenlightened Views of Women

Both male and female writers criticized the failure of some Enlightenment thinkers to view ideas about women with the same skepticism and rationalism that they brought to other subjects. One of the earliest was the Englishwoman Mary Astell (1666–1731). In this excerpt from **Some Reflections on Marriage (1700),** *Astell criticizes, in an ironic tone, negative assessments of women's capacities, Locke's separation of the public and private spheres, and the denial to women of the rights that men enjoy in public life.*

'Tis true, through want of learning, and that of superior genius which men, as men, lay claim to, she [the author] was ignorant of the natural inferiority of our sex, which our masters lay down as self-evident and fundamental truth. She saw nothing in the reason of things to make this either a principle or a conclusion, but much to the contrary.

If they mean that some men are superior to some women, this is no great discovery; had they turned the tables, they might have seen that some women are superior to some men. . . .

Again, if absolute sovereignty be not necessary in a state, how comes it to be so in a family? Or if in a family why not in a state, since no reason can be alleged for the one that will not hold more strongly for the other? If the authority of the husband, so far as it extends, is sacred and inalienable, why not that of the prince? The domestic sovereign is without dispute elected and the stipulations and contract are mutual; is it not then partial in men to the last degree to contend for and practice that arbitrary dominion in their families which they abhor and exclaim against in the state? For if arbitrary power is evil in itself, and an improper method of governing rational and free agents, it ought not to be practiced anywhere.

Source: Moira Ferguson, ed., *First Feminists* (Bloomington: Indiana University Press, 1985), pp. 191–193.

rejected the institutional brakes on state authority proposed by Locke and Montesquieu. Also, the demands of citizenship in such a political order, in contrast to simple obedience under a monarchy, necessitated, for Rousseau, the subordination of women's lives to those of male citizens.

Rousseau's emphasis on the private emotional life anticipates the romanticism of the early nineteenth century. It also reflects Rousseau's own experience as the son of a humble family, always sensing himself an outcast in the brilliant world of Parisian salons. He had a love-hate relationship with this life, remaining attached to several aristocratic women patrons even as he decried their influence. His own personal life did not match his prescriptions for others. He completely neglected to give his own four children the nurturing and education that he argued were vital; indeed, he

abandoned all of them to a foundling home. He was nevertheless influential as a critic of an elite society still dominated by status, patronage, and privilege. Rousseau's work reflects to an extreme degree the tensions in Enlightenment thought generally: It was part of elite culture as well as its principal critic.

The Growth of Public Opinion

It is impossible to understand the significance of the Enlightenment without an analysis of how it was a part of public life. Most of the philosophes were of modest origin. They influenced the privileged elite of their day because of the social and political environment in which their ideas were elaborated. Indeed, the clearest distinguishing feature of the Enlightenment may be the creation of

Rousseau Discusses the Benefits of Submitting to the General Will

In this excerpt from his **Social Contract,** *Rousseau describes the relationship of individuals to the general will. Notice the wider-ranging benefits Rousseau believes men will enjoy in society as he envisions it; Rousseau is clearly interested in intellectual, moral, and emotional well-being.*

I assume that men reach a point where the obstacles to their preservation in a state of nature prove greater than the strength that each man has to preserve himself in that state. Beyond this point, the primitive condition cannot endure, for then the human race will perish if it does not change its mode of existence. . . .

"How to find a form of association which will defend the person and goods of each member with the collective force of all, and under which each individual, while uniting himself with the others, obeys no one but himself, and remains as free as before." This is the fundamental problem to which the social contract holds the solution. . . .

The passing from the state of nature to the civil society produces a remarkable change in man; it puts justice as a rule of conduct in the place of instinct, and gives his actions the moral quality they previously lacked. . . . And although in civil society man surrenders some of the advantages that belong to the state of nature, he gains in return far greater ones; his faculties are so exercised and developed, his mind is so enlarged, his sentiments so ennobled, and his whole spirit so elevated that . . . he should constantly bless the happy hour that lifted him for ever from the state of nature and from a stupid, limited animal made a creature of intelligence and a man. . . .

For every individual as a man may have a private will contrary to, or different from, the general will that he has as a citizen. His private interest may speak with a very different voice from that of the public interest; his absolute and naturally independent existence may make him regard what he owes to the common cause as a gratuitous contribution, the loss of which would be less painful for others than the payment is onerous for him; and fancying that the artificial person which constitutes the state is a mere fictitious entity (since it is not a man), he might seek to enjoy the rights of a citizen without doing the duties of a subject. The growth of this kind of injustice would bring about the ruin of the body politic.

Hence, in order that the social pact shall not be an empty formula, it is tacitly implied in that commitment—which alone can give force to all others—that whoever refuses to obey the general will shall be constrained to do so by the whole body, which means nothing other than that he shall be forced to be free; for this is the necessary condition which, by giving each citizen to the nation, secures him against all personal dependence, it is the condition which shapes both the design and the working of the political machine, and which alone bestows justice on civil contracts—without it, such contracts would be absurd, tyrannical and liable to the grossest abuse.

Source: Jean-Jacques Rousseau, *The Social Contract,* trans. Maurice Cranston (London: Penguin Books, 1968), pp. 59–60, 63–65.

an informed body of public opinion that stood apart from court society.

Increased literacy and access to books and other print media are an important part of the story. Perhaps more important, the kinds of reading that people favored began to change. We know from inventories made of people's belongings at the time of their death (required for inheritance laws) that books in the homes of ordinary people were no longer just traditional works such as devotional literature. Ordinary people now read secular and contemporary philosophical works. As the availability of such works increased, reading itself evolved from a reverential encounter with traditional material to a critical encounter with new material. Solitary reading for reflection and pleasure became more widespread.

Habits of reading and responding to written material changed not only because there were increased opportunities to read but also because there were changes in the social environment. In the eighteenth century, forerunners of the modern lending libraries made their debut. In Paris, for a fee, one could join a *salle de lecture* (literally, a "reading room") where the latest works were available to any member. Booksellers, whose numbers increased dramatically, found ways to meet readers' demands for inexpensive access to reading matter. One might pay for the right to read a book in the bookshop itself. In short, new venues encouraged people to see themselves not just as readers but as members of a reading public.

Among the most famous and most important of these venues were the Parisian salons, where Voltaire and others read their works in progress aloud and discussed them. Several Parisian women—mostly wealthy, but of modest social status—invited courtiers, bureaucrats, and intellectuals to meet in their homes at regular times each week. The *salonnières* (salon leaders) themselves read widely in order to facilitate the exchange of ideas among their guests. This mediating function was crucial to the success and the importance of the salons. Manners and polite conversation had been a defining feature of aristocratic life since the seventeenth century, but they had largely been means of displaying status and safeguarding honor. The leadership of the salonnières and the protected environment they provided away from court life enabled a further evolution of "polite society" to occur: Anyone with appropriate manners could participate in conversation as an equal. The assumption of equality, in turn, enabled conversation to turn away from maintaining the status quo to questioning it.

The influence of salons was extended by the wide networks of correspondence salonnières maintained. Perhaps the most famous salonnière in her day, Marie-Thérèse Geoffrin (1699–1777) corresponded with Catherine the Great, the reform-minded empress of Russia, as well as with philosophes outside of Paris and with interested would-be participants in her salon. The ambas-

sador of Naples regularly attended her salon before returning to his native city, from which he exchanged weekly letters with her. He reflected on the importance of salon leaders like Geoffrin when he wrote from Naples, lamenting,

> [our gatherings here] are getting farther away from the character and tone of those of France, despite all [our] efforts. . . . There is no way to make Naples resemble Paris unless we find a woman to guide us, organize us, *Geoffrinise* us.[1]

Various clubs, local academies, and learned and secret societies copied some features of the salons of Paris. Hardly any municipality was without a private society that functioned both as a forum for political and philosophical discussion and as an elite social club. Here mingled doctors, lawyers, local officials—some of whom enjoyed the fruits of the political system in offices and patronage. In Scotland, universities were flourishing centers of Enlightenment thought, but political clubs in Glasgow and Edinburgh enriched debate and the development of ideas.

Ideas circulated beyond the membership of even the many far-flung clubs by means of print. Newsletters reporting the goings-on at salons in Paris were produced by some participants. Regularly published periodicals in Great Britain, France, and Italy also served as important means for the dissemination of enlightened opinion in the form of reviews, essays, and published correspondence. Some of these journals had been in existence since the second half of the seventeenth century, when they had begun as a means to circulate the new scientific work. Now, subscribers included Americans anxious to keep up with intellectual life in Europe. Europeans who could not afford the annual subscriptions could peruse the journals in the newly available reading rooms and libraries. In addition to newsletters and journals, newspapers, which were regularly published even in small cities throughout western and central Europe, circulated ideas.

In all these arenas, Enlightenment ideas became the encouragement for and the legitimation of a type of far-reaching political debate that had never before existed, except possibly in England during the seventeenth century. Understanding the Enlightenment involves understanding the milieu in which these ideas were received. The first and greatest impact of the Enlightenment,

The Growth of the Book Trade Book ownership dramatically increased in the eighteenth century, and a wide range of secular works—from racy novelettes to philosophical tracts— was available in print. In this rendering of a bookshop, shipments of books have arrived from around Europe. Notice the artist's optimism in the great variety of persons, from the peasant with a scythe to a white-robed cleric, who are drawn to the shop by "Minerva" (the Roman goddess of wisdom). *(Musée des Beaux-Arts de Dijon)*

particularly in France, was not the creation of a program for political or social change but the creation of a culture of politics that could generate change.

Art in the Age of Reason

The Enlightenment reverberated throughout all aspects of cultural life. Just as the market for books and the reading public expanded, so did the audience for works of art in the growing leisured urban circles of Paris and other great cities. The modern cultured public—a public of concertgoers and art-gallery enthusiasts—began to make its first appearance. The brilliant and sophisticated

courts around Europe continued to sponsor composers, musicians, and painters by providing both patronage and audiences. Yet some performances of concerts and operas began to take place in theaters and halls outside the courts and were more accessible to the public.

Beginning in 1737, one section of the Louvre palace in Paris was devoted annually to public exhibitions of painting and sculpture (though by royally sponsored and approved artists). In both France and Britain, public discussion of art began to take place in published reviews and criticisms: The role of art critic was born. Works of art were also sold by public means, such as auctions. As works became more available by such means, demand grew and production increased.

The Cult of Sensibility in Art
This painting, *The Swing*, by the Frenchman Fragonard, depicts a moment of playful and sensuous intimacy. This style of painting was an elaboration of baroque style known as *rococo*. It began to be considered too excessive and lighthearted and was replaced by the more serious neoclassical style as the century wore on. *(Wallace Collection/Bridgeman Art Library/Art Resource, NY)*

In subject matter and style these various art forms exhibited greater variety than works in preceding centuries had shown. We can nevertheless discern certain patterns and tendencies in both the content and the form of eighteenth-century European art. Late baroque painters contributed to an exploration of private life and emotion sometimes called the "cult of sensibility." Frequently, they depicted private scenes of upper-class life, especially moments of intimate conversation or flirtation.

The cult of sensibility was fostered by literature as well. The private life of emotion was nurtured by increased literacy, greater access to books, and the need to retreat from the elaborate artifice of court life. The novel became an increasingly important genre as a means of exploring human problems and relationships. In English literature the novels of Samuel Richardson (1689–1761)—*Pamela* (1740) and *Clarissa* (1747–1748)—explored personal psychology and passion. Rousseau followed Richardson's lead in structuring his own novels *La Nouvelle Héloïse* (1761) and *Emile* (1762). The cult of sensibility was not mere entertainment; it also carried the political and philosophical message that honest emotion was a "natural" virtue and that courtly manners, by contrast, were irrational and degrading. The enormous popularity of Rousseau's novels, for example, came from the fact that their intense emotional appeal was simultaneously felt to be uplifting.

A revival of classical subjects and styles after the middle of the century evoked what were thought to be the pure and timeless values of classical heroes. This revival revealed the influence of Enlightenment thought by assuming the educability of its audience by means of example. Classical revival architecture illustrated a belief in order, symmetry, and proportion. Americans are familiar with its evocations because it has been the architecture of their republic, but even churches were built in this style in eighteenth-century Europe. The classical movement in music reflected both the cult of sensibility and the classicizing styles in the visual arts. Embodied in the works of Austrians Franz Josef Haydn (1732–1809) and Wolfgang Amadeus Mozart (1756–1791), this movement saw the clarification of musical structures, such as the modern sonata and symphony, and enabled melody to take center stage.

Another trend in art and literature was a fascination with nature and with the seemingly "natural" in human culture—less "developed" or more historically distant societies. One of the most popular printed works in the middle of the century was the supposed translation of the poems of Ossian, a third-century Scots Highland poet. Early English, German, Norse, and other folktales were "discovered" (in some cases invented) and published. Many of these went through several editions during the century.

The fact that folk life, other cultures, and untamed nature itself began to be celebrated just when they were being more definitively conquered is very revealing. (See the feature, "Weighing the Evidence: Gardens," on pages 694–695.) The early poetry of Scotland, for example, was celebrated just as the Scottish Highlands were being punished and pacified by the English because of the clans' support for a rival claimant to the English throne. Once purged of any threat, the exotic image of another culture (even the folk culture of one's own society) could be a source of imagination and create a sense of distance from which to measure one's own sophistication. Thus, both ancient and exotic subjects reinforced a sense of dominance and control.

EUROPEAN RULERS AND EUROPEAN SOCIETY

Mindful of the lessons to be learned from the revolution in England and the achievements of Louis XIV, European rulers in the eighteenth century continued their efforts to govern with greater effectiveness. Some, like the rulers of Prussia and Russia, were encouraged in their efforts by Enlightenment ideas that stressed the need for reforms in law, economy, and government. In the main they, like Voltaire, believed that monarchs could be agents for change. In Austria, significant reforms, including the abolition of serfdom, were made. The changes were uneven, however, and at times owed as much to traditional efforts at better government as to enlightened persuasion.

In all cases, rulers' efforts to govern more effectively meant continual readjustments in relationships with traditional elites. Whether or not elites could formally participate in the governing process by means of established institutions such as the English Parliament, royal governments everywhere were still dependent on their participation. Enlightened monarchs were changing their view of themselves and their image from the diligent but self-aggrandizing image of Louis XIV to that of servant of the state. In this way, monarchs actually undermined the dynastic claim to rule by refounding it on a utilitarian basis. The state was increasingly seen as separate from the ruler.

France During the Enlightenment

It is one of the seeming paradoxes of the era of the Enlightenment that critical thought about society and politics flourished in France, an autocratic state with institutionally privileged elites. Yet in France there was a well-educated elite, a tradition of scientific inquiry, and a legacy of cultured court life that, since the early days of Louis XIV, had become the model for all Europe (see pages 592–594). French was the international intellectual language, and France was the most fertile center of elite cultural life. Both Adam Smith and David Hume, for example, spent portions of their careers in Paris and were welcomed into the salons. In fact, the French capital was an environment that encouraged debate and dissent precisely because of the juxtaposition of the new intellectual climate with the difficulties the French state was facing and the institutional rigidities of its political system—a system that excluded many talented and productive members of the elite from its privileged circles.

In the last decades of the reign of Louis XIV (d. 1715), many thoughtful French people criticized the direction the French state was taking. They began to question the point of foreign wars that yielded ever diminishing returns. The intoxicating blend of stability, effective government, national interest, and the personal glory of the monarch began to dissolve.

Louis XIV was followed on the throne by his 5-year-old great-grandson, Louis XV (r. 1715–1774). During the regency, nobles clamored for the establishment of councils so that they could become more active partners in government. Likewise, the supreme law courts, the parlements, reclaimed the right of remonstrance—the right to object to royal edicts and thus to exercise some control over the enactment of law. Throughout Louis XV's reign, his administration often locked horns with the parlements, particularly as royal ministers coped with France's financial crises. Louis XIV had exhausted the nation financially—in need of more money and of new and more reliable ways to get money. During Louis XV's reign the pressures of further wars intensified the need for wholesale reform.

Louis XV's government continued some of the rationalizing policies of Louis XIV by which relics of the decentralized medieval economy were abolished. Roads were improved and more and more internal customs barriers eliminated. The Crown did not challenge the Catholic church's privileged status or property, which would have been welcomed by many elites. Nor was Louis XV able, for most of his reign, to undercut the power of the parlements in order to reform the fiscal system.

By the late 1760s, the weight of government debt from foreign wars finally forced the king into action. He threw his support behind the reforming schemes of his chancellor, Nicolas de Maupeou. Maupeou dissolved the parlements early in 1771 and created new law courts whose judges would not enjoy independent power.

Public opinion was split over this conflict between the monarch and the parlements. A number of ministers under Louis XV and his successor, Louis XVI (r. 1774–1792), shared Enlightenment views of the efficiency of creating economic change from the top and the rationality of doing away with privileges such as the exemption of the nobility from taxation. However, the role of consultative bodies and the separation of powers beloved of Montesquieu, himself a parlementaire, were much prized, and the parlements were the only institutions that could legitimately check monarchical powers. Ordinary property holders, such as provincial nobles, who had little in common with privileged officeholders, might nevertheless see the parlementaires' privileges as the best guarantor of their own.

Further hampering reform efforts was the character of the king himself. Louis XV displayed none of the kingly qualities of his great-grandfather. He was not pleasant or affable, and he was lazy. By the end of his reign, he was roundly despised. He did not give the "rationality" of royal government a good name.

Not surprisingly, from about the middle of the century, enlightened public opinion, nurtured in salons and other new settings, began proposing a variety of ways to enhance representation, consultation, and reform. There were calls to revive the moribund Estates General, the cumbersome representative assembly last called in 1614, as well as for the establishment of new councils or local, decentralized representative assemblies. The workability of these proposals is less important than the simple fact that they were made.

The Crown lost control of reform in 1774, when Louis XV died. His grandson, Louis XVI, well meaning but insecure, allowed the complete restoration of the parlements. Further reform efforts, sponsored by the king and several talented ministers, came to naught because of parlementary opposition. The French crown had lost the chance to reform royal government from above. By the time an Estates General was finally called in the wake of further financial problems in 1788, the enlightened elites' habit of carrying on political analysis and criticism of government outside the actual corridors of power had given rise to a volatile situation.

Monarchy and Constitutional Government in Great Britain

After the deaths of William (d. 1702) and Mary (d. 1694), the British crown passed to Mary's sister, Anne (r. 1702–1714), and then to a collateral line descended from Elizabeth (d. 1662), sister of the beheaded Charles I. Elizabeth had married Frederick, elector of the Palatinate (and had reigned with him briefly in Bohemia at the outset of the Thirty Years' War; see page 575), and her descendants were Germans, now electors of Hanover. The new British sovereign in 1714, who reigned as George I (r. 1714–1727), was both a foreigner and a man of mediocre abilities. Moreover, his claim to the throne was immediately contested by Catholic descendants of James II, who attempted to depose him in 1715, and later his son, George II (r. 1727–1760), in 1745.

This second attempt to depose the Hanoverian kings in 1745 was more nearly successful. The son of the Stuart claimant to the throne, Charles (known in legend as Bonnie Prince Charlie), landed on the west coast of Scotland, with French assistance, and marched south into England with surprising ease. Most of the British army, and George II himself, was on the continent, fighting in the War of Austrian Succession (see page 682).

Scotland had been formally united with England in 1707 (hence the term *Great Britain* after that time), and Charles found some support among Scots dissatisfied with the economic and political results of that union.

But the vast majority of Britons did not want the civil war that Charles's challenge inevitably meant, especially on behalf of a Catholic pretender who relied on support from Britain's great commercial and political rival, France. Landholders and merchants in lowland Scotland and northern England gathered militia to oppose Charles until regular army units returned from abroad. Charles's army, made up mostly of poor Highland clansmen, was destroyed at the Battle of Culloden in April 1746. Charles fled back to France, and the British government used the failed uprising as justification for the brutal and forceful integration of the still-remote Highlands into the British state.

Traditional practices, from wearing tartans to carrying the accustomed personal daggers and

The Destruction of the Highlanders Although English rulers had previously attacked individual clans, Highland culture maintained its independence until the uprising of 1745. For the first time, clansmen were decisively beaten in battle by British troops, who used the tactics of volley fire and disciplined bayonet charge. *(The Royal Collection © 1993 Her Majesty Queen Elizabeth II)*

even playing bagpipes, were forbidden. Control of land was redistributed to break the social and economic bonds of clan society. Thousands of Highlanders died at the battle itself, in prisons or deportation ships, or by deliberate extermination by British troops in the aftermath of the battle.

Despite this serious challenge to the new dynasty and the brutal response it occasioned, the British state, overall, enjoyed a period of relative stability as well as innovation in the eighteenth century. The events of the seventeenth century had reaffirmed both the need for a strong monarchy and the role of Parliament in defending elite interests. The power of Parliament had recently been reinforced by the Act of Settlement, by which the Protestant heir to Queen Anne had been chosen in 1701. By excluding the Catholic Stuarts from the throne and establishing the line of succession, this document reasserted that Parliament determined the legitimacy of the monarchy. In addition, the act claimed greater parliamentary authority over foreign and domestic policy in the wake of the bellicose William's rule (see pages 602–603).

Noteworthy in the eighteenth century were the ways in which cooperation evolved between monarchy and Parliament as Parliament became a more sophisticated and secure institution. Political parties—that is, distinct groups within the elite favoring certain foreign and domestic policies—came into existence. Two groups, the Whigs and the Tories, had begun to form during the reign of Charles II (d. 1685). The Whigs (named derisively by their opponents with a Scottish term for horse thieves) had opposed Charles's pro-French policies and his efforts to tolerate Catholicism and had wholly opposed his brother and successor, James II. Initially, the Whigs favored an aggressive foreign policy against continental opponents, particularly France. The Tories (also derisively named—for Irish cattle rustlers) tended to be staunch Anglicans uninterested in Protestant anti-Catholic agitation. They tended to have a conservative view of their own role, favoring isolationism in foreign affairs and an attitude of deference toward monarchical authority. Whigs generally represented the interests of the great aristocrats or wealthy merchants or gentry. Tories tended to represent the interests of provincial gentry and the traditional concerns of landholding and local administration.

The Whigs were the dominant influence in government through most of the century to 1770. William and Mary as well as Queen Anne favored Whig religious and foreign policy interests. The loyalty of many Tories was called into question by their support for a Stuart, not Hanoverian, succession at Anne's death in 1714. The long Whig dominance of government was also ensured by the talents of Robert Walpole, a member of Parliament who functioned virtually as a prime minister from 1722 to 1742.

Walpole (1676–1745) was from a minor gentry family and was brought into government in 1714 with other Whig ministers in George I's new regime. An extremely talented politician, he took advantage of the mistakes of other ministers over the years and, in 1722, became both the first lord of the treasury and chancellor of the exchequer. There was not yet any official post or title of "prime minister," but the great contribution of Walpole's tenure was to create that office in fact, if not officially. He chose to maintain peace abroad where he could and thus presided over a period of recovery and relative prosperity that enhanced the stability of government.

Initially, Walpole was helped in his role as go-between for king and Parliament by George I's own limitations. The king rarely attended meetings of his own council of ministers and, in any case, was hampered by his limited command of English. Gradually, the Privy Council of the king became something resembling a modern Cabinet dominated by a prime minister. By the end of the century the notions of "loyal opposition" to the Crown within Parliament and parliamentary responsibility for policy had taken root.

In some respects, the maturation of political life in Parliament resembled the lively political debates in the salons of Paris. In both cases, political life was being legitimized on a new basis. In England, however, that legitimation was enshrined in a legislative institution, which made it especially effective and resilient.

Parliament was not yet in any sense representative of the British population, however. Because of strict property qualifications, only about 200,000 adult men could vote. In addition, representation was very uneven, heavily favoring traditional landed wealth. Some constituencies with only a few dozen voters sent members to Parliament.

Many of these "pocket boroughs" were under the control of (in the pockets of) powerful local families who could intimidate the local electorate, particularly in the absence of secret ballots.

Movements for reform of representation in Parliament began in the late 1760s as professionals, such as doctors and lawyers, with movable (as opposed to landed) property and merchants in booming but underrepresented cities began to demand the vote. As the burden of taxation grew—the result of the recently concluded Seven Years' War (see page 682)—these groups felt increasingly deprived of representation. Indeed, many felt kinship and sympathy with the American colonists who opposed increased taxation by the British government on these same grounds and began a revolt in 1775.

However, the reform movement faltered over the issue of religion. In 1780, a tentative effort by Parliament to extend some civil rights to British Catholics provoked rioting in London (known as the Gordon Riots, after one of the leaders). The riots lasted for eight days and claimed three hundred lives. Pressure for parliamentary reform had been building as Britain met with reversals in its war against the American rebels, but this specter of a popular movement out of control temporarily ended the drive for reform.

"Enlightened" Monarchy

Arbitrary monarchical power might seem antithetical to Enlightenment thought, which stressed the reasonableness of human beings and their capacity to discern and act in accord with natural law. Yet monarchy seemed an ideal instrument of reform to Voltaire and to many of his contemporaries. The work of curtailing the influence of the church, reforming legal codes, and eliminating barriers to economic activity might be done more efficiently by a powerful monarch than by other means then available, particularly because there was great confidence in the power of education to transform an individual (in this case, a ruler) and in the accessibility of the principles of reason. Historians have labeled a number of rulers of this era "enlightened despots" because of the arbitrary nature of their power and the enlightened or reformist uses to which they put it.

"Enlightened despotism" aptly describes certain developments in the Scandinavian kingdoms in the late eighteenth century. In Denmark, the Crown had governed without significant challenge from the landholding nobility since the mid-seventeenth century. The nobility, however, like its counterparts in eastern Europe, had guaranteed its supremacy by means of ironclad domination of the peasantry. In 1784, a reform-minded group of nobles, led by the young Crown Prince Frederick (governing on behalf of his mentally ill father), began to apply Enlightenment remedies to the kingdom's economic problems. The reformers encouraged freer trade and sought, above all, to improve agriculture by improving the status of the peasantry. With improved legal status and with land reform, which enabled some peasants to own the land they worked for the first time, agricultural productivity in Denmark rose dramatically. These reforms constitute some of the clearest achievements of any of the "enlightened" rulers.

In Sweden, in 1772, Gustav III (r. 1771–1796) staged a coup with army support that overturned the dominance of the Swedish parliament, the Riksdag. In contrast to Denmark, Sweden had a relatively unbroken tradition of noble involvement in government, stemming in part from its marginal economy and the consequent interest of the nobility in participation in the Crown's aggressive foreign policy. Since Sweden's eclipse as a major power after the Great Northern War (see pages 607–608), factions of the Riksdag, not unlike the rudimentary political parties in Great Britain, had fought over the reins of government. After reasserting his control, Gustav III began an ambitious program of reform of the government. Bureaucrats more loyal to parliamentary patrons than to the Crown were replaced, restrictions on trade in grain and other economic controls were liberalized, the legal system was rationalized, the death penalty was strictly limited, and legal torture was abolished.

Despite his abilities (and his charm), Gustav III suffered the consequences of the contradictory position of advancing reform by autocratic means in a kingdom with a strong tradition of representative government. Gustav eventually tried to deflect the criticisms of the nobility by reviving grandiose—but completely untenable—schemes for the reconquest of Baltic territory. However, in

Frederick the Great is pictured here returning from military maneuvers. Frederick's self-imposed work as king included arduous travel throughout his domains to check on local conditions and monitor local governments. *(Staatliches Schlösser und Gärten, Potsdam-Sans Souci)*

1796 he was mortally wounded by an assassin hired by disgruntled nobles.

Another claimant to the title "enlightened" monarch was Frederick II of Prussia (r. 1740–1786), "the Great." Much of the time, Frederick resided in his imperial electorate of Brandenburg, near his capital, Berlin. His scattered states, which he extended by seizing new lands, are referred to as "Prussia," rather than as "Brandenburg-Prussia," because members of his family were now kings of Prussia thanks to their ambitions and the weakness of the Polish state of which Prussia had once been a dependent duchy. In many ways, the Prussian state *was* its military victories, for Frederick's bold moves and the policies of his father, grandfather, and great-grandfather committed the state's resources to a military presence of dramatic proportions. Prussia was on the European stage only due to the degree of that commitment.

The institutions that constituted the state and linked the various provinces under one administration were dominated by the needs of the military. Frederick II's father, Frederick William (r. 1713–1740), had added an efficient provincial recruiting system to the state's central institutions, which he also further consolidated. But in many other respects, the Prussian state was in its infancy. There was no tradition of political participation—even by elites—and little chance of cultivating any. Nor was there any political or social room for maneuver at the lower part of the social scale. The rulers of Prussia had long ago acceded to the aristocracy's demand for tighter control over peasant labor on their own lands in return for their support of the monarchy. The rulers relied on nobles for local administration and army commands. Thus, there was a stark limit to the kinds of social, judicial, or political reforms that Frederick could personally hope to carry out.

Frederick tried to introduce improved agricultural methods and simultaneously to improve the condition of peasants, but he met stiff resistance from noble landholders. He did succeed in abolishing serfdom in some regions. He tried to stimulate the economy by sponsoring state industries and trading monopolies, but there were not enough resources or initiative from the tightly controlled merchant communities to create much economic expansion. Simplifying and codifying the inherited jumble of local laws was a goal of every ruler. A law code published in 1794, after Frederick's death, was partly the product of his efforts.

Frederick's views of the role of Enlightenment thought reflect the limitations of his situation. One doesn't have to lead a frontal assault on prejudices consecrated by time, he thought; instead, one must be tolerant of superstition because it will always have a hold on the masses. Perhaps his most distinctive "enlightened" characteristic was the seriousness with which he took his task as ruler. He was energetic and disciplined to a fault. In his book *Anti-Machiavel* (1741) he argued that a ruler has a moral obligation to work for the betterment of the state. He styled himself as the "first servant" or steward of the state. However superficial this claim may appear, in his energy and diligence he compares favorably to Louis XV of France, who, having a much more wealthy and flexible society to work with, did much less.

Describing Frederick as "enlightened," however, masks the degree to which his activities reflected as much the traditional goals of security and prosperity as the impetus of "enlightened" thinking. Indeed, some of the most thoroughgoing administrative, legal, and economic reforms were accomplished in rival Austria entirely within such a traditional framework, during the reign of Maria Theresa (r. 1740–1780), the daughter of Emperor Charles VI (r. 1711–1740).

Maria Theresa was a remarkable ruler in her diligence and determination. She overcame difficulties that surrounded her accession, survived the near dismemberment of Austrian territories in the wars that marked her reign, and embarked on an energetic reform program to shore up the weaknesses in the state that the conflicts had revealed. The Austrian monarchy was still a highly decentralized state. Maria Theresa worked to streamline and centralize administration, finances, and defense. She created new centralized governing councils and, above all, reformed the assessment and collection of taxes so that the Crown could better tap the wealth of its subjects. She established new courts of justice and limited the exploitation of serfs by landlords. In general, she presided over an effort to bypass many of the provincial and privatized controls on government still in the hands of great nobility. She accomplished all of this without being in any way "enlightened." For example, she had a traditional fear of freedom of the press and insisted on orthodoxy in religious matters.

Her son, Joseph, is an interesting contrast. Self-consciously "enlightened," Joseph II (r. 1780–1790) carried out a variety of reforms that his mother had not attempted, including freedom of the press and limited freedom of religion. Some of his reforms were particularly dramatic, such as drastic curtailment of the death penalty and encouragement of widespread literacy. Like Frederick the Great, Joseph regarded himself as a servant of the state. During his ten-year reign, the political climate in Vienna began to resemble that in Paris, London, and other capitals where political life was no longer confined to court life.

Many of Joseph's reforms, however, were simply extensions of his mother's. For example, he extended further legal protection to peasants and eventually abolished serfdom in all Habsburg lands. And in some ways he was less successful than Maria Theresa had been. Though persuaded of the benefits of enlightened government, he was by temperament an inflexible autocrat, whose methods antagonized many of his most powerful subjects. In the name of "rational" administration, he tried to extend Austrian institutions to the kingdom of Hungary—including the use of the German language for official business. He also tried to bypass the authority of the representative Estates in the Austrian Netherlands in order to achieve some of his aims. In this action reminiscent of his ancestor Philip II of Spain, Joseph II revealed that the curious blend of "enlightenment" and traditional absolutism was not greater than the sum of its parts. Joseph's policies provoked simmering opposition and open revolt in a number of his lands, and some of his reforms were repealed even before his death.

Catherine the Great and the Empire of Russia

Another ruler with a claim to the title "enlightened despot" was Catherine, empress of Russia (r. 1762–1796). Catherine was one of the ablest rulers in the eighteenth century and perhaps

Catherine the Great Catherine was a German princess who had been brought to Russia to marry another German, Peter of Holstein-Gottorp, who was being groomed as heir to the Russian throne. There had been several Russian monarchs of mixed Russian and German parentage since the time of Peter the Great's deliberate interest in and ties with other European states. *(The Luton Hoo Foundation)*

the single most able of all the rulers of imperial Russia. She combined intelligence with vision, diligence, and skill in handling people and choosing advisers. Her intelligence and political acumen were obvious early in her life in Russia simply from the fact that she survived at court. In 1745 she had been brought to Russia from her native Germany to marry the heir to the Russian throne. She was brutally treated by her husband, Tsar Peter III. In the summer of 1762, Catherine engineered a coup against him. Peter was overthrown and killed, and Catherine ruled alone as empress for most of the rest of the century.

Catherine the Great, as she came to be called, was the true heir of Peter the Great in her abilities,

policies, and ambitions. Under Catherine, Russia committed itself to general European affairs in addition to its traditional territorial ambitions. In situations involving the major European powers, Russia tended to ally with Britain (with which it had important trading connections, including the provision of timber for British shipbuilding) and with Austria (against their common nemesis, Turkey), and against France, Poland, and Prussia. In 1768, Catherine initiated a war against the Turks from which Russia gained much of the Crimean coast. She also continued Peter's efforts to dominate the weakened Poland. She was aided by Frederick the Great, who proposed the deliberate partitioning of Poland to satisfy his own territorial

Map 18.1 The Partition of Poland and the Expansion of Russia Catherine the Great
acquired modern Lithuania, Belarus, and Ukraine, which had once constituted the
duchy of Lithuania, part of the multi-ethnic Polish kingdom.

ambitions as well as those of Russia and Austria, with which he competed. In 1772, portions of Poland were gobbled up in the first of three successive "grabs" of territory (Map 18.1). Warsaw itself eventually landed in Prussian hands, but Catherine gained all of Belarus, Ukraine, and modern Lithuania—which had constituted the duchy of Lithuania. Thus, like any successful ruler of her age, Catherine counted territorial aggrandizement among her chief achievements.

Nevertheless, Catherine also counted herself a sincere follower of the Enlightenment. While young, she had received an education that bore the strong stamp of the Enlightenment. Like Frederick, she attempted to take an active role in the intellectual community, corresponding with Voltaire over the course of many years and acting as patron to Diderot. One of Catherine's boldest political moves was the secularization of church lands. Although Peter the Great had extended government control of the church, he had not touched church lands. Catherine also licensed private publishing houses and permitted a burgeoning periodical press. The number of books published in Russia tripled during her reign. This enriched cultural life was one of the principal causes of the flowering of Russian literature that began in the early nineteenth century.

The stamp of the Enlightenment on Catherine's policies is also clearly visible in her attempts at legal reform. In 1767 she convened a legislative commission and provided it with a guiding document, the *Instruction*, which she had authored. The commission was remarkable because it included representatives of all classes, including peasants, and provided a place for the airing of general grievances. Catherine hoped for a general codification of law as well as reforms such as the abolition of torture and capital punishment—reforms that made the *Instruction* radical enough to be banned from publication in other countries. She did not propose changing the legal status of serfs, however, and class differences made the commission unworkable in the end. Most legal reforms were accomplished piecemeal and favored the interests of landed gentry. Property rights were clarified and strengthened, and judicial procedures were streamlined but constructed to include legal privileges for the gentry.

Like the Austrian rulers, Catherine undertook far-reaching administrative reform to create more effective local units of government. Here again, political imperatives were fundamental, and reforms in local government strengthened the hand of the gentry. The legal subjection of peasants in serfdom was also extended as a matter of state policy to help win the allegiance of landholders in newly acquired areas—such as Ukrainian territory gained in the partition of Poland. Gentry in general and court favorites in particular, on whom the stability of her government depended, were rewarded with estates and serfs to work them.

In Russia as in Prussia and Austria, decline of the peasantry occurred because the monarch wanted to win the allegiance of the elites who lived from their labor. The cooperation of elites was particularly valued by Catherine because the Russian state was in a formative stage in another sense as well. It was trying to incorporate new peoples, such as the Tatars in the Crimea, and to manage its relationship with border peoples such

as the Cossacks. Catherine's reign was marked by one of the most massive and best-organized peasant rebellions of the century. Occurring in 1773, the rebellion expressed the grievances of the thousands of peasants who joined its ranks and called for the abolition of serfdom. The revolt took its name, however, from its Cossack leader, Emelian Pugachev (d. 1775), and reflected the dissatisfaction with the Russian government of this semiautonomous people.

The dramatic dilemmas faced by Catherine illustrate both the promise and the costs of state formation throughout Europe. State consolidation permitted the imposition of internal peace, of coordinated economic policy, of reform of justice, but it came at the price of greater—in some cases much greater—control and coercion of the population. Thus, we can see from the alternative perspective of Russia the importance of the political sphere that was opening up in France and was being consolidated in England. It was in that environment, rather than in Russia, that the Enlightenment philosophy could find most fertile ground.

STATES IN CONFLICT

In the eighteenth century a new constellation of states emerged to dominate politics on the Continent. Along with the traditional powers of England, France, and Austria were Prussia in central Europe and Russia to the east (see Map 18.1). Certain characteristics common to all these states account for their dominance. None is more crucial than their various abilities to field effective armies. Traditional territorial ambitions accounted for many wars in the eighteenth century, but the increasing significance of overseas trade and colonization was the most important source of conflict between England and France.

A Century of Warfare: Circumstances and Rationales

The large and small states of Europe continued to make war on each other for both strategic and dynastic reasons. The expense of war, the number of powerful states involved, and the complexities of their interests meant that wars were preceded and carried out with complex systems of alliances and were followed by the adjustments of many borders and the changing control of many bits of territory. We can distinguish certain consistent interests of the major states, however, and some of the circumstances within which all of the states acted.

States fought over territory that had obvious economic and strategic value. A fight over the Baltic coastline, for example, absorbed Sweden and Russia early in the century (see pages 605–608). Often these conflicts were carried out in arbitrary ways that revealed the dynastic view of territory that still existed. Although rational and defensible "national" borders were important, collecting isolated bits of territory was also still the norm. The wars between European powers thus became extremely complex strategically. France, for example, might choose to strike a blow against Austria by invading an Italian state in order to use the conquered Italian territory as a bargaining chip in eventual negotiations.

Dynastic claims were not merely strategic ploys but also major causes of war. Indeed, the fundamental instability caused by hereditary rule accounts for many of the major wars of the eighteenth century. The century opened with the War of Spanish Succession, and later the succession of the Austrian Habsburgs would be the cause of a major continental war.

The state of military technology, tactics, and organization also shaped the outcomes of conflicts. In the eighteenth century, weapons and tactics became increasingly refined. More reliable muskets were used. A bayonet that could slip over a musket barrel without blocking the muzzle was invented. Coordinated use of bayonets required even more assured drill of troops than volley fire alone to ensure disciplined action in the face of enemy fire and charges. Artillery and cavalry forces were also subjected to greater standardization of training and discipline in action. Increased discipline of forces meant that commanders could exercise meaningful control over a battle for the first time, but such battles were not necessarily decisive, especially when waged against a comparable force.

One sure result of the new equipment and tactics was that war became a more expensive proposition than ever before and an ever greater burden on a state's resources and administration. It became increasingly difficult for small states such as

Sweden to compete with the forces that others could mount. Small and relatively poor states, such as Prussia, that did support large forces did so by means of an extraordinary bending of civil society to the economic and social needs of the army. In Prussia, twice as many people were in the armed forces, proportionally, as in other states, and a staggering 80 percent of meager state revenue went to support the army.

Most states introduced some form of conscription in the eighteenth century. In all regions, the very poor often volunteered for army service to improve their lives. However, conscription of peasants, throughout Europe but particularly in Prussia and Russia, imposed a significant burden on peasant communities and a sacrifice of productive members to the state. Governments everywhere supplemented volunteers and conscripts with mercenaries and even criminals, as necessary, to fill the ranks without tapping the wealthier elements of the community. Thus, common soldiers were increasingly seen not as members of society but as its rejects. Said Frederick II, "Useful hardworking people should [not be conscripted but rather] be guarded as the apple of one's eye," and a French war minister agreed that armies had to consist of the "scum of people and of all those for whom society has no use."[2] Brutality became an accepted tool for governments to use to manage such groups of men. From the eighteenth century, the army increasingly became an instrument of social control used to manage and make use of individuals who otherwise would have had no role in society.

But the costs of maintaining these forces had other outcomes as well. Wars could still be won or lost not on the battlefield but on the supply line. Incentive still existed to bleed civilian populations and to exploit the countryside. Moreover, when supply lines were disrupted and soldiers not equipped or fed, the armies of a major power could be vulnerable to the small and "unmodernized" armies of lesser states. Finally, neither good generalship nor the discipline of soldiers could be guaranteed, yet both were crucial to success. Culloden, in 1746 (see page 673), was the first battle in which the British army was able decisively to defeat the fierce charge and hand-to-hand fighting of Highland clansmen by holding its position and using disciplined volley fire. Warfare became increasingly professional but was still an uncertain business with unpredictable results.

The Power of Austria and Prussia

Major continental wars had a marked impact on the balance of power among states in western and central Europe. The first of these, now known as the War of Austrian Succession, began in 1740. Emperor Charles VI died that year without a male heir, and his daughter, Maria Theresa, succeeded him. Charles VI had worked to shore up his daughter's position as his heir by means of an act called the Pragmatic Sanction, first issued in 1713. He had negotiated carefully to persuade allies and potential opponents to accept it. The question was not whether a woman could rule, for many women had ruled and did rule other states. However, a new ruler about whom there was any doubt—a woman, child, or any distant relative—opened the door for rival dynastic claims. In 1740, Frederick II of Prussia took advantage of Habsburg vulnerability by invading the wealthy Habsburg province of Silesia (see Map 18.1), to which he had a hereditary claim of sorts.

Maria Theresa proved a much more tenacious opponent than Frederick had anticipated. In the end, he was lucky to be able to hold onto Silesia, which was at some distance from Maria Theresa's other territories. Although Austrian forces were never able to dislodge Frederick, they did best most of the forces ranged against them by their perpetual opponent, France, and by other German states allied with Frederick. In a preliminary peace signed in 1745, Frederick was confirmed in possession of Silesia, but the throne of the Holy Roman Empire was returned to the Habsburgs—given to Maria Theresa's husband, who reigned as Francis (Franz) I (r. 1745–1765). A final treaty in 1748 ended all the fighting that had continued since 1745, mostly by France on the Continent and simultaneous fighting by France and Britain overseas.

The gainers were Prussia and Austria. Austria came out ahead because its succession had not been disrupted and its lands had not been dismembered. Prussia, because of the annexation of Silesia and the psychological imprint of victory, emerged as a power of virtually equal rank to the Habsburgs in Germany. Frederick II was now well placed to make further territorial gains.

Not surprisingly, the power of Prussia provoked the outbreak of the next major war. Indeed, the unprecedented threat that Austria now felt from Prussia caused a veritable revolution in alliances across Europe. So great in Austrian minds was the change in the balance of power that Austria was willing to ally with France, its traditional enemy, in order to isolate Prussia. In the years before what would later be known as the Seven Years' War (1756–1763), Austrian officials began to approach France to propose a mutual defensive alliance—a move that became known as the Diplomatic Revolution. Sweden and Russia, with territory to gain at Prussia's expense, joined the alliance system. Sweden wanted to regain territory along the Baltic Sea, and Russia coveted East Prussia, which bordered Russian territory.

Frederick initiated hostilities in 1756, hoping, among other outcomes, to prevent consolidation of the new alliances. Instead, he found that he had started a war against overwhelming odds. What saved him was limited English aid. The English, engaged with France in the overseas conflict known as the French and Indian War, wanted France to be heavily committed on the Continent. Also helpful to Frederick was Russia's withdrawal from the alliance against him when a new ruler took the throne there in 1762. Prussia managed to emerge intact—though strained economically and demographically.

The results of the war confirmed Prussia and Austria as the two states of European rank in German-speaking Europe. Their rivalry would dominate German history until the late nineteenth century. The war also demonstrated how fragile even successful states could be and revealed something about what it took for them to be successful. Military victory and the reputation that went with it— even at great cost—could allow a ruler a place on the European stage. The nearness of Prussia's escape also revealed that fortune had a great deal to do with the rise of this state.

The Atlantic World: Trade, Colonization, Competition

The importance of international trade and colonial possessions to the states of western Europe grew dramatically in the eighteenth century. Between 1715 and 1785, Britain's trade with North America rose from 19 to 34 percent of its total trade, and its trade with Asia and Africa rose from 7 to 19 percent of the total. By the end of the century, more than half of all British trade was carried on outside of Europe; for France, the figure was more than a third.

European commercial and colonial energies were concentrated in the Atlantic world in the eighteenth century, because there the profits were greatest. The population of British North America grew from about 250,000 in 1700 to about 1.7 million by 1760. The densely settled New England colonies provided a market for manufactured goods from the mother country, though they produced little by way of raw materials or bulk goods on which traders could make a profit. The colonies of Maryland and Virginia produced tobacco, the Carolinas rice and indigo (a dyestuff). England re-exported all three throughout Europe at considerable profit.

The French in New France, numbering only 56,000 in 1740, were vastly outnumbered by the British colonists. Nevertheless, the French successfully expanded their control of territory in Canada. Settlements sprang up between the outposts of Montreal and Quebec on the St. Lawrence River. Despite resistance, the French extended their fur trapping—the source of most of the profits that New France generated—west and north along the Great Lakes, consolidating their hold as they went by building forts. They penetrated as far as the modern Canadian province of Manitoba, where they cut into the British trade run out of Hudson Bay to the north. The French also contested the mouth of the St. Lawrence River and the Gulf of St. Lawrence with the British. The British held Nova Scotia and Newfoundland, the French held parts of Cape Breton Island, and both states fished the surrounding waters.

The commercial importance of all of these holdings, as well as those in Asia, was dwarfed by the European states' Caribbean possessions, however. The British held Jamaica and Barbados; the French, Guadeloupe and Martinique; the Spanish, Cuba and San Domingo; and the Dutch, a few small islands. Sugar produced by slave labor was the major source of profits, along with other cash crops such as coffee, indigo, and cochineal (another dyestuff). The concentration of shipping to this region indicates the region's importance.

Tobbaco Label This shipping label for American-grown tobacco fancifully depicts slaves enjoying a smoke. *(The Granger Collection, New York)*

By the 1760s, the British China trade occupied seven or eight ships. In the 1730s, British trade with Jamaica alone drew three hundred ships. The tiny Dutch possession of Guiana on the South American coast required twice as many visits by Dutch ships as the Dutch East India Company sent into Asia.

The economic dependence of the colonies on slave labor meant that the colonies were tied to their home countries not with a two-way commercial exchange but with a three-way "triangle" trade (Map 18.2). Certain European manufactures were shipped to western ports in Africa, where they were traded for slaves. The enslaved Africans were then transported to South America, the Caribbean, or North America, where planters bought and paid for them with profits from their sugar and tobacco plantations. (See the box, "Encounters with the West: An African Recalls the Horrors of the Slave Ship.") Sugar and tobacco

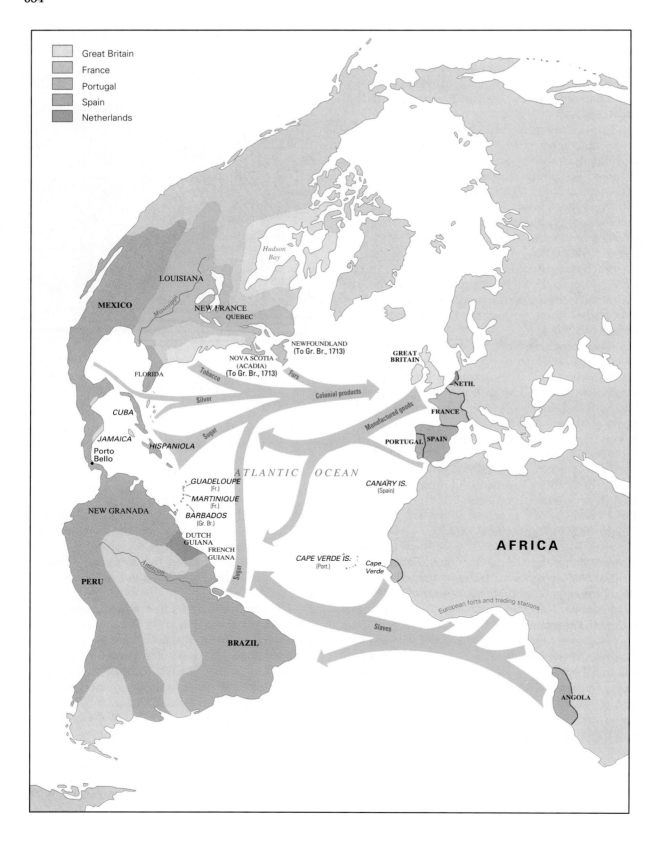

∼ ENCOUNTERS WITH THE WEST ∼

An African Recalls the Horrors of the Slave Ship

Olaudah Equiano (ca. 1750–1797) was one of the few Africans sold into slavery in the Americas to leave a written record of his experiences. An Ibo from the Niger region, he first experienced slavery as a boy when kidnapped from his village by other Africans. But nothing prepared him for the brutality of the Europeans who bought and shipped him to Barbados, in the British West Indies. He eventually regained his freedom and received an education.

The first object which saluted my eyes when I arrived on the [African] coast was the sea and a slaveship . . . waiting for its cargo. . . . When I was carried on board I was immediately handled, and tossed up, to see if I were sound, by some of the crew. . . . I was soon put down under the decks, and there I received such a salutation in the nostrils as I had never experienced in my life; so that, with the loathsomeness of the stench . . . I became so sick and low that I was not able to eat. . . . I now wished for the last friend, death, to relieve me; but soon, to my grief, two of the white men offered me eatables; and, on my refusing to eat, one of them held me fast by the hands and laid me across, I think, the windlass, and tied my feet while the other flogged me severely.

One day, when we had a smooth sea and a moderate wind, two of my wearied countrymen, who were chained together, preferring death to such a life of misery, somehow made through the nettings and jumped into the sea; immediately another dejected fellow who [was ill and so not in irons] followed their example. . . . Two of the wretches were drowned, but they got the other and afterwards flogged him unmercifully for thus attempting to prefer death to slavery. In this manner we continued to undergo more hardships than I can now relate. Many a time we were near suffocation for want of fresh air. . . . This, and the stench of the necessary tubs, carried off many.

Source: Philip D. Curtin, *Africa Remembered* (Madison: University of Wisconsin Press, 1967), pp. 92–96.

were then shipped back to the mother country to be re-exported at great profit throughout Europe. A variety of smaller exchanges also took place. For example, timber from British North America was traded in the Caribbean for sugar or its byproducts, molasses and rum. Individual planters in the colonies were not the only ones whose fortunes and status depended on these networks. Merchants in cities such as Bordeaux in France and

Map 18.2 The Atlantic Economy, ca. 1750 The "triangle trade" linked Europe, Africa, and European colonies in the Americas. The most important component of this trade for Europe was the profitable plantation agriculture that depended on enslaved Africans for labor.

Liverpool in England were also heavily invested in the slave trade and the re-export business.

The proximity and growth of French and British settlements in North America ensured conflict (see Map 18.3). The Caribbean and the coasts of Central and South America were strategic flashpoints as well. At the beginning of the eighteenth century, several substantial islands remained unclaimed by any power. The British were making incursions along the coastline claimed by Spain and were trying to break into the monopoly of trade between Spain and Spain's vast possessions in the region. Public opinion in both Britain and France became increasingly sensitive to colonial issues. For the first time, tensions abroad would fuel major conflicts between two European states.

Great Britain and France: Wars Overseas

In the eighteenth century, England became the dominant naval power in Europe. Its navy protected its far-flung trading networks, its merchant fleet, and the coast of England itself. England had strategic interests on the Continent as well, however. England's interest lay in promoting a variety of powers on the Continent, none of which (or no combination of which) posed too great a threat to England, to its coastline, or to its widespread trading system. From across the Channel, the French appeared a particular threat. They assembled a fleet on more than one occasion and actually dispatched one fleet to aid the cause of the Stuart claimants to the British throne (see page 673).

A second, dynastic consideration in continental affairs was the electorate of Hanover, the large principality in western Germany that was the native territory of the Hanoverian kings of England. Early in the century especially, the interests of this German territory were of importance to the Hanoverian kings and were a significant factor in British foreign policy. Unable to field a large army, given their maritime interests, the British sought protection for Hanover in alliances and subsidies for allies' armies on the Continent. The money for these ventures came from the profits on trade.

After the death of Louis XIV in 1715, England's energies centered on colonial rivalries with France, its greatest competitor overseas. There were three major phases of conflict between England and France in colonial regions. The first two were concurrent with the major land wars in Europe: the War of Austrian Succession (1740–1748) and the Seven Years' War (1756–1763). The third phase coincided with the rebellion of British colonies in North America—the American Revolution—beginning in the 1770s. France was inevitably more committed to affairs on the Continent than were the British. The French were able to hold their own successfully in both arenas during the 1740s, but by 1763, though pre-eminent on the Continent, they had lost many of their colonial possessions to the English.

In the 1740s, France was heavily involved in the War of Austrian Succession while Britain vied with Spain for certain Caribbean territories. Both France and England also tested each other's strength in scattered colonial fighting, which began in 1744 and produced a few well-balanced gains and losses. Their conquests were traded when peace was made in 1748.

Tension was renewed almost immediately at many of the strategic points in North America. French and British naval forces harassed each

French Fort Builders in North America
The French, whose settlements in North America were sparsely populated, tried to secure the vast territories they claimed with a series of strategically placed forts. The imagined fortifications in this contemporary engraving, which probably mocks the French effort, were far too elaborate for American conditions, where simple wooden palisades were the rule. (*Colonial Williamsburg Foundation*)

other's shipping in the Gulf of St. Lawrence. The French reinforced their encirclement of British colonies with more forts along the Great Lakes and the Ohio River. When British troops (at one point led by the colonial commander George Washington) attempted to strike at these forts, beginning in 1754, open fighting between the French and the English began.

In India, meanwhile, both the French and the British attempted to strengthen their commercial footholds by making military and political alliances with local Indian rulers. The disintegration of the Mogul Empire facilitated this move, heightening competition among Indian rulers, and sparked a new level of ambition on the part of the European powers in their struggle with each other. A British attack on a French convoy provoked a declaration of war by France in May 1756, three months before fighting in the Seven Years' War broke out in Europe. For the first time, a major war between European nations had started and would be fought in their empires, signifying a profound change in the relation of these nations to the world.

The French had already committed themselves to an alliance with Austria and were increasingly involved on the Continent after Frederick II initiated war there in August 1756. Slowly, the drain of sustaining war both on the Continent and abroad began to tell, and Britain scored major victories against French forces after an initial period of balanced successes and failures. The French lost a number of fortresses on the Mississippi and Ohio Rivers and on the Great Lakes and, finally, also lost the interior of Canada with the fall of Quebec and of Montreal in 1759 and 1760, respectively (Map 18.3).

In the Caribbean, the British seized Guadeloupe, the main French sugar-producing island. Superior resources in India enabled the British to take several French outposts there, including Pondicherry, the most important. The cost of involvement on so many fronts meant that French troops were short of money and supplies. They were particularly vulnerable to both supply and personnel shortages—especially in North America—not only because they were weaker than the British at sea but also because the territory they had occupied and fortified remained sparsely settled and dependent on the mother country for food.

By the terms of the Peace of Paris in 1763, France regained Guadeloupe. In India, France re-

tained many of its trading stations but lost its political and military clout. British power in India was dramatically enhanced not only by French losses but also by victories over Indian rulers who had allied with the French. In the interior Britain now controlled lands that had never before been under the control of any European power; British political rule in India, as opposed to merely a mercantile presence, began at this time. The British now also held Canada. They emerged as the preeminent world power among European states.

ECONOMIC EXPANSION AND SOCIAL CHANGE

The eighteenth century was an era of dramatic change, though that change was not always apparent to those who lived through it. The intellectual and cultural ferment of the Enlightenment laid the groundwork for domestic political changes to come, just as British victories in the Seven Years' War shifted the balance of power abroad. More subtle and potentially more profound changes were occurring in the European countryside, however: Population, production, and consumption were beginning to grow beyond the bounds that all preceding generations had lived within and taken for granted.

More Food and More People

Throughout European history, there had been a delicate balance between available food and numbers of people to feed. Population growth had accompanied increases in the amount of land under cultivation. From time to time, however, population growth surpassed the ability of the land to produce food, and people became malnourished and prey to disease. In 1348 the epidemic outbreak of bubonic plague known as the Black Death struck just such a vulnerable population in decline.

There were few ways to increase the productivity of land. Peasants safeguarded its fertility by alternately cultivating some portions while letting others lie fallow or using them as pasture. Manure provided fertilizer, but during the winter months livestock could not be kept alive in large numbers. Limited food for livestock meant limited fertilizer, which in turn meant limited production of food for both humans and animals.

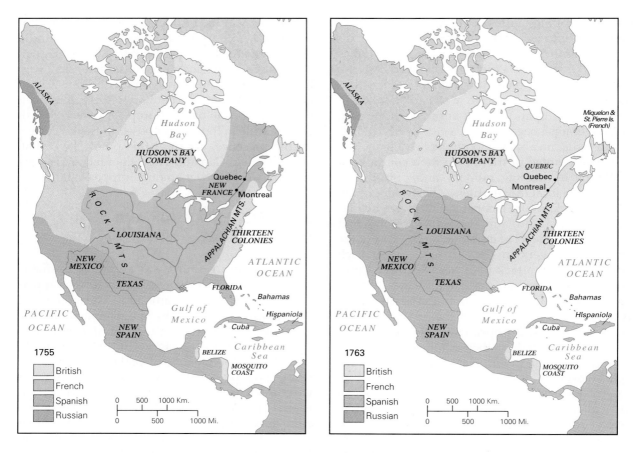

Map 18.3 British Gains in North America The British colonies on the Atlantic coast were effective staging posts for the armies that ousted the French from North America by 1763. However, taxes imposed on the colonies to pay the costs of the Seven Years' War helped spark revolt—the American Revolution—a decade later.

After devastating decline in the fourteenth century, the European population experienced a prolonged recovery, and in the eighteenth century the balance that had previously been reached began to be exceeded for the first time. Infant mortality remained as high as ever. No less privileged a person than Queen Anne of England outlived every one of the seventeen children she bore, and all but one of them died in infancy. Population growth occurred because of a decline in the death rate for adults and a simultaneous increase in the birthrate in some areas owing to earlier marriages.

Adults began to live longer partly because of a decline in the incidence of the plague. However, the primary reason adults were living longer, despite the presence of various epidemic diseases, was that they were better nourished and thus bet-

ter able to resist disease. More and different kinds of food began to be produced. The increase in the food supply also meant that more new families could be started.

Food production increased because of the introduction of new crops and other changes in agricultural practices. The cumulative effect of these changes was so dramatic that historians have called them an "agricultural revolution." The new crops included fodder, such as clover, legumes, and turnips, which did not deplete the soil and could be fed to livestock over the winter. The greater availability of animal manure, in turn, boosted grain production. The potato, introduced from the Americas in the sixteenth century, is nutrient-dense and can feed more people per acre than can grain. In certain areas, farming families produced potatoes to feed themselves while they grew grain to be sold and shipped elsewhere.

More food being produced meant more food available for purchase. The opportunity to buy food freed up land and labor. A family that could purchase food might decide to convert its farm into a dairy farm. In such a case, many families might be supported from a piece of land that had supported only one family when used for traditional agriculture. Over a generation or two, a number of children might share the inheritance of what had previously been a single farm, yet each could make a living from his or her share, and population could grow as it had not done before.

Farmers had known about and experimented with many of the crops used for fodder for centuries. However, the widespread planting of these crops, as well as other changes, was long in coming and happened in scattered areas. A farmer had to have control over land in order to institute change. In the traditional open-field system, peasants had split up all the land in each community so that each family might have a piece of each field. Making dramatic changes was hard when an entire community had to act together. Most important, changing agriculture required capital for seed and fertilizer and for the greater number of people and animals needed to cultivate the new crops. Only prosperous farmers had spare capital. Few were inclined to take risks with the production of food and trust the workings of the market. The bad condition of roads alone was reason enough not to rely on distant markets.

Yet where both decent roads and growing urban markets existed, some farmers—even entire villages working together—were willing to produce for urban populations. Capital cities, like London and Amsterdam, and trading centers such as Glasgow and Bordeaux were booming. These growing cities demanded not only grain but also specialized produce such as dairy products and fruits and vegetables. Thus, farmers had an incentive to make changes such as to dairy farming. Urbanization and improved transportation networks also encouraged agriculture because human waste produced by city dwellers—known as "night soil"—could be collected and distributed in the surrounding agricultural regions to further increase soil fertility. By the late eighteenth century, pockets of intensive, diversified agriculture existed in England, northern France, the Rhineland

in Germany, the Po Valley in Italy, and Catalonia in Spain.

In other areas, changes in agriculture were often accompanied by a shift in power in the countryside. Wealthy landlords began to invest in change in order to reap the profits of producing for the new markets. Where the traditional authority of the village to regulate agriculture was weak, peasants were vulnerable. In England, a combination of weak village structure and the attraction of urban markets created a climate that encouraged landlords to treat land speculatively. To make their holdings more profitable, they raised the rents that farmers paid. They changed cultivation patterns on the land that they controlled directly. They appropriated the village common lands, a process known as "enclosure," and used them for cash crops such as sheep (raised for their wool) or beef cattle. Among other ramifications, the clans of Scotland completely disintegrated as meaningful social units as markets for beef, wool, and other Highland commodities drew chieftains' resources and turned what remained of their traditional relationships with dependent clansmen into exploitative commercial ones.

Thus, although the agricultural revolution increased the food supply to sustain more people in Europe generally, it did not create general prosperity. The growth of population did not mean that most people were better off. Indeed, many rural people were driven off the land or made destitute by the loss of the resources of common lands. Peasants in eastern Europe produced grain for export to the growing urban centers in western Europe, but usually by traditional methods. In both eastern and western Europe, the power and profits of landlords were a major force in structuring the rural economy.

The Growth of Industry

Agricultural changes fostered change in other areas of economic and social life. As more food was grown with less labor, that labor was freed to do other productive work. If there was enough work to be had making other products that people needed, then the nonagricultural population could continue to grow. If population grew, more and more consumers would be born, and the demand for more goods would help continue the cycle of population growth, changes in production, and economic expansion. This is precisely what happened in the eighteenth century. A combination of forces increased the numbers of people who worked at producing a few essential materials and products (Map 18.4).

There was a dramatic expansion in the putting-out system, also known as cottage industry, in the eighteenth century, for reasons that were closely related to the changes in the agricultural economy (see page 620). All agricultural work was seasonal, demanding intensive effort and many hands at certain times but not at others. The labor demands of the new crops meant that an even larger number of people might periodically need nonfarm work in order to make ends meet. Rural poverty, whether as a result of traditional or new agricultural methods, made manufacturing work in the home attractive to more people.

Overseas trade stimulated the expansion of production by spurring the demand in Europe's colonies for cloth and other finished products and increasing the demand at home for manufactured items, such as nails to build the ships on which trade depended. The production of cloth expanded also because heightened demand led to changes in the way cloth was made. Wool was increasingly combined with other fibers to make less expensive fabrics. By the end of the century wholly cotton fabrics were being made cheaply in Europe from cotton grown in America by slave labor.

Steady innovation in production played an important part in the expansion of production because it meant that products were being aimed at a broad market. In the Middle Ages, weavers produced a luxury-quality cloth, and their profits came not from demand, which was relatively low, but from the high price that consumers paid. In the eighteenth century, cloth production became a spur to a transformed industrial economy because cheaper kinds of cloth were made for mass consumption. Producing more became important, and innovations that promoted productivity were soon introduced.

A crucial innovation was increased mechanization. The invention of machines to spin thread in the late eighteenth century brought a marked increase in the rate of production and profound changes to the lives of rural workers who had been juggling agricultural and textile work according to season and need. The selected areas of England, France, and the Low Countries where

the new technologies were introduced stood, by the end of the century, on the verge of a massive industrial transformation that would have dramatic social consequences.

Control and Resistance

The economic changes of the century produced both resistance and adaptation by ordinary people and, at times, direct action by state authorities. Sometimes ordinary people coped in ways that revealed their desperation. In many cities, numbers of abandoned children rose greatly because urban families, particularly recent immigrants from the countryside, could not support their offspring. The major cities of Europe put increasing resources into police forces and city lighting schemes. Charitable institutions run by cities, churches, and central governments expanded. By 1789, for example, there were more than two thousand *hôpitaux*—poorhouses for the destitute and ill—in France. The poor received food and shelter but were forced to work for the city or to live in poorhouses against their will. Men were sometimes taken out of poorhouses and forced to become soldiers.

Resistance and adaptation were particularly visible wherever the needs of common people conflicted with the states' desire for order and for revenue. The states' desire for order and revenue on the high seas, for example, led to the suppression of piracy. Piracy had been a way of life for hundreds of Europeans and colonial settlers since the sixteenth century. From the earliest days of exploration, European rulers had authorized men known as privateers to commit acts of war against specific targets; the Crown took little risk and was spared the cost of arming the ships but shared in the plunder. True piracy—outright robbery on the high seas—was illegal, but in practice the difference between piracy and privateering was often small. As governments' and merchants' desire for regular trade began to outweigh that for the irregular profits of plunder, and as national navies developed in the late seventeenth century, a concerted effort to eliminate piracy began.

Life on the seas became an increasingly vital part of west European economic life in the eighteenth century, and it began to resemble life on land in the amount of compulsion it included. English-speaking seamen alone numbered about thirty thousand around the middle of the eighteenth

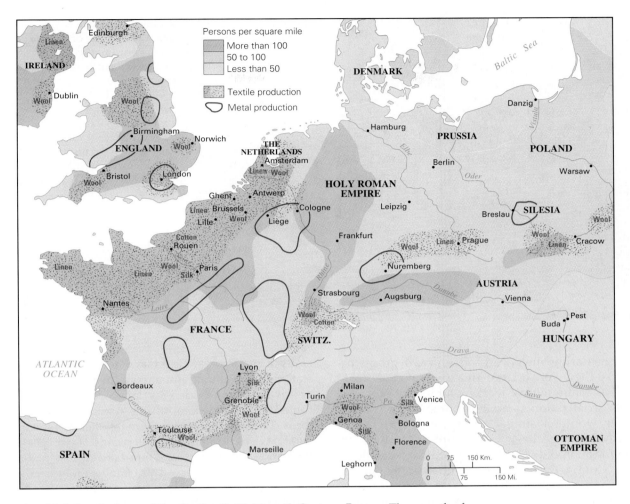

Map 18.4 Population and Production in Eighteenth-Century Europe The growth of cottage industry helped to support a growing population. With changes in agriculture, more land-poor workers were available in the countryside to accept work as spinners, knitters, and weavers.

century. Sailors in port were always vulnerable to forcible enlistment in the navy by impressment gangs, particularly during wartime. A drowsy sailor sleeping off a night of celebrating with new-gotten wages could wake up to find himself aboard a navy ship. Press gangs operated throughout England and not just in major ports, for authorities were as interested in controlling "vagrancy" as in staffing the navy. Merchant captains occasionally filled their crews by such means, particularly when sailing unpopular routes.

Like soldiers in the growing eighteenth-century armies, sailors in the merchant marine as well as the navy could be subjected to brutal disci-pline and appalling conditions. Merchant seamen attempted to improve their lot by trying to regulate their relationship with ships' captains. Contracts for pay on merchant ships were becoming more regularized, and seamen often negotiated their terms very carefully, including, for example, details about how rations were to be allotted. Sailors might even take bold collective action aboard ship. The English-language term for a collective job action, *strike,* comes from the sailing expression "to strike sail," meaning to lower the sails so that they cannot fill with wind. Its use dates from the eighteenth century, from "strikes" of sailors protesting unfair conditions.

An Idle Apprentice Is Sent to Sea, 1747 In one of a series of moralizing engravings by William Hogarth, the lazy apprentice, Tom, is sent away to a life at sea. The experienced seamen in the boat introduce him to some of its terrors: On the left dangles a cat-o'-nine-tails, and on the distant promontory is a gallows, where pirates and rebels meet their fate. *(From the Collections of Lauinger Library, Georgetown University)*

Seafaring men were an unusual group because they were a large and somewhat self-conscious community of workers for wages. Not until industrialization came into full swing a century later would a similar group of workers exist within Europe itself (see Chapter 21). But economic and political protest by ordinary people on the Continent also showed interesting parallel changes, even though strike activity itself would await the large wage labor force of industrialization. Peasant revolts in the past had ranged from small-scale actions against local tax officials to massive uprisings suppressed by an army. The immediate goals of the rebels were usually practical. They aimed not to eliminate taxation altogether but to limit its extent or to protest the collection of a particularly burdensome tax. The political rationale behind such actions was not a hope that the system could be eliminated but rather a hope that it could be adjusted to operate more fairly. Where there was a revolutionary vision, it was usually a utopian one—a political system with no kings, landlords, taxes, or state of any kind.

Peasant revolts continued to be commonplace and to follow those patterns in the eighteenth century. They were also driven by the localized unemployment caused by agricultural reforms or by objections to press gangs. In certain cases, however, peasants, like sailors, began to confront the

state in new ways. Peasants often attacked not state power but the remnants of the various powers over them wielded by landlords, including forced labor and compulsory use of landlords' mills. They also increasingly marshaled whatever legal devices they could to keep control over their land and thwart landlords' efforts to enclose fields and cultivate cash crops. This change, though subtle, was important because it signaled an effort to bring permanent structural change to economic and legal relationships and was not simply a temporary redress of grievances. (See the box, "The Condition of Serfs in Russia.")

Both the old and the new approaches to resisting authority are evident in the Pugachev rebellion of 1773, during the reign of Catherine in Russia (see page 677). The movement began among the Ural Cossacks but eventually included thousands of people with traditional grievances against the regime: Cossacks resisting absorption by the state, miners and other poor workers, peasants, and rebellious dissidents. The rebels thus represented a mixture of traditional grievances and acted under the rubric of "tsarist" legitimacy. Pugachev, in fact, proclaimed himself the legitimate tsar and set up a quasi-imperial court. The rebels' demands were utopian—the elimination of all landlords, all state officials, and all taxation. Less idealistic and more modern were their de-

The Condition of Serfs in Russia

*Generally, the condition of agricultural workers was worst in eastern Europe, where political and economic forces kept them bound in serfdom. In **A Journey from St. Petersburg to Moscow** (1790), the reform-minded nobleman Alexander Radishchev (1749–1802) describes an encounter with a serf who, like most serfs, was forced to work the lord's lands at the expense of his own.*

A few steps from the road I saw a peasant plowing a field. It was now Sunday, [about midday]. The ploughing peasant, of course, belonged to a landed proprietor, who would not let him pay a commutation tax. The peasant was plowing very carefully. The field . . . was not part of the master's land. He turned the plow with astonishing ease.

"God help you," I said, walking up to the ploughman, who, without stopping, was finishing the furrow he had started. . . . "Have you no time to work during the week, then, and can you not have any rest on Sundays, in the hottest part of the day, at that?"

"In a week, sir, there are six days, and we go six times a week to work on the master's field; in the evening, if the weather is good, we haul to the master's house the hay that is left in the woods. . . . God grant that it rains this evening. If you have peasants of your own, sir, they are praying for the same thing."

"But how do you manage to get food enough [for your family] if you have only the holidays free?"

"Not only the holidays, the nights are ours too."

"Do you work the same way for your master?"

"No, sir, it would be a sin to work the same way. On his fields there are a hundred hands for one mouth, while I have two for seven mouths: you can figure it out for yourself."

Source: Alexander Radishchev, *A Journey from St. Petersburg to Moscow,* trans. Leo Wiener, ed. Roderick Page Thaler (Cambridge, Mass.: Harvard University Press, 1958); quoted in Robert and Elborg Forster, eds., *European Society in the Eighteenth Century* (New York: Harper and Row, 1969), pp. 136–139.

mands to end serfdom and their attempts to set up an alternative administration in the areas they controlled. They also tried to form a creditable army—inevitably the weak spot of popular uprisings.

SUMMARY

It is important not to exaggerate the degree to which circumstances of life changed in the eighteenth century. The economy was expanding and the population growing beyond previous limits, and the system of production was being restructured. But these changes happened incrementally over many decades and were not recognized for the fundamental changes they were.

Most of the long-familiar material constraints were still in place. Roads, on which much commerce depended, were generally impassable in bad weather. Shipping was relatively dependable and economical—but only relatively. Military life likewise reflected traditional constraints. Despite technological changes and developments of the administrative and economic resources of the state to equip, train, and enforce discipline, the conduct of war was still hampered by problems of transport and supply that would have been familiar to warriors two centuries before.

Similarly, though some rulers were inspired by precepts of the Enlightenment, all were guided by traditional concerns of dynastic aggrandizement and strategic advantage. One new dimension of relations between states was the importance of conflict over colonies abroad, but the full economic and strategic impact of British colonial gains would not be felt until the next century.

The most visible change would happen first in politics, where goals and expectations
(continued on page 696)

GARDENS

What is a garden? We first think of intensely culti-vated flower gardens, such as the famous Rose Garden at the White House. We usually don't think of the yards around houses as gardens, yet that is what they are. The landscaping around most ordinary American homes derives from Eng-lish landscape gardening of the eighteenth cen-tury and after—a fact that is reflected in the British custom of calling the "yards" around their homes "gardens." Like most of the art forms that we see habitually, the garden, reproduced in the Ameri-can backyard, is difficult to analyze or even to think of as an art form. Like the buildings they surround, however, gardens have much to tell us about human habits and values. Let us examine their eighteenth-century ancestors for evidence of contemporaries' attitudes toward nature and their relationship with it.

Look at the two English-style gardens illus-trated here. The first is next to the Governor's Mansion in Williamsburg, the capital of the Eng-lish colony of Virginia. Construction of this garden began at the end of the seventeenth century; the photograph shows the restored gardens that tourists may visit today. The second garden, from the private estate of West Wycombe in England, looks very different—much more like a natural landscape. The engraving reproduced here dates from the 1770s. The two gardens represent distinct epochs in the development of the garden, hence the differences between them. However, each of these gardens in its own way celebrates human domination of nature.

This symbolic domination of nature is more ob-vious to us in the Williamsburg garden. The lawns and hedges are trimmed in precise geometrical shapes and are laid out, with the walkways, in straight lines. This "palace garden" was a small English variant of the classical garden developed in France—most spectacularly at Versailles Palace—and then imitated throughout Europe during the seventeenth century. At Versailles, the garden is so vast that at many points all of nature visible to the eye is nature disciplined by humans.

We can think of such gardens as pieces of ar-chitecture, because that is how they were origi-nally conceived: The design originated in the en-closed courtyard gardens of the homes of classical antiquity. The straight lines and squared shapes of these gardens mimic the buildings they are at-

The Governor's Mansion and Formal Gardens at Williamsburg, Virginia *(© Robert Llewellyn)*

Landscape Garden at West Wycombe, England *(Courtesy of the Trustees of the British Museum)*

tached to. In fact, these seventeenth- and eigh-teenth-century gardens were usually laid out as an extension of the building itself. Notice the wide staircase that descends from the central axis of the Governor's Mansion into the central walkway of the garden. Other architectural details, such as the benches positioned at the ends of various walk-ways, add to the sense of the garden as an exterior room. Elsewhere, this sense was enhanced by the construction of devices such as grottoes, such as that at Versailles. The garden symbolizes the tam-ing of nature into a pleasing vision of order and regularity.

The later, eighteenth-century garden repre-sents even greater confidence in the human rela-tionship with nature, although it does not appear to do so at first glance. The extensive gardens at first seem to be nature itself plus a few added de-tails, such as the statuary, and a few improve-ments, such as the grass kept trim by the workers in the foreground. Our familiarity with such land-scapes—in our own suburban yards—keeps us from immediately perceiving how contrived such a landscape is. Nature, however, does not inter-sperse dense stands of trees or clumps of shrub-bery with green expanses of lawns. Nor does na-ture conveniently leave portions of a hillside bare of trees to provide a view of the water from the palatial house, to the left on the hill. Note also that the waterfall cascading over rocks and statu-ary flows from an artificial lake, neatly bordered by a path.

This kind of garden reflects Enlightenment optimism about humans' ability to understand and work with nature. Such gardens were asym-metrical: Paths were usually curved, and lakes and ponds were irregularly shaped, as they would be in nature. Trees and shrubs were allowed to maintain their natural form. Nevertheless, this landscaping conveys a powerful message of order. Humans cannot bend or distort nature to their own ends, but they can live in harmony with it as they manage it and enjoy its beneficence. People were freed from regarding nature as hostile and needing to be fought. In this garden, one lives with nature but improves upon it. The workers cutting the grass do not detract from the engrav-ing but rather make the scene more compelling.

This brand of landscape gardening appeared in English colonies across the Atlantic by the end of the eighteenth century. One of the best exam-ples is at Monticello, Thomas Jefferson's Virginia estate, first designed in the 1770s and constructed and improved over the remainder of Jefferson's life (1743–1826). If you tour Monticello, you will notice a curving garden path bordered by flowers in season, with mature trees scattered here and there. Jefferson, we know, planned every inch of this largely random-looking outdoor space, just as he planned the regimented fruit and vegetable garden that borders it. The older classical style of the Williamsburg garden is partly explained by its earlier date and also because this more aggres-sively controlling style lasted longer in the Amer-ican colonies than in Europe, perhaps because "nature" seemed more wild and still more formi-dable in the New World. You might wish to con-sider the curious blend of "nature" and order that is evident in the landscapes we create and live with today. ✦

nurtured by Enlightenment philosophy clashed with the rigid structure of the French state and triggered the French Revolution. The Enlightenment was not simply an intellectual movement that criticized society. It also encompassed the public and private settings where "enlightened" opinion flourished. The revolutionary potential of Enlightenment thought came from belief in its rationality and from the fact that it was both critical of its society and fashionable to practice.

NOTES

1. Quoted in M. S. Anderson, *Europe in the Eighteenth Century, 1713–1783*, 3d ed. (London: Longman, 1987), pp. 218–219.
2. Dena Goodman, *The Republic of Letters: A Cultural History of the French Enlightenment* (Ithaca: Cornell University Press, 1994), p. 89.

SUGGESTED READING

General Surveys
Anderson, M. S. *Europe in the Eighteenth Century, 1713–1783.* 3d ed. 1987.
Doyle, William. *The Old European Order, 1660–1800.* 1978.
Treasure, Geoffrey. *The Making of Modern Europe, 1648–1780.* 1985. Three general histories covering political, social, economic, and cultural developments; each has an extensive bibliography.

The Enlightenment
Chartier, Roger. *The Cultural Uses of Print in Early Modern France.* 1987. A discussion of changes in reading habits and in the uses of printed materials throughout the eighteenth century in France.
Darnton, Robert. *The Literary Underground of the Old Regime.* 1982. One of several important works by Darnton on the social history of print culture.
Gay, Peter. *The Enlightenment: An Interpretation.* 2 vols. 1966–1969. A detailed study of Enlightenment thought by one of its foremost modern interpreters.
———. *Voltaire's Politics.* 1959. A lively introduction to Voltaire's career as a political and social reformer.
Goodman, Dena. *The Republic of Letters: A Cultural History of the French Enlightenment.* 1994. Indispensable for understanding the social context of the enlightenment and the role of women.
Hampson, Norman. *The Enlightenment.* 1968. A useful general survey.
Hazard, Paul. *The European Mind.* 1935. An older but still useful interpretation that depicts a European intellectual crisis between 1680 and 1715.

State Building and Warfare
Carsten, F. L. *The Origins of Prussia.* 1982. An introduction to the growth of the Prussian state in the seventeenth and eighteenth centuries.
Colley, Linda. *Britons: Forging the Nation, 1707–1837.* 1992. A history of the British that emphasizes the interrelationships of political, social, and cultural history.
Devine, T. M. *Clanship to Crofters' War: The Social Transformation of the Scottish Highlands.* 1994. A brief and readable study that follows the destruction and transformation of Highland culture from the Late Middle Ages to the nineteenth century.
Ford, Franklin. *Robe and Sword.* 1953. A path-breaking though controversial study of the consolidation of aristocratic power in France in the eighteenth century.
Gagliardo, John. *Enlightened Despotism.* 1968. A general introduction to the concept and to the rulers of the era.
Hubatsch, Walter. *Frederick the Great.* 1981. A recent biography that illuminates Frederick's system of government.
Kennedy, Paul. *The Rise and Fall of British Naval Mastery.* 1976. The authoritative work on the rise of British seapower from the sixteenth century to modern times.
Madariaga, Isobel de. *Russia in the Age of Catherine the Great.* 1981. The best recent biography of Catherine.
See also the works by Evans, Howard, Parker, Riasanovsky, and Vierhaus cited in Chapters 15 and 16.

Early Modern Economy and Society
Cipolla, Carlo. *Before the Industrial Revolution.* 1976. The most comprehensive single treatment of the development of the European economy and technology through this period.
De Vries, Jan. *The Economy of Europe in an Age of Crisis, 1600–1750.* 1976. Essential reading for understanding the changes in Europe's economy and in its trade and colonial relationships throughout the world.
Gullickson, Gay. *Spinners and Weavers of Auffay.* 1986.
Gutman, Myron P. *Toward the Modern Economy.* 1988. Two works that focus on specific communities in western Europe and thus provide compelling, detailed analyses of the changes in the European economy in the seventeenth and eighteenth centuries.
Hufton, Olwen. *The Poor of Eighteenth-Century Paris.* 1974. An analysis of the lives of the poor and the responses of the state.
Laslett, Peter. *The World We Have Lost.* 1965. An innovative study of premodern society and culture, emphasizing the differences in habits and values that separate our society from preindustrial times.
Parry, J. H. *Trade and Dominion: The European Overseas Empires in the Eighteenth Century.* 1971. A reliable survey of developments.

Revolutionary Europe, 1789–1815

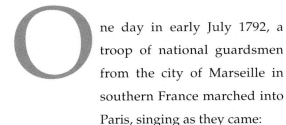

One day in early July 1792, a troop of national guardsmen from the city of Marseille in southern France marched into Paris, singing as they came:

Allons enfants de la patrie,	(Come, children of the nation)
Le jour de gloire est arrivé	(The day of glory is at hand)
Contre nous de la tyrannie	(Against us is raised)
L'étendard sanglant est levé!	(The bloody standard of tyranny!)

Their song quickly became famous as the "Marseillaise," and three years later was officially declared the French national anthem. This choice is appropriate, for the French Revolution, which was unfolding that July, profoundly shaped the growth and character of modern France.

Today the Revolution is considered the initiation of modern European as well as modern French history. The "Marseillaise" had been composed some months earlier by a French army captain in Alsace, where French troops were facing Austrian and German forces. Events in France reverberated throughout Europe because the overthrow of absolute monarchy threatened other monarchs. Revolutionary fervor on the part of ordinary soldiers compensated for inexperience, and France's armies unexpectedly bested many of their opponents. By the late 1790s the armies of France would be led in outright conquest of other European states by one of the most talented generals in European history: Napoleon Bonaparte. What he brought to the continental European nations that his armies eventually conquered was a fascinating amalgam of imperial aggression and revolutionary fervor. Europe was transformed both by the changing balance of power and by the spread of revolutionary ideas.

Léon Cogniet, *The National Guard of Paris leaves to join the army in September 1792* (detail).

Understanding the French Revolution means understanding not only how it began but also the complicated course it took and why, together with the significance of those events. Part of the Revolution's importance lay in the power of symbols, such as the "Marseillaise," to challenge an old political order and to legitimate a new one. Challenges to the power of the king were not new, but the Revolution overthrew his right to rule at all. The notion that the people constituted the nation, were responsible as citizens, and had some right to representation in government replaced a system of government by inherited privilege. Louis XVI was transformed from the divinely appointed father of his people to an enemy of the people, worthy only of execution. But on the day in 1792 the men from Marseille marched into Paris, none of this was clear.

BACKGROUND TO REVOLUTION

"I am a citizen of the world," wrote John Paul Jones, a captain of the fledgling United States Navy, in 1778. He was writing to a Scottish aristocrat, apologizing for the conduct of men under his command who had raided the lord's estate while conducting coastal raids against the British Isles during the American Revolution. Jones (1747–1792) himself was a Scotsman, who had begun a life at sea as a boy. He was one of the thousands of cosmopolitan Europeans who were familiar with European cultures on both sides of the Atlantic. As a sailor, Jones literally knew his way around the Atlantic world. He was a "citizen of the world" in another sense as well. When the Scotsman, Lord Selkirk, wrote back to Jones, he expressed surprise that his home had been raided because he was sympathetic to the American colonists. Like Jones, he said, he was a man of "liberal sentiments."[1] Both Jones and Lord Selkirk felt they belonged to an international society of gentlemen who recognized certain principles regarding just and rational government that grew out of the Enlightenment.

In the Atlantic world of the late eighteenth century, both practical links of property and trade and shared ideals about "liberty" were important shaping forces. The strategic interests of the great European powers were also always involved. Thus, when the American colonists actively re-

sisted British rule and then in 1776 declared their independence from Britain, there were many consequences: British trading interests were challenged, French appetites for gains at British expense were whetted, and illusive notions of "liberty" seemed more plausible and desirable. The victory of the American colonies in 1783, followed by the creation of the United States Constitution in 1787, further heightened the appeal of liberal ideas elsewhere. There were attempts at liberal reform in several states, including Ireland, the Netherlands, and Poland. However, the American Revolution had the most direct impact on later events in France because the French had been directly involved in the American effort.

Revolutionary Movements Around Europe

While the British government was facing the revolt of the American colonies, it also confronted trouble closer to home. The war against the American colonies was not firmly supported by Britons. Like many Americans, many Britons had divided loyalties, and many others were convinced that the war was being mismanaged. The prosecution of the war against the American colonies proceeded amid calls for reform of the ministerial government. In this setting, a reform movement in Ireland began to spring up in 1779. The reformers demanded greater autonomy from Britain. Like the Americans, Irish elites felt like disadvantaged junior partners in the British Empire. They chafed over British policies that favored British imperial interests over those of the Irish ruling class: for example, the exclusion of Irish ports from much trade in favor of English and Scottish ports and the granting of political rights to Irish Catholics so that they might fight in Britain's overseas armies.

Protestant Irish landlords, threatened by such policies, expressed their opposition not only in parliamentary but also in military ways. Following the example of the American rebels, middle- and upper-class Anglo-Irish set up a system of locally sponsored voluntary militia to resist British troops if necessary. The Volunteer Movement was undercut when greater parliamentary autonomy for Ireland was granted in 1782, following the repeal of many restrictions on Irish commerce. Unlike the Americans, the Irish elites faced an internal challenge to their own authority—the Catholic population whom they had for centuries dominated. That challenge forced them to reach an accommodation with the British government.

Meanwhile, a political crisis with constitutional overtones was also brewing in the Netherlands. Tensions between the aristocratic stadtholders of the House of Orange and the merchant oligarchies of the major cities deepened during the American Revolution, because the Dutch were then engaged in a commercial war against the British, to whom the stadtholder was supposed to be sympathetic. The conflict ceased to be wholly traditional for two reasons. First, the representatives of the various cities, calling themselves the Dutch "Patriot" party, defended their position in the name of the traditional balance of powers within the Netherlands as well as with wider claims to "liberty," like those of the American revolutionaries. Second, the challenge to traditional political arrangements widened when middling urban dwellers, long disenfranchised by these oligarchies, demanded "liberty," too—that is, political enfranchisement within the cities—and briefly took over the Patriot movement. Just as many Irish rebels accepted the concessions of 1782, many "Patriot" oligarchs in the Netherlands did nothing to resist an invasion in 1787 that restored the power of the stadtholder, the prince of Orange, and thereby ended the challenge to their own control of urban government.

Both the Irish "volunteers" and the Dutch "Patriots," though members of very limited movements, echoed the American rebels in practical and ideological ways. Both were influenced by the economic and political consequences of Britain's relationship with its colonies. Both were inspired by the success of the American rebels and their thoroughgoing claims for political self-determination.

Desire for political reform flared in Poland as well during this period. Reform along lines suggested by Enlightenment precepts was accepted as a necessity by Polish leaders after the first partition of Poland in 1772 had left the remnant state without some of its wealthiest territories (see Map 18.1 on page 679). Beginning in 1788, however, reforming gentry in the *sejm* (representative assembly) went further; they established a commission to write a constitution, following the American example. The resulting document, known as the May 3 (1791) Constitution, was the first codified constitution in Europe; it was read and admired by George Washington.

The Constitution established a constitutional monarchy in which representatives of major towns as well as gentry and nobility could sit as deputies. The *liberum veto*, which had allowed great magnates to obstruct royal authority at will, was abolished. However, Catherine the Great, empress of Russia, would not tolerate a constitutional government in place so close to her own autocratic regime; she ordered an invasion of Poland in 1792. The unsuccessful defense of Poland was led by a veteran of the American Revolution, Tadeusz Kościuszko (1746–1817). The second, more extensive partition of Poland followed, to be followed in turn in 1794 by a widespread insurrection against Russian rule, again led by Kościuszko. The uprising was mercilessly suppressed by an alliance of Russian and Prussian troops. Unlike the Americans from whom they drew inspiration, the Poles' constitutional experiment was doomed by the power of its neighbor.

The American Revolution and the Kingdom of France

As one of Britain's greatest commercial and political rivals, France naturally was drawn into Britain's struggle with its North American colonies. The consequences for France were momentous for two reasons. First, the cost of French aid for the American rebels was so great that it helped accelerate a financial crisis in the French monarchy. Second, French involvement directly exposed many French aristocrats and common soldiers to the "enlightened" international community to which John Paul Jones felt he belonged, though the absolute monarchy of France turned a cold shoulder toward "liberal" ideas.

Rivalry with Great Britain gave France a special relationship with the American colonies and their fight for independence. In the Seven Years' War (1756–1763), the French had lost many of their colonial settlements and trading outposts to the English (see page 687). Stung by this outcome, certain courtiers and ministers pressed for an aggressive colonial policy that would regain for France some of the riches in trade that Britain was threatening to monopolize. The American Revolution seemed to offer the perfect opportunity. The French extended covert aid to the Americans from the very beginning of the conflict in 1775. After the first major defeat of British troops by the

Americans—at the Battle of Saratoga in 1777—France formally recognized the independent United States and established an alliance with them. The French then committed troops as well as monetary support for American forces. John Paul Jones's most famous ship, the *Bonhomme Richard,* was purchased and outfitted in France at French government expense, as were many other American naval vessels during the war. French support was decisive. In 1781 the French fleet kept reinforcements from reaching the British force besieged at Yorktown by George Washington. The American victory at Yorktown effectively ended the war; the colonies' independence was formally recognized by the Treaty of Paris in 1783.

The effect on France of the alliance with the American colonies was complicated. Aid for the Americans saddled France with a debt of about 1 million *livres* (pounds), which represented as much as one-quarter of the total debt that the French government was trying to service. A less tangible impact of the American Revolution was also important. About nine thousand French soldiers, sailors, and aristocrats participated in the war. The best known is the Marquis de Lafayette, who became an aide to George Washington and helped to command American troops. For many humble men, the war was simply employment. For others, it was a quest of sorts. For them, the promise of the Enlightenment—belief in the rationality of men, natural rights, and natural laws by which society should be organized—was brought to life in America.

Exposure to the American conflict occurred at the French court, too. Beginning in 1775, a permanent American mission to Versailles lobbied hard for aid and later managed the flow of that assistance. The chief emissary of the Americans was Benjamin Franklin (1706–1790), a philosophe by French standards, whose writings and scientific experiments were already known to French elites. His talents—among them, a skillful exploitation of a simple, Quaker-like demeanor—succeeded in promoting the idealization of America at the French court.

The United States Constitution and the various state constitutions and the debates surrounding them were all published in Paris and were much discussed in salons and at court, where lively debate about reform of French institutions had been going on for decades. America became the prototype of what Enlightenment philosophy

said was possible. It was hailed as the place where the irrationalities of inherited privilege did not prevail. A British observer, Arthur Young (1741–1820), believed that "the American revolution has laid the foundation of another in France, if [the French] government does not take care of itself."[2]

By the mid-1780s there was no longer a question of whether the French regime would experience reform but rather what form the reform would take. The royal government was almost bankrupt. A significant minority of the politically active elite was convinced of the fundamental irrationality of France's system of government. Nevertheless, the cataclysmic proportions that the French Revolution eventually reached raise questions about why less drastic change did not happen. A dissatisfied elite and a financial crisis—even with the encouragement of a successful revolt elsewhere—do not necessarily lead to revolution. Why did the French government—the *Ancien Régime,* or "Old Regime," as it became known after the Revolution—not take care of itself?

The Crisis of the Old Regime

The Old Regime was brought to the point of crisis in the late 1780s by three factors: (1) an antiquated system for collecting revenue, as well as old and recent debts; (2) institutional constraints on the monarchy that defended privileged interests; and (3) elite public opinion that envisioned thoroughgoing reform and pushed the monarchy in that direction. Another factor was the ineptitude of the king, Louis XVI (r. 1774–1793).

Louis came to the throne in 1774, a year before the American Revolution began. He was a kind, well-meaning man better suited to carry out the finite responsibilities of a petty bureaucrat than to be king. The queen, the Austrian Marie Antoinette (1755–1793), was unpopular. She was regarded with suspicion by those for whom the alliance with Austria had never felt natural. She, too, was politically inept, unable to negotiate the complexities of court life, and widely rumored to be selfishly wasteful of royal resources despite the realm's financial crises.

The fiscal crisis of the monarchy had been a long time in the making and was an outgrowth of the system in which the greatest wealth was protected by traditional privileges. At the top of the social and political pyramid were the nobles, a legal grouping that included warriors and royal officials. In France, nobility conferred exemption from much taxation. Thus, the royal government could not directly tax its wealthiest subjects.

This situation existed throughout much of Europe, a legacy of the individual contractual relationships that had formed the political and economic framework of medieval Europe. Unique to France, however, was the strength of the institutions that defended this system. Of particular importance were the royal law courts, the parlements, which claimed a right of judicial review over royal edicts. All the Parlementaires—well-educated lawyers and judges—were noble and loudly defended the traditional privileges of all nobles. Louis XV (d. 1774), near the end of his life, had successfully undermined the power of the parlements by a bold series of moves. Louis XVI, immediately after coming to the throne, buckled under pressure and restored the parlements to full power.

Deficit financing had been a way of life for the monarchy for centuries. After early efforts at reform, Louis XIV (d. 1715) had reverted to common fund-raising expedients such as selling offices, which only added to the weight of privileged investment in the old order. England had established a national bank to free its government from the problem, but the comparable French effort early in the century had been undercapitalized and had failed. Late in the 1780s, under Louis XVI, one-fourth of the annual operating expenses of the government was borrowed, and half of all government expenditure went to paying interest on its debt.

Short-term economic crises added to the cumulative problem of government finance. During Louis's reign there were several years of disastrously poor harvests, and throughout the reign there was a downturn in the economy. The weakness of the economy proved to be a crucial component in the failure of overall reform.

The king employed able finance ministers who tried to institute fundamental reforms, such as replacing the tangle of taxes with a simpler system in which all would pay and eliminating local tariffs, which were stifling commerce. The parlements and many courtiers and aristocrats, as well as ordinary people, resisted these policies. Ordinary people did not trust the "free market" (free from traditional trade controls) for grain; most feared that speculators would buy up the grain supply and people would starve. Trying

Criticism of Marie Antoinette In a satirical engraving from 1787, the queen toasts the dismissal of a reforming minister. She wears a famous diamond necklace that had caused scandal and widespread criticism of the monarchy two years before; it was a gift from a cardinal with whom the queen was wrongly accused of having an affair. *(Musée Carnavalet/Jean-Loup Charmet)*

to implement such reforms in a time of grain shortage almost guaranteed their failure. Moreover, many supported the parlements out of self-interest and because they were the only institution capable of standing up to the monarchy. Yet not all members of the elite joined the parlements in opposing reform. The imprint of "enlightened" public opinion shaped in salons and literary societies was apparent in the thinking of some aristocrats, who believed that the government and the economic system as a whole needed reform and debated the nature and extent of reform needed.

In 1787 the king called an "Assembly of Notables"—an ad hoc group of elites—to support him in facing down the parlements and proceeding with some reforms. He found little support even among men known to be sympathetic to reform. Some did not support particular reforms, and many were reluctant to allow the monarchy free rein. Others, reflecting the influence of the American Revolution, maintained that a "constitutional" body such as the Estates General, which had not been called since 1614, needed to make these decisions.

Ironically, nobles and clergy who were opposed to reform supported the call for the Estates General, for they assumed that they could control its deliberations. The three Estates met and voted separately by "order"—clergy (First Estate), nobles (Second Estate), and commoners (Third Estate). It was thus assumed that the votes of the clergy and nobles would nullify whatever the Third Estate might propose.

In 1788 popular resistance to reform in the streets of Paris and mounting pressure from his courtiers and bureaucrats induced Louis to summon the Estates General. On Louis's orders, deputies to the Estates General were elected by intermediate assemblies chosen by wide male suffrage. Louis assumed there was widespread loyalty to the monarchy in the provinces, and he wished to tap into it by means of this voting. Louis also agreed that the Third Estate should have twice as many deputies as the other two Estates, but he did not authorize voting by head rather than by order, which would have brought about the dominance of the Third Estate. Nevertheless, he hoped that the specter of drastic proposals put forth by the Third Estate would frighten the aristocrats and clergy into accepting some of his reforms.

Louis faced a critical situation when the Estates General convened in May 1789. As ever, he faced immediate financial crisis. He also faced a constitutional crisis. There was already a sense of legitimacy about the Estates General, about the role of the Third Estate, and about the authority of the Third Estate to enact change. Political pamphlets abounded arguing that the Third Estate deserved enhanced power because it carried the mandate of the people. The most important of them was *What Is the Third Estate?* (1789) by Joseph Emmanuel Sieyès (1748–1836), a church official from the diocese of Chartres. The sympathies of Abbé Sieyès, as he was known, were with the Third Estate: His career had suffered because he was not noble. Sieyès argued that the Third Estate represented the nation because it did not reflect special privilege.

Among the deputies of the first two Estates—clergy and nobility—were men, like the Marquis de Lafayette (1757–1834), who were sympathetic to reform. More important, however, the elections had returned to the Third Estate a large majority of deputies who reflected the most radical political thought possible for men of their standing. Most were lawyers and other professionals who were functionaries in the government but, like Sieyès, of low social rank. They frequented provincial academies, salons, and political societies. They were convinced of their viewpoints and determined on reform and had little stake in the system as it was. When this group convened and met with resistance from the First and Second Estates and from Louis himself, they seized the reins of government and a revolution began.

1789: The Revolution Begins

The three Estates met at Versailles, but the opening of the Estates General was celebrated first in Paris with a solemn procession and religious services attended by all the participants—the last public ritual of the Old Regime. The three Estates marched separately—the clergy arrayed in magnificent vestments, the nobles decked out in furs and velvet, the "commoners" dressed in simple black, bringing up the rear. Neither this staged portrayal of social distinctions, nor the spectacularly presented king and queen, nor the religious symbolism that linked monarchy to divine order could conceal the political conflicts.

As soon as the three Estates began to meet, the conflicts surfaced. The ineptness of the Crown was immediately clear. On the first day of the meetings, Louis and his ministers failed to introduce a program of reforms for the deputies to consider. This failure raised doubt about the monarchy's commitment to reform. More important, it allowed the political initiative to pass to the Third Estate. The deputies challenged the Crown's insistence that the three Estates meet and vote separately. Deputies to the Third Estate refused to be certified (that is, to have their credentials officially recognized) as members of only the Third Estate rather than as members of the Estates General as a whole.

For six weeks the Estates General was unable to meet officially, and the king did nothing to break the impasse. During this interlude, the determination of the deputies of the Third Estate strengthened. More and more deputies were won over to the notion that the three Estates should meet together and that the reform process must begin in the most systematic way: France must have a written constitution.

By the middle of June, more than thirty reformist members of the clergy were sitting jointly with the Third Estate, which had invited all deputies from all three Estates to meet and be certified together. On June 17 the Third Estate simply declared itself the National Assembly of France. At first, the king did nothing, but when the deputies arrived to meet on the morning of June 20, they discovered they had been locked out of the hall. Undaunted, they assembled instead in a nearby indoor tennis court and produced the document that has come to be known as the "Tennis Court Oath." It was a collective pledge to meet until a written constitution had been achieved. Only one deputy refused to support it. Sure of their mandate, the deputies had assumed the reins of government.

The king continued to handle the situation with both ill-timed self-assertion and attempts at compromise. As more and more deputies from the First and Second Estates joined the National Assembly, Louis "ordered" the remaining loyal deputies to join it, too. Simultaneously, however, he ordered troops to come to Paris. He feared disorder in the wake of the recent disturbances throughout France and believed that any challenge to the legitimacy of arbitrary monarchical authority would be disastrous.

The Tennis Court Oath It was raining on June 20 when the deputies found themselves barred from their meeting hall and sought shelter in the royal tennis court. Their defiance created one of the turning points of the Revolution; the significance was recognized several years later by this painting's artist. *(Photographie Bulloz)*

Storming the Bastille The crowd was convinced that the Bastille held political prisoners as well as a large supply of arms. In fact, it held neither. Thousands of Parisians—including artisans and shopkeepers and not merely desperate rabble—surrounded the fortress and forced the garrison to surrender. *(Photographie Bulloz)*

This appeal for armed assistance stirred unrest in the capital. Paris, with a population of about 600,000 in 1789, was one of the largest cities in Europe. There were thousands of workers in all trades plus thousands more—perhaps one-tenth of the inhabitants—jobless recent immigrants from the countryside. Paris was the political nerve center of the nation; it was the site of the publishing industry, salons, the homes of Parlementaires and royal ministers. The city was both extremely volatile and extremely important to the stability of royal power. The king's call for troops aroused Parisians' suspicions. Some assumed that there was a plot afoot to

starve Paris and destroy the National Assembly. Already they considered the Assembly to be a guarantor of acceptable government.

It took little—the announcement of the dismissal of a reformist finance minister—for Paris to erupt in demonstrations and looting. Crowds besieged City Hall and the royal armory, where they seized thousands of weapons. A popular militia formed as citizens armed themselves. Armed crowds assailed other sites of royal authority, including the huge fortified prison, the Bastille, on the morning of July 14. The Bastille now held only a handful of petty criminals, but it still remained a

Declaration of the Rights of Man and the Citizen

Each of the articles of the 1789 Declaration was a response to some feature of Old Regime society or law that was now deemed unacceptable.

Preamble: The representatives of the French people, organized as a National Assembly, believing that the ignorance, neglect, or contempt of the rights of man are the sole cause of public calamities and the corruption of governments, have determined to set forth in a solemn declaration the natural, inalienable, and sacred rights of man. . . .

(1) Men are born and remain free and equal in rights. Social distinctions may be founded only upon the general good.

(2) The aim of all political association is the preservation of the natural and imprescriptible rights of man. These rights are liberty, property, security, and resistance to oppression.

(3) The principle of all sovereignty resides essentially in the nation. No body or individual may exercise any authority which does not proceed directly from the nation.

(6) Law is the expression of the general will. Every citizen has the right to participate personally, or through his representative, in its formation. It must be the same for all. . . . All citizens, being equal in the eyes of the law, are equally eligible to all dignities and to all public positions and occupations, according to their abilities, and without distinction except that of their virtues and talents.

(11) The free communication of ideas and opinions is one of the most precious rights of man. . . .

(13) A common contribution is essential for the maintenance of the public forces and for the cost of administration. This should be equitably distributed among all the citizens in proportion to their means.

Source: James Harvey Robinson, *Readings in European History* (Boston: Ginn, 1906), pp. 409–411.

potent symbol of royal power and, it was assumed, held large supplies of arms. Like the troops at the armory, the garrison at the Bastille had not been given firm orders to fire on the crowds if necessary. After leading a hesitant defense, the garrison commander decided to surrender after citizens managed to secure cannon and drag them to face the prison. Most of the garrison were allowed to go free, although several officers, including the commander, were murdered by the crowd.

The citizens' victory was a great embarrassment to royal authority. The king immediately had to embrace the popular movement. He came to Paris and in front of crowds at City Hall donned the red and blue cockade worn by the militia and ordinary folk as a badge of resolve and defiance. This symbolic action signaled the legitimation of politics based on new principles.

Encouraged by events in Paris, inhabitants of cities and towns around France staged similar uprisings. In many, the machinery of royal government completely broke down. City councils, officials, and even Parlementaires were thrown out of office. Popular militias took control of the streets. There was a simultaneous wave of uprisings in rural areas. Most of them were the result of food shortages, but their timing added momentum to the more strictly political protests in urban areas. These events forced the members of the National Assembly to work energetically on the constitution and to pass legislation to satisfy popular protests against economic and political privileges.

On August 4 the Assembly issued a set of decrees abolishing the remnants of powers that landlords had enjoyed since the Middle Ages, including the right to compel peasants to labor for them and the bondage of serfdom itself. Although largely symbolic, because serfdom and forced labor had been eliminated in much of France, these changes represented a dramatic inroad into the property rights of the elite as they had been traditionally construed. They were hailed as the "end of feudalism." A blow was also struck at established religion by abolishing the tithe. At the end of August, the Assembly issued a Declaration of the Rights of Man and the Citizen. It was a bold assertion of principles condemning the old order. (See the box, "Declaration of the Rights of Man and the Citizen.")

In September, the deputies debated the king's role in a new constitutional government. Deputies known as "monarchists" favored a government rather like England's, with a two-house legislature, including an upper house representing the hereditary aristocracy and a royal right to veto legislation. More radical deputies favored a single legislative chamber and no veto power for the king. After deliberation, the Assembly reached a compromise. The king was given a three-year suspensive veto—the power to suspend legislation for the sitting of two legislatures. This was still a

formidable amount of power but a drastic limitation of the king's formerly absolute sovereignty.

Again, Louis resorted to troops. This time, he called them directly to Versailles, where the Assembly sat. News of the troops' arrival provoked outrage, which heightened with the threat of another grain shortage. Women in street markets in Paris, early on the morning of October 5, noticed food shortages and took immediate collective action. "We want bread!" they shouted at the steps of City Hall. Women often led protests over bread shortages, because they procured food for their families. This protest, however, went far beyond the ordinary. A crowd of thousands gathered and decided to go all the way to Versailles, accompanied by the popular militia (now called the "National Guard"), to petition the king directly for sustenance.

At Versailles, they presented a delegation to the National Assembly, and a joint delegation of the women and deputies was dispatched to see the king. Some of the women fell at the feet of the king with their tales of hardship, convinced that the "father of the people" would alleviate their suffering. He did order stored grain supplies distributed in Paris, and he also agreed to accept the

Women's March on Versailles The Parisian marketwomen marched the twelve miles to Versailles, some provisioning themselves with tools, stolen firearms, and horses as they left the capital. *(Jean-Loup Charmet)*

A Young Woman Recounts the March to Versailles

In the months after the women's march of October 1789, the municipal council in Paris, suspicious of such popular action, questioned some of the participants. These depositions present problems as historical sources because the witnesses' words were not recorded verbatim and, in any case, each witness would have been very careful in her testimony. The following document comes from the questioning of a 20-year-old Marie-Rose Barré, a lace worker.

[Marie-Rose Barré] . . . [d]eposes that on October 5 last, at about eight o'clock in the morning, going to take back some work, she was stopped at the Pont Notre Dame by about a hundred women who told her that it was necessary for her to go with them to Versailles to ask for bread there. Not being able to resist this great number of women, she decided to go with them. At the hamlet at the Point-du-Jour, two young men, unknown to her, who were on foot and going their way, told them that they were running a great risk, that there were cannon mounted at the bridge at Saint-Cloud. This did not prevent them from continuing on their way. . . . The two young men of whom she spoke met them near Viroflay and told them that they had escaped at Saint-Cloud but that at Versailles they would be fired on. But they continued on their way. At Versailles they found the King's Guards lined up in three ranks before the palace. A gentleman dressed in the uniform of the King's Guard . . . came to ask them what they wanted of the King, recommending peaceful behavior on their part. They answered that they were coming to ask him for bread. This gentleman was absent for a few minutes and then returned to take four of them

to introduce them to the King. The deponent was one of the four. . . .

They spoke first to M. de Saint-Priest, and then to His Majesty, whom they asked for bread. His Majesty answered them that he was suffering at least as much as they were, to see them lacking it, and that so far as he was able he had taken care to prevent them from experiencing a dearth. Upon the King's response, they begged him to be so good as to arrange escorts for the flour transports intended for the provisioning of Paris, because according to what they had been told at the bridge in Sèvres by the two young men of whom she spoke earlier, only two wagons out of seventy intended for Paris actually arrived there. The King promised them to have the flour escorted and said that if it depended on him, they would have bread then and there. They took leave of His Majesty and were led, by a gentleman in a blue uniform with red piping, into the apartments and courts of the palace to the ranks of the Flanders regiment, to which they called out, "Vive Le Roi!" It was then about nine o'clock. After this, they retired into a house on Rue Satory and went to bed in a stable.

Source: Philip Dawson, ed., *The French Revolution* (Englewood Cliffs, N.J.: Prentice-Hall, Inc., 1967), pp. 66–67.

constitutional role that the Assembly had voted for him. (See the box, "A Young Woman Recounts the March to Versailles.")

The march ended on an odd note as the National Guard replaced much of the royal guard around the person of the king. That night the National Guard saved the king's life when members of the crowd broke into the palace and managed to kill two members of the royal guard still in atten-

dance outside the queen's chamber. The king agreed to return to Paris, so that he could reassure the people. But the procession back to the city was a curious one. The entire royal family was escorted by militia and city people, and the severed heads of the killed guardsmen were carried on pikes.

The king was now in the hands of his people. Already, dramatic change had occurred as a result of a complex dynamic among the three Estates, the

Crown, and the people of Paris. The king was still assumed to be the fatherly guardian of his people's well-being; but his powers were now limited, and his authority was badly shaken. The Assembly had begun to govern in the name of the "nation" and, so far, had the support of the people.

THE FRENCH REVOLUTIONS

The French Revolution was a complicated affair. It was a series of changes, in a sense a series of revolutions, driven not by one group of people but by several groups. Even among elites convinced of the need for reform there was a wide range of opinion. The people of Paris continued to be an important force for change. Country people also became active, primarily in resisting changes forced on them by the central government.

All of the wrangling within France was complicated by foreign reaction. Managing foreign war soon became a routine burden for the fragile revolutionary governments. In addition, there were the continuing problems that had precipitated the Revolution in the first place: the indebtedness of the government, economic difficulties, and recurrent shortages of grain. Finally, the Revolution itself was an issue in that momentum for further change was created once the traditional arrangements of royal government had been altered.

The First Phase Completed, 1789–1791

At the end of 1789, Paris was in ferment, but for a time the forward progress of change blunted the threat of disastrous divisions between king and Assembly and between either of those and the people of Paris. The capital continued to be the center of lively political debate. Salons continued to meet; academies and private societies proliferated. Deputies to the Assembly swelled the ranks of these societies or helped to found new ones. Several would be important throughout the Revolution—particularly the Jacobin Club, named for the monastic order whose buildings the members used as a meeting hall.

These clubs represented a wide range of revolutionary opinion. Some, in which ordinary Parisians were well represented, focused on economic policies that would directly benefit common people. Women were active in a few of the more

radical groups. Monarchists dominated other clubs. At first similar to the salons and debating societies of the Enlightenment era, the clubs increasingly became both sites of political action and sources of political pressure on the government. A bevy of popular newspapers also contributed to the vigorous political life in the capital.

The broad front of revolutionary consensus began to break apart as the Assembly forged ahead with decisions about the constitution and with policies necessary to remedy France's still-desperate financial situation. The largest portion of the untapped wealth of the nation lay with the Catholic church, an obvious target for anticlerical reformers. The deputies did not propose to dismantle the church, but they did make sweeping changes. They kept church buildings intact and retained the clergy as salaried officials of the state. They abolished all monasteries and pensioned the monks and nuns to permit them to continue as nurses and teachers where possible. The Assembly seized most of the vast properties of the church and declared them national property (*biens nationaux*) to be sold for revenue.

Economic and political problems ensued. Revenue was needed faster than the property could be inventoried and sold, so government bonds (*assignats*) were issued against the eventual sale of church properties. Unfortunately, in the cash-strapped economy, the bonds were treated like money, their value became inflated, and the government never realized the hoped-for profits. A greater problem was the political divisiveness generated by the restructuring of the church. Many members of the lower clergy, living as they did near ordinary citizens, were among the most reform-minded of the deputies. These clergy were willing to go along with many changes, but the required oath of loyalty to the state challenged clerical identity and seemed overly intrusive.

The Civil Constitution of the Clergy, as these measures were called, was passed by the Assembly in July 1790 because the clerical deputies opposing it were outvoted. More than half of the clergy did take the oath of loyalty. Those who refused, concentrated among the higher clergy, were in theory thrown out of their offices. A year later (April 1791) the pope declared that clergy who had taken the oath were suspended from their offices. Antirevolutionary sentiment grew among thousands of French people, particularly among rural people, to whom the church was still important. This religious opposition helped to undermine the legitimacy of the new government.

Meanwhile, the Assembly proceeded with administrative and judicial reform. The deputies abolished the medieval provinces as administrative districts and replaced them with uniform *départements* (departments). They declared that local officials would be elected—a revolutionary dispersal of power that had previously belonged to the king.

As work on the constitution drew to a close in the spring of 1791, the king decided that he had had enough. Royal authority and government had been virtually dismantled. Louis had always lived in splendid isolation in Versailles, but he now was a virtual prisoner in the Tuileries Palace in the very heart of Paris. Afraid for himself and his family, he and a few loyal aides worked out a plan to flee France. The king and the members of his immediate family set out incognito on June 20, 1791. However, the royal party missed a rendezvous with a troop escort and was stopped along the way—and recognized—in the town of Varennes, near the eastern border of the kingdom.

Louis and his family were returned to Paris and now lived under lightly disguised house arrest. The circumstances of his flight were quickly discovered. He had intended to invade France with Austrian troops if necessary. He and the queen had sent money abroad ahead of themselves. He had left behind a document condemning the constitution. Thus, in July 1791, just as the Assembly was completing its proposal for a constitutional monarchy, the constitution it had created began to seem unworkable because the king was not trustworthy.

Editorials and popular demonstrations against the monarchy echoed these sentiments. In an incident known as the Massacre of the Champ (Field) de Mars, government troops led by Lafayette charged citizens gathered in a public demonstration organized by certain clubs against the monarchy. The government of the National Assembly fired on the demonstrators, and about fifty men and women died. This incident both reflected and heightened tensions between moderate reformers satisfied with the constitutional monarchy, such as Lafayette, and those, including increasing numbers of Parisian citizens, who were openly republican and hoping to eliminate the monarchy.

THE FRENCH REVOLUTION, 1789–1791

May 5, 1789	Meeting of Estates General
June 17, 1789	Third Estate declares itself the National Assembly
June 20, 1789	Tennis Court Oath
July–August 1789	Storming of the Bastille (July 14); abolition of feudalism (August 4); Declaration of the Rights of Man and of the Citizen (August 27)
October 5–6, 1789	Women's march on Versailles; Louis XVI's return to Paris
July 1790	Civil Constitution of the Clergy
June 1791	Louis XVI attempts to flee Paris; is captured and returned
September 1791	New constitution is implemented; Girondins dominate newly formed Legislative Assembly

On September 14 the king swore to uphold the constitution. He had no choice. The event became an occasion for celebration, but the tension between the interests of the Parisians and the provisions of the new constitution could not be glossed over. Though a liberal document for its day, the constitution reflected the views of the elite deputies who had created it. The right to vote, based on a minimal property qualification, was given to about half of all adult men. However, these men only chose electors, for whom the property qualifications were higher. The electors in turn chose deputies to national bodies and also local officials. Although in theory any eligible voter could be an elected deputy or official, the fact that elite electors voted candidates into office reduced the likelihood that ordinary citizens would be national deputies or local officials. The Declaration

Declaration of the Rights of Woman

Authored in 1791 by Olympe de Gouges (1748?–1793), a butcher's daughter from southwestern France, this document and its author's career reflect the complexity of political life during the Revolution. Gouges's advocacy of women's rights represents the extension to women of the broad-based challenge to tradition that the Revolution embodied. Gouges dedicates the Declaration to the queen, drawing on the tradition of aristocratic patronage. Ironically, given Article 10, Gouges died on the scaffold for her revolutionary sympathies.

Man, Are you capable of being just? It is a woman who poses the question; you will not deprive her of that right at least. Tell me, what gives you sovereign empire to oppress my sex? . . . Bizarre, blind, bloated with science and degenerated—in a century of enlightenment and wisdom—into the crassest ignorance, he wants to command as a despot a sex which is in full possession of its intellectual faculties; he pretends to enjoy the Revolution and to claim his rights to equality in order to say nothing more about it.

(1) Woman is born free and lives equal to man in her rights. Social distinctions can be based only on the common utility.

(2) The purpose of any political association is the conservation of the natural and imprescriptible rights of woman and man; these rights are liberty, property, security, and especially resistance to oppression.

(4) Liberty and justice consist of restoring all that belongs to others; thus, the only limits on the exercise of the natural rights of woman are perpetual male tyranny; these limits are to be reformed by the laws of nature and reason.

(10) No one is to be disquieted for his very basic opinions; woman has the right to mount the scaffold; she must equally have the right to mount the rostrum. . . .

Source: Darlene Gay Levy, Harriet Branson Applewhite, and Mary Durham Johnson, *Women in Revolutionary Paris, 1789–1795* (Urbana: University of Illinois Press, 1979), pp. 87–91.

of Rights that accompanied the constitution reflected a fear of the masses that had not existed when the Declaration of the Rights of Man and the Citizen was promulgated in 1789. Freedom of the press and freedom of assembly, for example, were not fully guaranteed.

Further, no political rights were accorded to women. Educated women had joined Parisian clubs such as the Cercle sociale (Social Circle), where opinion favored extending rights to women. Through such clubs, these women had tried to influence the National Assembly. But the Assembly granted neither political rights nor legal equality to women, nor did it pass other laws beneficial to women such as legalizing divorce or mandating female education. The prevailing view of women

among deputies seemed to reflect those of the Enlightenment philosophe Rousseau, who imagined women's competence to be entirely circumscribed within the family. A Declaration of the Rights of Woman was drafted by a woman named Olympe de Gouges to draw attention to the treatment of women in the constitution. (See the box, "Declaration of the Rights of Woman.")

Very soon after the constitution was implemented, the fragility of the new system became clear. The National Assembly declared that its members could not serve in the first assembly to be elected under the constitution. Thus, the members of the newly elected Legislative Assembly, which began to meet in October 1791, lacked any of the cohesiveness that would have come from collective experience. Also, unlike the previous National Assembly, they did not represent a broad range of opinion but were mostly republicans.

In fact, the Legislative Assembly was dominated by republican members of the Jacobin Club. They were known as Girondins, after the region in southwestern France from which many of the club's leaders came. The policies of these new deputies and continued pressure from the ordinary citizens of Paris would cause the constitutional monarchy to collapse in less than a year.

The Second Revolution and Foreign War, 1791–1793

An additional pressure on the new regime soon arose: a threat from outside France and a war to counter the threat. Antirevolutionary aristocratic émigrés, including the king's brothers, had taken refuge in nearby German states and were planning to invade France. The emperor and other German rulers did little actively to aid the émigrés. Austria and Prussia, however, in the Declaration of Pilnitz of August 1791, declared, as a concession to the émigrés, that they would intervene if necessary to support the monarchy in France.

The threat of invasion, when coupled with distrust of the royal family, seemed more real to the revolutionaries in Paris than it actually was. Many deputies actively wanted war. They assumed that the outcome would be a French defeat, which would lead to a popular uprising that would rid them, at last, of the monarchy. In April 1792, under pressure from the Assembly, Louis XVI declared war against Austria. From this point, foreign war would be an ongoing factor in France's revolution—not only because of the threat of foreign invasion but also because of deliberate decisions to take war abroad in order to safeguard the revolution at home.

At first, the war was a disaster for France. The army had not been reorganized into an effective fighting force after the loss of many aristocratic officers and the addition of newly self-aware citizens. On one occasion, troops insisted on putting an officer's command to a vote. The French lost early battles in the Austrian Netherlands, but the Austrians did not press their advantage and invade France because they were preoccupied with problems in eastern Europe.

THE FRENCH REVOLUTION, 1792–1793	
April 1792	France declares war on Austria
August 10, 1792	Storming of the Tuileries; Louis XVI arrested
September 21, 1792	National Convention declares France a republic
January 21, 1793	Louis XVI is guillotined

Louis XVI in 1792 The king, though a kindly man, had neither the character nor the convictions necessary to refashion royal authority symbolically as the Revolution proceeded. When Parisian crowds forced him to wear the "liberty cap," the monarchy was close to collapse. *(Metropolitan Museum of Art, The Elisha Whittelsey Collection, The Elisha Whittelsey Fund, 1962)*

The defeats heightened criticism of the monarchy and pressure for dramatic change. Under the direction of the Girondins, the Legislative Assembly began to press for the deportation of priests who had been leading demonstrations against the government. The Assembly abolished the personal guard of the king and ordered provincial national guardsmen, including those from Marseille, to come to Paris. The king's resistance to these measures, as well as fears of acute grain shortages owing to a poor harvest and the needs of the armies, created further unrest. Crowds staged dramatic marches near the king's palace, physically confronted him, and forced him to don the "liberty cap," a symbol of republicanism. The king's authority and prestige were now thoroughly undermined.

By July 1792, tensions had become acute. The grain shortage was severe, Austrian and Prussian troops committed to saving the royal family were threatening to invade, and, most important, the populace was better organized and more determined than ever before. In each of the forty-eight "sections"—administrative wards—of Paris a miniature popular assembly thrashed out all the events and issues of the day just as deputies in the nationwide Legislative Assembly did. Derisively called *sans-culottes*, "without knee pants," because they could not afford elite fashions, the ordinary Parisians in the section assemblies included shopkeepers, artisans, and laborers. Their political organization enhanced their influence with the Assembly, the clubs, and the newspapers in the capital. By late July most sections of the city had approved a petition calling for the exile of the king, the election of new city officials, the exemption of the poor from taxation, and other radical measures.

10 August 1792 One of the turning points of the Revolution is captured by the contemporary painter François Gérard. The Parisian crowds have just successfully stormed the Tuileries Palace and now confront members of the Legislative Assembly. Notice the sympathetic portrayal of the people, accomplished in part by the inclusion of figures of children. The royal family, having just taken refuge in the Assembly's meeting hall, is visible behind the grille. *(Louvre © R.M.N.)*

In August they took matters into their own hands. On the night of August 9, after careful preparations, the section assemblies sent representatives who constituted themselves as a new city government with the aim of "saving the state." They then proceeded with an organized assault on the Tuileries Palace, where the royal family was living. In the bloody confrontation, hundreds of royal guards and citizens died. After briefly taking refuge in the Legislative Assembly itself, the king and his family were imprisoned in one of the fortified towers in the city, under guard of the popularly controlled city government.

The storming of the Tuileries inaugurated the second major phase of the Revolution: the establishment of republican government in place of the monarchy. The people of Paris now physically dominated the Legislative Assembly. Some deputies had fled. Those who remained agreed under pressure to dissolve the Assembly and make way for another body to be elected by universal manhood suffrage. On September 20, that assembly—known as the National Convention—began to meet. The next day, the Convention declared the end of the monarchy and began to work on a constitution for the new republic.

Coincidentally, on the same day French forces won their first real victory over the allied Austrian and Prussian forces that had attempted to invade France. Though not a decisive battle, it was a profound psychological victory. A citizen army had defeated the professional force of a ruling prince. The victory bolstered the republican government and encouraged it to put more energy into the wars. Indeed, maintaining armies in the field became increasingly a factor in the delicate equilibrium of revolutionary government. The new republican regime let it be known that its armies were not merely for self-defense but for the liberation of all peoples in the "name of the French Nation."

The Convention faced the divisive issue of what to do with the king. Louis had not done anything truly treasonous, but some of the king's correspondence, discovered after the storming of the Tuileries, provided the pretext for charges of treason. The Convention held a trial for him, lasting from December 11, 1792, through January 15, 1793. He was found guilty of treason by an overwhelming vote (683 to 39), reflecting the fact that the republican government would not compromise with monarchy. Less certain was the sentence:

THE FRENCH REVOLUTION, 1793–1794

February 1793	France declares war on Britain, Spain, and the Netherlands
June 1793	Radical Jacobins purge Girondins from the Convention
July 1793	Robespierre assumes leadership of Committee of Public Safety
July 1793–July 1794	Reign of Terror
July 1794	Robespierre is guillotined

Louis was condemned to death by a narrow majority, 387 to 334.

The consequences for the king were immediate. On January 21, 1793, Louis mounted the scaffold in a public square near the Tuileries and was beheaded. The execution split the ranks of the Convention and soon resulted in the breakdown of the institution itself.

The Faltering Republic and the Terror, 1793–1794

In February 1793, the republic was at war with virtually every state in Europe, except the Scandinavian kingdoms and Russia. Moreover, the regime faced massive and widespread counterrevolutionary uprisings within France. Vigilance against internal as well as external enemies seemed necessary. Nevertheless, for a time, the republican government functioned adequately. In May 1793, for example, it passed the first Law of the Maximum, which tried to fix the price of grain and ensure adequate supplies of bread flour, so that urban people could afford their staple food.

The Convention established an executive body, the Committee of Public Safety. In theory, this executive council was answerable to the Convention as a whole. As the months passed, however, it acted with greater and greater autonomy not only to institute various policies but also to

Robespierre Justifies the Terror

In this excerpt from a speech before the Convention in December 1793, Robespierre justifies the revolutionary government's need to act in an extraconstitutional manner. He echoes Rousseau's notion of a highly abstract sense of the public good. He also warns against challenges to the Revolution within France posed by foreign powers.

The defenders of the Republic must adopt Caesar's maxim, for they believe that "nothing has been done so long as anything remains to be done." Enough dangers still face us to engage all our efforts. It has not fully extended the valor of our Republican soldiers to conquer a few Englishmen and a few traitors. A task no less important, and one more difficult, now awaits us: to sustain an energy sufficient to defeat the constant intrigues of all the enemies of our freedom and to bring to a triumphant realization the principles that must be the cornerstone of public welfare. . . . Revolution is the war waged by liberty against its enemies; a constitution . . . crowns the edifice of freedom once victory has been won and the nation is at peace. . . . The principal concern of a constitutional government is civil liberty; that of a revolutionary government, public liberty. [A] revolutionary government is obliged to defend the state itself against the factions that assail it from every quarter. To good citizens revolutionary government owes the full protection of the state; to the enemies of the people it owes only death.

Is a revolutionary government the less just and the less legitimate because it must be more vigorous in its actions and freer in its movement than ordinary government? . . . It also has its rules, all based on justice and public order. . . . It has nothing in common with arbitrary rule; it is public interest which governs it and not the whims of private individuals.

Thanks to five years of treason and tyranny, thanks to our credulity and lack of foresight . . . Austria and England, Russia, Prussia, and Italy had time to set up in our country a secret government to challenge the authority of our own. . . . We shall strike terror, not in the hearts of patriots, but in the haunts of foreign brigands.

Source: George Rudé, ed., *Robespierre* (Englewood Cliffs, N.J.: Prentice-Hall, 1967), pp. 58–63.

eradicate internal and external enemies. The broadly based republican government represented by the Convention began to disintegrate.

The first major narrowing of control came in June 1793. Pushed by the Parisian sections, a group of extreme Jacobins purged the Girondin deputies from the Convention and arrested many of them. The Girondins were republicans who favored an activist government in the people's behalf, but they were less radical than the Jacobins, less insistent on central control of the Revolution, and less willing to share power with the citizens of Paris. After the purge, the Convention still met, but most authority was held by the Committee of Public Safety.

New uprisings against the regime began. Added to counterrevolutionary revolts by peasants and aristocrats were new revolts by Girondin sympathizers. As resistance to the government mounted and the foreign threat continued, a dramatic event in Paris led the Committee of Public Safety officially to adopt a policy of political repression. A well-known figure of the Revolution, Jean Paul Marat (1743–1793), publisher of a radical republican newspaper very popular with ordinary Parisians, was murdered on July 13 by Charlotte Corday (1768–1793), a young aristocratic woman who had asked to meet with him. Shortly afterward, a long-time member of the Jacobin Club, Maximilien Robespierre (1758–1794), joined the

A Citizen of Paris Suffers Under the Terror

The apparatus of the Terror meant that ordinary citizens could be arrested for the slightest offense. Here, a woman describes her arrest, which led to months of grim imprisonment. (She was eventually released only because she persuaded the authorities that she was pregnant.)

For a long time I have had to feed the members of my household on bread and cheese and . . . tired of complaints from my husband and my boys, I was compelled to go wait in line to get something to eat. For three days I had been going to the same market without being able to get anything, despite the fact that I waited [all day]. After the distribution of butter on the twenty-second, . . . a citizen came over to me and said I was in a very delicate condition [and I answered] "You can't be delicate and be on your legs for so long . . ." He replied that I needed to drink milk. I answered that I had men in my house and couldn't nourish them on milk [and that] if he . . . was sensitive to the difficulty of obtaining food, he would not vex me so, and that he was an imbecile and wanted to play despot, and no one had that right.

I was arrested [on the spot and] was led to the Revolutionary Committee [of the section] where I was called a counterrevolutionary and was told I was asking for the guillotine because I told them I preferred death to being treated ignominiously. . . . I was asked if I knew whom I had called a despot . . . and I was told that he was the commander of the post. I said he was more [a commander] beneath his own roof than anyone, given that he was there to maintain order and not to provoke bad feelings. For [these] answers, I was told that I had done three times more than was needed to get the guillotine and that I would be explaining myself before the Revolutionary Tribunal.

Source: Darlene Gay Levy, Harriet Branson Applewhite, and Mary Durham Johnson, *Women in Revolutionary Paris, 1789–1795* (Urbana: University of Illinois Press, 1979), pp. 267–268.

Committee and called for "Terror"—the systematic repression of internal enemies. He was not alone in his views. Radicals in the section assemblies of Paris led demonstrations to pressure the government into making Terror the order of the day.

Robespierre himself embodied all the contradiction of the policy of Terror. He was an austere, almost prim, man who lived very modestly—a model, of sorts, of the virtuous, disinterested citizen. The policies followed by the government during the year of his greatest influence, from July 1793 to July 1794, included generous, rational, and humane policies to benefit ordinary citizens as well as the policy of official Terror. (See the box, "Robespierre Justifies the Terror.")

Terror meant the use of intimidation to silence dissent. Since the previous autumn, the guillotine had been at work against identified enemies of the regime, but now a more energetic apparatus of terror was instituted. A Law of Suspects was passed that allowed citizens to be arrested simply on vague suspicion of counterrevolutionary sympathies. (See the box, "A Citizen of Paris Suffers Under the Terror.") Revolutionary tribunals and an oversight committee made arbitrary arrests and rendered summary judgment. In October a steady stream of executions began, beginning with the queen, imprisoned since the storming of the Tuileries the year before. The imprisoned Girondin deputies followed, and then the process continued relentlessly. In Paris there were about 2600 executions from 1793 to 1794.

Around France, approximately 14,000 executions were the result of verdicts from revolutionary tribunals. Another 10,000 to 12,000 people died in prison. Ten thousand or more were killed,

Robespierre the Incorruptible A lawyer who had often championed the poor, Robespierre was elected to the Estates General in 1789 and was a consistent advocate of republican government from the beginning of the Revolution. His unswerving loyalty to his political principles earned him the nickname "the Incorruptible." *(Musée des Beaux-Arts, Lille)*

usually by summary execution, after the defeat of counterrevolutionary uprisings. For example, 2000 people were summarily executed in Lyon when a Girondin revolt collapsed there in October. The repression in Paris, however, was unique because of the city's role in the nation's political life. The aim of the repression was not merely to stifle active resistance; it was also to stifle simple dissent. The victims in Paris included not merely aristocrats or former deputies but also sansculottes. The radical Jacobins wanted to seize control of the Revolution from the Parisian citizens who had helped them to power.

The Terror notwithstanding, the government of the Committee of Public Safety was effective in providing direction for the nation at a critical time. It instituted the first mass conscription of citizens into the army (*levée en masse*), and an effective popular army came into existence. In the autumn of 1793, this army won impressive victories. Accomplishments in domestic policy included an extended Law of the Maximum (September 1793) that applied to necessary commodities other than

bread. Extensive plans were made for a system of free and universal primary education. Slavery in the French colonies was abolished in February 1794. Divorce, first legalized in 1792, was made easier for women to obtain.

In the name of "reason," traditional rituals and rhythms of life were changed. One reform of long-term significance was the introduction of the metric system of weights and measures. Although people continued to use the old, familiar measures for a very long time, the change was eventually accomplished, leading the way for change throughout Europe. Equally "rational" but not as successful was the elimination of the traditional calendar. The traditional days, weeks, and months were replaced by forty-day months and *decadi* (ten-day weeks with one day of rest). All saints' days and Christian holidays were eliminated. The years had already been changed—Year I had been declared with the founding of the republic in the autumn of 1792.

Churches were rededicated as "temples of reason." Believing that outright atheism left people with no basis for personal or national morality, Robespierre sought instead to promote a cult of the Supreme Being. The public festivals organized around either principle were solemn civic ceremonies intended to ritualize and legitimize the new political order. These and other innovations of the regime were not necessarily welcomed. The French people generally resented the elimination of the traditional calendar. In the countryside, there were massive peasant uprisings over loss of poor relief, community life, and familiar ritual.

Divorce law and economic regulation were a boon, especially to urban women, but women's participation in sectional assemblies and in all organized political activity—which had been energetic and widespread—was banned in October 1793. The particular target of the regime was the Society of Revolutionary Republican Women, a powerful club representing the interests of female sans-culottes. By banning women from political life, the regime helped to ground its legitimacy, since the seemingly "natural" exclusion of women might make the new system of government appear part of the "natural" order. (See the feature, "Weighing the Evidence: Political Symbols," on pages 734–735.) Elimination of women's clubs and women's participation in section assemblies also eliminated a source of popular power, from which the regime was now trying to distance itself.

The Committee and the Convention were divided over religious and other policies, but the main policy differences concerned economic matters: how far to go to assist the poor, the unemployed, and the landless. Several of the temperate critics of Robespierre and his allies were guillotined because they differed with them on policy and on the continuing need for the Terror itself. Their deaths helped to precipitate the end of the Terror because Robespierre's power base shrank so much that it had no further legitimacy.

Deputies to the Convention finally dared to move against Robespierre in July 1794. French armies had scored a major victory over Austrian troops on June 26, so there was no longer any need for the emergency status that the Terror had thrived on. In late July (the month of Thermidor, according to the revolutionary calendar), the Convention voted to arrest Robespierre, the head of the Revolutionary Tribunal in Paris, and their closest associates and allies in the city government. On July 28 and 29, Robespierre and the others—about a hundred in all—were guillotined, and the Terror ended.

Thermidorian Reaction and the Directory, 1794–1799

After the death of Robespierre, the Convention reclaimed many of the executive powers that the Committee of Public Safety had seized. The Convention dismantled the apparatus of the Terror, repealed the Law of Suspects, and forced the revolutionary tribunals to adopt ordinary legal procedures. The Convention also passed into law some initiatives, such as expanded public education, that had been proposed in the preceding year but not enacted. This phase of the Revolution that followed the Terror is called the "Thermidorian Reaction" because it began in the revolutionary month of Thermidor (July 19–August 17).

The stability of the government, however, was threatened from the outset. Counterrevolutionary uprisings in western France during the autumn of 1794 were joined by landings of émigré troops the following June. These challenges were put down. There were also popular uprisings against the Terror throughout France. Officials of the previous regime were lynched, and pro-revolutionary groups were massacred by their fellow citizens.

The people of Paris tried to retain influence with the new government. With the apparatus of Terror dismantled, the Convention was unable to enforce controls on the supply and price of bread. Thus, economic difficulties and a hard winter produced famine by the spring of 1795. In May crowds marched on the Convention, chanting "Bread and the Constitution of '93," referring to the republican constitution drafted by the Convention but never implemented because of the Terror. The demonstrations were met with force and were dispersed.

Fearful of a renewed, popularly supported Terror, or even of desperate popular support for a royalist uprising, the Convention drafted a new constitution that limited popular participation, as had the first constitution of 1791. The new plan allowed fairly widespread (but not universal) male suffrage, but only for electors, who would choose deputies for the two houses of the legislature. The property qualifications for being an elector were very high, so all but elite citizens were effectively disenfranchised.

THE FRENCH REVOLUTION, 1794–1799

August 1794	Thermidorian reaction begins
October 1795	Directory is established
November 1799	Napoleon seizes power

In the fall of 1795, as the Convention was preparing to dissolve so that new elections might proceed, a final popular uprising shook Paris. The Convention anticipated the trouble, and when a crowd of twenty thousand or more converged on the Tuileries Palace, the officer in charge ordered his troops to fire. Parisian crowds never again seriously threatened the government, although living conditions worsened as food prices soared. The army officer who issued the command to fire was Napoleon Bonaparte.

A new government began under the provisions of the new constitution. It was called the Directory for the executive council of five men chosen by the upper house of the new legislature. To avoid the concentration of authority that had produced the Terror, the members of the Convention had tried to enshrine separation of powers in the new system. However, because of unsettled conditions throughout France, the governments under the Directory were never stable and never free from attempted coups and extraconstitutional maneuvering.

The most spectacular challenge, the Conspiracy of Equals, was led by extreme Jacobins who wanted to restore popular government and aggressive economic and social policy on behalf of the common people. The conspiracy ended with arrests and executions in 1797. When elections in 1797 and 1798 returned many royalist as well as Jacobin deputies, the Directory resorted to force to forestall challenges to its authority: Many deputies were arrested, sent into exile, or denied seats.

By 1799, conditions had once again reached a critical juncture. France was again at war with a coalition of states and was faring badly in the fighting. The demands of the war effort, together with other economic woes, brought the govern-

ment again to the brink of bankruptcy. The government seemed to be losing control of the countryside; there were continued royalist uprisings and local political vendettas as well as outright banditry.

Members of the Directory had often turned to sympathetic army commanders to carry out the arrests and purge of the legislature. They now invited General Napoleon Bonaparte to help them form a government that they could more strictly control. Two members of the Directory plotted with Napoleon and his brother, Louis Bonaparte, to seize power on November 9, 1799.

THE NAPOLEONIC ERA

Napoleon Bonaparte (1769–1821) was the kind of person who gives rise to myths. He was talented, daring, and ruthless. He was also charming and charismatic. His audacity, determination, and personal magnetism enabled him to profit from the political instability and confusion in France and ensconce himself in power. Once in power, he stabilized the political scene by enshrining in law the more conservative gains of the Revolution. He also used his power and his abilities as a general to continue wars of conquest against France's neighbors.

Napoleon's troops, in effect, exported the Revolution when they conquered most of Europe. Law codes were reformed, governing elites were opened to talent, and public works were undertaken in most states under French control. Yet French conquest also meant domination, pure and simple, and involvement in France's rivalry with Britain. The Napoleonic era left Europe an ambiguous legacy—war and its complex aftermath yet also revolution and encouragement to further change.

Napoleon: From Soldier to Emperor, 1799–1804

Napoleon was from Corsica, a Mediterranean island that had passed from Genoese to French control in the eighteenth century. The second son of a large gentry family, he was educated at military academies in France, and he married the politically well-connected widow Joséphine de Beauharnais (1763–1814), whose aristocratic husband had been a victim of the Terror.

Napoleon Crossing the Great St. Bernard This stirring portrait by the great neoclassical painter Jacques-Louis David memorializes Napoleon's 1796 crossing of the Alps before his victorious Italian campaign, as a general under the Directory. The painting depicts the moment heroically rather than realistically (Napoleon wisely crossed the Alps on a sure-footed mule, not a stallion), in part because it was executed in 1801–1802. Napoleon, as First Consul, wanted images of himself that would justify his increasingly ambitious claims to power. *(Louvre © R.M.N.)*

Napoleon steered a careful course through the political turmoil of the Revolution. By 1799, however, he was well known and popular because of his military victories. He demonstrated his reliability and ruthlessness in 1795 when he ordered troops guarding the Convention to fire on the Parisian crowd, but his greatest victories had been against France's foreign opponents. In 1796 and 1797 he had conquered all of northern Italy, forcing Austria to relinquish that territory as well as to cede control of the Austrian Netherlands, which revolutionary armies had seized in 1795. He then commanded an invasion of Egypt in an attempt to strike at British influence and trade connections in the eastern Mediterranean. The Egyptian campaign failed in its goals, but individual spectacular victories during the campaign ensured Napoleon's military reputation. In addition, Napoleon had demonstrated his widening ambitions. He had taken leading scientists and skilled administrators with him to Egypt in order to export the seeming benefits of French civilization as well as to buttress military victory with more lasting military authority.

Napoleon's partners in the new government after the November coup in 1799 soon learned of his great political ambition and skill. In theory, the new system was to be a streamlined version of the Directory: Napoleon was to be first among equals in a three-man executive—First Consul, according to borrowed Roman terminology. But Napoleon soon asserted his primacy among them and began not only to dominate executive functions but also to bypass the authority of the various legislative bodies in the new regime.

Napoleon was careful to avoid heavy-handed displays of power. He cleverly sought ratification of each stage of his assumption of power through national plebiscites (national referendums in which all eligible voters could vote for or against proposals)—one plebiscite for a new constitution in 1800 and another when he claimed consulship for life in 1802. Perhaps most important to the success of his increasingly authoritarian regime was his effort to include, among his ministers, advisers, and bureaucrats, men of many political stripes—Jacobins, reforming liberals, even former Old Regime bureaucrats. He welcomed many exiles back to France, including all but the most ardent royalists. He thus stabilized his regime by healing some of the rifts among ruling elites.

Napoleon combined toleration with ruthlessness, however. Between 1800 and 1804 he imprisoned, executed, or exiled dozens of individuals for alleged Jacobin agitation or royalist sympathies. His final gesture to intimidate royalist opposition came in 1804 when he kidnapped and coldly murdered a Bourbon prince who had been in exile in Germany.

By the terms of the Treaty of Amiens in 1802, Napoleon made peace with Britain, France's one remaining enemy. The fragile and short-lived peace only papered over the two countries' commercial and strategic rivalries, but it gave Napoleon breathing room to establish his rule more securely in France. One of the most important steps had been accomplished a year earlier by means of the Concordat of 1801. The aim of this treaty with the pope was to solve the problem of church-state relations that for years had caused antirevolutionary rebellions. The agreement allowed for the resumption of Catholic worship and the continued support of the clergy by the state, but also accepted the more dramatic changes accomplished by the Revolution. Church lands that had been sold were guaranteed to their new owners. Protestant churches were also allowed and their clergy was paid, although Catholicism was recognized as the "religion of the majority of Frenchmen." Later, Napoleon granted new rights to Jews also. Nonetheless, the Concordat removed one of the most important grounds for counterrevolutionary upheaval in the countryside and undermined royalist resistance to the new regime from abroad.

The law code that Napoleon established in 1804 was much like his accommodation with the church in its limited acceptance of revolutionary gains. His Civil Code reflected the revolutionary legacy in its guarantee of equality before the law and its requirement for the taxation of all social classes; it also enshrined modern forms of property ownership and civil contracts.

But neither the code nor Napoleon's political regime fostered individual rights, especially for women. Women lost all of the rights they had gained during the Revolution. Fathers' control over their families was enhanced. Divorce was no longer permitted except in rare instances. Women lost all property rights when they married, and they generally faced legal domination by fathers and husbands.

Napoleon helped to put the regime on better financial footing by establishing a national bank. The Bank of France, modeled on the Bank of England, provided capital for investment and could help the state manage its money and return to a system of hard coinage. Napoleon also further streamlined and centralized the administrative system, set up by the first wave of revolutionaries in 1789, by establishing the office of prefect to govern the départements. All prefects and their subordinates were appointed by Napoleon.

Some of these legal and administrative changes occurred after the final political coup that Napoleon undertook—declaring himself emperor. This was a bold move, but Napoleon approached it dexterously. For example, long before he declared himself emperor, Napoleon had begun to sponsor an active court life appropriate to imperial pretensions. The empire was proclaimed in May 1804 with the approval of the Senate; it was also approved by another plebiscite. Members of Napoleon's family were given princely status, and a number of his favorites received various titles and honors. The titles brought no legal privilege but signaled social and political distinctions of great importance. Old nobles were allowed to use their titles on this basis.

Many members of the elite, whatever their persuasions, tolerated Napoleon's claims to power because he safeguarded a number of revolutionary gains and reconfirmed their own status. War soon resumed against political and economic enemies—principally Britain, Austria, and Russia—and, for a time, Napoleon's success in the field continued. Because military success was central to the political purpose and self-esteem of elites, Napoleon's early successes as emperor further enhanced his power.

Conquering Europe, 1805–1810

Napoleon maintained relatively peaceful relations with other nations while he consolidated power at home, but the truces did not last. Tensions with the British quickly re-escalated when Britain resumed aggression against French shipping in 1803, and Napoleon countered by seizing Hanover, the ancestral German home of the English king. Then Napoleon seized several Italian territories and extended his influence in other German states. By 1805, all the states of Europe were threatened. Austria was alarmed by his power in Italy. England was at war on the high seas with Spain and the Netherlands, which Napoleon had forced to enter the fray. Napoleon began to gather a large French force on the northern coast of France, with which he could invade England.

The British fleet, commanded by Horatio Nelson (1758–1805), intercepted the combined French and Spanish fleets that were to have been the invasion flotilla and inflicted a devastating defeat off Cape Trafalgar in southern Spain (see Map 19.1) on October 21, 1805. The victory ensured British mastery of the seas and, in the long run, contributed to Napoleon's defeat. In the short run, the defeat at Trafalgar paled for the French beside Napoleon's impressive victories on land. Even as the French admirals were preparing for battle, Napoleon had abandoned the plans to invade England and in August had begun to march his army east through Germany.

In December 1805, after some preliminary, small-scale victories, Napoleon's army confronted a Russian force near Austerlitz, which is north of Vienna (see Map 19.1). Tsar Alexander I (r. 1801–1825) led his own troops into a battle that he ought to have avoided. Austrian reinforcements could not reach him in time, and French armies shattered the Russian force. The Battle of Austerlitz was Napoleon's most spectacular victory. Austria sued for peace. In further battles in 1806, French forces defeated Prussia as well as Russian armies once again.

Prussia was virtually dismembered by the subsequent Treaty of Tilsit (1807), but Napoleon tried to work out terms to make Russia into a contented ally. His hold on central Europe would not be secure with a hostile Russia, nor would the anti-British economic system that he envisioned—the Continental System (see page 725)—be workable without Russian participation.

French forces were still trying to prevail in Spain, which had been a client state since its defeat by revolutionary armies in 1795 but was resisting outright rule by a French-imposed king. In 1808, however, Napoleon turned his attention to a more fully subduing Austria. Napoleon won the Battle of Wagram in July 1809 but did not totally defeat Austria. Like Russia, Austria accepted French political and economic hegemony in a sort of alliance. By 1810 Napoleon had transformed most of Europe into allied or dependent states (see Map 19.1). The only exceptions were Britain and the parts of Spain and Portugal that continued to resist France with British help.

The states least affected by French hegemony were its reluctant allies: Austria, Russia, and the Scandinavian countries. Denmark had allied with France in 1807 only for help in fending off British naval supremacy in the Baltic. Sweden had reluctantly made peace in 1810 after losing control of Finland to Napoleon's ally, Russia. Sweden only minimally participated in the Continental System. At the other extreme were territories that had been incorporated into France. These included the Austrian Netherlands, territory along the Rhineland, and territories in Italy that bordered France. These regions were occupied by French troops and were treated as though they were départements of France itself.

In most other regions, some form of French-controlled government was in place, usually headed by a member of Napoleon's family. In both northern Italy and, initially, the Netherlands, where "sister" republics had been established after French conquests under the Directory, Napoleon imposed monarchies. Rulers were also imposed in the kingdom of Naples and in Spain. Western German states of the Holy Roman Empire that had allied with Napoleon against Austria were organized into the Confederation of the Rhine, with Napoleon as its "Protector." After a thousand years, the Holy Roman Empire ceased to exist. Two further states were created, largely out of the defeated Prussia's territory: the kingdom of Westphalia in western Germany and the duchy of Warsaw in the east (see Map 19.1).

Napoleon's domination of these various regions had complex, and at times contradictory,

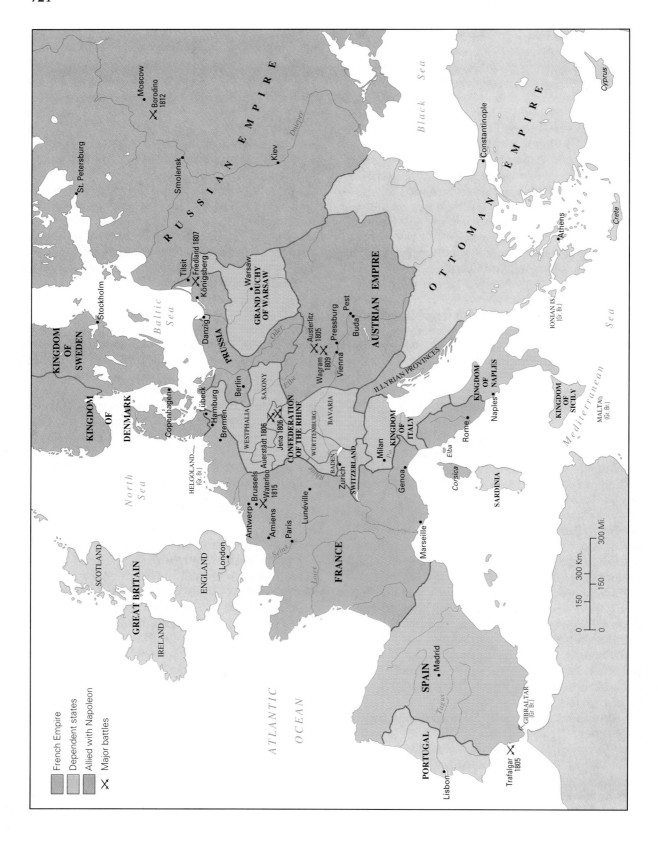

RUSSIAN EMPIRE

OTTOMAN EMPIRE

Black Sea

Moscow
• Borodino
1812

• St. Petersburg

• Kiev

• Smolensk

Constantinople •

Baltic Sea

Stockholm •

Tilsit •
✗ Friedland 1807
Königsberg •

Warsaw •

GRAND DUCHY
OF WARSAW

Danzig •

PRUSSIA

Austerlitz
✗ 1805
✗ Pressburg •
Wagram Vienna •
1809

Pest •
Buda •

AUSTRIAN EMPIRE

IONIAN IS.
(Gr. Br.)

Mediterranean Sea

Athens •

Crete

Cyprus

KINGDOM
OF
SWEDEN

KINGDOM
OF
DENMARK

Copenhagen •

Lübeck •
Hamburg •
Bremen •

Berlin •

SAXONY

WESTPHALIA
Jena 1806 ✗✗
Auerstädt 1806

CONFEDERATION
OF THE RHINE

BAVARIA

WÜRTEMBURG
BADEN

Elbe

ILLYRIAN PROVINCES

KINGDOM
OF
ITALY

Milan •

KINGDOM
OF
NAPLES

Naples •

KINGDOM
OF
SICILY

MALTA
(Gr. Br.)

North Sea

HELGOLAND
(Gr. Br.)

Antwerp •
Waterloo ✗ Brussels •
1815

Amiens • Paris •
Lunéville •

Zurich •
SWITZERLAND

Genoa •

Rome •

Elba

Corsica

SARDINIA

SCOTLAND

GREAT BRITAIN

ENGLAND
London •

IRELAND

Seine

Loire

FRANCE

Marseille •

Po

Tagus

ATLANTIC
OCEAN

300 Mi.

300 Km.

150

150

0

0

SPAIN
Madrid •

PORTUGAL

Lisbon •

GIBRALTAR
(Gr. Br.)

Trafalgar ✗✗
1805

French Empire

Dependent states

Allied with Napoleon

✗ Major battles

consequences. On the one hand, Napoleonic armies literally exported the French Revolution, in that French domination brought with it political and economic reform akin to that of the early phases of the Revolution, now enshrined in the Napoleonic Civil Code. Equality before the law was decreed following the French example; this meant the end of noble exemption from taxation in the many areas, like France, where it existed. In general, the complex snarl of medieval taxes and tolls was replaced with straightforward property taxes from which no one was exempt. As a consequence, tax revenues rose dramatically—by 50 percent in the kingdom of Italy, for example. Serfdom and forced labor were also abolished, as they had been in France in August 1789.

In most Catholic regions, the church was subjected to the terms of the Concordat of 1801. The tithe was abolished, church property seized and sold, and religious orders dissolved. Though Catholicism remained the state-supported religion in these areas, Protestantism was tolerated and Jews were granted rights of citizenship. Secular education, at least for males, was encouraged.

On the other hand, Napoleon would countenance only those aspects of France's revolutionary legacy that he tolerated in France itself. Just as he had suppressed any meaningful participatory government in France, so too did he suppress it in conquered regions. This came as a blow in states like the Netherlands, which had experienced its own democratizing "Patriot" movement and which had enjoyed republican self-government after invasion by French armies during the Revolution itself. Throughout the Napoleonic Empire, many of the benefits of streamlined administration and taxation were offset by the drain of continual warfare; deficits rose three- and fourfold, despite increased revenues. In addition, one of the inevitable costs of empire was political compromise to secure allies. In the duchy of Warsaw, reconstituted from lands Prussia had seized in the eighteenth century, Napoleon tampered little with either noble privileges or the power of the church. And, throughout Europe, Napoleon randomly al-

Map 19.1 Napoleonic Europe, ca. 1810 France dominated continental Europe after Napoleon's victories. Though French control would collapse quickly after defeats in Russia and Spain in 1812, the effects of French domination were more long-lasting.

lotted lands to reward his greatest generals and ministers, thereby exempting those lands from taxation and control by his own bureaucracy.

If true self-government was not allowed, a broad segment of the elite in all regions was nevertheless won over to cooperation with Napoleon by being welcomed into his bureaucracy or into the large multinational army, called the Grande Armée. Their loyalty was cemented when they bought confiscated church lands.

The impact of Napoleon's Continental System was equally mixed. Under this system, the Continent was in theory closed to all British shipping and British goods. The effects were widespread but uneven, and smuggling to evade controls on British goods became a major enterprise. Regions heavily involved in trade with Britain or its colonies or dependent on British shipping suffered in the new system, as did overseas trade in general when Britain gained dominance of the seas after Trafalgar. Peasants and landlords in many regions that produced grain for export suffered, and some cities dependent on overseas trade experienced catastrophic decline. However, the closing of the Continent to British trade, combined with increases in demand resulting from the need to supply Napoleon's armies, spurred the development of continental industries, at least in the short run. This industrial growth, enhanced by the improvement of roads, canals, and the like, formed the basis for further industrial development.

Defeat and Abdication, 1812–1815

Whatever its achievements, Napoleon's empire was ultimately precarious because of the hostility of Austria and Russia, as well as the belligerence of Britain. Austria resented losing the former Austrian Netherlands and lands in northern Italy to the French. Russia was a particularly weak link in the chain of alliances and subject states because Russian landowners and merchants were angered when their vital trade in timber for the British navy was interrupted and when supplies of luxury goods, brought in British ships, began to dwindle. A century of close alliances with German ruling houses made alliance with a French ruler extremely difficult politically for Tsar Alexander I.

It was Napoleon, however, who ended the alliance by provoking a breach with Russia. He suddenly backed away from an arrangement to marry one of Alexander's younger sisters and accepted the Austrian princess Marie Louise instead. (He had reluctantly divorced Joséphine in 1809 because their marriage had not produced an heir.) In addition, he seized lands along the German Baltic seacoast belonging to a member of Alexander's family. When Alexander threatened rupture of the alliance if the lands were not returned, Napoleon mounted an invasion. Advisers warned him about the magnitude of the task he seemed so eager to undertake—particularly about the preparations needed for winter fighting in Russia—but their warnings went unheard.

Napoleon's previous military successes had stemmed from a combination of strategic innovations and audacity. Napoleon divided his forces into independent corps. Each corps included infantry, cavalry, and artillery. Organized in these workable units, his armies could travel quickly by several separate routes and converge in massive force to face the enemy. Numbers were important to success, but so were discipline, control of troop movements, and determination to follow up initial gains. Leadership on the battlefield came from a loyal and talented officer corps that Napoleon had fashioned by welcoming returning aristocrats and favoring rising new talent. The final ingredient in the success formula was the high morale of French troops under Napoleon. Napoleon's English nemesis, Arthur Wellesley (1769–1852), duke of Wellington, once remarked that Napoleon's presence on a battlefield was worth forty thousand men.

The campaign against Russia began in June 1812. It was a spectacular failure. Napoleon had gathered a force of about 700,000 men—about half from France and half from allied states—a force twice as large as Russia's. The strategy of quickly moving independent corps and assembling massive forces could not be implemented because simply assembling so many men along the border was already the equivalent of gathering them for battle. Also, sustaining them thereafter was beyond the capacity of the supply system, which had always been Napoleon's weakness. Bold victories had often enabled Napoleon's troops to live off the countryside while they waited for supplies to catch up with them. But when the enemy attacked supply lines, when the distances traveled were very great, when the countryside was impoverished, or when battles were not decisive, Napoleon's ambitious strategies proved unwork-

able. In varying degrees, these conditions prevailed in Russia.

By the time the French faced the Russians in the principal battle of the Russian campaign—at Borodino, west of Moscow (see Map 19.1)—the Grande Armée had been on the march for two and a half months and stood at less than half its original strength. After the indecisive but bloody battle, the French occupied and pillaged Moscow but found scarcely enough food and supplies to sustain them. When Napoleon finally led his troops out of Moscow late in October, after an uncharacteristic period of indecisiveness, the fate of the French forces was all but sealed. The army marched south to reach the warmer and better-provisioned Ukraine but was turned back by Russian forces. The French then retreated north and west out of Russia, the way they had come. French soldiers who had not died in battle died of exposure or starvation or were killed by Russian peasants when they wandered away from their units. Of the original 700,000 French and allied troops, fewer than 100,000 made it out of Russia.

Napoleon left his army before it was fully out of Russia. A coup attempt in Paris prompted him to return to his governing duties before the French people realized the extent of the disaster in Russia. The collapse of his reign had begun, spurred by a coincidental defeat in Spain. Since 1808, Spain had been largely under French domination, with Napoleon's brother, Joseph, as king. A rebel Cortes (assembly), however, continued to meet in territory that the French did not control, and British troops were never expelled from the Iberian Peninsula. In 1812, as Napoleon was beginning his move against Russia, the collapse of French control accelerated. By the time Napoleon got back to Paris at the turn of the new year, Joseph had been expelled from Spain, and an Anglo-Spanish force led by the duke of Wellington was poised to invade France.

Napoleon's most able generals rallied what remained of his troops and held off Prussian and Russian forces in the east until he returned from France in April 1813 with a new army of raw recruits. Napoleon lost his last chance to stave off a coalition of all major powers against him when he refused an Austrian offer of peace for the return of conquered Austrian territories. With Britain willing to subsidize the allied armies, Tsar Alexander determined to destroy Napoleon, and the Austrians now anxious to share the spoils, Napoleon's empire

The French Army Flees Russia Napoleon's engineers built bridges for a night crossing of the Berezina River (in Belarus), which blocked the French retreat. The remainder of the army was saved from annihilation, but as in the rest of the Russian campaign, the cost was high: wagons and provisions, as well as thousands of wounded soldiers, were abandoned on the Russian side. Many of the engineers died of exposure. (*Musée de l'Armée*)

began to crumble. Napoleon's forces were crushed in a massive "Battle of Nations" near Leipzig in October, during which some of his troops from German satellite states deserted him on the battlefield. The allies were able to invade France and forced Napoleon to abdicate on April 6, 1814.

Napoleon was exiled to the island of Elba, off France's Mediterranean coast, but was still treated somewhat royally. He was installed as the island's ruler and was given an income drawn on the French treasury. Meanwhile, however, the restored French king was having his own troubles. Louis XVIII (r. 1814–1824) was the brother of the executed Louis XVI; he took the number eighteen out of respect for Louis XVI's son, who had died in prison in 1795. He had been out of the country and out of touch with its circumstances since the

beginning of the Revolution. In addition to the delicate task of establishing his own legitimacy, he faced enormous practical problems, including pensioning off thousands of soldiers now unemployed and still loyal to Napoleon.

Napoleon, bored and almost penniless on his island kingdom (the promised French pension never materialized), took advantage of the circumstances and returned surreptitiously to France on February 26, 1815. His small band of attendants was joined by the soldiers sent by the king to prevent him from advancing to Paris. Louis XVIII abandoned Paris to the returned emperor.

Napoleon's triumphant return lasted only one hundred days, however. Though many soldiers welcomed his return, many members of the elite were reluctant to throw in their lot with Napoleon again. Many ordinary French citizens had also become disenchanted with him since the defeat in Russia, and with the high costs, in conscription and taxation, of raising new armies. In any case, Napoleon's reappearance galvanized the divided allies, who had been haggling over a peace settlement, into unity. Napoleon tried to strike first, but he lost against English and Prussian troops in his first major battle, at Waterloo (in modern Belgium; see Map 19.1) on June 18, 1815. When Napoleon reached Paris after the defeat, he discovered the government in the hands of an ad hoc committee that included the Marquis de Lafayette. Under pressure, he abdicated once again. He was exiled to the tiny, remote island of St. Helena in the South Atlantic, from which escape would be impossible. He died there in 1821.

THE IMPACT OF REVOLUTION ON FRANCE AND THE WORLD

The process of change in France between 1789 and 1815 was so complex that it is easy to overlook the overall impact of the Revolution. Superficially, the changes seemed to come full circle—with first Louis XVI on the throne, then Napoleon as emperor, and then Louis XVIII on the throne. Even though the monarchy was restored, however, the Revolution changed the fundamental premises of political life in France and served to catalyze challenges to the existing order elsewhere.

The Significance of Revolution in France

The French monarchy was restored in 1815, but the Revolution had discredited absolute monarchy in theory and practice. The restored constitutional monarchy governed with only a small group of representatives of the elite, but their participation slowly widened during the nineteenth century. An important legacy of the Revolution was thus new principles on which to base a government: the right of "the people," however narrowly defined, to participate in government and to enjoy due process of law.

There was fundamental disagreement, however, about which people were worthy of inclusion in the political process and the degree to which the government might govern in their interests. There was a significant philosophical differ-

ence between many republicans and the reformers who had supported the Revolution in its initial stages. The latter argued for access to government only by the politically sophisticated elite and for the freeing of the economy from traditional constraints. The more inclusive view and the more activist posture regarding the appropriate role of government would be reinstated by revolutionary action later in the nineteenth century (see Chapter 20). Neither notion included a vision of women as citizens coequal with men.

Other legacies of the Revolution and the Napoleonic era included a centralized political system. The nation was divided into départements rather than provinces. For the first time, a single code of law applied to all French people. Most officials—from département administrators to city mayors—were appointed by the central government until the late twentieth century. The conscientious attention of the government, at various stages of the Revolution, to advances for France generally reflects the positive side of this centralization. The government sponsored national scientific societies, a national library and archives, and a system of teachers' colleges and universities. Particularly under Napoleon, there was a spate of canal- and road-building.

Napoleon's legacy, like that of the Revolution itself, was mixed. His self-serving reconciliation of aristocratic pretensions with the opening of careers to men of talent helped to ensure the long-term success of revolutionary principles from which the elite as a whole profited. His reconciliation of the state with the Catholic church helped to stabilize his regime and to ensure some revolutionary gains. The restored monarchy could not renege on these gains. But Napoleon could not eliminate the antirevolutionary bent of the church as a whole, and the church continued to be a reactionary force in France. The Napoleonic Code was a uniform system of law for the nation. But although it guaranteed equality under the law for men, it enshrined political and legal inferiority for women.

Whatever the concrete gains of the Revolution and Napoleon's rule, Napoleon's overthrow of constitutional principles worsened the problem of political instability. Napoleon's return to power in 1815, though brief, was nevertheless important. It reflects the degree to which his power was always rooted in military adventurism and in the loyalty of soldiers and officers. His bravado suggests the importance of personal qualities to the success of an authoritarian regime. But the swiftness of his collapse suggests that although the empire under Napoleon may have seemed an enduring solution to the political instability of the late 1790s, its legitimacy and security were as uncertain as the legitimacy and security of the revolutionary governments.

Although Louis XVIII acknowledged the principle of constitutionalism at the end of the Revolution, it rested on fragile footing. Indeed, the fragility of new political systems was one of the most profound lessons of the Revolution. There was division over policies, but even greater division over legitimacy—that is, the acceptance by a significant portion of the politically active citizenry of a particular system or of a particular government's right to rule.

Politics, the Revolution revealed, takes place in part on a symbolic level. What is acceptable and what is legitimate are expressed not only in words but also symbolically. The symbols are effective because they link a specific political system to a broader, fundamental system of values. The religious symbolism used by the monarchy, for example, linked royal government to divine order. Similarly, the public cults of reason and of the Supreme Being that Robespierre promoted during the Terror were attempts to link patriotism and support of the government to universal principles. Other, more limited, symbols were constantly in use: the red and blue cockades that supporters of the National Assembly put in their caps; the "liberty cap" that Louis XVI donned on one occasion; various representations of the abstract notion of "Liberty" in newspapers and journals widely available at the time.

Before the Revolution started, there was a significant shift in notions about political legitimacy. The deputies who declared themselves to be the National Assembly in June 1789 already believed that they had a right to do so. In their view, they represented "the nation," and their voice had legitimacy for that reason. The shift reflects not the innate power of ideas but the power of ideas in context. The deputies brought to Versailles not only their individual convictions that "reason" should be applied to the political system but also their experience in social settings where those ideas were well received. In their salons, clubs, and literary societies, they had experienced the fa-

miliarity, trust, and sense of community that are essential to effective political action.

The deputies' attempt to transplant their sense of community into national politics was not wholly successful. Factions, competing interests, and clashes of personality can be fatal to an insecure system. The National Assembly had scarcely inaugurated a secure system when its deputies undermined its workability by making themselves ineligible to hold office under the new constitution. The king also actively undermined the system because he disagreed with it in principle. The British parliamentary system, by comparison, though every bit as elitist as the narrowest of the representative systems during the French Revolution, had a long history as a workable institution for lords, commoners, and rulers. This shared experience was an important counterweight to differences over fundamental issues, so that Parliament as an institution both survived political crises and helped solve them.

The Revolution thus left a powerful yet ambiguous legacy for France. Politics was established on a new footing, yet still lacking were the practical means to achieve the promise inherent in the new principles.

The Impact of the Revolution Overseas

Throughout Europe and overseas, the Revolution left a powerful and complex legacy. French conquests in Europe were the least enduring of the dramatic changes of the revolutionary era. Nevertheless, French domination had certain lasting effects: Elites were exposed to modern bureaucratic management, and equality under the law transformed social and political relationships. Although national self-determination had an enemy in Napoleon, the breaking down of ancient political divisions provided important practical grounding for later cooperation among elites in nationalist movements. In Napoleon's kingdom of Italy, for example, a tax collector from Florence for the first time worked side by side with one from Milan. The example of the Revolution also helped inspire the uprising against Russian domination of Poland in 1794 (see page 701). This insurrection included not only educated elites, such as its leader Kościuszko, but also artisans and peasants; indeed, Catherine the Great was appalled when the rebels hanged members of a Russian-supported puppet government and vowed to crush the Polish "Jacobins."

European colonies overseas felt the impact of the Revolution and subsequent European wars in several ways. The British tried to take advantage of Napoleon's preoccupation with continental affairs by seizing French colonies and the colonies of the French-dominated Dutch. They were largely successful. In 1806 they seized the Dutch colony of Capetown—crucial for support of trade around Africa—as well as French bases along the African coast. In 1811 they grabbed the island of Java. In the Americas, French sugar colonies in the Caribbean were particularly vulnerable to English seapower. The British readily seized Martinique, Guadeloupe, and other islands while Napoleon was executing his brilliant victories on the Continent after 1805. The sugar island of Haiti was an exception to this pattern of French losses because British aggression there occurred in the context of a local revolution.

In Haiti the Revolution itself, and not merely the strategic moves of great powers, had an impact. The National Assembly in Paris delayed abolishing slavery in French colonies, despite the moral appeal of such a move, because of pressure from the white planters on Haiti and out of fear that the financially strapped French government would lose some of its profitable sugar trade. But the example of revolutionary daring in Paris and confusion about ruling authority that occurred as the Assembly and the king wrangled invited challenges to authority in the colonies.

Many white planters hoped to seize the opportunity the Revolution provided to gain political and economic independence from France. White planter rule in Haiti was challenged, in turn, by wealthy people of mixed European and African descent and then by a full-fledged slave rebellion, beginning in 1791. (See the box, "Encounters with the West: A Planter's Wife on the Haitian Slave Revolt.") Britain sent aid to the rebels when it went to war against the French revolutionary government in 1793. Only when the republic was declared in Paris and the Convention abolished slavery did the Haitian rebels abandon alliances with France's enemies and attempt to govern in concert with the mother country.

France, however, never regained control of Haiti. Led by a former slave, François Dominique Toussaint-Louverture (1743–1803), the new gov-

ernment of Haiti tried to run its own affairs, though without formally declaring independence from France. Napoleon, early in his rule, decided to tighten control of the profitable colonies by re-instituting slavery and ousting the independent government of Haiti. In 1802 French forces fought their way onto the island. They captured Toussaint-Louverture, who died shortly thereafter in prison. But in 1803 they were forced to leave by another rebellion prompted by the threat of renewed slavery.

The French Revolution and Napoleonic rule had a great impact on Spanish colonies in the Americas also, and for many of the same reasons as in Haiti. The confusion of authority in Spain enabled some Spanish colonies to govern themselves independently in all but name. Like the British North American colonies, the Spanish colonies wanted freedom from the closed economic ties the mother country tried to impose.

The liberal ideas that had helped spawn the French Revolution spurred moves toward independence in Spanish America. There were also echoes of radical republican ideology in some of the events in Spanish America. For example, participants in two major rebellions in Mexico espoused the end of slavery and generally championed the interests of the poor against local and Spanish elites. The leaders of these self-declared revolutions were executed (in 1811 and 1815), and their movements were crushed by local elites in alliance with Spanish troops. The efforts of local elites to become self-governing—the attempted liberal revolutions—were little more successful. Only Argentina and Paraguay broke away from Spain at this time. But as in Europe, a legacy remained of both limited and more radical revolutionary activity.

The View from Britain

Today the city of Paris is dotted with public monuments that celebrate Napoleon's victories. One of the main train stations is the Gare (Station) d'Austerlitz. A column in a city square, crowned with a statue of Napoleon, was made from the metal of enemy cannon captured at Austerlitz.

In London, another set of events and another hero is celebrated. In Trafalgar Square stands a statue of Lord Nelson, the British naval commander whose fleet destroyed a combined French and

∼ ENCOUNTERS WITH THE WEST ∼

A Planter's Wife on the Haitian Slave Revolt

The following are excerpts from two letters of Madame de Rouvray, a wealthy planter's wife living in the French colony of Saint-Domingue (the western half of the island of Hispaniola), to her married daughter in France. The decree of May 15, 1791, that Madame de Rouvray mentions in her first letter granted civil rights to free persons of mixed race. The decree affected only a few hundred persons on Saint-Domingue (many of whom themselves owned slaves), but white planters feared any breach in the barriers between the races. Tensions between white planters, on the one hand, and mulattos and modest white settlers who favored revolutionary changes, on the other, enabled the well-organized slave rebellion to be dramatically successful. It began in late August 1791 and is the backdrop to Madame de Rouvray's second letter. Madame de Rouvray and her husband fled the island—renamed Haiti, the Native American term for Hispaniola, after the revolt—for the United States in 1793.

July 30, 1791   I am writing to you from Cap [a city on the island] where I came to find out what the general mood is here. . . . All the deputies who make up the general assembly [of the colony] left here the day before yesterday to gather at Léogane [another city]. If they conduct themselves wisely their first action should be to send emissaries to all the powers who have colonies with slaves in order to tell them of the decree [of May 15] and of the consequences that will follow from it, and ask for help from them in case it happens that the National Assembly actually abolishes slavery too, which they will surely do. After their decree of May 15, one cannot doubt that that is their plan. And you understand that all the powers who have slave colonies have a common interest in opposing such a crazy plan because the contagion of liberty will soon infect their colonies too, especially in nearby Jamaica. It is said that [the English] will send a ship and troops [which] would be wonderful for us. Your father thinks it won't be long before the English take control here.

September 4, 1791   If news of the horrors that have happened here since the 23rd of last month have reached you, you must have been very worried. Luckily, we are all safe. We can't say whether our fortunes are also safe because we are still at war with the slaves who revolted [and] who have slaughtered and torched much of the countryside hereabouts. . . . All of this will gravely damage our revenues for this year and for the future, because how can we stay in a country where slaves have raised their hands against their masters? . . . You have no idea, my dear, of the state of this colony; it would make you tremble. Don't breathe a word of this to anyone but your father is determined, once the rebels have been defeated, to take refuge in Havanna.

Source: M. E. McIntosh and B. C. Weber, *Une Correspondance familiale au temps des troubles de Saint-Domingue* (Paris: Société de l'Histoire des Colonies Françaises et Librairie Larose, 1959), pp. 22–23, 26–28. Trans. by Kristen B. Neuschel.

Spanish fleet in 1805. Horatio Nelson was a brilliant tactician, whose innovations in maneuvering ships in the battle line resulted in stunning victories at Trafalgar and, in 1798, at the Nile Delta, which limited French ambitions in Egypt and the eastern Mediterranean.

Trafalgar looms large in British history in part because Nelson was mortally wounded during the battle. More significant, the battle ensured British mastery of the seas, which then forced Napoleon into economic policies that strained French ties to France's allies and satellites. Virtually

The Funeral of Lord Nelson, January 8, 1806 Nelson had been mortally wounded on the deck of his flagship at the Battle of Trafalgar in October. Rather than being buried at sea, as was the custom, his body was returned to London for an impressive state funeral, commemorated here in a contemporary engraving. *(National Maritime Museum, London)*

unchallenged seapower enabled the British to seize colonies formerly ruled by France and its allies.

Britain's seizure of French possessions expanded British trading networks overseas. The struggles against Napoleon also enhanced British trading networks and strategic dominance closer to home, particularly in the Mediterranean. As long as the British had been involved in trade with India, the Mediterranean had been important for economic and strategic reasons: It marked the end of the land route for trade from the Indian Ocean. Especially after Napoleon's aggression in Egypt, the British redoubled their efforts to control important strategic outposts in the Mediterranean, such as ports in southern Italy and on the island of Malta.

Since the late eighteenth century, the British had steadily made other gains abroad. In 1783, Britain had lost control of thirteen of its North American colonies; however, it had more successfully resolved the Irish rebellions. Similarly, in the Caribbean, British planter families, like Irish elites, were willing to accept tighter rule from the mother country in return for greater security against their subject population. In regions of India, the East India Company was increasing its political domination, and hence its economic stranglehold on Indian manufacture and trade.

The British economy would expand dramatically in the nineteenth century as industrial production expanded. The roots for that expansion were laid in this period in the countryside of Britain, where changes in agriculture and in production were occurring. These roots were also laid in Britain's overseas possessions by the profits made there and also, increasingly, by the control of sources of raw materials, notably raw cotton raised in India. The export of Indian cotton expanded significantly during the revolutionary period as part of an expanding trading system that included China, the source of tea.

However, economic expansion was not the sole motive for British aggression. In fact, economic expansion was often the product of increased British control of particular regions or sea-lanes, and the reasons for it were as much strategic as economic. Not every conquest had direct economic payoffs, but British elites were sure that strategic domination was a desirable step, wherever it could be managed. One Scottish landholder, writing in the opening years of the nineteenth century, spoke for many when he said that Britain needed an empire to ensure its greatness and that an empire of the sea was an effective counterweight to Napoleon's empire on land. Much as the French were at that moment exporting features of their own political system, the British, he said, could export their constitution wherever they conquered territory.

Thus, England and France were in fact engaged in similar phases of expansion in this period. In both, the desire for power and profit drove policy. In each, myths about heroes and about the supposed benefits of domination masked the state's self-interest. In both, the effects of conquest would become a fundamental shaping force in the nineteenth century.

SUMMARY

The French Revolution was a watershed in European history because it successfully challenged the principles of hereditary rule and political privilege by which all European states had hitherto been governed. The Revolution began when a financial crisis forced the monarchy to confront the desire for political reform by a segment of the French elite. Political philosophy emerging from the Enlightenment and the example of the American Revolution moved the French reformers to action. In its initial phase, the French Revolution established the principle of constitutional government and ended many of the traditional political privileges of the Old Regime.

The Revolution moved in more radical directions because of the intransigence of the king, the threat of foreign invasion, and the actions of republican legislators and Parisian citizens. Its most radical phase, the Terror, produced the most effective legislation for ordinary citizens but also the worst violence of the Revolution. A period of unstable conservative rule that followed the Terror ended when Napoleon seized power.

Though Napoleonic rule enshrined some of the gains of the Revolution, it also subjected France and most of Europe to the great costs of wars of conquest. After Napoleon, the French

monarchy was restored but forced to accept many limitations on its power as a result of the Revolution. Indeed, hereditary rule and traditional social hierarchies remained in place in much of Europe, but they would not be secure in the future. The legacy of revolutionary change would prove impossible to contain in France or anywhere else.

NOTES

1. Quoted in Samuel Eliot Morison, *John Paul Jones: A Sailor's Biography* (Boston: Little, Brown, 1959), pp. 149–154.
2. Quoted in Owen Connelly, *The French Revolution and Napoleonic Era* (New York: Holt, Rinehart and Winston, 1979), p. 32.

SUGGESTED READING

General Surveys
Connelly, Owen. *French Revolution/Napoleonic Era.* 1979. A clear and readable survey that devotes equal time to the Revolution and to Napoleon.
Sutherland, D. M. G. *France, 1789–1815.* 1986. A dense and detailed treatment, with extensive bibliography, that emphasizes the revolutionary over the Napoleonic period.
Thompson, John. *The French Revolution.* 1951. A classic liberal interpretation of the Revolution, useful for its clarity and detail.

Recent Interpretations of the Revolution
Baker, Keith Michael, ed. *The French Revolution and the Creation of Modern Political Culture.* 1987. A collection of essays by diverse scholars emphasizing the Revolution as a period of change in political culture.
Furet, François. *Interpreting the French Revolution.* 1981. The major work by the outstanding French scholar of the Revolution of the current generation, written in reaction to liberal and Marxist interpretations.
Hufton, Olwen. *Women and the Limits of Citizenship in the French Revolution.* 1992. A series of essays by the leading scholar on the history of women in the Revolution.
Hunt, Lynn. *The Family Romance of the French Revolution.* 1992. A study of political ideology and symbolic politics emphasizing the vast cultural consequences of killing the king and queen.
———. *Politics, Culture and Class in the French Revolution.* 1984. A survey and assessment of other interpretations of the Revolution, emphasizing the role of symbols and symbolic politics.
Kennedy, Emmet. *A Cultural History of the French Revolution.* 1989. An ambitious interpretation of the Revolution as a period of cultural change.

(continued on page 736)

POLITICAL SYMBOLS

During the French Revolution, thousands of illustrations in support of various revolutionary (or counterrevolutionary) ideas were reproduced on posters, on handbills, and in pamphlets. Some satirized their subjects, such as Marie Antoinette, or celebrated revolutionary milestones, such as the fall of the Bastille. The etching here of the woman armed with a pike, dating from 1792, falls into this category. Other pictures, such as the representation from 1795 of Liberty as a young woman wearing

An Armed Citizen, ca. 1792 *(Bibliothèque Nationale, Cabinet des estampes)*

the liberty cap, symbolized or reinforced various revolutionary ideals.*

Political images like these are an invaluable though problematic source for historians. Let us examine these two images of women and consider how French people during the Revolution might have responded to them. To understand what they meant to contemporaries, we must know something about the other images that these would have been compared to. We must also view the images in the context of the events of the Revolution itself. Immediately, then, we are presented with an interpretive agenda. How ordinary and acceptable was this image of an armed woman? If women were not citizens coequal with men, how could a woman be a symbol of liberty? What, in short, do these political images reveal about the spectrum of political life in their society?

The woman holding the pike stares determinedly at the viewer. Many details confirm what the caption announces: This is a French woman who has become free. In her hat she wears one of the symbols of revolutionary nationhood: the tricolor cockade. The badge around her waist celebrates a defining moment for the revolutionary nation: the fall of the Bastille. Her pike itself is inscribed with the words "Liberty or death!"

The woman appears to be serving not merely as a symbol of free women. She comes close to being the generic image of a free citizen, willing and able to fight for liberty—an astonishing symbolic possibility in a time when women were not yet treated equally under the law or granted the same

*This discussion draws on the work of Joan Landes, "Representing the Body Politic: The Paradox of Gender in the Graphic Politics of the French Revolution," and Darlene Gay Levy and Harriet B. Applewhite, "Women and Militant Citizenship in Revolutionary Paris," in Sara E. Melzer and Leslie W. Rabine, eds., *Rebel Daughters: Women and the French Revolution* (New York: Oxford University Press, 1992), pp. 15–37, 79–101.

political rights as the men of their class. Other images prevalent at the time echo this possibility. Many contemporary representations of the women's march on Versailles in 1789 (see page 708) show women carrying arms, active in advancing the Revolution. By the time this image was created (most likely in 1792), many other demonstrations and violent confrontations by ordinary people had resulted in the creation of dozens of popular prints and engravings that showed women acting in the same ways as men.

Repeatedly during 1792, women proposed to the revolutionary government that they be granted the right to bear arms. Their request was denied, but it was not dismissed out of hand. There was debate, and the issue was in effect tabled. Nevertheless, women's actions in the Revolution had created at least the possibility of envisaging citizenship with a female face.

The image of liberty from 1795 does not reflect the actions of women but rather represents their exclusion from political participation. It is one of a number of images of Liberty that portray this ideal as a passive, innocent woman, here garbed in ancient dress, surrounded by a glow that in the past had been reserved for saints. Liberty here is envisaged as a pure and lofty goal, symbolized as a pure young woman.

Late in 1793, during the Terror, women were excluded from formal participation in politics with the disbanding of women's organizations. Nor did they gain political rights under the Directory, which re-established some of the limited gains of the first phase of the Revolution. The justification offered for their exclusion in 1793 was borrowed from Rousseau: It is contrary to nature for women to be in public life (see page 665). Women "belong" in the private world of the family, where they will nurture male citizens. Women embody ideal qualities such as patience and self-sacrifice; they are not fully formed beings capable of action in their own right.

"Liberty" as a Young Woman, ca. 1795 *(S. P. Avery Collection, Miriam and Ira D. Wallach Division of Art, Prints, and Photographs, The New York Public Library, Astor, Lenox, and Tilden Foundations)*

Such notions made it easy to use images of women to embody ideals for public purposes. A woman could represent Liberty precisely because actual women were not able to be political players.

The two images shown here thus demonstrate that political symbols can have varying relationships to "reality." The pike-bearing citizen is the more "real." Her image reflects the way actual women acted, and it represents a way of thinking about politics that became possible for the first time because of their actions. The other woman reflects not the attributes of actual women but an ideal type spawned by the use of arbitrary gender distinctions to legitimize political power. In these images we can see modern political life taking shape: the sophistication of its symbolic language, the importance of abstract ideas such as liberty and nationhood—as well as the grounding of much political life in rigid distinctions between public and private, male and female. ✤

Landes, Joan. *Women and the Public Sphere in the Age of the French Revolution.* 1988. An analysis of the uses of gender ideology to fashion the new political world of the revolutionaries.

Manceron, Claude. *The Age of the French Revolution.* 1986. An innovative, multivolume study of the experience of the Revolution, beginning in the 1770s, told by means of biographical vignettes.

Origins and Preconditions of the Revolution

Censer, Jack, and Jeremy D. Popkin. *Press and Politics in Pre-Revolutionary France.* 1987. A work that is helpful in understanding the context of opposition to the monarchy before the outbreak of the Revolution.

Chartier, Roger. *The Cultural Origins of the French Revolution.* 1991. An interpretation of intellectual and cultural life in the eighteenth century with a view to explaining its revolutionary results; has a good bibliography.

Lefebvre, Georges. *The Coming of the French Revolution.* Translated by R. R. Palmer. 1947. The greatest of several works by this French historian; a readable Marxist interpretation that remains useful.

Palmer, R. R. *The Age of Democratic Revolution.* 2 vols. 1959. A study of the American and European revolutionary movements and their reciprocal influences; detailed, erudite, but immensely readable.

The Phases of Revolution, 1789–1791

Godeschot, J. *The Taking of the Bastille, July 14, 1789.* 1970. An explanation of the circumstances and significance of the seizure of the Bastille.

Rudé, George. *The Crowd in the French Revolution.* 1959. A classic Marxist assessment of the importance of common people to the progress of the Revolution.

Tackett, Timothy. *Priest and Paris in Eighteenth-Century France.* 1977. A study of rural Catholic life before the Revolution and after the impact of the Civil Constitution of the Clergy.

The Phases of Revolution, 1791–1794

Jordan, D. P. *The King's Trial.* 1979. A thorough and readable study of Louis XVI's trial and its importance.

Palmer, R. R. *Twelve Who Ruled.* 1941. A study of the principal figures of the Terror by one of the greatest American historians of the French Revolution.

Patrick, A. *The Men of the First French Republic.* 1972. A study of the Girondins—their identity and their coherence as a political faction.

Soboul, Albert. *The Sans-Culottes.* 1972. A study of the workers of Paris who were active in the Revolution, by Georges Lefebvre's successor as the foremost Marxist historian of the Revolution.

The Phases of Revolution, 1795–1799

Barton, H. Arnold. *Scandinavia in the Revolutionary Era, 1760–1815.* 1986. Treats the Scandinavian countries' response to and involvement in revolutionary movements and the Napoleonic wars.

James, C. L. R. *The Black Jacobins.* 1938. The classic study of the Haitian revolution in the context of events in Europe.

Sydenham, M. *The First French Republic, 1792–1804.* 1974. A useful survey of the relatively neglected phases of the Revolution.

Napoleon and Napoleonic Europe

Bayly, C. A. *Imperial Meridian.* 1989. A new study of the developing British Empire in the context of both European and world affairs; has an extensive bibliography.

Connelly, Owen. *Blundering to Glory: The Campaigns of Napoleon.* 1992. A new assessment of Napoleon's military achievements by an expert on Napoleonic warfare.

Lyons, Martyn. *Napoleon Bonaparte and the Legacy of the French Revolution.* 1994. A clear, readable, and up-to-date synthesis of scholarship on Napoleon.

Markham, Felix. *Napoleon.* 1963. The best biography in English of Napoleon.

Chapter Opener Credits

Chapter 11: Staatliche Museen zu Berlin, Preussischer Kulturbesitz Kunstgewerbemuseum. Photo: Mues-Funke
Chapter 12: Erich Lessing/Art Resource, NY
Chapter 13: Bridgeman Art Library
Chapter 14: Scala/Art Resource, NY

Chapter 15: Musée Cantonal des Beaux-Arts, Lausanne
Chapter 16: Scala/Art Resource, NY
Chapter 17: Erich Lessing/Art Resource, NY
Chapter 18: Photographie Bulloz
Chapter 19: Château de Versailles/Hubert Jones

Text Credits

Chapter 11: Page 399: "Saint Catherine and The Avignon Papacy" from *Babylon on the Rhone: A Translation of Letters by Dante, Petrarch, and Catherine of Siena on the Avignon Papacy* by Robert Coogan. Copyright © 1983 by Robert Coogan. Reprinted by permission of the author. **Page 417:** "The Black Death" from *The Decameron* by Giovanni Boccaccio, translated by Mark Musa and Peter Bondanella. Translation copyright © 1982 by Mark Musa and Peter Bondanella. Reprinted by permission of Dutton Signet, a Division of Penguin Books USA Inc. **Page 424:** "The Rising of 1381" from *Peasant's Revolt of 1381, The Anoniimalle Chronicle* by R. B. Dobson. Copyright © 1970 by The Macmillan Press Ltd. Reprinted by permission of Macmillan Press Ltd. **Page 428:** "A European View of Constantinople" from *Pursuit of Power* by James C. Davis. English translation copyright © 1970 by James C. Davis. Reprinted by permission of HarperCollins Publishers, Inc.

Chapter 12: Page 453: Poem by Michelangelo from *The Italian Renaissance Reader* by Julia Bondanella and Mark Musa. Copyright © 1987 by Julia Conaway Bondanella and Mark Musa. Reprinted by permission of Dutton Signet, a division of Penguin Books USA Inc. **Page 443:** "Petrarch Responds to His Critics" from *The Renaissance Philosophy of Man* by Ernst Cassirer, Paul Oskar Kristeller, and John H. Randall. Copyright 1948 The University of Chicago Press. Reprinted by permission of the publisher. **Page 445:** "Cassandra Fedele Defends Liberal Arts for Women" from *Her Immaculate Hand: Selected Works By and About the Women Humanists of Quattrocento Italy* (Binghamton, N.Y.: Center for Medieval and Early Renaissance Studies, State University of New York, 1983). Reprinted by permission. **Page 447:** "Rabbi Mordecai Dato Criticizes the Humanists" from *Rabbi's and Jewish Communities in Renaissance Italy* edited and translated by Robert Bonfil, Oxford University Press 1990. Reprinted by permission of Oxford University Press: England. **Page 465:** "Isabella d'Este Orders Art" from *Patrons and Artists in the Italian Renaissance* by David S. Chambers. Copyright 1970 by Macmillan Ltd. Reprinted by permission of the publisher. **Page 467:** "Giovanni della Casa on the

Perfect Gentleman" from *The Portable Renaissance Reader* edited by James Bruce Ross and Mary Martin McLaughlin. Copyright 1953, renewed © 1981 by Viking Penguin Inc. Reprinted by permission of Viking Penguin, a division of Penguin Books USA Inc.

Chapter 13: Page 479: "Pegalotti on Travel to the East" from *Medieval Trade in the Mediterranean World,* edited by Robert S. Lopez and Irving W. Raymond. Copyright © 1990 by Columbia University Press. Reprinted by permission of the publisher. **Page 485:** "Albuquerque Defends the Portugese Empire" from *Albuquerque: Caesar of the East.* Copyright © 1990 by Aris and Phillips. Reprinted by permission of the publisher. **Page 495:** "An Inca Nobleman Defends His Civilization" from *Letter to a King, a Picture History of the Inca Civilization* by Huáman Poma. Originally published by Unwin Hyman Ltd., a division of HarperCollins Ltd.: London 1978. **Page 503:** "The New World and the Old" from *The Florentine Codex: General History of the Things of New Spain* by Fray Bernardino de Sahagún. Introductory Volume, pp. 96–97. Translated by Arthur J. O. Anderson and Charles E. Dibble. Copyright 1982 by the School of American Research, Santa Fe and The University of Utah, Salt Lake City. Reprinted by permission of the School of American Research.

Chapter 14: Page 515: "Martin Luther's Address to the Christian Nobility of the German Nation" from *The American Edition of Luther's Works.* Copyright © 1943 Muhlenberg Press. Reprinted by permission of Augsburg Fortress. **Page 537:** "Ignatius Loyola's Spiritual Exercises" from *Culture and Belief in Europe, 1450–1600: An Anthology of Sources,* edited by David Englander, Diana Norman, Rosemary O'Day, and W. R. Owens. (Basil Blackwell in association the Open University, 1990). Reprinted by permission of Blackwell Publishers.

Chapter 15: Page 566: "Richelieu Supports the Authority of the State" from *The Political Testament of Cardinal Richelieu: The Significant Chapters and Supporting Selections* edited and trans-

Index